THE OXFORD HANDBOOK OF
CARE IN MUSIC EDUCATION

THE OXFORD HANDBOOK OF CARE IN MUSIC EDUCATION

Edited by
KARIN S. HENDRICKS

OXFORD
UNIVERSITY PRESS

OXFORD
UNIVERSITY PRESS

Oxford University Press is a department of the University of Oxford. It furthers the University's objective of excellence in research, scholarship, and education by publishing worldwide. Oxford is a registered trade mark of Oxford University Press in the UK and certain other countries.

Published in the United States of America by Oxford University Press
198 Madison Avenue, New York, NY 10016, United States of America.

© Oxford University Press 2023

All rights reserved. No part of this publication may be reproduced, stored in a retrieval system, or transmitted, in any form or by any means, without the prior permission in writing of Oxford University Press, or as expressly permitted by law, by license, or under terms agreed with the appropriate reproduction rights organization. Inquiries concerning reproduction outside the scope of the above should be sent to the Rights Department, Oxford University Press, at the address above.

You must not circulate this work in any other form and you must impose this same condition on any acquirer.

Library of Congress Cataloging-in-Publication Data
Names: Hendricks, Karin S., 1971– editor.
Title: The Oxford handbook of care in music education / Karin S. Hendricks.
Description: [1.] | New York : Oxford University Press, 2023. |
Series: Oxford handbooks series | Includes index.
Identifiers: LCCN 2023017643 (print) | LCCN 2023017644 (ebook) |
ISBN 9780197611654 (hardback) | ISBN 9780197611685 |
ISBN 9780197611678 (epub)
Subjects: LCSH: Music—Instruction and study—Social aspects. |
Music—Instruction and study—Psychological aspects. |
Music—Instruction and study—Political aspects. |
Music—Instruction and study—Philosophy.
Classification: LCC MT1 .O925 2023 (print) | LCC MT1 (ebook) |
DDC 780.71—dc23/eng/20230517
LC record available at https://lccn.loc.gov/2023017643
LC ebook record available at https://lccn.loc.gov/2023017644

DOI: 10.1093/oxfordhb/9780197611654.001.0001

Printed by Integrated Books International, United States of America

Contents

List of Figures   xi
List of Tables   xiii
Foreword   xv
Preface   xvii
Acknowledgments   xxi
Contributors   xxiii

SECTION 1   PHILOSOPHICAL PERSPECTIVES ON CARE AND MUSIC EDUCATION—CARE-ING IN THE MUSIC PEDAGOGICAL MOMENT: NAVIGATING CHALLENGES

Section Foreword: *Panagiotis A. Kanellopoulos*

1. A Call for Care and Compassion in Music Education   5
   KARIN S. HENDRICKS

2. On Caring for Music Education in Troubled Times   22
   ESTELLE R. JORGENSEN

3. Caring About Caring for Music Education   31
   MARISSA SILVERMAN

4. An Ethic of Expectation Surrounding the Virtual Performance   44
   BRENT C. TALBOT AND CARA FAITH BERNARD

5. Compassion During Musical Engagement with Young Children   56
   DIANA R. DANSEREAU

6. *Convivencias* and a Web of Care   69
   KEVIN SHORNER-JOHNSON, MARTHA GONZALEZ, AND DANIEL J. SHEVOCK

7. The Hospitality of Wonder and Its Relation to Care and Compassion in Music Education — 79
JUNE BOYCE-TILLMAN

8. Disability, Lifelong Musical Engagement, and Care — 91
DAVID BAKER

9. Caring Through Dialogical Relations in Community Music Settings — 103
LAURA BENJAMINS

10. The Politics of Care in the Education of Children Gifted for Music: A Systems View — 115
GUADALUPE LÓPEZ-ÍÑIGUEZ AND HEIDI WESTERLUND

11. Ways of Caring in Music Education Through the Lens of Classic Confucianism and Classic Daoism — 130
C. VICTOR FUNG

12. Caring with the Earth, Community, and Co-Learners for the Health of Biological, Social, and Musical Ecosystems — 141
TAWNYA D. SMITH

SECTION 2 CO-CREATING CARING RELATIONSHIPS—*CARE*: FINGER POINTING AT THE MOON

Section Foreword: *Liora Bresler*

13. The Musical Circle of Care: A Framework for Relationship Building and Healing Through Musicing — 157
JANELIZE MORELLI

14. (Re)Imagining Intersectionality: Holistic Acceptance in Music Education — 168
LATASHA THOMAS-DURRELL

15. Accompanying LGBTQIA+ Students in the Music Classroom — 179
JUSTIN MCMANUS AND BRUCE CARTER

16. Compassion and Care Through Musical Social Emotional Learning — 192
SCOTT N. EDGAR, KARA IRELAND D'AMBROSIO, AND ELISE HACKL-BLUMSTEIN

17. Empathy and Deep Listening in Jazz Improvisation 205
    TROY DAVIS

18. Facilitating Trust and Connection Through Musical Presencing: Case Study of a Conflict Transformation Facilitator 217
    KARIN S. HENDRICKS, DELANEY A. K. FINN, CHERYL M. FREEZE, AND JESSANDRA KONO

19. Sometimes I Just Crawl Under the Covers and Hide: Caring by, for, and with Community Music Leaders During Crises 231
    FIONA EVISON

20. "This Guitar Hurts!": Empathy and Caring in Inclusive Ensembles 245
    KIMBERLY A. MCCORD

21. Fostering Reciprocal and Responsive Musical Relationships in a Youth Instrumental Ensemble: One Guest Conductor's "Caring With" Approach 256
    ALLEN R. LEGUTKI, KARIN S. HENDRICKS, TAWNYA D. SMITH, AND KRISTI N. KING

22. Singing and Caring 268
    ELIZABETH CASSIDY PARKER AND JENNIFER C. HUTTON

23. Developing Trust and Empathy Through Peer Mentoring in the Music Classroom 280
    ANDREW GOODRICH

24. Using the Lens of Psychological Safety to Understand the Effects of Bullying Within the School-Based Music Ensemble Classroom 292
    JARED R. RAWLINGS

SECTION 3 CARING FOR WELLBEING AND HUMAN FLOURISHING

Section Foreword: *Susan A. O'Neill*

25. The Vulnerability in Being Heard: Care in the Supervision of Music Students 307
    TIRI BERGESEN SCHEI

26. Student and Teacher Mental Health: Nurturing Wellbeing Within a Climate of Trust 318
RACHEL L. DIRKS

27. Mindfulness, Self-Compassion, and Gratitude in Music Teaching and Learning 328
FRANK M. DIAZ

28. Self-Care and the Music Educator 339
BRIDGET SWEET

29. Somatic Self-Care for Music Educators 350
STEPHEN A. PAPARO

30. Music's Relational Imperative: Wellbeing, Music-Making, and the Interconnections Between Music Therapy and Music Education 361
ELIZABETH MITCHELL

31. Music as a Vehicle for Caring for Students with Learning Differences 373
RYAN M. HOURIGAN

32. Trauma: A Compassionate Lens for Music Teaching 384
SHANNAN HIBBARD AND ERIN PRICE

33. Caring Connection, Music Participation, and Quality of Life of Older Adults 395
LISA J. LEHMBERG AND C. VICTOR FUNG

34. Reconsidering Musical Ability Development Through the Lens of Diversity and Bias 408
KARIN S. HENDRICKS AND GARY E. MCPHERSON

35. Conveying Pupil Access to Wellbeing Through Relational Care in Music Education 421
KARI HOLDHUS

36. Fostering Care Through Core Reflection 433
MARGARET H. BERG

SECTION 4 CARE, SOCIAL ACTIVISM, AND CRITICAL CONSCIOUSNESS

Section Foreword: *Cathy Benedict*

37. The Sounds of Hope: Music Homeplaces and Compassionate, Abolitionist Music Teaching — 449
    EMILY GOOD-PERKINS

38. Critical Race Theory and Care in Music Education — 463
    AMY LEWIS

39. Call Me by MY Name: Knowing Our Students' Names as Intercultural Sensitivity — 471
    KÍNH T. VŨ

40. Critical Listening and Authorial Agency as Radical Practices of Care — 482
    KELLY BYLICA

41. Love, Care, Revolution, and Justice: Loving Oneself and Loving One's Students — 494
    GARETH DYLAN SMITH, BRANDI WALLER-PACE, MARTIN URBACH, AND BRYAN POWELL

42. "I Just Wanna Live My Life Like It's Gold": Prioritizing Anti-Racist Music Education — 504
    ALICE A. TSUI, JULIET HESS, AND KARIN S. HENDRICKS

43. Music-Making in Prisons and Schools: Dismantling Carceral Logics — 517
    REBECCA D. SWANSON AND MARY L. COHEN

44. Popular Music Education, Aesthetic Judgment, and Gender Relations in Hungary — 530
    EMÍLIA BARNA

45. Caring About Deaf Music in Culturally Responsive Music Education — 542
    WARREN N. CHURCHILL AND CLARE HALL

46. In Search of Meaning, Joy, and Justice in Music Education: Teachers Matter — 554
    GRAÇA MOTA

47. Cultural Humility and Ethics of Caring in Multicultural Settings of Music Teacher Education 566
AMIRA EHRLICH

48. Policy Practice as Citizenship Building: From Duty to Care to Solidarity in Music Education 580
PATRICK SCHMIDT

Index 593

Figures

7.1.	The spiritual experience in music (Boyce-Tillman, 2016).	86
18.1.	Layers of presence.	223
18.2.	The process of being true to oneself (musically and otherwise) leading to trust in self and others.	225
19.1.	Participants' emotions varied but were often expressed in negative terms.	238
19.2.	Routes of care in noncrisis times.	241
19.3.	Alternate routes of care in crisis times.	241
26.1.	AIR—Framework of music educators' experiences with adolescent mental health concerns (adapted from Dirks's [2020] preliminary framework).	323
34.1.	Differentiated model of giftedness and talent (adapted from Gagne, 2009, p. 64).	411
39.1.	Developmental Model of Intercultural Sensitivity (DMIS) (Bennett, 1986, p. 182).	473
39.2.	Ethnorelative stages from developmental model of intercultural sensitivity (DMIS).	478
43.1.	Compass of compassion-based activism, copyright 2018, Frank Rogers Jr., Center for Engaged Compassion.	521
47.1.	Self-portraits.	572
47.2.	A student group of three (secular woman of Russian descent; Christian-Arab woman; and Jewish Orthodox woman) teach the class a Jewish Ethiopian prayer chant: *Salam Licha Ir* ("Hello [Holy] City").	573
47.3.	A secular Jewish student leads the class in an improvised folk dance to a traditional tune being shared by a Muslim student on the piano.	574
47.4.	A student ensemble including a Muslim man on piano, a secular Jewish man on electric guitar, an Ultraorthodox Jewish woman on darbuka drum, and a Muslim woman on oud. The illustrative recording depicts a similar ensemble playing Mosh Ben Ari's Israeli pop song *Salam* ("Bring Peace upon Us").	574

Tables

1.1. Chapter Themes and Connections Across the Handbook. — 10
17.1. From Seddon, F. A. (2005). Modes of communication during jazz improvisation. *British Journal of Music Education*, 22(1), p. 53. https://doi.org/10.1017/S0265051704005984 — 212
33.1. Benefits of Music Participation Relating to Caring Connection in Older Adults (Post-2015 Publications). — 400

Foreword

Lucy Green

The concept of "care" in music education is a Pandora's box—but in a good way, in a fantastic way, in a way that is exciting and enticing—potentially for all music educators. Open the box and a whole host of questions, puzzles, challenges, problems, and possibilities come flying out, many of which I would suggest most of us in music education have not properly considered before. While the concept of care may be, at least implicitly, part of an age-old tradition of ethics in philosophy, and while it has been applied to various aspects of educational studies over the last several decades, it is a relatively recent addition to music education studies. I believe this book both heralds and is part of a sea change caused by the advent of this concept and its application to a range of music education contexts.

The Oxford Handbook of Care in Music Education introduces a plethora of standpoints from which to explore the multifaceted question of what is meant by "care" in music education, and what implications this concept carries for us as music education researchers, theorists, and practitioners. In community music studies, the concept of care, or commensurate concepts, possibly have a longer history than in music education studies—but now we need to grapple with the massive crossovers that can be perceived between those two fields: The concept of "care" surely is a unifying concept across both music education and community music. Such crossovers are abundant in many threads running through the current volume.

The concept of care of course goes along with many other commensurate terms including for example compassion, empathy, sympathy, humaneness, and many more, all of which are brought into play and interrogated in the book. Yet, while the editor has allowed individual expression and the articulation of manifold meanings of care to emerge, at the same time her strong editorial hand, along with the obvious communication that has gone on among the authors, have ensured focus and clarity concerning the main backbone of the book throughout. The authors have engaged with each other's work in such a way as to reveal both synergies and differences between interpretations and applications of care in their various fields. Through this close teamwork, they have put the concept of care into practice—caring for, about, and with each other's views, and supporting the editor and each other to produce what is a very fine volume indeed.

For so long, music educators took for granted a teacher-led, directive approach to educating students in music, an approach which rarely or never questioned the superiority of the teacher's knowledge of appropriate curriculum content, and of how to deliver that content through pedagogy. Music education theory and practice have undergone waves of change in this respect during the last few decades, and it is now widely accepted that we music educators need to be more aware of our students' needs, backgrounds, skills, and prior knowledge, individually and collectively, and that we are not the sole possessors of all that is important about our subject. We now interrogate the notion of "child-centered" music teaching, a notion that for a long time *appeared* to put the child at the center of the process, but very often nonetheless pursued a teacher-centered notion of what the child's central needs were, without really delving into the child's perspective. We recognize that not only students themselves but also their parents, wider families, and communities possess huge amounts of knowledge about and skills in different types of music and musical engagement, which they bring to our classes, projects, rehearsals, and other contexts. Yet the concept of care and other commensurate concepts tended to be missing from these discussions and revelations.

Now, thanks to the work of many authors in this volume and in the last few years, we can frame such questions by the concept of care, in a way which I think many music educationalists will find refreshing.

Preface

KARIN S. HENDRICKS

Hardly a person would suggest that there is currently sufficient care in this world. Where people may be more likely to disagree is in what the essence of care is, and how care might be best enacted for the common good. Within the field of music education, many are quick to assert that care is fundamental to student-centered approaches, yet "care"—not to mention the term "student-centered"—remains a nebulous notion with numerous interpretations and countless practical manifestations. In this volume, Liora Bresler draws on Buddhist thought to describe writings on care like a finger pointing to the moon: They are only descriptions or guides for something that is much too elusive for words and is best understood through experience. Yet care—all too often discounted or diminished in discussions of music education—is critical to understand if we are serious about striving toward human flourishing. As Susan O'Neill articulates, caring, "as a deep form of authentic connection," is necessary to impact the quality of people's lives.

There are 48 chapters and 4 forewords in this handbook, but an even greater number of conceptualizations and perspectives on what it means to "care" in music education. As editor I have made no effort to restrict various conceptualizations of care, nor to prescribe one approach to practicing it. Although authors share a common vision about the *need* for care in music education, each chapter and foreword offers a unique perspective on the meaning of care, and chapters situate these diverse meanings within a variety of educational, performance, and therapeutic contexts. Whereas some authors problematize notions of caring for, about, and with other music-makers (and music), other authors provide practical illustrations of what care might look like in certain instances of relational music engagement.

This handbook is intended for an audience of scholars in addition to practicing or preservice music educators in a broad range of settings, spanning from early childhood to adult learning. Chapter authors write in a variety of styles, with a broad range of voices, perspectives, and approaches. I have welcomed and embraced this kind of complementarity in the handbook, eschewing a more traditional approach to philosophical uniformity that would contradict the unique and context-specific enactments of care that are proposed and presented throughout.

The volume is international and intercultural. It includes perspectives from over 18 countries and spans a broad range of music-making contexts. Many chapters feature collaborations between seasoned and emerging scholars, school and community music teachers, and music students. The handbook includes and embraces voices of minoritized (e.g., African-American, Latinx, Asian, disabled, LGBTQ+) music makers, both in its authorship and as one of its primary content aims.

Chapters were written through continued verbal dialogue among authors, not only within co-authored chapters but also between chapters through peer review and international, small-group dialogue clusters that I curated in early stages of the project. By engaging in dialogue clusters with authors from other chapters, *OHCME* contributors were encouraged to challenge one another's assumptions and biases and to move conversations forward in new directions.

Although handbook chapters focus primarily on conceptualizations and practices of care, they also raise other questions, including: How do we learn to care? Can care be taught? Does everyone care to care? Here, again, there are no simple answers.

I remember an experience as a young teacher, as I took one of my violin students to have a lesson with a teacher whom I held in high esteem. After the teacher listened "carefully" to the student perform, he looked her squarely in the eye and said, "You have a gift of expressiveness. This is something that cannot be taught." I remember how conflicted I felt inside as I registered his words. It seemed to me, despite my limited experience at the time, that musicianship was far more complex than simply something that students possessed or did not possess. If the musicianship equation were indeed reduced to a simple binary of "musicians" versus "non-musicians," I was left wondering what my purpose was as a teacher. I have since learned (with thanks to many wonderful research mentors) about the abundance of scholarship addressing complexities of musical expression and engagement, offering practical implications for music teachers that extend beyond what space allows here. This volume extends on these previous conversations by considering the ways in which music educators might take care to nurture and amplify students' expressions—not only musical ones but also expressions of their identity and personhood.

Caring in music teacher education might be considered in a similar way: Can music teachers *learn* how to care? Does one simply either care, or not care? Marissa Silverman offers that there are certain actions or behaviors that "caring teachers know-to-do and feel-to-do"—yet how does a music teacher become caring in the first place? Many chapters in this volume engage with these questions through a variety of philosophical, psychological, and sociological lenses. As Cathy Benedict suggests in her foreword, it may be a question of understanding what one means by care, because the "care" we take to conceptualize "care" drives subsequent actions.

I am inspired by the chapters in this handbook to be "careful" in honoring the dignity and intentions of others whose manifestations of care might appear different than mine. Human relations are much too complex to be understood or divided into categories of care versus uncare; what feels like care to me may be experienced very differently by someone else. My deep wish for this handbook, then, is to open a dialogue about the multifarious ways that care might be evident in music learning spaces, and to share a broad palette of ideas, conceptualizations, and visions of care, from which music educators might sample, select, and adapt to what fits their needs and propensities at any given time. However, as Panos Kanellopoulos notes, these various, multifaceted, and often subversive treatments of care are perhaps not best "handled with care." Instead, they are to be troubled, challenged, and questioned by the reader, as each grapples with their own understandings and interpretations of the ways that they might uniquely care for, about, and with other music learners, as well as themselves.

Acknowledgments

This handbook is a product of collaborative care, with deeply thoughtful and reflective contributions from 70 authors who interacted with one another from start to finish through co-authorship, small-group dialogue clusters, and formal chapter reviews. It has been sheer joy to interact with each of you, to learn from your work, and to be inspired by your ideas for implementing caring practices. It is not an exaggeration to say that I have changed both as a scholar and person through my associations with you.

Each chapter had at least three reviewers, including the editor and at least two other internal or external readers from the following list: David Baker, Emília Barna, Betty Bauman, Laura Benjamins, Margaret H. Berg, Cara Faith Bernard, June Boyce-Tillman, Kelly Bylica, Bruce Carter, Dustin Cates, Warren N. Churchill, Mary L. Cohen, Kara D'Ambrosio, Diana Dansereau, Troy Davis, Frank M. Diaz, Rachel Dirks, Scott N. Edgar, Amira Ehrlich, Fiona Evison, Sommer Forrester, C. Victor Fung, Scott Goble, Emily Good-Perkins, Andrew Goodrich, Lucy Green, Clare Hall, Jonathan Hall, Suzanne Hall, Juliet Hess, Shannan Hibbard, Kari Mette Holdhus, Ryan M. Hourigan, Kaitlyn S. Leahy, Allen R. Legutki, Lisa J. Lehmberg, Amy Lewis, Guadalupe López-Íñiguez, Kimberly A. McCord, Justin McManus, Gary E. McPherson, Elizabeth Mitchell, Janelize Morelli, Graça Mota, Stephen A. Paparo, Elizabeth Cassidy Parker, Bryan Powell Erin Price, Jared R. Rawlings, James Ray, Tiri Bergesen Schei, Patrick Schmidt, Daniel J. Shevock, Kevin Shorner-Johnson, Marissa Silverman, Darryl Singleton, Gareth Dylan Smith, Tawnya D. Smith, Bridget Sweet, Brent C. Talbot, Latasha Thomas-Durrell, Kính T. Vũ, and Heidi Westerlund.

Many thanks to the Oxford University Press team who brought this volume to fruition. I am particularly grateful to Suresh Perumal for seeing the project through to final edits and to Michelle Chen, who received the proposal and was tremendously helpful and informative in guiding the handbook from beginning to end. Thank you to everyone at OUP for your vision, professionalism, and encouragement.

There are insufficient ways to express gratitude to Boston University graduate assistant Cheryl Freeze, who edited each chapter and foreword with utmost care. I join many handbook authors who have acknowledged her keen eye and meticulous attention to detail, while also thanking her personally for her tremendous generosity of time and spirit. I remember walking through the Boston University College of Fine Arts student lounge more than once to find Cheryl sitting with a laptop and hard copy of the APA manual at her side. Her efforts are evident in every chapter.

On behalf of the contributors, I acknowledge the music teachers and learners around the world who have inspired this work, and hope that the handbook may have a genuine place in conversations of music, education, and care in the future.

Contributors

David Baker is Associate Professor at University College London, where he leads the Music Education MA and has been Academic Head of Learning and Teaching. In the past, David has taught at Reading University and Trinity Laban Conservatoire of Music. David has assisted in developing new degree courses and modules across a range of education disciplines, and he has been external assessor for periodic program reviews, including at the Royal Academy of Music. His published research has encompassed instrumental teaching; work on Lucy Green's informal learning "Ear playing project" (Esmée Fairbairn Foundation, 2011–12); the life histories of internationally renowned classical soloists; disability; and assistive technology development; etc. David was principal investigator for "Visually-Impaired Musicians' Lives" (Arts and Humanities Research Council, 2013–15), which led to his co-authored book, *Insights in Sound* (2017). His work has taken him as a presenter to Australia, India, Norway, Sweden and the United States.

Emília Barna, PhD, is Associate Professor at the Budapest University of Technology and Economics, and Head of the Cultural Industries specialization. She is a sociologist and popular music scholar. She completed a Popular Music Studies PhD program in 2011 at the University of Liverpool. Her main research areas are the music industries and digitization, popular music, technology and gender, cultural labor, and music and politics. With Tamás Tófalvy, she co-edited the books *Made in Hungary: Studies in Popular Music* (2017) and *Popular Music, Technology, and the Changing Media Ecosystem: From Cassettes to Stream* (2020). She is a member of the International Association for the Study of Popular Music (IASPM) and the Working Group for Public Sociology "Helyzet."

Cathy Benedict is currently a lecturer in the faculty of Curriculum and Teaching at Teachers College, Columbia University. After teaching elementary music for 15 years, she has taught university at both the undergraduate and graduate levels in the United States and Canada and guest taught courses in Beijing, Guatemala, and Ecuador. As codirector of Western's Kodály Certification program, she has also taught both musicianship and Kodály pedagogy at the university level. Her publications can be found in the *Canadian Music Educator, Journal of the American Academy of Audiology, Philosophy of Music Education Review, Music Education Research, Research Studies in Music Education, Action, Criticism and Theory for Music Education, British Journal of Music Education, Journal of Curriculum Theorizing*, and the Brazilian journal *ABEM*. She co-edited *The Oxford Handbook of Social Justice and Music Education* (2015) and her recent book, *Music and Social Justice: A Guide for Elementary Educators* is available through Oxford University Press.

Laura Benjamins is a PhD candidate in Music Education at Western University, Canada. Her doctoral research, funded by the Social Sciences and Humanities Research Council of Canada, examines worship music-making practices from a sociological perspective. Laura holds undergraduate degrees in Piano Performance and Education (Redeemer University), an ARCT in Piano Performance (Royal Conservatory of Music, Toronto), and a MMus in Music Education (Western University). She works as a music course instructor at Laurier University and Redeemer University. Laura's research interests include informal music learning, church music, community music facilitation, and reflective practice. Laura has presented on these and other topics at national and international conferences including the Research in Music Education (RiME) conference and the International Symposium on the Sociology of Music Education (ISSME) conference. Several of Laura's papers can be found in journals such as the *International Journal of Music Education* and *Arts and Humanities in Higher Education*.

Margaret H. Berg is Professor of Music Education and Associate Dean for Graduate Studies at the University of Colorado, where she teaches undergraduate and graduate courses in music education and string pedagogy. She is co-author of the book *The ASTA String Curriculum: Assessment Companion*, as well as numerous book chapters and articles focused on sociology of music education, music teacher mentoring, music teacher education, and school orchestra and applied studio curriculum and assessment. She has presented at the American Educational Research Association Conference, NAfME Music Research and Teacher Education National Conference, Society for Music Teacher Educators Symposium, and the ASTA National Conference. Margaret has served on the editorial board for the *Bulletin of the Council for Research in Music Education*, *Journal of Music Teacher Education*, and *String Research Journal*. In addition, she served on the National ASTA Executive Board and was awarded the ASTA String Researcher Award.

Cara Faith Bernard is Associate Professor of Music Education at the University of Connecticut, where she teaches courses in choral and elementary methods and curriculum. As a conductor, Cara prepared choruses for performances at Carnegie Hall and Lincoln Center. Cara's research areas include music teacher evaluation, policy, curriculum, and social justice. She serves on the editorial committees of *Music Educators Journal*, *Arts Education Policy Review*, and *Journal of Popular Music Education*, and is associate editor of *Visions of Research in Music Education*. She is co-author of the book *Navigating Teacher Evaluation: A Guide for Music Teachers*, published by Oxford University Press.

June Boyce-Tillman, MBE, read music at Oxford University and is Professor Emerita of Applied Music, University of Winchester, United Kingdom. She has published widely in the area of education and music, often on spirituality/liminality and eudaimonia. Her research into children's musical development has been translated into five languages and supported the development of improvisatory activities in the classroom.

She held visiting fellowships at Indiana University and the Episcopal Divinity School in Massachusetts, United States. She is an international performer, especially in the work of Hildegard of Bingen. She has written hymns and large scale works for cathedrals involving professional musicians, community choirs, people with disabilities, and school children. She is the convenor of Music, Spirituality and Wellbeing international (www.mswinternational.org) and the international improvising Peace Choir. She is editor of the Peter Lang Music and Spirituality series. She is an Extra-Ordinary Professor at North West University, South Africa and is an ordained Anglican priest.

Liora Bresler is Professor Emerita at the University of Illinois, Champaign. She is the editor of the book series Landscapes: Aesthetics, the Arts and Education (Springer) and the co-founder of the *International Journal of Education and the Arts* (2000–). Her authored and edited books on the arts in education, include *Knowing Bodies, Moving Minds* 2004), the *International Handbook of Research in Arts Education* (2007), and the co-edited *International Handbook of Creative Learning* (2011). Awards include The AERA Outstanding Lifetime Achievement in Arts and Learning SIG (2021); Lifetime Achievement Award by SEMPRE (Society for Education and Music Psychology research) (2019); and Distinguished Fellow, the National Art Education Association (2010–). Teaching awards include University of Illinois Campus Award for Excellence in Graduate Teaching (2005); and the University of Illinois Campus Award for Excellence in Mentoring (2018). Her work was translated to German, French, Portuguese, Spanish, Hebrew, Lithuanian, Finnish, Korean, and Chinese.

Kelly Bylica is Assistant Professor of Music Education at Boston University, where she works with both undergraduate and graduate students. Originally from Chicago (United States), Kelly taught middle school and K-8 general and choral music throughout the Midwestern United States and has also served on the teaching faculty of several community-based youth music programs. Kelly's research agenda is focused on middle school musical experiences, curriculum and policy, and critical pedagogy. Kelly has presented on these and other topics at regional, national and international conferences. She has also published chapters in several edited volumes as well as articles in *Music Education Research, Bulletin of the Council for Research in Music Education, Journal for Popular Music Education, British Journal of Music Education*, and *Arts & Humanities in Higher Education*, among others. Kelly holds a PhD in Music Education from the University of Western Ontario.

Bruce Carter is a music educator and researcher, whose work focuses on issues of creativity and the intersections of social justice, technology, and arts participation. Dr. Carter is Visiting Research Professor at New York University, where his work centers on redesigning pedagogies of string instruments through new technologies. Additionally, he is founder of Repetivo, a company that designs innovative musical instruments bridging traditional musical instruments with innovative technology-based pedagogy.

Warren N. Churchill, EdD, is Lecturer of Music and Coordinator of Musical Performance at New York University Abu Dhabi, in the United Arab Emirates. He has presented on the topic of disability and music making in the Deaf community in numerous music education conferences. He teaches a core curriculum course at NYUAD titled "dis/Abilities in Musical Contexts," which invites students to deeply reflect on relations of power and ethics that come to the fore in regard to how we make meaning of peoples' varied musical capacities. This work is heavily influenced by interdisciplinary synergies between the field of Music Education and Disability Studies. His research has been published in *Research Studies in Music Education* and the *Philosophy of Music Education Review*. In addition, he has contributed chapters to books published by Routledge, Intellect, and the Oxford Handbook series.

Mary L. Cohen is Associate Professor of Music Education at the University of Iowa. She works to build relationships and support individual and collective wellbeing through research on music-making, songwriting, and peacebuilding. She has initiated international efforts toward prison abolition and has cowritten *Music-Making in U.S. Prisons: Listening to Incarcerated Voices*. In 2009, she founded the Oakdale Prison Community Choir (http://oakdalechoir.lib.uiowa.edu/). In 2010 she started the Oakdale songwriting workshop, where now over 150 songs are available with the Creative Commons License. She has been a keynote speaker for conferences in Germany, Canada, Portugal, and the United States. Her research is published in the *International Journal of Research in Choral Singing*, *Journal of Research in Music Education*, *Australian Journal of Music Education*, *Journal of Historical Research in Music Education*, *The Prison Journal*, *Journal of Correctional Education*, the *International Journal of Community Music*, *International Journal of Music Education*, and in numerous book chapters.

Diana R. Dansereau is Assistant Professor of Music Education at Boston University and focuses her scholarship on early childhood music education and music education research. She is co-editor of *Pluralism in American Music Education Research* and has presented her work in *Psychology of Music*, *Journal of Research in Music Education*, *Bulletin of the Council for Research in Music Education*, *Journal of Music Teacher Education*, *International Journal of Music in Early Childhood*, *International Journal of Community Music*, *The Music Educators Journal*, *Perspectives: Journal of the Early Childhood Music & Movement Association*, and *Massachusetts Music News*. Diana is the founding editor of the *International Journal of Music in Early Childhood* (Intellect) and serves on the editorial board of the *Journal of Music Teacher Education*. She received the BM degree from the Eastman School of Music; MME from the Pennsylvania State University; and PhD from Georgia State University.

Kara Ireland D'Ambrosio holds three degrees in Music Education: BM from the University of New Hampshire, MM (Kodaly) from Holy Names University (Oakland), and DMA from Boston University. Kara also earned her National Board Certification in Early/Middle Childhood Music Education (2004) and continues to keep it renewed. Kara also teaches music (TK-8) at Woodside School, where she won a Grammy Gold in 2002 for Excellence in Music Education. Her teaching philosophy includes employing SEL practices to create an inclusive, caring environment for learning. Kara served two terms on Bay Section CMEA Board (Special Representative for Classroom music, 2006–2010 and Higher Ed Representative 2017–2021). At San Jose State University, Dr. Ireland D'Ambrosio teaches Music Education Methods, VAPA Arts Integration and is the Secondary Field Placement Coordinator in Teacher Education. Kara has special interest in intercultural educational practices, antiracist arts, social-emotional learning, preservice education, and interventions for income inequality.

Troy Davis is Director of Instrumental Music and Jazz Studies at West Valley College in Saratoga, California. He is also the Camp Director at Hayward La Honda Music Camp, Director Emeritus of the Oakland Municipal Band, and guest conducts many regional honor bands, orchestras, and jazz bands. Dr. Davis was honored as the California Music Educators Association (CMEA) "Music Educator of the Year" in 2017 and as a "Distinguished Music Educator" by Yale University in 2011. He earned his doctoral degree in music education from Boston University, master's degree in music education from Notre Dame de Namur University, and his bachelor of music in oboe performance from the San Francisco Conservatory of Music.

Frank M. Diaz is Associate Professor of Music at the Indiana University Jacobs School of Music. An active scholar and teacher in the field of contemplative science. Frank is also the founder and former director of the Institute for Mindfulness-Based Wellness and Pedagogy (MBWP), an organization founded to facilitate collaboration among artists, educators, and scholars interested in disseminating research and best practices on the art of mindful living, teaching, and performance. He has taught meditative practices to thousands of students through courses and workshops at educational, religious, and nonprofit institutions across the United States, and leads several mindfulness initiatives through partnerships with the Jacobs School of Music, IU Lifelong Learning, and the Eskenazi Museum of Art. As a scholar, Diaz focuses on mixed-methods investigations of meditative practices and on developing theoretical models that might effectively deal with existing gaps between scientific and humanistic approaches to understanding contemplative practices.

Rachel L. Dirks is Director of Orchestral Studies and Assistant Professor of Music at Kansas State University and is an active conductor, clinician, and educator. She has made written contributions to the *American String Teacher* journal, ASTA, NAfME, and TMEA online resources, and volumes 1, 2, and 4 of the *Teaching Music Through Performance in Orchestra* series. Dr. Dirks has conducted all-state and regional orchestras throughout the United States, including appearances in New York, Georgia, Nevada, Kentucky, Oregon, Illinois, and Kansas. As a featured clinician, she has been invited to present conference sessions for the American String Teachers Association, the Midwest International Band and Orchestra Clinic, the National Association for Music Education, and numerous state music education conferences. Dr. Dirks currently serves as chairperson of the National ASTA Health and Wellness Committee, where she hopes to further the discussion surrounding mental health and well-being in the music classroom.

Scott N. Edgar (*he/him*) has dedicated his career to highlighting the potential music education and educators have to build life skills students will use long after they leave the classroom. As a notable authority on music education and social-emotional learning, he is the author of *Music Education and Social Emotional Learning: The Heart of Teaching Music*, *The ABCs of My Feelings and Music* (co-authored with his wife, Stephanie), and editor of *Portraits of Music Education and Social Emotional Learning*. Dr. Edgar prioritizes facilitating spaces where people can explore their identity, build a sense of belonging, and experience agency. He is Associate Professor of Music at Lake Forest College, and serves as Director of Practice and Research for The Center for Arts Education and Social Emotional Learning. Striving for work/life balance, he enjoys grilling, exercising, and spending time with his wife Steph, their son, Nathan.

Amira Ehrlich is Dean of the Faculty of Music Education at Levinsky College of Education, Tel Aviv, and a faculty member of Mandel Leadership Institute's Program for Ultraorthodox women in Jerusalem. Amira is a music educator with more than 20 years' experience in the field of music, as a teacher, producer, and researcher. Her published writings explore sociological and cultural aspects of music education. Between 2015 and 2020 Amira has been a member of the international research team of Global Visions Through Mobilizing Networks: Co-Developing Intercultural Music Teacher Education in Finland, Israel, and Nepal research project funded by the Academy of Finland. Since 2020 Amira has been the chair of the International Society of Music Education's special interest group for spirituality in music education.

Fiona Evison is completing a Music Education PhD at Western University in London, Ontario, Canada, and a lifelong community musician who wants to use her creativity to enable community music-making. Her research interests include community music leadership, community composition, and community singing. Her novel research on the role of community composers will be reported in the *Oxford Handbook of Community Singing*, and continues to investigate the COVID-19 pandemic's impact on music and arts communities. Fiona holds an MA in Community Music (Wilfrid Laurier University) and a Bachelor of Church Music (Heritage College). She is a member of the Royal Canadian College of Organists, and is a community music director, conductor, and accompanist, who is privileged to make music with participants of all ages. She is a board member of the Association of Canadian Women Composers, and is editor of the ACWC *Journal*.

Delaney A. K. Finn is a current undergraduate student at Boston University pursuing a BM in Music Education. She has taught music students for the past seven years as a tutor, private instructor, and classroom teacher. Her experience with teaching started during high school, and she continues to teach throughout her preparation for music teacher licensure. In the summer of 2021, with funding from the Boston University Undergraduate Research Opportunities Program, Delaney Finn (alongside Dr. Karin Hendricks, MM student Cheryl Freeze, and MM alum Jessandra Kono) researched the seven facets of trust through a case study of a musician working in conflict areas (e.g.,

Palestine, Belfast). This formative experience led to the continuation of her research the following year alongside Dr. Karin Hendricks, where they delved deeper into vulnerability and agency in the music classroom.

Cheryl M. Freeze is currently completing her Master of Music degree in Music Education at Boston University. Originally from the Netherlands, where she completed her bachelor of music in Education at Codarts Rotterdam, she relocated to the United States on a Fulbright scholarship to study the intersections of music, community, and social justice. Cheryl has a background teaching elementary and middle school general music, working with youth choirs, and facilitating community music workshops for and with people with a refugee background. She currently co-teaches *Introduction to Music Teaching and Learning* at Boston University, co-presented research on trust in music education at the *Cultural Diversity in Music Education* conference in October 2021, and has been the graduate assistant to BU's Chair of Music Education since 2020. Cheryl's interests also include compassionate music teaching, community music, LGBTQIA+ studies in education, and the role music plays in supporting people with a refugee background.

C. Victor Fung is Professor of Music Education and Director of Center for Music Education Research, University of South Florida. His research areas include social psychological, philosophical, and international perspectives in music education. He is author of *A Way of Music Education* (2018, Chinese translation forthcoming), co-author of *Music for Life* (2016, Chinese translation published in 2021) and *Music, Senior Centers, and Quality of Life* (2023), and co-editor of *Meanings of Music Participation: Scenarios in the United States* (2023). He has contributed to various book chapters and refereed journals. He has reviewed for 16 research journals and served as editor for 3. He has given open lectures and seminars at 32 institutions and over 100 presentations at professional conferences across 4 continents. He was a Fulbright Researcher in Japan (2018) and a board member for the College Music Society, Florida Music Education Association, and International Society for Music Education.

Martha Gonzalez is a Chicana artivista (artist/activist) musician, feminist music theorist, and Associate Professor in the Intercollegiate Department of Chicana/o Latina/o Studies at Scripps/Claremont College. Born and raised in Boyle Heights Gonzalez is a Fulbright, Ford, Woodrow Wilson, and McArthur Fellow. Her academic interests have been fueled by her own musicianship as a singer/songwriter and percussionist for Grammy Award winning band Quetzal. Gonzalez's first manuscript, *Chican@ Artivistas: Music, Community, and Transborder Tactics in East Los Angeles*, was published by the University of Texas Press in 2020.

Andrew Goodrich is Assistant Professor of Music Education at Boston University, Boston, MA. Research interests include peer mentoring, community music, jazz education, and preservice music teacher preparation. Goodrich has published research in the leading music education journals including the *Journal of Research in Music Education*, *Music Education Research*, the *International Journal of Music Education*, the *Journal of*

Music Teacher Education, the *Bulletin of the Council for Research in Music Education*, and *Update: Applications of Research in Music Education*. Recent chapter publications appear in *Teaching School Jazz: Perspectives, Principles, and Strategies* (2019), *The Oxford Handbook of Preservice Music Teacher Education* (2019), and co-authored with Keith Kelly in *Listening to Voices Seldom Heard: Perspectives and Narratives in Music Education* (2020). He is author of the monograph *Peer Mentoring in Music Education: Developing Effective Student Leadership* (2023).

Emily Good-Perkins has presented, performed and taught in the United States, Cuba, Austria, Italy, Sweden, Azerbaijan, England, China, UAE, Oman, Jordan, Saudi Arabia, Malaysia, and Indonesia. She has published in *PMER* and *IJME* and contributed to the book *Humane Music Education for the Common Good*. Additionally, her book *Culturally Sustaining Pedagogies in Music Education: Expanding Culturally Responsive Teaching to Sustain Diverse Musical Cultures and Identities* was published in September 2021. Emily received her doctor of education and master of education degrees in Music Education from Columbia University. She also received master of music and bachelor of music degrees in Voice Performance from the University of Arizona and Temple University. Currently she is enjoying her work as dissertation supervisor for Boston University and as the new owner of The Music Playhouse in Carmel, Indiana. She continues her social justice in music education work with her nonprofit organization, Voicing Futures.

Elise Hackl-Blumstein (she/her) is a neurodivergent-accessible music teacher and accessibility coach in the northwest suburbs of Chicago, working with neurodiverse individuals from preschool through adulthood. Elise is a proud alum of Illinois State University (BS in Music and Special Education '14), Concordia University Chicago (MA '17, MMEd with Principal Certification '22), and Wichita State University (MME '19). Elise's main focus in her research is training and preparation for accessible classrooms. In 2018, Elise was nominated for the Illinois State Board of Education "Those Who Excel" Teacher of the Year program. Elise's contributions can be found in music journals, podcasts, texts, and social media around the world. Elise currently serves as the director of the International Championships of High School (ICHSA) and judge of Collegiate a Cappella. In order to help make music more accessible for all, Elise has an accessible music store designed with financial and neuro/physical diversity in mind (shorturl.at/rzEP4) and often shares lessons and activities on her teacher Instagram page @accessiblemusicroom.

Clare Hall, PhD, is Lecturer in Performing Arts, Monash University, Australia. Her research, educational, and artistic practice coalesces around music, sound, and performance to promote creative arts engagements across the lifespan. Her interdisciplinary scholarship bridges boundaries between the arts, education, and sociology, with her key contribution to date in music and masculinity. Her work is driven by issues of social justice in music teaching and learning, which underpins her contribution to the ARC funded project "Diversifying Australian Music: Gender Equity in Jazz and Improvisation" and her co-leadership of the Decolonising and Indigenising Music

Education Special Interest Group for ISME. She is the sole author of *Masculinity, Class and Music Education* (2018) and co-editor of *Sociological Thinking in Music Education* (2021), and *Decolonising and Indigenising Music Education* (2022).

Karin S. Hendricks is Associate Professor of Music and Chair of Music Education at Boston University. As a university professor and former K-12 orchestra teacher, she has received numerous teaching awards at local, state, and national levels. In 2023 she was awarded Boston University's Metcalf Cup and Prize, the university's highest faculty honor. Karin is a frequent orchestra clinician, adjudicator, and workshop presenter and is president-elect of the American String Teachers Association (ASTA). She serves on the editorial committees for the *Journal of Research in Music Education* and the *Bulletin of the Council for Research in Music Education*. She has published dozens of book chapters and over 50 journal articles related to student motivation and engagement. She was the 2018 recipient of the ASTA "Emerging Researcher" Award. Karin is committed to presenting research to music teachers in meaningful and approachable ways. She has published six books, including *Compassionate Music Teaching*.

Juliet Hess is Associate Professor of Music Education at Michigan State University, having previously taught elementary and middle school music in Toronto. Her book *Music Education for Social Change: Constructing an Activist Music Education* explores the intersection of activism, critical pedagogy, and music education. Her second book, *Trauma and Resilience in Music Education: Haunted Melodies*, is an edited volume co-edited with Deborah Bradley. The volume acknowledges the ubiquity of trauma in our society and its long-term deleterious effects while examining the singular ways music can serve as a support for those who struggle. Juliet received her PhD in Sociology of Education from the Ontario Institute for Studies in Education at the University of Toronto. Her research interests include antioppression education, trauma-informed pedagogy, activism in music and music education, music education for social justice, disability and Mad studies, and the question of ethics in world music study.

Shannan Hibbard is Assistant Professor of Vocal Music Education at Wayne State University. She teaches undergraduate music education courses and coordinates student teaching experiences in vocal and general music. Shannan's research centers on relationships in the music classroom with focus on trauma awareness, social justice ally development, creativity, and spirituality. She is published in a number of journals and has contributed chapters in *Trauma and Resilience in Music Education*, *Narratives and Reflections in Music Education*, *The Oxford Handbook of Preservice Music Teacher Education*, and *Giving Voice to Democracy in Music Education*. She received her undergraduate, masters, and PhD in music education from the University of Michigan and serves as president-elect of the Michigan Music Education Association. A student of abolition, Shannan advocates for music education's potential to foster connection, joy, justice, freedom, and expression.

Kari Holdhus is Professor of Music Education at the Western Norway University of Applied Sciences. Her research and teaching interests are relational pedagogy, dialogic musical encounters, creative teaching and learning, and pedagogical improvisation. Holdhus explicitly studies communication processes between musicians, teachers, and pupils in visiting music practices and musical partnerships. In the years 2017–2021 Kari was project leader of an innovation project on Norwegian professional visiting concerts, called School and Concert—From Transmission to Dialogue. The project aimed at developing alternative forms of music visits in schools by emphasizing dialogic encounters between musicians, teachers and pupils, allowing pupils' agency and creativity. Holdhus was engaged as a researcher in "Music teacher education for the Future" (FUTURED 2019–2022), exploring potential development and change in Norwegian general teacher education in music. She chaired the Nordic Network for Music Education Research (NNRME) in the years 2019–2023.

Ryan M. Hourigan is Professor of Music Education at Ball State University. Dr. Hourigan holds degrees from Eastern Illinois University (BM), Michigan State University (MM Wind Conducting), and the University of Michigan (PhD). Hourigan is the co-author (with Alice Hammel) of *Teaching Music to Students with Special Needs: A Label-free Approach*, currently in its second edition. This is a comprehensive text written by practicing music educators, music teacher educators, and researchers in the field. Hourigan and Hammel's second book, *Teaching Music to Students with Autism*, is also in its second edition. In 2009, Hourigan cofounded the Prism Project. This program provides an opportunity for Ball State students to gain skills in the area of teaching students with special needs. This program has expanded to other cities around the United States since 2014. Dr. Hourigan is also on the National Roster and National Speakers Bureau with the John F. Kennedy Center in Washington DC.

Jennifer C. Hutton, PhD, is a Lecturer in Choral Music Education at the Peck School of the Arts at University of Wisconsin-Milwaukee. She previously served as Music Department Chair and Director of Choirs at Cheltenham High School. Her research interests include connection during group singing, culturally responsive vocal pedagogy, and teacher–student relationships in music classrooms. Her writing may be found in the *Journal of Music Teacher Education*, *ChorTeach*, and the *Pennsylvania Music Educators Association News*, and she has shared her work at international, national, and state conferences. She has taught PreK-12 students in general and choral music in varied public school, independent school, and community settings. She holds degrees in Psychology, Women's and Gender Studies, Music Education, and Choral Conducting, and she is a certified Estill Master Trainer through Estill Voice International.

Estelle R. Jorgensen is Professor Emerita of Music (Music Education) at Indiana University Jacobs School of Music, United States. Contributing faculty at Walden University, United States, and editor of the *Philosophy of Music Education Review*. The founding co-chair of the International Society for the Philosophy of Music Education, she has edited two essay collections *Philosopher-Teacher-Musician: Contemporary Perspectives on Music Education*, and (with Iris Yob) *Humane Music Education for the Common Good*, and authored *In Search of Music Education, Transforming Music*

Education, The Art of Teaching Music, Pictures of Music Education, Values and Music Education, and numerous articles in music educational journals and book chapters internationally. She is the recipient of two honorary doctoral degrees in music and the 2020 Senior Researcher Award by the National Association for Music Education in the United States.

Panagiotis (Panos) A. Kanellopoulos is Professor of Music Education at the University of Thessaly, Greece. Active as a researcher and a music maker, Panos is particularly interested in politicophilosophical, theoretical, and field-based explorations of creative music making, its educative uses, misuses, and potentialities. His work has been published in major international journals, such as *Philosophy of Music Education Review, Action, Criticism, and Theory for Music Education, British Journal of Music Education, Educational Philosophy and Theory, Research Studies in Music Education, European Journal of Philosophy in Arts Education*, and edited volumes. Recently he co-edited *The Routledge Handbook to Sociology of Music Education* (2021), together with Ruth Wright, Patrick Schmidt, and Geir Johansen.

Kristi N. King currently teaches music at Exuma Christian Academy in Exuma, Bahamas. Prior to that appointment she taught music at Imagine School North Manatee in Palmetto, Florida, United States. Kristi has completed doctoral coursework in music education at the University of Illinois at Urbana-Champaign, and holds a master's degree from the University of Reading in the United Kingdom, and an undergraduate degree from Fisk University in the United States.

Jessandra Kono is a cellist and music educator. She obtained her bachelor's degrees in Cello Performance and Educational Sciences from the University of California, Irvine. Since then, she obtained her master's of Music Education and teaching credential from Boston University, where she worked as a research assistant with Dr. Karin Hendricks and was the collegiate representative for the Massachusetts chapter of the American String Teachers Association. In the interim before her teaching position, Jessandra worked on a podcast exploring the effects of the COVID-19 crisis in music classrooms. She also worked as a writing contributor for College Prep for Musicians Careers in Music, a multiplatform resource for young musicians looking to use their musical skills in their careers. Currently, she lives in California, where she is a general music teacher at two Chula Vista Elementary Schools and a string teaching artist with the San Diego Youth Symphony.

Allen R. Legutki is Associate Professor of Music Education at Benedictine University, where he advises the music education degree program, teaches music education methods courses, and directs the wind ensemble, concert band, and athletic bands. Dr. Legutki's research interests include motivation, performer identity, equity and access in music education, and school governance. He serves as state research chair for the Illinois Music Education Association, and is an active speaker, panelist, and guest instructor at national and international conferences and college programs. Dr. Legutki is also a frequent guest conductor, adjudicator, and clinician for school music programs, and is an active performer and conductor in community ensembles in the Chicago area. He was Benedictine University's 2016 recipient of the Distinguished Faculty Award for Service, and the 2021 recipient of the Distinguished Faculty Award for Teaching.

Lisa J. Lehmberg is Professor and Coordinator of Music Education at the University of Massachusetts Amherst. She holds a PhD in music education and bachelor's and master's degrees in piano performance. Her recent research on older adult music participation and quality of life is published in the co-authored books *Music, Senior Centers, and Quality of Life* (2023), *Music for Life: Music Participation and Quality of Life of Senior Citizens* (2016, Chinese translation published in 2021), and the co-edited book *Meanings of Music Participation: Scenarios from the United States* (2023). Lisa also has extensive experience as a PreK-12 school music practitioner and is certified in the Orff Schulwerk approach. She serves on the International Society for Music Education (ISME) Publications Committee and the editorial boards of the *International Journal of Music Education* and the *Journal of the Association for Technology in Music Instruction*.

Amy Lewis is the daughter of Jayne McShann Lewis and Bennie Lewis and is the granddaughter of Frances McShann Shelton and jazz pianist Jay McShann. Dr. Lewis is currently Assistant Professor and former Anna Julia Cooper Fellow at the University of Wisconsin–Madison, where her research is focused on systemic oppression, equity, and racism in music education. As a public music teacher, she taught K-1; 6-8 general music, beginning band, middle school choir, and jazz band in the Chicagoland suburbs. She received the 2022 Compass Visionary Award, the 2019 Black Faculty, Staff, and Administrators Association Emerging Leader Award and was also named the 2015 Illinois Education Association Teacher of the Year. She earned her BME degree from DePaul University, MA from Concordia University, and PhD from Michigan State University. Her work is published in *The Bulletin for the Council of Research in Music Education*; *Action, Criticism, and Theory in Music Education*; and *Michigan Music Educator Journal*, and she is on the editorial board of the *Research and Issues in Music Education Journal*.

Guadalupe López-Íñiguez has a Doctorate in Psychology from the Autonomous University of Madrid and is a cellist specializing in historical performance practice. She is Associate Professor of Music Education at the Sibelius Academy of the University of the Arts Helsinki, Finland, and Honorary Senior Fellow at Melbourne Conservatorium of Music, Australia. Her research includes the study of psychological processes inherent in music learning and teaching, the optimization of interpretation, lifelong learning and employability, musical identities and learner identities, giftedness and talent, and the theories of emotion. Guadalupe is co-editor-in-chief of ISME's *Revista Internacional de Educación Musical*, and co-chair for the International Society for Music Education (ISME) Commision for the Education of the Professional Musician (CEPROM). Guadalupe has published over 50 scholarly publications in international journals and books and is the co-editor of *Learning and Teaching in the Music Studio: A*

Student-Centred Approach (2022). She regularly gives concerts as a soloist and has recorded the complete works of Gabrielli, Scarlatti, and Mendelssohn for cello.

Kimberly A. McCord is Professor Emerita of Music Education at Illinois State University and Adjunct Professor of Music Education at New York University. Her books include *Teaching the Postsecondary Music Student with Disabilities, Exceptional Pedagogy for Children with Exceptionalities: International Perspectives, Accessing Music: Using UDL to Enhance Student Learning in the General Music Classroom, Chop Monster, Jr.,* and *Together We Can Improvise*. She is the past chair of the ISME Commission on Music in Special Education, Music Therapy and Music Medicine and the founder and past chair of the National Association for Music Education Special Research Interest Group on Children with Exceptionalities. She is the founder and director of Just Accessible Music (JAM), an equity-based music school in Connecticut.

Justin McManus is Director of Athletic Bands and Assistant Professor of Music at the University of Connecticut, where he directs the marching band and pep bands, and conducts other ensembles in the music department. Previously, he served as Assistant Director of University Bands at the University of Notre Dame. A strong advocate for diversity, equity, and inclusion in band programs, Dr. McManus completed a dissertation that centered the experiences of transgender and gender-expansive collegiate marching band members. Dr. McManus has served as a guest clinician, presenter, and conductor in the United States and abroad. He holds a DMA in music education from Boston University, and MM, BA, and BS degrees from the University of Connecticut.

Gary E. McPherson studied Music Education at the Sydney Conservatorium of Music, before completing a master of music education at Indiana University, a Doctorate of Philosophy at the University of Sydney and a Licentiate and Fellowship in trumpet performance through Trinity College, London. In 2021, he was the recipient of an Honorary Doctorate—*Artium Doctorem Honoris Causa*—from Lund University Sweden. Gary is the Ormond Professor of Music at the Melbourne Conservatorium of Music and has served as president of the Australian and International societies for music education. His most important research examines the acquisition and development of musical competence, and motivation to engage and participate in music from novice to expert levels. With a particular interest in the acquisition of visual, aural, and creative performance skills, he has attempted to understand more precisely how music students become sufficiently motivated and self-regulated to achieve at the highest level.

Elizabeth Mitchell holds a Master of Music Therapy from Wilfrid Laurier University in Waterloo, Ontario, and a PhD in Music Education from Western University in London, Ontario. A registered psychotherapist and certified music therapist, Liz has extensive experience working in mental health treatment settings with children, adolescents, and adults. In 2020, Liz was appointed Assistant Professor at Wilfrid Laurier University, where she currently coordinates the Bachelor of Music Therapy program. Since 2019, Liz has served as the Ethics Chair for the Canadian Association of Music Therapists. Outside of music therapy, Liz holds an ARCT (Associate of the Royal Conservatory of

Toronto) in piano performance. To fill up her musical soul, she sings professionally with the Canadian Chamber Choir.

Janelize Morelli holds a PhD in Music Education from NYU Steinhardt School of Culture, Education, and Human Development. Janelize's research interests include the ethics of community music practices in South Africa, relational ethics, and arts-based inquiry. She is currently a senior lecturer in Community Music at the School of Music, North-West University in South Africa. Janelize is a member of the Musical Arts in Southern Africa: Resources and Applications research entity. Through community music workshops and prolonged programs, Janelize focuses on building reciprocal relationships between the university and various community partners. She has published in journals such as *The International Journal of Community Music* and *Psychology of Music*. She is also the author of various book chapters and co-editor of *Ritualised Belonging: Musicing and Spirituality in the South African Context*.

Graça Mota, pianist, Master in Music Education, Boston University, United States; PhD in Psychology of Music, University of Keel, United Kingdom, has been for more than 30 years engaged in music teacher's education at the Music Department of the School of Education in the Polytechnic of Porto in Portugal. Currently, she is a senior researcher of the CIPEM (Research Centre in Psychology of Music and Music Education) branch of INET-md (Institute of Ethnomusicology—studies in music and dance) at the Polytechnic of Porto. Her research is concerned with musical practice and social inclusion, music in the community, and women in philharmonic bands. This research has been published in Portugal, Spain, Brazil, the United States, the United Kingdom, and Latvia. She was chair of the ISME Sistema Special Interest Group 2014–2016. She is a Board member and cofounder of the international research platform SIMM (Social Impact of Making Music, www.simm-platform.eu).

Susan A. O'Neill is Professor and Head of Learning and Leadership at the Institute of Education in the Faculty of Education and Society, University College London. Previously, she was Dean of Education at Simon Fraser University in Vancouver, Canada, President of the International Society for Music Education (ISME), and a member of the Presidential Council of the World Alliance for Arts Education (WAAE). Her interdisciplinary background includes degrees in music performance (BMus, MA), education (MA), and psychology (PhD). For 30 years, she has taught at universities in Canada, Hong Kong, Portugal, the United Kingdom, and the United States, and held visiting fellowships at the University of Michigan (2001–2003), University of Melbourne (2012), and Trinity College Dublin (2015). Her current research includes studies of young people's music engagement and music learning ecologies, intercultural communication and creative practice, and intergenerational multimodal curricula. An intergenerational arts program she developed received a provincial award for Excellence in Public Education.

Stephen A. Paparo is Associate Professor of Music Education at the University of Massachusetts Amherst and conductor of the University Chorale. He holds degrees from Michigan State University, Syracuse University, and Ithaca College, and is a Guild Certified Practitioner of the Feldenkrais Method® of somatic education. He regularly presents at international, national, and state conferences and is active as guest conductor for honor and festival choirs at all levels. He is a member of the editorial board for the *International Journal of Research in Choral Singing*. His research interests include the application of the Feldenkrais Method in choral music education, non-traditional choral ensembles, and LGBTQ studies in music education. He is published in a number of leading journals and has contributed chapters in the *Oxford Handbook of Music Performance*; *Meanings of Music Participation: Scenarios from the United States*; *Somatic Voice: From Practice to Praxis*; and *Musicianship: Composing in Choir*. His compositions for beginning choirs are published by Alfred Music.

Elizabeth Cassidy Parker is Associate Professor of Music Education at the Boyer College of Music and Dance at Temple University. Prior to Temple University, Parker taught at the Schwob School of Music at Columbus State University and held PreK-12 school positions in New York, Nebraska, and Georgia. Parker is also co-artistic director of the Commonwealth Youthchoirs, a community choral program with 600 singers located in the greater Philadelphia area. Her research interests include the social, vocal, and philosophical development of adolescent musicians and preservice music educator identity. Parker sits on three editorial boards including the *Journal of Research in Music Education*, the *Journal of Music Teacher Education*, and the *International Journal of Research in Choral Singing*. In addition to peer-reviewed journal and chapter publications, Parker is the author of *Adolescents on Music*.

Bryan Powell is Assistant Professor of Music Education and Music Technology, and Coordinator for the Recording Arts and Production degree at Montclair State University. Bryan is also the Interim Senior Director of Programs for Music Will (formerly known as Little Kids Rock), and former Director of Programs for Amp Up NYC. Bryan is the founding co-editor of the *Journal of Popular Music Education*, co-author of *Popular Music Pedagogies: A Practical Guide for Music Teachers*, series co-editor for *Contemporary Music Making and Learning*, and editor of *The Modern Band Handbook*. He serves as the Executive Director of the Association for Popular Music Education and is a past chair for the NAfME Popular Music Education Special Research Interest Group.

Erin Price, DMA, is an Adjunct Professor of Music Education (Department of Music Education and Therapy) at West Chester University of Pennsylvania. Additionally, Dr. Price is a special education music teacher and researcher in the Greater Harrisburg area. Prior to teaching general music and elementary special education music for a Pennsylvania public cyber charter school, Dr. Price worked in multiple Pennsylvania Approved Private Schools for students with emotional disturbance, where she served students aged 5–21 with advanced inpatient and outpatient behavioral support needs. Dr. Price holds a BM in Music Education from West Chester University of Pennsylvania and MM and DMA degrees in Music Education from Boston University. An advocate for equity and increased access points in music education, she frequently contributes journal articles and presents research on trauma-informed music pedagogy and the intersections of trauma and emotional/behavioral disorders.

Jared R. Rawlings, PhD, was appointed tenured Professor of Music and Director of the School of Music at the University of Missouri on July 1, 2023. Previously, Rawlings served as Associate Dean for Faculty & Academic Affairs at the University of Utah College of Fine Arts as well as holding administrative appointments as the Associate Director of the School of Music, Music Education Area Head and Director of Undergraduate Studies. Rawlings consistently works with scholars, master pedagogues, and performing artists of varied disciplines. His research, which appears in leading research journals and texts, focuses on issues related to arts-in-health and promoting an inclusive learning environment within school music programs. In particular, he explores the application of behavioral and ecological approaches to preventing youth violence within arts education classrooms and how to translate these empirical findings to arts teachers. School–university partnerships are integral to his creative work.

Tiri Bergesen Schei is Professor in Music Education and leader of the strategic research program "Arts, Creativity and Cultural Practices" at Western Norway University of Applied Sciences (HVL). Schei is an experienced music teacher, singer, and academic supervisor. As a researcher she has explored emotional, relational, and cultural aspects of vocal performance, by elucidating the perceived norms that govern what it means to be "a real professional singer," and how "voice shame" may lead to self-censorship, conformity, and stage fright. Her recent research targets the functions of art in early childhood education. Schei is also engaged in facilitating research education for PhD students. She was a co-founder of the Grieg Research School in Interdisciplinary Music Studies (GRS) in 2010. She has been affiliated with Harvard University (2004–2005) as a visiting fellow and McGill University (2016–2017) as a visiting scholar.

Patrick Schmidt is Professor of Music and Music Education at Teachers College, Columbia University. Recent publications can be found in various journals focused on education, music, and policy. Schmidt led consulting and evaluative projects for the National Young Arts Foundation and the New World Symphony. He co-edited the *Oxford Handbook of Music Education and Social Justice* (2015), a two-volume book on *Leadership in Higher Music Education* (2020), and the 2021 *Routledge Handbook for the Sociology of Music Education*. His books *Policy and the Political Life of Music Education* and *Policy as Practice: A Guide for Music Educators* were released by Oxford University Press in 2017 and 2020, respectively.

Daniel J. Shevock is a Music Education Philosopher whose scholarship blends creativity, ecology, and critique. He is the author of the monograph *Eco-Literate Music Pedagogy* (2017), and a blog at eco-literate.com, where he wrestles with ideas such as sustainability, place, culture, race, gender, and class. Having grown up in rural Central Pennsylvania, he currently serves as a steering committee member for the MayDay Group, and is a music teacher at Central Mountain Middle School in Mill Hall, Pennsylvania.

Kevin Shorner-Johnson is Professor of Music Education and the Dean of the School of Arts and Humanities at Elizabethtown College. His scholarship focuses on the intersection of peacebuilding and music education. As a teacher and scholar, he has applied his interests in ethics, spirituality, philosophy, ethnomusicology, and psychology to the study of artistic peacebuilding. His work has been published in the *Philosophy of Music Education Review*, *Music Educators Journal*, *Journal of Medical Humanities*, *International Journal of Music Education*, and *Advances in Music Education Research*. In 2018, Dr. Shorner-Johnson was named a "Peacemaker in our Midst" by the World Affairs Council of Harrisburg. His on-the-ground peacebuilding scholarship focuses on curating the Music & Peacebuilding podcast to build sonic explorations of mutuality, agency, and imagination.

Marissa Silverman is Professor at the John J. Cali School of Music, Montclair State University, New Jersey. A Fulbright Scholar, she is author of *Gregory Haimovsky: A Pianist's Odyssey to Freedom* (2018) and co-author of *Music Lesson Plans for Social Justice: A Contemporary Approach for Secondary School Teachers* (2022) as well as the 2nd edition of *Music Matters: A Philosophy of Music Education* (2015). She is co-editor of *Eudaimonia: Perspectives for Music Teaching and Learning* (2020), *The Oxford Handbook of Philosophical and Qualitative Assessment in Music Education* (2019), *Artistic Citizenship: Artistry, Social Responsibility, and Ethical Praxis* (2016), and *Community Music Today* (2013).

Gareth Dylan Smith is Assistant Professor of Music, Music Education, at Boston University. His research interests include drum kit studies, popular music education, sociology of music education, and punk pedagogies. His first love is to play drums. Recent music releases include progressive smooth jazz with The New Titans, the *Sun Sessions* EP with Stephen Wheel, and the *Ignorant Populists* EP with Build a Fort. Gareth is working on an album of duets titled *Permission Granted*, a concept album with Stephen Wheel called *Tinker, Tailor, Soldier, Rock*, and a new wave album with Black Light Bastards. Gareth's recent scholarly publications include *Eudaimonia: Perspectives for Music Learning* (with Marissa Silverman) and a monograph, *Magical Nexus: A Philosophy of Playing Drum Kit*. Gareth is a founding co-editor of the *Journal of Popular Music Education*. He is on the steering committee of the International Society for the Sociology of Music Education.

Tawnya D. Smith is Assistant Professor of Music Education at Boston University. She teaches graduate courses in research, curriculum, arts integration, and undergraduate courses in healthy classroom dynamics, and arts and the environment. She has published in *Action, Criticism and Theory for Music Education*, *Frontiers in Education*, *Gender and Education*, *International Journal of Education and the Arts*, *International Journal of Music Education*, *Journal of Applied Arts and Health*, *Journal of Music Teacher Education*, *Journal of Popular Music Education*, *Music Educators Journal*, and *String Research Journal*. Her book chapters appear in *The Oxford Handbook of Musical Performance*; *Trauma and Music Education*; *Art as Research, Key Issues in Arts Education*; *Queering*

Freedom: Music, Identity, and Spirituality; and *Authentic Connection: Music, Wellbeing, and Spirituality*. Tawnya is co-author of the book *Performance Anxiety Strategies* and co-editor of *Narratives and Reflections in Music Education: Listening to Voices Seldom Heard*. Her research focus includes arts integration, trauma and mental health, and ecojustice education. She currently serves as Senior Editor of the *International Journal of Education and the Arts*.

Rebecca D. Swanson completed a Bachelor of Arts in Music Education and a Bachelor of Music in Organ Performance with an Honors in Education in May 2022 at the University of Iowa. She currently teaches fifth–eighth grade general music and seventh and eighth grade choir at West Liberty Middle School in West Liberty, Iowa. In her undergraduate program, Swanson was a research fellow and studied peacemaking circles, prison abolition, self-compassion, and participated in creative scholarship in the Oakdale Prison with the songwriting workshop, group piano classes, and leadership with the Oakdale Choir. She has presented at an Undergraduate Research Festival and "Remember: Be Love: Choral Singing, Songwriting, Peacebuilding, and Group Piano in Prison" online for students from eight different countries in the National Institute of Political Science University in Paris, France. She served as the general music representative for the University of Iowa Collegiate Chapter of the National Association for Music Education.

Bridget Sweet is Associate Professor of Music Education at the University of Illinois in Urbana-Champaign, where she teaches choral methods and literature, middle-level music education pedagogy, graduate research, and a course focused on the development of healthy practices for all musicians. Dr. Sweet has worked extensively with adolescent singers as a teacher, clinician, and conductor. She wrote the books *Growing Musicians: Teaching Music in Middle School and Beyond* (2016) and *Thinking Outside the Voice Box: Adolescent Voice Change in Music Education* (2019). Her research interests include middle-level choral music education, female and male adolescent voice change, empowering music educators, health and wellness, and intersections of diversity and the music classroom. She is earning licensure to be a Body Mapping Instructor through the Association for Body Mapping Education.

Brent C. Talbot has been a leading voice for change in the field of music education. A prolific author and frequent presenter, Talbot's work examines power, discourse, and issues of justice in varied settings for music learning around the globe. He is the editor of *Marginalized Voices in Music Education*; the curator of an indigenous-centering resource, *Gending Rare: Children's Songs and Games from Bali*; and co-author of *Education, Music, and the Lives of Undergraduates: Collegiate A Cappella and the Pursuit of Happiness*. Talbot is Professor and Head of the Department of Music at the University of Illinois Chicago. For more information, visit www.brentctalbot.com.

Latasha Thomas-Durrell is Assistant Professor and the Coordinator of Music Education at the University of Dayton, where she teaches music education courses and serves as supervisor for music education student teachers. Her research interests center around culturally responsive pedagogy and understanding the intersections of identity and their impact on music education, with specific focus on race, faith, socioeconomic status, and sexuality. Her work is published in *Trauma and Resilience in Music Education* and *Music Education Research*. Dr. Thomas-Durrell holds a music performance degree from the University of Central Arkansas and music education degrees from Michigan State University, the University of North Carolina at Greensboro, and the University of Tennessee at Martin. Her public school teaching experience includes middle and high school band positions, elementary general music, and choir. She is an avid traveler, a foodie, a social butterfly, and is working toward becoming trilingual.

Alice A. Tsui 徐晓兰 (pronounced TSOY) is an Asian American/Chinese American pianist, Grammy Finalist music educator, scholar, activist, dog mom, and lifelong Brooklyn, New Yorker. Alice is the founding music educator and arts coordinator at PS 532 New Bridges Elementary, an arts-integrated public elementary school in Crown Heights, Brooklyn. She graduated from New York University with a bachelor of music in Piano Performance and a master of arts in Music Education, and is currently a doctoral candidate (ABD) in music education at Boston University. As a product of the NYC public school system, Alice is passionate about decolonizing, ABAR (anti-bias, anti-racist), abolitionist public music education, and empowering the individual and collective voices of youth through music as expression. Learn more about Alice and her work at https://www.alicetsui.com and on Instagram @musicwithmissalice.

Martin (pronounced mar-TEEN) **Urbach**, drummer/percussionist, is a Latine immigrant, educator, activist, and youth organizer. His work in the classroom is based on facilitating brave spaces for young folks to fall in love with music and to promote social justice through music making in their community. He holds a BA in jazz performance from the University of New Orleans, a MA in jazz arts from the Manhattan School of Music, and an Advanced Certificate in Music Education from Brooklyn College. He is currently a Doctoral candidate in Urban Education at the CUNY Graduate Center. Currently, he serves as music educator and Restorative Justice Dean of Students at Harvest Collegiate High School in New York City. In addition, Martin is currently a "Vocal Justice Fellow" as well as an "Academy For Teachers" fellow. Martin is a thrice nominated Grammy Music Educators Award and he contributes to Decolonizing The Music Room as well as PBS, and NPR as education consultant on issues of Restorative Justice, Social Justice activism, and Critical pedagogy.

Kính T. Vũ is Assistant Professor of Music at Boston University, where he teaches music education courses in general music methods, instrumental music, history, and philosophy. Focusing his teaching model on global citizenship and intercultural literacy, Kính's pedagogy is community-based, with partnerships emerging in Boston and Việt Nam. His newest research is centered on transnational and transracial adoption issues in which Asian American music educators and preservice teachers navigate the conundrum of being othered in both their birth country and in the United States.

Kính's co-edited book with André de Quadros, *My Body Was Left on the Street: Music Education and Displacement*, was published in 2020.

Brandi Waller-Pace is an artist, educator, and scholar/activist. She is Founder and Executive Director of the nonprofit Decolonizing the Music Room, and Founder and Organizer of the Fort Worth African American Roots Music Festival and the Black, Brown, Indigenous, and Asian Music Education Symposium. Brandi holds a BM and MM in Jazz Studies from Howard University and is pursuing a PhD in Music Education at the University of North Texas. An 11-year veteran music educator, she has written district elementary music curriculum and from 2019 and 2020 served on the Texas African American Studies Course Curriculum Advisory Team, which helped formulate curriculum standards for the first state-approved African American History course. Her work focuses on topics including decolonizing and antiracist philosophies, Black feminist thought, U.S. roots music, Afrofuturism, and Sankofa. Brandi's writing can be found in the *The Orff Echo*, *The Illinois Music Educator Journal*, *The Music Educators Journal*, and on the "Decolonizing the Music Room" website.

Heidi Westerlund is Professor at the Sibelius Academy, University of the Arts Helsinki, Finland, where she is responsible for music education doctoral studies. She is also Adjunct Professor of Research at Monash University, Sir Zelman Cowen School of Music and Performance, Faculty of Arts, Australia. She has published widely in international journals and books and she is the co-editor of *Collaborative Learning in Higher Music Education* (2013/2016); *Music, Education, and Religion: Intersections and Entanglements* (2019); *Visions for Intercultural Music Teacher Education* (2020); *Politics of Diversity in Music Education* (2021); and *Expanding Professionalism in Music and Higher Music Education* (2021). Her research interests include higher arts education and professionalism in music, music teacher education, collaborative learning, cultural diversity, and democracy in music education. She is currently leading the Music Education, Professionalism, and Eco-Politics (2021–2025) project, funded by the Academy of Finland.

FOREWORD TO SECTION 1

PHILOSOPHICAL PERSPECTIVES ON CARE AND MUSIC EDUCATION

Care-ing in the Music Pedagogical Moment: Navigating Challenges

PANAGIOTIS A. KANELLOPOULOS

How could music education navigate the challenges posed by market-informed misappropriations of "learner-centered" education, cultivating an approach to practice that is based on authenticity, criticality, social responsibility, creativity and compassion? Adopting distinct philosophical perspectives, the chapters in Section 1 of *The Oxford Handbook of Care in Music Education* address several dimensions that underpin this general theme, flooding the reader with questions that touch the core of music education, and which, like the unsettling melodies of my beloved Manos Hadjidakis (1988), "may become yours and be brought home, so that your sleep is cut short and your peace of mind is lost forever" (p. 33). Even when the chapters seem to arrive at possible answers as a result of a careful argumentative line, these, in the end, function only as pathways for new problematizations, paving the way for new questions. This is an example of how, away from the superficial "music-benefits-this-or-that" modes of discourse that overwhelm music education advocacy approaches, careful scholarly work might offer a critical outlook that directly engages with difficult issues of exclusion, violence, silence, and injustice. Paraphrasing Stuart Hall, one could say that music education scholarly thought is critical "or it is nothing" (as cited in Gökarıksel, 2022, p. 188).

At the same time, the chapters in this section cultivate a stance of *care* toward the subject of their critical engagement. Which leads us to ask: Can one "care" for something "inanimate?" Can one care for a form of human practice, like music? For an idea(l), like equality, justice? Or should care be retained for speaking about human relationships only? If the answer to this last question is "yes," are we not throwing Winnicott and his "transitional object" (Litt, 1986) out of the window, and on a different level, are we not continuing to regard "Man" (*sic*) as the center of the world, thus foreclosing the possibility of "an appreciation of nonhuman agents . . . as intelligent life forms with the ability to communicate," that, as a result "might help humans to conceive of alternative modes of being and to cease consigning non-humans to the status of mere resources?" (Oksanen, 2019, p. 79).

Care seems to be an imperative, a much-cherished quality of human and therefore of educational relationships, but also of the ways in which human beings relate to the world as part of this world. In everyday linguistic contexts, care moves between notions of protection (one takes care *of* someone else) and affective and meaning investment (one cares *about* or *for* some*one* or some*thing*). Issues of power, domination, equality and inequality, issues related to the complex entanglement between the politics of care and the ethics of vulnerability are integral in any critical examination of issues of care (see Browne et al., 2021). Care . . . oh yes. But care for what? Care for whom? In whose interest? And how do each of these three questions come into the other? Does care for or about music, or better, for specific musical practices, necessarily induce caring for those that participate in the study of this musical practice? If the answer is "not necessarily," what is it that would make this possible? How could we initiate a nuanced discussion about how to avoid becoming musical caretakers that guard quality by performing (mis)educative acts on the basis of "saving" the music? From another angle, if we think of music education more as culture-*making*, showing deep care about developing or students' voice, how could we avoid the trap of self-eulogizing our doings, and how could we seriously grapple with the question of "what" this music, this piece, this musical idea, this technical issue, is "asking of me?" (Biesta, 2018, p. 154).

I am watching violinist Andrew Manze teaching a masterclass (USC Thornton School of Music, 2015): The tender kindness with which he makes comments to the student's performance is striking; as is his insistence that his opinions are just that: personal opinions. On a closer look though, and as one hears how the tone of his voice becomes suddenly sharp when he justifies his views by emphasizing the definiteness of the archival evidence on which they are grounded, one can see how his care for what he sees as much cherished musical values stands above everything else. One could say that he cares for the aesthetic imperatives of classical virtuoso performance more than anything else. However, although he does not seem "to care" for the individual student and her/his personality as such, can one so easily say that his approach to music teaching does not show "a sense of care" for the student and her education?

Phil, an 11-year-old boy, plays an improvisation duet with his teacher; on mandolins. The playing is adventurous, at times quite messy, but betrays sense of deep commitment. Discussing the process afterward, Phil says: "When I was seeing that Mr. Panagiotis was stuck, what would I do? Would I leave him on his own? No, I would 'cover' for him" (as cited in Kanellopoulos, 2011, p. 105). Phil feels responsible for the unfolding of the music, exercising agency on the basis of equality, but somehow this responsibility to the musical process induces a mode of musical thinking that creates a distinctive relationship with his coplayer, who, most importantly, is his teacher. It seems to me that here we begin to glimpse a quite distinctive sense of care, that Karin Hendricks (2018), inspired by Buber, refers to as "care with": an experience of caring with the other induces compassion, a notion that, for Hendricks, points toward a "shared human experience between equals" (p. 5) that creates "a common sense of purpose" (Hendricks, 2021, p. 246). Note that in this improvisation vulnerability emerges as a strength, for it creates space for caring with the other, not merely about the other. Most significantly, from a pedagogy perspective, in this example the distinction between care for the music and care for the student and his learning evaporates, as in this moment of "caring with," musical action *itself* molds relationships to the self, to the other and to music in a unified manner.

Music education practices that celebrate meritocratic approaches to learning, guarding traditions and standards of excellence, may find this description unsettling, even dangerous. The same might be true for the chapters you are about to read. Their perspectives on care not only do not mask the need for struggle against injustice and inequality in music, music education, and beyond (as much past discourse about care has done), but, on the contrary, they are making inroads toward such goals. In this sense, their perspectives on care in music education are not at all meant to be "handled with care."

References

Biesta, G. (2018). Walking the museum: Art, artists and pedagogy reconsidered. In C. Naughton, G. Biesta, & D. R. Cole (Eds.), *Art, artists and pedagogy: Philosophy and the arts in education* (pp. 147–156). Routledge.

Browne, V., Danely, J., & Rosenow, D. (Eds.). (2021). *Vulnerability and the politics of care: Transdisciplinary dialogues*. Oxford University Press.

Gökarıksel, S. (2022). University embodied: The struggle for autonomy and democracy. *South Atlantic Quarterly*, 121(1), 188–198. https://doi.org/10.1215/00382876-9561643

Hadjidakis, M. (1988). *O kathreftis ke to macheri* [The mirror and the knife]. Ikaros.

Hendricks, K. S. (2018). *Compassionate music teaching*. Rowman & Littlefield.

Hendricks, K. S. (2021). Authentic connection in music education. In K. S. Hendricks & J. Boyce-Tillman (Eds.), *Authentic connection: Music, spirituality, and wellbeing* (pp. 237–253). Peter Lang.

Kanellopoulos, P. A. (2011). In pursuit of musical freedom through free improvisation: A Bakhtinian provocation to music education. In J. White & M. Peters (Eds.), *Bakhtinian pedagogy: Opportunities and challenges for research, policy and practice in education across the globe* (pp. 91–116). Peter Lang.

Litt, C. J. (1986). Theories of transitional object attachment: An overview. *International Journal of Behavioral Development*, 9(3), 383–399. https://doi.org/10.1177/016502548600900308

Oksanen, S. (2019). Museum-as-compost: Matter, rhythms, and the non-human. In S. Hacklin & S. Oksanen (Eds.), *Co-existence: Human, animal, and nature in Kiasma's collections* (71–95). Museum of Contemporary Art Kiasma.

USC Thornton School of Music. (2015, September 24). *Andrew Manze—violin masterclass—YuEun Kim* [Video]. Youtube. https://www.youtube.com/watch?v=cdRgWbZ7JJg

CHAPTER 1

A CALL FOR CARE AND COMPASSION IN MUSIC EDUCATION

KARIN S. HENDRICKS

CARE HANDBOOK TOPICS

Co-creating caring relationships
Philosophical perspectives
Social activism and critical consciousness
Wellbeing and human flourishing

MUSIC educators are currently teaching in an age of previously unimaginable virtual connection, juxtaposed with intense political division and emotional and physical isolation. When I wrote *Compassionate Music Teaching* (Hendricks, 2018) I was concerned about our rapidly shifting world, where globalization and advancements in technology were changing nearly everything we experienced, including music education. I was interested in the unique ways in which new generations of students would need to be taught—what it meant to learn and make music together, and to learn from one another. I recognized a shift not only in what it meant to be a music learner and teacher but also what it meant to be musical. I wrote about maintaining and fostering human relationships: teacher and student, student and student, within and between musical communities, and even the relationships we nurture within ourselves. I wrote of the need for human connection, and the unique ways in which exercising compassion in music-learning settings can catalyze authentic relationships and authentic expression.

In only a few years, the need for care and connection has amplified in our world. The various technologies that connect humans virtually, from any part of the world, have both illuminated and facilitated civil discord. We have endured the fear and isolation associated with a global pandemic, with its social distance protocols that kept us from making synchronous music together at a time we might have needed it most. Compounded on fears of health and safety, we have also witnessed a rise in oppressive political self-interests that have brought age-old social inequities and centuries-old systemic racism to the forefront of our attention. Various institutions holding social power have invested deeply into educational politics as a result (see Bylica & Hendricks, under review). In the United States, for example, teachers—who are already exhausted from the extra care they must take for the wellbeing of their students and themselves—carry the brunt of political fallout due to hasty changes in laws and policies that threaten to monitor and control their every action and word.

Music classrooms and pedagogies must change even more rapidly now, in parallel with sudden shifts in society, technology, and—perhaps most notably—the dynamism of music learners' inner worlds. Since March 2020, approximately one in four young adults has contemplated suicide, and three in four have experienced at least one adverse symptom of mental health (St. Amour, 2020). Drug-related deaths were also rising in the United States at a record-breaking amount for the second year in a row (National Center for Health Statistics, 2020). Many young people are consumed with concerns over environmental degradation, economic insecurity, and the senseless and unnecessary deaths of their human family members (including, but not limited to COVID-19, drug abuse, and police brutality).[1] Educational institutions are facing an unprecedented need to provide students, faculty, and staff with psychological support and counseling, not only considering current crises but also due to rising awareness of sexual abuse and other traumas. Music teachers must be equipped to work with students experiencing trauma and mental health concerns while simultaneously managing their own distresses (Dirks et al., in press; Smith, 2021b).

It is unrealistic to assume that music learning can occur in a studio, rehearsal space, or community setting that is somehow sealed off from the rest of the world. Those who maintain a need to "keep politics out of music education" and attempt to teach as they have in the past may be more likely than ever to confront students with blank stares and hollow expressions, or a blatant resistance to focus on mundane facts that do not relate to the global concerns youth find to be much more pressing (Hendricks, 2022). Radical shifts taking place in the world at large, and in each learner's inner world, require radical shifts in music learning and teaching.

Fear-based motivational approaches have never served us in music education (Allsup & Benedict, 2008; Forsyth et al., 2011; Hendricks, 2018), but it is time to rid them from our repertoire for once and for all. To forge and maintain authentic musical connections, we have no choice but to grapple with the various potential distractions (both within and beyond the music-learning space) that inhibit music learners from being fully present, fully engaged, and fully expressive. It is a moment to meet students with deeper

---

[1] Examples of youth movements concerned with environmental justice include the global climate strike (see https://fridaysforfuture.org) and the Sunrise Movement (see https://www.sunrisemovement.org).

levels of care—not as some way of "selling out on quality," "lowering standards," or "softening" more traditional music-learning approaches. On the contrary. Notions of care, as outlined here, compel us as music teachers to revisit not only what we do but also who we are, and to be *fiercely demanding* of the things that truly matter to our students within and across our shared musical communities.

Educational systems will likely continue to change rapidly, requiring music teachers to remain remarkably flexible and adaptive to new pedagogical and technical approaches while also refining practices of compassion, human connection, and expression. The *Oxford Handbook of Care in Music Education* (OHCME) addresses ways in which music teachers act as co-learners and facilitate spaces of authenticity, improvisation, risk-taking, and an openness to vulnerability. It is intended as a resource for music teachers at all ages and stages as we navigate new terrain and become better able to understand one another, as well as ourselves. The aim of this text is to provide a space to reconsider and re-envision our own positions and places in the various human interactions that are essential and ever-present in music education.

Conceptualizations of Care in Music Education

Care may be defined as demonstrations of benevolence, concern, compassion, or even love in relation to others. It has been described as a universal human need (Edgar, 2014) and a moral imperative for music educators (Allsup & Shieh, 2012). However, the notion of caring is sometimes misunderstood in practical contexts within music education—equated simply with kindness or associated with lowered expectations—and is often dismissed without consideration of its full value to music learning and teaching.

When viewed through a student deficit perspective, the concept of care might evoke unnecessary pity or a sense of rescue, thereby positioning music teachers and learners in a superior/inferior relationship that may be unhealthy and/or unhelpful for either person (Hendricks, 2018, 2021a). Similarly, many well-meaning approaches to care do not fully account for the ways in which a teacher also continues to learn and develop (Parker, 2016). As Richerme (2017) has argued, "if teachers and students provide others care without acknowledging their own limitations and vulnerabilities, they risk propagating paternalistic attitudes" (p. 418).

A more empowering conceptualization of care in music education might involve sharing—sharing experience, sharing passion, sharing excitement, sharing music-learning goals, and sharing humanness. The OHCME addresses ways in which music teachers and students can interact as co-learners and forge authentic relationships with one another (and with music) through collective music-making experiences. Authors offer approaches to care that intersect with a broad range of topics set within the context of music teaching and learning. They extend previous conceptions of care to meet the needs of contemporary music learners and the teachers who care for, about, and with them.

Topics, Perspectives, and Contexts of Care in Music Education

The *Oxford Handbook of Care in Music Education* addresses the essence of caring relationships in music education from a variety of perspectives and/or contexts, including anti-racism and anti-sexism; bullying and harassment prevention; critical perspectives; dialogic education; disability/ability; eco-justice; gender identity and sexual orientation; inclusivity of a range of musical styles and genres; intercultural sensitivity; mindfulness; musical creativity (including composition and improvisation); music technology (e.g., access, inclusion in mixing and production, online/remote learning); non-violent communication; pedagogy as a culturally sustaining force; self-care; social emotional learning; transgressive pedagogy for critical consciousness; and trauma-sensitive pedagogies.

This collection contains chapters written by leading and emerging scholars, as well as contributions from practicing music teachers in a broad range of music-learning settings. It also features voices of music students with a variety of backgrounds, identities, and interests. The aim of the volume is to provide a space for music educators to re-envision our own positions and practices of care in the various human interactions that are essential and ever-present within music teaching and learning.

Chapters uniquely address any of the following six questions:

- What philosophical perspectives relate to care in music education?
- How can caring relationships be co-created in music-learning spaces?
- What is the role of care in supporting students' musical development?
- How might music educators support students' identity expressions with care?
- How does care in music education contribute to wellbeing and human flourishing?
- How might care in music education promote social activism and critical consciousness?

Relevant topics are listed at the top of each chapter. Chapters have been organized in the handbook according to one of four primary topics: (a) philosophical perspectives on care and music education; (b) co-creating caring relationships; (c) caring for wellbeing and human flourishing; and (d) care, social activism, and critical consciousness.[2] Of course authentic caring relationships are not (nor should not be) confined to one

---

[2] The OHCME was originally divided into all six areas. However, I realized that most authors deemed "musical development" as critical, but not primary, to their aims—whereas chapters whose authors had articulated "identity expressions" as their major focus tended to address systematically excluded people (e.g., students with disabilities, LGBTQ+ persons). Thanks to a helpful conversation with Juliet Hess, I

dimension of care. Therefore, Table 1.1 displays how the chapters reach across various themes to create a more holistic expression of care in music education. Each of the four major themes is introduced in the sections that follow.

Philosophical Perspectives on Care and Music Education

Concepts of care addressed in the OHCME stem from philosophies of relationship (Buber, 1970), feminist and relational ethics (Gilligan, 1982; Noddings, 1984, 2013; Tronto, 1998), musical meaningfulness (Silverman, 2012, 2013), and compassionate music teaching (Hendricks, 2018, 2021a). Together, these philosophies highlight the essence of authentic relationships and shared experiences between teachers and learners, as they apply to a variety of music-making contexts. These philosophies are detailed below.

Care Ethics

Buber's (1970) approach to relationship emphasizes the ways in which an intimate encounter with another creates an experience of engrossment where "I" and "You" are integrated. In Buber's "I-You"[3] conceptualization, any "It" qualities about "I" or "You" are subsumed by the spiritual experience of being fully present with one another. Noddings's (1984, 2013) ethic of care draws on Buber's philosophy to articulate differences between caring *about* things and people, versus caring *for* them. It inspires a shift in educational thought from merely teaching concepts and ideas, to a state of presence and human connection.

Similar to the work of Gilligan (1982), who criticized male-normative psychological understandings of moral development, Noddings's earlier writing associated ethics of care unabashedly with femininity.[4] This was not to suggest that they believed only

---

made the decision to place "identity expressions" chapters into other sections throughout the handbook according to other topics mentioned by the authors, thereby avoiding marginalization of topics related to people for whom authors in this text were advocating inclusion.

[3] Although English speakers more commonly reference Buber's philosophy using "I-Thou" pronouns, I join Walter Kaufmann (translator of the 1970 version) to use I and You, which more aptly reflects the familiar language of "Ich und Du" pronouns in Buber's original German.

[4] Care ethicists such as Noddings and Gilligan have often been criticized for their emphasis on the feminine/masculine dichotomy, with critics stating (among other things) that such divisions serve to reinforce stereotypes about men and women, assign caring as women's work, and encourage self-sacrifice of women while leaving men out of the equation. See the Preface to Noddings (2013)—in which the author explains her change from the title "feminine approach" to "relational approach"—as well as Silverman (2012) for more extended discussions of these critiques.

Table 1.1 Chapter Themes and Connections Across the Handbook

Author(s)	Social Activism and Critical Consciousness	Wellbeing and Human Flourishing	Philosophical Perspectives	Musical Development	Identity Expressions	Co-Creating Caring Relationships
Benjamins	X		***			X
Baker	X		***	X	X	X
Barna	***					
Berg		***				
Boyce-Tillman			***			
Bylica	***			X		
Churchill & Hall	***				X	
Dansereau			***		X	X
Davis						***
Diaz		***				
Dirks		***				X
Edgar, D'Ambrosio, & Hackl	X	X			X	***
Ehrlich	***				X	
Evison		X	X	X		***
Fung			***			
Good-Perkins	***				X	
Goodrich						***
Jorgensen			***			
Hendricks	X	X	***			X
Hendricks, Finn, Freeze, & Kono						***
Hendricks & McPherson	X	***		X	X	
Hibbard & Price		***				
Tsui, Hess, & Hendricks	***					
Holdhus		***				
Hourigan	X	***			X	
Legutki, Hendricks, Smith, & King				X		***

Table 1.1 Continued

Author(s)	Social Activism and Critical Consciousness	Wellbeing and Human Flourishing	Philosophical Perspectives	Musical Development	Identity Expressions	Co-Creating Caring Relationships
Lehmberg & Fung		***				
Lewis	***				X	X
López-Íñiguez, & Westerlund	X	X	***	X	X	
McCord					X	***
McManus & Carter	X			X	X	***
Mitchell		***	X			X
Morelli		X				***
Mota	***				X	X
Paparo		***				
Parker & Hutton		X	X			***
Rawlings						***
Schei		***	X			
Schmidt	***					
Shorner-Johnson, Gonzalez, & Shevock	X		***			
Silverman			***			
G Smith, Waller-Pace, Urbach, & Powell	***				X	
T Smith	X	X	***			
Swanson & Cohen	***	X				
Sweet		***				
Talbot & Bernard			***	X		
Thomas-Durrell						***
Vu	***				X	

X = Related topic
*** = Assigned section

women can or should care for others.[5] Rather, their intent was to balance the scales of scholarly conversations on ethics from an overly patriarchal or disembodied emphasis on so-called universal[6] principles of justice or morality, to more fully embrace ethical behavior that is relational, contextual, and situational (Noddings, 2002). In other words, from the perspective of care ethics, one engages in actions that benefit others not because it is the "right thing to do," but because one is attuned to the needs of another and responds according to those perceived needs.

The focus in Noddings's work is relational yet primarily unidirectional, with the "one-caring" exercising empathy in human interactions to interpret and meet the needs of the "cared-for," who reciprocates by acknowledging that their needs have been met. In these circumstances, a young person who is well cared for can then learn to care for others (Noddings, 2005). Tronto (1998) divides steps of relational care into "caring about," or having an awareness of needs; caring "for" as assuming responsibility to attend to those needs; "caregiving" as engaging in acts of care; and "care receiving" as the acknowledgment of met needs.

Musical Meaningfulness and Compassionate Care in Music Education

Silverman (2012, 2013) applies Noddings's (1984) ethic of care to music-making settings to explain how meaningful musical connections can be forged as individuals care for and about each other—while engaging in musical experiences that have shared meaning. In the essence of musical meaningfulness, Buber's compound pronoun "I-You" is depicted with a conceptualization of "we" or "us," where "the 'self' [is] actually a part of the larger 'us'" (Silverman, 2012, p. 102). The collective experience within musical meaningfulness resonates with the notion of "caring connection" or "compassionate mutuality" (Martela, 2012), in which a caring relationship involves mutual validation, a state of presence with one another, an openness to feelings and emotions, affection, and acts of care that are received with gratitude (see Lehmberg & Fung, this volume).

Similar to the conceptualization of musical meaningfulness, compassionate music teaching (Hendricks, 2018), or compassionate care, extends beyond teachers caring *for* and *about* students, to an experience of learners and teachers caring *with* one another in music-learning settings (Hendricks, 2021a). Whereas much of care ethics stems from a

---

[5] Boyce-Tillman (2000) argues how societal perceptions of men's and women's roles (with women as caregivers and men as embarking on "heroic" individualist quests) have been hurtful to both men and women, limiting opportunities for women while also abrogating men's responsibility—and underestimating men's ability—to care for others. In her later writing, Boyce-Tillman (2018) articulates how the "queering" of gender and gender roles allows for a liberating, healing, and holistic approach to living as well as to musicking, as any person is provided space to "juggle" and express their own unique array of multiple identities, including in caring contexts.

[6] Surely, principles that have guided much of educational thought are not truly universal but determined by those in power (Freire, 2018).

resistance to standards of morality based on male-normative philosophies and psychological inquiries (Noddings, 2002), this conceptualization of compassionate care stems from a problem in practice: It is offered as an alternative to the top-down, hierarchical approaches to music education that have permeated much of our history.

In *Compassionate Music Teaching* I argue[7] that overly teacher-centered approaches in our field have stymied creativity, stifled expressiveness, and interfered with possibilities for authentic connections with others, with self, and with music (Hendricks, 2018). I have further described how pedagogies involving a "maestro" or "master teacher" who imparts musical traditions and imposed standards of perfection to others, runs parallel with societal notions of supremacy (Hendricks, 2021a). Revisiting the work of Buber (1970), I propose that music educators contemplate how the I-You relationship represents "spiritual communion rather than roles to be performed, and where neither I nor You need be superior nor inferior" (Hendricks, 2021a, p. 246). *Compassionate Music Teaching* applies research in motivation, empathy, trust, and inclusion to describe how music teachers can act as co-learners with students to welcome individual expressions, and to foster a collective sense of purpose and musical engagement (Hendricks, 2018). The framework is centered around six qualities of teaching and learning (trust, empathy, patience, inclusion, community, authentic connection) that are both enacted and modeled by music teachers as they practice compassion.

Compassionate care aligns with writings of Boyce-Tillman (2000) to challenge the "hero narrative," particularly as it is applied to music educators. In other words, compassionate care suggests that placing the teacher on a "pedestal" (or podium) of grandeur, or in a posture of reaching down to help students with alleged deficits, can (a) create a false sense of separation between teachers and students, (b) abrogate the responsibility or opportunity of students to be agents their own learning, and (c) deny the teacher permission to continue learning as well. Drawing from Buddhist understandings of compassion (Chödrön, 2004), I describe how teachers and learners might be viewed as equals in a humanitarian sense, each bringing strengths, weaknesses, and aspirations to their collaborative musical endeavors (Hendricks, 2018). Further:

> Although these equals may bring different . . . experiences to a music learning space (such as in the case of an adult and child), they are neither greater nor lesser than one another, and they connect through a common sense of purpose. This essence of caring about, for, *and* with, in a music learning context, is also reflective of musical meaningfulness . . . and plays a role in the pursuit of human flourishing. (Hendricks, 2021a, p. 246)

Compassionate care in music education involves an understanding of how music educators might hold students to the highest expectations, but in relation to students' identities, interests, and goals (see Hendricks, 2018, 2021a; O'Neill, 2015). Such caring involves being attuned not only to learners' feelings and needs but also to their values

---

[7] As have others; see, for example, Allsup (2016).

and worldviews (Hendricks, 2018). As OHCME authors explain, understanding care as a catalyst toward connection and empowerment might inspire music teachers to practice persistent curiosity, and to open themselves to a state of presence and authentic engagement with others, with self, and with music.

Co-Creating Caring Relationships

Several OHCME authors describe ways in which teachers exercise trust and empathy to co-create caring relationships with their students. Trust in music learning may be present in one-on-one relationships, as well as collectively, such as in an ensemble's shared belief in their ability to accomplish a musical task. Trust within educational settings—musical and otherwise—is correlated with high levels of achievement (J. Ray & Hendricks, 2019; Tschannen-Moran & Hoy, 2000) and can be developed and manifested through seven facets: willingness to experience vulnerability, confidence, benevolence, reliability, competence, honesty, and openness (Tschannen-Moran & Hoy, 2000).

Although each facet of trust is addressed throughout the handbook, willingness to experience vulnerability receives considerable attention. Practicing radical hospitality and nurturing trusting relationships might mean that teachers "risk vulnerability in terms of our own teaching, curriculum, and perceived authority" (Hendricks, 2018, p. 127). On the other hand, hegemonic enactments of care (in which there is an oppressive power differential) often involve the one-caring attempting to cover up their own vulnerabilities. Music teachers interested in co-creating caring relationships may find it necessary to grapple with the ways in which their own weaknesses as teachers or musicians may be exposed, especially in instances where they are out of their "comfort zone" and trying new things. However, as Hourigan (this volume) emphasizes, "trying is also caring." Exercising the "courage to teach" (Palmer, 2017) in ways that might make teachers vulnerable calls for an equal share of self-compassion. As Noddings (1984) writes: "As I care for others and am cared for by them, I become able to care for myself" (p. 67).

Trust in a student's potential can be viewed in terms of what Noddings (1984) calls *confirmation*, which occurs "when we attribute the best possible motive consonant with reality" to that student (p. 202). Confirmation involves visualizing and affirming those characteristics of another that help to bring out their ideal self (Hendricks, 2018, p. 165). Understanding that ideal self, however, requires understanding individuals' lives beyond the immediate music-learning context, in part through an experience of empathy.

Empathy is the ability to understand what other people are experiencing by thinking and/or feeling along with them (Hendricks, 2018). Various types of empathy addressed in this handbook include cognitive, affective, mature, compassionate, and musical empathy and empathetic attunement. Contrary to popular opinion, empathy is not innately positive. For example, one can feel or understand the needs of others without necessarily choosing to do anything about it. Furthermore, it is possible for people to use the information they gain about others' feelings to manipulate them in unhealthy ways, or for people to focus on their own discomfort to justify their own morality and maintain a superior stance above those who are suffering (Hendricks, 2021b; Hess, 2021). Mature empathy, however, involves added awareness of another's values and worldviews, promoting action or support that is truly warranted or wanted by another (Hendricks, 2018).

Noddings (2013) draws on Buber's (1970) concept of "engrossment" to describe something akin to mature empathy. Here, one resists the notion to insert any sort of agenda into the act of "feeling with," and instead becomes fully receptive and attuned to the needs, feelings, and experiences of another. Engrossment reduces the propensity toward shallow "othering" that might be associated with a less sophisticated form of empathic connection (Noddings, 1984). Engrossment leads to teachers discerning feelings and needs of students to make informed choices about the most appropriate ways to act (Hoffman, 2001).

Mature empathy requires authentic listening, or the art of seeking to understand. Truly listening will likely reveal disagreements with others, which—although often avoided or viewed as a sign of trouble—can, in fact, be positive catalysts for authentic connection when coupled with a genuine desire to appreciate another's perspective (Hendricks, 2018). Many chapters in this handbook address the art of listening to understand, rather than listening merely to respond. They further celebrate how teachers might transgress beyond listening for a "right" or "best" sound or answer and invite musical and verbal dialogue that represents the complexity and variety of student experience.

CARING FOR WELLBEING AND HUMAN FLOURISHING

Topics of wellbeing and mental health are rising rapidly in music education, education, and society more broadly. Until recently, topics of trauma and mental health have received relatively little attention in music education research, which is surprising given how critical thoughts and emotions are to music learning and performance. However, a composite of recent events (including the COVID-19 pandemic, escalating concerns with climate change, rising racial and political tensions, and social comparison via social media) has created what Dirks (this volume) calls "a pressure cooker of stress in which today's youth are navigating their lives."

Arguably, conversations on mental health in music performance have been limited in part due to the stigma associated with mental health in society at large, and the individualist drive for "survival of the fittest" in competitive cultures (McGrath et al., 2016). As Bradley (2020) notes, the lack of attention to trauma in music education may have less to do with lack of interest or irrelevance, but rather with the tendency to avoid contentious topics—a common practice from those "who view the inclusion of musical context as extra-musical and thus unnecessary" (p. 4). Yet music education, when offered in a caring way, can offer a unique avenue for bearing witness to trauma, processing ineffable thoughts and emotions, facilitating human connections (from intimate relationships to cross-cultural understandings), and promoting emotional healing. Mental health has become less taboo in society and people have begun to speak more openly about various traumas at the same time that we have experienced further global catastrophes, including civil unrest, devastating superstorms, and health crises. These recent concerns have made the need for this topic even more apparent.

The importance of recognizing both the dignity and contribution of each music learner is becoming more critical as music technology and virtual musicking make a rapid entry into our learning spaces. While music teachers have faced new teaching realities and practices, we have also been introduced to a variety of technological tools and possibilities for virtual music-making that raise a new set of concerns and questions: How does a teacher continue to exercise compassion and care in situations where students are not physically present? How might authentic connections be forged through "virtual" music? Authors in this handbook address questions regarding access, community, and ethics to promote authenticity, connection, and agency in virtual music settings that can lead to human flourishing.

As teachers nurture caring relationships, it is possible—particularly in the case when teachers experience affective empathy—to become so caught up in the experiences, feelings, and/or needs of others that one can lose one's own sense of self and become unable to help someone else in effective or appropriate ways. As Noddings (1984) cautioned, "there is a characteristic and appropriate mode of consciousness in caring" (p. 51). Many OHCME authors advocate for teachers to learn and practice appropriate personal and professional boundaries to maintain healthy levels of caring. Authors provide evidence for the effectiveness of reflection, self-care, and mindfulness in music education, and offer specific practices and approaches for readers to try on their own.

Care, Social Activism, and Critical Consciousness

As argued above, authentic, anti-hegemonic care requires that music teachers revisit pedagogical practices, music teacher identities and priorities; and remain fiercely demanding of the things that truly matter to our students and within our shared musical communities. Smith and colleagues (this volume) state, "When we tell our students we love them without embedding in our practices a deep ethic of love that includes justice, we are simply perpetuating a surface-level understanding of what love is." Schmidt (this volume) goes further to argue that, "[as] with any educational endeavor that aims to be inclusive, equity oriented, and even transformational, practices of . . . care often carry with them (or must employ) a disruptive kind of ethics" and a recognition of a music educator's role in decolonial work. Many handbook authors address ways in which authentic, anti-hegemonic care is enacted through social activism and critical consciousness at all levels of a teacher's influence, from one-on-one interactions with students based on individual needs, to effecting change for the common good at broader institutional and societal levels.

Inclusive pedagogy accounts for, and incorporates strengths from, every person within a music-learning space (Florian & Linklater, 2010). Notions of diversity and inclusion can, if misunderstood or misused, lead to false separations between humans and provide those in power a vantage point wherewith to maintain that power. For example, efforts toward inclusion can be problematic when viewed as a means of diversifying a current organization in name or identity only, without considering what strengths new group members might bring (V. Ray, 2019). True inclusion is possible only in instances of full participation, embrace of diverse interests, and shared power (Spellers, 2006). Similarly, as several handbook authors acknowledge, diversity in terms of access and representation is moot when learners are severed from their own cultures, backgrounds, and interests as students are accepted into institutions that do not make place for music-making experiences that are relevant or important to them.

Several OHCME authors take a critical lens to envision inclusive pedagogy and radical welcome in music education. They address caring relationships relating to a variety of topics including: access and representation, culturally sustaining pedagogy, intercultural sensitivity, cultural humility, abolitionist pedagogy, anti-racist music education, intersectionality and holistic acceptance, dismantling symbolic violence and carceral logics, policy practice and solidarity, eco-justice education, and pedagogies of love. Instead of merely "making space for" or "allowing" minoritized individuals to the table (practices that keep the power with the powerful), authors argue that radical inclusion is embodied in a truly diverse community where a collective range of individuals not only learn from and celebrate one another but also work toward one another's liberation and empowerment.

Radical inclusion requires a community and its gatekeepers to engage in a process of continual evolution (Spellers, 2006)—a potentially frightening but emancipatory possibility Many authors challenge the term "safe space" in music performance and relational interactions, noting how the term "safety" has sometimes been misused to maintain the status quo, from societal politics to individual moments of expressive trepidation in music performance. They discuss the concept of "brave spaces" to envision how students might feel encouraged to take risks musically and in dialogue with others. Authors offer ways by which educators might help students (a) become better attuned to their individual needs, interests, and values; (b) learn how to assert and express those needs; (c) listen to and respect the expressions of others; and (d) forge authentic connections with others and with the music they make.

Conclusion

Writings on care have spanned several decades, having first emerged as care scholars became disillusioned by dualistic theories of moral development that relied too heavily on abstract and universal reasoning (Gilligan, 1982). An interest in care ethics deepened in education fields as teachers and students faced violence and mistreatment in schools (Noddings, 2002). Now, in this precarious age of civil unrest, climate catastrophes, and diminished physical and emotional health, it appears that we need care more fully and deeply than ever before—not just on an individual level from teacher to student, but in ways that extend to collective care for the common good.

To rephrase words of Greta Thunberg, it is time to *care* "as if the house was on fire"[8]—not only to survive but also to thrive as a species (Smith, 2021a). Care ethics offer a vision for individualized yet holistic, relational decision-making possibilities wherein music educators can practice presencing with students and meet their needs in ways that matter most to them and to their communities—in music-learning spaces and beyond. Caring for, about, and with students can lead music teachers and learners beyond instances of self-actualization to what Motschnig-Pitrik and Barrett-Lennard (2010) call "co-actualization," or collective thriving (Mitchell, this volume).

Noddings (1984) asserted that happiness is the purpose of life, and that education should be a preparation for such a well-lived life. The OHCME offers a further argument: Education is both a preparation for a well-lived life, and a distinctive and critical element of students' lived experiences in the present moment. "Real life" is already occurring all around music learners of all ages. If music is a reflection of life, then music education should not only prepare students for vocational success but also support them—in the present—to experience collective thriving. It is my hope that this volume might support music teachers in their efforts to practice care with their students and similarly care for themselves. In so doing, music teachers may be better positioned to continually revisit pedagogical practices and priorities toward co-actualization, and to foster meaningful, authentic connections in all the ways that music makes possible.

References

Allsup, R. E. (2016). *Remixing the classroom: Toward an open philosophy of music education*. Indiana University Press.

Allsup, R. E., & Benedict, C. (2008). The problems of band: An inquiry into the future of instrumental music education. *Philosophy of Music Education Review, 16*(2), 156–173. https://www.jstor.org/stable/40327299

Allsup, R. E., & Shieh, E. (2012). Social justice and music education: The call for a public pedagogy. *Music Educators Journal, 98*(4), 47–51. https://doi.org/10.1177/0027432112442969

---

[8] https://www.youtube.com/watch?v=RjsLm5PCdVQ

Boyce-Tillman, J. (2000). *Constructing musical healing: The wounds that sing.* Jessica Kingsley Publishers.

Boyce-Tillman, J. (2018). The myths we live by. In K. S. Hendricks & J. Boyce-Tillman (Eds.), *Queering freedom: Music, identity, and spirituality* (pp. 3–34). Peter Lang.

Bradley, D. (2020). We are all haunted: Cultural understanding and the paradox of trauma. *Philosophy of Music Education Review, 28*(1), 4–23. https://www.muse.jhu.edu/article/753770

Buber, M. (1970). *I and Thou* (W. Kaufmann, Trans.). Simon & Schuster. (Original work published 1937)

Bylica, K., & Hendricks, K. S. (under review). Preservice music teacher education: Learning with Gaga feminism. In M. Silverman & N. Niknafs (Eds.), *The Oxford handbook of feminism and music education.* Oxford University Press.

Chödrön, P. (2004). *Start where you are: A guide to compassionate living.* Shambhala Publications.

Czeisler, M. É., Lane, R. I., Petrosky, E., Wiley, J. F., Christensen, A., Njai, R., Weaver, M. D., Robbins, R., Facer-Childs, E. R., Barger, L. K., Czeisler, C. A., Howard, M. E., & Rajaratnam, S. (2020). Mental health, substance use, and suicidal ideation during the COVID-19 pandemic—United States, June 24–30, 2020. *Morbidity and Mortality Weekly Report, 69*(32), 1049–1057. https://doi.org/10.15585/mmwr.mm6932a1

Delpit, L. (Ed.). (2019). *Teaching when the world is on fire.* New Press.

Dirks, R. L., Smith, T. D., González-Moreno, P. A., & Phelps, A. (in press). Mental health in string education: Identifying concerns within the American String Teachers Association community. *String Research Journal.*

Edgar, S. N. (2014). An ethic of care in high school instrumental music. *Action, Criticism, and Theory for Music Education, 13*(2), 111–137. http://act.maydaygroup.org/articles/Edgar13_2.pdf

Florian, L., & Linklater, H. (2010). Preparing teachers for inclusive education: using inclusive pedagogy to enhance teaching and learning for all. *Cambridge Journal of Education, 40*(4), 369–386. https://doi.org/10.1080/0305764X.2010.526588

Forsyth, P. B., Adams, C. M., & Hoy, W. K. (2011). *Collective trust: Why schools can't improve without it.* Teachers College Press.

Freire, P. (2018). *Pedagogy of the oppressed* (M. B. Ramos, Trans.; 50th anniversary ed.). Continuum. (Original work published 1970)

Gilligan, C. (1982). *In a different voice: Psychological theory and women's development.* Harvard University Press.

Hendricks, K. S. (2018). *Compassionate music teaching.* Rowman & Littlefield.

Hendricks, K. S. (2021a). Authentic connection in music education: A chiastic essay. In K. S. Hendricks & J. Boyce-Tillman (Eds.), *Authentic connection: Music, spirituality, and wellbeing* (pp. 237–253). Peter Lang.

Hendricks, K. S. (2021b). Counternarratives: Troubling majoritarian certainty. *Action, Criticism, and Theory for Music Education, 20*(4), 58–78. https://doi.org/10.22176/act20.4.5

Hendricks, K. S. (2022). Contexts and conceptualizations of care in music education. In C. Randles & P. Burnard (Eds.), *The Routledge companion to creativities in music education* (pp. 404–415). Routledge.

Hess, J. (2021). When narrative is impossible: Difficult knowledge, storytelling, and ethical practice in narrative research and pedagogy in music education. *Action, Criticism, and Theory for Music Education, 20*(4), 79–113. https://doi.org/10.22176/act20.4.79

Hoffman, M. L. (2001). *Empathy and moral development: Implications for caring and justice.* Cambridge University Press.

Martela, F. (2012). *Caring connections—compassionate mutuality in the organizational life of a nursing home* [Doctoral dissertation, Aalto University]. Aalto University Publication Series. http://urn.fi/URN:ISBN:978-952-60-4848-2

McGrath, C., Hendricks, K. S., & Smith, T. D. (2016). *Performance anxiety strategies.* Rowman and Littlefield.

Motschnig-Pitrik, R., & Barrett-Lennard, G. (2010). Co-actualization: A new construct in understanding well-functioning relationships. *Journal of Humanistic Psychology, 50*(3), 374–398. https://doi.org/10.1177/0022167809348017

National Center for Health Statistics. (2020, October 15). *Provisional drug overdose death counts.* Centers for Disease Control and Prevention. https://www.cdc.gov/nchs/nvss/vsrr/drug-overdose-data.htm

Noddings, N. (1984). *Caring: A feminine approach to ethics and moral education.* University of California Press.

Noddings, N. (2002). *Educating moral people.* Teachers College Press.

Noddings, N. (2005). *The challenge to care in schools* (2nd ed.). Teachers College Press.

Noddings, N. (2013). *Caring: A relational approach to ethics and moral education* (2nd ed.). University of California Press.

O'Neill, S. A. (2015). Youth empowerment and transformative music engagement. In C. Benedict, P. Schmidt, G. Spruce, & P. Woodford (Eds.), *The Oxford handbook of social justice in music education* (pp. 388–405). Oxford University Press.

Palmer, P. (2017). *The courage to teach: Exploring the inner landscape of a teacher's life* (3rd ed.). John Wiley & Sons.

Parker, E. C. (2016). The experience of creating community: An intrinsic case study of four midwestern public school choral teachers. *Journal of Research in Music Education, 64*(2), 220–237. https://doi.org/10.1177/0022429416648292

Ray, J., & Hendricks, K. S. (2019). Collective efficacy belief, within-group agreement, and performance quality among instrumental chamber ensembles. *Journal of Research in Music Education, 66*(4), 449–464. https://doi.org/10.1177/0022429418805090

Ray, V. (2019). A theory of racialized organizations. *American Sociological Review, 84*(1), 26–53. https://doi.org/10.1177/0003122418822335

Richerme, L. K. (2017). A feminine and poststructural extension of cosmopolitan ethics in music education. *International Journal of Music Education, 35*(3), 414–424. https://doi.org/10.1177%2F0255761416667470

Silverman, M. (2012). Virtue ethics, care ethics, and the good life of teaching. *Action, Criticism, and Theory for Music Education, 11*(2), 96–122. http://act.maydaygroup.org/articles/Silverman11_2.pdf

Silverman, M. (2013). A conception of "meaningfulness" in/for life and music education. *Action, Criticism, and Theory for Music Education, 12*(2), 20–40. http://act.maydaygroup.org/articles/Silverman12_2.pdf

Smith, T. D. (2021a). Music education for surviving and thriving: Cultivating children's wonder, senses, emotional wellbeing, and wild nature as a means to discover and fulfill their life's purpose. *Frontiers in Education, 6.* Article 648779. https://doi.org/10.3389/feduc.2021.648799

Smith, T. D. (2021b). Teaching through trauma: Compassion fatigue, burnout, or secondary traumatic stress? In D. Bradley & J. Hess (Eds.), *Trauma and resilience in music education* (pp. 49–63). Routledge.

Spellers, S. (2006). *Radical welcome.* Church Publishing.

St. Amour, M. (2020, August 17). Pandemic increasing suicidal ideation. *Inside Higher Ed.* https://www.insidehighered.com/news/2020/08/17/suicidal-ideation-rise-college-aged-adults-due-covid-19-pandemic

Tronto, J. C. (1998). An ethic of care. *Generations: Journal of the American Society on Aging, 22*(3), 15–20. https://www.jstor.org/stable/44875693

Tschannen-Moran, M., & Hoy, W. K. (2000). A multidisciplinary analysis of the nature, meaning, and measurement of trust. *Review of Educational Research, 70*(4), 547–593. https://doi.org/10.3102/00346543070004547

CHAPTER 2

ON CARING FOR MUSIC EDUCATION IN TROUBLED TIMES

ESTELLE R. JORGENSEN

Care Handbook Topics

Philosophical perspectives

IN this chapter, I reflect briefly on the moment in which we find ourselves as musician teachers and sketch three principles of caring that address what and how to transform music education for the common good (Yob & Jorgensen, 2020).[1] By caring, I think of what Nel Noddings (1984) describes as a "feminine approach to ethics and moral education" that highlights the relational nature of caring and the way in which women often see the world and are involved as caregivers and caretakers.[2] Caring goes well beyond matters that concern formal subject matter to reach beyond the school out into the community and wider society. One cannot care for everyone and everything equally, and given limited energy and time, difficult choices need to be made by teachers about who,

---

[1] An earlier version of this writing was presented as a Keynote to the National Association for Music Education National Assembly, June 27, 2021.

[2] Noddings (2013) titled the second edition of her original treatise on caring (1984) a "relational" approach to caring, claiming that her original subtitle invoking a "feminine approach" did not capture the wider import of her ideas and was misleading. For me, something of the import of women's perspectives on ethics and education is lost in the subtitle of the second edition. I am inclined to the view that Noddings's original title highlights different ways in which women see the world ethically. It resonates with Carol Gilligan's (1982) earlier insight that women often construe ethical issues in relational terms that differ from male ethical perspectives—a position that invariably situates them uncomfortably in what Madeline Grumet (1988) refers to as their "master's house." For bell hooks (1994), their discomfort and alienation inevitably prompt women in solidarity with their sisters to transgress ethical norms in pursuit of a liberatory education.

what, for, and how much they are able to care. Music educators make choices that affect the life of music and the arts, the decent societies that democratic countries aspire to be, the welfare of their musical and cultural institutions, and the individual happiness of their citizens and inhabitants. These choices are rooted in and expressions of those things about which musicians and teachers care. Times of war, strife, plague, violence, discontent, and discouragement focus the mind on those things that are of greatest importance in creating a better future and benefiting humankind. In considering the things about which music educators need to care, I see these principles as of greatest importance for musicians, teachers, their students, and their publics.

We have come through a dark time (see Abramo et al., 2022) that William Shakespeare (1653) might describe figuratively as "the winter of our discontent."[3] A global plague of historic proportions that has upended lives and livelihoods has unfolded against the backdrop of worldwide natural and human disasters—fire, flood, storm, famine, displacement, dispossession, incivility, oppression, corruption, violence, war, terror—that have torn the fabric of civil and decent societies. The rise of mediated disinformation, misinformation, anti-intellectualism, ignorance, economic inequality, autocratic thinking, conspiracy theories, and the devaluation of and disregard for education, truth, wisdom, expertise, and intellectual prowess have only exacerbated these problems. During this pandemic, the United States and other countries in the West have been shaken by a profound racial awakening and outrage, political extremism, and violence that has brought home the imperative of rediscovering and rethinking our common humanity and the ties that bind us together and sustain our democratic way of life with its ideals of life, liberty, and the pursuit of happiness. We cannot go back to the way things once were before these events occurred and pretend that they never happened. Rather, as music educational policy makers we now have work before us of rethinking our mission, tending to the life of music, taking greater care of ourselves and all those we lead, binding up the nation's wounds, and collectively working toward a better future.[4] This moment provides us with opportunities to reconsider what we have done in the past and reshape music education in ways that better meet our present realities.[5]

---

[3] Notwithstanding that the opening line of *Richard III*, "Now is the winter of our discontent" should be read together with the second line, "made glorious summer by this sun of York," Shakespeare aptly encapsulates our riven time.

[4] This task necessitates recognizing the role of trauma and the need for resilience in a music education that hopes to understand the many cultures of the world. Deborah Bradley (2020) explores the paradoxical nature of trauma and contributors to Bradley and Hess (2021) examine the intersection of trauma and resilience in music education.

[5] At "How Education Fared During the First Wave of COVID-19 Lockdowns? International Evidence," a forum convened by the American Educational Research Association (AERA) and the Organisation for Economic Cooperation and Development (OECD) and moderated by Felice J. Levine, Executive Director of AERA, November 29, 2021, 9:30–11:00 am ET, 15:30–17:00 CET, speakers discussed an OECD report, *Schooling during a Pandemic*, published on October 18, 2021. This report focused on statistical evidence of the impact of the pandemic on schooling during March–June 2020 from France, Germany, Ireland, the United Kingdom, and the United States. Speakers sought to envision this pandemic as one of possibility rather than unmitigated loss. They suggested that educators have opportunities to build on strategies, techniques, and skills that worked well during this period of

Thinking about transforming music education illustrates the resilience of musician-educators—our tendency as a community to hope, to be unbowed by difficulties in our way, and to courageously consider what we believe and should do in the future. This resilience has been manifested by the response of music teachers at every level to the urgency of learning how to navigate virtual online instructional spaces during a pandemic, often with little time for preparation, especially in those places where face-to-face education effectively ceased. For music teachers and students alike, the challenges wrought by seeking new ways to engage musically with each other in the face of the threat of a deadly and mutating virus that some did not take seriously, physical isolation even from family members, the absence of live musical and social events, and social and political upheaval have been profound and unlike anything we have faced in a lifetime. Mere survival through this time was an achievement. Reviewing the dossiers of nominees for the Grammy Outstanding Teacher of the Year award, I saw evidence of music teachers who realized anew their crucial roles in creating a sense of community in their schools where the virtual world had rendered so many teachers and students isolated. They became bastions of hope, comfort, and consolation for faculty and students and their families alike. They mounted food drives and pantries to feed students and their families when schools closed, drove by student homes and kept in contact with them on social media, composed and arranged songs and instrumental pieces that brought the school community together, and gave voice to the loss, distress, pain, suffering, and grief that they now confronted. They created ensemble protocols to keep musicians safe and virtual and socially distanced instruction and performances. It was a wonder to see and hear this riot of divergent music-making that seemed to take on renewed urgency in difficult circumstances.

Even as we rightly celebrate the accomplishments of music educators internationally in surviving this dark period, there is still much to do. The isolation during the pandemic combined with the absence of high-speed Internet in underserved areas only exacerbated the difficulties for indigenous communities, students of color at all educational levels who fell behind or disappeared from schools and programs despite the earnest efforts of teachers and administrators to keep them involved in their schooling. In the United States, public and private schools, especially in areas that served the poor and people of color often lacked resources to reopen safely, and long-standing inequities in the distribution of music education only exacerbated the problems in returning to live face-to-face schooling. Likewise, the nation's tertiary institutions were stressed, and some closed, unable to weather the roiling impact of loss of financial support. Faculty

dislocation and outcomes that were positive rather than negative, and rethink ways in which education needs to be undertaken in the future. With the emergence of studies of the impact of COVID-19 on music education and other aspects of musical life, for example, in Germany (Roese & Merrill, 2021), Spain (Nusseck & Spahn, 2021), the United Kingdom (Levstek et al., 2021), and the United States (Parkes et al., 2021), opportunities present for collaborative research between OECD and music education researchers to frame music educational interests within a wider economic and cultural focus and foreground music education research as an important window into cultural socialization.

lost their positions, face-to-face professional and scholarly conferences on which many depended were upended, and new virtual formats needed to be created. The social movements of the past years also brought home clearly the need for more representative and diverse music education faculty, students, and programs, and urgent attention to a pervasive and persistent lack of funding for faculty, support staff, schools, colleges, music programs, scholarship, and publication.

Sometimes, change in music education occurs slowly as the system transforms incrementally over time. Other times, dramatic changes are forthcoming in response to greatly altered realities. It remains to be seen what the long-term effects of our recent disruption will be. Nevertheless, the dramatic events of the recent past, the claims of addressing the changing demographics and the "multiplicities and pluralities" of Western societies (Greene, 1988); the redressing of inequities, promoting equality, and including heretofore marginalized people within music education; the challenges of a mediated ecosphere and matters of actuality and virtuality; and the importance of providing the musical glue that can help generate a shared collective, national, and global identity and purpose, create a sense of urgency for a broad vision that meets this moment.

In considering these prospects for change, it is also crucial to remember that transformation is also grounded in tradition. Music educational policy makers confront important questions of what to hold onto from the past and what to embrace that is new and different. For me, tradition and transformation are two sides of a coin. Tradition offers continuity, stability, and continued development that builds on the contributions of the past. Transformation challenges tradition and seeks to change, unsettle, and critique it, whether incrementally or drastically. The difficult challenge for musicians, teachers, students, and their publics is to determine how to navigate the fraught terrain between the two. We need tradition as we also need transformation, and it becomes necessary to ask how we may keep the best of what we have done in the past while also seeking to transform music education toward humane ends.

As we reflect on our current predicament and determine what we should do, it is essential to keep our eyes fixed on matters of greatest importance. I want to briefly sketch three of these principles. First, *we need to take care of music*. Our reason for being is music. We are heirs to musical traditions that we hope to bequeath to our students. We seek individually and collectively to employ our skills in bringing people of all ages and in multiple contexts and cultures to a love of musics that sustain them for a lifetime and enable them to express themselves effectively and truthfully in a variety of musical ways.[6]

---

[6] In Chapter 3 of this volume, Marissa Silverman seeks answers to the question of why music educators should care about caring about music education. For me, the answer to this question is grounded in musical and pedagogical claims in service of humanity. If one wishes for a humane musical education, one must necessarily care for music that is an expression of people's imaginations just as one needs to care about how to bring people to a wider, deeper, and richer understanding of music. Both musical and pedagogical caring are expressions of the value one places not only on the music one

In his book, *The Responsibility of the Artist*, Jacques Maritain (1960/1972) argues that artists' first responsibility is to their art. For much of recorded history, music has been a phenomenal and material activity—taking place in the physical world of acoustic sound and sight. In the recent past, it has become increasingly immaterial, transmitted, and accessed technologically through electronic means. Joseph Abramo (2021) argues that music's growing immateriality has contributed to its commodification and exploitation for economic ends—a reality that potentially undermines its value and renders it object rather than subject.[7] This pandemic and the loss of access to live musicking in social settings around the nation has revealed music's vulnerability, shattered musicians' livelihoods and the financial viability of musical institutions, and reminded us of its social and psychological importance in our lives. It is now abundantly clear that people need live, face-to-face musicking and educating. We might be thankful for the technologies that have enabled our work over the recent past and that have opened new possibilities of teaching and learning, scholarship, and musicking, but the limits of this virtuality are now stark. To keep music flourishing requires musicians and audiences. We cannot expect to bring music alive in the material world and teach it effectively unless we are first musicians, skilled exponents of the traditions we practice. We owe it to our students and colleague music teachers to offer them nothing short of our very best. The difficult time through which we have passed has taught us of music's crucial role as an expression of our inner selves, and of its purpose in giving voice to our individual and collective experience of the panoply of human existence, whether it be joy, grief, longing, desire, reverence, wonder, or whatever else. In remembering this, we now understand more clearly that notwithstanding all the things that music may be good for and all the goods that we might seek as music educators, it is first and foremost our responsibility to take care of the music.

Second, and paradoxically, if we are to take care of music, *we need to take care of ourselves and those with whom we work*. Ours is a people-centered undertaking, about and for people. Thinking about first principles, and given the experience of these past years, we reflect constructively on what we are attempting to do for and with these people. We might ask: Is it possible to accomplish more with less and remove the clutter of potentially worthwhile activities that together create a perpetual busyness and treadmill existence that prevents us from reflecting on those things of greatest importance and living balanced, happy, and productive lives? During this pandemic, some have rediscovered the value of quietness, slowness, and having unstructured time for play unburdened by perpetual duties; others have found themselves stressed, depressed, and exhausted by offering virtual instruction. It takes time to care about oneself and others and focusing

---

teaches but also on those one seeks to educate. I begin with musical caring because this is our specific educational expertise and reason for being as music educators.

[7] Abramo's argument resonates with Karin Hendricks's (2021) proposal couched differently in terms of "authentic connections" and drawing on Buber's notion of *I-Thou* in which subjects are mutually regarded with respect, even reverence. As relationships have become objectified, reflecting an *I-It* focus, Hendricks sees a loss of authentic connections between people, music, and each another.

on fewer and more crucial tasks might open more time for the most important activities that allow all of us to build the house of music education together more happily. Some musician teachers are fearful, resistant to change, and prefer the comfort of tried-and-true methods. They have often spent years cultivating sets of skills and prefer to continue doing that which they already love to do. Other adventurous teachers are eager to try new ideas and practices and ready to embrace change.

As leaders of music teachers, if we are to both inspire them and keep them with us, we cannot continue to add expectations of them without taking others away. We shall always have transformational and traditional teachers with us, and it is important that all are welcomed and see a place for themselves in the community of music education. Accomplishing this objective requires a thoughtful and person-centric approach that values multiple perspectives on musical education and empowers musician teachers to make crucial decisions close to the ground of their practical situations. Caring for people may mean valuing slowness and time for reflection more than we have done in the past and refocusing our efforts on fewer and most important tasks (see Berg & Seeber, 2016).

Third, *we need to bind up society's wounds, and act toward civility, justice, and truth to value the one and the many who make up today's multicultural societies.* How are we to do this? As music teachers, we cannot change society and culture alone. Our mission is specifically musical and educational. Still, we can constitute a metaphor for humane musicking and educating. We can "leaven the lump" of society and culture. Our influence can seep out beyond the situations in which we teach and learn music. By embodying a search for truth in all our musicking, encouraging our students to express themselves musically and providing them with the skills to do so, their hearts and minds may be enriched in ways that ripple out into their families and communities. Whether it be a cry of rage, distress, longing, fear, joy, or ecstasy, music transforms feeling in powerful ways from mere self-exposure into musical self-expression. It can give voice to all, including those who have been marginalized and excluded from opportunities in society.[8]

The history of American music education, as in other countries, illustrates the principle that one of the most effective ways to accomplish this is through the power of example.[9] If you demonstrate a transformative principle and show how it can be accomplished, others will want it too. Change occurs when people show examples of its operation in practice, and ideas and practices catch fire by osmosis as others seek to adopt them. In this way, what happens musically spills out into the school, the community, and

---

[8] Contributors to Yob and Jorgensen (2020) tease out some of the ways in which music education can accomplish these ends. They critique and clarify how humane music education that seeks the common good is evidenced, illustrate pedagogical principles that apply in practice, offer ways in which more inclusive approaches to music education may be undertaken, and reflect on how music education could be different when humanity and the common good are crucial considerations. For example, Eleni Lapidaki (2020) considers the importance of trust and intimacy as crucial aspects of music education—a theme that is echoed in a study by Karin Hendricks and her students in chapter 18 of this handbook.

[9] This principle can be seen at the outset of music education in American publicly supported schools (see Jorgensen, 1983).

wider cultural and political life as people sing and play their way into different beliefs and practices. Music offers profound ways to bridge differences, awaken understandings, and meld the one and the many. If we are to transform music education and impact the wider society, we shall need to find music that can accomplish this, hone an ability to bring it alive, and show others how to do this by our example.

The big ideas I have suggested—how we can best care for music, for each other, and influence the wider society through the power of our example—clarify what is of greatest importance and refocus our task and energies. They also raise a host of more specific issues including diversifying the musics taught and learned, and the musicians who make them, including indigenous people, people of color, and newer immigrants; better serving poor communities and distributing music education more equitably; reshaping the theoretical foundations and practices of music education for this time; challenging the marginalization and minimization of school time and resources to music; rethinking school music and lifelong music education; revisioning advanced programs of music education and systems of music educational scholarship and publication; designing more effective "green" music educational approaches that care for the environment and the health and wellbeing of musicians, teachers and students; and weaving a tapestry of musical and educational approaches that can bring us together as a people in this land and also represent our diversity.[10]

As we seek to care for the musics, for ourselves, and for those with whom we work, and to influence the wider public whom we seek to benefit in myriad ways, we may individually and collectively transform music education for the common good. Doing this dignifies our task and humanizes it. Such an approach repudiates the rampant individualism, materialism, and technologization of our age, and resists the desire for immediate gratification and self-promotion that fuel greed and incivility. Instead, such carefulness fosters spiritual as well as physical health, wellbeing, and happiness; refocuses our efforts on things of greatest consequence; and brings joy and fulfillment in service of others. Focusing on caring for those things of greatest importance removes the clutter of busywork that becomes drudgery, frees time and energy to play and savor the present moment and go more slowly, and energizes and inspires us to transcend the ordinary and humdrum and find added meaning in our lives.

References

Abramo, J. (2021). Whence culture and epistemology? Dialectical materialism and music education. *Philosophy of Music Education Review.* 29(1), 155–173. https://doi.org/10.2979/philm usieducrevi.29.2.03

[10] See June Boyce-Tillman's (2004) ground-breaking essay, "Towards an ecology of music education." Tawnya Smith (2021) mines this ecological approach to music education in her approach to surviving and thriving; in chapter 12 of this handbook, Smith highlights caring for the earth, ecosystems, and wellbeing.

Abramo, J., Allsup, R. E., Benedict, C., & Kanellopoulos, P. A. (2022). Symposium: "Music education in times of darkness: Possibilities of resistance." *Philosophy of Music Education Review, 30*(2), 111–162. https://doi.org/10.2979/philmusieducrevi.30.2.02

Berg, M., & Seeber, B. K. (2016). *The slow professor: Changing the culture of speed in the academy.* University of Toronto Press.

Boyce-Tillman, J. (2004). Towards an ecology of music education. *Philosophy of Music Education Review, 12*(2), 102–125. https://doi.org/ 10.1353/pme.2005.0013

Bradley, D. (2020). We are all haunted: Cultural understanding and the paradox of trauma. *Philosophy of Music Education Review, 28*(1), 4–23. https://doi.org/10.2979/philmusieducrevi.28.1.02

Bradley, D., & Hess, J. (Eds.). (2021). *Trauma and resilience in music education: Haunted melodies.* Routledge.

Gilligan, C. (1982). *In a different voice: Psychological theory and women's development.* Harvard University Press.

Greene, M. (1988). *Dialectic of freedom.* Teachers College Press.

Grumet, M. R. (1988). *Bitter milk: Women and teaching.* University of Massachusetts Press.

Hendricks, K. S. (2021). Authentic connection in music: A chiastic essay. In K. S. Hendricks & J. Boyce-Tillman (Eds.), *Authentic connection: Music, spirituality, and wellbeing* (pp. 238–253). Peter Lang.

Hooks, B. (1994). *Teaching to transgress: Education as the practice of freedom.* Routledge.

Jorgensen, E. R. (1983). Engineering change in music education: A model of the political process underlying the Boston School Music Movement (1829–1838). *Journal of Research in Music Education, 31*, 65–75. https://doi.org/10.2307/3345111

Lapidaki, E. (2020). Toward the discovery of contemporary trust and intimacy in higher music education. In I. M. Yob & E. R. Jorgensen (Eds.), *Humane music education for the common good* (pp. 261–273). Indiana University Press.

Levstek, M., Barnby, R. M., Pocock, K. L., & Banerjee, R. (2021). "It all makes us feel together": Young people's experiences of virtual group music-making during the COVID-19 pandemic. *Frontiers in Psychology, 12*, Article 703892. https://doi.org/10.3389/fpsyg.2021.703892

Maritain, J. (1960/1972). *The responsibility of the artist.* Gordian Press.

Noddings, N. (1984). *Caring: A feminine approach to ethics and moral education.* University of California Press.

Noddings, N. (2013). *Caring: A relational approach to ethics and moral education* (2nd ed.). University of California Press.

Nusseck, M., & Spahn, C. (2021). Musical practice in music students during COVID-19 lockdown. *Frontiers in Psychology, 12*, Article 643177. https://doi.org/10.3389/fpsyg.2021.643177

Organization of Economic and Cultural Development (OECD). (2021, October 18). *Schooling during a pandemic: The experience and outcomes of schoolchildren during the first round of COVID-19 lockdowns.* https://www.oecd.org/health/schooling-during-a-pandemic-1c78681e-en.htm

Parkes, K. A., Russell, J. A., Bauer, W. I., & Miksza, P. (2021). The well-being and instructional experiences of K-12 music educators: Starting a new school year during a pandemic. *Frontiers of Psychology, 12*, Article 701189. https://doi.org/10.3389/fpsyg.2021.701189

Roese, N. A., & Merrill J. (2021). Consequences of the COVID-19 lockdown in Germany: Effects of changes in daily life on musical engagement and functions of music. *International Journal of Environmental Research in Public Health, 18*(19), Article 10463. https://doi.org/10.3390/ijerph181910463

Shakespeare, W. (1994). *King Richard the Third*. In *The complete works of William Shakespeare*. Project Gutenberg. https://www.gutenberg.org/ebooks/100 (Original work published 1623).

Smith, T. D. (2021). Music education for surviving and thriving: Cultivating children's wonder, senses, emotional wellbeing, and wild nature as a means to discover and fulfill their life's purpose. *Frontiers in Education*, 6, Article 648799. https://doi.org/10.3389/feduc.2021.648799

Yob, I. M., & Jorgensen, E. R. (Eds.). (2020). *Humane music education for the common good*. Indiana University Press.

CHAPTER 3

CARING ABOUT CARING FOR MUSIC EDUCATION

MARISSA SILVERMAN

CARE HANDBOOK TOPICS

Philosophical perspectives

WHY should we care *for* music education? Or, more fundamentally, why should we care *about* caring *for* music education? This chapter examines how an understanding of "care" and therefore care ethics (e.g., Noddings, 1984; Tronto, 2013, 2015) can frame potentials for our students and our profession through, fundamentally, a better understanding of our responsibilities and therefore our relationships with those around us. Additionally, this chapter argues that music *education*—holistically conceived—is an *ethical* engagement with/for communities of people. Relatedly, explanations of why and how music making, creating, listening, and sharing contribute to many kinds of identity formation—including musical, personal, social, cultural, gendered, and ethical identity development—should be framed from a "care"—caring, care-filled, and careful—perspective.

PRELIMINARY CONSIDERATIONS

The English language contains nearly 150 prepositions. Needless to say, prepositions matter. We have prepositions of direction, time, place, location, spatial relationships; some prepositions follow verbs, while others follow adjectives. In short, the differences among all prepositions hinge on intent. Because of that intent, prepositions and their usage forge particular kinds of relationships. For now, and with the reader's indulgence, I'd like to clarify the following prepositions: "through," "with," "about," and "for."[1]

- *Through*; primarily a preposition of "spatial relationships" and "time," notably, from one end to another—"We walked through the woods"; "I celebrate my birthday through the month of June." Additionally, "as a result of"; "I learned of my teacher's passing through an obituary in the newspaper."
- *With*; a preposition of "company," "method," "relationships," or "description," and more; "She went to Hawaii with her best friend"; "Wrap this present with scotch tape"; "She is fighting with my sister"; or "I speak with a Long Island accent, especially when I'm emotional."
- *About*; a preposition "on the subject of" or relating to "connection"; "This book is about a multilayered character"; "I worry about the future."
- *For*; a preposition of "intention," "purpose," "relation," or "responsibility" or more; "There is a package for you in the mailroom"; "These books are for sale"; "She felt nothing but love for her"; "The decision about her future is not for me to make."[2]

The above-mentioned prepositions all play out in discussions within care ethics. But how?

Care Ethics

Despite the work of female philosophers in ancient Greece and the Vedic traditions, as well as the work of feminist ethicists in the 1700s,[3] most scholars argue that care ethics emerges from the work of Carol Gilligan (for a detailed analysis, see Kittay & Meyers, 1987; Kroeger-Mappes, 1994; Sevenhuijsen, 1998). Gilligan's (1982) book, *In a Different Voice: Psychological Theory and Women's Development*, brought "women's voices into psychology," rather than assimilate "women's voices" into male-dominated theoretical frameworks (Gilligan, 1995, p. 120). From Gilligan's work, care ethics develops depending on the context of its engagement (e.g., education, Nel Noddings, 1984;

---

[1] Prepositional usage taken from the *Cambridge Dictionary*. In Silverman (2015), I distinguish between the preposition "to" and "for," specifically "listening-to" versus "listening-for."

[2] These prepositional distinctions were made after consulting the following: https://www.macmillandictionary.com/us/dictionary/american/about; https://dictionary.cambridge.org/us/grammar/british-grammar/about; https://www.itepexam.com/everything-you-need-to-know-about-prepositions/.

[3] Feminist approaches to ethics trace back thousands of years. See Waithe (1987) for a rich historical framing of feminist ethics. From ancient times through today, women from around the world have sought to redefine concepts of liberty and justice by means of poetry, drama, and academic prose (see Rogers, 2004; Waithe, 1987). Feminist ethics has sought to rethink ethics in relation to women's moral experience (e.g., Butler, 1990; Nussbaum, 1992; Ruddick, 1980; Walker, 2007). Accordingly, while there is neither a "single" feminist ethic, nor a unified feminist moral theory, feminist ethics is a discipline within the much broader field of moral philosophy.

philosophy, Virginia Held, 1993; political science, Joan Tronto, 1994). "Care ethics," in most philosophical circles, is typically subsumed under the larger category of "virtue ethics." Though some scholars believe care ethics warrants its own ethical category (see Silverman, 2012), I will not pursue this line of investigation here.

Any examination of "care ethics" must begin with an understanding of the word "care."[4] As obvious as this may seem, according to Reich (1995), the history of the word "care" did not get its due examination in the work of early care ethicists.[5] Whether used as a noun or a verb, "care" derives from the Old English *caru, cearu*, "sorrow, anxiety, grief," as well as "burdens of mind; serious mental attention." In late Old English, it also connoted "concern, anxiety caused by apprehension of evil or the weight of many burdens." And from the Proto-Germanic *karō*, we find influences of "lamentation" and "grief." More modern uses of the word equate care with "oversight, attention or heed with a view to safety or protection" (c. 1400), with additional meanings such as "object or matter of concern"; to *take care of* "take in hand, do"; and *take care*, as in to "be careful" (all c. 1580s).[6] Also, particular uses of "care" have found way into mythological traditions, Ancient Roman literature, and more modern narratives, as well as existentialist and phenomenological examinations in philosophy (see Reich, 1995). Thus, "care" has many meanings. For present purposes, let us follow Bernice Fisher and Joan Tronto (1990) who state:

> care is a species activity that includes everything we do to maintain, continue, and repair our world so that we may live in it as well as possible. That world includes our bodies, our selves, and our environment, all of which we seek to interweave in a complex, life-sustaining web. (p. 40)

Given this sense of care, how might "caring" connect to music[7] and music education depending on the specific prepositions[8] we use? What follows delineates particular

---

[4] The nature of "care," especially when used in its verb-form, is as interesting as it is informative about its practice. "To care" can either be a transitive or intransitive verb. By way of review, a transitive verb connects a direct object to the verb; the action of the verb is transmitted to someone or something (e.g., "I love nature"; or "I care about nature"). An intransitive verb does not necessitate a direct object; it might only involve a subject (e.g., "The bird soared in the sky" or "Do you care if the bird soars in the sky?").

[5] https://theology.georgetown.edu/research/historyofcare/classicarticle/

[6] https://www.etymonline.com/word/care#etymonline_v_33875

[7] When using the word (and therefore concept) "music," I mean to include the following relational dimensions: (a) people (globally) who engage in (b) musical processes—all forms of music making and listening—to create (c) musical products (e.g., vocal and instrumental improvisations; compositions and arrangements; musical-spiritual rituals; music-dance performances; digital musicing; music-film productions; presentational, participatory musicing, etc.), in and for (d) people who live and make music in particular settings (e.g., specific cultural, gendered, geographic, economic, political, technological, religious, and other contexts) for (e) a wide variety of values, as determined by the people who are involved (to various degrees as music makers or listeners) in specific "*musical communities*" (e.g., Irish traditional fiddle music, bebop jazz, EDM, West African drumming, singing, and dancing, etc.), or musical-social praxes (adapted from Elliott & Silverman, 2015, p. 51).

[8] Joan Tronto (1994) specifies "four phases of caring": Caring about, taking care of, care-giving, and care receiving. She notes that these phases, while "analytically separate" should be acknowledged as

"relationships" of caring. It should be noted at the outset that oftentimes, caring *through*, caring *with*, caring *about*, and caring *for* can and do intersect, overlap, and inform the ways in which caring "shows up" in music making and music teaching and learning. However, sometimes such intersections and overlaps do not necessarily occur. Because of this, I am, treating them separately.

"Caring Through"

The preposition "through" yields particular understandings and relationships. When we care *through* music and music education, we engage music teaching and learning to achieve goals beyond "the music," whether or not we're consciously using music for such ends. In such instances, music and music education are used to illustrate and experience ourselves as one caring. Consider the ways in which drumming circles, playing in ensembles (large and small), and singing with others can afford the values that stem from care: connection and connectivity, friendship and fellowship, spirituality and belonging. This can occur because we are synchronized and coordinated with one another when *we*—collectively—are fully present in moments of music making; this synchronization extends through our mirroring abilities that are ignited if/when we bond through music making and listening. Thus, caring through music and music education instantiates that music teaching and learning is the vehicle for which caring can,[9] and often does, occur. It also allows for the possibility that when musicing,[10] we can be our caring bests.

"Caring With" or "With Care"

The preposition *with* is somewhat different. When we engage in a particular pursuit with care, we find ourselves connected to the "noun" form of this word "care." Specifically, we "pay attention." We are more present and therefore aware of potential mishaps, mistakes, errors, or damage to be done. The verb form of "caring with" maintains some of the same focus. Caring *with* music (as well as music *with* caring) and caring *with* music education (as well as music education *with* caring) yields a starting point of attentiveness, responsibility, competency, and responsivity[11] to all those involved in and affected by

---

"interconnected." In this chapter, I am not considering "phases" of care, but rather attitudes, dispositions, and relationships of care.

[9] When music teaching and learning are not "care directed," care may not be a result. Musical engagement does not automatically yield care-full and care-filled relationships.

[10] "Musicing" is a contraction for "music making." In this chapter, I use the concept "musicing" as coined by David Elliott (1995; Elliott & Silverman, 2015), acknowledging there are important distinctions to be made between this concept and Christopher Small's (1998) "musicking."

[11] Tronto (2015) states we should image someone who is "attentive, responsible, competent, and responsive"; "caring with" takes these dispositions one step further by imagining a "polity . . . engaged in a lifetime of commitment to and benefitting from these principles" (p. 14).

our musical experiences (whether through teaching and learning, or not). Therefore, "caring *with*" denotes vulnerability and transformation. Caring with is, as Tronto (2015) states, a "democratic ideal" (p. 14). Why a democratic ideal? Caring *with* music and caring *with* music education also denotes a group effort in which all are "committed" in the effort of caring together. In particular, the preposition *with* helps us understand how *we* are stakeholders in the process, who possess voice toward the ultimate goal of caring (Hendricks, 2018).

"Caring About"

The preposition "about" is different yet again when connected with caring. Tronto (2015) states: "In the first place . . . care *requires* caring about: identifying caring needs" (p. 5, italics mine).

Noddings (e.g., 1984, 2010) states that "caring *about*" may serve us well, especially when considering issues of justice. Because care is relational, and because we cannot care directly for everyone, we need to think about how we would treat societal issues. Noddings (2010) writes, "When there is no provision for direct encounter and reception" with persons, places, and institutions, "we try to employ some form of justice in our policies. Justice does not become irrelevant when we embrace an ethic of care" (p. 50).

Caring *about* music and music education acknowledges there is a "need" (or needs) to be met. Indeed, wherever there is music and music teaching and learning, there are people. And wherever there are people, there are implicit and explicit needs. Still, societal issues demand we consider the *needs* and *rights* of others differently. Any discussion about "rights" seems to imply "obligation"; whereas discussion about "needs" yields "responsibility." The hard truth is we all possess both needs and rights. Yet, when we start from a framework of justice, we run the risk of "equality" being the measure by which to distribute resources, whether they be financial or emotional (see Tronto, 1994, 2013).[12] There is a fatal flaw, though, in this line of thinking. When caring remains a "subordinate activity" (Tronto, 2013, p. 101), inequities erupt, and progress—across a number of domains, including health and education—becomes impossible for many. As Tronto (2013) explains, we must rethink our responsibilities by caring *about* care: "We have to think differently about how we value the time we spend caring, and that means first noticing it as time we're spending doing worthwhile activities" (p. 29).

Tronto (1994) cites Jeffrey Blustein, noting that caring about caring maintains an emotional investment in being one who cares: "to care about caring is to care about one's ability to care deeply about things and people . . . to invest oneself in and devote oneself

---

[12] Within the sphere of education, neoliberal agendas have hijacked public care in schools by demanding "accountability," and linking funding to "standardized" evaluative measures regardless of school needs.

to something (or someone) or other" (p. 118). However, as Tronto notes, we must move beyond "emotional attitudes" and recognize the active components of caring.

For example, if I am a music teacher and I care *about* music, I will ask and answer the following question again and again, and adapt classroom curriculum accordingly: What does it mean to *musically* teach students? If I am a music teacher and I care *about* music teaching and learning, I will ask and answer the following question—with students—again and again: What does it mean to musically *educate*[13] students? If I care *about* music education (the profession) I will not only ask this question often; I will pause and feel through the weight of it.

The simple truth is this: As a profession, and as professional teachers, we can always be better at caring. The best way to be better at caring is to care more, not less (Tronto, 2015, p. 30). And as Noddings (2010) writes, "*caring about* may inspire *caring for*" (p. 51).

"Caring For"

Some critics might argue that "caring for" places those in receipt of caring into a subordinate position (e.g., Pettersen, 2011; Tronto, 1994). Other critics might note that "caring for" is "maternal" and "altruistic," and, potentially, creates spaces of co-dependence (e.g., Kittay & Meyers, 1987). However, and by way of example, if we recognize that we must care *for* ourselves—as in self-care—in order to properly care for others, we might not consider our own care as "co-dependent." Therefore, it stands to reason that how we conceptualize care—as related to the contexts (i.e., people, places, time, and spaces) where care abounds—is of significance to the ways it is practiced and, therefore, understood/felt.

Notably, the accepting of responsibility is crucial for caring *for* music and music education. As Tula Brannelly (2015) writes, "responsibility is a call to action based on needs identified through attentiveness. [It] is forward looking and based in action" (p. 226). On some level, this happens when we connect with people, given the ways in which our body's systems function through somatic, affective, and cognitive empathy. Somatic empathy occurs when we mimic sensory output of another (e.g., our own facial expressions change). Affective empathy refers to "feeling as if" we experience another's internal state. Cognitive empathy occurs when we "consider" another's experiences (e.g., Hendricks, 2018, p. 56). So, caring *for* involves more conscious attention and direction. A metacognitive awareness that we are caring plays into this.

For example, we can experience somatic, affective, and cognitive empathy when we connect with a song, its lyrics, or a particular performer's interpretation of a specific song (say, through autobiographical associations). Indeed, some listeners "feel" more attuned to Sarah Vaughan, Billie Holiday, Ella Fitzgerald, or Sam Cooke singing

---

[13] For an important distinction made between "training" and "education," see Bowman (2004) and Elliott and Silverman (2015).

"Summertime"; or some listeners connect with conductor Carlos Kleiber's version of Beethoven's 7th Symphony more than they do Simon Rattle's interpretation of the same work (and vice versa); or some listeners think Aretha Franklin's version of "A Song for You" is more authentic or meaningful than Ray Charles's version (and vice versa).

Additionally, we experience somatic, affective, and cognitive empathy when we are *caregiving* and, most importantly, *care-receiving* (Tronto, 2015, pp. 6–7). Caregiving and care-receiving are habits, dispositions, and abilities. So, how might we examine empathy related to caregiving and care-receiving as connected to caring for, and how might we consider further connections to music and music teaching and learning?

EMPATHY

"Thinking-with and feeling-with" persons, places, things, experiences, and phenomena (including musics); this is the cornerstone of relational being in music education. For now, there are a few ways to understand the importance of "empathy" as a means toward caring. First, and notably, the "self" can only be understood in its relation to others. No other, no sense of self (e.g., Buber, 1970; Elliott & Silverman, 2015; Silverman, 2020; Thompson, 2007). Second, empathy allows us to be and become someone who is sensitive to the feelings, thoughts, difficulties, needs, and desires of others. Third, "thinking-with and feeling-with" connotes somatic, affective, and cognitive dimensions of empathy (e.g., Elliott & Silverman, 2015; Hendricks, 2018); therefore, to empathize in one or more of these ways often is—and more often than not can be—embodied, embedded, extended, and enacted (e.g., Silverman, 2020) in, with, and through others and their worlds depending on the ways in which we "pay attention." Viewing "empathy" this way reminds us that empathy, when felt, is "receptive"; it is not like sympathy, which asks that we project ourselves onto another. Empathy is receptive, insofar as we become one who *listens*[14] actively and intently to expressed—whether verbally or not—needs.

Educative, empathetic, compassionate caring for music education asks us to be aware of and alert to how school and community music participants feel about how they're learning to make and listen to music, how they feel about and respond to what we're doing as educators, how others in their learning community respond to them, or not, and how we can improve students' experiences in these regards (e.g., Hendricks, 2018; Silverman, 2012). Viewing teaching and learning music through this intersubjective, relational, caring lens, rather than a purely objective, knowledge-focused lens, is essential if teachers want to teach music musically, effectively, and meaningfully.

Caring for music education includes the development of students' awareness of their ever-changing sense of self, the enhancement of students' creative and academic growth, their personal wellbeing, and more. In fact, it seems unlikely that any of these goods can

---

[14] For more on "listening" and the kind implied here, see Silverman (2015).

grow, develop, or thrive in an uncaring or unempathetic environment (see Hendricks, 2018; also, Elliott & Silverman, 2015; Silverman, 2012). As Wayne Bowman (2009a) says, education is, first and foremost, *relational*.[15] Moreover, because music education is relational, it depends on feelings and emotions, for emotional reactions are central (or should be) in guiding action in interpersonal situations and scenarios. Rather than being liabilities, feelings help us determine what is best to do. So in what ways does justice factor into this?

As Nicki Ward (2015) warns, identifying as a carer or cared-for may seem more "natural" for some than others; in the context of "identities of 'carer' and 'cared for' the two are often seen as immutable" (p. 67). However, this is not always the case. Importantly, ethical, social, and political issues require we recognize "roles and relationships" of care as experienced and developed within "the broader sociopolitical contexts" of the people and contexts where caring occurs (p. 67). And since all we are and all we do sit within frames of social, cultural, and political norms and values, we must do our best not to impose our own realities on those we attempt to care for, and "recognize the experience of intersectionality within this" (p. 68). This is yet another reason why listening and empathy are so crucial to caring for an-other (Hendricks, 2018; Silverman, 2012).

"Mature care," a term coined by Gilligan, might be helpful in situating the above issue about the give-and-take that completes empathetic caregiving and care-receiving. About this, Tove Pettersen (2011) states: "mature care seeks to highlight the relational aspect of the persons involved in the caring relationship, their equal worth as well as the wider web of relationships of which each of them partakes" (p. 11).

LOVE AND IDENTITY-MAKING THROUGH MUSIC AND MUSIC EDUCATION

What do we do when we find ourselves in situations that do not support such caring states? "Love is something that can take us . . . beyond the whole idea of morality" to an "ethical outlook"[16] (Chappell, 2011, p. 223). Given this, it is difficult to fully conceive of teaching and learning without an ethical outlook, without an ethic of love, without a sense of *caring for*. What does this mean for us?

If COVID-19 taught us anything, it is just how we need each other; how we need to feel and be needed; how we need to care more about caring *for* ourselves, each other, our worlds. Teaching remotely, making music virtually, and being separated from one another taught us how valuable care and connection are for our thriving, if not our

---

[15] According to most iterations of care ethics and feminist ethics, a "relational engagement" assumes an "ethical engagement"; see, for example, Buber's "I-Thou."

[16] Chappell completes this claim about "getting beyond the whole moral outlook" with these words: "though to say that love *transcends* the moral need not be to say that love is *immoral*."

survival. So to say, "I care for you" means, more or less according to Tronto (2013), "I love you." Because of this, I do not find it obtuse to ask: How dare we not be better about bringing *more* care and love into our worlds and work?

A music teacher who practices love-as-care engages with students as persons who are in the process of developing toward full personhood. In other words, a music teacher loves and therefore treats a student in relation to an "ideal of personhood" (Chappell, 2011, p. 9). "The interpersonal attitude," and a relational stance, "always involves a degree of idealization" (Chappell, 2011, p. 13). Because of this, caring for a student in class or in an ensemble involves an act of idealization that includes the assumption that her hopes and dreams and your hopes and dreams for her are achievable simply because she is a person. Still, however unrealistic some hopes and dreams may seem, it is essential that music teachers find ways to help, support, and keep hope alive for each and all. This is what caring teachers know-to-do and feel-to-do (Elliott & Silverman, 2015, p. 167).

Addressing the role of our being and becoming more human—i.e., caring and loving—and more ourselves through, with, about, and for music and music education—and therefore through, with, about, and for an ethic of caring and love—allows us to more fully face our humanity. These considerations are critical to engage in educational praxes for ourselves and for those we teach.

How does this "play out," given the contexts and content of the "what" we teach, namely (about, in, and through) "musics"? Since music "moves" temporally and phenomenologically; and because people suggest or feel as if music seems "alive"; and since people express that they "love" their musics, it may be that people interpret musical pieces and processes with a "principle of charity," making musical experiences feel like an interaction with another person:

> [I]n addition to many other human processes that make it possible for music to arouse and express a very wide range of the same emotions we feel in everyday life, it may be that *we make it true* that specific pieces or musical-social events possess a special kind of personhood that we respond to empathetically and emotionally. (Elliott & Silverman, 2015, p. 190; italics mine)

Further, as Bowman (2009b) argues, musicing can be "a rich, wonderful way of knowing and being in a phenomenally unique state with tremendous pedagogical and motivational potency" (p. 144). Why and how can musicing be so educationally potent and valuable?[17] Engaging in the world musically

> is a living in and through music. It is a unique kind of event, an experientially concrete way of being where the remarkable sense captured in T. S. Eliot's memorable

---

[17] It is beyond the scope of this chapter to discuss the potential harm musical engagements can do (Elliott & Silverman, 2015; Turino, 2008); still, it would be a mistake to suggest that all music and music making is innocuous and beneficent, because it isn't (e.g., Elliott, Silverman, & Bowman, 2016).

phrase "you are the music while the music lasts"[18] is neither metaphorical nor occasional, but physically actual and always the rule. (Bowman, 2009b, p. 147)

Thus, when *caring for* music education, performing, improvising, arranging, composing, leading, conducting, dancing (and so forth), or musicing—regardless of the musical praxis—includes phronesis and, therefore, a disposition to care for others *ethically*. Musicing can engage us in one of the deepest values of music: making ourselves (Elliott & Silverman, 2015; Small, 1977, 1998). Through the ethical idealization of musicers in acts of musicing with and for others, we constitute others as persons (Elliott & Silverman, 2015). For these reasons, when musicing is taught musically and carried out expressively and ethically, we find ourselves performing and re-performing ourselves in relation to others (Bowman, 2009b; Stubley, 2002). Thus, caring musically is "a process of mutual formulation and reformulation: an exquisite and vivid sense of . . . 'identity in the making,' . . . not just in a dyadic relation to a musical other, but in a rich and often complex web of relations with sounds and musically-sounding others" (Bowman, 2009b, p. 148; Elliott & Silverman, 2015, p. 242).

Let's take this one step further and wonder: Is it possible that one reason we're emotionally moved by certain pieces, performances, or performers is that we engage with music in ways that resemble or "mirror" how we affirm and validate other persons through acts of idealization—by taking a charitable stance toward the singer who sings her song for us? We often hear people say things like "That's my song!" or "That's my music!" or "I adore her voice." If it is true that personhood includes the propensity to empathize with others, then why wouldn't the same thing apply to our phenomenological experiences of music, or our actual and vicarious relationships with performers, composers, and improvisers? Is it possible that just as "self and other enact each other reciprocally through empathy" (Elliott & Silverman, p. 186), you and a musical "other"—a performer, a performance, an expressive performance of a piece—enact each other reciprocally through empathy, which often includes other affective, empathetic interactions?

More, music makers—especially those who find themselves dedicating lots of time, energy, and care into music making—idealize instruments, too. Think about the many guitar players who name their guitars; or the trombone players who prefer a particular brand of trombone; or the drummer who collects drums as souvenirs when she travels (see Alperson, 2008). Such acts are idealizations of instruments; of things. But these instruments are not just "things"; they are part of the identifying fabric of the people who make music with these instruments.

In addition to all the other processes that can arouse people's emotions while connecting with the music they make, "listeners engage in the same kinds of idealization and emotional-charitable stances they enact with and for others they care about" (Elliott & Silverman, 2015, pp. 329–330). As music teachers of music makers and listeners, we

---

[18] T. S. Eliot, 1988, "Dry Salvages," *Four Quartets* (Harcourt, Brace, Jovanovich).

must recognize this charitable stance our students potentially frame their musical experiences through, with, about, and for; they need and therefore deserve this kind of care and love.

Final Thoughts

Given the above, then, foundationally, music education should be "needs based" and therefore "care based." Music teaching and learning environments should be founded on reciprocity between the carer and the cared-for, despite the asymmetrical relationships of teachers and students. A central aim should be "mutual respect, attention, and recognition of equal worth" through which, Pettersen (2011) suggests, both the carer and the cared-for "contribute to the caring relationship" (p. 16).

Music educators who understand that identity formation and the interrelatedness of self-and-other does not reside solely "in the head" recognize that selfhood is "of the world" of personal relationships. Moreover, the interrelatedness of musical, social, emotional, and biological identities emerge from collaborative processes of music making and music listening. Facilitating caring relationships through music making and sharing in collaborative classrooms enhances opportunities for life-changing affective experiences, as well as for personal, communal, and democratic agency.

Because music education can potentially create pathways for identity building, we might be better poised to acknowledge that, as a profession, we would do better by *caring more about caring*. More specifically, *caring for* music education necessitates caring through, with, about, and for all the stakeholders that are affected by the profession's reach. We hold a great deal of responsibility as well as possibility across our educational encounters. Caring more about caring is cornerstone for doing well through music education.

If these points are valid, perhaps we need to acknowledge that we've got things backward. Perhaps the key to teaching and learning music well—because it is the key to living well—is for our profession to be "care-filled." We all—stakeholders in music education—need to feel we are "cared for well by others" when needed, feel able to care for ourselves, and possess the room to provide for "the care of other people," the environment, animals, institutions, and the "ideals" that fill our lives with "particular meaning" (Tronto, 2015, p. 38). Because of this, care must become a central value in our schools and music classrooms.

References

Alperson, P. (2008). The instrumentality of music. *Journal of Aesthetics and Art Criticism, 66*, 37–51. https://doi.org/10.1111/j.1540-594X.2008.00286.x

Bowman, W. (2004). Cognition and the body: Perspectives from music education. In L. Bresler (Ed.), *Knowing bodies, moving minds: Toward embodied teaching and learning* (pp. 29–50). Kluwer Academic Press.

Bowman, W. (2009a). The community in music. *International Journal of Community Music*, 2(2 & 3), 109–128. https://doi.org/10.1386/ijcm.2.2-3.109_1

Bowman, W. (2009b). Why musical performance? Views praxial to performative. In D. J. Elliott (Ed.), *Praxial music education: Reflections and dialogues* (pp. 142–164). Oxford University Press.

Brannelly, T. (2015). Mental health service use and the ethics of care: In pursuit of justice. In M. Barnes, T. Brannelly, L. Ward, & N. Ward (Eds.), *Ethics of care: Critical advances in international perspectives* (pp. 219–232). Polity Press.

Buber, M. (1970). *I and Thou* (W. Kaufmann, Trans.). Charles Scribner's Sons.

Butler, J. (1990). *Gender trouble: Feminism and the subversion of identity*. Routledge.

Chappell, T. (2009). Ethics beyond moral theory. *Philosophical Investigations*, 32(3), 206–243. https://doi.org/10.1111/j.1467-9205.2009.01374.x

Chappell, T. (2011). On the very idea of criteria for personhood. *Southern Journal of Philosophy*, 49(1), 1–27. https://doi.org/10.1111/j.2041-6962.2010.00042.x

Elliott, D. J. (1995). *Music matters: A new philosophy of music education*. Oxford University Press.

Elliott, D. J., & Silverman, M. (2012). Why music matters: Philosophical and cultural foundations. In R. MacDonald, G. Kreutz, & L. Mitchell (Eds.), *Music, health and wellbeing* (pp. 29–39). Oxford University Press.

Elliott, D. J., & Silverman, M. (2015). *Music matters: A philosophy of music education* (2nd ed.). Oxford University Press.

Elliott, D. J., & Silverman, M. (2017). Identities and musics: Reclaiming personhood. In R. MacDonald, D. Hargreaves, & D. Miell (Eds.), *Handbook of musical identities* (pp. 27–45). Oxford University Press.

Elliott, D. J., Silverman, M., & Bowman, W. (Eds.). (2016). *Artistic citizenship: Artistry, social responsibility, and ethical praxis*. Oxford University Press.

Fisher, B., & Tronto, J. C. (1990). Toward a feminist theory of caring. In E. K. Abel & M. Nelson (Eds.), *Circles of care* (pp. 35–54). SUNY Press.

Gilligan, C. (1982). *In a different voice: Psychological theory and women's development*. Harvard University Press.

Gilligan, C. (1995). Hearing the difference: Theorizing the connection. *Hypatia*, 10(2) 120–127. https://doi.org/10.1111/j.1527-2001.1995.tb01373.x

Held, V. (1993). *Feminist morality: Transforming culture, society, and politics*. University of Chicago Press.

Hendricks, K. (2018). *Compassionate music teaching*. Rowman & Littlefield.

Kittay Feder, E., & D. Meyers (Eds.). (1987). *Women and moral theory*. Rowman & Littlefield.

Kroegger-Mappes, J. (1994). The ethic of care vis-à-vis the ethic of rights: A problem for contemporary moral theory. *Hypatia*, 9(3), 108–131. https://doi.org/10.1111/j.1527-2001.1994.tb00452.x

Noddings, N. (1984). *Starting at home: Caring and social policy*. University of California Press.

Noddings, N. (2007). Caring as relation and virtue in teaching. In R. L. Walker & P. J. Ivanhoe (Eds.), *Working virtue: Virtue ethics and contemporary moral problems* (pp. 40–60). Oxford University Press.

Noddings, N. (2010). *The maternal factor: Two paths to morality*. University of California Press.

Nussbaum, M. C. (1992). Human functioning and social justice: In defense of Aristotelian essentialism. *Political Theory*, 20(2), 202–246. https://doi.org/10.1177/0090591792020002002

Pettersen, T. (2011). Conceptions of care: Altruism, feminism, and mature care. *Hypatia*, 27(2), 366–389. https://doi.org/ 10.1111/j.1527-2001.2011.01197.x

Reich, W. T. (1995). Classic article: History of the notion of care. In W. T. Reich (Ed.), *Encyclopedia of Bioethics* (Rev. ed., pp. 319–331). Simon & Schuster Macmillan.

Rogers, D. (2004). Before "care": Marietta Kies, Lucia Ames Mead, and feminist political theory. *Hypatia, 19*(2), 105–117. https://doi.org/10.1111/j.1527-2001.2004.tb01291.x

Ruddick, S. (1980). Maternal thinking. *Feminist studies, 6*, 342–367. https://doi.org/10.2307/3177749

Sander-Staudt, M. (2006). The unhappy marriage of care ethics and virtue ethics. *Hypatia, 21*(4), 21–39. https://doi.org/10.1111/j.1527-2001.2006.tb01126.x

Sevenhuijsen, S. (1998). *Citizenship and the ethics of care: Feminist considerations on justice, morality, and politics.* Routledge.

Silverman, M. (2012). Virtue ethics, care ethics, and "The good life of teaching." *Action, Criticism, and Theory, 11*(2), 96–122. http://act.maydaygroup.org/articles/Silverman11_2.pdf

Silverman, M. (2015). Listening for social justice. In L. DeLorenzo (Ed.), *Giving voice to democracy in music education* (pp. 157–175). Routledge.

Silverman, M. (2020). Sense-making, meaningfulness, and instrumental music education. *Frontiers: Psychology, 11*(837), 1–10. https://doi.org/10.3389/fpsyg.2020.00837

Small, C. (1977). *Music, society, education: An examination of the function of music in western, eastern and African cultures with its impact on society and its use in education.* Schirmer Books.

Small, C. (1998). *Musicking: The meanings of performing and listening.* University Press of New England.

Stubley, E. V. (2002). Studies of the musical work. *Canadian Music Educator, 44*(2), 6–7.

Thompson, E. (2007). *Mind in life.* Harvard University Press.

Tronto, J. C. (1994). *Moral boundaries: A political argument for an ethic of care.* Routledge.

Tronto, J. C. (2013). *Caring democracy: Markets, equality, and justice.* New York University Press.

Tronto, J. C. (2015). *Who cares? How to reshape a democratic politics.* Cornell University Press.

Turino, T. (2008). *Music and social life: The politics of participation.* University of Chicago Press.

Waithe, M. E. (1987). *Ancient women philosophers, 600 B.C.–500 A.D.* M. Nijhoff; Distributors for the United States and Canada.

Walker, M.U. (2007). *Moral understanding: A feminist study in ethics* (2nd ed.). Oxford University Press.

Ward, N. (2015). Care ethics, intersectionality and poststructuralism. In M. Barnes, T. Brannelly, L. Ward, & N. Ward (Eds.), *Ethics of care: Critical advances in international perspectives* (pp. 57–68). Polity Press.

CHAPTER 4

AN ETHIC OF EXPECTATION SURROUNDING THE VIRTUAL PERFORMANCE

BRENT C. TALBOT AND CARA FAITH BERNARD

CARE HANDBOOK TOPICS

Musical development
Philosophical perspectives

TEACHERS may often hear—or say—that they are doing something "for the greater good." Some might even call such a pursuit for the greater good on the basis of ethics. Yet, we wonder, "Good for whom?" Music educators' teachings and decisions often come out of habits or standards that are learned or inherited from previous experiences, teachers, traditions, oneself or outside influences. However, "educating ethically leads us to face and reconsider deeply ingrained tendencies of social living: the tendency to generalize, to codify into norm, and to assert" (Schmidt, 2012, p. 149). Although music educators' habits and standards may seem like a pursuit of the greater good, such choices may not always be ethical—or good for all.

Take the following, for example: An administrator or parent sees a virtual ensemble performance shared on social media or on a morning television show. The performance seems effortless and sounds polished. Out of good intentions the administrator or parent sends it to the music teacher saying, "Did you see this? We should do something like this for *our* school." For this viewer, the performance might be perceived as a model to be replicated in the ensemble program. In these moments, parents and administrators—in pursuit of the greater good to highlight the music program and school—might overlook the process taken to make musical products meaningful for students, including the social, personal, and pedagogical values and intentions of teachers and the program.

Hendricks (2018) reminds that such moments might put teachers in a difficult situation of having to choose between pleasing parents and administrators and doing what they deem valuable for young people to learn: "It's hard when you feel as though someone else is controlling your teaching and you feel as if you can't advocate for your own passions, goals, and values, let alone those of your students" (p. 8). We call this tension an *ethic of expectation*. An ethic of expectation serves an external desire (determined by an administrative action, curricular mandate, community member, or even the music teacher themself) for the greater good without necessarily serving the needs or wants of the students. Regelski (2012) notes that ethics in teaching are about more than pleasing the public:

> [J]ust as a "good legal practice" is not a matter of size, earnings, public notice, and the like but a matter of regularly serving the legal needs of clients well, a "good music program" is an ethical responsibility for clearly functional and beneficial results owed to the students, the community, and society. (p. 297)

The virtual performance setting might be one instance where music educators experience an ethic of expectation, or tension between the greater good and "simultaneous, customized information" (Bowen, 2012, p. 49). As Bowen has articulated, "Getting the balance of humanity and technology right is everyone's new mission, but we often want both and we want it now. This drive for both simultaneous and customized information may be a defining characteristic of human expectation" (p. 49). Our intention is not to argue that virtual performances and the use of technology are "bad" or "not valuable." We recognize that, in many realities, the virtual performance serves as an indicator that the teacher is doing quality work, or that the students are working toward a common goal.

Despite extant research on creating and producing virtual performances, the ethics surrounding inequities such as access to recording equipment as well as the sound manipulation and muting of student submissions have not been discussed. Such issues are central to music educators' ethical decisions. What are the ethical dilemmas surrounding the preparation and process of creating a shareable product? When one's decisions are made or influenced by external parties (administrators, parents, or other stakeholders), the ramifications "can quickly lead to misguided educative actions that may emphasize social inequity, skill over understanding, and the development of aesthetically narrow music 'doing,' rather than creative production" (Schmidt, 2012, p. 151). How might music educators cultivate connections with students and members of the community? What elements of one's humanity might be lost or gained within these tensions?

In this chapter, we examine the tensions and ethics surrounding the often perceived and/or (in)directly communicated expectation music teachers might face by administrators, parents, and others for creating and producing a virtual ensemble.

Framed through what we term an *ethic of expectation*, we consider ways music educators might build connections, promote student agency, and model compassion within various tensions surrounding the virtual ensemble.

Virtual Ensembles

The rise of virtual ensembles has become one popular approach for musicians to connect and make music at a distance. Researchers in music education have found benefits to virtual participation, noting that virtual ensembles mirror participation in live ensembles (Cayari, 2018; Talbot & Paparo, 2013; Thibeault, 2012; Waldron, 2018).[1] In their study on the Eric Whitacre Virtual Choir, Talbot and Paparo (2013) found that participation in a virtual ensemble can accomplish multiple aims, including (a) a fulfillment of musical, social, and personal aspirations; (b) extended musical engagement and learning beyond the classroom; (c) opportunities for self-critique and self-reflection; and (d) further development of musicianship skills. The structure of virtual ensembles provides anyone with a digital device the access to musical participation. Additionally, virtual ensemble participants see virtual ensembles as a "place" where social connections are strengthened (Jenkins, 2009; Konewko, 2012).

Research has shown that the process of engaging in musical and social experiences differs from in-person experiences. Talbot and Paparo (2013) described that some participants did not feel virtual musical processes provided the same embodied feelings of in-person music-making. For these ensemble members, the act of receiving feedback, hearing the entire ensemble, and adjusting to musical dynamics or blending was lost. Participants also missed the social connections that can occur before or after a live rehearsal. However, Carvalho and Goodyear (2014) and Konewko (2012) described that these connections might be achieved through social media including chat functions in online meeting platforms.

Though the virtual ensemble setting can provide a myriad of opportunities for singers, music teachers must be cautious when facilitating this learning space. Tensions may arise, including (a) access to material resources and labor to edit and produce virtual performances, including student access to technology and physical spaces for recording; (b) the added teacher role of editor/producer of content; (c) and the dilemma of manipulating other people's voices to create a final product—such as muting or changing their singing or playing. There are also external expectations to produce high-quality recorded performance products without displaying an in-person process. And, amid these tensions lies a possibility that the virtual ensemble performance might become the benchmark model toward which music educators are expected to strive, and

---

[1] For more information on how-tos regarding the creation of a virtual ensemble, see Cayari (2021).

on which music educators might be evaluated. In the following section, we explore how the ethic of expectation manifests a series of tensions in virtual ensemble settings.

Tensions Surrounding the Virtual Ensemble

Though any performance requires a great deal of labor and shared processes, there is a marked difference between preparing musicians to perform live versus preparing them to submit recording tracks to be edited and stitched together. For example, in both rehearsals and performances where musicians gather in person, musicians can make immediate adjustments and respond to conducting cues that facilitate blend, intonation, and change of expressive qualities, including dynamics, articulation, and tempo changes. Likewise, they can draw from visual and aural cues from one another to make sonic adjustments. In a virtual setting, musical decisions are made ahead of time in order to align the recorded material later. The pre-determined musical decisions—from tempi to dynamics—remove opportunity for rich discussions and group decision-making. As a result, musical choices may often become absolute, bound to a click track that provides calculated metric tempi to execute such decisions—which can stifle student agency.

Additional tensions include logistical responsibilities and specific roles that may lead educators to question the purpose or end goals of the music rehearsal. Music teachers typically support students' musical development in live settings by assessing their musicianship needs (i.e., rhythmic, tonal, or expressive components). In doing so, they may place students near other musicians who complement these components, immersing students in a sonic bubble that supports their development. Such expectations cannot be replicated in the same ways when students record alone in their own spaces. Thus, music teachers might consider the ethics surrounding their choices including how students access and execute recording assignments, and how teachers manipulate or adjust students' recorded submissions.

Access to Material Resources and Labor

The COVID-19 pandemic amplified music educators' struggles with having to orchestrate logistics surrounding a virtual performance, including facilitating an easy process for students to record, collecting student audio tracks and videos, and finding editors and producers to put together the performance.[2] Take, for example, this scenario:

---

[2] Virtual ensembles are not new; however, their usefulness became apparent during the pandemic, when the majority of instruction occurred through online learning platforms. We acknowledge that, under these extreme circumstances, teachers did not have a choice of in-person instruction, and thus embraced the virtual ensemble as a primary way to connect with students and communities. However, we feel the usefulness as well as the expectations to produce digital content from both singers and community members will remain a part of music teaching practices beyond the pandemic. We situate this chapter within a classroom space that considers both in-person and virtual experiences. Though our scenarios reflect the dilemmas of balancing in-person instruction amid a virtual world, we hope to elucidate the strategies and processes that might be used in virtual, hybrid, and in-person settings.

Ms. Bautista's assistant principal approaches her with the suggestion to create a virtual performance video to showcase the music department's work: "My daughter's school just did one and everyone loved it. It would really show the community how strong the kids perform." Upon assigning students to audio and video record one of their recent pieces, Ms. Bautista discovers that only eight out of thirty-six turned in their audio and video recordings. During the following rehearsal Ms. Bautista asks the class, "How can I help you to complete this task? What are the challenges you are facing?" Students first volunteer a variety of technological concerns such as: "I did it, but it kept saying the file was too large to upload, so I gave up"; "I left my good headphones at my dad's house"; and "I can't find a quiet space to record." Ms. Bautista addresses these specific issues but it becomes clear that this still doesn't account for the vast number of students. At the end of class a few students linger behind to share more reasons for not turning in their recordings: "There are six people living in my house and my neighbors next door have a baby—making music will distract everyone"; "My mom is a nurse and she works nights; I have to be quiet when she's home sleeping." Lastly, one student remarks, "I just hate doing this, it feels like a chore. I prefer singing with people." Ms. Bautista notes that there is a general feeling that the students do not enjoy the virtual performance experience because of these struggles. She too finds it taxing; because she has no budget to hire an engineer, it takes her hours to mix student recordings together. But she knows that her school expects to see some sort of virtual performance and finds herself in what Patrick Schmidt calls "a restless interaction between constant motion and adaptability" (Schmidt, 2012, p. 149).

Ms. Bautista recognizes that there are logistical barriers in place that may prevent students from turning in their recordings. Her students have varied access to material resources: Some students have only a phone to record while others have a microphone and digital audio workstation (DAW). Also, students come from varied living situations that may not be conducive to recording. Some do not feel comfortable video recording themselves; others cannot find space and time to record successfully. Additionally, some students remarked that they did not enjoy recording on their own and wanted to make live music in person with others instead. Ms. Bautista's assistant principal wants her to create a video because she sees other districts gaining positive feedback and exposure on social media. Yet, the pressure to create this final product for the community almost inhibits Ms. Bautista from being responsive to her students and adaptable in her teaching. Additionally, because Ms. Bautista was not expected to engineer recordings as part of her degree program, she finds her role as editor/producer to be cumbersome and distracting to her planning and teaching. Does she continue on the path of virtual performance despite the students' concerns and realities for the sake of showcasing a product and appeasing her administrators?

Manipulating Recorded Submissions

Likewise, manipulating one's recorded submissions for the virtual ensemble—such as muting or changing their singing or playing—is a serious ethical dilemma with which music teachers must reckon. Music educators might encounter having to alter a performer's tone, pitch, volume, or other expressive qualities on a recording. Take this second scenario:

> Acclaimed choral director Mx. Stevenson is working on blending all the voices in the DAW and observes in the recordings that a few students are not matching pitch well; a few other singers have poor breath support; and two students are holding the "s" too long while another singer places the "s" too early. Mx. Stevenson reflects that, in a live setting, upon hearing these sounds, "I would put these students next to other singers who have a stronger sense of pitch and who model good breath support in order to blend and balance the group." Additionally, Mx. Stevenson acknowledges the importance of visual cues, recognizing they would typically use conducting gestures or some movement to show better breath support or to indicate exactly where the "s" is to be placed. They elaborate, "I want students' hard work to be represented well." Mx. Stevenson struggles with continuing their legacy of lauded performances: "How am I to accomplish this without overly altering, silencing, or muting the students' voices?" In this virtual performance setting, Mx. Stevenson struggles with how to utilize and represent all singers' voices without having to manipulate their recordings.

Here, Mx. Stevenson's ethic of expectation is self-ignited to continue producing great performances. Their tension is one of altering a student's sound quality or deciding not to include a student's recording all together. Again, despite scaffolding ways for students to record and listen for potential pitch and other musical discrepancies, some students still submit recordings with multiple errors. Mx. Stevenson debates the options, noting that muting and silencing voices might be similar to asking a student to mouth the words during a live performance (see Hendricks, 2018, pp. 103–105). They question if it is ethical to alter or remove a student's recording when the student is expecting to hear themself as part of the ensemble.

Though these issues might have been ameliorated in a live setting, Mx. Stevenson must make an ethical decision. Given the need for a consonant, quality sounding choral recording, does Mx. Stevenson manipulate the recorded submissions? Do they take the stronger singers' recordings and duplicate them for a stronger, more in tune, precise sound? Do they mute certain voices but highlight their video so they are still represented? Or, do they accept the performance with various issues knowing that this will impact their reputation for excellence?

Virtual Performance as a Benchmark for Quality and Evaluation

The scenarios of Ms. Bautista and Mx. Stevenson illustrate struggles around the choices music teachers make when producing virtual performances—begging more inquiry into *how* best to balance the pedagogical, personal, and social goals with the expectations presented by administrators and community members. Some students may have access to better recording equipment and technology, whereas others may just not have the technical acumen to execute such an assignment on their own.

A recorded performance sets up an anticipation that the product is going to be of particular quality, something polished, mixed, and mastered. A recording is something that can be returned to, whereas a live performance is fleeting. Any preserved recording of a live setting contains nuances associated with being in a live space, including audience whispers, creaking of chairs, rustling of concert programs, or coughs. This product can be viewed and shared by parents, administrators, and community members. One inherent tension is that if the expectations of quality are not met through this recording, stakeholders might express their disappointment and pass judgement on what is being taught in the music classroom. Such snapshots may affect a music teacher's yearly evaluation in some states, even though the process of teaching and learning was not demonstrated in the performance. The virtual ensemble performance, then, as depicted through Ms. Bautista and Mx. Stevenson, might become the benchmark model toward which music educators are expected to strive and on which music educators might be evaluated. In order to meet the satisfactory requirements, teachers might make decisions that favor efficiency and routine (Bernard, 2015), with pre-determined learning criteria. In these moments, the virtual ensemble structure serves community stakeholders more than those participating in music-making processes. The technical challenges and external expectations in this regard overlook the human element of musical learning.

Resolving Tensions

Hendricks's (2018) model for care and compassion may be one way for music educators to resolve some of the aforementioned tensions. She describes compassion as "experience-sharing" which leads to action (p. 5). In other words, to teach with compassion is to "teach in the way that is best for each student or each class in each particular moment" (p. 5). So, instead of embracing expectations that appease the "greater good," music educators may focus more centrally on students' needs. As Hendricks (2018) reminds, moments like these "allow learning to naturally unfold, negotiating with our students the 'ifs' and 'whys' and 'hows' that likely will—with a bit of patience and creativity—eventually lead back to where we both wanted to go anyway" (p. 6). Such focus can flip the ethic of expectation from one of logistics and benchmarks to one of possibility. In a music classroom setting, ethics "can only be regained at the moment in which music becomes the medium through which the individual enacts *her* voice" (Schmidt, 2012, p. 160). When music teachers defy tensions surrounding the ethic of expectation, they may become open to more compassionate and ethical ways of approaching music learning. In the following discussion, we provide some strategies Ms. Bautista and Mx. Stevenson developed to address their ethical dilemmas.

Flexible Musical Choices

Compassionate approaches to teaching—which are more empathetic, flexible, and student-centered—are not cop outs, nor are they a "pass" to share poor quality playing or singing (Hendricks, 2018). Rather, they are moments where students might take action to respond musically to the conditions of the world around them and to create a product that is musically comfortable and attainable. Recall that Ms. Bautista's students found virtual performance preparation a chore, citing lack of places to record. Some students had only a smartphone, whereas others had higher-quality recording equipment. Together with the students, Ms. Bautista developed solutions and alternatives that facilitated compassionate-based outcomes rather than appeasing external expectations for a product. Ms. Bautista arranged for the students to record at school before or after classes, at a friend's house, or at a public space like a library or community arts center.

> Noting that some students did not enjoy the burden of recording parts, Ms. Bautista acknowledges that this virtual performance needs to be less about replicating an in-person experience but an opportunity to create something new that meets the realities, interests, and abilities of her students. To do this, she incorporates more comprehensive music making approaches to their virtual performance such as arranging and composing a piece, giving additional options for students who do not enjoy recording their parts. Ms. Bautista also chooses an open source, non-copyrighted piece that provides a foundation for added arrangements. During rehearsals, students discuss the meaning of the piece and ways it relates to their lives. Students liken their feelings to sounds, using rain sticks, shakers, and thunder tubes as a soundscape to personify a storm.
>
> Additionally, students work in small groups to create ostinati based on the text. Ms. Bautista incorporates the ostinati into the piece, arranging them in thirds throughout repeated musical sections. She layers them in as an introduction and uses them as a bass line and descant. As part of the recording process, students write reflections about the piece, providing context of the learning process and choices they made, priming the audience to listen deeply to the construction of the piece. Ms. Bautista weaves these descriptions together carefully as a reel preceding the musical presentation.
>
> Lastly, while compiling audio and video recordings, Ms. Bautista makes a conscious decision not to highlight herself conducting. Whereas teachers might feel the need to show the role of a conductor to administrators and parents to validate their employment, Ms. Bautista chooses instead to focus on displaying her participation in the musical process. She adds a short 30-second video at the end of the piece, building off the students' narratives and performance from the teacher's perspective. Her contribution provides a cohesiveness of the learning process—one that focuses on the students' needs rather than the community expectation.

Being more intentional with programming repertoire or arranging an existing tune may help music educators shift the expectation of a polished performance to something more focused on the process of learning. Inviting students to add in parts that are more pertinent to their existing lives and situations can facilitate greater student input. We advocate that choosing repertoire that may be less difficult than what might be programmed for an in-person performance (e.g., repetitive, memorable melodic, pieces in a smaller and more comfortable range with metronomic piano parts for easy learning and moments to solo) might afford time for discussion and working with the ideas and musical material in a more meaningful way. Through these choices, music educators like Ms. Bautista can demonstrate compassion by being responsive to conditions of students' worlds, thus creating a flexible musical product that is stronger and ultimately represents the students' and teacher's learning and growth.

Negotiating the "Ifs, Whys, and Hows"

As displayed with Ms. Bautista above, compassionate music teaching in any setting may acknowledge and resolve the differing conditions for musical participation.

> Worried about maintaining their program's excellent reputation, Mx. Stevenson debates how to accomplish creating a performance that truly represents all the singers, while also maintaining the high level of quality for which the choir is known. As Mx. Stevenson considers this dilemma, they realize that the technology is an impediment rather than an enhancer to the goals and processes to which they have become accustomed. In a live rehearsal or performance Mx. Stevenson would never ask a student to mouth the words or to not sing. However, stitching students' voices together in a DAW makes Mx. Stevenson question the ethics of this endeavor, leaving them with an uneasy feeling about how to address the disparities of acoustic spaces and errors in the recorded submissions.

Hendricks (2018) reminds music educators that a central responsibility of modeling compassion is to *trust* the students. She warns: "when we over-function for students—including providing loads of information and/or incessantly checking up on them—we demonstrate a lack of trust in their ability to learn and to work things out on their own" (p. 39).

> Conscious that their decisions might lead to over-functioning for the students, Mx. Stevenson decides to play the aligned yet unaltered tracks for the students in the homophonic sections and center them in the decision making. Collaboratively, students name and negotiate the "ifs and whys and hows" of how they, as a group, want to proceed with the project. They consider how the changing conditions of a recording warrant a different set of expectations and actions, including how a live performance more easily welcomes errors in a one-off listening session versus a recorded effort where audience members expect the highest of quality and can return to the source for multiple listenings. Mx. Stevenson poses the ethical dilemma of muting, silencing, or autotuning voices to the students and they discuss the ramifications, deciding that acting upon these choices would not represent the group's personality. Mx. Stevenson also offers the option for the group to not share the piece as a public product.
>
> The students describe that the ensemble typically performs unaccompanied works; however, one student with amateur recording skills suggests that within the recorded environment, adding accompaniment might facilitate better blend of disparate acoustic spaces and cover up some of the non-aligned breaths and sustained singing. As a group, they decide to add a piano and strings accompaniment that will help cover up some of the issues discussed, as well as improve the blend of the acoustic space.
>
> Students also suggest that anyone is welcome to re-record their part. One of the students volunteers to create a new practice track with two full measures of them

count-singing the meter and providing a starting pitch, establishing a strong tonal and rhythmic center for recording. Students could then submit a portion of the piece each week for feedback. Mx. Stevenson would listen to each voice individually and consider ways to scaffold the recording process to better address pitch issues, vowel unification, tone production, phrase shaping.

In pursuit of advocating that the program is "good" or holding oneself accountable to a particularly high performance standard, music teachers can lose sight of their own autonomy (Schmidt, 2012, p. 150), and in turn, their students' autonomy. When music teachers act with compassion, they can help students develop musical skills that avoid pitfalls of ethical decisions. Instead of "over-functioning" for the students by manipulating their recordings or autotuning their pitches, Mx. Stevenson approached the situation with trust and competence in their singers, speaking with them first about the best approaches to honor each of their voices. Incorporating students into these decisions provides pause for them to look and see if they are content with their choices and sound. When music educators trust students, students build confidence in their learning—this trust and confidence serves and centers the learner rather than the external expectation for the "greater good."

Resituating the Ethic of Expectation

When music educators trouble tensions inherent in the ethic of expectation, they can better understand their own contradictions (Schmidt, 2012, p. 150). In the cases of Ms. Bautista and Mx. Stevenson, shifting the external ethic of expectation to an internal, more collaborative expectation, honored the needs, situations, and interests of their students while also creating a quality virtual performance. Approaching something like a virtual performance through a model of compassion rather than an ethic of expectation driven by external pressures can help achieve the aims of social and musical fulfillment, and reflective space (Talbot & Paparo, 2013). Moreover, it centers the musical participants in the music-making process, spotlighting one's humanity over a benchmark product.

Ms. Bautista, Mx. Stevenson, and their students were able to create and produce virtual performances that were reflective of students' needs in their programs. Again, these small shifts reimagined the ethic of expectation, transforming the virtual performance into a place where all participants' voices could be heard and honored. Regelski (2012) reminds that

> the ethical virtue of school music is not a matter of simply claiming to have implemented a "good music program" (e.g., highly practiced select ensembles, a generous schedule of music classes, abundant resources) but is seen in (a) what the "program" actually does to enhance the musical functioning of the individual students

for whom it exists, and (b) its functional impact on the changing world of music in a rapidly changing society. (p. 286)

As Regelski notes, the focus should be less about building a "good" program and more about building a program that is good for the students' wellbeing and musicianship. When music educators work compassionately toward shifting the virtual *space* to a virtual *place*, students are given possibilities to flourish and belong (Hendricks, 2018).

Redefining the ethic of expectation is more about serving the needs of the students, acting for the "good" of the students, in "self critical and self directed parameters" (Schmidt, 2012, p. 150). In turn, this redefinition helps students to recognize how to respond to more individual or group needs of a changing society.

We return to the opening quote by Bowen (2012) regarding the intersection of technology and expectations. We argue that a more internal, customized expectation will lead to longer, sustainable change for students. "Becoming more compassionate," Hendricks (2018) writes, "is a lifelong journey for all of us" (p. 138), one where compassion is the act; a process of becoming flourishing musicians and meaningful members of a community. Redefining an external ethic of expectation not only promotes sustainable change for musical participation but also models what tenets of care and compassion might look like. Students may take such tenets and practice them in their own lives—what were custom, internal, personal expectations of care and compassion might then be modeled and given back to the greater good in more humanistic ways.

REFERENCES

Bernard, C. F. (2015). *Ensemble educators, administrators, and evaluation: Support, survival, and navigating change in a high-stakes environment* (Publication No. 3704455) [Doctoral dissertation, Teachers College, Columbia University]. Proquest Dissertations Publishing.

Bowen, J. A. (2012). *Teaching naked: How moving technology out of your college classroom will improve student learning*. John Wiley & Sons.

Carvalho, L., & Goodyear, P. (Eds.). (2014). *The architecture of productive learning networks*. Routledge.

Cayari, C. (2018). Connecting music education and virtual performance practices from YouTube. *Music Education Research*, 20(3), 360–376. https://doi.org/10.1080/14613808.2017.1383374

Cayari, C. (2021). Creating virtual ensembles: Common approaches from research and practice. *Music Educators Journal*, 107(3), 38–46. https://doi.org/10.1177/0027432121995147

Hendricks, K. S. (2018). *Compassionate music teaching*. Rowman & Littlefield.

Jenkins, H. (2009). *Confronting the Challenges of Participatory Culture: Media Education for the 21st Century*. MIT Press.

Konewko, M. (2012). Actual connections in a virtual world: Social capital of Eric Whitacre's virtual choir. *ATINER Conference Paper Series*, Article 2012-0205. http://www.atiner.gr/papers/ART2012-0205.pdf

Regelski, T. A. (2012). Musicianism and the ethics of school music. *Action, Criticism, and Theory for Music Education*, 11(1), 7–42. http://act.maydaygroup.org/articles/Regelski11_1.pdf

Schmidt, P. (2012). Ethics or choosing complexity in music relations. *Action, Criticism, and Theory for Music Education*, 11(1), 149–169. http://act.maydaygroup.org/articles/Schmidt11_1.pdf

Talbot, B. C., & Paparo, S. A. (2013, April 4–7). *Real voices, virtual performing: Phenomena of digitally mediated choral singing* [Conference session]. National Association for Music Education Eastern Division Conference, Hartford, CT.

Thibeault, M. D. (2012). Music education in the postperformance world. In G. McPherson & G. Welch (Eds.), *The Oxford handbook of music education* (Vol. 2, pp. 517–529). Oxford University Press.

Waldron, J. L. (2018). Online music communities and social media. In B. D. Bartleet & L. Higgins (Eds.), *The Oxford handbook of community music* (pp. 109–140). Oxford University Press. https://doi.org/10.1093/oxfordhb/9780190219505.013.34

CHAPTER 5

COMPASSION DURING MUSICAL ENGAGEMENT WITH YOUNG CHILDREN

DIANA R. DANSEREAU

Care Handbook Topics

Philosophical perspectives
Co-creating caring relationships
Identity expressions

To be compassionate is to recognize the suffering of others and respond by taking action (Peterson, 2017). Compassionate teachers, therefore, recognize the suffering that the education enterprise can inflict on students and actively seek to remedy it. According to Hendricks (2018), power imbalances or struggles within a classroom may be particularly painful to students and thwart their learning. To counter this, music teachers are encouraged to adopt a compassionate approach, which entails "shared music-making with others whom, despite their usually younger age and lesser experience in certain areas, we recognize to be equal to us" (p. 3). On the surface, the positioning of students and teachers as equal partners in the learning environment would seem to be somewhat common and readily attainable; however, such equality may be more difficult to achieve relative to young children (birth to age 8), and any difficulty likely stems from cultural and historical conceptualizations of children that position them as inchoate, lesser adults. The purpose of this chapter is to bring these cultural and historical conceptualizations to light, explore a reconceptualization of childhood, and envision practices for early childhood musical engagement that reflect progressive conceptualizations of both childhood and compassionate teaching.

"The Element They Live In": Conceptualizations of Childhood That Impede Compassionate Teaching

In referencing how humans are often oblivious to the technologies influencing their environments, McLuhan and Fiore (1968) stated, "one thing about which fish know exactly nothing is water, since they have no anti-environment which would enable them to perceive the element they live in" (p. 175). The way childhood is conceptualized by those surrounding a young child profoundly affects the elements that child lives within—including their relationships and learning environments (Dahlberg et al., 2013). An adult's conceptualization of childhood is likely acquired organically from birth and gleaned from the modeling, behaviors, and discourse of previous generations. Consequently, that conceptualization of childhood may be considered universal and absolute, and without awareness of an anti-environment, it remains unrecognized and unquestioned by the adult. Then, that conceptualization is passed onto the child and the cycle continues.

Should such conceptualizations be interrogated, however, it becomes clear that they are not in fact universal, but culturally and temporally specific (Waller, 2012). They can evolve and shift and are often tied to larger economic and political trends. Once aware of the conceptualizations an individual holds, they can consider them critically and then reconceptualize to adopt a view that is better aligned with a goal—in this case, the goal of becoming a more compassionate educator. This chapter begins with a discussion of three commonly held conceptualizations of childhood that run counter to the principle of compassionate teaching that holds that students and teachers are equal. The three conceptualizations are (a) children as lesser adults, adults as interveners; (b) children as lesser adults, adults as protectors; and (c) children as labor threats, adults as managers. I draw from the work of Dahlberg et al. (2013), Bruce (2015), and others, and situate these conceptualizations within US political discourse. I acknowledge that they are not universal, nor is this an exhaustive inventory of conceptualizations of childhood.

Children as Lesser Adults; Adults as Interveners

In the 17th century, John Locke suggested that a human is a tabula rasa (blank slate) at birth. This notion became a key principle of an empiricist view of education—an outgrowth of the work of behavioral psychologists such as Watson and Skinner (Bruce, 2015). According to empiricists, the child is "a knowledge, identity and culture reproducer" (Dahlberg et al., 2013, p. 47) who is an empty vessel waiting to be filled by an adult with more knowledge, skills, and dominant cultural values that are pre-determined by the adult and socially approved. As such, this conceptualization of childhood represents an inherently deficit view of children. That is, childhood is the beginning of a process of realization from the incomplete and insufficient state of being a child, to the full human status of adulthood (Bruce, 2015; Dahlberg et al., 2013). Children are seen as needing to constantly climb from skill to skill and stage to stage; they are in a perpetual state of becoming.

This conceptualization is apparent in the words and actions of political leaders who, when faced with a global economy that is becoming more and more competitive, are worried about their country's economic productivity (Kagan & Cohen, 1996). They often see education as the primary opportunity to provide the specific knowledge, skills, and cultural values that will equip children to become effective global competitors as adults. To this end, they seek ways to shape and lengthen children's educational experiences. As an example, in a 2021 address to the US Congress, President Biden stated:

> We're in competition with China and other countries to win the 21st century.... To win that competition for the future, in my view, we also need to make a once-in-a-generation investment in our families and our children ... adding two years of universal, high-quality preschool for every 3-year-old and 4-year-old, no matter what background they come from, puts them in the position of being able to compete. (Biden, 2021, paras. 18, 40)

Although universal preschool may be a beneficial outcome for children in the United States, the conceptualization that underlies the effort—that children are insufficiently becoming adults who are capable of competing—reflects a deficit view of childhood and a fear that children's blank slates will not be properly filled. Accordingly, children are seen as lesser adults who require interventions into their childhoods to ensure that predetermined outcomes are achieved.

Children as Lesser Musical Adults; Adults as Musical Interveners

This conceptualization of childhood may be reflected in music classrooms where step-by-step skill development is foregrounded. It also appears to underlie the 2014 Music Standards (National Coalition for Arts Standards, 2014) that are endorsed by the National Association for Music Education (NAfME). NAfME (2014) depicts these grade-by-grade standards as serving to help teachers move children closer and closer to an image of musicianship that has been observed in adults across time:

> The standards emphasize conceptual understanding in areas that reflect the actual processes in which musicians engage. The standards cultivate a student's ability to carry out the three Artistic Processes [that] are the processes that musicians have followed for generations. (Para. 1)

An overemphasis on children becoming musical adults discredits the child's existing musicianship and positions the child as musically deficient to the adult. Adult intervention is needed to prepare the child for the complete and coveted state of musical adulthood. Such a perspective runs in contrast to a compassionate view of music education in which teachers recognize children as equals.

Children as Lesser Adults; Adults as Protectors

Another conceptualization of childhood that may impede compassionate teaching grew from the work of Jean-Jacques Rousseau, who positioned childhood as the golden age of life and the innocent period of one's existence (Dahlberg et al., 2013). In this conceptualization, the child is viewed as virtuous and perhaps a bit primitive. There is a belief that children have an "innate will to seek out Virtue, Truth and Beauty; it is society which corrupts the goodness with which all children are born" (Dahlberg et al., 2013, p. 48).

This conceptualization also suggests that humans have an innate, biological propensity to develop in particular ways (Bruce, 2015), and aligns with the work of developmental psychologists such as Erikson. Sociocultural aspects are seen to have less influence on a child's development than what is biologically pre-programmed (Bruce, 2015). Adult intervention into childhood runs counter to the fundamentals of this conceptualization; however, adults who embody this perspective often show an inclination to shield the child from the society in which they live—to shelter and protect in order for the natural development of childhood to unfold.

An example of this conceptualization—and the associated inclination to protect children from the society in which they live (including schools)—can be found in legislation recently passed in the state of Arizona that prohibits sexuality education for children in kindergarten through fourth grades (Christie, 2021). The legislation also requires parents to opt-in to any instruction for students related to sexuality, sexual orientation, or gender identity. In celebrating his signing of the legislation, Governor Doug Ducy stated, "This is a no-brainer piece of legislation that protects our children from learning materials that aren't suited for them. Every family has their own priorities for their children's education, and parents should get to weigh in" (Office of the Governor Doug Ducey, 2021, para. 2).

This legislation represents an attempt to shield children on the part of three adult-controlled entities: state government that bans particular sexuality education from elementary schools, schools that determine to what degree associated topics are presented to children (if at all), and parents who must grant permission for their children to encounter any such topics. Shielding children from information that relates or will relate directly to their lives, bodies, and orientations represents a supposition of child naivety. Such a conceptualization discredits the child's own awareness of themselves and their world, reflects a fear of perceived societal threats on the part of the adult, and again positions the child as deficient to the adult. Like the previous conceptualization, viewing a child as a lesser adult who requires protection from ideas and information runs counter to a pedagogy built on equality.

Children as Lesser Musical Adults; Adults as Musical Protectors

The conceptualization of children as lesser musical adults with adults serving as musical protectors is evident when children are shielded from the musical culture in which they live. For example, a focus on music that has been commercially produced specifically for children—which often represents sanitized or musically watered-down versions of popular or folk music—in lieu of original, authentic, or musically complete versions, may reflect this view and the associated desire to protect children. While perhaps well-intentioned, pedagogical decisions such as this can have detrimental outcomes. According to Dahlberg et al. (2013), "if we hide children away from a world of which they are already a part, then we not only deceive ourselves but do not take children seriously and respect them" (p. 49). As with the view of adults as interveners, this view wherein adults are protectors similarly positions the child as in a deficit state of becoming and runs counter to compassionate teaching.

Children as Labor Threats; Adults as Managers

A third conceptualization of childhood that is influential to the care and education of young children is thinking of a child as a "labour market supply factor" (Dahlberg et al., 2013, p. 50). The US economy requires that mothers—particularly those in their prime working years (and also child-bearing years)—maintain jobs, and therefore that care is shared. Within this conceptualization of childhood, the emphasis and attention are not primarily on the health and development of the child, but on the health and development of the economy. Children, accordingly, must be managed. This management comes in a direct form when adults provide the actual care to children (e.g., grandparents, babysitters, nannies) but also indirectly, when government and market entities create systems, structures, and spaces to occupy children while parents contribute to the labor market (e.g., companies providing onsite childcare services).

This conceptualization of children as labor threats can be observed in statements pertaining to government efforts to institute early childhood care. For example, a recent press release detailing the Biden administration's American Jobs Plan stated:

> Lack of access to child care makes it harder for parents, especially mothers, to fully participate in the workforce. In areas with the greatest shortage of child care slots, women's labor force participation is about three percentage points less than in areas

with a high capacity of child care slots, hurting families and hindering U.S. growth and competitiveness. (The White House, 2021, para. 51)

As with the "children as lesser adults, adults as interveners" view of childhood, this conceptualization links children with US competitiveness and economic growth. In the former view, childhood is viewed as a necessary training stage for adults who will hopefully compete well on the global stage. In the latter view, childhood is an impediment to a complete workforce needed for competition and economic growth. In both views, childhood is seen as an obstacle to the success of the society.

Children as Labor Threats; Adults as Musical Managers

Music education has played a role in managing children while parents are otherwise engaged in work. While this goal may not be explicitly articulated, after-school music programs often position themselves as alternatives to the undesirable behaviors children may confront and engage in while under- or unsupervised by parents. For example, the El Sistema movement—an instrumental music education program that provides lessons and ensemble experiences primarily to poor children—has been said to provide "an alternative offer [to children and youth] that could be more attractive than gangs, drug-dealing, and violence" (Majno, 2012, p. 57). Organizations such as this may speak to goals of social improvement and nurturing promising futures for children and youth; however, implicit in this is a message that such programs would not be necessary if parents (namely mothers) were available to provide an alternative offer to derelict behavior.

Commonalities Among Conceptualizations of Childhood That Impede Compassionate Teaching

As indicated earlier, these three conceptualizations of childhood share commonalities, the most salient of which is the perception of childhood as a deficit state of personhood. Akin to implicit sexism, racism, and ableism—which reflect hierarchical thinking favoring men over women, white people over people of color, people who are abled versus those who have disabilities—a hierarchy favoring adults over children serves to bolster adults and reinforce their positioning (Alderson, 2005; Duhn, 2018). According to Duhn (2018), "Childhood, the domain of the child as the incomplete and unstable subject and thus in need of adult governance, strengthens and normalises adulthood as the domain of the self-governing adult subject" (p. 36). Further, as stated by Dahlberg et al. (2013), viewing children as "weak, passive, incapable, under-developed, dependent, and isolated" (p. 51) actually results in children who embody those characteristics. Consequently, a cycle is established and maintained wherein adults conceptualize children as requiring protection, delayed responsibility, and dependency, treat children accordingly, and in so doing, bolster their own views of self. The ethical concerns that such a cycle provoke are deepened when one considers that attempts on the part of the child to transcend this positioning may be met with punishment (Alderson, 2005). It is not difficult to see how viewing children through these lenses and the associated cycle of deficit treatment runs counter to—and in fact undermines—common principles and goals of education in general, and compassionate teaching specifically.

Influences of Problematic Conceptualizations on Musical Engagement

Lisa sits in a circle on the carpet with eight 4-year-old children who have just arrived for music class. She begins the class by greeting the children:

Lisa: Good morning!
Children: Good morning.
Lisa: You can do better than that! Let me hear your enthusiasm! Good morning!
Children: (louder) Good morning!
Lisa: I can't hear you!
Children: (shouting) Good morning!!!
Lisa: Much better! Now, we are going to begin our class by learning a song about my favorite animal. Can anyone guess what my favorite animal might be? I'll give you a hint: it likes to jump.
Michael (one of the children): A frog?
Lisa: Not a frog...
Amalia (another of the children): A grasshopper?
Lisa: No, not a grasshopper.
Kareem: A rabbit?
Lisa: Nope! Not a rabbit! Okay, I'll tell you. My favorite animal is a kangaroo and our first song is about a kangaroo.

>   Lisa sings the song for the children and then passes shaker eggs to each child, instructing them to keep the beat by shaking the eggs while singing the song. The children follow her instructions and appear to enjoy playing the shaker eggs. Michael explores shaking his eggs to the microbeat. Lisa pauses to correct Michael and reminds him that they are to be shaking on the macrobeat. When the song is finished, Lisa collects the eggs. Kyana holds her shaker eggs tightly, not wanting to return them. Lisa explains that it is time to move on and Kyana reluctantly, with a sad expression on her face, gives Lisa her shaker eggs.

As indicated earlier, the three deficit conceptualizations about childhood can permeate the music classroom, leading to an environment of protection, delayed responsibility, and dependence. Specifically, children may be shielded from particular repertoires or genres of music. They may be positioned as in a state of perpetual musical development—that is, viewed as musical becomings rather than musical beings. Music educators may seek to control the classroom and thus delay responsibility for children, and they may unwittingly encourage musicianship that is dependent on the educator. Teachers might employ management strategies that strengthen the adult–child hierarchy, and/or embody and portray themselves as all-knowing. In critiquing problematic, yet widespread conceptualizations of childhood, Dahlberg and Moss (2004) wrote:

> All [conceptualizations] view the teacher as someone who knows the one right answer to every question, as the privileged voice of authority with a privileged relation to the meaning of knowledge; and the complementary image of children as receptacles for the teacher's explanation and transmission of preconstituted and unquestionable knowledge.... All, in short, make the Other into the Same and remove the possibility of otherness, through the exercise of power and grasping the child. (pp. 95–96)

Music educators may strive to make the "Other" into the "Same" by moving the child closer to the educator's own profile of musicianship, and because the child does not yet wholly reflect that conceptualization of musicianship, the child is seen as deficient.

The musical experience described at the beginning of this section contains several indicators of a problematic conceptualization of childhood that obstructs a compassionate approach. Beginning with the greeting, Lisa establishes an asymmetrical power dynamic. The children respond to her greeting more quietly than she would prefer, so without a clear pedagogical goal apparent, she shapes the volume of their response until she is satisfied. This does not acknowledge, nor honor, the emotional or psychological condition that the children may have been experiencing when entering the room.

Lisa then engages the children in an exchange regarding her favorite animal. In this exchange, she centers herself and her particular preferences, and establishes a problematic power dynamic wherein the children are being told to exert effort to learn information about their teacher. Lisa possesses the single correct answer and the children must attempt repeatedly to find it. They offer thoughtful responses to her prompt, but those responses are not validated. Because there is no clear educational objective to this exchange, one might assume that the purpose was to reinforce the notion that the teacher is all-knowing and the children have a knowledge deficiency.

Lisa has a specific idea of how the children should respond musically to the kangaroo song and does not permit Michael's musical behaviors that differ from her intent. In this way, she fails to see Michael's musicianship as Other-but-equal. She possesses and commands the shaker eggs, and distributes or collects them entirely according to her wishes and without flexibility when a child expresses upset nonverbally. These actions further reinforce the power differential Lisa has established, delay the responsibility the children might otherwise have related to the instruments, reveal a deficit conceptualization of childhood, and thwart a child's attempt at agency.

The Anti-Environment: A Reconceptualization of Childhood That Reflects Principles of Compassionate Teaching

Although evidence of the aforementioned conceptualizations of childhood is widespread, new perspectives (including the reconceptualization that I will discuss here) are appearing and beginning to influence early childhood practice and policy. The shift to a more progressive view of childhood has largely been an outgrowth of changes in fields such as psychology, sociology, and childhood studies; and the move is largely led by European—notably Scandinavian—countries (Dahlberg et al., 2013).

Children as Interactors; Adults as Interactors

The "children as interactors; adults as interactors" reconceptualization of childhood is spurred by postmodernism, which has led to deconstructions of existing ideas about childhood (Bruce, 2015; Dahlberg et al., 2013) and the positioning of adults and children as equals. In terms of psychology, the reconceptualization is an outgrowth of interactionism—the notion that children learn via interactions with what is external to them (e.g., people, culture, physical experiences) as well as via interactions internal to the child through the senses and across parts of the brain (Bruce, 2015). Interactions between adults and children are key to meaningful growth for all parties and in demonstrating equality.

Those who embrace a reconceptualization of childhood understand that children are extraordinarily competent from birth, and therefore reject a deficit view and the idea of tabula rasa. They acknowledge that children are "both part of, but also separate from, the family, with their own interests that might not always coincide with those of parents or other adults" (Dahlberg et al., 2013, p. 52). Given this, the child is both similar to the adult, but also an Other with differences acknowledged an honored. According to Dahlberg and Moss (2004),

> There is an apparent paradox . . . the importance of being together with the Other; and, at the same time, the importance of an infinite separation, a distance to enable the possibility of difference. The child becomes a complete stranger, not a known quantity through classificatory systems and normative practices whose progress and development must be steered to familiar and known ends. (p. 93)

Children are considered to be a distinct social group, with their own rights and recognized as full members of society—an idea supported by the United Nations

Convention on the Rights of the Child[1] (Clark, 2005; UN General Assembly, 1989). They should have the means to participate "in constructing and determining their own lives, but also the lives of those around them and the societies in which they live" (Dahlberg et al., 2013, pp. 52–53). According to Hill et al. (2004), children have historically been socially excluded, having no input into local or national policies, and participation is the antidote to this. They define participation as "the direct involvement of children in decision-making about matters that affect their lives, whether individually or collectively" (Hill et al., 2004, p. 83) and distinguish this from consultation, which is the collection of input from children with no guarantees that it will inform decisions.

In this reconceptualization, it is acknowledged that power transactions are integral to relationships between adults and children, and that these transactions should be noted and examined (Dahlberg et al., 2013). In particular, "it is necessary to take account of the way in which adult power is maintained and used, as well as of children's resilience and resistance to that power" (Dahlberg et al., 2013, p. 53). In this perspective, children and adults are now actively viewed and working as co-equals—a key principle in establishing a compassionate educational context.

Children as Musical Interactors; Adults as Musical Interactors

Mya sits on the carpet as eight 4-year-old children enter the classroom. The children notice the photographs on the carpet in front of Mya which depict the songs and activities that the children have experienced in previous music classes. Some photos show props that the children have used to accompany music-making, some are images of the children moving in ways that align with particular activities, others help the children remember song characters. Each child chooses one or two photos and hands them to Mya, who adheres them to the felt board at the front of the room. The pictures will guide the content of the class and the order that the content will be experienced. Mya has also prepared a new song to share, which she will introduce toward the middle of the class.

The familiar song depicted in the first photograph involves shaker eggs, so the children and Mya move to the basket of shaker eggs which is stored on a shelf that is accessible to the children. All musicians take their two eggs and return to the carpet. Mya begins to sing the song and the children play along. At the end of the song there is a pause and James begins the song again. All musicians join James for three additional repetitions of the song. At one point, Annie chooses a scarf from a basket on the materials shelf and performs a flowing movement to accompany the singing.

After the last note, Mya sings SOL-DO and waits should a child choose to respond. Lizzie repeats Mya's pattern, so Mya sings it again to Lizzie. Ben jumps in and sings

---

[1] As of the time this chapter was written, 196 countries have ratified the United Nations Convention on the Rights of the Child, including all members of the United Nations with the exception of the United States (United Nations Human Rights Office of the High Commissioner, 2021).

SOL-MI-DO, which Mya also repeats. Ben sings SOL-MI-DO again and Mya sings MI-RE-DO.

Hakim: That sounds like a song my mom sings to me!
Mya: Neat! Could you sing the song for us?
Hakim: [sings song]
Mya: Hakim, I have never heard that song before. Would you mind singing it again so that we can all learn it?
Hakim sings and Mya makes a mental note to create a photograph depicting the song for the next class. She will work with Hakim and the other children to build on the song, perhaps adding movements or instruments.
Mya then says: I suggest we move on to our next activity. Remember that we decided hand drums work well for this one.
Thalia grips her shaker eggs tightly, appearing unwilling to return them yet.
Mya: Thalia, do you think our next song would sound nice with some shaker eggs also?
Thalia: I want to try!
The other musicians retrieve hand drums, Mya begins the second song, and Thalia plays along with her shaker eggs. Lizzie says "again!" after they finish so they repeat the song.

In reconceptualizing children and adults as co-equal interactors, musical engagement shifts from a teacher-centered approach to a more egalitarian context. Those embracing this reconceptualization rethink musical knowledge as universal, unchanging, and absolute; and consider how music is indeed culturally and individually specific. Music educators acknowledge the fallibility of their own musical knowledge and embark with children on explorations into musics that may be unfamiliar to them. Early childhood music educators emphasize individualization and provide a space where new musical and movement possibilities can be uncovered, honored, and explored. The teaching approach becomes a pedagogy of relationships, wherein the communication of the child and the adult as well as between the child and adult is key.

Consistent with a pedagogy of relationships built on communication is an emphasis on listening, which should include the various verbal and nonverbal methods of communication that children select (Clark, 2005). Inherent in this definition is musical communication, but also the physical cues that infants, toddlers, and children offer, which can indicate their levels of engagement and enjoyment. Conscientious adults notice these cues and identify them as indicators of children's firsthand involvement in the decisions that will affect their lives (Hill et al., 2004). They adjust their musical offerings to honor the children's expression of agency, make their collaborative intent apparent, and further and deepen the musical engagement.

This reconceptualization of childhood related to music involves the presumption of children's musical competence. Children often turn out to be far more musically capable than thought, and the presumption of competence can reveal even more capabilities.

An early childhood music educator's conceptualization of childhood affects large-scale decisions such as the structure of classes, curriculum, and materials to be provided; however, it also deeply impacts small moments and microinteractions. In the description of musical engagement above, Mya demonstrated her willingness to remain open and flexible and allow the course of the musical engagement to unfold in response to the children. This flexibility reflects Rinaldi's (1993) caution that "The potential of the child is stunted when the endpoint of their learning is formulated in advance" (p. 104). Though Mya made decisions regarding the songs and activities the children experienced in previous music classes, with the activities now familiar to the children, the children chose which would be included in the class. A song that Hakim introduced during class was treated as carefully as others, and it will become part of the class repertoire. Mya encouraged individual expression, showed empathy toward Thalia, and honored the musical behaviors that the children demonstrated.

The educational priority in a music classroom that reflects a reconceptualization of childhood is the full and free expression of children as musical beings, rather than their continuous climb to become adult musicians. Within this conception, teachers actively seek to minimize power imbalances that stem from deficit views of childhood. They acknowledge that both children and adults are on a developmental journey, yet all in the learning environment are sufficient persons and full members of our collective humanity. By resisting the formation of an endpoint of learning for children, conceptualizing children as Other and equal, and conscientiously listening to children as full participants in the learning experience, the music classroom becomes one imbued with compassion.

References

Biden, J. R. (2021, April 29). *Address to a joint session of congress* [Speech audio recording]. *New York Times.* https://www.nytimes.com/2021/04/29/us/politics/joe-biden-speech-transcript.html

Alderson, P. (2005). Children's rights: A new approach to studying childhood. In H. Penn (Ed.), *Understanding early childhood: Issues and controversies* (pp. 127–141). Open University Press.

Bruce, T. (2015). *Early childhood education* (5th ed.). Hodder Education.

Christie, B. (2021, April 14, 2021). Conservatives propose revised sex ed rules in LGBTQ pushback. *Associated Press.* https://apnews.com/article/parental-rights-gay-rights-arizona-gender-identity-sex-education-1f19f7a1aad2d2be7de934aa9807e9c6

Clark, A. (2005). Listening to and involving young children: A review of research and practice. *Early Child Development and Care, 175*(6), 489–505. https://doi.org/10.1080/03004430500131288

Dahlberg, G., & Moss, P. (2004). *Ethics and politics in early childhood education.* Routledge.

Dahlberg, G., Moss, P., & Pence, A. (2013). *Beyond quality in early childhood education and care: Languages of evaluation.* Routledge.

Duhn, I. (2018). Governing childhood. In M. Fleer & B. van Oers (Eds.), *International Handbook of Early Childhood Education* (pp. 33–46). Springer. https://doi.org/https://doi.org/10.1007/978-94-024-0927-7_2

Hendricks, K. S. (2018). *Compassionate music teaching.* Rowman & Littlefield.

Hill, M., Davis, J., Prout, A., & Tisdall, K. (2004). Moving the participation agenda forward. *Children & Society, 18*(2), 77–96. https://doi.org/10.1002/chi.819

Kagan, S. L., & Cohen, N. E. (1996). *Reinventing early care and education: A vision for a quality system*. Jossey-Bass.

Majno, M. (2012). From the model of El Sistema in Venezuela to current applications: Learning and integration through collective music education. *Annals of the New York Academy of Sciences, 1252*(1), 56–64. https://doi.org/10.1111/j.1749-6632.2012.06498.x

McLuhan, M., & Fiore, Q. (1968). *War and peace in the global village*. McGraw-Hill.

National Association for Music Education. (2014). *National Core Arts Standards*. https://nafme.org/my-classroom/standards/

National Core Arts Standards. (2014). *National Coalition for Arts Standards*. Rights administered by Young Audiences, Inc. New York, NY https://www.nationalartsstandards.org

Office of the Governor Doug Ducey. (2021, July 9). *Governor Ducey signs legislation to protect transparency in education* [Press release]. https://azgovernor.gov/governor/news/2021/07/governor-ducey-signs-legislation-protect-transparency-education

Peterson, A. (2017). *Compassion and education: Cultivating compassionate children, schools and communities*. Palgrave Macmillan.

Rinaldi, C. (1993). The emergent curriculum and social constructivism. In C. Edwards, L. Gandini, & G. Forman (Eds.), *The hundred languages of children: The Reggio Emilia approach to early childhood education* (pp. 101–111). Ablex Pub.

UN General Assembly. (1989). Convention on the Rights of the Child. *United Nations, Treaty Series, 1577*(3), 1–164. https://treaties.un.org/doc/Treaties/1990/09/19900902%2003-14%20AM/Ch_IV_11p.pdf

United Nations Human Rights Office of the High Commissioner. (2021). *Status of Ratification: Convention on the Rights of the Child*. https://indicators.ohchr.org/

Waller, T. (2012). Modern childhood: Contemporary theories and children's lives. In C. Cable, L. Miller, & G. Goodliff (Eds.), *Working with Children in the Early Years* (pp. 102–115). Routledge.

The White House. (2021, March 31). *Fact sheet: The American jobs plan* [Press release]. https://www.whitehouse.gov/briefing-room/statements-releases/2021/03/31/fact-sheet-the-american-jobs-plan/

CHAPTER 6

CONVIVENCIAS AND A WEB OF CARE

KEVIN SHORNER-JOHNSON, MARTHA GONZALEZ,
AND DANIEL J. SHEVOCK

Care Handbook Topics

Philosophical perspectives
Social activism and critical consciousness

STEMMING from the Spanish words *con* and *vivir*, or "to live with," *convivencia* is "the mindfulness of presence with others." The *fandango* from Veracruz, Mexico, and the *son jarocho* music it produces is enacted via convivencia, which challenges the notion of a "music" that exists outside of human relationship. Rooted within the equality and shape of a circle, convivencia as a value and aesthetic within the fandango gathering has become an invaluable code of ethics that extend beyond its cultural practice.

Fandangos happen through sites of convivencia via music that represent an indigenous understanding and embodiment of the kind of living and presence it inspires beyond its practice. In many ways care is like the value system that resides in convivencia, as humans are beckoned together under the guise of music-making to respond to the bio/ethical responsibilities of being present to each other in mind, body, and spirit. To be near one another, create music, and share undivided attention is a radical act of care, especially in modern contexts of digital distraction and isolation (see Bates et al., 2021). From this understanding, we examine histories of care and ask why the shape and study of care matters and how this may relate to music education.

In the spirit of relational understandings of convivencia and ecology, we propose diverse countermelodies of music, music-making, and music education that may deepen, challenge, and test the boundaries of what we understand "care" to be. Our personal and scholarly investments in music, ecological care, and indigenous perspectives lead us to epistemologies that are intersectional, relational, and rooted in natural relationships much like the ones embedded in soil (see also Smith, this volume). We acknowledge that contextual and place-based epistemologies are often in tension with scholarly desires to extract universalized definitions and phenomena from observational study. Rooted within Gustavo Esteva and Suri Prakash's (2014) framework of soil, we explore the problems of universalized definitions and how rational-objective frameworks distort shapes of care and caring into dyads that can be readily theorized and wielded for power. Feeling the dissonance of bidirectional care and caring, we problematize how idealized care is often an empathetic illusion that ignores the influences and interests of economic, anthropocentric, and social systems. In this time of great strife and questioning of all things and likeness to white supremacy, we seek to bring new voices and sources into conversation with the study of music education that lie outside traditional and privileged halls of conversation.

Like the diversity of musics across the world, the earth's soil-human conversations are richer in their diversity. We trust in the reader's open mindedness as our countermelodies may seem dissonant in some moments. With the promise to resolve in time, we hope the reader bears patience with this dissonance. The dissonance is descriptive. For our goal is to converse with new perspectives that envision (and en-*hear* the possible) emancipatory music educations where collective futures are richer in a diversity of soundings.

Care and Caring as an Object of Study

Gilligan (1982) and later Noddings (2013) point to how the language of care challenged patriarchal norms of principle-based ethics with contextually situated ethics, or care ethics. Drawing on a critique of male-normed developmental psychology, Gilligan noted that many developmental theorists pointed to cooperative tendencies as a disordered weakness that stymied competitive strength. Gilligan wrote that a "concern with relationships appears as a weakness of women rather than a human strength" (p. 17). Care ethics raised the profile of dilemma-based morality within found relations, or the unchosen relations of family and place. A mother cares for her child on a rich set of contextual interactions that are evaluated within a contextual framework of love (Dalmiya, 2016).

Noddings's (2013) theorized caring acts and caring relations between the "one-caring" and the "cared for." In her text, she explores presence, mutuality, engrossment, receptivity, and an empathetic displacement of interest, when we "see the other's reality as a possibility for us." That vision moves us "to reduce pain, to fill the need, to actualize the dream" (p. 14). The ethic of care presented by Noddings added complexity and mutuality to previous theories that focused on largely one-directional constructs of caring. The move to a theory of care offered new ways to dialogue, debate, and study the relation of care within dyads or bidirectional relationships. However, we note that in the process of building a theory of caring, theorists traded universals of principle-based ethics for universals of action and role. Care became a universal bidirectional interaction that could be studied, theorized, and reduced to constituent parts.

Studies of interactional synchrony have used dyads to study prosocial human interactions, especially the interactions between care-giver and cared-for (Golen & Ventura, 2015; Pasiak & Menna, 2015; Radesky et al., 2014). In controlled studies, dyads were a useful tool that revealed actions and dispositions that lead to synchrony, shared affect, and prosocial behavior. The presence of eye contact, perspective taking, and aroused attention, for example, is a necessary foregrounding that is the fertile soil from which care takes root (Miller & Hastings, 2019).

Though Buber's (1970) seminal text could be misconstrued as an exploration of dyads, his notion of *Ich und Du* is one that breaks the boundaries of isolated actors into the complexity and messiness of relational reality. Within dharma traditions, Dalmiya (2016) seemed to also sense a necessary blurring between boundaries of equality and mutuality if caring is to become a sustainable practice. Fung (this volume) notes a similar blurring of lines that is brought about by selflessness and non-egoistic being within Taoist traditions to attain an equality of care. Shirch (2005) and Pranis (2014) advocate for rituals of care that take place within the equality and interconnections of a circle. Such a shape breaks past reductionist transactional models toward lived expressions of circular, interconnected realities.

Problematizing the Idealization of the "Caring Act"

Dyadic studies of caring come from ontological and epistemological beliefs in the importance of abstracting universal principles from observation and study. This tradition should be held in tension with an understanding that abstractions can become "distortions of reality" that may colonize others and uproot Truths from soil (Esteva & Prakash, 2014, p. 127). In a recent critique, Hendricks (2021) noted that abstraction can empower supremacist beliefs and promotes a distancing that blunts empathy, particularly within racialized abstractions.

The rational-objective tradition is a human construction that has pioneered many "discoveries" and abstractions that are rooted in colonization and Newtonian cause and effect. Drawing on comparisons of Newtonian and quantum mechanics, Pranis (2014) writes of how circular systems cannot be reduced to cause/effect and observer/observed dualisms. Circular acts are irreducible systems of interdependence. In the same way that a harmony or melody resides within an interconnected realm of meaning, we argue that situated caring is circular and irreducible from interdependent relations.

Historical Problems of Dyadic Altruistic Care and Its Relation to Gender and Race

A survey of diverse histories of caring may point to how idealized, dyadic caring can intentionally or unintentionally become acts of transaction or domination. Nakano-Glen (2012) notes that a prominent narrative of care throughout the 19th century centered white women as "moral guardians" who could wield altruism to reform the fringes of society (p. 43). Nineteenth-century caring efforts within the Carlisle Indian School, convict rehabilitation, and immigrant communities were instances in which "caring" was sometimes used to intervene in Otherness that diverged too far from societal norms. Interventions were often problematically racialized as one-directional interactions that reinforced hero narratives of reform, rescue, and progress, identified by Flaherty (2016) as the roots of a savior mentality.

Hero narratives were often empowered by an imagined norm of caring that worked from an aspirational, white, middle-class, heterosexual model that was rooted in a theory of colorblindness (Audrey, 2004; Smith, this volume). Audrey (2004) noted "the idealism, individualism, and colorblindness of White ethical and educational traditions contrasts markedly with the political and communal pragmatism of Black traditions of justice and caring" (p. 34). Historical theories of teacher care dreamed that a teacher could cultivate the innocence of a child without considerations of race or culture (Obidah et al., 2004).

Notions of altruistic care had the additional disadvantage of devaluing entire economies of caring labor. If citizens viewed care as the work of selfless altruism, citizens believed care should not be compensated because it was the calling of a moral human being. However, this became problematic as more and more caring labor became the undercompensated or uncompensated work of women. In a chapter on the "feminization of teaching," Goldstein (2014) notes how 19th-century teaching was devalued in market systems as it became associated with women's altruism.

The United States also built entire economies around the unpaid or underpaid "caring" labor of immigrants and women of color. According to Nakano-Glenn's (2010) analysis, care workers are predominantly women (91.8%), disproportionately immigrants (24.9%), and are often people of color (49.7%). Dyadic caring became a tool of oppression on diverse communities and recursively on the gendered roles that were expected to provide care.

Writing from her own experience as a Chicana woman of color, co-author Martha Gonzalez writes:

> Care is a loaded term for me. I cannot uproot my subjectivity (as a Chicana) from a term that holds so much historical meaning in relation to labor. I understand care as a commodity, one that many women of color like myself have provided for white women and their children for centuries now. My own mother provided this kind of labor for many white women for over 15 years in order to provide for our family. As women of color in this country we have been paid little to no money to provide care or other related services, for wealthy, often white families.

As we seek to restore the dyad to become a circle, we do so knowing that linear, idealized shapes of care have a raced, gendered, and economic history that played a role in systematic oppressions throughout US history.

A Rerooting Care in Soil

In her seminal text, *Silent Spring*, Rachel Carson (2002) introduces the language of a "web of life" to invite humans into an ecological sense of circular mutuality. Aghast at the human capacity to inject harmful chemicals into waterways and along roadsides, Carson reminded readers of the "interwoven strands that lead from microbes to man" (p. 69). Embracing circular, interconnected ecological relationships as a web of caring, might we imagine that likewise, new forms of music education demonstrate a web of listening, a moving, and a sounding? A reciprocal gift of musicking with Mother Earth, and not merely the extraction of resources (Smith, this volume; see also Smith, 2021).

In rerooting music education to the likeness of soil, Shevock (2018) builds a vision of eco-literate music-making that is an interspecies balance of listening and sounding within a specific, localized soil. Rerooting is also remembering, or re-membering, as we are *members* of ecological bodies born of and returning our bodies to soil—facts we in industrial culture have forgotten. The language of soil carries with it a deeply embodied experience of digging our hands into the richness of our place. In his text on care, Boff (2008) speaks to reframing "care" as "caress" in an attempt to translate abstractions of care into tangible expressions of physical touch. This can be a multi-sensoral musical caress, reciprocating among diverse organisms and soil.

In the caress of soil, eco-literate music-making is rooted in a sense of care that resists monocultures of industrial and uniform music education (Shevock, 2018, p. 106). Modern forms of music education build one-way soundings into acoustically treated and ecologically sterile environments of perfect resonance.

To exemplify, Levin and Süzükei's (2006) ethnomusicological treatise on Tuvan soundscapes may point to indigenous understandings about how circles of listening-sounding are genuine forms of relationality and care. Levin and Süzükei note that Tuvan singers often stop at streams, caves, and sacred natural dwellings to listen to the polyphonic resonance within a particular place. Using techniques such as *borbangnadyr*, Tuvan musicians create a pulsating imitation of water with voice, singing to the water in a cyclical listening-sounding recognition of the sacred, caring relationship between place and species. It may be that the only way to re-member music practices with ecological being in modern American music education is to escape our uprooted, institutional notions of music education and enter a circular embrace with unmediated listening-sounding in a local place (see Shevock, 2016).

Convivencia as a System of Care by Martha Gonzalez

In my text *Chican@ Artivistas: Music, Community and Transborder Tactics in East Los Angeles* (2020), I ground my study of a reclamation of music as a radical act of caring through conviviencia and its significance in the community ritual of fandango; and how it has influenced Chicanx artivista (artist/activist) communities. As a participatory music, dance and poetic practice native to the state of Veracruz, Mexico, Fandango is not a performance but rather a transgenerational convivial space where community gives birth to the music of the son jarocho.

Rooted in a history of colonization, labor exploitation, and resistance, the music, poetry, and dance of fandango is a unique cultural mixture of African, Indigenous, and Spanish (Andalusia) influences. Mostly prominent in the region currently known as southern Veracruz, Mexico, fandango is currently exercised as ritual celebration in honor of a town's patron saint or as part of other community celebrations such as weddings, baptisms, and funerals. The music born in fandango-son jarocho is manifested and maintained through everyday practice of the *jaraneros* (musicians who play a small, eight-string five course guitar called a *jarana*), *versadores* (poets), *bailadoras* (dancers), and the greater community including children of all ages and the elderly.

Importantly, the fandango ritual takes place in the shape of a circle. Singular or concentric, complete or spiraled, the circle mirrors the praxis and value system of reciprocity in fandango-convivencia. As we began this essay above, "to live with" or convivencia is the mindfulness of presence with others. Our participation in fandango communities, and experiences in a cultural process of learning and participating in fandangos, has emancipated us to new ways of being in music and how it can exist in our lives. That is to say, convivencia within fandango has become an invaluable code of ethics in *artivista* philosophy—one that uproots our understanding of music solely as a product for consumption or music skillset to acquire with a desire to professionalize.

Decentering music as commodity made us focus on the relationships one must build in the learning and participation of fandango. Relationship building is a central and most important part of acquiring knowledge in the practice. Indigenous Cree nation scholar Shawn Wilson (2008) might refer to this as centering the values of "relationality," which results from moments of sharing and healing. Citing relationality as part and parcel to an Indigenous ontology, Wilson states that "rather than viewing ourselves as being *in* relationships with other people or things, we *are* the relationships that we hold and are a part of" (p. 80). Relationship building within the fandango community and the care that one gives to the respected elders, women and children in the tradition is part of learning the craft and in so doing we earn our place and identity within it.

Circling back to the importance of land and soil, the extensive repertoire in fandango is rooted in an appreciation, care, and commitment to land, for the tradition was born in, and has been informed by life in the *campo*, or the countryside. Many *sones* bare names of animals such as "*La Guacamaya*" (the macaw), "*El Balaju*" (sword fish), "*La Iguana*" (iguana), and "*El Toro Zacamadu*" (the bull) for example, for they are all animals needed for survival or sustenance. Furthermore, the poetics (lyrics) of the sones are deliberate sites of critical reflection about all things related to humanity and our cosmic and/or ecological role to each other and the earth.

Finally, fandango and particularly the convivencia inherent in the practice incites multiple dialogues among the community and its constituents, which can lead to greater analysis of society and one's role in it. It is no coincidence that we see more than one fandango community harness the music (son jarocho) and fandango, to build around social justice issues and struggles. In Santa Ana, California, for example, the community in Centro Cultural de Mexico and their son jarocho collective *Son del Centro* has used son jarocho and fandango practice in support of immigrant rights, May Day marches, the Immokalee workers strike, and other related local and international struggles. In Seattle, Washington, the Seattle Fandango Project (SFP) organizes fandangos and workshops in women's shelters, food justice events, preschool, elementary and high schools. In San Diego the "*Fandango Fronterizo*" or Border Fandango is a yearly event initiated in 2008 at the US-Mexican border, whereby two *tarimas* are placed on each side of the fence as US and Mexican participants engage in a transnational fandango. By managing to hold a fandango at the border, the sociality of sound temporarily wills the border out of existence. Indeed, in the case of the Fandango Fronterizo, embodied practices are what performance studies scholar Diana Taylor (2003) might cite as, "an episteme, a praxis, a way of knowing as well as a way of storing and transmitting cultural knowledge and identity that is not adherent to political or nation-state boundaries" (p. xv).

This brief example of the fandango music world, and the care one takes in the learning and acquisition of skillsets, stands in stark contrast to the academy—which has the tendency to extract information (i.e., skillsets, technique) from communities. Often, we regretfully forget the importance of care and relationship building but also the cultural contexts and values rooted in the music that inform the practice. In this way, we miss the deep history that gives rise to music, which are often the most important and organic learning opportunities that may enrich one's overall practice.

A Convivencia of Circular Caring

In her texts, Hendricks (2018, 2021) notes that we need to upend the heroic journey model if we wish to form deeper communities within music education. In a sense we need to enter an "atmosphere of caring" that upends traditional dyadic power structures in which the music teacher acts on students (p. 125). We believe that enacting convivencia of music teaching breaks down roles of caregiver and cared-for and, in so doing, builds sound-listening exchanges within a web of circular relations.

When we enter a circular care for musical place in all its lived diversity, we enter a state of being where we will always be the "one-caring" and the "cared for" at the same time. The vulnerability of circular space resists our pull to domination and may re-member our being into local ecologies. Vulnerability is the center of entering into authentic relationship (Hendricks, 2021) and leans into the softness and flexibility necessary to care (see Fung, this volume). From this exploration, we encourage a resistance to universalize caring, and a resistance to reductionist bidirectional models of caring. We recognize the mutuality of relation and non-egoistic action that is found within rich philosophical traditions of interdependence (see Fung, this volume). Sounding the circle that is found in so many musical traditions, we enter a circular web of relationality that breaks the audience-performer dyad that is so common in modern economies of music.

So as bailadoras feet strike the *tarima* and the circular interlaced community responds with the multisonic polyrhythmic strums of the jaranas, *requintos*, and *leonas*, we experience the ecosystem. We understand that the poetic prose of the versadores is informed by its rooted history as well as the lived present. We lean into an understanding of music rooted to a deep web of life, allowing us to awaken to the cycles of our soundings. We trust the process and learn by participating and listening with the promise that we may be mutually responding to each other's calls, to those caring and those cared for, continuously, at the same time.

REFERENCES

Audrey, T. (2004). Caring and colortalk: Childhood innocence in white and black. In V. S. Walker & J. R. Snarey (Eds.), *Race-ing moral formation: African American perspectives on care and justice* (pp. 23–37). Teachers College Press.

Bates, V. C., Shevock, D. J., & Prest, A. (2021). Cultural diversity, ecodiversity, and music education. In A. A. Kallio, H. Westerlund, S. Karlsen, K. Marsh, & E. Sæther (Eds.), *The politics of diversity in music education* (pp. 163–174). Springer.

Boff, L. (2008). *Essential care: An ethics of human nature*. Baylor University Press.

Buber, M. (1970). *I and thou*. Simon & Schuster.

Carson, R. (2002). *Silent spring*. Houghton Mifflin.

Dalmiya, V. (2016). *Caring to know: Comparative care ethics, feminist epistemology, and the Mahabharata* (pp. 41–86). Oxford University Press. https://doi.org/10.1093/acprof:oso/9780199464760.001.0001

Esteva, G., & Prakash, M. S. (2014). *Grassroots post-modernism: Remaking the soil of cultures* (2nd ed.). Zed Books.

Fallace, T. D. (2011). *Dewey and the dilemma of race: An intellectual history (1895–1922)*. Teachers College Press.

Flaherty, J. (2016). *No more heroes: Grassroots challenges to the savior mentality*. AK Press.

Gilligan, C. (1982). *In a different voice: Psychological theory and women's development*. Harvard University Press.

Goldstein, D. (2014). *The teacher wars: A history of America's most embattled profession*. Doubleday.

Golen, R. P., & Ventura, A. K. (2015). What are the mothers doing while bottle-feeding their infants? Exploring the prevalence of maternal distraction during bottle-feeding interactions. *Early Human Development, 91,* 787–791. https://doi.org/10.1016/j.earlhumdev.2015.09.006

Gonzalez, M. (2020). *Chican@ Artivistas: Music, community, and transborder tactics in East Los Angeles.* University of Texas Press.

Hendricks, K. S. (2018). *Compassionate music teaching.* Rowman & Littlefield.

Hendricks, K. S. (2021). Authentic connection in music education: A chiastic essay. In K. S. Hendricks & J. Boyce-Tillman (Eds.), *Authentic connection: Music, spirituality, and wellbeing* (pp. 237–253). Peter Lang.

Hove, M. J., & Risen, J. L. (2009). It's all in the timing: Interpersonal synchrony increases affiliation. *Social Cognition, 27*(6), 949–960. https://doi.org/10.1521/soco.2009.27.6.949

Kimmerer, R. W. (2013). *Braiding sweetgrass.* Milkweed Editions.

Levin, T., & Süzükei, V. (2006). *Where rivers and mountains sing: Sound, music, and nomadism in Tuva and beyond.* Indiana University Press.

Miller, J. G., & Hastings, P. D. (2019). Parenting, neurobiology, and prosocial development. In D. J. Laible, G. Carlo, & L. M. Padilla-Walker (Eds.), *Oxford handbook of parenting and moral development* (pp. 130–144). Oxford University Press.

Nakano-Glenn, E. (2012). *Forced to care: Coercion and caregiving in America.* Harvard University Press.

Noddings, N. (2005). What does it mean to educate the whole child? *Educational Leadership, 63*(1), 8–13.

Noddings, N. (2012). *Peace education: How we come to love and hate war.* Cambridge University Press.

Noddings, N. (2013). *Caring: A relational approach to ethics and moral education.* University of California Press.

Nunes, M. R., van Es, M. M., Schindelbeck, R., James Ristow, A., & Ryan, M. (2018). No-till and cropping system diversification improve soil health and crop yield. *Geoderma, 328,* 30–43. https://doi.org/10.1016/j.geoderma.2018.04.031

Obidah, J. E., Jackson-Minot, M., Monroe, C. R., & Williams, B. (2004). Crime and punishment: Moral dilemmas in the inner-city classroom. In V. S. Walker & J. R. Snarey (Eds.), *Race-ing moral formation: African American perspectives on care and justice* (pp. 111–129). Teachers College Press.

Pasiak, C., & Menna, R. (2015). Mother–child synchrony: Implications for young children's aggression and social competence. *Journal of Child and Family Studies, 24,* 3079–3092. https://doi.org/10.1007/s10826-015-0113-y

Pranis, K. (2014). *The little book of circle processes: A new/old approach to peacemaking.* Simon & Schuster.

Radesky, J. S., Kistin, C. J., Zuckerman, B., Nitzberg, K., Gross, J., Kaplan-Sanoff, M., Augustyn, M., & Silverstein, M. (2014). Patterns of mobile device use by caregivers and children during meals in fast food restaurants. *Pediatrics, 133*(4), 843–849. https://doi.org/10.1542/peds.2013-3703

Shevock, D. J. (2016). Music educated and uprooted: My story of rurality, whiteness, musicing, and teaching. *Action, Criticism, and Theory for Music Education, 15*(4), 30–55. http://dx.doi.org/10.22176/act15.4.30

Shevock, D. J. (2018). *Eco-literate music pedagogy.* Routledge.

Shirch, L. (2005). *Ritual and symbol in peacebuilding.* Kumarian Press.

Smith, T. D. (2021). Music education for surviving and thriving: Cultivating children's wonder, senses, emotional wellbeing, and wild nature as a means to discover and fulfill their life's purpose. *Frontiers in Education*, 6(648799). http://dx.doi.org/10.3389/feduc.2021.648799

Taylor, D. (2003). *The archive and the repertoire: Performing cultural memory in the Americas*. Duke University Press.

Wilson, S. (2018). *Research is ceremony: Indigenous research methods*. Fernwood Publishing.

CHAPTER 7

THE HOSPITALITY OF WONDER AND ITS RELATION TO CARE AND COMPASSION IN MUSIC EDUCATION

JUNE BOYCE-TILLMAN

CARE HANDBOOK TOPICS

Philosophical perspectives

INTRODUCTION

This chapter will base care and compassion in music education within the reestablishment of the element of wonder in music education. It will see the uncertainty implicit in wonder as allowing for openness to the Other, particularly within the notion of difference. It will chart the philosophical origins of wonder, its place in an educational system based in certainty, its relationship with virtues including care and compassion, and its role in child development. It will see how wonder opens us to be compassionate toward different ways of knowing and the role music education may play in this. It is illustrated throughout with practical examples.

A PHILOSOPHY OF WONDER

In Aristotle's view, philosophy begins in wonder. This wonder establishes a sense of sacred in the world. Humanity's fundamental relationship with the world is via wonder.

It is part of the loss of wonder in our concept of knowledge that has colored how we interact with the human and other-than-human world. In wonder there is a place for not knowing and uncertainty, which is the deepest fear in an educational world filled with facts and figures and certainties which may be false or at least only partly true. Our educational systems have become a means of keeping uncertainty at bay. But this chapter will set out how the end of the search for certainty is fundamentalisms of various kinds, which are often violent and disrespectful of difference. It will argue that wonder gives dignity to the Other and approaches other aspects of the cosmos in an open humane way rather than one colored by stereotyping and prejudice. This is an area where teachers can potentially learn from the younger children's natural embracing of wonder where there can be mutual learning. It will argue that the arts that both confront us with uncertainties and also give us ways of handling them. H. M. Evans (2012) attempts a definition of wonder as a special kind of transfiguring encounter between us and something other than us, characterized by a very particular attitude of special attentiveness. In it the ordinary is transfigured by and suffused with something extraordinary in an experience that transforms the wonderer. This transformation can engender compassion.

Wonder and the Unknown

The philosopher Mary Jane Rubinstein (2008) asks "what it might mean to stay with the perilous wonder that resists final resolution, simple identity, and sure teleology" (p. 24). Jerome Miller (1992) sees knowledge as currently conceived in education systems as the process of gaining control over the world of wonder. For him, knowledge is a way to escape the inferior position in which wonder places us when it both transcends and terrifies us. Both Heidegger (1994) and Otto (1923) see terror as a significant part of wonder. To surrender to wonder means "allowing oneself to be cast into the abyss of the unknown instead of trying to find a way to secure oneself from that vertiginous possibility" (Miller, 1992, pp. 4–5). This is part of the composer Pauline Oliveros's (2005) idea of deep listening:

> The practice is intended to expand consciousness to the whole space/time continuum of sound/silences. . . . Creativity means the formation of new patterns. . . . Compassion (spiritual development) and understanding comes from listening impartially to the whole space/time continuum of sound. (p. xxv)

Approaching music with wonder opens us up to compassion with the journey of the composer that can help us with our own journey. Anthony Rooley (1990), for example, gives an account of the cathartic effect of performances of John Dowland's *The Songs of Mourning* for people who have suffered a bereavement. The compassion generated by listening extends to the caring action of choosing listening material appropriate for the situation of listener. Rik Palieri (2008) describes the power of his song "Fathers and Sons," which he wrote to heal violent abuse by his father (p. 201) by showing compassion for him. A song—written to heal the relationship with my mother after her death—has helped people in their processes of compassion based on an understanding of the Other; it ends with the lines:

> Now we are separate, living's turned easy;
> I find forgiveness in wounds that can heal. (Boyce-Tillman, 2006, p. 110)

Compassion for the Other can be expressed through song itself, as Catherine Pestano (2021) illustrates with her song "Take a Risk," which helped her "to re-find compassion for someone with whom there was a complicated, difficult working relationship":

> When your mind just makes me wrong an' shatters all sense of belongin'
> It takes away all safety for the things you dread to face with me. (p. 200)

This often requires compassion for the less explored areas of our self (Pestano, 2021, p. 202) and an openness to vulnerability that accompanies it (Hendricks, 2018, 2021). Galtung (2008) describes how music achieves such reconciliations in which compassion plays a part: "Art, like peace, has to overcome such false dichotomies by speaking to the heart and to the brain, to the compassion of the heart and construction of the brain" (p. 60).

Wonder and Virtue

The ancient Greek process of psychagogia describes the calling of the compassionate teacher (Boyce-Tillman, 2016, p. 13), leading the soul by means of words performed with love—love of the forms and love of those to whom they speak (McCoy, 2007). Sam Keen (1973) links the desire for certainty that characterizes the contemporary world with violence, and wonder with both gratitude and unknowing—the disposition to exercise the virtues of compassion and care in the face of things and people. Ruth Illman (2009) asks for the development of a new set of tools to overcome violent trends in contemporary culture of which music may be one. This call for compassion and empathy in the way in which we listen characterizes improvisational activity:

> I wish to show that improvisation is best accomplished when attunement takes place by all of the voices being attuned to one another. In *that* sense, it is a spiritual exercise that requires empathy for those with whom one is improvising. Further, empathy requires both humility and trust. The point of humility is that, apart from opening oneself up to the other, I can only remain in tune with *myself*. Yet, opening oneself up to the other requires a kind of trust that others with whom I'm improvising are willing to listen to *one another*. (Benson, 2021, p. 35)

This capacity can lead to caring. I remember an improvising group of nine-year-olds, in which one member of the group had to hold a steady pulse on a drum, while the other members improvised in turn on their instruments. A nine-year-old boy had the drum to hold the pulse and played loudly throughout. At the end of the piece we discussed any problems with the improvisation. "The girls were too soft," he said. "What should we do?" I asked. "Well, they must play louder," he replied. The girls had small glockenspiels; so I asked him if he could think of another solution. He could think of nothing. "Perhaps you could play softer?" I suggested. We did the exercise again, and he proved to be an incredibly sensitive accompanist to other people's offerings. It had simply never occurred to him to be more sensitive. He develop the capacity to exercise care in relation to others in the group. I think that music lesson taught him far more about awareness of other people—especially in the area of gender—than any discussion might have done. So his openness through musicking was a place of encounter, in which he could take a new risk in the area of improvisation (Boyce-Tillman, 2016, p. 178).

Openness to wonder leads to the valuing of care and compassion in the processes of musicking. Julie Shaw (2021) describes the Florecer project in her school, linking this with the writings of the founders of the school:

> Moreover, true human flourishing indicates a process filled with movement and change. It has within it an understanding of thriving, growth, productivity, and fertility ... it is not value free but contains "virtues"—what the sisters of CoMOL would term "gospel values" (Company of Mary Our Lady, 2011, p. 19). . . . Celebration helps the girls to identify ways in which they are flourishing, marking successes large and small, kindnesses, manners, good behavior, as steps on the learning journey. (p. 175)

She describes how care for the girls is exercised here in the openness to mistake-making as an important part of the process to be honored. A nursery rhyme played on a recorder is valued equally with a more complex piano piece.

Ruth Debrot (2021) describes a similar process with her compassionate and caring teacher Constantine Cassolas at the City College of New York, who led forth her overall vocal agility and her range of nearly three octaves, which relates to Ruth Illman's work: "[S]pirituality can be envisioned both as a 'dialogue of souls' and as an 'incarnating encounter' (Illman, 2012, p. 60). Both people are transformed in this interaction, so that it becomes an I/Thou rather than an I/It encounter (Buber, 1970, p. 57). Chris Roberts (2021) explains his quest to transform participatory care home concerts from what Buber (1970) termed an "I-It" relationship into one of "I-Thou"—where mutual engagement bridging the divide between performers and audience is the essence of compassion. Levinas drew on Buber's work in his work on otherness for his concept of infinity, which is produced in a caring relationship that does not reduce the Other to the Same (Levinas, 1969, pp. 63–65). So hospitality to wonder is to engender compassion and care toward the Other and is an antidote to prejudice (Rubenstein, 2006, pp. 11–17; see also Hendricks, 2021).

This quality of care is essential in multicultural education, including both the alterities within and beyond the self. Siraj-Blatchford and Clarke (2000) looked for a truly inclusive pedagogy valuing multiple identities. Here hospitable wonder needs to be articulated and discussed (Brown, 1998). This returns us to Rubenstein's (2008) assertion that wonder encourages acceptance and compassion toward diverse ways of knowing. Keith D. Thomasson (2021) describes the qualities in musicking in the Alabare community:

> Central to this are the four values of care, compassion, generosity, and respect agreed by those involved in the charity, staff, clients, and wider family members. It is because of its Christian ethos that there is a commitment to inclusiveness where the gifting of all and the worldviews of all enrich Alabare's commitment to serving those who are vulnerable. (p. 116)

So the musical experience, seen as encounter, invites care and compassion among the participants. It enables us to access compassion generated by a mutual vulnerability as in this 10-year-old girl who sings a setting of an African prayer every night: "I felt close to the people in Africa whose prayer we sang. Now I continue to sing it and think of them." In my two collections of songs from various cultures, I give the background to the songs–contextualizing the material (Tillman, 1987a, 1987b) enabling compassion with the cultures in which the songs originated.

Music is able to handle the paradoxes set up by feeling mixed and contradictory emotions that are embedded in its structure (Langer, 1953). Vegar Jordanger (2007), in his work with warring parties in Crimea, used this notion to interrogate the complexity of emotional tensions by using music to take participants to a place of collective vulnerability where compassion became a possibility: "The group processes initiated touched directly and involved very deeply the affective layers of the participants. A reconfiguration of human relations resulted" (p. 144). This can lead them to a place of empathy often regarded as an extension of compassion (Laurence, 2008). Pat and Kathie Debenham (2008) describe this in a dance project *Beyond Words* bringing deaf and hearing people together which "engendered ways to build respect for difference, compassion, understanding and a sense of being connected to the greater themes of life" (p. 52).

Although classical literature is filled with stories embodying the potential power of music to engender compassion, the linkage with wonder is often not spelled out. It is still there in government documents in the United Kingdom, where the spiritual is sometimes linked with the delivery of the citizenship agenda, including religious, moral, cultural, personal, social, and health issues (Rubenstein, 2008). Here there is an important role for music.

Wonder and Children

Wonder is often associated with childlike states (Chazan, 2002; Laub-Novak, 1976; Winnicott, 1971). This is because it is a regular part of the child's way of seeing the world:

> For trailing clouds of glory do we come
> From God, who is our home:
> Heaven lies about us in our infancy!

> Shades of the prison-house begin to close
> Upon the growing Boy. (Wordsworth, 1919)

Children have a certain freedom because they are not yet trapped by a particular culture. Tagore asks for an educational environment of freedom for children to stay in touch "with the still small voice within" (Tagore & Elmhirst, 1961, pp. 83–84). The history of European thought sees the transformation from the view of children as "imps of Satan" into romantic views elaborated by poets. A somewhat naïve innocence was exalted, finally finding its expression in Barrie's (1904/2008) *Peter Pan, or the Boy Who Wouldn't Grow Up*. The dilemma for caring and compassionate education is how to keep the sense of wonder alive at the same time as teaching the vernacular of a particular culture.

Ways of Knowing

Musicians in the area of justice and peace are often very clear about their compassionate intention (Boyce-Tillman, 1996, 2001, 2007; Urbain, 2007). Examples include Paul Simon (1994) in his recording *Graceland* in the context of apartheid in South Africa. Guy Claxton (2002) calls for the restoration of the psyche in current educational systems and models, characteristic of which would be an unusually strong sense of *aliveness*—a heightened sense of vitality, clarity and strength of perception. Another he calls *belonging*—a sense of being at home in the world—which is a restoration of anima mundi. As the aesthetic and analytical became dominant value systems in Western culture, compassionate values such as connecting with the natural world, healing, peace and reconciliation became subjugated—indeed the notion of intention in musicking became marginalized and its link with caring and compassion diminished.

Educational systems have limited the ways of knowing; instead, in schools we find a habitus that seeks to promote affirming "one view of reality against others" (Evans, 2012, p. 5). This way of knowing—perpetuated in schooling—can deny the possibility of a compassionate relationship to the natural world, such as the ways of the seagull, fish, and worm: "The world supports all of these experiences simultaneously—and, for each experiencer, exclusively—shows that none of us has nor could have, even in principle, anything more than a minutely partial experience of the world" (Evans, 2012, p. 5).

Education has become an initiation into a particular way of seeing—a cultural or human norm—but it needs to keep alive the possibility of other ways of knowing (Smith, 2021, this volume). We perceive the world in the way that we are trained to see it (Evans, 2012, p. 5). Tagore therefore sees the importance of play in keeping the realm of other possibilities alive (Tagore & Elmhirst, 1961, p. 68).

The dominant culture of the European-American centered classroom may be at odds with the ways of knowing of children who are minoritized because of their ethnic group. Lubeck (1996) shows how early childhood practices help to maintain social inequality by reinforcing the ways of knowing of the dominant classes. An individualized, discrete view of knowledge has downplayed the corporate and communal that is characteristic of Other cultures such as those of indigenous peoples. Small's concept of musicking included the restoration of the communal element to music, which needs reflecting in caring and compassionate music education (Cohen, 2000). Peter Abbs (2003) sees arts education as a powerful antidote to a differentiated, separated way of knowing. The situating of education in the market economy has devalued ethical and creative dimensions and with them compassion and care. He draws on poetry, literature, and visual art to develop a passionate argument for the developing of authenticity and imagination. Encouraging wonder in a classroom will lead to an appreciation a variety of intelligences and a compassionate approach to them (Gardner, 1983/1993). Gonzales-Mena (1998) argues that "the independence and interdependence approaches represent two different ways of looking at getting needs met" and engenders a culture of care (p. 229). The valuing of wonder will embrace children from backgrounds where, for example, the religious experience is more valued, and encourage others to be caring and understanding toward those who come from different backgrounds.

The Musical Experience and Wonder

The four domains of musical experience (Boyce-Tillman, 2016; Figure 7.1) can all be framed with wonder. These are the diverse awarenesses that characterize the relationship between the experiencer and the experienced (Marton & Booth, 1997, pp. 112–113). Focusing on a limited form of knowing has led to a musicological concentration on a single domain (Construction) often taught in a way devoid of wonder.

Young children naturally approach the materials of sound, whether these are musical instruments or their own body, with wonder. Evelyn Glennie (2016) described how for her first percussion lesson she was simply given a side drum to take home and explore. She rejoiced that she did not start by being told how far to stand away from the drum and how to hold the sticks. The basis of her love and care for the instrument resided in this first wondrous exploration. So often instrumental lessons start with the vernacular (Tillman, 1987c) of an instrument—how a culture has decided to play it—rather from the basic wonder at the sound. It is possible to keep a delight in the tonal possibilities alive while teaching the vernacular patterns—often done by the inclusion of improvised exploration.

Here the body and the natural world are brought into relationship. We could include wondering at the tree that gave its wood to the violin and engender care for the environment. We can also explore our embodiment—our body size, the length of our limbs and vocal chords, the volume of our lungs—that makes particular resonances natural and comfortable for us both tonally and rhythmically (Evans, 2013, p. 887), enabling self-care. Students need time for deep engagement with sound (the basis of all musical wonder), which Schopenhauer saw as giving a glimpse of a world beyond (Evans, 2013, p. 887).

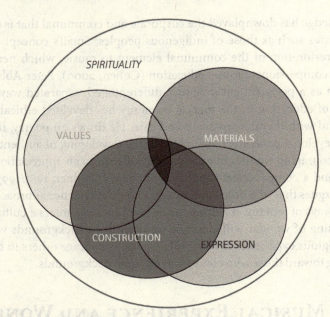

FIGURE 7.1 The spiritual experience in music (Boyce-Tillman, 2016).

Emotion and feeling characterize the domain of expression, which has been devalued in music education. Yet by honoring the personal experience of musicking, including associations locked on to particular pieces, we have weakened the contribution music might make to

> psychological fluency and vitality. The benefit may stop when the music stops, or it may persist . . . but in either case it arises, surely, out of a more strongly resonant fit between the organic fabric of agency and the imagination, brought about by music's deep engagement with the sorts of creatures we are. (Evans, 2013, p. 887)

This connection with our humanity encourages compassion. Patricia St John describes introducing the aria of the Queen of the Night from *The Magic Flute*. A four-year-old boy commented, "If it is like you say it is, it is going to be very beautiful." The framing of musical experiences imaginatively is crucial for compassionate emotional engagement with them and through that with the wider world. Autobiographies explore powerfully the role of music in identity formation and accommodating Otherness, as in Ruth Westheimer's (2003) use of music to connect her with her fragmented Jewishness, to develop self-care.

The domain of Construction has dominated music curricula. The "structured playfulness in sound" can be killed by the teaching of isolated tones, intervals, forms, and rhythms (Evans, 2013, p. 887). It is possible to present these in a way that wonders at the way these elements have arisen and been constructed. A local music teacher in the United Kingdom allows her pupils to play a C major scale in a concert if that is what they want to play. We can frame a simple scale as the remarkable phenomenon that has underpinned so much of Western culture. Young children delight in finding patterns. When the author introduced the pattern of ternary form to seven-year olds, they found the pattern all over their world, such as house structures and flowers. This domain often marks the entry into a cultural vernacular. The growing child abandons less shaped improvised songs and delights in singing songs like "London's Burning" (Tillman, 1987c). Although their horizons are being limited by cultural presuppositions, they are avoiding the Peter Pan syndrome in music. Wonder can frame the appreciation of the shapes and forms that a particular culture has validated and develop a compassionate approach to the patterns developed by other cultures.

The Values underpinning a musical culture have often been ignored by the individual constructivist model of education (Cohen, 2000), which is being rediscovered in research such as St John (2004), where "awareness of others was integral to the facilitation and maintenance of optimal experience" (Custodero, 2005). We have seen how this will support compassionate and caring behavior where intention in musicking is honored, positive interactions are encouraged, and attention paid to constructive ways of handling difference (Hendricks, 2018). Wonder-infused introduction to a variety of musical cultures can facilitate this.

Approaching each of these domains with a "wondering" approach makes what Turner (1974) called the liminal experience more likely (Boyce-Tillman, 2016):

> You lose grasp of time and to a certain extent of space too, in the sense that the whole room I am lying in starts to revolve. In the fortissimo on the dominant in the last bars, it is like a light passes over my closed eyes, fading out more and more in the following diminuendo. (Gabrielsson, 2011, p. 175)

The liminal/spiritual space is potentially transformative because it heightens the intuitive faculties bringing an awareness of hidden areas (alterities) within the self, enables compassion in a space of collective vulnerability, forges new relationships, and brings an aliveness that leads to acts of caring in the everyday world (Boyce-Tillman, 2016, p. 138; see also Hendricks, 2021).

Conclusion

This chapter has set out the importance of wonder in education in engendering a culture of compassion and care. This involves challenging the prevailing values underpinning Western curricula and embracing uncertainty alongside certainty. This is an easier experience for young children who have not yet been fully enculturated into the Western adult experience of separation from surrounding objects. It has set out some ways in which to keep this wondering experience—with its relationship to compassion and care—alive, alongside the more rational, less intuitive adult view of the world of objects.

It has suggested ways of valuing it while teaching the vernacular of a culture and ways in which this will contribute to a society that is hospitable to Otherness—open to engage with the different ways of knowing that infuse our world with care and compassion.

References

Abbs, P. (2003). *Against the flow: The arts, postmodern culture and education*. Routledge.
Barrie, J. M. (2008). *Peter Pan*. Union Square Kids. (Original work published 1904)
Benson, B. E. (2021). Improvisation as spiritual exercise: The improvisational virtues of empathy, humility, and trust. In K. S. Hendricks & J. Boyce-Tillman (Eds.), *Authentic connection: Music, spirituality, and wellbeing* (pp. 33–45). Peter Lang.
Boyce-Tillman, J. (1996). A framework for intercultural dialogue in music. In M. Floyd (Ed.), *World musics in education* (pp. 43–94). Scolar.
Boyce-Tillman, J. (2001). Sounding the sacred: Music as sacred site. In K. Ralls-MacLeod & G. Harvey (Eds.), *Indigenous religious musics* (pp. 136–166). Scolar.
Boyce-Tillman, J. (2006). *A rainbow to heaven*. Stainer & Bell.
Boyce-Tillman, J. (2007). Peace making in educational contexts. In O. Urbain (Ed.), *Music and conflict transformation: Harmonies and dissonances in geopolitics* (pp. 212–228). I. B. Tauris. https://doi.org/10.5040/9780755619955
Boyce-Tillman, J. (2016). *Experiencing music—Restoring the spiritual: Music as well-being*. Peter Lang.
Buber, M. (1970). *I and Thou* (W. Kaufmann, Trans.). Charles Scribner's Sons. (Original work published 1937)
Brown, B. (1998). *Unlearning discrimination in the early years*. Trentham Books.
Chazan, S. (2002). *The profiles of play*. Hamish Hamilton.
Cohen, M. (1992). *A constructivist approach to elementary school music learning experiences with reference to the ideas of John Dewey* [Master's thesis, University of Kansas]. KU ScholarWorks. https://kuscholarworks.ku.edu/handle/1808/29357
Cohen, M. L. (2000). *Christopher Small's concept of musicking* [Doctoral dissertation, University of Kansas]. KU ScholarWorks. https://kuscholarworks.ku.edu/bitstream/handle/1808/29289/Cohen_2007_Christopher_Small.pdf?isAllowed=y&sequence=3
Claxton, G. (2002, October 21). *Mind expanding: Scientific and spiritual foundations for the schools we need* [Public lecture]. University of Bristol.
Custodero, L. A. (2005). Observable indicators of flow experience. *Music Education Research*, 7(2), 185–209. https://doi.org/10.1080/14613800500169431
Debenham, P., & Debenham, K. (2008). Experiencing the sacred in dance education: Wonder, compassion, wisdom and wholeness in the classroom. *Journal of Dance Education*, 8(2), 44–45. https://doi.org/10.1080/15290824.2008.10387358
Debrot, R. A. (2021). Singing the good life. In J. Boyce-Tillman & K. S. Hendricks (Eds.), *Living song: Singing, spirituality, and wellbeing* (pp. 219–234). Peter Lang.
Evans H. M. (2010). Music, medicine, and embodiment. *Lancet*, 375(9718), 886–887. https://doi.org/10.1016/S0140-6736(10)60376-5
Evans, H. M. (2012, June 14). *Transfigurings: Beauty, wonder and the noumenal* [Paper presentation]. Transfigurings: The world, wonder and beauty. Durham University, Centre for Medical Humanities and Institute of Advanced Studies. https://dro.dur.ac.uk/9726/

Gardner, H. (1993). *Frames of mind: The theory of multiple intelligences*. Basic Books. (Original work published in 1983)

Glennie, E. (2016, July 25). *How to truly listen* [Keynote lecture]. The 32nd World Conference of the International Society for Music Education, Royal Conservatoire of Scotland, Glasgow.

Galtung, J. (2008). Peace, music and the arts: In search of interconnections. In O. Urbain (Ed.), *Music and conflict transformation: Harmonies and dissonances in geopolitics* (pp. 53–60). I. B. Tauris. https://doi.org/10.5040/9780755619955

Gabrielsson, A. (2011). *Strong experiences with music: Music is much more than just music* (R. Bradbury, Trans.). Oxford University Press.

Gonzales-Mena, J. (1998). *Foundations: Early childhood education in a diverse society*. Mayfield Publishing Company.

Hendricks, K. S. (2018). *Compassionate music teaching*. Rowman & Littlefield.

Hendricks, K. S. (2021). Authentic connection in music education: A chiastic essay. In K. S. Hendricks & J. Boyce-Tillman (Eds.), *Authentic connection: Music, spirituality, and wellbeing* (pp. 237–253). Peter Lang.

Heidegger, M. (1994). *Basic questions of philosophy: Selected "problems" of "logic"* (R. Rojcewicz & A. Schuwer, Trans.). Indiana University Press.

Illman, R. (2009). Momo and Ibrahim—"Thus-and-otherwise": A dialogical approach to religious difference. *Journal of Contemporary Religion*, 24(2), 157–170. https://doi.org/10.1080/13537900902816640

Illman, R. (2012). Incarnating encounters. In G. Giordan & E. Pace (Eds.), *Mapping religion and spirituality in a postsecular world* (pp. 43–62). Brill.

Jordanger, V. (2007). Healing cultural violence: "Collective vulnerability" through guided imagery with music. In O. Urbain (Ed.), *Music and conflict transformation: Harmonies and dissonances in geopolitics* (pp. 128–146). I. B. Tauris.

Keen, S. (1973). *Apology for wonder*. Harper & Row.

Langer, S. (1953). *Feeling and form: A theory of art*. Routledge and Kegan Paul.

Laub-Novak, K. (1976). Creativity and children. *Momentum*, 7(1), 13–19.

Laurence, F. (2008). Music and empathy. In O. Urbain (Ed.), *Music and conflict transformation: Harmonies and dissonances in geopolitics* (pp. 13–25). I. B. Tauris.

Levinas, E. (1969). *Totality and infinity: An essay on exteriority* (A. Lingis, Trans.). Duquesne University Press. (Original work published 1961)

Lubeck, S. (1996). The politics of developmentally appropriate practice. In B. L. Mallory & R. S. New (Eds.), *Diversity and developmentally appropriate practices: Challenges for early childhood education* (pp. 17–43). Teachers College Press.

McCoy, M. (2007). *Plato on the Rhetoric of Philosophers and Sophists*. Cambridge University Press. https://doi.org/10.1017/CBO9780511497827.007

Marton, F., & Booth, S. (1997). *Learning and Awareness*. Lawrence Erlbaum Associates.

Miller, J. (1992). *The throe of wonder: Intimations of the sacred in a post-modern world*. State University of New York Press. http://www.salisbury.edu/philosophy/faculty/Miller.html

Oliveros, P. (2005). *Deep listening: A composer's sound practice*. iUniverse.

Otto, R. (1923). *The idea of the holy: An inquiry into the non-rational factor in the idea of the divine and its relation to the rational*. Oxford University Press.

Palieri, R. (2008). Working in the trenches: Surviving conflicts through folk music and tales. In O. Urbain (Ed.), *Music and conflict transformation: Harmonies and dissonances in geopolitics* (pp. 187–200). I. B. Tauris.

Pestano, C. (2021). A time of change: An autoethnographic account. In J. Boyce-Tillman & K. S. Hendricks (Eds.), *Living song* (pp. 195–209). Peter Lang.

Roberts, C. (2021). Re-imagining ritual, creating communitas. In K. S. Hendricks & J. Boyce-Tillman (Eds.), *Authentic connection* (pp. 319–334). Peter Lang.

Rooley, A. (1990). *Performance: Revealing the Orpheus within*. Element Books.

Rubenstein, M. (2006). A certain disavowal: The pathos and politics of wonder. *Princeton Theological Review*, 12(2), 11–18. http://mrubenstein.faculty.wesleyan.edu/files/2008/11/a-certain-disavowal.pdf

Rubenstein, M. (2008). *Strange wonder: The closure of metaphysics and the opening of awe*. Columbia University Press.

St. John, P. A. (2004). *A community of learners: An investigation of the relationship between flow experience and the role of scaffolding in a Kindermusik classroom* [Unpublished doctoral dissertation]. Teachers College, Columbia University.

Shaw, J. (2021). Florecer, faith, and music living song. In J. Boyce-Tillman & K. S. Hendricks (Eds.), *Living song* (pp. 166–181). Peter Lang.

Simon, P. (1994). *Graceland* [Album]. Warner Bros.

Siraj-Blatchford, I., & Clarke, P. (2000). *Supporting identity, diversity and language in the early years*. Open University Press.

Smith, T. D. (2021). Music education for surviving and thriving: Cultivating children's wonder, senses, emotional wellbeing, and wild nature as a means to discover and fulfill their life's purpose. *Frontiers in Education*, 6, Article 648779. https://doi.org/10.3389/feduc.2021.648799

Tagore, R., & Elmhirst, L. K. (1961). *Rabindranath Tagore, pioneer in education: Essays and exchanges between Rabindranath Tagore and L. K. Elmhirst*. John Murray.

Thomasson, K. D. (2021). Creative spirit conversations that accompany creativity in the lives of young people who are at risk of homelessness. In K. S. Hendricks & J. Boyce-Tillman (Eds.), *Authentic connection* (pp. 111–127). Peter Lang.

Tillman, June B. (1987a). *Light the candles*. Cambridge University Press.

Tillman, June B. (1987b). *The Christmas search*. Cambridge University Press.

Tillman, June B. (1987c). *Towards a model of the development of musical creativity: A Study of the compositions of children aged 3–11* [Unpublished doctoral dissertation]. University of London.

Turner, V. (1974). *The ritual process: Structure and anti-structure*. Penguin Books.

Urbain, O. (Ed.). (2007). *Music and conflict transformation: Harmonies and dissonances in geopolitics*. I. B. Tauris.

Westheimer, R. K. (2003). *Musically speaking: A life through song*. University of Pennsylvania Press.

Winnicott, D. (1971). *Playing and reality*. Tavistock.

Wordsworth, W. (1919). Ode: Intimations of immortality from recollections of early childhood. In A. T. Quiller-Couch (Ed.), *The Oxford book of English verse: 1250–1900* (pp. 349–353). Oxford University Press.

CHAPTER 8

DISABILITY, LIFELONG MUSICAL ENGAGEMENT, AND CARE

DAVID BAKER

CARE HANDBOOK TOPICS

Co-creating caring relationships
Identity expressions
Musical development
Philosophical perspectives
Social activism and critical consciousness

INTRODUCTION

This chapter explores care in the lifelong musical engagement of disabled people. This engagement can happen within the formal learning of mainstream or special schools, and within school curricula, but can also occur through participation facilitated in communities and into adult life. In some countries too, since the 1960s, children with disabilities, but without severe learning disabilities, have been increasingly educated in mainstream schools, along with putting "reasonable adjustments" in place (e.g., Ruddock & Bishop, 2006, on Australia; Atkin et al., 2003, on Canada; and the Individuals with Disabilities Education Act, 1997, on the United States). UNESCO's 1994 Salamanca statement recommended that "those with special educational needs must have access to regular schools which should accommodate them within a child-centered pedagogy capable of meeting these needs" (p. viii). The engagement discussed in this chapter is about people making music together or the participant learning with an educator, rather than merely listening to music or being an audience member.

Disability and how it is experienced is so diverse that the chapter makes unapologetically broad observations and reflections, at times touching on the author's own research into blind and partially sighted musicians (Baker, 2014, 2021; Baker & Green, 2016, 2017, 2018; Baker et al., 2019). This is simply as a starting point for readers' exploration of specific disability types. It begins by defining disability, looking at causes and commonplace categories, but also the terminology used and its connotations for how society understands disabled people's care. It then considers how disabled musicians' social history frames their identities, leading to reified social scripts about musical capacities and appropriate pedagogies. Three commonplace models of disability are then discussed. The chapter subsequently reflects on care deemed as accessible and socially inclusive practice, also noting some of the sizable challenges that exist. Nel Noddings's (2003, 2005, 2013) concepts of "caring about" and reciprocal care are then discussed in light of disabled people in music. Finally, Virgina Hel's (2018) "distributive justice" is posited as a way to avoid care that fails to consider the disabled musician and music learner's authentic experience.

Understanding Disability

Disability is caused by genetics, environmental factors (e.g., disease, infection), injury, ageing, and sometimes mysterious causes. It sometimes has complex, non-discrete interactions too. An example is diabetic retinopathy, whereby a person's genetics affects his or her responses to diet (an environmental factor), which results in impaired vision or blindness alongside other health issues. Disability can be *physical*, i.e., relating to the poor functioning or underdevelopment of the body, even the absence of a body part. It can be *sensory*, thus referring to auditory or visual perception. Disability can be *cognitive*, that is, relating to perception and understanding. Or, it can be *neurological*, that is, about atypical brain and nervous system functioning leading to loss of bodily control. Disability can also be *intellectual*, affecting, e.g., problem-solving, memory, communication, and learning. It can be *psychiatric*, so concerned with the emotions, thought-processes, and behaviors. Disability is also sometimes *congenital* (i.e., appearing in the prenatal child or first months after birth), *lifelong*, or it can occur unexpectedly (as in resulting from an accident), and it is sometimes *episodic* (as in some mental health conditions).

Worldwide, disability is categorized variously in terms of its severity, sometimes referring to independence in living and the ability to learn. Terms are used such as Specific Learning Difficulties (SpLDs) (e.g., dyslexia, dyscalculia, dyspraxia), Severe Learning Difficulties (or SLDs), and Profound and Multiple Learning Difficulties (PMLDs) (see Learning Disabilities Association of America, 2021; Royal College of Psychiatrists, 2021). Most people will be disabled at some point in their life and, if not for other reasons, it will be due to ageing and the deterioration of the body and mind. Disability, therefore, is a normal part of being a human.

Disability may be underreported due to: different benchmarks and policies in countries worldwide; variable national diagnosis and healthcare systems in addition to how these manage preventable conditions (i.e., consider cataracts in poorer countries); and, also, stigma, or perceived stigma, and people not wanting to disclose their disability. Some disability is more easily *hidden*, e.g., as in a person wearing a discrete prosthetic or hearing aid. The World Health Organization (2021) estimates that there are over a billion people worldwide with some form of disability, which corresponds to approximately 15% of the world's population. Moreover, the organization states that as many as 190 million people of 15 years of age or over have significant difficulties in functioning, with levels increasing due to ageing populations (World Health Organization, 2021). Owing to the huge diversity of disability, in terms of health, experience and other factors, the extent to which disabled people can exercise agency in their care lies on a very broad spectrum.

Commonplace terminology can also lead to a particular tenor to care. Largely, societies have discarded terms that many would find offensive such as "handicapped," i.e., alluding to having a cap in one's hand, being incapable of employment, and begging. However, "*dis*-ability," "*dis*-abled," "visually *impaired*," "hearing *impaired*," or "*typical*" versus "*atypical* functioning," suggest capability deficits against the norm. These terms are used in the chapter, but only because they are widely employed. It is not because the author supports a perspective of lacking or inherent helplessness in every disabled person. Nonetheless, there are underlying assumptions in the words we use that imply "abnormality," i.e., that the person must fit into, or adapt to "normal" society, with no moral compunction for society to accommodate him or her. This seems strange, given the earlier observation that disability is experienced by almost everyone and thus is a normal part of being human.

Historical Traditions and Three Disability Models

Religious Model

The "religious model" of disability (see Baker, 2021) draws on the social history of disabled people worldwide. Heightened musical and spiritual capacities were deemed "special dispensations" for the atypical body in the past, with disability a punishment or test of faith. Blind Ukrainian minstrels c. 1850–1930 (Kononenko, 1998) and Shinto lute priests from the medieval period (De Ferranti, 2009; Groemer, 2012; Isaki, 1987; Lubet, 2011) were thought conduits of God's word (also see Ottenberg, 1996, on African tribal musicians). The lore on blind people's musical "specialness" was continued and strengthened in US ragtime, jazz, gospel, and blues. A long-standing US tradition exists of blind performers such as "Blind Tom" Wiggins (1849–1908), George Shearing (Shearing & Shipton, 2005), and Stevie Wonder (Ribowsky, 2010). The Blind Boys of Alabama are a gospel vocal ensemble from the 1930s that remains within this spiritual tradition today (Blind Boys of Alabama, 2021; Fuqua, 2011). Owing to this history, some people today infer that blind people are mysteriously and innately "gifted" musically, or have better hearing, or that they are predisposed to music. This thinking, correct or otherwise, has led to supposedly appropriate professions, such as blind piano tuners in the United Kingdom (e.g., Association of Blind Piano Tuners, n.d.).

Baker and Green (2017) interviewed music teachers working with blind and partially sighted learners in a variety of educational settings. The educators believed blind and partially sighted learners had better aural capacities than others and, therefore, the most appropriate learning was predominantly by ear (i.e., without notation). This was their perspective even when those learners had no intellectual difficulties that might prevent music reading in some form (e.g., music Braille, large print, modified stave notation). The interviewees were less inclined to support the use of assistive technologies for accessing scores (e.g., Braille hardware devices, screen reader software, or digital magnification). A key point is that these music educators were not aware of research in support of heightened aural or other musical capacities in this learner group (e.g., Dimatati et al., 2012; Welch, 1988). This was purely the reified lore described above.

Music educators can, therefore, make powerful pedagogical choices that are neither informed nor shaped by needs disabled learners express to them, or those articulated by surrounding carers. Pedagogy can be wrought from potentially flawed thinking and expediency given insufficient knowledge or resourcing. Belief in learning by ear as the sole modus operandi has ramifications for the blind learner as it risks limiting his or her ability to access music genres and ensembles where notation is routinely used. It also reduces the learner's chances of participating in ensembles alongside sighted peers and defies music's ability to assist with integration into wider society.

Medical Model

The "medical model" considers disability and its experience purely as the result of an abnormal, defective human body (i.e., from disease or trauma) (see Beaudry, 2019; Smart, 2004). A connotation is that treatment, therapy, adaptive devices and rehabilitation are best decided by empowered medical professionals, specialists, and social services to compensate for the disabled person's abnormality. However, this model proffers the abnormal person who is less able to make apt life decisions than the non-disabled expert. The potential agency of some disabled people, depending on their particular health and intellectual circumstances, in making care decisions is disregarded. This is non-consultative, hierarchical, and it disempowers the disabled person. The assumptions embedded within this model extend beyond medical treatment and rehabilitation, for instance, to the manner in which non-disabled people might exercise power in the facilitation of musical opportunities.

Baker and Green (2017, 2018) have written about those who put together disabled adults in "special" (segregated) music ensembles formed and led by non-disabled facilitators. These "disability ensembles" (Baker, 2018) are assumed to create a healthy, therapeutic environment (or a type of remedial action or treatment) for disabled people. There are a number of these "disability ensembles" worldwide including the United Kingdom's Inner Vision Orchestra, or the Para-orchestra, which is conducted by Charles Hazelwood (Baker & Green, 2017, 2018).

The authors found that this remedial action was considered well intentioned by many of their blind and partially sighted respondents. However, some noted it made potentially incorrect assumptions about their social networks lacking social abnormality, and the need for social adjustment. It is important to recognize, however, that the study tapped into a particular respondent type, i.e., articulate, without intellectual disability; and there are blind disabled music learners with, e.g., SLD and PMLD (see Ockelford, 2000). There were arguments on both sides from the disabled musicians, with some considering these groups to emanate a damaging identity. The detractors argued that they belonged to a low-incidence disability group and, as such, the skills of the overall ensemble membership, their learning strategies and the instrumentation would be extremely variable. This equated to poor-quality performances in hybrid ensembles, they argued. Some contended that the experience diminished from their musical identity.

Assistive device development is another way that empowered non-disabled people wield power in caring. Researchers working with electronic engineers develop prototype devices for "sonification" and "haptification" (e.g., Brewster & Brown, 2004; Csapó et al., 2015). Sonification for the blind involves e.g., translating information normally conveyed visually, e.g., in text or keystrokes in computing, into sounds, whereas the latter is concerned with tactile signals. Baker, Fomukong-Boden, and Edwards (2019) developed a Bluetooth ring worn by a sighted conductor and a "haptic vest" worn by blind adult ensemble performers. The latter contained a matrix of vibration controllers across the wearer's chest (similar to those in a mobile phone). Testing illustrated that a two-dimensional tracking of the conductor's swing across the vest was far too challenging for blind performers to interpret. They were unable to keep in time with audio tracks with tempo changes. The performers involved in the testing commented they had no visual experience of conductors and, therefore, could not understand what the haptic signaling meant.

A supposition in their care, then, was that mirroring the sighted developer's visual experience as faithfully as possible in two dimensions would be in their best interests. This approach to creating new devices imagines that redressing the absence of something in the sighted person's sensory world is apt, rather than valuing the disabled person's own experience. Baker, Fomukong-Boden, and Edwards (2019) conclude that, to avoid ableism, it would have been better to start with their "voice" to design technologies that provide the specific cues they desired. These authors ponder a "troubling question": "Is a 'sighted perspective' on technology development another way in which disabled people are marginalized?" (p. 311).

Social Model

The 1960s gave rise to a "social model" that challenged the ableist view (Barnes & Mercer, 2004; Beaudry, 2019; Pickard, 2021; Purtell, 2013). Disability was to be a positive identity, with the disabled individual inherently normal potentially with high agency to shape his or her life. Challenges they faced, rather than being blamed on insurmountable bodily abnormalities were, instead, deemed due to incorrect social organization e.g., of the built environment, policy, of people's attitudes, or financial resourcing, etc. (Beaudry, 2019). Straus (2011) has endeavored to take a more cultural, social perspective on disabled musicians' identities. Caring for disabled people, in view of this model, means we need to look to "insider" experiences (e.g., of individuals, their care networks and family, and the educators working with them) to better understand where society needs to change.

REFLECTING ON DISABILITY AND CARE

Richerme (2017) asks: "Who is in our local community and what unmet needs do they have? How might we foster direct musically-based interactions with those individuals and groups? How might we facilitate spaces where people can receive and respond to our care?" (p. 417). These are substantial questions when considering care for disabled musicians, but they are not without broader considerations. If we take a lifelong learning perspective (e.g., Myers, 1995; Roulston, 2010), then the identification of disabled people who might participate in music may be challenging. This rests on knowledge of available participants by facilitators, but there is also the potential for some not to wish to participate due to social and healthcare pressures, or because it means disclosing themselves. Then, there are challenges relating to resourcing for and of physical spaces. So funding, societal attitudes, legal obligations, and the built environment all come into play. There is also the disabled learner's confidence and level of independent mobility, the surrounding support needed, and even simply where the person lives in relation to opportunities (Baker, 2021).

Care as Accessible and Inclusive Practice

The social model seeks to "normalize" disability and most would agree on the extensive benefits of musical participation (e.g., Hallam, 2015). Owing to the high diversity of health conditions, capacities, backgrounds, aims and aspirations of disabled people, musical participation may have differing foci. It can be concerned with aesthetic awareness, or gaining social skills and socializing, or becoming an accomplished instrumental performer or composer. It can benefit those with less severe disability like dyslexics (see Oglethorpe, 2002; Overy, 2000; Reifinger, 2019). Likewise, for those with severe learning difficulties, it can be "for the pleasurable sensory and emotional responses [it] can engender" (Ockelford, 2000, p. 202). Advocates for normalizing disability would likely argue that it is simply ethical that musical participation should be as accessible and inclusive for all. From their perspective, *where reasonable and feasible*, apt care for disabled music participants would mean, rather than e.g., segregating them in "special" musical experiences or within special educational contexts, they would participate to mutual social benefit alongside the non-disabled. From this perspective, exclusive practices and experiences would be seen as a failing by wider society. But how realistic is that intention?

This view both assumes that disabled people themselves desire and feel competent to be integrated into musical experiences with the non-disabled, which may not always be the case. The Inner Vision Orchestra is a world music ensemble of disabled London musicians who have come together as a "campaigning tool to encourage recognition of the particular problems facing blind or visually impaired performers" (Clerk, 2014, p. 18). Its founder, Baljui Shrivastav, believes insufficient confidence, social isolation, mobility issues, and musical approaches that fit less easily in sighted ensembles, have led to the formation of this self-supportive "campaigning" group (Baker & Green, 2017, 2018).

Integration as an aspect in the care of disabled musicians has further challenges because societies, their musical instruments, and their practices have developed across history in ways that include some while excluding others. For example, Eurocentric traditions of classical music have prized music literacy and sight-reading, troubling participation, e.g., by a blind music Braille reader who cannot sight-read. That musician may need to iterate between touching and playing an instrument to memorize their score ahead of rehearsals. Symphony orchestras are inflexible in instrumentation too, which can prevent participation by a physically disabled person using a non-standard or adapted instrument. The University of Nebraska Kearney's (2021) One-Handed Woodwinds program has sought to alleviate this problem with toggle-key instruments that can be played with one hand. However, where physical disability is more severe, creative solutions to instrument design have led to entirely new instruments, but these can only be accommodated in non-standard ensembles and certain genres (e.g., jazz, popular music, hybrid or new music, etc.). Clarence Adoo (n.d.), for example, who is paralyzed from the shoulders down, plays Headspace, a digital instrument operated by his neck movements and a blowing tube.

Caring "About"

Noddings (2013) remarks: "'Caring about' always involves a certain benign neglect. One is attentive just so far. One acknowledges. One affirms. One contributes five dollars and goes on to other things" (p. 12). "Benign neglect" can occur in the lives of disabled musicians and music learners where, for example, donations are made to charities by people without further engagement by them, or where there are short-term assistive technology development projects for music by researchers, but without attention to meaningful relationships and understanding "insider" needs. Endeavors concerned with "caring about" may be well intentioned, but neglect reciprocal, longer-term dimensions to caring relationships.

Care and Reciprocal Relationships

Noddings (2003, 2005) notes an important central relational aspect to care in that it often involves the "carer" and "cared for" in a reciprocal relationship, with the "cared for" also having some responsibility to the former. Yet, Noddings acknowledges that relationships can be relatively equal or unequal. In music education, we might, e.g., consider the extent to which the learner him- or herself is responsible for articulating specific learning needs to their teacher, or for feeding back what is working well personally, or for conveying aspirations or pressures experienced outside the teaching room, i.e., to shape learning processes. Through this dialogue, the learner is caring for and enhancing the educator's work to mutual benefit. Edgar (2014) observes, however, in unequal relationships, only one party holds responsibility to the other. Richerme (2017) agrees, warning that:

> Solely working towards "caring for" others . . . has the potential to foster a sustained power imbalance. . . . If teachers and students provide others care without acknowledging their own limitations and vulnerabilities, they risk propagating paternalistic attitudes. (p. 418)

Hendricks (2018, 2021; also Tsui et al., this volume) concurs that compassionate teaching involves shifting from "caring about" or "for," with potentially problematic notions of pity, superiority and inferiority, to "caring with" students.

Care and Distributive Justice

Hel (2018) writes about "distributive justice." In asking "What makes a society fair?," she notes that, in recent decades, there has been focus on "values of care seen most clearly in the contexts of family and friendship but then extended to politics and society" (para. 2). She remarks: "When we look at a society, we can see that most of its rich pattens of relatedness and interdependence and mutual pursuit of interests proceed without the intervention of the law. . . . They especially concern themselves in meeting needs, building trust, and doing so in ways that reflect mutuality" (para. 5). Barnes (2012) also calls for "the need to consider lived experience of giving and receiving care, and how the context, conflicts and power impact the . . . practical tasks of care" (p. 40). The emphasis, therefore, should be starting from the perspectives of, e.g., disabled people themselves where practical, and their parents, partners, music educators, and caregivers, to better understand the specifics of relationships, pressures, and specific needs. Thus, policy, practices, and resourcing for music education can be formulated accordingly.

Baker and Green (2017) adopted this lens by exploring blind and partially sighted musicians' life histories. They encountered, for example, a partially sighted musician who reflected she had disengaged from music in her mainstream primary school due to having a teaching assistant alongside her in class, appearing different, and consequently being bullied. Other instances included participants inhibited by living in rural areas.

Considering "distributive justice," accounting for "insider" perspectives, and thus contemplating care accordingly can potentially offer valuable insights to drive social and educational change. Contrariwise, the imposition of policy, practice, and care in music education through hierarchy of the medical model (i.e., imposition "from above"), ableism (Campbell, 2009), or merely by observing interactions in the teaching room, risks missing authentic experience. It fails to ascertain and appreciate genuine care needs for the lifelong music engagement of the disabled.

References

Adoo, C. (n.d.). *Headspace*. Retrieved July 7, 2021, from http://www.clarenceadoo.co.uk/headspace.html

Association of Blind Piano Tuners. (n.d.). *Association of Blind Piano Tuners (ABPT)*. Retrieved July 7, 2021, from https://www.piano-tuners.org/

Atkin, M. -M., Holbrook, C., MacCuspie, A., Mamer, L., McConnell, D., McConnell, R., Muller, C., Nagel, K., Rannelli, P., Sitar, D., & Studholme, L. (2003). *Canadian national standards for the education of children and youth who are blind or visually impaired, including those with additional disabilities*. National Coalition for Vision Health.

Australian Government Department of Education, Skills and Employment. (2021, April 15). *Disability standards for education 2005*. Retrieved March 17, 2022, from https://www.education.gov.au/disability-standards-education-2005

Baker, D. (2014). Visually-impaired musicians' insights: Narratives of childhood, lifelong learning and musical participation. *British Journal of Music Education, 31*(2), 113–135. https://doi.org/10.1017/S0265051714000072

Baker, D. (2021). Additional needs and disability in musical learning: Issues and pedagogical considerations. In A. Creech, D. A. Hodges, & S. Hallam (Eds.), *Routledge international handbook of music psychology in education and the community* (pp. 351–366). Routledge.

Baker, D., Fomukong-Boden, A., & Edwards, S. (2019). "Don't follow them, look at me!": Contemplating a haptic digital prototype to bridge the conductor and visually impaired performer. *Music Education Research, 21*(3), 295–213. https://doi.org/10.1080/14613808.2019.1605344

Baker, D., & Green, L. (2016). Perceptions of schooling, pedagogy and notation in the lives of visually-impaired musicians. *Research Studies in Music Education, 38*(2), 193–219. https://doi.org/10.1177%2F1321103X16656990

Baker, D., & Green, L. (2017). *Insights in sound: Visually impaired musicians' lives and learning*. Routledge.

Baker, D., & Green, L. (2018). Disability arts and visually impaired musicians in the community. In L. Higgins & B.-L. Bartleet (Eds.), *The Oxford handbook of community music* (pp. 477–502). Oxford University Press. https://doi.org/10.1093/oxfordhb/9780190219505.013.1

Barnes, C., & Mercer, G. (Eds.). (2004). *Implementing the social model of disability: Theory and research*. The Disability Press.

Barnes, M. (2012). *Care in everyday life: An ethic of care in practice*. Polity Press.

Beaudry, J.-S. (2019). Theoretical strategies to define disability. In A. Cureton & D. T. Wasserman (Eds.), *The Oxford handbook of philosophy and disability* (pp. 3–21). Oxford University Press. https://doi.org/10.1093/oxfordhb/9780190622879.013.3

Blind Boys of Alabama. (n.d.). Retrieved July 7, 2021, from http://www.blindboys.com/

Brewster, S. A., & Brown, L. M. (2004). Tactons: Structured tactile messages for non-visual information display. *Proceedings of the Fifth Conference on Australasian User Interface, 28*, 15–23. https://dl.acm.org/doi/10.5555/976310.976313

Campbell, F. K. (2009). *Contours of ableism: The production of disability and ableness*. Palgrave Macmillan.

Clerk, C. (2014). *The Inner Vision national tour, England, June–October 2013*. Baluji Music Foundation.

Csapó, A., Wersényi, G., Nagy, H., & Stockman, T. (2015). A survey of assistive technologies and applications for blind users on mobile platforms: A review and foundation for research. *Journal of Multimodal User Interfaces, 9*(4), 275–286. https://doi.org/10.1007/s12193-015-0182-7

De Ferranti, H. (2009). *The last biwa singer: A blind musician in history, imagination and performance*. Cornell University Press.

Department for Education. (2012). *Support and aspiration: A new approach to special educational needs and disability: Progress and next steps*. Department for Education (UK). http://dera.ioe.ac.uk/id/eprint/14455

Department for Education and Skills. (2001a). *Inclusive schooling: Children with special educational needs*. DfES Publications. http://dera.ioe.ac.uk/id/eprint/4552

Department for Education and Skills. (2001b). *Special educational needs: Code of practice*. DfES Publications.

Dimatati, M., Heaton, P., Pring, L., Downing, J., & Ockelford, A. (2012). Exploring the impact of congenital visual impairment on the development of absolute pitch using a new online assessment tool: A preliminary study. *Psychomusicology: Music, Mind and Brain, 22*(2), 129–133. https://psycnet.apa.org/doi/10.1037/a0030857

Edgar, S. N. (2014). An ethic of care in high school instrumental music. *Action, Criticism, and Theory for Music Education, 13*(2), 112–137. http://act.maydaygroup.org/articles/Edgar13_2.pdf

Fuqua, C. S. (2011). *Alabama musicians: Musical heritage from the heart of Dixie*. The History Press.

Groemer, G. (2012). *The spirit of tsugaru: Blind musicians, Tsugaru-Jamisen and the folk music of northern Japan* (2nd ed.). Tsugaru Shobo Hirosaki.

Hallam, S. (2015). *The power of music: A research synthesis of the impact of actively making music on the intellectual, social and personal development of children and young people*. Music Education Council and International Music Education Research Centre.

Hel, V. (2018). The ethics of care. In S. Olsaretti (Ed.), *The Oxford handbook of distributive justice* (pp. 213–234). Oxford University Press. https://doi.org/10.1093/oxfordhb/9780199645121.013.12

Hendricks, K. S. (2018). *Compassionate music teaching*. Rowman & Littlefield.

Hendricks, K. S. (2021). Authentic connection in music education. In K. S. Hendricks & J. Boyce-Tillman (Eds.), *Authentic connection: Music, spirituality, and wellbeing* (pp. 237–253). Peter Lang.

United States Department of Education. (1997). *Individuals with disabilities education act*. Retrieved March 17, 2022, from https://sites.ed.gov/idea/about-idea/

Isaki, M. (1987). Japanese music and the blind. *British Journal of Visual Impairment*, 5(3), 103–105. https://doi.org/10.1177%2F026461968700500307

Kononenko, N. (1998). *Ukrainian minstrels: And the blind shall sing*. M. E. Sharpe.

Learning Disabilities Association of America. (n.d.). *Types of learning disabilities*. Retrieved July 7, 2021, from https://ldaamerica.org/types-of-learning-disabilities

Lubet, A. (2011). *Music, disability, and society*. Temple University Press.

Myers, D. E. (1995). Lifelong learning: An emerging research agenda for music education. *Research Studies in Music Education*, 4(1), 21–27. https://doi.org/10.1177%2F1321103X9500400104

New Zealand Parliamentary Counsel Office. (2020, August 1). *Education act 1989*. http://www.legislation.govt.nz/act/public/1989/0080/latest/whole.html#DLM177470

Noddings, N. (2003). *Caring: A feminine approach to ethics and moral education*. University of California Press.

Noddings, N. (2005). *The challenge to care in schools* (2nd ed.). Teachers College Press.

Noddings, N. (2013). *Caring: A relational approach to ethics and moral education* (2nd ed.). University of California Press.

Ockelford, A. (2000). Music in the education of children with severe or profound learning difficulties: Issues in current UK provision, a new conceptual framework, and proposals for research. *Psychology of Music*, 28(2), 197–217. https://doi.org/10.1177%2F0305735600282009

Oglethorpe, S. M. (2002). *Instrumental music for dyslexics: A teaching handbook* (2nd ed.). Whurr.

Ottenberg, S. (1996). *Seeing with music: The lives of three blind African musicians*. University of Washington Press.

Overy, K. (2000). Dyslexia, temporal processing and music: The potential of music as an early learning aid for dyslexic children. *Psychology of Music*, 28(2), 218–229. https://doi.org/10.1177%2F0305735600282010

Pickard, B. (2021). A framework for mediating medical and social models of disability in instrumental teaching for children with down syndrome. *Research Studies in Music Education*, 43(2), 110–128. https://doi.org/10.1177%2F1321103X19855416

Purtell, R. (2013). Music and the social model of disability. In J. Williams (Ed.), *Music and the social model: An occupational therapist's approach to music with people labelled as having learning disabilities* (pp. 26–32). Jessica Kingsley.

Royal College of Psychiatrists. (n.d.). *Specific learning disabilities*. Retrieved July 7, 2021, from https://www.rcpsych.ac.uk/mental-health/parents-and-young-people/information-for-parents-and-carers/specific-learning-disabilities-for-parents-and-carers

Reifinger, J. L. (2019). Dyslexia in the music classroom: A review of literature. *Update: Applications of Research in Music Education*, 38(1), 9–17. https://doi.org/10.1177%2F8755123319831736

Ribowsky, M. (2010). *Signed, sealed, and delivered: The soulful journey of Stevie Wonder*. John Wiley and Sons.

Richerme, L. K. (2017). A feminine and poststructural extension of cosmopolitan ethics in music education. *International Journal of Music Education*, 35(3), 414–424. https://doi.org/10.1177%2F0255761416667470

Roulston, K. (2010). "There is no end to learning": Lifelong education and the joyful learner. *International Journal of Music Education*, 28(4), 341–352. https://doi.org/10.1177%2F0255761410381822

Ruddock, P., & Bishop, J. (2006). *Disability standards for education 2005*. Commonwealth of Australia.

Shearing, G., & Shipton, A. (2005). *Lullaby of birdland: The autobiography of George Shearing*. Bloomsbury.

Smart, J. (2004). Models of disability: The juxtaposition of biology and social construction. In T. Riggar & D. Maki (Eds.), *Handbook of rehabilitation counselling* (pp. 25–49). Springer.

Straus, J. N. (2011). *Extraordinary measures: Disability in music*. Oxford University Press.

UK Government. (2001, May 11). *SENDA: Special educational needs and disability act*. https://www.legislation.gov.uk/ukpga/2001/10/2001-05-11

UK Government. (n.d.). *Disability rights: Education*. Retrieved July 7, 2021, from https://www.gov.uk/rights-disabled-person/education-rights

UNESCO and Ministry of Education, Spain. (1994). *The Salamanca statement and framework for action on special needs education (adopted by the World Conference on Special Needs Education: Access and Quality)*. https://unesdoc.unesco.org/ark:/48223/pf0000098427

University of Nebraska Kearney. (n.d.). *UNK one-handed woodwinds program*. Retrieved July 7, 2021, from http://www.unk.edu/academics/music/unk-one-handed-winds-program.php

Üstün, T. B., Kostanjsek, N., Chatterji, S., & Rehm, J. (Eds.). (2010). *WHO disability assessment schedule 2.0*. World Health Organization.

Welch, G. F. (1988). Observations on the incidence of absolute pitch (AP) ability in the early blind. *Psychology of Music*, 16(1), 77–80. https://doi.org/10.1177%2F0305735688161009

World Health Organization. (2021, November 24). *Disability and health*. Retrieved January 26, 2022, from https://www.who.int/news-room/fact-sheets/detail/disability-and-health

CHAPTER 9

CARING THROUGH DIALOGICAL RELATIONS IN COMMUNITY MUSIC SETTINGS

LAURA BENJAMINS

CARE HANDBOOK TOPICS

Co-creating caring relationships
Philosophical perspectives
Social activism and critical consciousness

> Joy is possible . . . only where I partake in being in a justified manner *through* the other and *for* the other, where I am passive and receive a bestowed gift. It is my otherness that rejoices in me, not I-for-myself.
> —Bakhtin (1990, p. 136)

INTRODUCTION

WITHIN music education settings, linearity of progress, a focus on successful outcomes, and limited conceptions of music's potential for sociality too often prevail (Kanellopoulos, 2011; Mitchell & Benedict, 2020), reducing the possibility of stepping into the unknown, cultivating authentic connections with others, and simply "being." The notion of *care* within a framework of compassionate music teaching (Hendricks, 2018) can be understood as an experience of caring *with* others through shared music-making, compassion, empathy, diversity, and inclusion. Community music is one form of music-making that has been seen to emphasize people, community, and participation through its diverse and inclusive modes of being (Higgins, 2012). With a distinct emphasis on facilitation and the process of its practice, community music constitutes "a form of thoughtful disruption" or "an encounter with 'newness' . . . towards moments of futural transformation" (Higgins, 2015, p. 446). Community music is not without its challenges, however, and several scholars suggest that it is too often understood as an ideal, as it also has the potential to reinforce social constraints, inequalities, and issues of hegemony (Boeskov, 2017; Kertz-Welzel, 2016).

In this chapter, I aim to address the notion of "care" in relation to musical and pedagogical practices within community music settings. Using Bakhtin's (1981) concept of dialogism, I explore how pedagogues and facilitators might "care with" fellow musicians, through their musical and pedagogical practices, toward participative dialogue and the encounter of Others. Bakhtin's concept of dialogism is particularly useful in addressing "care" in music-making through his emphasis on the act or utterance. He both addresses the direct implications of any act of dialogue, considering the self in relation to the Other, while also recognizing the historical and social significance of any act in relation to a living "text" or social field. I extend Bakhtin's theory to community music-making, placing a direct emphasis on the responsibility of the facilitator in creating spaces conducive to musicians' engagement in dialogue. I address places of church worship as a particular case in which such a concept is demonstrated, noting the complexities of the social field and beliefs at hand.

Dialogue Within Music Education and Community Music

Dialogue "cannot exist . . . in the absence of a profound love for the world and for people. The naming of the world, which is an act of creation and re-creation, is not possible if it is not infused with love. Love is at the same time the foundation of dialogue and dialogue itself" (Freire, 2005, p. 89). Throughout this chapter, I use the term "encounter" at various points to describe a sense of meeting or relational engagement between an individual and an Other, driven by love or care. Some have linked the concept of encounter directly to the arts, understood to hold and express meaning separate from everyday life (Yob, 2011). At times, scholars have connected the notion of spirituality to relational spaces particularly within the musical experience (Boyce-Tillman, 2007; van der Merwe & Habron, 2015; Yob, 2011). I further explore concepts of spirituality and relational meeting in music classroom elsewhere (Benjamins, 2021a). Although I write about musicians meeting the Other through encounters or engagement in relational dialogue throughout this chapter, I am not referring to a spiritual "experience" but rather encounters of dialogue with Others (other individuals, musics, theological beliefs, and so on) that may result in a sense of discomfort, a new understanding, or shift in the way in which one approaches their musical engagement.

The notion of dialogue has been addressed in community music scholarship by scholars who address dialogue in terms of musical collaboration (de Bruin, 2016) and an exploration into the dialogic space of participatory music (Camlin, 2015). Mitchell and Benedict (2020) examine the relational musical engagement from music education and music therapy perspectives, acknowledging that music has inherent personal and relational affordances that should be considered when making distinctions between the "music itself" and "non-musical benefits." The authors engage in dialogue with one another, considering music's relational imperative outside the boundaries of music education and music therapeutic perspectives alone. They encourage genuine dialogue between disciplines, allowing one to hear the other and "open [them]selves to transformation" (p. 55). Meeting the Other through words, actions, silence, and music, each as components of dialogue, involves an act of inviting the Other in, with a readiness to respond with one's whole being.

Garred (2001) provides a particularly useful dialogical view of music in music therapy that can also be applied to other community music contexts. Using Buber's (1970) concept of the *I-Thou* relation, he recognizes the reciprocal, accepting relation between *I* and *You*, as well as music's role in mediating the relation between the two. *I-Thou* relations involve a living encounter with another being, leaving all fixed preconceptions behind. Garred suggests that music's value is ultimately found in and through its interrelations, unable to be "reduced or determined purely on a physical basis" (para. 14). From a community music perspective, one might similarly understand music's value to be found in its dialogical nature; music reveals unique experiences and encounters through its interrelations. Along with a broader understanding of music's role in dialogical relations, however, a framework that properly accounts for the significance of performed acts of dialogue and utterances is necessary to consider in this conversation.

BAKHTIN'S CONCEPT OF DIALOGISM

Russian philosopher and literary theorist, Mikhail M. Bakhtin's (1895–1975) theory of dialogism (1981) provides a useful framework in which to understand the significance of one's utterances or acts in dialogical relation to an Other. Within dialogism, one's capacity to have consciousness is ultimately based on otherness (Holquist, 2002). Otherness is found in the differential relation between the center and all that is not the center. For Bakhtin, the "self" is dialogic, engaging in relationships such as system/history, signifier/signified, text/context, and speaking/writing. In order for one to understand the "self" and become an object of their own perception, they must do so from the outside, "authoring" themselves. The self, therefore, consists of a phenomenon of multiple elements: a center (I-for-itself), a not-center (the not-I-in-me), and the relation between them. Relationships are not static, but are constantly being "made" or "unmade" (Holquist, 2002) and in a mode of transition.

Scholars such as Morson and Emerson (1990) have addressed three different ways in which Bakhtin conceptualizes dialogue. These include (a) an understanding of dialogue as an essential attribute of every utterance, considering the socioideological contexts wherein words live; (b) a conceptualization of dialogue in terms of a speaker's awareness of the sources of their words and translating those sources to a listener; and (c) dialogue as a philosophical idea, as an "inter-subjective quality of all meaning" (Hirschkop, 1999, p. 4). For the purposes of this chapter, I focus primarily on the first element of dialogue listed, in order to problematize one's practices in music-making settings, considering the specific socioideological context at hand.

Dialogism of Authoring

In one's shared relation with the other, the "self" responds to addressivity, forming unique responses according to their particular life existence and situationality (Holquist, 2002). These responses or dialogues tend to have a pattern, forming a text that ultimately makes up one's life. Bakhtin (1993) understands every human thought, along with its content, as an act or a deed that one performs. These performed acts or "texts" and lived-experiences are constituent moments in life, connected to historical contexts. Every word or utterance that we speak, according to Bakhtin, reflects a valuative attitude toward an object and "sets it in motion toward that which is yet-to-be-determined about it" (pp. 32–33). Our words or utterances become a participant in a greater ongoing event, entering into a relationship "within the unity of the ongoing event encompassing us" (p. 33). "Texts" or acts are therefore "historically located, socially placed, and individually enacted," meaning there is a "continual dialogue between text and context" (Mackinlay, 2002, p. 32).

Elsewhere, Bakhtin (1981) highlights the embodiment of speech acts or utterances, and their active participation in living heteroglossia. Heteroglossia, for Bakhtin, is the simultaneous use of different dialogues or utterances within a specific text or encounter. At any given time, social, historical, and physiological conditions impact a word's meaning according to a particular time and place (p. 263). All utterances operate under a matrix of forces in tension and conflict with one another, shaping a word's meaning in an original manner. Heteroglossia accounts for the contingency in the conditions that impact each utterance (Hess, 2018). Utterances do not only answer requirements of their own individualized embodiment, but they "answer the requirements of heteroglossia as well" (Bakhtin, 1981, p. 272).

Scholars such as Mackinlay (2002) extend Bakhtin's concept of dialogue to a classroom context as a dialectic and discursive space. Similar to Mackinlay's use of dialogism to analyze multiple speaking positions within shifting and differing subjectivities within the classroom, I understand educational settings as polyphonic and discursive in nature, consisting of a variety of forms of cultural production and "texts." Bakhtin

(1986) defines language as "any sign system" (p. 106), which can be broadly understood as a subset of culture—such as musical culture—that engages listeners and performers in performative acts. Music and the arts demand responses from audience members as participants and/or observers. Community music, and more specifically, church music, blurs the boundaries of "participants" and "observers," creating a discourse between them. Mackinlay specifically examines the Indigenous performance classroom as a type of cultural production rooted in a language or "text." In the study, students and Indigenous performers engage in and maintain dialogue between, within, and outside multiple subjectivities while contributing to cultural production. Various settings of music-making—formal, non-formal, and informal—similarly produce culture through the "text" in which the music-making is located and in terms of the utterances expressed through performative acts.

Several scholars have extended Bakhtin's theory specifically to music educational contexts in relation to the notion of the text. Kanellopoulos (2011), for example, proposes a Bakhtinian conception of improvisation, emphasizing an attitude of consciousness that views musical improvisation as "an obligation to explore the unknown" (p. 113). Improvisation, Kanellopoulos argues, is dialogic because it is "characterized by unfinalizability and openness" (p. 113). In using Bakhtin as a framework to approach improvisation, improvisation is regarded as a problem-positing approach rather than a problem-solving method. Such an approach "counter[s] monologue [in the classroom] by allowing the flourishing of a polyphony of unmerged voices" (Kanellopoulos, 2011, p. 114), shifting the overall attitude and "text" in the classroom setting away from one set way of knowing and being. Bakhtin's framework allows for an understanding of both the immediate, dialogic aspects of the musical action, as well as a historical, situated understanding of each musical gesture.

Encountering the Other

Bakhtin has been seen by scholars to have a thoroughly relational view of human subjectivity that emphasizes its irreducibility (Kanellopoulos, 2011). For Bakhtin, the self has no absolute meaning in itself; it is "dependent for its existence on the other" (Holquist, 2002, p. 34). Through the event of an utterance, a simultaneous unity of differences occurs, where the self and the other partake in dialogue (Holquist, 2002).

Hess (2018) employs Bakhtin's concept of dialogism to examine one's encounter of the Other within musical encounters. In considering such encounters, Hess recognizes the "pedagogy of discomfort" that occurs when we, as humans, encounter an epistemology—both musical and otherwise—that is different from our own. Dialogism includes the presence of multiple voices, or polyphony, where ideologies meet and encounter Others as subjects yet maintain their own independence. Through one's participation in the encounter, ideologies are placed into conversation with each other dialogically, without requiring the acceptance of other ideologies.

In carnivalistic spaces (see Bakhtin, 1984) where encounters are possible, "people appear for a moment outside the usual conditions of their lives . . . and there opens up another—more genuine sense of themselves and of their relationships to one other" (Bakhtin, 1984, p. 145). One comes to know themselves through an encounter with Others and the familiar is made strange (Hess, 2018). As evident in Bakhtin's writings, "any encounter with the other is by definition an encounter with the self" (Gasbarrone, 1994, p. 10). Similar to Kanellopoulos's (2011) observations of improvisation with dialogism, Hess (2018) reminds the reader that encounters are not fixed; rather, they are relational and responsive, open to a plethora of possibilities.

Understanding Bakhtin's Theory Within Community Music-Making

There are several elements of Bakhtin's theory that I wish to apply to community music-making contexts. Bakhtin's work addresses both the dialogic aspect of particular moments in relation to, or encountering, the Other, as well as how one's utterances or dialogue contribute to an overarching "text" located in specific social and historical contexts (i.e., heteroglossia). If musical gestures are to be understood as performative utterances or acts, then each act of dialogue with Others engages both an immediate relation, while also contributing to an even greater sociocultural and contextual situatedness.

Similar to Bakhtin's theory of dialogism where individuals understand the "self" in relation to Others, possibly encountering a sense of "disruption" or discomfort (Hess, 2018), community music has been described as "a form of thoughtful disruption" or an "encounter with 'newness,'" contributing to moments of "futural transformation" (Higgins, 2015, p. 446). Community music facilitators encourage this sense of open dialogue, encouraging "conversation" between different individuals with differing perspectives (Higgins, 2012). With an emphasis on active participation, equality of opportunity, and sensitivity to context, facilitators welcome musicians in, encouraging them toward creative music-making (Higgins, 2008). Community musicians tend to employ pedagogical approaches focused on negotiation through collaboration, co-authorship, and group work, learning through a "bottom up" approach (Higgins, 2015). The facilitative process therefore opens up possibilities to venture collaboratively into the unknown, putting faith, trust, and responsibility into relationships (Higgins, 2012).

As Bakhtin (1990) described in his understanding of the self, individuals are dependent for their existence on their relationship with Others (Holquist, 2002). In accordance with an ethic of care (Noddings, 2013), community music facilitators consciously strive to cultivate spaces of trust and respect through "an overarching desire to hear others' voices" (Higgins, 2012, p. 161). While the facilitator holds the responsibility as the leader of the process, community music "blurs the boundaries" through its polyphony of perspectives and voices. Rather than a hierarchical, monological way of being, facilitators and participants engage with others in a multiplicity of ways through acts of hospitality, active listening, and relational encounters.

Bakhtin understood ethics in terms of a manner of knowing what to do in particular occasions, rather than following a distinct set of rules (Morson, 2002). Musical facilitators have a specific task of open-endedness wherein a sense of wisdom is required. There is a frightening sense of openness required in dialogism where the musical action is not decided beforehand. Practically, such a concept might be enacted through the alteration of traditional spaces toward openness and diversity. Perhaps marginalized voices might be privileged above those that are dominant, unsettling traditional and historical frameworks (Hess, 2018). The pedagogue or facilitator may invite musicians into practices of active and contemplative listening through multiple roles as musicians, listeners, and audience members. Boundaries become blurred and a tapestry of polyphonic voices emerges.

A consideration of the social context or field in which one is located is also necessary when acknowledging the significance of utterances or dialogical acts in music-making. When examining community music through the lens of a theory of practice (Bourdieu, 1977), Phelan (2008) seeks to address how principles of community music are enacted through decisions, actions, and choices—planned, improvised, conscious, or unconscious. Music-making activities, Phelan writes, are strategic in that the "act of acting" involves a decision-making "towards a finite, expressed reality" (p. 148). As Phelan articulates, it is important to consider "how music-making can implicitly strategize behaviours such as inclusivity, accessibility, or empowerment . . . through repertoire, modes of performance (e.g. improvisation) . . . and through participative choices related to gender, age, race, or ability" (p. 148).

For community music, then, one might consider how a facilitator generates values through their music-making practices, actions, and decisions. As facilitators cultivate spaces of dialogue and encounter for diverse voices, not only are they generating immediate values and moments of relation to others, but also they are contributing to overarching "texts" and the greater social field (i.e., the community's values, identity, ways of being). Through practices or dialogic acts, meaning is generated within particular social/cultural/political contexts. As a leader or facilitator, it is critical to think about how a sense of care might be enacted for others in cultivating such as space of dialogue, while also considering how one's actions contribute to overarching social "texts" and ways of being.

Case Study: Places of Christian Worship

I extend the concepts addressed above within a Christian church worship context as a form of community music-making and facilitation. My dissertation research (Benjamins, forthcoming) explores the role of a church worship leader's participative decisions and actions in creating a space of encounter with others—referring to both other worshippers and God. Drawing on Bourdieu's (1977) *Theory of Practice*, I consider how a church's music-making practices may both reflect and respond to the musical and theological fields in which it is located. I examine how and why worship leaders and musicians, as agents, strategize their musical behaviors in different church settings, and whether these musical behaviors reflect and shape habitus both institutionally and individually.

The worship leader, typically the lead vocalist or instrumentalist in evangelical Christian church settings, plays a particular role in the selection and facilitation of musical repertoire (Ingalls, 2018). Elsewhere, I have written about the role of the worship leader as a pedagogue and facilitator (Benjamins, 2019, 2021b). Similar to a community music facilitator who leads musical experiences, guiding musicians in their music-making engagements (Higgins, 2008), worship leaders' decisions and actions could be seen to affect musicians and congregants' overall musicking experiences. As I have argued, the worship leader often has a responsibility to decipher the formative impact that lyrics and musical practices overall have on musicians and the greater congregation (Benjamins, 2021b).

Church worship is diverse in nature, and within any specific congregational setting, worshippers encounter differences as they engage in dialogue with Others. Such an encounter with Others might include other musician-worshippers, musics, theological beliefs, understandings of worship, among others. Worship leaders, as facilitators, have a responsibility to perform theology that reflects the beliefs of the church, contributing to the overall promotion of unity rather than division (Boyce-Tillman, 2013). Engaging in music-making within a worship context can be transformational (Boyce-Tillman, 2013); therefore, one's engagements in worship must be intentional and thoughtful as they lead to the formation of the unconscious (Smith, 2013; Strawn & Brown, 2013).

Within places of worship, I suggest that notions of care may be enacted through leaders' musical and pedagogical practices. Caring involves compassion, a relationship of "experience-sharing," based on a "shared understanding of feelings, hopes, and/or desires" (Hendricks, 2018, p. 5). As Noddings (2013) states, caring-for involves listening, rather than just "telling" or assuming we know what others need. Specifically, within religious contexts, it can be difficult to invite musicians into participative dialogue, placing their differences into conversation with one another. Because of a church's particular social field or location, intertwined with theological beliefs, differences may not be welcomed. In encountering others through such a dialogism that Bakhtin encourages does not result in a resolution of sorts, but it is "responsive, relational, and filled with possibilities" (Hess, 2018, p. 32). Rather than a finality of a closed product or "end" to dialogue, community musicians or worship leaders might instead consider their processes of engagement or attitude of consciousness (Bakhtin, 1993).

Dialogue in places of worship is a particularly interesting phenomenon because of the various layers of relationships that exist. Musicians encounter other musicians, worshippers, the greater congregation, as well as God. I have described this in more detail elsewhere using Buber's (1970) framework of the *I-Thou* relationship (Benjamins,

2021b). Church musicians engage in meeting or dialogue with God and one another, resulting in a sense of meaning. They engage in an element of self-critical questioning such as confession and self-examination, "re-orienting themselves to God" (Benjamins, 2021b, p. 11). A final "answer" is not reached; rather, meaning is found in one's engagement in dialogue or meeting (worship) of God. The worship leader, then, has a responsibility to cultivate spaces of community, encouraging dialogue, encounter, and meeting among fellow worshippers.

Lingering Thoughts and Considerations

In considering the broader picture of dialogical relations in community music settings, several key considerations should be addressed. This chapter has framed dialogical relations in a positive light, and as Hess (2018) reminds readers, encounters do, indeed, act on us. At their best, "they foster epistemological possibilities and create spaces for potential growth" (p. 27). Yet at their worst, encounters certainly have the potential to destroy, producing defensiveness and "reinscribe dominant power structures" (p. 27). Although notions of care may be enacted through facilitators and worship leaders' practices, the opposite might also occur. If encounters or spaces for dialogue are not approached carefully, dominant relationships might increase in power, further reducing the polyphony of voices into a monological, hierarchical structure. There is also a concern when encounters are assimilated into traditional or "comfortable" frameworks. Active processes of reflection and awareness, as part of an overarching framework of care, could be beneficial for pedagogues or facilitators, as they critically question their contribution to the facilitation of dialogue and spaces of authentic connection consisting of trust, empathy, inclusion, and community (Hendricks & Boyce-Tillman, 2021) between musickers.

Although community music has transformative potential, relationships or meanings generated in community music practices are not always positive or "ideal" (Boeskov, 2017). There tends to be a misconception that community music practices inherently result in joyful, empowering practices that "counter experiences of marginalization and exclusion" (p. 88). In accordance with Bakhtin's theory, because "texts" or processes of dialogue are located within specific social and historical contexts, musical acts are performative, affirming and transforming individuals in ambiguous and, at times, conflicting ways (Boeskov, 2017). The framework provided in this chapter encourages facilitators in all music-making settings to further consider their actions, decisions, and practices in relation to "caring for" fellow musicians. As the quotation at the beginning of the chapter reminds readers, joy is found in one's concern and care for, about, and with others. Practices of, and engagement in, dialogism is a purely relational view of humanity; for as Bakhtin believed, the self has no absolute meaning in itself; it is ultimately "dependent for its existence on the other" (Holquist, 2002, p. 34). May readers continue to live into this concern, relying on, and caring for and with the other in the world in which they find themselves living.

REFERENCES

Bakhtin, M. M. (1981). *The dialogic imagination: Four essays* (M. Holquist, Ed.; C. Emerson & M. Holquist, Trans.). University of Texas Press.

Bakhtin, M. M. (1984). Problems of Dostoevsky's poetics. In C. Emerson (Ed.), *Theory and history of literature* (Vol. 8). University of Minnesota Press.

Bakhtin, M. M. (1986). *Speech genres and other late essays* (C. Emerson & M. Holquist, Eds.; V. McGee, Trans.). University of Texas Press.

Bakhtin, M. M. (1990). *Art and answerability: Early philosophical essays by M. M. Bakhtin* (V. Liapunov & M. Holquist, Eds.; V. Liapunov, Trans.). University of Texas Press.

Bakhtin, M. M. (1993). *Toward a philosophy of the act* (V. Liapunov & M. Holquist, Eds.; V. Liapunov, Trans.). University of Texas Press.

Benjamins, L. (2019). Learning through praise: How Christian worship band musicians learn. *Journal of Popular Music Education*, 3(3), 417–433. https://doi.org/10.1386/jpme_00004_1

Benjamins, L. (2021a). Facilitating relational spaces of musicking: A music educator's practice of care. In K. Hendricks & J. Boyce-Tillman (Eds.), *Authentic connection: Music, spirituality, and wellbeing* (pp. 219–236). Peter Lang.

Benjamins, L. (2021b). Musicking as liturgical speech acts: An examination of contemporary worship music practices. *Studia Liturgica*, 51(2), 143–158. https://doi.org/10.1177/0039320721 1033993

Benjamins, L. (forthcoming). *Musical behaviours, dispositions, and tendencies: Exploring church music-making through a theory of practice* [Unpublished doctoral dissertation, Western University].

Boeskov, K. (2017). The community music practice as cultural performance: Foundations for a community music theory of social transformation. *International Journal of Community Music*, 10(1), 85–99. https://doi.org/10.1386/ijcm.10.1.85_1

Bourdieu, P. (1977). *Outline of a theory of practice* (R. Nice, Trans.). Stanford University Press.

Boyce-Tillman, J. (2007). Spirituality in the musical experience. In L. Besler (Ed.), *International handbook of research in arts education* (pp. 1405–1422). Springer.

Boyce-Tillman, J. (2013). Tune your music to your heart: Reflections for church music leaders. In M. Ingalls, C. Landau, & T. Wagner (Eds.), *Christian congregational music: Performance, identity and experience* (pp. 49–66). Ashgate.

Buber, M. (1970). *I and Thou* (W. Kaufmann, Trans.). Simon & Schuster. (Original work published 1937)

Camlin, D. A. (2015). "This is my truth, now tell me yours": Emphasizing dialogue within participatory music. *International Journal of Community Music*, 8(3), 233–257. https://doi.org/10.1386/ijcm.8.3.233_1

de Bruin, L. R. (2016). Journeys in jazz education: Learning, collaboration and dialogue in communities of musical practice. *International Journal of Community Music*, 9(3), 307–325. https://doi.org/10.1386/ijcm.9.3.307_1

Freire, P. (2005). *Pedagogy of the oppressed* (M. B. Ramos, Trans.). Continuum. (Original work published 1970)

Garred, R. (2001). The ontology of music in music therapy. *Voices: A World Forum for Music Therapy*, 1(3). https://voices.no/index.php/voices/article/view/1604/1363

Gasbarrone, L. (1994). "The locus for the Other": Cixous, Bakhtin, and women's writing. In K. Hohne & H. Wussow (Eds.), *A dialogue of voices: Feminist literary theory and Bakhtin* (pp. 1–19). University of Minnesota Press.

Hendricks, K. (2018). *Compassionate music teaching*. Rowman & Littlefield.

Hendricks, K. S., & Boyce-Tillman, J. (2021). Music, connection, and authenticity. In K. S. Hendricks & J. Boyce-Tillman (Eds.), *Authentic connection: Music, spirituality, and wellbeing* (pp. 3–15). Peter Lang.

Hess, J. (2018). A "discomfortable" approach to music education: Re-envisioning the "Strange Encounter." *Philosophy of Music Education Review*, 26(1), 24–45. https://doi.org/10.2979/philmusieducrevi.26.1.03

Higgins, L. (2008). The creative music workshop: Event, facilitation, gift. *International Journal of Music Education*, 26(4), 326–338. https://doi.org/10.1177/0255761408096074

Higgins, L. (2012). One-to-one encounters: Facilitators, participants, and friendship. *Theory into Practice*, 51(3), 159–166. https://doi.org/10.1080/00405841.2012.690297

Higgins, L. (2015). Hospitable music making: Community music as a site for social justice. In C. Benedict, P. Schmidt, G. Spruce, & P. Woodford (Eds.), *The Oxford handbook of social justice in music education* (pp. 446–455). Oxford University Press.

Hirschkop, K. (1999). *Mikhail Bakhtin: An aesthetic for democracy*. Oxford University Press.

Holquist, M. (2002). *Dialogism: Bakhtin and his world* (2nd ed.). Routledge.

Ingalls, M. (2018). *Singing the congregation: How contemporary worship music forms Evangelical community*. Oxford University Press.

Kanellopoulos, P. A. (2011). Freedom and responsibility: The aesthetics of free musical improvisation and its educational implications—a view from Bakhtin. *Philosophy of Music Education Review*, 19(2), 113–135. https://doi.org/10.2979/philmusieducrevi.19.2.113

Kertz-Welzel, A. (2016). Daring to question: A philosophical critique of community music. *Philosophy of Music Education Review*, 24(2), 113–130. https://doi.org/10.2979/philmusieducrevi.24.2.01

Mackinlay, E. (2002). Engaging with theories of dialogue and voice: Using Bakhtin as a framework to understand teaching and learning Indigenous Australian women's performance. *Research Studies in Music Education*, 19, 32–45. https://doi.org/10.1177%2F1321103X020190010501

Mitchell, E., & Benedict, C. (2020). Lives in dialogue: Shared musical-relational engagements in music therapy and music education. *European Journal of Philosophy in Arts Education*, 5(1), 33–67. https://www.ejpae.com/index.php/EJPAE/article/view/22/31

Morson, G. S. (2002). Contingency and the literature of process. In R. Bracht Branham (Ed.), *Bakhtin and the classics* (pp. 250–272). Northwestern University Press.

Morson, G. S., & Emerson, C. (1990). *Mikhail Bakhtin: Creation of a prosaics*. Stanford University Press.

Noddings, N. (2013). *Caring: A relational approach to ethics and moral education* (2nd ed.). University of California Press.

Phelan, H. (2008). Practice, ritual and community music: Doing as identity. *International Journal of Community Music*, 1(2), 143–158. https://doi.org/10.1386/ijcm.1.2.143_1

Smith, J. K. A. (2013). *Imagining the Kingdom: How worship works*. Baker Academic.

Strawn, B. D., & Brown, W. S. (2013). Liturgical animals: What psychology and neuroscience tell us about formation and worship. *Liturgy*, 28(4), 3–14. https://doi.org/10.1080/0458063X.2013.803838

Van der Merwe, L., & Habron, J. (2015). A conceptual model of spirituality in music education. *Journal of Research in Music Education, 63*(1), 47–69. https://doi.org/10.1177/0022429415575314

Yob, I. (2011). If we knew what spirituality was, we would teach for it. *Music Educators Journal, 98*(2), 41–47. https://doi.org/10.1177/0027432111425959

CHAPTER 10

THE POLITICS OF CARE IN THE EDUCATION OF CHILDREN GIFTED FOR MUSIC

A Systems View

GUADALUPE LÓPEZ-ÍÑIGUEZ AND
HEIDI WESTERLUND

CARE HANDBOOK TOPICS

Identity expressions
Musical development
Philosophical perspectives
Social activism and critical consciousness
Wellbeing and human flourishing

INTRODUCTION

The decades-long and ongoing popularity of positivistic research on gifted children's[1] musical education is today confronted by a growing awareness of the discriminating

---

[1] Following François Gagné's (2021) Differentiating Model of Giftedness and Talent (DMGT; see Figure 34.1 in Hendricks & McPherson, this volume) we assume that children can be considered *gifted for music* when they display unusually precocious "intellectual, creative and/or physical maturity well before the majority of their peers" (Gagné, 2021, p. 77).

power of "ableism" in the discipline of music education. Ableist music education that assumes normality and completeness, particularly in terms of students' motoric abilities and sensitivity together with elitism and meritocracy, forms a power structure in which the elite presents itself as a select group of people attributed with certain intrinsic qualities and special skills, or experience that is judged as merit (Ilmola et al., 2021). As such, meritocracy is claimed to be the defining feature of the entire education system of modern democratic societies, in its belief that social class and other social categories have been declared to be irrelevant to an individual's life prospects, which should now only depend on talent and effort. Yet, a vast body of research shows that in a democracy "the professed equality of rights of all citizens contrasts sharply with the very real inequality of living conditions" (Piketty, 2014, p. 361). Hence, a meritocratic education system "grants excessive value to people who stand out in a given field—more often than not socioeconomically—at the expense of those who occupy lower positions in that field" (Gagné, 2021, p. 67). Thus, in gifted education stakeholders face a pressing need to support children from lower socioeconomic strata instead of those already better situated, as precocious children from more challenged backgrounds might not ever get a chance to fully achieve their potential, or even have their gifts recognized. However, whereas ableist music education puts talent on a pedestal the critical anti-ableist stance is reluctant to admit any fundamental differences between individual students (Slote, 2013).

In this chapter we distance ourselves from any conception of equality that assumes sameness or talent-related unfairness by recognizing the existence of *giftedness* in the domain of music—albeit when viewed through the critical lenses of care, justice, and democracy (see also Slote, 2013). In our attempt to overcome the polarizing tendencies and Stigma of the Giftedness Paradigm (SGP; Cross & Coleman, 2005), we will highlight how children gifted for music—*because of* their giftedness and potential for being "able" and "selected" to perform at expert levels—can also be vulnerable and at risk in "ableist" and elitist meritocratic music education systems. Once their potential is identified (e.g., Haroutounian, 2002), these children tend to be treated as future professionals; they are prone to being used as showcases and national priorities in order to enhance socio-educational ecosystems' prestige (Borland, 1989) and therefore lack the preconditions for becoming thriving agents of their own lives "here and now."

Despite a large number of biographical accounts and studies of the cognitive-motoric skill development of children gifted for music (e.g., McPherson, 2016)—which have been used to support the existence of acceleration programs to maximize their potential in private and public music schools, conservatoires, and music universities[2]—there are

---

[2] Formal acceleration programs for precocious underage children—in which "access is controlled through a quota of limited available places" (Gagné, 2021, p. 97)—are common in Western music institutions. These programs are aimed at accelerated progression in music for children who pursue a regular curriculum in a condensed manner, with the main options being (a) entering official youth programs specifically aimed at talent development and professionalism in/outside higher music education, or (b) pursuing two or more academic years at the same time (or skipping a grade) at any institution not particularly oriented toward talent development.

also vivid descriptions of the lifelong trauma and abuse that children gifted for music have faced within (but also outside) special programs for talent development in music education systems (e.g., MacNamara et al., 2016). With a history that includes the brutal physical abuse through castration of young boys by the Roman Catholic Church in the service of artistic achievement (Siegel, 2020), as well as more commonplace parental oppression and exploitation (Gordon, 1988; Kijas, 2016) and the authoritarian behaviors of teachers (López-Íñiguez, 2019), music cannot be said to be a field that self-evidently nurtures the welfare of the musically precocious child and follows the legal codes of the United Nations Convention on the Rights of the Child (UN General Assembly, 1989). However, questions concerning a child's welfare and self-determination, needs and interests, and their exposure to public scrutiny are complex. For instance, in matters such as child labor, children's rights to protection and provision should be prioritized over their right to participation (Wyness et al., 2004). Yet, in light of the literature to date, it is obvious that a simple norm or generalized rule disconnected from reality cannot direct how parental or educational power is exerted in the education of children gifted for music—or any music education for that matter.

We argue that the education of children gifted for music can be seen as a special case in terms of social justice and children's rights, requiring professional care and reflexivity from these children's music teachers and educational institutions. More specifically, we argue for a transformative *politics of care*, not only focused on the typical master-apprentice setting that surrounds children gifted for music but also expanding the normative professional frames of the entire music education system in Western countries. Based on the premise of relational ontology, the politics of care stresses responsibility for human relationships by accepting that in care ethics "no aspect of human life is unshaped by the political" (Greenswag, 2019, p. 914). Care ethics thus recognizes the complexity of relational ethical life by approaching situations from multiple perspectives. This includes a collective concern for others as well as care and solidarity at the institutional and societal levels (Urban, 2020), and recognizing an individual's rights not only to personal autonomy *for* decision-making regarding their bodies and minds, and their roles in societies, but also freedom *from* the public struggle for recognition and shared vulnerabilities (Dean, 2009).

In constructing the lens for a politics of care in music education for the gifted, we first lay the theoretical grounds for expanding the currently technically oriented talent education and view of music professionalism to encompass a moral-political endeavor characterized by epistemic respect, empathy, needs interpretation, and deliberation as well as the public ethic of care. We then discuss how a care ethics approach can support a just education for children gifted for music and balance the common elitist approaches to their educational programs. By drawing from Gagné's work on giftedness and talent development (e.g., Gagné, 2021; in music, e.g., Gagné & McPherson, 2016), we illustrate how care ethics can provide a more holistic frame for educating children gifted for music and for defending the acceleration programs of talent development in a fair manner. Furthermore, we call for *systems reflexivity* that integrates the ethics of care into a critical analysis of the social systems of music education, arguing that through such reflexivity it is possible to transform the entire education system so that it can recognize its unwanted outcomes—such as ableism, abuse, and elitism—and establish an agenda of care in music education. As a whole, we aim to reposition music in contemporary societies by engaging in the reconciliation of the over century-old tension between cognitive/rational educational efficacy views and moral theories in arts education, and recognizing professional work in music—even at its highest level of expert development—as a moral and political endeavor.

Theorizing Care Ethics in Morally Oriented Music Education

A Moral Turn

In their recent work, Westerlund and Gaunt (2021) underline that in contemporary societies, professional practice in music needs to be conceptualized as positioned at the nexus of artistic, creative, technical, ethical, democratic, and socially responsible dimensions, and that this work revolves around the capacity to engage in *morally principled association*. In such a professional practice, attaining specialized expert knowledge in music is not seen as the final goal but, rather, a mediating means in the service of human good that needs to be guided by moral wisdom (*phronesis*). As Carr (2014) writes,

> any theoretical or technical knowledge which professional agents may indeed require for the effective prosecution of the various moral ends or goals of professional service are at least normatively secondary to or subservient of such ends. (p. 21)

Such a professional practice requires reflexivity that recognizes how professional work cannot be practiced "simply by applying value-free, technically defined authoritatively prescribed competences" (Cribb & Gewirtz, 2015, p. 73). Rather, "[t]ricky ethical and political dilemmas should properly be seen as falling within rather than outside the remit of professional ethics" (p. 73) and, as we argue, the music education of children gifted for music can be seen as one of these ethical dilemmas—often manifested in educational contexts that can be characterized as "ableist" and elitist. Leaning on Sennett (2008), we see a parallel between the care one invests in practices of craftsmanship and the care that is involved in making human relationships: "the craft of making physical things provides insight into the techniques of experience that can shape our dealings with others. Both the difficulties and the possibilities of making things well apply to making human relationships" (p. 289). However, children gifted for music, when selected for advanced programs, may enter an "ableist" regime of technically defined and authoritatively prescribed musical competence goals instead of being cared for as genuine partners in human relationships and authors of their own lives.

Hence, one might relate the aspects of care, responsibility, and morality in music with the traditional image of the independent, autonomous, rational, and highly skilled expert musician who invests their knowledge and skills in leading their students into their own craftsmanship, while knowing from experience what it takes to be and become skilled at a high level. As Sennett (2008) notes, one can sense a deep care and responsibility for the musical tradition and craftsmanship one represents. However, this image easily overlooks the pluralist educational reality of human dependence and the morality for which it calls and, instead, instrumentalizes the student in pedagogical settings to serve a professional realm of specific craftsmanship, represented by the teacher as the highest representative of the hierarchy (e.g., Gaunt et al., 2021; Pozo et al., 2022). Good work in music teaching in all its aspects therefore also requires *relational expertise* (Edwards, 2010) in which one is always in dialogue not just with one's disciplinary issues and own performative excellence, but also with people and various complex issues of social life.

Epistemic Respect: Turning Points in Learning and Professional Pathways

As an approach to moral philosophy, care ethics recognizes the complexity of relationality. By acknowledging multiple experienced realities, care ethics "implies and justifies the epistemic virtue of open mindedness, and ... a kind of epistemic humility" (Slote, 2013, p. 80). Slote (2013) argues that failing to be open to other perspectives and to take into account the wellbeing of others *from the perspective of others* is a failure of epistemic empathy. Relational expertise can therefore be said to require *epistemic* respect:

> Some people claim to be concerned about the welfare of others but also tend to impose their own ideas of what is good for them on the others they purportedly want to help. This is disrespectful, and so in defending an ideal of empathic concern for others, the sentimentalist care ethicist is criticizing not only certain kinds of indifference or malice toward others, but also the sort of disrespect(fulness) that consists in not taking the other's point of view into account (and in a caring way). (p. 51)

Hence, in insisting on always knowing what a child's best interest is, and not being able to shift one's perspective toward accepting and offering multiple paths of being a student gifted for music, implies a failure of epistemic empathy and a lack of relational expertise. In this challenging scenario, an opportunity arises when considering the turning points in these children's professional learning pathways, as every person has "undoubtedly experienced ... key moments that transformed [thei]r trajectory, for better or worse" (Gagné, 2021, p. 107). Supporting the ability and opportunity of children gifted for music to reflect critically on their own journeys can enable them to create meanings and understandings of the (typically neglected and at times unsettling) critical incidents that differently catalyzed their pathways. However, engaging in such a process requires empathetic behaviors in both the public and domestic spaces surrounding these children, and in reality the socio-educational systems might fail to adapt and realign to meet their basic psychological needs (Davidson & Faulkner, 2013).

Empathy, Needs Interpretation, and Deliberation

Traditionally, care ethics has been considered to be a matter of private life that lies outside the scope of the questions concerning wider political landscapes (Morgan, 2020; Urban & Ward, 2020). This tendency has been fortified by policies concerning children that tend to emphasize the role of family and parents in care. However, according to Wyness et al. (2004), the emphasis on private life in terms of care "is at odds with children's membership of more variegated kin and community networks and their involvement in more public adult-oriented environments" (p. 90). This also pertains to children gifted for music, who are often given (semi-)professional roles in institutions and talent development programs. Here, we adhere to theorization that approaches caring as a social practice and also places care, vulnerability, and interdependency in the public domain (e.g., Greenswag, 2019; Urban & Ward, 2020).[3] In this view, the ethical and the political are intrinsically intertwined with one another, and care and justice, emotion and rationality, are brought together beyond the domain of domestic care. However, in this kind of *ethics of care* empathy can still be central, as Morgan (2020) explains:

> The emphasis on empathy in care ethics ... does not eschew rationality and purpose; it critiques any allegedly pure notion of reason that does not conjoin with emotion, while simultaneously rejecting any argument that would diminish the necessity of rational grounding and application. ... What moves us to act comprises an admixture of emotional-affective transformation and rational understanding. (p. 111)

Such an ethics of care highlights the importance of paying attention to the diversity of needs and the required "politics of needs interpretation" (Fraser, 1987) and deliberation (Urban & Ward, 2020). Although care ethics typically acknowledges social and political inclusion and equal individual possibilities to resist processes of marginalization and exclusion (e.g., Smith, 2006), a politics of care may address a similar mechanism in the abuse of children gifted for music when the child is given no choice and the expert teacher and educational institution use their power to limit alternatives and impose on the child their view of what the child's future will be like. A politically formulated ethics

---

[3] See Tronto's (1993) argument for a political ethic of care and Fisher and Tronto's (1990) broad definition of caring as a social practice.

of care stresses that a social order, such as an official educational program with specific traditions and hierarchies, must acknowledge care in order to be just to all (Urban & Ward, 2020). Yet, matters of needs are complex when looked at from the relational perspective of dependencies: The child should have the freedom to resist a social order while also being recognized as having a need to belong. In the education of children gifted for music, this translates into an imperative to offer high quality, tailor-made, inclusive, and caring tuition that truly meets the educational needs and intrinsic interests of these students, while (a) letting them decide when and in which ways they can safely share their developed competencies and expertise with the world (e.g., when to attend competitions, when to be remunerated for public concerts or recordings, when to appear in a live TV show or radio broadcast); and (b) supporting their development as rounded, caring citizens in all areas of life rather than merely the cognitive domain. "Caring for" students in this way requires an awareness of the entire spectrum of sociocultural influences affecting these people's lives (parents, teachers, peers), as well as institutional efforts.

Toward a "Public Ethic of Care" in Music Education Institutions

According to Urban (2020), an institutional approach in care ethics addresses values such as reconciliation, reciprocity, diversity, and responsibility, and envisions and institutes social justice as a matter of "caring solidarity" and collective responsibility for care in order to do justice to the idea that people are differently situated (Urban & Ward, 2020). Urban (2020) points out how American philosopher Nel Noddings's seminal views on the ethics of care situated institutions as responsible only for "care-about:, i.e., addressing concerns about something and recognizing existing needs and rights; in this view, institutions cannot "care-for," at least directly. Institutions can only facilitate translating their caring-about into caring-for by providing and supporting the conditions under which actual persons can engage in genuine caring-for (Noddings, 2015). Instead of separating care-about and care-for, however, Urban (2020) argues that:

> caring and the dependence on care must be incorporated into what is said to count as the "normal" subject of politics [and] that we need to rethink the role and responsibility of larger social and political structures, such as the state and its institutions, in securing care as a public value. (p. 284)

Such a rethinking of collective institutional responsibilities can be called a public ethic of care in music education. A public ethic of care challenges the still common patriarchal and elitist ethos of the education of children gifted for music, while seriously considering alternative, mutually negotiated educational paths for serving the wellbeing of these children. A public ethic of care does not refer to an administrative state only, but to a common space in which it is possible to openly debate values and choices from multiple perspectives. In this way, it also addresses the controversial issues of the education of children gifted for music and its deep groundedness in "ableism" in music scholarship "in which human sciences are compelled to surrender to a medicalised and biological gaze" (Odendaal et al., 2020). Indeed, Fraser (1997) claims that only through struggle and debate can a society engage in needs interpretation, and that only by making the needs public can one influence inequalities. Importantly, a public ethic of care does not assume consensus, but rather takes the concerns and care as an ongoing, case-by-case struggle.

Although institutional contexts for the education of children gifted for music differ globally, it may therefore not be an overstatement to claim that all music education contexts would benefit from consciously creating a "public sphere" for the politics of care, because expert education in music is known to still take place within a "conservatory culture" (Gaunt & Westerlund, 2013; Pozo et al., 2022) with limited communicative openness, critical discussion, and collaboration.

The Politics of Care in Educational Programs for Children Gifted for Music

In contemporary societies, gifted children's education can, however, be like "the elephant in the room." On the one hand, differentiated music education seems necessary for providing effective education early enough for these children, and in this way for sustaining a high level of professional life. Gifted children's education can also be seen as part and parcel of democratic, student-centered efforts, since it is based on knowledge according to which children with potential are "bored, unmotivated, and unchallenged" in normal classes (Cross, 2013, p. 116). On the other hand, differentiated education is uncomfortably elitist, sometimes even feeding the narcissistic features of contemporary celebrity culture. It creates an undemocratic polarization toward the top of the hierarchy and in this way strengthens the "ableism" against which contemporary institutions and societies should fight.

Similarly, as with gifted education in general (see Cross, 2013; Gagné, 2021), differentiated music education programs are often based on an unfair and unreflected meritocracy. The programs seem not to represent the ethnic, racial, and socioeconomic diversity of societies, and they even poorly serve those of the highest ability. For instance, the official programs for talent development in Western countries can be rather expensive for many students—either in terms of high enrollment fees or the necessity of sustaining the living standards of developed countries—and not all such programs are supported by scholarships or bursaries. Hence, in music, the access to education by the gifted falls within the concept of "chance." What grounds are there, then, to consider the education for children gifted for music from the perspective of care ethics?

First, care ethics would pay attention to the potential epistemic disrespect and imposed futures (cf. Slote, 2013) that are common in gifted children's programs in general. In these programs, as Cross (2013) argues, adults are "more familiar with the consequences of high ability—higher educational attainment and ultimate occupational status" (p. 117). Teachers and parents that value this continuum turn "the horizontal plane into a vertical one [in which] the ability continuum becomes a status hierarchy" (p. 117). Over time, this straightforward occupational continuum may be adopted by the children, but such unrequested pressure and external requirements might lead to the development of the unethical-unempathetic mindsets and self-damaging behaviors typically prevalent among talented students—particularly as they grow up and their "novelty" wears off (Seider et al., 2009). Care ethics—with its imperative for openness, epistemic respect, and ethicoprosocial attitudes—provides a critical, morally oriented framework for a more holistic understanding of these children's sociodevelopmental process and the importance of the child to be given voice and agency in this process.

These aspects of care ethics also resonate with the research on differentiated instruction. For instance, Gagné's (2021) differentiated model emphasizes the "developmental" nature of talent and distinguishes between natural abilities or aptitudes and systematically developed abilities or skills at the high level of expertise, such as musical expertise. For Gagné, giftedness refers to the possession of outstanding natural abilities or aptitudes, whereas talent refers to the outstanding mastery of systematically developed abilities or competencies, comprising knowledge and skills. Educational programs that follow this model should aim to create a structured, systematic, deliberate, and ongoing and progressive process to develop gifts into talents (i.e., abilities into competences) in order to achieve excellence in musical performance (e.g., McPherson, 2016; McPherson & Williamon, 2016).

Importantly, however, Gagné's model emphasizes that intrapersonal and environmental factors function as mutually constituting catalysts impacting positively or negatively on the talent development process, and in particular that the intrapersonal factors (the child's motivation) filter the environmental catalysts. Hence, the role of the educational environment is also significant in the education of the gifted for music. Gagné (2008) claims that "natural abilities are NOT innate," but rather developed over the whole course of a person's life (p. 3, emphasis in the original). Based on the relational and lifelong nature of this development, Gagné proposes that the programs for children who are gifted should have customized and accelerated pacing for progress, and that the children should have *personal* excellence goals (Gagné, 2015, p. 287; cf. Gagné, 2011, p. 12). Thus, from the perspective of the education for children gifted for music, it seems important that the education should be individually tailor-made, that care should be invested in monitoring the child's motivation, and that this monitoring should be made in dialogue *with* the child by providing the possibility for the child to express alternative goals (in line with López-Íñiguez et al., 2022). As such, acceleration and setting personal goals could in principle be easily included in one-to-one instrumental studies, compared to group-based school education in other subjects.

A second issue that supports the perspective of care ethics in programs for children gifted for music is related to the public ethic of care, and how the educational institution sees itself in terms of supporting democratic and equity processes (in line with Gagné, 2011; McPherson, 1997). While perhaps trying to best serve the child's vertical developmental continuum toward professional life, institutions "are caught in the societal struggle for dominance of the status hierarchy" (Cross, 2013, p. 117). They unconsciously create unwanted public politics and unfair societal presence. With a more conscious care ethics approach, the educational institution can remind itself, its educational environment, teachers, and administrators, as well as the children and their parents, of the positive freedom (e.g., Greene, 1988) of every child to choose their own future. With care ethics, music education institutions and programs for children gifted for music can nurture a practice of negotiation where the children can also understand the existence of alternatives and be taken as partners in deliberation. This, in essence, would mean a real reconciliation of the tension between cognitive/rational educational efficacy views and moral theories in arts education.

Moreover, by refusing to accept and fighting against "ableist," elitist, and meritocratic discourses—according to which the gifted children deserve the highest-level music education whereas the non-gifted can be taught with less quality or not at all—the institution can resist producing structural inequality. Indeed, Cross (2013) argues that gifted education in general plays to varying degrees into "the maintenance of the hierarchical structure that undeniably exists in our society" (p. 117). In order to be truly fair, the differentiating programs should recognize how a seemingly democratic program can at the same time produce inequality and strengthen the unwanted elitist public image of the institution. It can therefore be argued that educational programs for children gifted for music require a conscious politics of care at multiple interactive levels of the educational system. Drawing from Urban (2020), such a politics of care at an institutional and administrative level can

1. reflect "not only expert judgment but a collaborative work that takes into account different viewpoints and lived experiences";
2. "use their discretionary authority not to accumulate more power but to reach out to the public and invite them to join a dialogue";
3. situate their administrative knowledge "in experience and dialogical reflection"; and
4. be "critically reflexive, willing to question and challenge their own values, assumptions and professional judgments" (p. 290).

In such a politics of care, care-*about*, care-*for*, and care-*with* are integrated, and professional work in music—at all levels of expertise—is recognized as a moral and political endeavor.

Toward Caring Music Education Systems

The critical mode of care ethics is "a method of discovery to uncover what underlying forces have contributed to the production and perpetuation of gross injustices" (Greenswag, 2019, p. 917), in this way aiming at transformation. We suggest that in order to increase the concreteness of the critical mode of care ethics, a politics of care should also call for a shift toward a more consciously socioecological and politically and morally oriented systems view, and what has been called *systems reflexivity* (Westerlund et al., 2021). As all educational phenomena can be seen as social systems (Väkevä et al., 2017), they can potentially transform their practices by constantly intervening and critically testing their prevailing epistemic frames against the purpose and function of the system.

When reflexivity as a "dialectic interplay between thought and action" (Gale & Molla, 2016, p. 249) and translation of critical thinking into action permeates the whole social system, we can talk about systems reflexivity. In other words, systems reflexivity allows us to see, interrogate, and reimagine the taken-for-granted structures that sustain the unwanted features and consequences of the system (Moore et al., 2018; Westerlund et al., 2021). Systems reflexivity provides the politics of care with a bigger operational stage on which to reflect on the fundamental grounds and values of the system as a whole. Indeed, through systems reflexivity it is possible to identify in what way a system acts as a social system, how it may produce unwanted consequences—for instance by privileging some and marginalizing others—and how the system could, through some conscious choices and different kinds of action, provide more just and fair understandings to the whole society. Hence, a systems view of care ethics emphasizes that epistemic issues are the foundation of any social system, and that some of our deep-rooted mental models can be the very source for unwanted, unfair consequences, even in a discipline such as music education.

The lack of care can be the consequence of our own mental models and conceptions, such as the inability to see beyond the "vertical-occupational path of learning music" (Väkevä et al., 2017) typically pre-determined for children gifted for music. A politics of care with systems reflexivity, therefore, points toward one's self *within* the system equally so as someone else *outside* it. In this sense, the politics of care is not possible unless one better understands oneself and the systemic function of the system itself. When the moral and emotional politics of care are paired with politically aware systems reflexivity, it is possible for an institution to be able to initiate the continuous struggle that any institutional change requires.

In sum, a politics of care is not simply an individual attitude in which a teacher cares for a child who is gifted, but rather can be understood as an institutional, multi-level capacity to rethink and reorganize practices and transform the institution's self-understanding of the purpose of the very social system. A politics of care that involves systems reflexivity does not reduce the consequences to individual students' wellbeing, but rather expands professional responsibility and care toward ongoing critical deliberation on the entire system while also making it possible to see how the system positions itself within wider society through its policies and legal regulations—such as those on children's rights. In this sense, when transformed through ethics of care, education for children gifted for music "can become a catalyst for greater equality; a vehicle for social improvement" (Cross, 2013, p. 121).

Concluding Thoughts

In this chapter we have explored the education for children gifted for music from the perspective of care ethics with a systems view, and claim that through care ethics it is possible to transform not just the education for children gifted for music but the entire music education system. We have suggested that by engaging with the politics of care with systems reflexivity, and by accepting ongoing struggle as a characteristic of such reflexive, morally oriented professional work, it is possible for a music education system to distance itself from "ableist," elitist, and meritocratic practices that support the status quo of musical expertise at the expense of democratization of the society. By engaging in politics of care it is then possible to overcome the view in which professional work in music is seen as a power-neutral niche operating outside of society's understanding of what is fair and right. Indeed, in an approach characterized by ethics of care, the education for children gifted for music can become a healthy test for the whole educational system's understanding of democracy, social justice, and fairness, and of the very purpose of music education in contemporary societies.

Acknowledgments

This research was undertaken as part of *The Politics of Care in the Professional Education of Children Gifted for Music* project [no. 348591] funded by the Academy of Finland. This work was also supported by the *ArtsEqual* [no. 314223] and *EcoPolitics* [no. 338952] projects, funded by the Academy of Finland and by the Center for Educational Research and Academic Development in the Arts (CERADA) at the University of the Arts Helsinki.

References

Ballam, N. (2019). Fostering resilience in "at-risk" gifted and talented young people. In S. R. Smith (Ed.), *Handbook of giftedness and talent development in the Asia-Pacific* (pp. 319–337). Springer.

Borland, J. H. (1989). *Planning and implementing programs for the gifted*. Teachers College Press.
Carr, D. (2014). Professionalism, profession and professional conduct: Towards a basic logical and ethical geography. In S. Billett, C. Harteis, & H. Gruber (Eds.), *International handbook of research in professional and practice-based learning* (pp. 5–27). Springer.
Cribb, A., & Gewirtz, S. (2015). *Professionalism*. Polity Press.
Cross, J. R. (2013). Gifted education as a vehicle for enhancing social equality. *Roeper Review*, 35(2), 115–123. https://doi.org/10.1080/02783193.2013.766962
Cross, T. L., & Coleman, L. J. (2005). School-based conception of giftedness. In R. J. Sternberg & F. E. Davidson (Eds.), *Conceptions of giftedness* (pp. 52–63). Cambridge University Press.
Davidson, J., & Faulkner, R. (2013). Music in our lives. In S. B. Kaufman (Ed.), *The complexity of greatness: Beyond talent and practice* (pp. 367–390). Oxford University Press.
Dean, H. (2009). Critiquing capabilities: The distractions of a beguiling concept. *Critical Social Policy*, 29(2), 261–278. https://doi.org/10.1177/0261018308101629
Edwards, A. (2010). *Being an expert professional practitioner: The relational turn in expertise*. Springer.
Fisher, B., & Tronto, J. C. (1990). Toward a feminist theory of caring. In E. K. Abel & M. K. Nelson (Eds.), *Circles of care: Work and identity in women's lives* (pp. 35–62). SUNY Press.
Fraser, N. (1987). Women, welfare and the politics of needs interpretation. *Hypatia: A Journal of Feminist Philosophy*, 2(1), 103–121. doi:10.1111/j.1527-2001.1987.tb00855.x
Fraser, N. (1989). *Unruly practices: Power, discourse and gender in contemporary social theory*. Polity Press.
Fraser, N. (1997). *Justice interruptus: Critical reflections on the "postsocialist" condition*. Routledge.
Freeman, J. (2010). *Gifted lives: What happens when gifted children grow up*. Routledge.
Gagné, F. (2008). *Building gifts into talents: Overview of the DMGT*. YUMPU. https://www.yumpu.com/en/document/read/43155487/building-gifts-into-talents-overview-of-the-dmgt-templetonfellows-
Gagné, F. (2011). Academic talent development and the equity issue in gifted education. *Talent Development and Excellence*, 3(1), 3–22. https://d-nb.info/1011435659/34
Gagné, F. (2015). Academic talent development programs: A best practices model. *Asia Pacific Education Review*, 16, 281–295. https://doi.org/10.1007/s12564-015-9366-9
Gagné, F. (2021). *Differentiating giftedness from talent: The DMGT perspective on talent development*. Routledge.
Gagné, F., & McPherson, G. E. (2016). Analyzing musical prodigiousness using Gagné's Integrative Model of Talent Development. In G. E. McPherson (Ed.), *Musical prodigies: Interpretations from psychology, education, musicology and ethnomusicology* (pp. 3–114). Oxford University Press.
Gale, T., & Molla, T. (2016) Deliberations on the deliberative professional. Thought-action provocations. In J. Lynch, J. Rowlands, T. Gale, & A. Skourdoumbis (Eds.), *Practice theory and education. Diffractive readings in professional practice* (pp. 247–262). Routledge.
Gaunt, H., López-Íñiguez, G., & Creech, A. (2021). Musical engagement in one-to-one contexts. In A. Creech, D. Hodges, & S. Hallam (Eds.), *Routledge international handbook of music psychology in education and the community* (pp. 335–350). Routledge.
Gaunt, H., & Westerlund, H. (Eds.). (2013). *Collaborative learning in higher music education*. Ashgate.
Gordon, E. E. (1988). Musical child abuse. *The American music teacher*, 37(5), 14–16. http://www.jstor.org/stable/43544151

Greenswag, K. (2019). Care ethics and public policy: A holistic, transformative approach. *Politics & Gender, 15*, 912–940. https://doi.org/10.1017/S1743923X18000521

Haroutounian, J. (2002). *Kindling the spark: Recognizing and developing musical potential*. Oxford University Press. http://dx.doi.org/10.1093/oso/9780195129489.001.0001

Ilmola-Sheppard, L., Rautiainen, P., Westerlund, H., Lehikoinen, K., Karttunen, S., Juntunen, M.-L., & Anttila, E. (2021). *ArtsEqual: equality as the future path for the arts and arts education services*. CERADA. https://urn.fi/URN:ISBN:978-952-353-043-0

Kijas, A. E. (2016). Teresa Carreño: "Such gifts are of God, and ought not to be prostituted for mere gain." In G. E. McPherson (Ed.), *The child as musician: A handbook of musical development* (2nd ed., pp. 621–637). Oxford University Press. https://doi.org/10.1093/acprof:oso/9780199685851.003.0027

López-Íñiguez, G. (2019). Epiphonies of motivation and emotion through the life of a cellist. *Action, Criticism, and Theory for Music Education, 18*(2), 157–189. https://doi.org/10.22176/act18.2.157

López-Íñiguez, G., Pérez-Echeverría, M. P., Pozo, J. I., & Torrado, J. A. (2022). Student-centred music education: Principles for improving learning and teaching. In J. I. Pozo, M. P. Pérez-Echeverría, G. López-Íñiguez, & J. A. Torrado (Eds.), *Learning and teaching in the music studio: A student-centred approach* (369–385). Landscapes: Arts, Aesthetics, and Education, vol. 3. Springer.

MacNamara, Á., Collins, D., & Holmes, P. (2016). Musical prodigies: Does talent need trauma? In G. E. McPherson (Ed.), *The child as musician: A handbook of musical development* (2nd ed., pp. 338–357). Oxford University Press.

McPherson, G. E. (1997). Giftedness and talent in music. *Journal of Aesthetic Education, 31*(4), 65–77. https://doi.org/10.2307/3333144

McPherson, G. E. (Ed.). (2016). *Musical prodigies: Interpretations from psychology, education, musicology, and ethnomusicology*. Oxford University Press.

McPherson G. E., & Williamon, A. (2016). Building gifts into musical talents. In G. E. McPherson (Ed.), *The child as musician: A handbook of musical development* (2nd ed., pp. 341–360). Oxford University Press.

Moore, M.-L., Olsson, P., Nilsson, W., Rose, L., & Westley, F. R. (2018). Navigating emergence and system reflexivity as key transformative capacities: Experiences from a Global Fellowship program. *Ecology and Society, 23*(2), Article 38. https://doi.org/10.5751/ES-10166-230238

Morgan, M. (2020). *Care ethics and the refugee crisis emotions, contestation, and agency*. Routledge.

Noddings, N. (2015). Care ethics and "caring" organizations. In D. Engster & M. Hamington (Eds.), *Care ethics and political theory* (pp. 72–84). Oxford Academic. https://doi.org/10.1093/acprof:oso/9780198716341.003.0005

Odendaal, A., Levänen, S., & Westerlund, H. (2020). The mnemonist's legacy: On memory, forgetting, and ableist discourse in 21st century inclusive music education. *Music Education Research, 22*(3), 360–370. https://doi.org/10.1080/14613808.2020.1759518

Phillipson, S. N., & McCann, M. (2007). *Conceptions of giftedness: Socio-cultural perspectives*. Routledge.

Piketty, T. (2014). *Capital in the twenty-first century*. Belknap Press.

Pozo, J. I., Pérez-Echeverría, M. P., López-Íñiguez, G., & Torrado, J. A. (Eds.). (2022). *Learning and teaching in the music studio. A student-centred approach*. Landscapes: Arts, Aesthetics. Springer.

Seider, S., Davis, K., & Gardner, H. (2009). Morality, ethics and good work: young people's respectful and ethical minds. In D. Ambrose & T. Cross (Eds.), *Morality, ethics and gifted minds* (pp. 209–222). Springer.

Senge, P. (1990). *The fifth discipline: The art and practice of the learning organization*. Century Business.

Sennett, R. (2008). *The craftsman*. Yale University Press.

Siegel., D. (2020). Castrati: Child abuse and the search for musical perfection. In D. Siegel & F. Bovenkerk (Eds.), *Crime and music* (pp. 55–71). Springer.

Slote, M. (2013). *Education and human values: Reconciling talent with an ethics of care*. Routledge.

Smith, C. M. M. (2006). *Including the gifted and talented: Making inclusion work for more gifted and able learners*. Routledge.

Tronto, C. J. (1993). *Moral boundaries. A political argument for an ethic of care*. Routledge.

UN General Assembly. (1989). Convention on the Rights of the Child. *United Nations, Treaty Series, 1577*(3), 1–164. https://treaties.un.org/doc/Treaties/1990/09/19900902%2003-14%20 AM/Ch_IV_11p.pdf

Urban, P. (2020). Organizing the caring society: Toward a care ethical perspective on institutions. In P. Urban & L. Ward (Eds.), *Care ethics, democratic citizenship and the state* (pp. 277–306). Palgrave Macmillan.

Urban, P., & Ward, L. (2020). Introducing the contexts of a moral and political theory of care. In P. Urban & L. Ward (Eds.), *Care ethics, democratic citizenship and the state* (pp. 1–27). Palgrave Macmillan.

Väkevä, L., Westerlund, H., & Ilmola-Sheppard, L. (2017). Social innovations in music education: Creating institutional resilience for increasing social justice. *Action, Criticism, and Theory for Music Education, 16*(3), 129–147. doi:10.22176/act16.3.129

Westerlund, H., & Gaunt, H. (Eds.). (2021). *Expanding professionalism in music and higher music education: A changing game*. Routledge; SEMPRE. https://doi.org/10.4324/9781003108337

Westerlund, H., Karttunen, S., Lehikoinen, K., Laes T., Väkevä, L., & Anttila, E. (2021). Expanding professional responsibility in arts education: Social innovations paving the way for systems reflexivity. *International Journal of Education & the Arts, 22*(8). http://doi.org/10.26209/ijea22n8

Wyness, M., Harrison, L., & Buchanan, I. (2004). Childhood, politics and ambiguity: Towards an agenda for children's political inclusion. *Sociology, 38*(1), 81–99. https://doi.org/10.1177/0038038504039362

CHAPTER 11

WAYS OF CARING IN MUSIC EDUCATION THROUGH THE LENS OF CLASSIC CONFUCIANISM AND CLASSIC DAOISM

C. VICTOR FUNG

CARE HANDBOOK TOPICS

Philosophical perspectives

A group of writers emerged since the 20th century who saw the importance of *care* in the field of education. Austrian-born philosopher Buber's (1923) influential book published in Leipzig, Germany, *Ich und Du*, later translated into English, *I and Thou*, in 1937 and in subsequent editions, included a twofold proposition in the world of humans: (a) relationship between humans, and (b) human's connection with objects. This work set up a foundation for a relational philosophy, addressing human's relationship with other humans and objects. Led by Gilligan (1977, 1979, 1993), who proposed a relational concept with a feminine approach, the idea of *care* grew in the United States. It evoked a stark contrast to the centuries-old masculine views and standards.

A prolific and leading US educational philosopher, Noddings (1984, 1995, 2013, 2016) continued by focusing on and refining how *care* should work in education, through engrossment, commitment, motivational displacement, and reciprocity. Noddings made it clear that she used the word "feminine" in her writing only with the understanding that "all of humanity can participate in the feminine," as she described (1984, p. 172; 2013, p. 161). As the ethic of care evolved, Noddings (2003) explained her use of the word "feminine" to "point to centuries of female experience and the tasks and values long associated with that experience" (p. 225), but it was meant to apply to everyone, not only females. "Feminine" referred "to a mode of experience [that men might share], not to an essential characteristic of women" (2013, p. xx). To extend further, she postulated that *care* did not only occur among humans but also animals, plants, things, and ideas. In her words, themes of care included "caring for self, for intimate others, for strangers and global others, for the natural world and its non-human creatures, for the human-made world, and for ideas" (Noddings, 1995, p. 675). Both the carer and the cared-for entered a reciprocal relationship and could be anyone.

Soon after, meanings and applications of an ethic of care in music education were developed (e.g., Bates, 2004; Edgar, 2014; Hendricks, 2018, 2021; Nourse, 2003; Silverman, 2012, 2013). This idea of *care* is more desirable than ever in the middle of a call for social justice, equality and equity, and the rights and voices of the marginalized at a crossroad with a global pandemic and an economic downturn of 2020-2021. Cultivating *care* in any setting may offer a glimpse of hope for everyone to move into a more positive direction for a greater good.

Although these conceptions of care appear to have roots in the Western scholarly tradition, they might have been embedded in other lasting traditional philosophies waiting to be uncovered. As I aim at exploring ways of caring in music education through the lens of Confucianism and Daoism, I see striking parallels between the development of care in music education in the United States and the underpinning concept of care in Confucian and Daoist terms. Uncovering Buber's (1923) relational way of thinking in humans' relationship with other humans reminds me of Confucians' emphasis on human relationships. Buber's query about the human connection with objects prompts me to think of Daoists' connection to the universe, including nature, the environment, and all living beings and non-living objects. As different chapters in this handbook focus on a variety of perspectives, I focus on discussing views of *care* in classic Confucian and classic Daoist terms.

The background of Confucianism and Daoism was set in an organismic worldview established around 2900 BCE, when Fuxi came up with the idea of *yin* and *yang* based on observations of nature and various phenomena in the universe. All things, human and non-human, and their phenomena were connected and worked together to move forward in constant changes with unchanging principles (e.g., appearances of the sun and the moon, the change of seasons). These concepts and principles were recorded with the help of simple symbols; Zhou Wen Wang documented these concepts extensively in the 11th century BCE, and the additional explanatory essays were believed to be written by Confucius and his followers around the 5th century BCE. These components were collected to become a key philosophical source *Yijing* (易經 or *Zhouyi* 周易, The Book of Changes).

Classic Confucianism and classic Daoism are two established and consolidated philosophic schools built on the foundation laid out in *Yijing* and have persisted till this day. The two schools are based on the work of key figures, Confucius (551–479 BCE) and Mencius (372–289 BCE) for classic Confucianism and Laozi (b. 570 BCE) and Zhuangzi (369–286 BCE) for classic Daoism. Influenced by folk religion, politics, and other philosophical schools, the two schools evolved into a great variety of branches and variants and some have been labeled with prefixes such as religious-, neo-, new-, and contemporary-. These diverse branches also persist to this day, but in this chapter, I only focus on the classic, "original, high-quality, definitive ideologies . . . [but not] those that diverged and evolved after this period" (Fung, 2018, p. 8). This way, a connection with the nature of being humans and the natural environment can be restored in its most basic and original form. I addressed the rationale to focus on the classics more fully in my 2018 publication, so I can focus on discussing *care* here.

The two classic philosophic schools are significant because (a) they form a philosophical ambience that has intertwined with many people's lives for about two and a half millennia; (b) their principles transcend time and space and "break boundaries set by language, ethnicity, and religion, and at the same time venerated by those who know them" (Fu, 2012, p. 3); (c) they are described as "mainstream" philosophical schools in China (Mou, 1974); (d) they work in complementarity to provide rich potential developments in different values, viewpoints, meanings, and life experiences (Dong, 2007; Li, 2002, pp. 166–177); (e) they provide a foundation for many subsequent philosophical, religious, and spiritual developments worldwide; and (f) they persist in many Chinese communities throughout the world to this day and have influenced the lives of many non-Chinese (e.g., some meditation practices, moral axioms). In the rest of this chapter, I address *care* through the lens of each school and explore ways to practice it in music education, hoping to uncover insights that might have been overlooked.

Care Through Classic Confucianism

Principles of classic Confucianism, including its branches and variants, have been discussed, interpreted, and debated extensively through two and a half millennia by numerous scholars who have written exclusively in Chinese. From the mid-19th century, some scholars and translators began to study this body of literature and publish in English. Without being excessively complex and detailed, I have chosen to focus on four key principles (Fung, 2018), while acknowledging other principles that could be considered as extensions or subsumed, when discussing the core of classic Confucianism. The concept of *care* permeates throughout much of these principles from the Confucian *dao*: sincerity, kindness, benevolence, and being an exemplary person.

Sincerity

Sincerity (*cheng* 誠) is primarily an internal state of mind that is often expressed externally through speech, action, or any artistic and expressive medium. It is free from hypocrisy, deception, or pretense. It demonstrates two features. First, it needs a personal decision to practice it and cultivate it for it to become habitual and reflected in all external means (i.e., speaking, behaving, and other expressive modes). Second, it needs conscious effort on the part of the individual to reject and prevent any invasion of evil thoughts that can lead to insincerity (*Wenyan, Yizhuan* in *Yijing* 《易經》《易傳》《文言》). From a *care* perspective, it is a way to care for the self, so there is confidence in being ethical, conscientious, righteous, and so forth. Classic Confucians make it clear that human action is a critical guiding force that follows the natural order and to achieve one's goal; nature alone, without any conscious effort in humans, is not sufficient to make things better (*Analects* 論語, 15.29). This principle, like others present in this chapter, is seen to transcend time and space, which means that it is still valid both within and outside of China. For example, humans have to take recycling action to preserve natural resources; without such deliberate action, nature is not able to care for its materials. Although *care* through this Confucian lens of sincerity focuses on the self and the interaction between people, it also includes human's relationship with all things. In this lens, it is necessary to practice sincerity in a way that moves outward in concentric circles to include the family, the nation, and the world (*Daxue* 大學 Great Learning, 2 & 3 in *Liji* 禮記 Book of Rituals).

Kindness

From a Confucian standpoint, sincerity must be coupled with kindness (*shan* 善), because sincerity can be used in unkind ways too. "To allow sincerity to work is the human way. . . . To allow sincerity to work is to *choose kindness* [emphasis added] and be persistent in it" (*Zhongyong* 中庸 20.5 in *Liji*). Furthermore, kindness (rather than being unkind) is seen as a natural human inclination which, like water, would naturally flow downward. Examples of exceptions to this rule would be created when humans use a hand to splash water upward or put barriers to make water flow upward. Similarly, unkind acts are due to situations created by humans (*Mencius* 孟子, 11.2). Kindness is "an act that follows the natural, innermost, and definite drive . . . [and it is] an inherent human potency" (Fung, 2018, p. 43). In an ethic of care, kindness is recognized as one of the stepping-stones toward "caring, competent, loving, and lovable people" with "a respect for the full range of human talents" and the ability to "lead lives of deep concern for others, for the natural world and its creatures, and for the preservation of the human-made world" (Noddings, 1995, p. 676). Although kindness does not equate with *care*, it is an essential step toward *care*. Care without kindness is despicable.

Benevolence

Benevolence (*ren* 仁), with connotations of compassion, altruism, generosity, and magnanimity, is seen to be a key to a peaceful and harmonious society. Leaders who rule with benevolence are seen as models for citizens, implying that benevolence is a reciprocal practice applicable to everyone regardless of roles or hierarchies. Benevolence is seen as the most important basis for everything human does, including music-making (*Analects*, 3.3). Benevolence is similar to sincerity and kindness, insofar as a person needs to make conscious efforts to practice it until it becomes habitual and integral to the individual's value and meaning in life. However, benevolence is different in that it is a manifesto of sincerity and kindness *in action* rather than simply focusing on the internal self. In other words, practicing benevolence is key in practicing *care*, in many contexts that include both carers and cared-fors.

Being an Exemplary Person

In classic Confucianism, exemplary persons (*junzi* 君子) are those who have committed to practice benevolence throughout the rest of their lives (*Analects*, 4.5). Although benevolence is built on sincerity and kindness, an exemplary person is expected to practice benevolence along with wisdom, courage, righteousness, and courteousness (*Analects*, 2.24, 14.4, 14.28; *Mencius*, 3.6, 13.21). They are supposed to read widely and have a high level of self-control as guided by rituals (*li* 禮), or proper behaviors established at the time (*Analects*, 6.27 & 12.15). Again, regardless of social roles and hierarchies, everyone needs to be on a path toward an exemplary person; once there, their next goal is to be a *better* exemplary person.

Self-reflection is an important process in improving the exemplary characteristic of a person (*Analects*, 14.42, 16.10; *Mencius*, 8.28). In this lens, exemplary persons are seen as role models and teachers for others and therefore have the responsibility of helping others to become exemplary persons. "Teaching everyone irrespective of the learner's background" (*Analects*, 15.39) is another expectation for exemplary persons and is an important Confucian axiom throughout the millennia. I have seen it engraved on campuses of teacher education institutions in various parts of China.

More importantly, exemplary persons are required to improve themselves throughout their lifetime, with the possibility of becoming a sage (*shengren* 聖人) (i.e., someone who has achieved perfection as an exemplary person). It is important to note that in classic Confucianism a sage is not a self-proclaimed title but an honor granted by others. Neither Confucius nor Mencius claimed the title of sage. More specific explanations of an exemplary person are extensive in various parts of the *Analects* (2.14, 4.11, 4.16, 7.37, 12.16, 12.19, 13.23, 13.25, 13.26, 14.6, 15.2, 15.21, 15.34, and 16.8). They mostly portray contrasts between an exemplary person and a villain, or an uneducated and an ill-developed person in terms of the standards expected of a human being. Numerous Chinese writers also presented their interpretations of the exemplary person (e.g., Liu, 2012). Given the different time and space, I am excited to see the possibility that these Confucian principles may transcend cultural and temporal boundaries. I still find these principles important and practical. The concepts of building on sincerity, kindness, benevolence, and being an exemplary person, seem to have tremendous value as reference points when developing *care* practices in the contemporary world.

Care Through Classic Daoism

Like classic Confucianism, classic Daoism has evolved into many branches and variants and its principles have been interpreted and addressed by generations of scholars who wrote exclusively in Chinese throughout the last two and a half millennia. Only since the 18th century have translators and scholars pioneered and spread their work in the West using Latin, German, English, and other languages. *Care* through the lens of classic Daoism works complementarily with that of classic Confucianism. The classic Daoist view offers a different but necessary and important perspective. To parallel my previous publication (Fung, 2018), I focus on four key principles here but keeping in mind other principles that could be extensions or subsumed. The key principles drawn from the Daoist *dao* are non-egoistic action, observation, equality, and flexibility.

Non-Egoistic Action

Wuwei (無為) is the Chinese term used in the literature since Laozi (b. 570 BCE) to today, and it is often translated as "non-action," which is literally accurate. However, it can easily be misconstrued as "doing nothing." Semantically and philosophically, it is not a complete translation. Given the Daoist emphasis in the nature and the progression of all things, the idea of *wuwei* entails *taking action* to support this natural way of progression, which is based on the guidance of *dao*, not the human self; it is *non-egoistic*. For this reason, I adopt *non-egoistic action* as a translation that does not deny all actions, and it makes better philosophical sense. From this, it is clear that *non-egoistic action* emphasizes a proactivity and is a way to *care* about the nature and the natural way of progression in all matters and phenomena. These human actions feature a reciprocity in *care*, because nature has been taking *care* of humans by providing food sources and other means of survival (e.g., clean air, water, and shelter). In other words, human and nature become carer and the cared-for, and their roles are reciprocal. Even between humans, the same principle still applies as seen in Confucian principles and those of Noddings.

Observation

Contemporary understanding of observation (*guan* 觀) tends to be yielding, passive, and unobtrusive. In a classic Daoist standpoint, however, observation is conceived in a refreshing perspective. One can understand all beings, things, and phenomena by observing from the perspective of the being observed (*Laozi* 老子, 54). This means that, to understand an individual, one should observe from the standpoint of that individual, which is similar to the idea of *mature empathy* that includes "an awareness for and acceptance of values and beliefs that might differ from their own" (Hendricks, 2018, p. 57). The same applies to a family, a nation, or the world. Zhuangzi goes further to specify the use of this principle for non-humans, such as a butterfly (*Zhuangzi* 2.17). In other words, humans can be "materialized" as anything to observe from that perspective and be able to understand the being observed. As humans can observe from any perspective, all beings and matters are equal with different values, perspectives, functions, strengths, weaknesses, behaviors, and images (*Zhuangzi* 17.5). When this Daoist way of observation is applied, it could represent a culture of *care* for whatever is being observed, human or non-human.

Equality

The idea of equality (*qiwu* 齊物) from the classic Daoist standpoint contains connotations different from common contemporary understandings. This is based on chapter 2 in the book *Zhuangzi* (莊子), named Theory of Equality (齊物論). The underlying concept for the theory is the necessity for a state of selflessness, to avoid bias in a judgement (*Zhuangzi*, 2.1). This fits well with *non-egoistic action* and *observation* described above, which also implies that it is selfless and unbiased. Because human and all things are unified as one under the auspices of *dao*, all things human and non-human are connected, valuable, relative, and working together. Judgments such as right and wrong, good and bad, and big and small are subjective and therefore relative and dependent on the context and the perspective used. All things, including humans, can become a "self" and an "other." Every "self" and every "other" can be both right and wrong, again, depending on the context and the perspective used (*Zhuangzi*, 2.6). Because the "self" and the "other" are equally important and the right can be wrong and vice versa, they should not be considered as opposites but as the center of a circle that can go in any direction equally well with adaptations to indefinite changes. Ultimately, in any circumstances, a flexible strategy can allow right and wrong to co-exist, as a means of reaching the goal of harmony (*Zhuangzi*, 2.7). In contemporary terms, I suggest that equity is incorporated within the flexible strategy involved in putting the Theory of Equality in practice. This way, *care* is extended to everyone and everything, including those with opposing views. In other words, the majority can become the minority and vice versa, depending on the context and the perspective used; there are ways to co-exist in harmony.

Flexibility

Although being flexible (*rou* 柔) is a distinctive core principle in classic Daoism, it is integrated with other mentioned principles. It also embraces the idea of being soft. Flexibility and softness are more desirable than being rigid, because of the constantly changing world as laid out in *Yijing*. Only by being flexible and soft can human beings respond to the constant changes, which is repeatedly stated in *Laozi* (36, 43, 76, & 78). Water is identified as the most flexible of all the elements (78), because it can be in any shape or state; it can penetrate and erode the hardest of stones through long periods of drips and also destroy a village in the large mass of a flood. Being flexible is not only in line with other classic Daoist principles; being flexible is the key to adapting to constant changes in the way to *care* and being *cared for*, which is extremely desirable in every music education setting.

Ways of Caring in Music Education

A main reason that classic Confucianism and classic Daoism have thrived continuously for two and a half millennia as two of the mainstream philosophic schools is that they have transcendental and immanent qualities. Their metaphysical principles appear to transcend time and space and can be applied regardless of culture, ethnicity, gender, economic status, location, climate, environment, and regime. The same principles are seen as being found anywhere, in all beings, objects, and phenomena. This means that they suggest many ways, and perhaps *more* ways to add to the existing literature on *caring* in music education. Through their lens, I present a few for consideration here. Throughout my studies on this topic, I realize that the principles suggested by these philosophic schools and the principles of *care* share a common character: They are based on the individual's choice to care, to be sincere, to be kind, to be non-egoistic, to observe from the standpoint of being observed, and so forth. These are all voluntary choices that can be guided, cultivated, and taught. This offers hope for a better and more inclusive, socially just, and ecologically friendly future that can be achieved through making changes in the education system.

Humans are undeniably part of the universe; therefore, humans should broaden their views to include the universe and the long-term future of the world as music and music education move forward. This is in accord with (a) Buber's (1923) dyadic philosophy for human relationships and their connection with objects; (b) Noddings's (2002, 2005) recommendations to organize curriculum around themes of care, be unapologetic about the goals of care, relax the impulse of control in schools, reduce testing, and get rid of hierarchies; and (c) suggestions many others who advocate for an ethic of care in education (e.g., Goldstein, 2002) have made. These directions reflect many recent developments in music education and can be incorporated more broadly and strategically in contemporary music education. For example, *care* and its different elements and processes can be a component in every music class or lesson. Examples are caring for the environment through caring for musical instruments, caring for self through sincere and kind musical expressions in a song-writing lesson, or mutual caring of ensemble members through logistics and musical communications in rehearsals. Music teachers may structure classes so students can make major decisions such as pacing, repertoire selection, and musical arrangements and interpretations. Classes could be designed so students of any skill and knowledge level would feel welcome. In all such activities, the core principles of classic Confucianism and classic Daoism should be used as guiding principles (e.g., sincerity, kindness, benevolence, being an exemplary person, non-egoistic action, observation, equality, and flexibility).

Noddings (2013) discusses "aesthetical caring" and suggests that "artistic receptivity" and "receptivity of caring" are not necessarily correlated. She cites some high commanding Nazis "who loved music and art and yet performed unbelievable cruelty on humans" (p. 21) as an example of such disconnect between the two. This example illustrates the need to use sincerity, kindness, benevolence, and being an exemplary person as the foundation for any aesthetic activity and experience. These core principles need to be cultivated early on. I suggest that this is prior to the mid-teen years, to enable practice and improvement in subsequent years. Confucius suggests that by age 15 years one should be committed to pursue exemplary personhood as a lifelong goal (*Analects*, 2.4). Furthermore, in the *Record of Music* (*Yueji* 樂記) (5), which is a part of *Liji*, Confucians state that an exemplary person should know that music created by humans has deeper meanings than sounds and tones. This idea not only manifests the core Confucian principles stated above but also has tremendous implications for music educators to reconsider their current practices. The music curriculum needs to include not only knowledge and skills about sounds and tones, but the development of ability to identify, appreciate, evaluate, and create *music*, not just sounds and tones. One can play or sing all notes accurately but there could be no *music*. According to a classic Confucian view, such a person does not meet the criteria of being an exemplary person.

It is possible that the use of the core Daoist principles as guides in music education could deepen humanity's connection with nature and objects. When setting up musical experiences such as classes and performances, being non-egoistic but ecological could trigger student's attention to the connection they have with nature, non-humans, and objects. Topics such as the sources of the raw materials of various musical instruments and the processes involved in making them, or the effect of musical instruments on the environment, could be discussed and investigated. What actions can musicians take to sustain the musical tradition and the environment? When an unfamiliar musical piece or tradition is introduced, how should the teacher guide students in observing the music makers and from whose perspective? How can musicians and educators treat the wide range of world musical traditions equally with equitable access? How might one set up a music curriculum in school so access to music learning is equitable? How can music teachers and students exercise their flexibility in the music teaching and learning process? Many more questions can be asked, and they offer a glimpse of some directions that music educators may explore using these principles. There are striking parallels between the core principles of the philosophic schools and the act of caring. Although the act of care may be "predictable in a global sense, . . . [but] unpredictable in detail [and] variation is to be expected" (Noddings, 2013, p. 23), the Daoist notion of flexibility will enable music teachers to adapt their practice in relation to a specific context and along with the other principles mentioned in this chapter.

In the same way as an ethic of care stems from the tradition of a "feminine mode of experience" but it is not intended for females only, classic Confucianism and classic Daoism have a Chinese origin but are not intended for Chinese people only. Both philosophic schools have visions for lifelong self-reflection, cultivation, and improvement, which is a demanding long-term goal for contemporary music educators. It is time for music educators, and other professionals too, to reclaim, repossess, and restore these long-overlooked traditions, so professional practices and people's broader lives can be enriched in ways that are constructive, desirable, sustainable, and transcendental across time and space.

REFERENCES

Bates, V. (2004). Where should we start? Indications of a nurturant ethic for music education. *Action, Criticism, and Theory for Music Education*, 3(3). http://act.maydaygroup.org/articles/Bates3_3.pdf

Buber, M. (1923). *Ich und Du* [I and Thou]. Insel Verlag.

Dong, P. 董平. (2007). Mutual complementary principle of Confucianism and Daoism "儒道互保"原論. *Journal of Zhejiang University (Humanities and Social Sciences)* 浙江大學學報(人文社會科學版), 37(5), 59–69.

Edgar, S. N. (2014). An ethic of care in high school instrumental music. *Action, Criticism & Theory for Music Education*, 13(2), 112–137. http://act.maydaygroup.org/articles/Edgar13_2.pdf

Fu, P. 傅佩榮. (2012). *Lunyu jiedu* 論語解讀 [The Analects reader]. New Century Publishing Co. 立緒文化事業有限公司.

Fung, C. V. (2018). *A way of music education: Classic Chinese wisdoms*. Oxford University Press.

Gilligan, C. (1977). In a different voice: Women's conceptions of self and of morality. *Harvard Educational Review*, 47(4), 481–517. https://doi.org/10.17763/haer.47.4.g6167429416hg5lo

Gilligan, C. (1979). Women's place in man's life cycle. *Harvard Educational Review*, 49(4), 431–446. https://doi.org/10.17763/haer.49.4.h1365735411313g463

Gilligan, C. (1993). *In a different voice: Psychological theory and women's development* (2nd ed.). Harvard University Press.

Goldstein, L. S. (2002). *Reclaiming caring in teaching and teacher education*. Peter Lang.

Hendricks, K. S. (2018). *Compassionate music teaching*. Rowman & Littlefield.

Hendricks, K. S. (2021). Authentic connection in music education: A chiastic essay. In K. S. Hendricks & J. Boyce-Tillman (Eds.), *Authentic connection: Music, spirituality, and wellbeing* (pp. 237–253). Peter Lang.

Li, Z. 李宗桂. (2002). *An introduction to Chinese culture* 中國文化導論. Guangdong Peoples Publishing House 廣東人民出版社.

Liu, L. 劉林睿. (2012). *Lunyu Zhong de junzi xingxiang* 《論語》中的"君子"形象 [Image of junzi in the Analects]. In Z. Li 李宗桂 & Z. Zhang 張造群 (Eds.), *Chuantong ruxue de lishi xingcha* 傳統儒學的歷史省察 [Reflections and observations of traditional Confucianism] (pp. 57–66). Flower City Publishing House 廣東花城出版社.

Mou, Z. 牟宗三. (1974). *Zhongguo zhexue di tezhi* 中國哲學的特質 [Special qualities of Chinese philosophy]. Student Book 學生書局.

Noddings, N. (1984). *Caring: A feminine approach to ethics & moral education*. University of California Press.
Noddings, N. (1995). Teaching themes of care. *Phi Delta Kappan, 76*(9), 675–679. https://www.jstor.org/stable/20405432
Noddings, N. (2002). *Educating moral people: A caring alternative to character education*. Teachers College Press.
Noddings, N. (2003). *Caring: A feminine approach to ethics and moral education* (2nd ed.). University of California Press.
Noddings, N. (2005). *The challenge to care in schools: An alternative approach to education*. Teachers College Press.
Noddings, N. (2013). *Caring: A relational approach to ethics and moral education* (2nd ed.). University of California Press.
Noddings, N. (2016). *Philosophy of education* (4th ed.). Westview Press.
Nourse, N. (2003). The ethics of care and the private woodwind lesson. *Journal of Aesthetic Education, 37*(3), 58–77. https://doi.org/10.1353/jae.2003.0024
Silverman, M. (2012). Virtue ethics, care ethics, and the good life of teaching. *Action, Criticism, and Theory for Music Education, 11*(2), 96–122. http://act.maydaygroup.org/articles/Silverman11_2.pdf
Silverman, M. (2013). A conception of "meaningfulness" in/for life and music education. *Action, Criticism, and Theory for Music Education, 12*(2), 20–40. http://act.maydaygroup.org/articles/Silverman12_2.pdf

CHAPTER 12

CARING WITH THE EARTH, COMMUNITY, AND CO-LEARNERS FOR THE HEALTH OF BIOLOGICAL, SOCIAL, AND MUSICAL ECOSYSTEMS

TAWNYA D. SMITH

CARE HANDBOOK TOPICS

Philosophical perspectives
Social activism and critical consciousness
Wellbeing and human flourishing

A complex and interrelated set of environmental challenges has been created by the overuse of natural resources, unchecked pollution, and unsustainable development of the wilds. For example, human-released greenhouse gases have caused rapidly escalating and damaging levels of global heating, and biodiversity loss and pollution has resulted in the extinction of 70% of the non-human species on the planet (Figueres & Rivett-Carnac, 2020). At a moment when more people are awakening to these and other human-caused environmental crises, it is becoming clearer that the only viable way forward is to stop *living on* the planet and start *living with* the earth.

To live with the earth requires that individuals and communities relinquish anthropocentric assumptions that humans are superior to other life forms, and exercise humility as a means consider sustainable relations and new lifeways (Smith, 2021). It requires that we *care with*—not simply care about or for—the earth. Hendricks (2021) defines "caring with" as a relationship that "is one of spiritual communion rather than roles to be performed, and where neither I nor You need be superior nor inferior" (p. 246). Caring with the earth would, then, necessitate that individuals and communities attune with the earth as an equal partner in discerning what care is needed for the biological ecosystem (see Shorner-Johnson et al., this volume).

Shifting from an anthropocentric worldview to one where humans and all other entities of the earth are seen as equal collaborators is likely to inspire profound changes in cultural ecosystems as well. Such a perspective might help us to understand the benefits of "caring with" in our human relations. For example, when humans learn to fathom the myriad ways that they are interconnected with the biological ecosystem, perhaps they will also learn to understand the unique niche that they occupy within the social ecosystem (Plotkin, 2008). In this way, humans might better understand the need to maintain relations within a web of caring (Shorner-Johnson et al., this volume). In this chapter, I argue that music education pedagogies that are mindful of caring with the earth are perhaps the most profound and powerful place to attend our energies if our goal is to address systemic barriers to equity, and to confront and transform the unsustainable thinking that negatively impacts our social relations and personal wellbeing.

"Caring With" the Earth vs. Saving the Planet: Embracing the Narrative of "Caring With"

Many in the environmental movement speak of how individuals must "save the planet" as if an individual alone could do such a thing. Such statements can induce feelings of guilt and shame as well as panic. These ideas stem from capitalist propaganda meant to convince individual consumers that they are the ones responsible for the multiple environmental crises humans now face—and that governments, multinational corporations, and the extremely wealthy are somehow not to be held accountable as well (Powell, 2021). The propaganda works by engaging one's egotistical wish to be a hero—a role that is often thought to be a noble path in our cultural narratives (as described in the next section) but one that I assert is harmful to the individual, their community, and the planet.

Holding the belief that it is one's responsibility to "save the planet" can cause isolation in three ways. First, given the complexity of the climate crisis, it can cause one to feel paralyzed in despair, unable to act as a hero or otherwise. Second, it can separate individuals from their local community including those who are working on local solutions. Most importantly, it can sever one's relationship with the earth. Believing in the hero narrative can preclude one's identity *as* the earth, or as an integral part of an intricate system of relations (Smith, 2021). Such separation can also lead to declines in mental and physical wellbeing when one is isolated from the nurturing energy of nature and community (Louv, 2012).

The Hero Narrative and Salvific Discourse

The hero narrative, as told through the ideology of Western individualism, is one where a male "asserts his individuality and 'finds himself' through the undertaking of a journey ... usually without a permanent companion ... after this, he returns home as a mature man, assured of his personhood" (Boyce-Tillman, 2000, p. 34). In some cases, his homecoming is for the purpose of saving the people deemed too weak or unable to save themselves. In these stories[1] the hero is isolated and does not have healthy relations with the community nor the earth-system; through his separation he may feel rejected from and/or superior to the community and earth.

In her critique of the hero narrative, Boyce-Tillman (2000) states that it imparts "an abrogation of responsibility for anyone but oneself, a denial of any responsibility for the results of one's actions and a confusion between the private and the public" (p. 34). Boyce-Tillman also points out that such a journey is often not open to women, the poor, and others with lower social status. For example, for women "the heroic quest was never a possibility" as many are torn between a society that values the type of individualism characterized in the hero's narrative and a "deep need for community and stability for the sake of their children or their family" (p. 34). The hero narrative precludes the more equitable option of "caring with" to create a just community, because it excludes most from the opportunity to gain full personhood, and its individualistic pull impedes on the impulse of those most inclined to value the creation and maintenance of community and the earth.

As Boyce-Tillman (2000) notes, the poor and those of lower status are also prohibited the opportunity to embark on the hero's journey. The hero's narrative is mired within

---

[1] From Boyce-Tillman (2000): "The need of human beings for community is to be found in many sources today—political, psychological and religious, to name but a few. The legacy in the UK of the Thatcher years is one of fragmentation and an excessive emphasis on the individual. But it is a process that started with the Enlightenment and its rediscovery of the epic of the heroic journey. The male hero narrative (based on Homer's *Odyssey* and Virgil's *Aeneid*) is of one who asserts his individuality and 'finds himself' through the undertaking of a journey. This is usually without a permanent companion (although with many temporary travelling associates who are often either embraced or killed). After this, he returns home as a mature man, assured of his personhood. This particular myth is at the very heart of Western civilisation" (p. 34).

a system of value hierarchies that are enacted through a system of dualisms (man/woman, culture/nature, mind/body, civilized/savage, etc.). As such, a greater amount of subjecthood is afforded to white, male, cisgendered, heterosexual, and able-bodied individuals (Plumwood, 1994, 2002). Such a system is one of control that is deeply embedded in Western language (Plumwood, 1994, 2002).

It is important to acknowledge that the same value hierarchy places humans above nature (Plumwood, 1994, 2002). Situated squarely within an anthropocentric worldview, humans are seen as the only entities considered to have subjecthood. Given the history of colonization and the imposition of Western thought across the world, such control likely influences most systems in which humans participate.

Value hierarchies devalue the inherent wisdom of persons of color and indigenous persons; women and gender non-conforming individuals; homosexual, bisexual, and asexual persons; those who are neurodiverse or have embodied differences; more-than-human creatures;[2] and the earth system herself. This unjust and unbalanced perspective lies at the foundation of the systems of thought that elevate one dominant narrative at the expense of all others, and that objectify both "low-status" humans and the earth-system to exploit, extract, and abuse. In music education, this hierarchical thinking is evident in philosophies, theories, and curricula that suppose that Western classical music has a civilizing capacity, or in situations where music is lauded as having "saving power" to correct some societal ill (Koza, 2006). Here music is seen figuratively as the hero.

In the context of music education, Hendricks (2021) proposes a "caring-with" perspective to replace the "music teacher as hero" narrative which, at best, reinforces a "caring about" or "for" perspective but does not fully value the contributions of music learners. Hendricks (2018) explains that the hero narrative can harm students when teachers exercise power over them, and it can harm teachers when they believe they must make inappropriate personal sacrifices for their students. Similarly, Koza (2006) critiques of the notion of "Saving the Music"—school music specifically—because of the "salvific impulse" at the root of such efforts. Historically such "salvific initiatives" have been justified because school music (and the typically Western classical canon taught there) could save "children's souls from eternal perdition, their morals from the ravages of 'trashy' music and undisciplined ways, and their taste from the corrosive effects of a supposedly deficit culture" (p. 26). When educators hold the attitude of caring about and for their students in order to save them from some perceived ill or deficit, they reinforce the very value hierarchies that have placed our students in what seems, through this perspective, to be a lesser-than position (Hendricks, 2021). As such, reinforcing such value hierarchies is both socially unsustainable and unjust.

---

[2] More-than-human is defined here as all flora and fauna, as well as the planetary and cosmic system of which humans are an interrelated part.

Occupying a Niche in the Biological and Cultural Ecosystems

Rather than understanding oneself as a hero or through the intersectional locations of an invented value hierarchy, Plotkin (2008), an ecopsychologist, suggests that individuals view themselves as occupying a niche in both social and ecological ecosystems. In this way, one can see one's actions as influencing the human and more-than-human entities with which one co-exists, and vice versa. Through such a perspective, the emphasis is not on control of one over the other, but rather on just, peaceful, and life-giving relations between individuals, among groups, and within a complex web of social and physical relationships. To the extent that one can imagine oneself as embodying a niche in an ecosystem, one might begin to embody a "caring with" attitude that honors one's unique creative gifts, skills, and purpose in life as well as the ways that one's contributions might simultaneously benefit oneself, others, and the more-than-human world.

As an oak tree is connected to the ecosystem of which it is a part through thousands of chemical relations—including the oxygen-carbon-dioxide cycle and networks of mycorrhizal fungi (to name a few)—so too is each human interconnected in many systems of relations. Musically one might consider one's relationship with the instruments or voice one uses to express oneself, with the various genres of music to which one has been exposed, and so forth. Learning to occupy one's niche in the musical ecosystem requires discernment of how much space one needs to thrive as well as the importance of sharing space and resources. Musically, it means learning when to listen and when to play—when to solo or accompany (see Boyce-Tillman, this volume).

To better understand how one currently occupies a niche in the more-than-human world, one can learn to "care with" the earth and her wisdom toward the co-creation and co-enactment of life-giving and sustainable living (Smith, 2021). In music education, for example, music students might co-create musically within a natural soundscape attuning to the musical intelligence of a particular ecosystem. In this case, the wisdom of the earth can be seen in the balance, form, and expressive qualities of the biophony (those made by the flora or fauna), and geophony (sounds made by weather or geological features) (Pijanowski et al., 2011). Musical co-creation with the earth's wisdom might occur when music makers attune to the biophony and geophony to co-create a soundscape responsively and dialogically.

Deep listening to the ecosystem might also help learners to cultivate their auditory and spatial senses, which might prevent the atrophying of such abilities—as is argued to occur when humans spend too much time indoors and/or using technology (Louv, 2012). Here the wisdom of the earth can be seen to educate one's body and mind, an important consideration given that humans evolved in outdoor spaces—and that auditory and spatial capabilities are the very ones that allowed humans to develop their ability to express musically. In the case of deep listening and attunement, a learner might also develop a deeper understanding of how their body and the more-than-human world are interdependent and relational.

To better understand how one occupies a niche in a just social world, one can learn to "care with" others in their communities to co-create peaceful and equitable structures, laws, policies, and cultural practices. In music education settings, one can "care with" other music makers to co-create musics that represent the musical heritages, experiences, and unique musical expressions of all involved. Paris and Alim (2017) refer to such an approach when they describe culturally sustaining pedagogies that decenter monocultural norms.

Decentering monocultural norms is essential for our survival. For biological ecosystems to be healthy, self-organizing, and sustaining they must contain a diverse array of plants—so too must our social ecosystems include diverse cultural expressions to survive and thrive (Shorner-Johnson et al., this volume). Such a pluralistic approach is quite different from the monocultural ones too often enacted in schools, which have been and continue to be a "largely assimilationist and often violent White imperial project, with students and families being asked to lose of deny their languages, literacies, cultures, and histories in order to achieve in schools" (Paris & Alim, 2017, p. 1). Pushes for standardization and conformity to one cultural norm are in essence no different than deforesting the Amazon to create a pasture for cattle or a palm oil plantation: The end result of such efforts are social ecosystems that are unsustainable because they are built on exploitive relationships.

To engage in a pluralist music education that helps an individual to understand their niche within the social ecosystem, I do not mean that one "learn their place" within a system of value hierarchies based on Western ideals. Rather, I mean that learners first be encouraged to explore the musical heritages important to their family, those of youth culture, and of other traditions that appeal to the learner. To explore one's own unique place requires a reciprocal inquiry that deepens one's self-identified musical culture(s) as it simultaneously exposes the learner to those of others.

Stated differently, "caring with" requires that one spend time deeply cultivating the ability to make music via one's own tradition(s) (Sarath, 2018) as well as learning cultural traditions other than one's own. Similarly, caring with co-learners requires that one spend time with others to better understand the gifts, traditions, and creative impulses that each individual (the self and other) brings to music-making. Similarly, investing time in relation with those of cultural traditions other than one's own can also be seen as a means toward being in relation with oneself—each learner understanding that they occupy a different strand in the web of human experience. In other words, pluralistic music education approaches that model themselves as an ecosystem are not hierarchical but relational, and they acknowledge that "engagement with culture is always shifting and dynamic" (Paris & Alim, 2017, p. 7).

Educators who can see themselves and their students as located in a web of relations—rather than occupying a rung in a singular hierarchy—might be able to free themselves from deficit thinking and see the value their own unique contributions as well as those of all others. For example, a high school choral teacher might consider a student as being deficient because she cannot read notation well. However, the same teacher could instead regard the student as an expert in gospel music and rely on her expertise to inform the performance of such repertoire. As such, each student can be seen to have unique and particular form of expertise in the tradition(s) in which they are well versed, as well as areas and traditions that are less developed. By focusing on the web of cultural relations within the ensemble, the teacher might better ascertain the cultural gifts that each student brings rather than measuring their worth by the criteria of only one tradition. To use an ecological analogy, instead of expecting every flower to be a lily, one might delight in the colors and shapes of all the plants in the ecosystem. Such a perspective is one that focuses on strengths rather than weaknesses.

Humility and openness are essential to break with value hierarchies that assume that Western music is superior. Breaking the habit of sizing up others to see where they stand in relation to Western classical standards can make way for new practices that lead to just and sustainable relations. Instead of comparing our students' collective achievement to that of the student achievements of other teachers, worrying that one lacks expertise in all musical genres, or being intimidated by musicians who hold skillsets that one has yet to master, educators could create a hospitable space of sharing and co-creation that celebrates the gifts of everyone. By focusing on what each musician might share with others rather than what each musician is lacking, educators might be able to unblock learning and free themselves and their students from the fear of judgment. Doing so might foster a more sustainable type of music-learning that is welcoming, inclusive, compassionate, and joyful.

Culture Bearing or Culture Making?

A culture-bearer can be defined as one who maintains and passes along a cultural tradition to the next generation. Music educators act as culture-bearers in instances when they are primarily concerned with helping children to listen to and engage in the music in which the teacher is well versed. Traditionally, school music has privileged the transmission of Western and European cultural traditions over all others, which has empowered Western classical culture-bearers and disenfranchised those bearing other traditions. In places where Western ideas have been imposed through settler colonialism, the result has been more than mere disenfranchisement: Western dominance has led to the intentional erasure of indigenous peoples, their languages, and their cultural traditions (Martusewicz, 2019).

To "care with" culture, it is necessary to acknowledge that there are multiple cultural traditions that co-inhabit the human musical ecosystem. Caring with cultures in music education settings means that we as educators honor and respect the multiple cultures that co-exist within our school and larger communities, privileging none over another—seeing each as an ecosystem and each occupying its own critical niche in the whole of our community. As mentioned above, this perspective allows us as music educators to relinquish our role as expert (Hendricks, 2018) and notions of superiority/inferiority (Hendricks, 2021). To use another ecological analogy, we must respect that we are but one species of tree in the forest if we have seen ourselves as a culture-bearer of a particular musical tradition.

Making way for culture-bearers of other traditions to occupy their rightful niche within the music education profession is an essential part of caring with our communities, because to care with others we must be willing to build relations. Preservice and in-service teachers need opportunities to critically examine ill-fitting roles in which educators have traditionally cared for learners as part of the project of "civilizing" those from "other" cultural traditions that are deemed inferior as viewed through the dominant system of value hierarchies (Plumwood, 1994, 2002). Instead, preservice and in-service professional development might be seen as collaborative ventures where teachers learn to embrace "caring with" attitudes that in some cases could lead to roles such as collaborator, culture maker, and facilitator—or new roles that are co-created and negotiated in each situation.

In keeping with Hendricks's (2021) definition of "caring with" as a function of eliminating value hierarchies in music-learning relationships, it will be important to relax expectations that music educators must fulfill particular roles at any given time, and instead open space for negotiating with others from moment to moment. The role of the culture-bearer will likely continue to be one of the roles that music educators might be called to embody in such negotiations. However, from a "caring with" perspective, that role would need to be enacted with recognition that all learners and community members who identify with that tradition have a mutual responsibility for maintaining the tradition, with equal investment and co-ownership of the process. For example, a high school orchestra director might partner with regional Bluegrass musicians, the fiddling community, their students, parents, and the venues that feature such music to ensure that tradition is maintained. The same director might also partner with the regional or city orchestra, chamber ensembles, soloists, community orchestra members, their students, parents, and audiences and work together to consider the ways that the Western orchestral tradition is experienced and maintained within that community.

"Caring with" might also be understood as a culture-making process. In order to create a space for communities to engage in music-making that respects and acknowledges the musical heritages, experiences, and creative impulses of all, musicians within the community might work to re-value collective community-based music to a greater extent. To support this notion, a culture-making approach might be embraced in schools where music is considered not only a subject worthy of study but also a means of bringing disparate voices to the table, to celebrate the cultural richness that might be created if deep respect and inclusion were practiced. For example, a music teacher might invite culture-bearers from the traditions represented within the community to ensure that each tradition is preserved and respected, and that each tradition is in musical dialogue with the others via intercultural exchanges. Such an exchange might include the musical fusions co-created in a way unique to that community (e.g., a country, hip-hop, mariachi, and Western classical musical dialogue).

In a culture-making approach students craft music with their community in a way that reflects the rich traditions, interests, and identity of those with whom they collaborate. In such a case, music is for the purpose of self and community expression, of bringing people together for community solidarity and resilience, and for celebrating all that is good about one's place of residence or bioregion. Alternatively, the music might convey what is problematic or needs to be changed in the community. It might involve sharing important information and even involve protest. In either case, individual and community interests are focused on simultaneously as a means to promote mutual thriving.

"Caring With" Learners: Nurturing Uniqueness and Soulcentric Maturation

Attunement with nature, or "soulcraft" can be seen as a means of building relationship with the earth as oneself (Plotkin, 2003). Such attunement differentiates from nature activities meant only to facilitate personal growth, which assumes an extractive and self-serving perspective instead of a relational one. Plotkin defines "soulcraft" as those activities that allow one to discern their place in the ecosystem. Such understanding transcends and includes one's occupational, familial, and cultural identities to consider the deeper metaphor one is enacting throughout one's life. For example, Plotkin—a psychologist—has identified that he lives the metaphor of a cocoon weaver, or a person who supports others through times of transition. According to Plotkin, understanding the metaphor of one's purpose is an essential quest of a human's maturation process, and it affects one's physical, emotional, mental, and spiritual wellbeing as well as one's relations with the earth and one's human communities. Unfortunately, current educational practices often fail to provide the type of personal reflection that would assist learners toward an ever-deepening understanding of their purposes because education has become too standardized and focused on career development (Robinson & Aronica, 2016).

Just as an oak tree cannot survive in the brackish waters where mangrove trees thrive, so it is that each of us must be in a biological and social ecosystem where we can flourish. Caring with learners is essential if educators see their role as one of assisting learners to better discern their rightness-of-fit in the biological and social ecosystems. Contrary to many of the assumptions that have forwarded notions of standardization in music education, caring with learners means that we do not force on them ways of learning and curricula that are ill-fitting and unsupportive as they seek their niche in the ecosystems.

Nature allows for multiple pathways for learning. For example, when fledgling birds first leave the nest, they sometimes flutter around wildly as they learn to use their wings. Some fly weakly but seem to understand immediately how to ascend into the canopy, whereas others fly more horizontally at first until they build the coordination to make an ascent. In music education, maintaining a stance of humility and curiosity is essential for educators to create the conditions needed to support learners in the testing, trying, and exploring that children and youth need to survive and thrive musically (see Boyce-Tillman, this volume; Dansereau, this volume), and to do so in such a way that does not sever their identity *as* earth (Smith, 2021, 2022).

Conclusion

As music educators consider ways to shift education so that it might promote a sustainable worldview, it is important that we acknowledge how anthropocentric approaches to learning have been harmful to both people and planet. Specifically, value hierarchies and standards imposed by the dominant social group have led to the exploitation and abuse of both the social and biological ecosystems, as the needs of the few at the top of the value hierarchy are prioritized over those of the rest. Such an emphasis has weakened relations within the interdependent biological and social ecosystems that all depend on for life.

To restore such relations, educators and learners alike might adopt a "caring with" approach to listen and attune carefully with one another and the more-than-human world. Through such an approach, all might learn to fully occupy their unique niche in the social and biological ecosystems. "Caring with" in music education ecosystems requires that all listen to and partner with one other. It also requires and that educators continually ensure that all learners have the resources that they need to thrive and that all students are valued for their contributions. Attempting the shift to a sustainable worldview might help educators and students to identify the unsustainable thinking that has negatively impacted our social relations and personal wellbeing. Perhaps together we can heal, restore, and create a just world as we create new and sustainable lifeways.

References

Boyce-Tillman, J. (2000). *Constructing musical healing: The wounds that sing*. Jessica Kingsley Publishers.

Figueres, C., & Rivett-Carnac, T. (2020). *The future we choose: Surviving the climate crisis*. Vintage.

Hendricks, K. S. (2018). *Compassionate music teaching*. Rowman & Littlefield.

Hendricks, K. S. (2021). Authentic connection in music education: A chiastic essay. In K. S. Hendricks & J. Boyce-Tillman (Eds.), *Authentic connection: Music, spirituality, and wellbeing* (pp. 237–253). Peter Lang.

Koza, J. (2006). "Save the Music"? Toward culturally relevant, joyful, and sustainable school music. *Philosophy of Music Education Review*, 14(1), 23–38. https://doi.org/10.1353/pme.2006.0006

Louv, R. (2012). *The nature principle: Reconnecting with life in a virtual age.* Algonquin Books.
Martusewicz, R. A. (2019). *A pedagogy of responsibility: Wendell Berry for ecojustice education.* Routledge.
Paris, D., & Alim, H. S. (Eds.). (2017). *Culturally sustaining pedagogies: Teaching and learning for justice in a changing world.* Teachers College Press.
Pijanowski, B., Villanueva-Rivera, L., Dumyahn, S. L., Farina, A., Krause, B., Napoletano, B. M., Gage, S. H., & Pieretti, N. (2011). Soundscape ecology: The science of sound in the landscape. *BioScience, 61*(3), 203–216. https://doi.org/10.1525/bio.2011.61.3.6
Plotkin, B. (2003). *Soulcraft: Crossing into the mysteries of nature and psyche.* New World Library.
Plotkin, B. (2008). *Nature and the human soul: Cultivating wholeness in a fragmented world.* New World Library.
Plumwood, V. (1994). *Feminism and the mystery of nature.* Routledge.
Plumwood, V. (2002). *Environmental culture: The ecological crisis of reason.* Routledge.
Powell, A. (2021, September 28). Tracing big oil's PR war to delay action on climate change: Harvard researchers chart evolution from denial to misdirection as House inquiry widens. *Harvard Gazette.* https://news.harvard.edu/gazette/story/2021/09/oil-companies-discourage-climate-action-study-says/
Robinson, K., & Aronica, L. (2016). *Creative schools: The grassroots revolution that's transforming education.* Penguin Publishing.
Sarath, E. (2018). *Black music matters: Jazz and the transformation of music studies.* Rowman & Littlefield.
Smith, T. D. (2021). Music education for surviving and thriving: Cultivating children's wonder, senses, emotional wellbeing, and wild nature as a means to discover and fulfill their life's purpose. *Frontiers in Education, 6,* Article 648779, 1–10. https://doi.org/10.3389/feduc.2021.648799
Smith, T. D. (2022). The trauma of separation: Understanding how music education interrupted my relationship with the more-than-human world. *Action, Criticism, and Theory for Music Education, 21*(1), 172–194. https://doi.org/10.22176/act21.1.172

FOREWORD TO SECTION 2

CO-CREATING CARING RELATIONSHIPS

Care: Finger Pointing at the Moon

LIORA BRESLER

The acknowledgment of care in education is both recent and ancient. Care in education is a charged concept, reintroduced in the early 1980s (Noddings, 1981). In a dichotomous worldview that highlights factual knowledge and simple evaluation measures, care has been regarded as soft yet threatening. As care is associated with the vulnerable (as if not all of us are), preschools, for example, distinguish themselves from daycares, emphasizing skills rather than enrichment. The chapters in this section, addressing care in diverse music education settings, exemplify the falsity of this dichotomy.

The recognition that care is integral to the human condition has consistently underlined the profession of teaching even as institutional structures and their reward system has undermined it. I witnessed this recognition when elementary classroom and arts teachers spoke about children's need for expression and refuge from the rigid academic curricula. Teachers contrasted the expressive qualities of the arts with ever-present hard accountability measures (Bresler, 1992). Teachers' care often had to resist a school culture that seemed hostile to the nurturing of children (and teachers). In the false yet prevalent dichotomy of skills and care, music education, of all school arts, had to negotiate a particularly thin line, given the skill level required by the traditions of music performance and competition.

Care ethics as a field of inquiry is a coming together of philosophers, political scientists, sociologists, anthropologists, and the medical humanities, among others, focusing on care as theory, care as practice, and care as ethics (Stake & Visse, 2021). Still, the quality of experience involved in care eludes definitions and prescriptions. Writing about care is akin to pointing to the moon, where the finger is only a guide. Care is practiced and modeled. I learned this first-hand back in my very first semester at Stanford in Spring 1983 during Nel Noddings's course, not through her writings but through her modeling (Bresler, 2012). Each student had to present a project related to a major theme discussed in the course. On that day, the presenter took us to the basement where she pre-arranged chairs in a maze-like constellation, asking for a volunteer. Blindfolding the volunteer, the presenter instructed her to walk around the room along the labyrinth of chairs, guided by class-members' directions on how to navigate. Suddenly, the experimenter motioned us to be quiet, and the directions stopped. The blindfolded student halted, not knowing where to proceed. I remember sensing her distress, and my own, stepping tentatively out to help, then back, worrying that I, a newcomer, would sabotage an important experiment. After many long seconds, Nel stepped in, held the volunteer's hand, and said in an even, measured tone: "I don't know what the purpose of this experiment is, but I need to do this." That was a lesson that no matter how inexperienced, I should always intervene when something didn't feel right. An exemplification rather than theorization, it has stayed with me as the most compelling learning experience in my education.

This episode captures the challenge of care in the midst of the "operational curriculum," not the ideal or the formal one. How do we bring aspirations and good intentions to specific situations, when pulled by different considerations? The gap between theory and practice, part of the human condition, and remarkably present in teaching music and the arts (Bresler, 1992), can be particularly poignant in relation to care.

The chapters in this section are grounded in complex, real settings of music education. They address, with sensitivity and insight, issues of care for different populations, including intersectionality as a holistic approach to care (Thomas-Durell); LGBTQIA+ music students (McManus and Carter); social emotional learning (Edgar et al.); bullying (Rawlings); community music (Evison); peer mentoring (Goodrich); special education (McCord); and trauma-informed care (Morelli). Based on compassionate music teaching (Hendricks, 2018), all these highlight the delicate balance of qualities involved (Hendricks et al.; Legutki et al.).

As musicians, we embody some of the qualities at the heart of care, including attuned listening and improvisation generated by that attunement (Bresler, 2005). Chapters focusing on listening (Troy) and voice as embodying singing-caring relationships (Cassidi-Parker & Hatton) alert us to qualities we already have. The interaction between musical qualities and caring relationships is not a given but requires attention and cultivation.

The institutional settings of these chapters point to the centrality of public policy in attending to care. Tronto's (2017) characterization of people as *homines curans*—caring people—argues for a democratic form of care that makes the reallocation of care responsibilities its central concern.

A common, dualistic assumption in our culture is that the more we care for others the less we care for ourselves and vice versa. Irwin (2007) makes the point that our formal roles as educators have become the focus of our existence and we have lost sight of our souls. Moving from our roles to our souls means giving attention to our need for connections within ourselves, as well as with others. Sweet's important observations on self-care (this volume) signify that the ability to care for others necessitates self-care. The chapters in this section do indeed point to a full moon—the importance of wise conceptualization, intention, and awareness for shining some light on the vital practice of care in music educational settings.

REFERENCES

Bresler, L. (1992). Visual art in primary grades: A portrait and analysis. *Early Childhood Research Quarterly, 7*, 397–414. https://doi.org/10.1016/0885-2006(92)90029-X

Bresler, L. (2005). What musicianship can teach educational research. *Music Education Research, 7*(2), 169–183. https://doi.org/10.1080/14613800500169399

Bresler, L. (2012). The day you intervened. In R. Lake (Ed.), *Dear Nel: Opening the circles of care (letters to Nel Noddings)* (pp. 98–99). Teachers College Press.

Hendricks, K. S. (2018). *Compassionate music teaching*. Rowman & Littlefield.

Irwin, R. (2007). Prelude: Plumbing the depth of being fully alive. In L. Bresler (Ed.), *The International handbook of research in arts education* (pp. 1401–1404). Springer.

Noddings, N. (1981). Caring. *Journal of Curriculum Theorizing, 3*(2), 130–148.

Stake, R., & Visse, M. (2021). *A paradigm of care*. Information Age.

Tronto, J. (2017) There is an alternative: *Homines curans* and the limits of neoliberalism, *International Journal of Care and Caring, 1*(1), 27–43. https://doi.org/10.1332/239788217X14866281687583

CHAPTER 13

THE MUSICAL CIRCLE OF CARE

A Framework for Relationship Building and Healing Through Musicing

JANELIZE MORELLI

CARE HANDBOOK TOPICS

Co-creating caring relationships
Wellbeing and human flourishing

MUSIC educators have become sensitized to the need to practice with care and compassion (Hendricks, 2018; Silverman, 2012; Walzer, 2021). Furthermore, music educators have become more aware of their role as ethical agents working within the political space of music education praxis (Elliott et al., 2016; Hess, 2019). However, despite this awareness, the current sociocultural climate, with social inequality reaching a boiling point, makes it simultaneously challenging and increasingly necessary for music educators to practice with compassion and care to foster young activists who can continue working toward social change (Hess, 2018).

To this end, music educators' practices can support a music education politics of hope, which may be mechanized to build solid relationships and enable relational healing to occur (Walzer, 2021). The musical circle of care is an example of a pedagogical ritual, which may be used within diverse contexts to meet the educator's and participants' needs. Furthermore, because this pedagogical ritual is adapted from trust-based relational interventions (Purvis et al., 2013), it may serve as a concrete structure for music educators to facilitate relationship building and healing through a trauma-informed lens.

The Context

The musical circle of care pedagogical framework is the culmination of my music education and community music praxes in South Africa. As a white music educator, raised and educated sheltered by privilege, I was initially shocked when confronted with the socioeconomic realities many students in my class faced. South Africa is a country marred by inequalities. These inequalities are mirrored in the education system to such an extent that Spaull (2013) suggests that there are two separate education systems in South Africa. In my community music praxis, I, alongside the undergraduate and postgraduate students enrolled in community music modules, mostly music[1] together with children who live lives filled with adverse childhood experiences including parental unemployment, food insecurity, lack of access to essential services such as running water and electricity, and domestic and gender-based violence. These experiences may lead to various adverse outcomes, including but not limited to relational trauma (Schore, 2013). For children who have experienced relational trauma, creating opportunities to build new, meaningful relationships may aid healing (Hughes et al., 2019; Purvis et al., 2007). However, as a music educator, I felt out of my depth during community music workshops I facilitated. There was no curriculum framework guiding me and many of the pedagogical strategies I employed in more formal education settings seemed out of place in these contexts. Therefore, it became increasingly important for me to build a community music pedagogical framework informed by the three pillars of trauma-informed care: safety, connection, and managing emotions (Bath, 2008).

The Musical Circle of Care

The musical circle of care is a pedagogical framework for music educators and community music facilitators informed by trauma-informed pedagogy and focused on relationship building and healing (Brunzell, 2021; McEvoy & Salvador, 2020; Purvis et al., 2013). Because vulnerable children are often in a heightened state of arousal, routine and predictability may aid in breaking the stress-response cycle (Purvis et al., 2013). The stress-response cycle refers to a state of heightened awareness (sometimes described as a fight-or-flight state) which is brought on by continuous exposure to stressful events or experiences. The musical circle of care seeks to address this heightened state of arousal by providing participants with a routine and predictability. This is achieved by organizing the music lesson or workshop as a ritual, which is comprises "activities composed of ordered sequences of acts or utterances that carry, encode, or generate

---

[1] I employ music as a verb instead of a noun, as this is true to the praxial view of music education (Elliott & Silverman, 2014) and in line with the ethics of community music (Higgins, 2012).

meaningful experience for participants" (Reynolds & Erikson, 2017, p. 2). This pedagogical framework is centered around the belief that music education and community music spaces provide an opportunity for interaction ritual chains (Collins, 2004).

The musical circle of care provides music educators and community music facilitators with a pedagogical framework that helps to frame their musicing as rituals of caring for and together with their participants and students. The five phases involved in the musical circle of care help establish bodily copresence, create permeable barriers to outsiders (while maintaining the felt safety for participants), facilitate a mutual focus of attention, and help create a shared mood (Collins, 2004). If the musical circle of care framework leads to successful caring rituals, there should be four outcomes: group solidarity, emotional effervescence, the creation of sacred objects or symbols, and standards of morality (Collins, 2004). It is important to note that many education activities are ritualized in traditional music education, but few of these rituals are filled with care. The rituals we enact in music education may lead to oppression and even retraumatize students (Bradley & Hess, 2021; Palmer, 2018; Scrine, 2016). Therefore, it is paramount for music educators and community musicians to explicitly find pedagogical frameworks and practices that will infuse the rituals practiced in their social space with care.

In my practice, the circle has been featured as a means to organize social space. Using the circle as an organizational strategy has become a recurring theme. I find myself moving tables and chairs, creating openness, space, and the ever-present circle. The circle also features meaningfully in public performances and rituals across the world (Stige, 2011; Stige & Aarø, 2011). The musical circle of care employs the circle both literally and metaphorically. The circle serves as a popular means to organize space in music education and community music practice alike. As an undergraduate student, I remember watching with amusement as time and time again the entire class started walking in a circle during Dalcroze workshops. Metaphorically, the circle is significant as it may refer to femininity, softness, warmth, and the cycles of life (Liu, 1997). However, the circle may also serve as a metaphor for how we understand, adhere to, and circumvent norms (Mendes de Oliveira, 2018).

In the following discussion, I lay out both how the musical circle may be organized through the sequential phases and how the musical circle of care may be seen as a foundation for cultivating caring norms through the building of reciprocal relationships. The musical circle of care comprises five phases:

1. welcoming one another,
2. extending hospitality,
3. becoming aware,
4. finding healing, and
5. taking leave.

It is important to note that the musical circle of care framework should not be seen as a prescriptive list of activities or a method for facilitating community music workshops. Rather, the musical circle of care is a pedagogical framework community music facilitators and music educators may employ to reflect on their current practice, plan workshops, and to build the foundation that will enable participants and facilitators to co-create musical interventions.

Welcoming One Another

The first phase in the musical circle of care framework is focused on extending a welcome (Higgins, 2015). The aim of this phase is to create felt safety (Huefner et al., 2020; Purvis et al., 2013). As community music facilitators, it is essential to remember that past traumatic experiences may lead to anxiety and uncertainty, even when the environment they find themselves in at the moment is objectively safe (Purvis et al., 2013). Students and participants are not free to participate fully in musicing, expressing themselves, becoming vulnerable, and learning together when they do not experience felt safety (McEvoy & Salvador, 2020). The activities included in the welcoming phase are focused on facilitating felt safety by creating initial opportunities for connection between the facilitator and participants as well as among participants. These opportunities are important to establishing the musical circle of care because they encourage playful engagement, self-awareness, and attunement among the group members (Purvis et al., 2013).

In my workshops I draw on Dalcroze-inspired techniques, such as those taught by Nivbrant Wedin (2011). During this phase of the musical circle of care, it is important to create an environment of felt safety; therefore, it is paramount to engage playfully in musicing activities that eliminate the pressure of musical performance and where failure is not possible. The following vignette illustrates one such activity:

> *It is the beginning of my workshops during gender awareness week. Gender awareness week is an initiative driven by the university's diversity and inclusion committee. During this week, staff and students collaborate and co-create workshops, lectures, and performances informed by pressing issues related to gender and sexuality. The majority of the participants in my workshop are not music students or staff. They come from across the humanities faculty, and the tension is palpable as I unpack the instruments. I do not think they view themselves as musicians—possibly not even as musical.*
>
> *I begin the workshop by playing "New Brighton" by queer artist Nkhane. During the first listening, I ask participants to find their way around the room. I am challenging them to experience the space differently, removing the safety and reassurance of the circle. I am hoping that by finding their own path they will experience the hall in a new way, perhaps circumventing the sanctity of the School of Music (or Conserv, as it is often referred to). I am also asking them to become more self-aware by removing the assurance of following in each other's footsteps.*
>
> *During the second listening, I ask them to continue finding their unique path while making eye contact with the other participants as they pass. I hope to facilitate a greater sense of attunement among the participants without adding the intensity of prolonged eye contact or the possible challenge of physical touch. During the third listening, I ask them to continue on their path, but this time to high-five participants as they pass each*

other. This time I am adding the socially acceptable form of safe touch. With each listening I engage fully with the participants. As we move through each listening, I notice a shift in the energy in the room. I notice more eye contact, a little nod here and there, even two participants briefly high-fiving. In general, I feel like there is more space to breathe in the room.

The vignette above illustrates the ways in which welcoming participants to the community musicing workshop may begin with the acknowledgment that we are finding ourselves on strange terrain. In this example, the Dalcroze-inspired activities gently guide an exploration of this terrain, introducing the space and guiding participants toward acceptable safe forms of touch (such as greeting each other with the high five).

Extending Hospitality

The second phase in the musical circle of care is focused on extending hospitality by defining the expectations set for group membership. Higgins (2012) describes hospitality as "a verb that describes the actions and desires of community musicians who seek to provide *authentic* music-making opportunities for people" (p. 137). Although hospitality is seen as one of the cornerstones of community music, absolute hospitality remains elusive (Higgins, 2012). In the musical circle of care, the facilitator needs to carefully balance the desire to extend an open welcome with the need to define conduct within the group. These rules can play an essential part in creating ecological strategies to empower participants (Purvis et al., 2015).

Although rules and routines make it easier for the participants to feel safe within the musical circle of care, the facilitator needs to carefully negotiate the perceived dichotomies of leadership and egalitarianism by facilitating a discussion (musical or verbal) of what is expected of group members. However, in the hands of a skilled facilitator, this phase of the musical circle of care can become a lively enactment of artistic citizenship (Silverman & Elliott, 2018). The process of defining group member responsibility through consensus may be a means to model active citizenship and show how caring societies react when group members violate the expectations set of members during the welcome phase (Effrat & Schimmel, 2003; Held, 2010). The following vignette illustrates what may happen when this phase of the musical circle of care is not established:

It was the first time I visited the community center. I did not know the children, and they did not know me. Their excitement sounded off as the room filled with chatter. Some children were also illustrating their excitement somatically, bumping into one another and dashing from one side of the small room to the other. As I placed the instruments on the floor, approximately 20 children eagerly descended on the boxes filled with recorders, ukuleles, and pitched and unpitched percussion. They also started rummaging through my files and purse. I felt violated in the moment and lacked the experience to respond tactfully to the situation. Instead, I stood there, frozen. I had failed to extend hospitality and illustrate the kind of citizenship I envisaged we would practice in the workshop. I had also failed to recognize that we had very different concepts of privacy and ownership. I had set them and myself up to fail by not negotiating the welcome clearly.

This vignette illustrates how extending hospitality is a reciprocal process. However, there was a mismatch between my expectations as the facilitator and the participants' expectations in this instance. The participants had expectations regarding musicing together and communal ownership of the musical resources (which included objects I considered personal property). I had expectations regarding acceptable conduct in a musicing space, which remained poorly communicated. There was also an interesting tension with regard to ownership of the space. The community center belonged to the participants, not to me, yet I had expectations about power distribution in the setting. Looking back at this instance, it is clear that the situation could have been remedied if I had focused on relationship-building prior to the musicing workshop. I can also acknowledge that this instance would have been an opportune moment to practice reflexivity in action and to take critically reflexive action (Silverman & Elliott, 2018). Practicing reflexivity would have allowed me to acknowledge my expectations. I might have been more open to other possible scenarios if I had acknowledged my expectations. This, in turn, could have made me more willing to cede my perceived power and practice extending hospitality.

Becoming Aware

The third phase of the musical circle of care builds on the self-awareness and attunement cultivated during the first two phases. During this phase the facilitator carefully guides participants through musicing to enhance and repair participants' regulatory capabilities. This phase may be focused on any combination of the following aspects: routine and rhythm, self-regulation, mindfulness, and de-escalation (Brunzell et al., 2016). Focusing on these aspects may help participants to enhance regulatory capabilities. Mindfulness remains an underused tool in music education but could potentially enhance musical understanding (Diaz, this volume; Falter, 2016). Although mindfulness is founded in spirituality, the kind of mindfulness I advocate for through the musical circle of care can be better defined as "training mental processes to be under greater intentional control, which enables one to be more attentive and aware of oneself and one's surroundings" (Falter, 2016, p. 20).

The mindfulness and self-regulation practices in the musical circle of care framework may be musical or extramusical activities. Initially, extramusical activities may seem easier to identify. These could include using an engine check-in, in which participants show on a placard how their engine—their internal state-of-being—is running. Generally, these placards make use of four different colors to show four different emotional states: Green means that everything is fine and the participant is ready to engage; yellow means that there is already a little too much energy; red indicates that the participant is feeling out of control or angry; and blue indicates that the participant is experiencing a lack of energy or feeling drained. One could also adapt these engine checks to become group improvisations, where participants express their current emotional state using instruments, their voices, or movement. The following vignette describes the process I followed during my first semester presenting group marimba workshops at a private girls school. This process helped me facilitate both awareness of their own inner state and awareness of those around them through musical improvisation.

> *I became increasingly aware that the girls were simply not paying enough attention to each other in the marimba band. Even though there was pressure to learn all the repertoire for the annual music competition, I decided to press hold on the formal rehearsals and first focus on addressing the lack of awareness I noticed in the ensemble. I devised an improvisation game where the participants stood behind their marimbas, waiting for me to walk past and show which notes they could use for their improvisation. This limited framework was initially employed to create safe boundaries for their expression and to remove any fear of failure.*
>
> *Next, I introduced switching. When I called out the switch command, participants moved to the next available spot in the band. They needed to start improvising again at the beginning of the next bar. The next step was to introduce self-initiated switches. I told the participants that they could switch with anyone in the band as long as they had managed to make eye contact and received a nonverbal affirmation from the other band member. An initial reluctance to switch would be followed by a movement toward complete chaos as all the band members hastily moved around the room.*
>
> *After each chaotic session, I would encourage them to reflect on when and why the music stopped. As a group, we realized that we needed to be more aware of each other and that playing marimba in the band required an intricate balance between my own need to express myself and the needs of the marimba community around me. They would request the switching game at many points throughout the term, and I happily obliged.*

Finding Healing

The fourth phase of the musical circle of care is focused on using the relationships built during the first three phases to promote healing. This phase may focus on either finding voice as an act of empowerment (Koon, 2009) or building compassion through kinesthetic empathy (Reynolds & Reason, 2012; Shuper Engelhard, 2019). In line with Koon (2009), I assert that participants in community music workshops founded on caring action can be empowered to express their own voice, develop interpersonal skills, build clearer communication channels, and experience enjoyment through musicing. Furthermore, during musicing, a focus on kinesthetic empathy may enable us to experience the world through someone else's eyes by moving together or observing their movements closely while musicing (Reynolds & Reason, 2012). In this regard, I find mirroring activities to be some of the most meaningful ways to experience deep empathy for the other and feel acknowledged when one sees oneself reflected in their movements.

> *As I stood in front of the tall male student, I could feel a sense of apprehension. We did not know each other, and I thought perhaps social conventions had taught us to fear the other. Yet here we were, standing less than an arm's length apart. I felt deeply aware of my Whiteness. I felt unsettled by the power dynamic between us.*
>
> *As the music started playing I held my hands up. This was our starting position. We held our hands close to each other without touching. I asked him to lead, knowing that this might be challenging. As I focused intently on mirroring his movements as closely as possible, I became more aware of the softness of his eyes. It was a strange feeling. As we moved along with the activity, I changed partners throughout until I could mirror every student in the group. On some level, I had gotten to know each of them better in those 15 minutes than I probably would throughout the rest of the semester.*

Taking Leave

The final phase in the musical circle of care is taking leave. Closing the ritual can be a sacred moment, but it can also be a moment filled with sadness. These moments may be filled with emotional effervescence or may require debriefing. It is essential for the facilitator in a musical circle of care to be attuned to the participants and to guide the process of taking leave in a manner that addresses both the group's expressed and implicit needs (Noddings, 2013).

During community musicing workshops with the elderly, I often experienced this deep sadness at the end of the workshop. Every time the workshop ended, I would feel a deep sense of sadness in the room. This sadness required space to breathe. Partnerships and educational community building require facilitators to hold space (Ostrowdun et al., 2020). In this space, artful facilitators can account for the life stories they witnessed unfolding during the education partnership and also for that which may still come into being. Holding space also requires facilitators to live with the messiness of the relationship.

> *I am not religious. I feel extremely uncomfortable with the heaviness of my Afrikaner heritage, but as the participants sang Amen in the Dutch Reformed Church's traditional arrangement, I felt a feeling of spaciousness I had not often experienced in churches and places of worship before.*

I often found closing rituals at these workshops for the elderly especially challenging. During the workshop I was focused on facilitating engagement. I was distracted from the feelings of discomfort due to the religious and cultural differences I experienced in the space. However, as we sang the version of the closing prayer prayed in the Dutch Reformed Church, I would remind myself to sit in the discomfort and allow myself, my fellow facilitators, and the participants the space to take leave from one another.

CONCLUSION

The musical circle of care is a malleable pedagogical framework. I created this framework as a means to develop my facilitation practices. During my interaction with undergraduate students, I realized that other facilitators and educators may struggle to express their caring intentions, especially when working alongside people who are hurting or living lives filled with trauma, rejection, and pain. This framework is informed by a worldview of relationality and grounded in the ethic of care (Noddings, 2013). The musical circle of care also employs trauma-informed pedagogy principles by emphasizing felt safety, connection, and managing emotions (Bath, 2008). It encourages a pedagogy of care, connection, empathy, and hope as fundamental to our practice (Hendricks, 2018). I hope this framework may invoke further dialogue and reflection on trauma-informed care and relationship-building in music education and community music spaces.

REFERENCES

Bath, H. (2008). The three pillars of trauma-informed care. *Reclaiming Children and Youth*, *17*(3), 17–21.

Bradley, D., & Hess, J. (2021). *Trauma and resilience in music education: Haunted melodies*. Routledge.

Brunzell, T. (2021). Trauma-aware practice and positive education. In M. L. Kern & M. L. Wehmeyer (Eds.), *The Palgrave handbook of positive education* (pp. 205–223). Springer International Publishing. https://doi.org/10.1007/978-3-030-64537-3_8

Brunzell, T., Stokes, H., & Waters, L. (2016). Trauma-informed flexible learning: Classrooms that strengthen regulatory abilities. *International Journal of Child, Youth and Family Studies*, *7*(2), 218–239. https://doi.org/10.18357/ijcyfs72201615719

Collins, R. (2004). *Interaction ritual chains*. Princeton University Press.

Effrat, A., & Schimmel, D. (2003). Walking the democratic talk: Introduction to a special issue on collaborative rule-making as preparation for democratic citizenship. *American Secondary Education*, *31*(3), 3–15.

Elliott, D. J., & Silverman, M. (2014). *Music matters: A philosophy of music education*. Oxford University Press.

Elliott, D. J., Silverman, M., & Bowman, W. (2016). Artistic citizenship: Introduction, aims, and overview. In D. J. Elliott, M. Silverman, & W. Bowman (Eds.), *Artistic citizenship: Artistry, social responsibility, and ethical praxis* (pp. 3–21). Oxford University Press.

Falter, H. E. (2016). Mindfulness: An underused tool for deepening music understanding. *General Music Today*, *30*(1), 20–24. https://doi.org/10.1177/1048371316641461

Held, V. (2010). Can the ethics of care handle violence? *Ethics and Social Welfare*, 4(2), 115–129. https://doi.org/10.1080/17496535.2010.484256

Hendricks, K. S. (2018). *Compassionate music teaching*. Rowman & Littlefield.

Hess, J. (2018). Revolutionary activism in striated spaces? Considering an activist music education in K-12 schooling. *Action, Criticism, and Theory for Music Education*, 17(2), 22–49. https://doi.org/10.22176/act17.2.21

Hess, J. (2019). *Music education for social change: Constructing an activist music education*. Routledge.

Higgins, L. (2012). *Community music: In theory and in practice*. Oxford University Press.

Higgins, L. (2015). Hospitable music making: Community music as a site for social justice. In C. Benedict, P. Schmidt, G. Spruce, & P. Woodford (Eds.), *The Oxford handbook of social justice in music education* (pp. 447–459). Oxford University Press.

Huefner, J. C., Ringle, J. L., Gordon, C., & Tyler, P. M. (2020). Impact of perception of safety on outcomes in the context of trauma. *Children and Youth Services Review*, 114, 1–8. Article 105060. https://doi.org/10.1016/j.childyouth.2020.105060

Hughes, D. A., Golding, K. S., & Hudson, J. (2019). *Healing relational trauma with attachment-focused interventions: Dyadic developmental psychotherapy with children and families*. W. W. Norton & Company.

Kroon, C. (2009). "Everybody should be heard; everybody has got a story to tell, or a song to sing." In M. S. Barrett & S. L. Stauffer (Eds.), *Narrative inquiry in music education* (pp. 135–152). Springer Netherlands. https://doi.org/10.1007/978-1-4020-9862-8

Liu, C. H. (1997). Symbols: Circles and spheres represent the same referents. *Metaphor and Symbol*, 12(2), 135–147. https://doi.org/10.1207/s15327868ms1202_3

McEvoy, C. A., & Salvador, K. (2020). Aligning culturally responsive and trauma-informed pedagogies in elementary general music. *General Music Today*, 34(1), 21–28. https://doi.org/10.1177/1048371320909806

Mendes de Oliveira, M. (2018). Cultural conceptualizations of business negotiations in the Expanding Circle. *World Englishes*, 37(4), 684–696. https://doi.org/10.1111/weng.12346

Nivbrant Wedin, E. (2011). *Playing music with the whole body: Eurhythmics and motor development*. Gehrmans.

Noddings, N. (2013). *Caring: A relational approach to ethics and moral education*. University of California Press.

Ostrowdun, C., Friendly, R., Matthews, K., De Bie, A., & Roelofs, F. (2020). Holding space and engaging with difference: Navigating the personal theories we carry into our pedagogical partnership practices. *International Journal for Students as Partners*, 4(1), 82–98. https://doi.org/10.15173/ijsap.v4i1.4093

Palmer, E. S. (2018). Literature review of social justice in music education: Acknowledging oppression and privilege. *Update: Applications of Research in Music Education*, 36(2), 22–31. https://doi.org/10.1177/8755123317711091

Purvis, K. B., Cross, D. R., Dansereau, D. F., & Parris, S. R. (2013). Trust-based relational intervention (TBRI): A systemic approach to complex developmental trauma. *Child & Youth Services*, 34(4), 360–386. https://doi.org/10.1080/0145935X.2013.859906

Purvis, K. B., Cross, D. R., & Sunshine, W. L. (2007). *The connected child: Bring hope and healing to your adoptive family*. McGraw Hill Professional.

Purvis, K. B., Razuri, E. B., Howard, A. R. H., Call, C. D., DeLuna, J. H., Hall, J. S., & Cross, D. R. (2015). Decrease in behavioral problems and trauma symptoms among at-risk adopted children following trauma-informed parent training intervention. *Journal of Child & Adolescent Trauma, 8*(3), 201–210. https://doi.org/10.1007/s40653-015-0055-y

Reynolds, C., & Erikson, E. (2017). Agency, identity, and the emergence of ritual experience. *Socius, 3*, Article 2378023117710881. https://doi.org/10.1177/2378023117710881

Reynolds, D., & Reason, M. (2012). *Kinesthetic empathy in creative and cultural practices*. Intellect Books.

Schore, A. N. (2013). Relational trauma, brain development, and dissociation. In D. J. Ford & C. A. Courtois (Eds.), *Treating complex traumatic stress disorders in children and adolescents: Scientific foundations and therapeutic models* (pp. 3–23). Guilford Press.

Scrine, E. (2016). Enhancing social connectedness or stabilising oppression: Is participation in music free from gendered subjectivity? *Voices: A World Forum for Music Therapy, 16*(2). https://doi.org/10.15845/voices.v16i2.881

Shuper Engelhard, E. (2019). Embodying the couple relationship: Kinesthetic empathy and somatic mirroring in couples therapy. *Journal of Couple & Relationship Therapy, 18*(2), 126–147. https://doi.org/10.1080/15332691.2018.1481801

Silverman, M. (2012). Virtue ethics, care ethics, and "The good life of teaching." *Action, Criticism, and Theory for Music Education, 11*(2), 96–122. http://act.maydaygroup.org/articles/Silverman11_2.pdf

Silverman, M., & Elliott, D. J. (2018). Rethinking community music as artistic citizenship. In B.-L. Bartleet & L. Higgins (Eds.), *The Oxford handbook of community music* (pp. 366–390). Oxford University Press.

Spaull, N. (2013). Poverty & privilege: Primary school inequality in South Africa. *International Journal of Educational Development, 33*(5), 436–447. https://doi.org/10.1016/j.ijedudev.2012.09.009

Stige, B. (2011). *Elaborations toward a notion of community music therapy*. Barcelona Publishers.

Stige, B., & Aarø, L. E. (2011). *Invitation to community music therapy*. Routledge.

Walzer, D. (2021). Fostering trauma-informed and eudaimonic pedagogy in music education. *Frontiers in Education, 6*, Article 647008. https://doi.org/10.3389/feduc.2021.647008

CHAPTER 14

(RE)IMAGINING INTERSECTIONALITY

Holistic Acceptance in Music Education

LATASHA THOMAS-DURRELL

CARE HANDBOOK TOPICS

Co-creating caring relationships

"Take care." "Be careful." "Tender loving care." These are phrases that people toss around in their day-to-day goings on. Though people sometimes flippantly use these phrases, what does the core concept of care expressed *really* mean? Though safety has multiple definitions and understandings, the word involves protection from danger or injury. To *take care* or to *be careful* is to have some regard for one's safety. When someone needs *tender loving care*, they need compassion and empathy in matters concerning their physical, mental, and emotional safety. How does this manifest in the classroom? How can teachers care for their students? How might embracing a philosophy of intersectionality help teachers provide care?

"Intersectionality" was coined by Kimberlé Crenshaw (1989, 1991), and its origins were created under the context of law. Crenshaw observed how multiple layers of identity such as class, race, and ability impacted Black women's experiences and therefore made their experiences different from most of the experiences feminist and legal scholars were writing about at the time—the experiences of White women. Crenshaw asserted that Black women's experiences were impacted by both sex and race. This impact, however, was not simply twice as complex as having to consider race with sex. Rather, Crenshaw introduced the term "intersectionality" to denote that Black women experienced the categories of their identities simultaneously, intersecting at many different places. Thus, intersectionality meant the multidimensional and intersecting nature of Black women's constructions of identity that must be taken into account in order to more fully grasp their experiences. In Crenshaw's (1989) words, intersectionality is the not "mutually exclusive categories of experience and analysis" (p. 139).

Since Crenshaw coined the term in 1989, people from different contexts have woven intersectionality into their philosophies, policies, and practices, including healthcare (Bowleg, 2021), education in general (Bešić, 2020), and more specifically, in music education (Escalante, 2020; Thomas-Durrell, 2019). In these writings, authors use intersectionality as a way to imagine better care for people about whom they are writing. Care is embedded in intersectionality, indeed part of intersectionality's very foundation. One understands this point from the ways in which Crenshaw (1991) writes about intersectionality as a whole, as well as structural, political, and representational intersectionality. Dill and Zambrana (2009) explicate intersectionality's core concepts as "centering the experiences of people of color, complicating identity, and unveiling power in interconnected structures of inequality" (pp. 5–7). This means that intersectionality is about foregrounding the lived experiences of people of color and about how race interacts with other layers of identity, understanding how these socially constructed categories influence each other as well as how power and privilege form and are maintained around these categories (Gardner & McKinzie, 2020; Jones & Wijeyesinghe, 2011). As one acknowledges how various power structures have functioned against marginalized populations—especially Black women—one can (re)imagine ways to affirm and care for those people (Greene, 1980).

I center Flavia Dzodan's (2011) quote, "My feminism will be intersectional or it will be bullshit" to tie intersectionality to music education. If one's feminism does not take into account the crisscrossing, overlapping, and interconnected ways that one exists in life, then it is fraudulent. If one does not embrace the whole picture of a person, then one is not embracing the person at all. Either an educator will teach with a philosophy built on intersectionality or the teacher's overall effect is to uphold white supremacy (Bonds & Inwood, 2015). Or as commonly quoted in the Black community, "You a lie, and the truth ain't in ya," meaning the person is lying to one's face (African American Proverb, 2014). For how can both be true? Either educators accept that students hold multiple intersecting layers of identity and embrace the responsibility of creating and affirming them or they really do not see students in their full humanity and embrace them holistically.

Music teachers often express the importance of establishing connections with students so that students feel understood and accepted. However, many may not realize what and how much those connections may genuinely require. As Miller (2021) explains, "teachers may value care, and believe they are demonstrating responsive care, but students may not recognize the care as such" (p. 117). The type of care that students are likely to recognize requires (a) an undetermined amount of time for connections to grow and flourish, and (b) a co-created learning space that is built on trust and empathy in which each person shares the role of learner. From those two overarching components come the sub-components of (a) embracing dissent, (b) fostering critical thinking and autonomy, (c) each person getting what they need, and (d) acceptance of the whole person. Of course, teaching with a philosophy of intersectionality cannot be achieved by a simple checklist, but the aforementioned actions help to (re)imagine and establish a classroom culture built on an approach to care that is built on a philosophy of intersectionality.

Care from a Co-created Learning Space

I extend the concept of compassion and care in music teaching, put forth by Hendricks (2018), by drawing on Valenzuela's (1999) idea of authentic care, a type of care in which teachers derive their modes of interaction from what students express or demonstrate (Noddings, 2005; Osterman, 2010). Students develop trust from teachers putting forth authentic care, and once students have grown to trust their environment, including the people in it, students can learn better (Held, 2006; Miller, 2021). Not only do students' show growth in classroom activities and work, but also they are more open to learning (Held, 2006). Several studies find that this greater propensity for learning influences school and personal life (Cohen et al., 2009; Glasser, 1998; Osterman, 2000; Resnick et al., 1997). Where music teachers employing a culturally responsive teaching approach in music education take into account students' cultural capital (Bourdieu, 1973; Thomas-Durrell, 2021), those who also employ an intersectional approach embrace that cultural capital. Embracing students' knowledge and experience is coupled with centering the perspectives of people of color, highlighting the complicated nature of experiences for people who embody multiply marginalized layers of identity, and paying attention to and deconstructing power dynamics (Dill & Zambrana, 2009; Jones & Wijeyesinghe, 2011).

Music teachers who embrace intersectionality do so in co-created learning spaces. A co-created learning space, according to Beaumont (1998) is "where the degree of collaboration is determined not only by participant shared goals, but also by participant attitudes, resources, and protocols that are specific to the academic, social, and cultural environments of [all] who engage in collaborative efforts" (p. 39). For a class to be truly co-created, it must affirm all the people involved and it must attend to the power dynamics inherent in student-teacher relationships. Freire (2000) explains:

> Through dialogue, the teacher-of-the-students and the students-of-the-teacher cease to exist and a new term emerges: teacher-student with students-teachers. The teacher is no longer merely the-one-who-teaches, but who is himself [sic] taught in dialogue with the students, who in turn while being taught also teach. (p. 80)

When all participants possess the same power, when their feelings have meaning, when their different ways of knowing and being are taken into account, then a new classroom emerges, new ways of understanding can emerge and grow because trust has been established (Hendricks, 2018; 2021). Embracing an intersectional approach to music teaching "enriches collaboration by facilitating a classroom community where a diverse range of identities and perspectives are utilized in learning processes.... [It] provides ways ... to simultaneously create and sustain inclusive and authentic classrooms" (Pliner et al., 2011, p. 44). From these connections, teachers are able to make transfers from known to unknown concepts.

In a word, embracing intersectionality in music teaching is care, and there are specific ways teachers can show care in the classroom: embracing dissent and fostering critical thinking and autonomy, ensuring that each student gets the care that they need, and accepting the whole of the students as more than the sum of their parts. These components are not strictly separated; they crisscross and overlap, and either of them could be considered the foundation. However, it is more accurate that a little of each component serves as the base from which teachers can build to help students achieve self-actualization as defined in the motivation theory of Maslow's hierarchy of needs (Heylighen, 1992; Maslow, 1943).

Embracing Dissent/Fostering Critical Thinking and Autonomy

A co-created learning space cannot exist without the expression of different, sometimes opposing, perspectives (Paavola et al., 2004). In this section about dissent, the focus is mostly on articulated dissent (Kassing, 1997), but there are many ways students may express or articulate their disagreement, both verbally and nonverbally. Goodboy (2011) writes that dissent in the classroom is the "expression of disagreement or contradictory opinions concerning policies or practices" (p. 297). Teachers do well to take into account students' direct disagreements, but sometimes student dissent is expressed more indirectly through statements of lived experience (London & Van Buskirk, 2018). For example, a student might say, "In my experience/culture/family, we (insert lived experience)." Centering this type of dissent will transform the classroom. "The classroom becomes transformed when ... tacit knowledge become[s] available and central to the work of the class ... the classroom then can be experienced as a community with true interdependence because neither expertise nor authority can be centralized in a single individual" (London & Van Buskirk, 2018, p. 1061).

At the core of an intersectional teaching approach is co-creating a space where all voices are acknowledged. By acknowledging all voices, the teacher–student power dynamic changes. One approach to shifting the power dynamic between students and teachers is through welcoming dissent. As students make their feelings and opinions known without negative repercussions, they begin to understand the role of power and privilege in the classroom. When students feel understood, they begin to trust that educators will take care not to harm their sense of self, that teachers will be empathetic and compassionate (Hendricks, 2018). Further, students can begin to see new ways of how they might inhabit the learning space (Dill, 2009), which makes them increasingly comfortable with their own voices. After feeling accepted and respected, students' ability and willingness to think critically blossoms. According to Hendricks (2018), "Students require a safe emotional environment where they can feel free to be vulnerable, take risks, and let their authentic selves come through" (pp. 155–156). When they are able to allow their thoughts to take up space, their confidence grows, encouraging them to think for themselves, even in the face of possibly opposing views.

At this stage, students are able to engage meaningfully and courageously in a wealth of different contexts. This is a point that Hendricks (2018) makes when she writes, "Compassionate teachers can help students feel confident enough in their own abilities and potential so that they are willing and interested in seeing their peers succeed as well" (p. 152). When teachers embed intersectionality into compassion and care, some of the contexts students will engage with will include interrogating how society constructs identity, deconstructing and (re)constructing power in the music classroom, and centering the experiences of people of color (Dill & Zambrana, 2009). "Because intersectional work validates the lives and stories of previously ignored groups of people, it is seen as a tool that can be used to help empower communities and the people in them" (p. 12). The acceptance and centering of people who have been downtrodden can demonstrate to students that even when society has deemed one unworthy of acknowledgment, the teacher and everyone in that collective space lavishes care on those rejected people even more. This is a supreme act of care, compassion, and empathy that embraces the notion that when one rises, everyone rises. With that type of support and care, students, confident in their own voices, begin to think critically, which can lead to autonomy. Therefore, fostering critical thinking and autonomy through dissent becomes possible when the teacher is committed to decentering their inherent power and (re)centering more balanced power among the class. In addition to autonomy, Mahat and Dollinger (2019) include greater student investment, better teacher–student connections, and greater productivity as by-products of a co-created learning space.

Each Person Gets What They Need

Though the dictionary defines "equity" as fairness and impartiality, I conceptualize equity as freedom from oppression and each person getting what they need. Although there are aspects of oppression that influence what happens in classrooms, the teacher may not be able to address all areas *from* the classroom. For example, a teacher can supply a meal for a student with no lunch, but cannot always address the larger issue of why that student has no food. However, the teacher can approach equity in that particular classroom by attending to what the student needs to function at that moment. Just as there is no single step to building a house, there is no single action to achieving equity. Rather, one can take a series of actions that approach equity. As such, equity is dually focused on (a) acknowledging that each person inhabits the world differently than the next person, and (b) changing policies and practices to account for varied ways of being.

When teachers engage in equitable practices in the classroom, they are committing to taking actions that both acknowledge students' lived experience and change their classroom policies to rid the space of oppression, "creating a space that values all voices requires clear understandings of privilege and oppression" (Hess, 2019, p. 100). Sometimes the best way to care for students is for teachers to manage the things in their direct control, i.e., their classrooms. Using a Freirean approach, teachers would start by articulating the oppression and privilege present in their classrooms, which would highlight avenues for change. These actions could lead students to understand the world differently, and therefore, navigate future oppressive situations and spaces better. At other times, teachers are able to expand the reach of their care. However, each situation is context-driven.

The attention to equitable actions is already anchored in intersectionality. Recall that intersectionality provides a lens through which we can examine the processes, practices, policies, and structures that increase the risk of students experiencing disadvantage or discrimination because of their intersecting identities (race, class, gender, sexuality, age, ability, etc.). This then focuses on the diverse experiences each individual carries rather than the experiences of a group of people. Therefore, an approach to teaching that is built on a philosophy of intersectionality would ensure that each person receives the care that they need by embracing all student voices, especially those voices that challenge authority and might emerge from a place of fear of retaliation. In the end, when teachers listen to student voices, they are able to facilitate the care that students need, which may engender greater trust and lead to deepening critical thinking and autonomy.

More Than the Sum of Their Parts/Acceptance of the Whole Person

In teachers' initial interpretations of teaching music with a philosophy of intersectionality, some teachers attempted to embrace the concept with additive measures, such as adding a song in a different language to the curriculum or adding a genre that the teacher associates with most of the students in their classroom (Jones & Wijeyesinghe, 2011). For instance, if the school or surrounding community had a large Hispanic population, sometimes the teacher assumed that those students would be interested in studying and learning about Mariachi. Because of this assumption, the teacher added Mariachi to their pre-set curriculum in order to seem more accepting and more intersectional in their approach to teaching. What teachers who do this fail to realize is that intersectional teaching requires more than a shallow embrace of students' identities, or assumed identities. Intersectionality necessitates that teachers form the basis of their understanding of students from students themselves, and blend that understanding with the knowledge and skills that they have learned from their teaching experiences and teacher preparation (Freire & Macedo, 1987; Hess, 2019). Only embracing a component or assumed component of students' identities often has deleterious consequences.

In the above scenario, the teacher likely thought, "Most of these students are Hispanic, so we need to cover Mariachi so they will be able to connect music in my class to the rest of their lives" (see Lechuga & Schmidt, 2018). But that same student has other layers of identity that complicate being Hispanic. Here I refer to "complicate" in the sense that aspects of identity cannot be fully understood by a single matrix, so that making sense of the student's Hispanic background can only make sense while also taking into account their age, immigration status, generation, etc. All of these components influence and determine who shows up in the classroom. Therefore, all layers of identity must be taken into account together (Carastathis, 2016; Davis, 2008). As I have written previously, it is impossible to fully understand any person without acknowledging the overlapping aspects of their identity because "all [people] continuously and simultaneously navigate all parts of their identities" (Thomas-Durrell, 2019, p. 129). Picking apart the pieces of one's identity, highlighting single components, is not caring for the person as a whole. It is more of regarding the person additively, as the sum of their parts (Gardner & McKinzie, 2020), which is the exact opposite of complicating identity (Dill & Zambrana, 2009; Jones & Wijeyesinghe, 2011)—a key component of intersectionality.

Trust is the very foundation of all connections, and that trust is comprised of respect and care, care that will be empathetic and compassionate (Hendricks, 2018). Teachers gain the trust of their students when they seek to understand each student's interlocking layers of identity, when they see each student holistically.

Conclusion

Students learn better from teachers whom they respect and trust. Therefore, teachers have a critical role to play in what is possible within a process of co-creating knowledge. The gate is open to (re)imagine (Greene, 1980) what learning opportunities are possible (Pliner et al., 2011) when educators take an intersectional approach to teaching; when they embrace dissent and foster critical thinking and autonomy, ensuring all students receive the care they need and are accepted for their multilayered identities. Though many educators have had the best of intentions, there have been many times when their intentions did not breathe care into the lives of students. Some of this likely stems from centuries of teacher training centered around the myth that teachers must maintain "control" of "their" classroom at all times, and that to not be in control is a sign of weakness, a point that Hendricks (2018) writes about at length. However, an approach to teaching built on intersectionality is not concerned with having all or most of the control in the classroom. This type of teaching philosophy is built on care and mutual respect for all class participants. It makes space for varying perspectives and centers the lived experiences of people who continue to be regarded as less than. This level of intentionality to care necessitates a change in focus from the current approach to education. A teaching philosophy built on intersectionality, one that "involves changes and modifications in content, approaches, structures and strategies" (UNESCO, 2005, p. 13), offers a deeper level of inclusion than perhaps has been commonly imagined. Teachers facilitate richer learning when they work alongside students, learn from the multiple perspectives present in the class, and highlight and center intersectionality in their classrooms (Bešić, 2020; García & Ortiz, 2013; UNESCO, 2005).

Self-actualization occurs when students begin to imagine and (re)imagine the possibilities of what their lives could be and how they might navigate their communities, cultures, and the world. Self-actualization is only possible when we are able to be our true selves openly. As Audre Lorde (1984) states,

> My fullest concentration of energy is available to me only when I integrate all the parts of who I am, openly ... without the restrictions of externally imposed definition. Only then can I bring myself and my energies as a whole to the service of those struggles which I embrace as part of my living. (pp. 120–121)

If music teachers' main goal is to assist students in achieving self-actualization, then it is critical for teachers to (re)imagine what is possible in the classroom, by establishing an environment of care and compassion through a philosophy built on intersectionality. Accepting students holistically includes embracing the intersecting layers of their identities instead of narrow conceptions of their identities. An additional part of teaching from an intersectional philosophy includes addressing how societal power and privilege influence education, which is accomplished by centering the experiences of people of color. Two specific ways educators can go about achieving holistic care in music teaching include (a) fostering critical thinking and autonomy by embracing verbal and nonverbal dissent, and (b) (re)establishing the classroom as a co-created space. Both of these approaches help develop the trust needed for genuine connections in intersectional teaching. Though the process of changing educational systems is a long-term goal that will not occur overnight, it is imperative for music educators to remain vigilant in adopting an intersectional approach to music teaching. By teaching with this approach of holistic acceptance, teachers truly demonstrate their care for students.

References

African American Proverbs. (2014, June 5). "*You a lie and the truth ain't in ya!*" https://blkproverbs.tumblr.com/post/87922418725/you-a-lie-and-the-truth-aint-in-ya

Beaumont, J. (1998). Administrator and researcher: Conflicting dual roles in directing a school-university partnership. *Urban Education*, 32(5), 645–660. https://doi.org/10.1177%2F0042085998032005007

Bešić, E. (2020). Intersectionality: A pathway towards inclusive education? *Prospects: Comparative Journal of Curriculum, Learning, and Assessment*, 49(3–4), 111–122. https://doi.org/10.1007/s11125-020-09461-6

Bonds, A., & Inwood, J. (2015). Beyond white privilege: Geographies of white supremacy and settler colonialism. *Progress in Human Geography*, 40(6), 715–733. http://doi.org/10.1177/0309132515611316

Bourdieu, P. (1973). Cultural reproduction and social reproduction. In R. Brown (Ed.), *Knowledge, education, and cultural change: Papers in the sociology of education* (pp. 71–112). Tavistock.

Bovill, C. (2013). Students and staff co-creating curricula: A new trend or an old idea we never got around to implementing? In C. Rust (Ed.), *Improving student learning through research and scholarship: 20 years of ISL* (pp. 96–108). University of Glasgow.

Bowleg, L. (2021). Evolving intersectionality within public health: From analysis to action. *American Journal of Public Health, 111*(1), 88–90. https://doi.org/10.2105/AJPH/2020/306031

Carastathis, A. (2016). *Intersectionality: Origins, contestations, horizons.* University of Nebraska Press.

Cohen, J., McCabe, E., Michelli, N. M., & Pickeral, T. (2009). School climate: Research, policy, practice, and teacher education. *Teachers College Record, 111*(1), 180–213. https://doi.org/10.1177%2F016146810911100108

Crenshaw, K. (1989). Demarginalizing the intersection of race and sex: A Black feminist critique of antidiscrimination doctrine, feminist theory and antiracist politics. *University of Chicago Legal Forum, 140,* 139–167.

Crenshaw, K. (1991). Mapping the margins: Intersectionality, identity politics, and violence against women of color. *Stanford Law Review, 43*(6), 1241–1299. https://doi.org/10.2307/1229039

Davis, K. (2008). Intersectionality as buzzword: A sociology of science perspective on what makes a feminist theory successful. *Feminist Theory, 9*(1), 67–85. https://doi.org/10.1177/1464700108086364

Dill, B. (2009). Intersections, identities, and inequalities in higher education. In B. Dill & R. Zambrana (Eds.), *Emerging intersections: Race, class, and gender in theory, policy, and practice* (pp. 229–252). Rutgers University Press.

Dill, B., & Zambrana, R. (2009). Critical thinking about inequality: An emerging lens. In B. Dill & R. Zambrana (Eds.), *Emerging intersections: Race, class, and gender in theory, policy, and practice* (pp. 1–21). Rutgers University Press.

Dzodan, F. (2011, October 10). *My feminism will be intersectional or it will be bullshit.* Tiger Beatdown. http://tigerbeatdown.com/2011/10/10/my-feminism-will-be-intersectional-or-it-will-be-bullshit/

Escalante, S. (2020). Exploring access, intersectionality, and privilege in undergraduate music education courses. *Journal of Music Teacher Education, 29*(2), 22–37. https://doi.org/10.1177/1057083719873981

Freire, P. (2000). *Pedagogy of the oppressed.* Bloomsbury.

Freire, P., & Macedo, D. (1987). *Literacy: Reading the word and the world.* Routledge.

García, S., & Ortiz, A. (2013). Intersectionality as a framework for transformative research in special education. *Multiply Voices for Ethnically Diverse Exceptional Learners, 13*(2), 32–47. https://doi.org/10.56829/muvo.13.1.x2u036p588087pu0

Gardner, J., & McKinzie, A. (2020). Embodying inequality: Using ethnographic data to teach intersectionality. *Teaching Sociology, 48*(3), 184–195. https://doi.org/10.1177/0092055X20922896

Glasser, W. (1998). *Choice theory in the classroom.* HarperCollins.

Goodboy, A. (2011). Instructional dissent in the college classroom. *Communication Education, 60*(3), 296–313. https://doi.org/10.1080/03634523.2010.537756

Greene, M. (1980). Notes on aesthetic education. In M. Greene (Ed.), *Variations on a Blue Guitar: The Lincoln Center Lectures on Aesthetic Education* (pp. 7–43). Teachers College Press.

Held, V. (2006). *The ethics of care: Personal, political, and global.* Oxford University Press.
Hendricks, K. S. (2018). *Compassionate music teaching.* Rowman & Littlefield.
Hendricks, K. S. (2021). Authentic connection in music education. In K. S. Hendricks & J. Boyce-Tillman (Eds.), *Authentic connection: Music, spirituality, and wellbeing* (pp. 237–253). Peter Lang.
Hess, J. (2019). *Music education for social change: Constructing an activist music education.* Routledge.
Heylighen, F. (1992). A cognitive-systemic reconstruction of Maslow's theory of self-actualization. *Behavioral Science, 37*(1), 39–58. https://doi.org/10.1002/bs.3830370105
Jones, S., & Wijeyesinghe, C. (2011). The promises and challenges of teaching from an intersectional perspective: Core components and applied strategies. *New Directions for Teaching and Learning, 125,* 11–20. https:/doi.org/10.1002/tl.429
Kassing, J. (1997). Articulating, antagonizing, and displacing: A model of employee dissent. *Communication Studies, 48*(4), 311–332. https://doi.org/10/1080/10510979709368510
Lechuga, C., & Schmidt, M. (2018). Cultural straddling: The double life of a mariachi music education major. In B. Talbot (Ed.), *Marginalized voices in music education* (pp. 80–98). Routledge.
London, M., & Van Buskirk, B. (2018). The co-created classroom: From teacher/student to mentor/apprentice. In J. Neal (Ed.), *Handbook of personal and organizational transformation* (pp. 1051–1080). Springer.
Lorde, A. (1984). *Sister outsider: Essays and speeches.* Crossing Press.
Mahat, M., & Dollinger, M. (2019). Mind the gap: Co-created learning spaces in higher education. In K. Fisher (Ed.), *The translational design of universities: An evidence-based Approach* (pp. 245–258). Sense Publishers.
Maslow, A. (1943). A theory of human motivation. *Psychological Review, 50*(4), 370–396. https://doi.org/10.1037/h0054346
Miller, K. (2021). A light in students' lives: K-12 teachers' experiences (re)building caring relationships during remote learning. *Online Learning, 25*(1), Article 1150134. https://doi.org/10.24059/olj.v25i1.2486
Noddings, N. (2005). *The challenge to care in schools* (2nd ed.). Teachers College Press.
Osterman, K. F. (2000). Students' need for belonging in the school community. *Review of Educational Research, 70*(3), 323–367. https://doi.org/10.3102/00346543070003323
Osterman, K. F. (2010). Teacher practice and students' sense of belonging. In T. Lovat, R. Toomey, & N. Clement (Eds.), *International research handbook on values education and student wellbeing* (pp. 239–260). Springer. https://doi.org/10.1007/978-90-481-8675-4_15
Paavola, S., Lipponen, L., & Hakkarainen, K. (2004). Models of innovative knowledge communities and three metaphors of learning. *Review of Educational Research, 74*(4), 557–576. https://doi.org/10.3102%2F00346543074004557
Pliner, S., Iuzzini, J., & Banks, C. (2011). Using an intersectional approach to deepen collaborative teaching. *New Directions for Teaching and Learning, 125,* 43–51. https://onlinelibrary.wiley.com/doi/pdf/10.1002/tl.432
Resnick, M., Bearman, P., Blum, R., Bauman, K. E., Harris, K., Jones, J., Tabor, J., Beuhring, T., Sieving, R., Shew, M., Ireland, M., Bearinger, L., & Udry, J. (1997). Protecting adolescents from harm. *JAMA, 278*(10), 823–832. https://doi.org/10.1001/jama.278.10.823
Thomas-Durrell, L. (2019). *"Like a double, triple hate": Music education at the intersections of race, religion, and sexuality in the Bible Belt* (Publication No. 22620429) [Doctoral dissertation, Michigan State University]. ProQuest Dissertations and Theses Global.

Thomas-Durrell, L. (2021). Unlearning academic music education: How music education erases already-present musical identities. In D. Bradley & J. Hess (Eds.), *Trauma and resilience in music education: Haunted melodies* (pp. 110–124). Routledge. https://doi.org/10.4324/9781003124207-7

UNESCO. (2005). *Guidelines for inclusion: Ensuring access to education for all.* UNESCO.

Valenzuela, A. (1999). *Subtractive schooling: U.S.-Mexican youth and the politics of caring.* State University of New York Press.

CHAPTER 15

ACCOMPANYING LGBTQIA+ STUDENTS IN THE MUSIC CLASSROOM

JUSTIN MCMANUS AND BRUCE CARTER

CARE HANDBOOK TOPICS

Co-creating caring relationships
Identity expressions
Musical development
Social activism and critical consciousness

OVER the past decade, research focused on LGBTQIA+ issues in music education has blossomed. Since Bergonzi (2009) called for a critical examination of heteronormative practices within the music classroom, scholars have explored the experiences, attitudes, and beliefs of LGBTQIA+ students, teachers, and preservice instructors. Educators play an important role in creating an affirming, welcoming, and compassionate environment for their students, particularly those who identify as a sexual and/or gender minority and face increased levels of bullying, harassment, and separation (Kosciw et al., 2020). LGBTQIA+ students may find the artistic expression and opportunities for social engagement within the music classroom as affirming and empowering. However, students may also face isolation, frequent micro- or macroaggressions, and heteronormative reinforcement within music spaces (Bergonzi et al., 2016; Carter, 2011). We therefore examine the role of the music educator in partnering and journeying with their LGBTQIA+ students within the context of *accompaniment*.

Accompaniment is ubiquitous in our music-making, from piano reductions carefully tailored for solo recitals to large ensemble performances. Both authors of this chapter have experienced the excitement, hesitation, and sense of vulnerability common in accompanied performance, an intimate relationship shared by many within the field. We similarly conceive of the relationship between student and teacher as a form of accompaniment, using our musical vocabulary in pursuit of a more empathetic, compassionate vehicle for understanding the musical experience. In accompanied performance, musicians engage in a nuanced partnership, critically listening for changes in style, phrasing, tempo, dynamic contrast, and articulation. When conditions allow, parties engage in active problem-solving, identifying areas of concern and offering solutions. Connections with our students must also be characterized by a critical, active listening that allows us to hear, interpret, and adjust to our students' needs and the conditions of their performance. Although it may be easiest to envision our role as *aiding*—or remedying problems for—our students, we offer the alternative of *accompanying*, or engaging in a longer-term relationship with our students:

> There's an element of mystery, of openness, of trust, in accompaniment. The companion, the accompagnateur, says: "I'll go with you and support you on your journey wherever it leads. I'll share your fate for a while"—and by "a while," I don't mean a little while. Accompaniment is about sticking with a task until it's deemed completed—not by the accompagnateur, but by the person being accompanied. (Farmer, 2013, p. 234)

Accompaniment between teacher and student would ideally result in fewer product- and task-driven activities and in a more *empathetic* experience for both parties, "acknowledging each individual's life experience and understanding of the world" (Taylor, 2018, p. 56). Such an understanding can be understood under the umbrella of compassion in music education as a form of "mature empathy" (Hendricks, 2018, p. 57), which calls on individuals to better understand worldviews and contexts rather than simply experiences or ways or thinking. The notion of accompaniment in music education also aligns with Hendricks's (2021) notion of educators and students *caring with* each other rather than a model in which a teacher *cares for* their students. The latter constructs a hierarchical relationship between teacher and student, whereas the former allows for a mutual journey of trust, compassion, and grace. For LGBTQIA+ students engaged in the musical experience, an accompanied journey may allow us to collectively move beyond the confines of the "safe" music classroom and into one of authenticity, grace, and empowerment.

We continue this chapter with a brief review of recent developments in LGBTQIA+ scholarship, including key terms and trends in education and music education. We then offer two vignettes, each an example of how support, care, partnership, and compassion impacted the experiences of LGBTQIA+ students in our respective careers. Next, we provide an analysis and discussion of each scenario through the lens of accompaniment, interrogating how students were or were not accompanied in their journey as a queer member of a music classroom. Finally, we present implications for educators who wish to engage in a more empathetic form of teaching in pursuit of a braver musical space.

Recent Developments in LGBTQIA+ Music Education Literature

We begin the next section by briefly examining recent developments in LGBTQIA+ scholarship within the field of music education. Areas of interest have included the experiences of LGBTQIA+ students and music educators, preservice teacher education programs, the inclusion of queer content in programming, and aspects such as concert attire and attendance rosters.

Save and Brave Spaces in the Music Classroom

Although earlier scholarship has rightfully focused on the music classroom as a "safe space" for LGBTQIA+ students, educators have been pushing for the concepts of authenticity, resilience, and courage for queer students and educators alike (e.g., Goodrich, 2020; Thomas-Durrell, 2019) in pursuit of building "brave spaces" in which students may contest, challenge, or subvert restrictive or oppressive conditions placed on them. Numerous gender and sexual minority students participate in school music programs (Kosciw et al., 2014), and often find their music-making serves as a "release" from their daily stresses, outlets for artistic creation, spaces for forming social relationships, and opportunities to explore their queerness (Hansen, 2016; Shane, 2020). However, music teachers may still reinforce hetero- and cisnormative practices and content that may be viewed as hurtful or exclusive to LGBTQIA+ students (Bergonzi, 2015).

Preservice Training and Professional Development

Music educators frequently cite largely positive attitudes toward working with LGBTQIA+ students, but often cite lack of preservice training and professional development as significant concerns (Garrett & Spano, 2017; Silveira & Goff, 2016). Some college music education resources may also reinforce heteronormative and cisnormative attitudes that are then passed along to preservice educators through a favoring of supposedly masculine repertoire selections, conflating gender identity with vocal register, and recommending traditionally gendered ensemble attire (McBride & Palkki, 2020). LGBTQIA+ music education majors may generally feel supported during their undergraduate education (Taylor et al., 2020), but often grapple with the intersection of their queer and educator identities and the decision of being "out" to their peers and students (Minette, 2018), as well as their desire for peer mentoring within the field (Talbot & Hendricks, 2016; see also Goodrich, 2020).

For many music students who identify as a sexual and/or gender minority, the inclusion of queer composers, song lyrics, and teaching language are important factors as they seek representation and positive expressions of LGBTQIA+ people in music (Hansen & Sears, 2019). Including resources and content about queer composers, performers, and music-makers generally may allow students to move beyond mere "safety" and experience possibilities for creation, joy, and affirmation important to their journey in a music classroom (Panetta, 2021).

A Word About Words

Before continuing, we feel it important to note that language related to sexual orientation and gender identity is constantly changing, which may be an unsettling or frustrating experience for educators who are still working to better understanding their LGBTQIA+ students. Even the acronym LGBTQIA+ (lesbian, gay, bisexual, transgender, queer/questioning, intersex, asexual, and others) as recommended by the American Psychological Organization is presented with the caveat that "there is not consensus about which abbreviation including or beyond LGBTQ to use" (American Psychological Association, 2020, p. 145).

Researchers have noted a generational shift in language, with many young adults identifying with the term "queer" to represent their sexual and gender identities more fully rather than disaggregrating them (Schreuder, 2021). For many students, the agency of choosing and using their own pronouns and names may help carve out that "braver" space, asserting their identity within a classroom and to their peers and teachers. Therefore, we move between specific LGBTQIA+ terms and use the word "queer" throughout this chapter to honor students' agency and suggest that accompaniment through language may take many forms.

VIGNETTES OF LGBTQIA+ ACCOMPANIMENT

In the following section, we present two vignettes of how we conceptualize *accompaniment* as representing the relationship between LGBTQIA+ students and their music teachers. In both cases, we describe the role of student and teacher in navigating mistakes, errors, and lack of communication to build a most positive, cohesive partnership in the music classroom. After each vignette, we offer a discussion of how the scenario impacted the educator and student, and how each may have gone differently given a more cohesive working knowledge and greater level of empathy.

Vignette 1

Mrs. Smith begins her day teaching in a hybrid model, sometimes utilizing Zoom, and occasionally holding classes in person. This morning, she begins this band class via

Zoom with students who have opted to not join in person due to the COVID-19 pandemic. Taking a quick sip of coffee, and gathering her energy to begin another long day, Mrs. Smith looks at the screen to call students' names to note attendance. After a few names, she calls the name of a student—Jarod—who then nervously whispers "here." It was then Mrs. Smith noted her mistake, she had called the roster according to the names displayed on Zoom, names that had been inputted into the records by the county, not the student. Immediately, she realized her mistake of calling Jarod a different name—by his dead name[1]—rather than utilizing his correct name.

Later in class, Mrs. Smith is rehearsing a piece of music and struggling to get the students to engage with the music. She tells a story of how, to her, the piece of music represents love, and the composer intended the work as a love song between a man and woman. But to connect with the student she extends the anecdote and describes how the work is deeply personal because it reflects the love and importance of her having children. She goes on to state that there is no love greater than that shared by a mother and a child, and relishes her connection and how she sees the connection between her feelings and the music they are rehearsing. Several of the students nervously twitch as her story unfolds. Finally, at the end of her story, Mrs. Smith realizes that she had assumed her language would engage and motivate, but to some, it did the opposite. One student, Sarah, raises her hand and states that not all great loves are between a man and woman, and that love can be found in same-sex couples, not just the heterosexual relationship as described. Natalie, a transgender student, raises her hand and states that not all women are capable of having children, some are trans, some women may have had chemo, and while it is moving that this love is important to her, it does nothing to help some of the students relate or engage with the work in a meaningful way. Mrs. Smith thanks the students for their comments and continues the rehearsal.

Discussion

We believe that the notion of *accompaniment* can be powerful and helpful for music teachers in a number of ways. In this vignette, Mrs. Smith has made some mistakes that some of the students either commented on or reacted to in deeply personal and emotional ways. The question now is, what next? In this case, Mrs. Smith calling the student by their dead name rather than their preferred was an honest mistake made in haste and due to the way the county controls the input of names. The student, Jarod, is well aware of Mrs. Smith's inclusivity and appreciates how she asks students at the beginning of the year for their preferred pronouns. Jarod also takes note of how Mrs. Smith shares the stories of past students, always mentioning that some students have transitioned, or that some students have same-sex partners, but never in a way that seemed different or forced. Rather, Jarod perceives her attempt to create a compassionate classroom as genuine and well-intentioned. Because of this trend of meaningful attempts at inclusivity

---

[1] A dead name is a name an individual receives at birth and no longer wishes to use (Lieberth, 2020). The use of a dead name may be traumatic for a student attempting to leave the name and its negative implications behind.

it is likely Mrs. Smith will apologize for making the mistake, and Jarod will graciously accept.

Part of the accompanist experience might include the notion of *grace*, that is to say a thoughtful and intentioned give and take during a performance. Additionally, as musicians know, no performance is ever perfect and often there is that moment of grace required where musicians have to flex to meet the needs of their musical partner. Music teaching has a similar push and pull, and the notion of grace can be important to teachers and students. In the case of Mrs. Smith, her stories or anecdotes were attempts to connect with students, but perhaps a bigger difficulty might be that, although personal stories might create connection, there is plenty of room for misinterpretation, misrepresentation, and overgeneralization. Mrs. Smith is likely offered grace by her students, because it is earned. She consistently makes an overt attempt to create a place of safety for students in her classroom. It is likely that the students, their parents, and the school administration are aware of Mrs. Smith's consistent work toward building a non-toxic classroom. Finally, the concept of grace goes both ways in both performing and in the classroom. The students too should be aware of the social capital[2] they are accruing through their actions and engagement in the classroom. We stress the need to move away from a "got you" culture that seeks to punish a mistake, but rather consider the multitude of variables required for a healthy classroom.

Vignette 2

Mr. Barrington becomes uncomfortable with gendered language after one of his students, Alex, comes out as non-binary to him in an email over the summer. He switches the name of the Women's Choir to the Treble Choir. Weeks before the end-of-semester concert, Mr. Barrington meets with members of the Treble Choir to discuss concert expectations and dress code. After Mr. Barrington commences the meeting by suggesting that students purchase their traditional, black full-length dresses, Alex raises their hand and asks, "may I wear a tuxedo for the concert?" Mr. Barrington and the other students sit in silence for a moment, and the choral director asks Alex to see him after the meeting. After a discussion with Alex and his department chairperson, Mr. Barrington announces that students will be invited to wear "power black" for the concert, including dresses and tuxedos.

In preparation for the school's concert, Mr. Barrington seeks input from students to select the final piece of their program. Wishing to include more diverse composers, Mr. Barrington asks if students have suggestions and lists several categories of underrepresented composers from whose works he would like to choose. Gesturing to Alex, Mr. Barrington adds, "and queer composers" before moving on. Alex is momentarily

---

[2] According to Jones (2010), social capital is defined as "is a disposition towards and practice of cooperating with others. Such cooperation is based on values and interpersonal skills that foster cooperation such as honesty, honour, empathy and trustworthiness" (p. 294). Accumulating social capital may allow a student to better understand the norms, expectations, and cultural knowledge critical to building and sustaining relationships with others.

startled by the distinction but does not say anything for the remainder of the meeting. Although Mr. Barrington wanted to signal to Alex that he deemed LGBTQIA+ composers to be an important part of his repertoire list, Alex felt isolated and embarrassed by the unexpected attention in front of their peers. Alex later sends an email to Mr. Barrington acknowledging that he meant well but requesting that he not single them out in future meetings or rehearsals.

Discussion

In the second vignette, we present another demonstration of how *accompaniment* plays an important role in the lives of music students who are navigating structures (e.g., repertoire selection and concert attire) that many non-LGBTQIA+ students and educators take for granted. As we noted earlier, to accompany someone is to journey with them beyond single events, collaborating and sharing in their experiences. After Alex came out to him as non-binary, Mr. Barrington listened critically and connected his student's stated need to a remedy. Mr. Barrington may have either not considered concert attire or was actively attempting to preserve a traditional element of his program, but in either case was willing to engage with his student. When Mr. Barrington requested that Alex speak with him after the full meeting, the caesura may have given both parties an opportunity to reflect on the request and formulate solutions.

When Mr. Barrington asks Alex to offer the names of queer composers for inclusion in the choir's concert program, he engages in a moment of both consonant understanding and dissonant spotlighting. The director understands the need for diversity and inclusion, again connecting his student's gender identity to a larger thread within music education: repertoire selection. However, Mr. Barrington's decision to openly ask Alex about queer composers may represent a form of misinterpretation and tension, putting Alex on the spot and asking them to engage in queer discourse when they may not have been prepared to do so. Mr. Barrington may have likely thought he was showing Alex grace and agency in asking them to be more engaged in the repertoire process, and Alex likewise expresses grace and gratitude for Mr. Barrington's good-faith effort while also making a firm recommendation for future interactions. Alex may have been more prepared to share their thoughts given a more discrete way of sharing or advance notice. Additionally, Alex's non-binary identity does not, in and of itself, indicate their knowledge of queer musicians or composers. Just as in any musical relationship defined by accompaniment, it is important for educators and students to seek to correct miscommunication; listen with the intent of adjusting; and offer solutions in a flexible, understanding manner.

Implications for Practice

Through the presentation and discussion of the above vignettes, we attempt to apply a concept familiar to many musicians, accompaniment, as a metaphor for relationship building and journeying with our LGBTQIA+ students for whom building shared experiences with faculty in a school setting may be particularly important. We now turn to implications for our field and best practices for how educators might best form and foster positive, affirming relationships with their LGBTQIA+ students. Continuing to borrow from our common musical vocabulary, we offer recommendations organized by the concepts of *critical listening*, *adaptability*, *communication*, and *feedback*. We then end the chapter with a brief summary.

Critical Listening

In accompanying our LGBTQIA+ students from safe spaces to braver ones, we must ensure we are listening to rather than simply hearing their voices. Petress (1999) asserted that "unlike hearing, which is a physiological passive activity, listening is an *active* cognitive process" (para. 2, emphasis added). During a musical engagement, accompanist and accompagnateur are constantly engaged in critical listening. Phrasing, style, and tempo are negotiated constantly, and parties hone in carefully on their partner(s) as the role of the "lead" is passed back and forth. Performers must not only maintain an active presence within the musical line but also anticipate the subsequent lines.

If a student feels safe enough to come out to and disclose their queer identity to their educator, the next step is *anticipating* how the words they speak or words they write impact the totality of the music classroom. For example, a student may volunteer their pronouns (e.g., "he/him" or "they/him") during a conversation. To hear that student may be to honor their pronouns on forms or documents, while to listen critically may prompt a thorough examination of gendered language (e.g., "good morning, ladies and gentlemen/boys and girls") to *all* students in their classroom. A student may also wish to equally engage in active, critical listening, and we encourage educators to share their own journey with learning about LGBTQIA+ issues. In the authors' experiences, students whose teachers disclose their own desire to learn, grow, and identify their own blind spots are generally shown tremendous grace and patience by their students. Teachers who display vulnerability and openness through genuine expressions of apology may foster more compassionate relationships between themselves and their students through "relational trust" (Hendricks, 2018, p. 49).

Conversely, critical listening applies to words spoken *about* or *around* our LGBTQIA+ students. Perhaps a student has not come out to their teacher, but is known to some or many of their peers. How do those students talk about queer issues in the music classroom? Students who feel comfortable engaging in homophobic or transphobic rhetoric in a music environment may effectively reclaim and weaponize that space's safety. In both of the earlier vignettes, teachers engaged in conversations with students with a desire to better understand the ways in which their instruction impacted their music students' experiences. Natalie, for instance, advised Mrs. Smith that, although her attempts to make her instruction more relatable through talking about relationships, the heteronormativity of those relationships might actually be harmful. Alex's email to Mr. Barrington addressed his potentially well-meaning statement about "queer composers" for its power to single out a queer student who may not wish to be identified. For a student unsure about the safety and welcome of a music classroom, observing an educator who listens to and then actively disrupts anti-LGBTQIA+ discourse may find it easier to live a more authentic version of themselves.

Adaptability

A feature of live, performed music is the tendency for things to go wrong. At any time, musical partners may miss a cue, skip a note, or endure a mechanical malfunction on their instrument. The lights in a recital hall may suddenly go out, or the air conditioning might suddenly break. It has been established that many music educators (and teachers of all subjects, to that point) lack a breadth of preservice and in-service training related to their LGBTQIA+ students. An adaptive educator will seek to be informed and apply that information to their teaching. That is not to say that even a better informed educator will not make mistakes—we have all been there—but rather that their desire to meet their students' changing needs drives their actions. The act of being adaptable to our students is considering *what* needs to be changed or altered and *why* such adjustments are needed in the first place. Attending to only the issue at hand, for instance a student's discomfort at language used during a lesson, addresses the symptom rather than underlying condition. Part of our adaptability and flexibility consists of examining why we may feel resistance toward change.

Although we are not advocating for a wholesale replacement of ensemble names (e.g., Men's Chorus), it may be helpful to interrogate why the *idea* of changing an ensemble name may feel difficult or uncomfortable. Conditions may require student and teacher alike to move far beyond their comfort zone, using language or addressing aspects of their musicking that had not previously been assessed. In the second vignette above, Mr. Barrington allowed Alex to wear a tuxedo for their ensemble concert, possibly disrupting the traditionally gendered expectations of student attire. Students may also need to be adaptable and flexible in understanding an individual teacher's constraints or honest mistakes, similar to Jarod's show of grace in acknowledging his teacher's good intentions despite being dead-named.

Communication

Communication during an accompanied musical performance takes many forms, from eye contact to a subtle gesture to indicate the length of a fermata. How we communicate our comfort with and support of our LGBTQIA+ students may also take myriad forms, many often taken for granted in our daily lives. Although we may feel comfortable speaking with an individual student, parent, peer teacher, or administrator, speaking more broadly about queer issues to a larger group may feel uncomfortable. Looking down, lowering one's voice, or turning away from a group when discussing LGBTQIA+ issues may signal our discomfort to our students. Similarly, we might note our students' body language and verbal communication for any signs of discomfort or distress. Perhaps an educator assumes that by speaking often of a queer composer or performing artist during class, they are honoring a gay or trans student. However, if that student suddenly bristles or appears anxious, that well-intended gesture may be doing more harm than good.

Feedback

After a rehearsal or sight-reading session, one of the most importance components of preparing for the subsequent performance is feedback. An honest, open conversation between all parties regarding the positives and negatives of each person's contribution may be uncomfortable, but allows for issues to be resolved while mitigating resentment or frustration. Similarly, teachers and their LGBTQIA+ students may wish to check in on a regular basis to discuss repertoire, logistics for field trips, or other issues within the school building. Educators may be unaware of changing trends in queer discourse (for instance, the use of the word "queer" at all!) and may want to seek resources from openly queer colleagues who are willing to engage in discussion, practitioner journals, and guides from organizations such as the Human Rights Campaign.

It will be important for educators to encourage students to be open about areas of concern (e.g., rehearsal language, bullying from peers, or name change procedures), so students are less likely to assume their teacher is disinterested or uncaring. If music teachers find having a direct conversation with their student(s) uncomfortable or difficult, an anonymous drop-box or online form may inform the instructor of concerns without outing or putting undue pressure on a student. It may also be helpful to keep a running list of concerns, moments of joy, and action items throughout a season or year. Educators may find receiving feedback from students as disconcerting or potentially undermining their authority in the classroom, resulting in what may be perceived as a defensive or dismissive attitude. However, Stone and Heen (2014) posit that seeking and incorporating feedback may be viewed positively, adding, "someone who's asking for coaching is more likely to take what is said to heart and genuinely improve" (p. 5). Although it may be common for teachers to get lost in concert planning, budgeting, and attendance, many students will remember if asked to repeat their same concerns or give the same feedback multiple times.

Each of the preceding four aspects of accompaniment with music teacher and music student are manifestations of compassionate musical interactions. Hendricks (2018) posited that "compassionate music teachers act as guides, supports, and champions of students' self-selected dreams, using the students' own aspirations for musical expression as a catalyst for emphasizing the practice of diverse technical skills" (p. 5). To that end, teachers may best show grace to their students in recognizing and celebrating numerous lived realities, and in turn may accept demonstrations of their students' grace toward them as both parties strive for a more empathetic and just music-learning environment.

SUMMARY

In this chapter, we used the metaphor of *accompaniment* to highlight the importance of relationship building with our LGBTQIA+ students. Although support and resources for queer students have grown exponentially over the past decades, it is imperative that we strive to move beyond creating spaces that are simply safe and foster spaces that inspire courage, action, and empowerment. By accompanying our students along their musical journey, we offer them and ourselves an opportunity to grow, experience support, and find their voice. We encourage educators of every grade level and musical environment to view their relationship with their LGBTQIA+ students as one of accompaniment, building more empathetic and compassionate musicking.

REFERENCES

American Psychological Association. (2020). *Publication manual of the American Psychological Association* (7th ed.).

Bergonzi, L. (2009). Sexual orientation and music education: Continuing a tradition. *Music Educators Journal, 96*(2), 21–25. https://www.jstor.org/stable/40666402

Bergonzi, L. (2015). Gender and sexual diversity challenges (for socially just) music education. In C. Benedict, G. Spruce, P. K. Schmidt, & P. Woodford (Eds.), *The Oxford handbook of social justice and music education* (pp. 221–237). Oxford University Press.

Bergonzi, L., Carter, B. A., & Garrett, M. L. (2016). Establishing identity, finding community, and embracing fluidity. *Bulletin for the Council of Research in Music Education*, (207–208), 9–23. https://doi.org/10.5406/bulcouresmusedu.207-208.0009

Carter, B. A. (2011). A safe education for all: Recognizing and stemming harassment in music classes and ensembles. *Music Educators Journal, 97*(4), 29–32. https://doi.org/10.1177%2F0027432111405342

Farmer, P. (2013). Accompaniment as policy: Harvard Kennedy School of Government commencement. In J. Weigel (Ed.), *To repair the world: Paul Farmer speaks to the next generation* (pp. 233–247). University of California Press.

Garrett, M. L., & Spano, F. P. (2017). An examination of LGBTQ-inclusive strategies used by practicing music educators. *Research Studies in Music Education, 39*(1), 39–56. https://doi.org/10.1177/1321103X17700702

Goodrich, A. (2020). Counterpoint in the music classroom: Creating an environment of resilience with peer mentoring and LGBTQIA+ students. *International Journal of Music Education, 38*(4), 582–592. https://doi.org/10.1177/0255761420949373

Hansen, E. M. (2016). *Roles of music making in the lives of sexual and gender minority youth* [Doctoral dissertation, University of Michigan]. Deep Blue. http://hdl.handle.net/2027.42/120873

Hansen, E. M., & Sears, C. A. Q. (2019). Gender and sexual diversity in music teacher education. In C. M. Conway, K. Pellegrino, A. M. Stanley, & C. West. *The Oxford handbook of preservice music teacher education in the United States* (pp. 575–602). Oxford University Press. https://doi.org/10.1093/oxfordhb/9780190671402.013.27

Hendricks, K. S. (2018). *Compassionate music teaching*. Rowman & Littlefield.

Hendricks, K. S. (2021). Authentic connection in music education: A chiastic essay. In K. S. Hendricks & J. Boyce-Tillman (Eds.), *Authentic connection: Music, spirituality, and wellbeing* (pp. 237–253). Peter Lang.

Jones, P. M. (2010). Developing social capital: A role for music education and community music in fostering civic engagement and intercultural understanding. *International Journal of Community Music*, 3(2), 291–302. https://doi.org/10.1386/ijcm.3.2.291_1

Kosciw, J. G., Clark, C. M., Truong, N. L., & Zongrone, A. D. (2020). *The 2019 National School Climate Survey: The experiences of lesbian, gay, bisexual, transgender, and queer youth in our nation's schools*. GLSEN. https://www.glsen.org/sites/default/files/2020-10/NSCS-2019-Full-Report_0.pdf

Kosciw, J. G., Greytak, E. A., Palmer, N. A., & Boesen, M. J. (2014). *The 2013 National School Climate Survey: The experiences of lesbian, gay, bisexual and transgender youth in our nation's schools*. GLSEN. https://www.glsen.org/sites/default/files/2020-03/GLSEN-2013-National-School-Climate-Survey-Full-Report.pdf

Lieberth, M. R. (2020). *What's in a name? Lived experiences of transgender college students using a preferred name policy* [Doctoral dissertation, Cleveland State University]. OhioLINK. http://rave.ohiolink.edu/etdc/view?acc_num=csu1607697772575963

McBride, N. R., & Palkki, J. (2020). Big boys don't cry (or sing) . . . still? A modern exploration of gender misogyny, and homophobia in college choral methods texts. *Music Education Research*, 22(4), 408–420. https://doi.org/10.1080/14613808.2020.1784862

Minette, S. M. (2018). *"Do I really want to do this now?": Negotiations of sexual identity and professional identity: An intergenerational collaboration with six gay and lesbian K-12 music educators* (Publication No. 10979676) [Doctoral dissertation, Arizona State University]. ProQuest Dissertations Publishing.

Panetta, B. J. (2021). Understanding an invisible minority: A literature review of LGBTQ+ persons in music education. *Update: Applications of Research in Music Education*, 40(1), 18–26. https://doi.org/10.1177/87551233211015730

Petress, K. C. (1999). Listening: A vital skill. *Journal of Instructional Psychology*, 26(4), 261–262.

Schreuder, M. C. (2021). Safe spaces, agency, and resistance: A metasynthesis of LGBTQ language usage. *Journal of LGBT Youth*, 18(3), 256–272. https://doi.org/10.1080/19361653.2019.1706685

Shane, S. L. (2020). *Queering the classroom: A study of performativity and musical engagement in high school* (Publication No. 27929869) [Doctoral dissertation, Boston University]. ProQuest Dissertations Publishing.

Silveira, J. M., & Goff, S. C. (2016). Music teachers' attitudes toward transgender students and supportive school practices. *Journal of Research in Music Education*, 64(2), 138–158. https://doi.org/10.1177/0022429416647048

Stone, D., & Heen, S. (2014, January). Finding the coaching in criticism: The right ways to receive feedback. *Harvard Business Review*, 108–111. https://hbr.org/2014/01/find-the-coaching-in-criticism

Talbot, B., & Hendricks, K. S. (2016, October 24–25). *Including LGBTQ voices: A narrative of two gay music teachers* [Paper presentation]. Diversity Research Symposium 2014: From Research to Action conference, Muncie, IN, United States. http://cardinalscholar.bsu.edu/bitstream/handle/123456789/200530/2014%20Diversity%20Research%20Symposium%20v7%20Article%202.pdf?sequence=1

Taylor, D. (2018). Research-to-resource: Dignity for all: LGBTQ students and empathetic teaching. *Update: Applications of Research in Music Education, 36*(3), 55–58. https://doi.org/10.1177/8755123318761914

Taylor, D. M., Talbot, B. C., Holmes, E. J., & Petrie, T. (2020). Experiences of LGBTQ+ students in music education programs across Texas. *Journal of Music Teacher Education, 30*(1), 11–23. https://doi.org/10.1177/1057083720935610

Thomas-Durrell, L. (2019). Being your "true self": The experiences of two gay music educators who teach in the Bible Belt. *Music Education Research, 22*(1), 29–41. https://doi.org/10.1080/14613808.2019.1703921

CHAPTER 16

COMPASSION AND CARE THROUGH MUSICAL SOCIAL EMOTIONAL LEARNING

SCOTT N. EDGAR, KARA IRELAND D'AMBROSIO, AND ELISE HACKL-BLUMSTEIN

Care Handbook Topics

Co-creating caring relationships
Identity expressions
Social activism and critical consciousness
Wellbeing and human flourishing

Introduction

The implicit connections between social emotional learning (SEL) and music education are becoming more explicit as teachers, researchers, and policymakers further a vision to collaboratively build artistic literacy and fluency, along with lifelong social and emotional competence (ArtsEdSEL, 2021).[1] Many motivators drive this increased attention, including student mental health, the prevalence and intensity of trauma, and amplified understanding that the arts provide a space for meaningful relationships and experiences conducive for SEL (Edgar & Morrison, 2020). All of these understandings position the student at the center of focus for musical instruction, necessitating care

---

[1] https://artsedsel.org/

and compassion focused on the needs of individual students. For SEL to deepen social emotional competence and nourish and advance the artistic processes (create, perform/present/produce, respond, and connect), it should be approached compassionately, intentionally, embedded into the musical instruction, and be sustained (ArtsEdSEL Framework, 2020).[2] The lines between SEL and music can be blurred to a point that casual observers (and students) do not know where one ends and the other begins. However, many music education models represent environments that are not caring and compassionate and do not nurture life skills. SEL does not automatically make a space caring; compassionate and caring SEL in music education must be a choice (Rizzuto, 2021).

Terms like "trauma-informed," "equity," "academic learning loss," and "emotional setbacks" saturate educational narratives. It is clear that certain competencies are needed for students and teachers to adapt to this tumultuous uncertainty. Strategies need to be embedded in school processes to help students and teachers forge a path forward built on caring relationships. SEL skills are seen as foundational to managing these collective difficulties. Implementation of SEL in K-12 schools is growing steadily, and key to its further expansion and effective delivery is the role of music educators.

SEL is defined as building capacity in the areas of self-awareness, self-management, social-awareness, relationship skills, and responsible decision-making (CASEL, n.d.). The objective is for students, teachers, and communities to better understand their emotions, and their root causes, and compassionately envision and enact productive actions from them. The language of SEL is purposeful. It is not *self-control*; instead, *self-management*. Control is silencing ("You shouldn't feel that way, control your emotions"); management is empowering. Typically, educational priorities may not have reflected students' needs. This priority is often discovered through engaging in caring relationships and dialogue (Edgar, 2014). The music classroom can be a place to foster and teach students to care through prioritizing the individual (Edgar, 2014): "We should want more from our educational efforts than adequate academic achievement, and we will not achieve even that meager success unless our children believe that they themselves are cared for and learn to care for others" (Noddings, 1995, p. 675–676).

SEL holds deep potential to move students and teachers past academic (musical) objectives to a place of artistry and humanity. Re-conceptualizing our educational aims should "encourage the growth of competent, caring, loving, and lovable people" (Noddings, 2002, p. 94). To achieve this, Noddings (2005) suggests: (a) organizing curriculum around themes of care; (b) being unapologetic about the goals of care; (c) keeping students and teachers together longer and in the same building; (d) relaxing the impulse of control in schools; and (e) addressing care daily.

All of these key tenets of care align with compassionate interpretations of SEL in music classrooms. Personal connection, school connectedness, and amplified student voice are necessary for meaningful music teaching and learning. Intentional, embedded,

[2] https://selarts.org/

and sustained attention to musical SEL in schools can help facilitate moving students to be competent, caring, loving, and lovable. Compassionate music teachers and teaching build on these key tenets with the mindset that the time together with their students is a "shared human experience between equals" (Hendricks, 2018, p. 5). They are aware of the feelings and needs of their students to make adjustments in their teaching to support a caring learning environment. This demonstration of caring for their students is a key component of trust and teacher credibility (Hendricks, 2018).

SOCIAL EMOTIONAL LEARNING IN MUSIC EDUCATION

The existing literature linking SEL and music education represents the arts broadly (Edgar, 2020), work in higher education (Edgar, 2019; Hellman & Milling, 2020), and the levels and layers of social emotional development (e.g., teacher social emotional competence, teacher pedagogical skill and efficacy, student learning). These levels start with the efficacy and disposition of teachers to implement such caring instruction (Edgar, 2013, 2014, 2015a, 2015b).

The primary variables creating the proper potential environment for SEL and care in the music classroom are the inherent social nature of group music-making, the social environment that a music classroom and teacher engender, the emotional involvement necessary for music-making, and the developmental relationships that build over multiple years of instruction (Edgar, 2014). As SEL increases in implementation, building awareness around the necessity to make social emotional instruction culturally relevant and sustaining is necessary to support a caring and compassionate environment for all. The unique setting of teaching the same students over several years provides a music teacher with the ability to develop personal relationships and communication styles that are culturally relevant to the students' needs (Lind & McKoy, 2016, pp. 65–66). They are able to create learning communities that set high expectations for all students, provide structure to leverage students' assets, and shift the culture of a school to promote diversity. The caring teacher, guide, and facilitator fosters a community of learners that are comfortable to express themselves through music (Hendricks, 2018, p. 3).

INTENTIONALLY USING SEL AND MUSIC FOR CARE AND COMPASSION

SEL = Identity, Belonging, and Agency

The work of SEL must be positioned as a collaborative effort *with* students so that classrooms do not become assumptive spaces where students' societal needs and challenges are dictated instead of explored. Similarly, without this level of co-learning and co-creation of academic/musical spaces, students and teachers will never fully realize the innate skills they bring with them to schools. The hallmark SEL competency-building of SELF (self-awareness & self-management), OTHERS (social-awareness & relationship skills), and DECISIONS is more important now than ever. When we approach students, colleagues, and ourselves with grace and empathy, classrooms become a place for growth and learning, both artistically and holistically.

The systemic challenges (e.g., racism, bigotry, individualism) saturating culture necessitate positioning SELF–OTHERS–DECISIONS within a new context: IDENTITY–BELONGING–AGENCY. Dr. Robert Jagers (CASEL) reframed SEL to be adapted for *all* students (Jagers et al., 2019). The result is a reconceptualization built on collaboration across communities with all having an equal voice in the process. Compassionate music teaching involves being open to the process of engaging students in choosing repertoire and musical experiences, thus providing a space for students to belong to the group and experience agency in the process of learning music. Being open and accepting to employ diverse music in their practice, the music teacher can demonstrate an ethos that values the various identities of their students. The students are able to work together as equally important parts of the song or learning experience. The process of learning music together becomes the wisdom that the whole class brings and obtains.

When prioritizing musical SEL, the process becomes equally as important as the product. This approach is a dramatic shift from defining musical work as outcome-based. As students and teachers reimagine music education through the process, amplifying student voice and facilitating choice emerge in a powerful and creative way. A central tenet of care is prioritizing the needs of each student (Noddings, 1995). Elevating each students' voice, facilitating a space of safety, and engaging students in a journey to explore their identities provides a strategic plan for achieving care and compassion in the music classroom.

Translating IDENTITY, BELONGING, and AGENCY for music education builds on the following points highlighting the beliefs that unify music education around the arts, a cultural necessity (ArtsEdSEL, 2021).[3]

Identity

SELF becomes more focused on IDENTITY. Who are we, what have been our experiences, and how do those inform our beliefs, mindsets, and biases? Skill sets include understanding personal and sociocultural identity, recognition of beliefs, mindsets, and biases, stress management, self-care, and perseverance. Translated for music education:

- Musical creation fosters self-awareness and allows for students to develop a greater sense of identity, autonomy, and emotional vocabulary.
- Musicians learn the necessity of personal goal-setting, self-assessment, and accountability as they develop high standards for artmaking and themselves.

---

[3] www.artsedsel.org

Belonging

OTHERS becomes centralized on creating spaces for BELONGING. Are music classrooms safe spaces for all of our students to be vulnerable and to take risks as they pursue their musical dreams? Skill sets include perspective-taking, empathy, collaborative problem solving, co-construction, and effective interpersonal communication. Translated for music education:

- The relationship built between teachers and students over multiple years of instruction fosters the caring environment necessary to help build school connectedness, foster empathy, and provide a sense of belonging.
- Collaborative music classrooms build connections between students, facilitate community engagement, and uplift and celebrate the cultural assets of students.
- Music classrooms necessitate vulnerability and facilitate a space where students can explore, tinker, envision, and grow.

Agency

DECISIONS expands to ensure that students' voices are heard, amplified, and can effect change in school and community contexts—AGENCY. Skill sets include: ethical responsibility, distributive justice, and collective wellbeing. Translated for music education:

- The collaborative community developed in the music classroom welcomes discussions and an awareness of acceptance and embracing diversity, resulting in a greater sense of agency and effecting meaningful change.
- Student voice is amplified through the musical process, providing an experience to develop personal and musical efficacy.
- The musical process necessitates editing of the product. This process builds student capacity to hone their beliefs and become flexible to represent themselves in concise and meaningful ways.

To advance student empowerment and agency, it often necessitates teachers taking a less direct role in music classrooms and assuming the role of facilitator so that students can tinker and envision their own journey. Intentional, embedded musical SEL can amplify every student's voice.

Setting the Stage for Compassion and Care Through SEL with UDL

As each individual student's voice is amplified in the music classroom, another guiding construct to ensure SEL does not become another avenue for control (Kaler-Jones, 2020) is universal design for learning (UDL). As SEL and music education align, building space for adaptation and flexibility is necessary to avoid a "one size fits all" model. Humans are neurodiverse, meaning that we *all* have differences in how our brains function. Neurodivergent people—those with a variety of conditions related to cognitive function—and neurotypical people both fall under the neurodiverse umbrella. It is important to remember that people do not perceive emotion, socialize, and feel comfortable being vulnerable in the same way. Therefore, developing strategies to adapt musical SEL instruction is necessary for all students and teachers to have their needs met through music. UDL focuses on providing multiple means across three areas: engagement, representation, and various options for demonstrating understanding (Basham et al., 2020, p. 5).

Educators focusing on compassionate music teaching using SEL do the same, ensuring that every student has multiple means for participation, engagement, and demonstration of knowledge. Using UDL in the classroom intentionally aids students in enhancing executive functions including the skill sets associated with identity, belonging, and agency. Executive functions are the processes that people use to plan and adjust to their environment, often completing tasks with a broad or specific goal (Vasquez & Marino, 2021). Understanding emotions, relationships, and enacting productive actions all require planning and adjusting to an environment, essential components of self-management. Executive functions empower students to be active members of their classroom, enhancing self-management, relationships to others, and decision-making. As students begin to enhance executive functions, they can begin to work toward establishing identity. The relationship between SEL and UDL is most tangibly noted in the intersection of executive function and social emotional competence (Edgar et al., 2021).

Respecting Individuality in the Music Classroom

Linguistics plays a large role in both acceptance and stigmatization. In order to ensure that identity and individuality are recognized, it is the duty of professionals to respect the terms of independent individuals. This awareness can be increasingly difficult when stereotypes, media, colleagues, and families disagree on preferred terminology. In 2016, when seeking data on the preferred terms of adults regarding their autism, researchers found that members disagreed on the use of terminology: Whereas most autistic adults and family members preferred the term "autistic," almost half of the professionals preferred the term "person with autism" (Kenny et al., 2016). However, Bury et al. (2020) suggested that "for many participants, their preferred terms reflect how they see themselves and choose to express their autism" (p. 5). The identity of students—what makes them who they are—must be at the forefront of instruction to adequately address SEL.

In the realm of neurodivergent students, the focus lies on two main aspects of linguistics: person-first language and identity-first language. Person-first language puts the focus on the person; for example, stating "an individual with autism." Identity-first language puts the focus on the identity, such as "autistic individual" (Bury et al., 2020).

All over the world, birth sex and gender norms play a large part in household roles, family models, and systematic bias. For queer students, language modeled by educators can demonstrate acceptance of gender identity or further stigmatize by misgendering, using incorrect pronouns, or using a person's dead name (see McManus & Carter, this volume). When it comes to linguistic identity, asking a student about their preferred terms, pronouns, and identity can provide validation, support, and continue a positive classroom culture of accepting student identity. "As cultural norms continue to be enforced through outgroup individual's actions, LGBTQ identifying members are silenced" (Samaroo, 2017, p. 26). Thus, it is vital to not only ask students their terminology, but also model its use. For the purpose of the examples in this chapter, many types of language are used to model terminology preferred by various students. This approach helps to set the stage for building safe spaces for our students—creating a sense of belonging, a key piece to embedding SEL into the classroom.

Implementation of Compassionate and Caring SEL

As students and teachers navigate collective values, common aims emerge; however, space for individual goals and self-assessment are needed to prioritize the individual within the group. The process of finely tuning melodies, harmonies, and accents with all elements coalescing together in equal balance, is the responsibility of all members. Compassionate SEL-informed music teaching encourages each member to have an identity in the process of learning the music while also belonging to the group. With care, the music teacher supports discussions that embrace the diversity of the class in order to make decisions for the process and product of the music. Prioritizing the musicians' individuality within the music classroom builds agency skills and effects meaningful social, emotional, and musical change.

Student Empowerment in Diverse Settings

When thinking of creating safe spaces, physical limitations that may exist in a room are primary; however, safety goes beyond the physical walls of the classroom. In the Charlotte Danielson (2013) model, teachers are evaluated on physical space in component 2: Organizing physical space. Danielson says that the physical surroundings in a classroom "have a material effect on interactions or structure of activities" (p. 37). This is true for all, but especially for neurodivergent students.

Physical spaces can heavily influence how comfortable students feel. It is important for the physical environment to enhance learning, with intention on the SEL component of belonging. When spaces are set up for collaboration, students are more likely to not only choose to collaborate, but to initiate peer conversations. Leaving space for communication is a large piece in student empowerment. There is no one correct way to communicate. Teachers who model and promote multiple communication methods bring space for each student's voice. For example, employing a communication board or a board with common terms and images in directives creates more opportunities for them to be part of the classroom and set goals for themselves. Providing a checklist for student instructions allows students to self-monitor their current state and music progress. If a student speaks a primary language that differs from the majority of the class, teachers can include visuals and their primary language in handouts and classroom labels. Such adaptations to communication methods can remove barriers to learning. In the following five vignettes, we highlight ways where music educators can actualize the concepts of care, SEL, and access.

> In my general music classroom, the physical classroom space is designed to keep student interests and needs at the forefront. Flexible seating that allows students to move when necessary provides comfort as well as a collaborative environment. When students have the ability to move around as they need to, they can engage and participate on their own terms, promoting independence (agency). When choosing resources to use in class, I ask myself three questions: First, is this resource appropriate for my students? Second, is this resource accessible for all students? If not, can I make adaptations to the resource that will serve the needs of my students? Third, does this resource fit the objective or purpose of what I would like the students to learn?
>
> Providing students with options for independence such as placing instruments and materials in an accessible location, along with labels, promotes autonomy. Students can establish their own routines, collaborate with peers, and share resources. Students can make decisions about how to use these resources effectively. This executive thinking skill is developed through intentional SEL.

Community

> Margaret, a 7th/8th band teacher, whose mission focused on SEL and community, was passionate about teaching music, but believed the process of music-making and development of community to be most important. Her hope was to develop SEL competencies such as: responsibility to the ensemble, understanding their personal role in the band, and finding a way that every child who wanted to be in the band experienced belonging. During one rehearsal, the teacher asked the students, "What if just three of you played wrong notes every measure? What would we sound like? Students identified the problem that when they did not play the right notes together the music doesn't sound good. The teacher facilitated an SEL problem-solving discussion with an end result of students feeling empowered to practice and be responsible to the band community.

The teacher in the vignette above endeavored to balance and connect identity and belonging. She observed a change in her students' sense of belonging and agency to actively and conscientiously contribute to the ensemble. She took the time to care and intentionally employ SEL strategies to create a safe, productive environment where students can pose questions and discuss challenges. Moreover, the teacher and students authentically collaborated to share and create together. The students cared for one another by taking responsibility to help each other learn. These circumstances amplified the students' voice and employed a caring and compassionate way to develop empathy for one another.

Care, SEL, and Culturally Relevant Pedagogy

I'll never forget my first job, teaching music in an urban elementary school. I was excited to have the gift to teach my students over the nine years they attended the school. I was able to create a cohesive music plan to spiral the curriculum (Bruner, 1960), connecting and deepening learning from prior years to set students up for success in the following years. As time went on, I realized the greatest value was my time to connect and grow strong relationships with my students. Although I appreciated their learning, I valued our year-after-year interactions and social development. Building the trust that is needed to take educational risks and be willing to grow was a powerful tool in my teaching. I soon realized the relationship needed to bridge to home. Communication with parents about my focus on social emotional and musicianship goals led to supportive parents who volunteered, shared their musical lives, and attended performances. When I connected with the parents, I was able to learn about cultural celebrations that influenced my students' learning styles. I was able to bring these aspects of culture into the classroom. Students were proud of their heritage and modern forms of musical expression. Their participation and collaboration was engaging for all. As one of the only teachers who taught the students all their years at this school, I used that time to develop relationships and create lessons that were culturally relevant and meaningful.

Caring teaching involves building trust through honest conversations and vulnerability, sharing how teachers too have encountered difficult situations that cultivated empathy. Overcoming adversity and persevering can prepare the learner for future challenges and work to establish an authentic connection, not a subordinate role, but one that embodies a collaborative relationship when an educator models a lifelong learning attitude.

Diverse music curricula offer one important way to employ culturally relevant pedagogy and learning opportunities. Although teaching music concepts through diverse multicultural repertoire in traditional ensembles such as band, orchestra, choir and classroom music is a good place to start, adding learning choices such as mariachi, buckets, drumline, modern/pop small music groups, guitar, banda, and electronic music (i.e., DJ, iPads) may be an excellent catalyst to opening up access to a comprehensive music education for all students while highlighting that the teacher cares about exploring musical interests of the collective class and not solely based on tradition (Ireland D'Ambrosio, 2015).

Student Choice and Amplifying Voice

The end of the school year is an exciting time for students to demonstrate what they have learned all year. In 4th grade recorder class, the students have a UDL-influenced Project-Based Learning composition activity. The learning objective is for students to demonstrate the melodic, rhythmic, and expression concepts they learned over the school year through composing their own song. They may write lyrics or not. They may use one staff or add more staffs for accompaniment. The project is scaffolded to provide variety for each student's assets and challenges. The final production may be a recorded or live performance. The student may share by speaking or writing about their experience creating their music, or they may only introduce their song. This flexible project is conceived to meet the students where they are and bring them forward to the next level. There are ample opportunities for student voice and peer support/mentoring. Moreover, the collaboration is a meaningful assessment.

When students feel cared for, they are empowered to ask for help, offer help, and take risks to explore their craft. Compassionate teaching includes being flexible with lesson plans. Drawing from UDL, students have choice, voice, and multiple means for accessing the knowledge, curriculum, and expression of understanding and assessment. It involves flexibility with the classroom environment, moving from large group instruction to small group discussion and stations. Varied learning activities allow the teacher to offer support when students need help. For example, compassionate music teaching may involve discussions about the changing voice and what can happen physiologically during the growth of middle school students. Intentionally engaging with SEL skill development builds support helping students exercise empathy with other students when adolescent vocal cracks occur. Instead, the students can learn to make decisions that have a positive impact on others.

Beyond Inclusion to Accessibility

Our peer buddy musical theater program is designed to ensure success for all students, regardless of age, status, gender, race, or disability. In order for this program to function successfully, every member of the community must buy in. This includes leadership from all students, and a sense of confidence in the program. This program was built on peer collaboration; however, during a performance, one of the mentors stopped showing up, which in turn left an imbalance in the participant-mentor pairs. This heavily impacted our community in the flow of rehearsals and the community we had built, which left us all thinking, "How ever will the participant learn to be part of this group?" After a few weeks of rehearsal, the participant started taking on more responsibility, memorized their lines, and became a leader in their own right. We were asking the wrong question. What we should have been noticing is that the participant was part of the group all along, and it was our idea of the performance that needed to change, not the participant.

When students are part of the conversation and given the opportunity to engage in responsible decision-making student agency is amplified. With student voices at the center of setting expectations, contributing to the community, and working together to design the outcome that fits their vision, a socially and emotionally accessible space can be created. Accessible spaces, performances, and communities happen when teachers are willing to take students as they are, and allow them to shine in the ways they do every day—through acceptance, understanding, and appreciation of who they are as individuals.

Conclusion

The effects of the COVID-19 education disruption have had a deep impact on how music education, as a profession, will function for the foreseeable future (Edgar et al., 2020). Centering relationships and connections between teachers, students, schools, and communities focusing on understanding identity, fostering belonging, and student empowerment furthers the ultimate goal of care and kindness in the music classroom. For more information on embedding SEL into the music classroom for all students, please see the following resources:

- The Center for Arts Education and Social Emotional Learning (ArtsEdSEL): www.artsedsel.org
- Music for All Teaching Social Emotional Learning Through Music: https://education.musicforall.org/sel/
- CAST: Universal Design for Learning Framework: https://www.cast.org/impact/universal-design-for-learning-udl
- Autism Self-Advocacy Network (ASAN): https://autisticadvocacy.org/about-asan/about-autism/
- Journey to Responsiveness (Culturally and Linguistically Responsive Teaching and Learning: https://www.culturallyresponsive.org/journeytoresponsiveness

When SEL and UDL are melded intentionally to create a compassionate and caring music classroom, the end result can be a productive space where students have the opportunity to explore, tinker, and envision what their musical future can look like. In the end, it just looks like great music teaching!

References

The Arts Education and Social Emotional Learning Framework. (2019). https://selarts.org/.

Basham, J. D., Gardner, J. E., & Smith, S. J. (2020). Measuring the implementation of UDL in classrooms and schools: Initial field test results. *Remedial and Special Education*, 41(4), 231–243. https://doi.org/10.1177/0741932520908015

Bury, S. M., Jellett, R., Spoor, J. R., & Hedley, D. (2020). "It defines who I am" or "It's something I have": What language do [autistic] Australian adults [on the autism spectrum] prefer? *Journal of Autism & Developmental Disorders*, 53(2), 1–11. https://doi.org/10.1007/s10803-020-04425-3

Bruner, J. (1960). *The Process of Education*. Harvard University Press.

The Center for Arts Education and Social Emotional Learning. (2021). https://artsedsel.org/

The Collaborative for Academic Social Emotional Learning (CASEL). (n.d.). https://casel.org/

Danielson, C. (2013). *The framework for teaching: Evaluation instrument*. The Danielson Group.

Edgar, S. N. (2013). Introducing social emotional learning to music education professional development. *Update: Applications of Research in Music Education*, 31(2), 28–36. https://doi.org/10.1177/8755123313480508

Edgar, S. N. (2014). An ethic of care in high school instrumental music. *Action, Criticism, and Theory for Music Education*, 13(2), 112–137. http://act.maydaygroup.org/articles/Edgar13_2.pdf

Edgar, S. N. (2015a). Preparing high school instrumental music educators to respond to the social and emotional challenges of students. *Journal of Music Teacher Education*, 24, 67–82. https://doi.org/10.1177/1057083713514980

Edgar, S. N. (2015b). Approaches of a secondary music teacher in response to the social emotional lives of students. *Contributions to Music Education*, 40, 91–110.

Edgar, S. N. (2017). *Music education and social emotional learning: The heart of teaching music*. GIA Publications.

Edgar, S. N. (2019). Music and the social and emotional challenges of undergraduate instrumental music students. *Update: Applications of Research in Music Education*, 37(3), 46–56. https://doi.org/10.1177/8755123319832067

Edgar, S. N. (Ed.). (2020). Social emotional learning and the arts: Policies, practices, and interpretations [Special issue]. *Arts Education Policy Review*, 122(3).

Edgar, S. N., & Edgar, S. L. (2020). *The ABCs of my feelings and music* (N. Bohm, Illus.). GIA Publications.

Edgar, S. N., & Elias, M. J. (2020). Setting the stage for social emotional learning (SEL) policy and the arts. *Arts Education Policy Review*, 122(3), 205–209. https://doi.org/10.1080/10632913.2020.1777494

Edgar, S. N., Hammel, A., Hackl-Blumstein, E., & Hernandez-Ruiz, E. (2021, December 8). *Supporting neurodiversity through SEL & music education* [Webinar]. Social Emotional Learning in Music Education. https://www.savethemusic.org/resources/sel-webinar/

Edgar, S. N., & Morrison, R. (2020). A vision for social emotional learning and arts education policy. *Arts Education Policy Review*, 122(3), 145–150. https://doi.org/10.1080/10632913.2020.1774830

Edgar, S. N., Schwartz Reichl, L., & Kick, F. (2021). The promise of artistic process: Social emotional learning (SEL) aligns the standards. *Teaching Music*, 28(3), 26–31. http://digitaleditions.walsworthprintgroup.com/publication/?m=61045&i=687550&view=articleBrowser&article_id=3839736&ver=html5

Farrington, C. A., Maurer, J., McBride, M. R. A., Nagaoka, J., Puller, J. S., Shewfelt, S., Weiss, E. M., & Wright, L. (2019). *Arts education and social-emotional learning outcomes among K–12 students: Developing a theory of action*. Ingenuity and the University of Chicago Consortium on School Research.

Hellman, D. S., & Milling, S. (2020). Social emotional learning in arts teacher education policy: A content analysis of assurance standards and course descriptions. *Arts Education Policy Review*, 122(3), 171–181. https://doi.org/10.1080/10632913.2020.1793251

Hendricks, K. S. (2018). *Compassionate music teaching*. Rowman & Littlefield.
Ireland D'Ambrosio, K. (2015). *The California music project teacher training program as an intervention in poverty and income inequality* (Publication No. 368609e2) [Doctoral dissertation, Boston University]. ProQuest Dissertations Publishing.
Jagers, R. J., Rivas-Drake D., & Williams, B. (2019). Transformative social emotional learning (SEL): Toward SEL in service of educational equity and excellence. *Educational Psychologist*, 54(3), 162–184. Https://doi.org/10.1080/00461520.2019.1623032
Kaler-Jones, C. (2020). *When SEL is used as another form of policing*. Medium. https://medium.com/@justschools/when-sel-is-used-as-another-form-of-policing-fa53cf85dce4
Kenny, L., Hattersley, C., Molins, B., Buckley, C., Povey, C., & Pellicano, E. (2016). Which terms should be used to describe autism? Perspectives from the UK autism community. *Autism: The International Journal of Research & Practice*, 20(4), 442–462. https://doi.org/10.1177/1362361315588200
Lind, V., & McKoy, L. (2016). *Culturally responsive teaching in music education*. Routledge Taylor & Francis Group.
Noddings, N. (1995). Teaching themes of care. *Phi Delta Kappan*, 76(9), 675–679.
Noddings, N. (2002). *Educating moral people: A caring alternative to character education*. Teachers College Press.
Noddings, N. (2005). *The challenge to care in schools* (2nd ed.). Teachers College Press.
Rizzuto, K. (2021, June). *Planning artistic social emotional learning: embedded, intentional, sustained*. The Center for Arts Education and Social Emotional Learning. https://artsedsel.org/wp-content/uploads/JUNE-2021-HotA_Final-for-Web.pdf.
Samaroo, A. (2017). Effects of an LGBTQ identity and support systems on mental health: A study of 4 theories. *Modern Psychological Studies*, 22(2), 20–27.
Vasquez, E., & Marino, M. T. (2021). Enhancing executive function while addressing learner variability in inclusive classrooms. *Intervention in School and Clinic*, 56(3), 179–185. https://journals.sagepub.com/doi/10.1177/1053451220928978

CHAPTER 17

EMPATHY AND DEEP LISTENING IN JAZZ IMPROVISATION

TROY DAVIS

CARE HANDBOOK TOPICS

Co-creating caring relationships

IN a study that I conducted involving four professional jazz musicians (Davis, 2020), I found that an important goal of these musicians was to foster empathy with one another while they were improvising. These musicians described improvisation as a form of conversational music-making akin to a deep, caring, verbal conversation in a co-created space. Such musical conversations were necessary for the musicians to create improvised music together and, further, were integral for the musicians to connect with one another, in order to foster a sense of care and understanding (Davis, 2020). These musicians represented an emotional understanding of each other through gestures of empathy, including supportive verbal feedback and utterances, nonverbal communication, and musical responses. In an earlier study, Seddon (2005) found that these same gestures were used to create a state of empathetic attunement among jazz musicians. Both studies (Davis, 2020; Seddon, 2005) involved musicians using skills related to empathy.

Jazz educators can also use gestures of empathy like those used by improvisers when teaching their students. Hendricks (2018) suggested that music teachers consider the following to foster empathy:

1. Model empathy and action.
2. Provide artistic experiences for perspective-taking.
3. Be sensitive to students' nonverbal messages. (p. 69)

In this chapter, I explore empathy and deep listening as potential strategies to support the musical growth of developing musicians. Specifically, I explore ways that jazz educators might model empathy to create the conditions for empathy and relational trust among students. I also consider ways that jazz educators might encourage students to interpret the nonverbal communication of other musicians, as this practice may enhance deep listening skills, which help to strengthen personal connections and build community (Kossak, 2007).

Background

> What I love about improvisation is that it is not just about you. You are influenced and choose to play things based on your "in the moment" reactions with the other musicians, as well as the overall vibe and feeling of the physical space you are performing in. (Davis, 2020, p. 93)

Music is often described as a means to communicate emotions (Juslin, 1997). Emotions are a way for humans to quickly adapt during interpersonal interactions, and emotions themselves and the expression of emotions are different facets of the human communication process. Musicians can convey distinct emotions through their performance, specifically through the use of expressive cues, such as "tempo, volume, timing, timbre, articulation, and intonation" (Juslin, 1997, p. 414). The emotional intent of musical performers can be interpreted by listeners with high accuracy (Juslin, 1997). By accurately interpreting emotional intent, listeners are effectively developing a sense of emotional understanding toward the performers. This type of emotional understanding is what Goleman (2000) described as empathy, or the ability to understand another person's point of view, from their perspective.

Empathetic Strategies

Perspective-taking is a form of care toward others and a higher-level thinking process that is required for someone to experience cognitive empathy for others (Batson et al., 1997; Davis, 1996; Feshbach, 1978; Hendricks, 2018). Two distinct forms of perspective-taking are first- and third-person (Leiberg & Anders, 2006). During first-person perspective-taking, one imagines how they might feel in another person's situation. During third-person perspective-taking, one imagines another person's thoughts and feelings. In the context of jazz education, third-person perspective-taking is a necessary skill for jazz musicians to experience what Seddon (2005) described as "empathetic creativity" (p. 48), which he argued, is the goal of musical communication during improvising. When musicians experience empathetic creativity, they take musical risks that require a sense of trust, care, and respect from fellow musicians, by imagining "things from other musical perspectives" (Seddon, 2005, p. 49).

When jazz musicians perform, they regularly experience an altered state of consciousness during which time seems to stand still and creativity flourishes, particularly when they are improvising (Jedelloh, 2003; Sarath, 2013). According to Csíkszentmihályi (1990), this concept is often referred to as "flow," or the mental state of operation in which a person performing an activity is fully immersed in a feeling of energized focus, full involvement, and enjoyment in the process of the activity. This experience causes increased output, creativity, levels of self-esteem and engagement, and overall wellbeing (Csíkszentmihályi, 1990). The flow state is often referred to as an important pillar in the art of collaboration (Mazzola & Cherlin, 1998) and can be achieved through empathic listening or "deep listening" among collaborators (Davis, 2020).

Deep listening is an intense form of nonverbal communication that serves as a way for people to build connections with one another (Kossak, 2007). Davis (2020) found that the practice of deep listening to one another conveyed a sense of connectedness among four professional jazz musicians. Further, these musicians felt that an emotional understanding helped them practice empathy and enter a flow state when making music together. According to the participants, this concentration was more manageable when they had established a sense of trust and emotional connection with one another.

"Empathetic attunement" (Seddon, 2005) is a term used to describe the collective flow state of musicians. During empathetic attunement, musicians have the opportunity for "exploration, risk-taking, and concentration" (Seddon, 2005, p. 48) and often exhibit "spontaneous musical utterances" (p. 50), or musical phrases played by the musicians that they have never practiced before. Seddon (2005) proposed that these spontaneous musical utterances were an example of the musicians communicating with deep levels of empathy and connection. Davis (2020) found that achieving empathetic attunement was a goal of jazz musicians while performing together.

Each of these strategies—perspective-taking, flow, deep listening, and empathetic attunement—are examples of empathic behaviors that are often used by jazz musicians. These strategies are also skills that can be incorporated into pedagogical situations to help support the growth of burgeoning musicians, as empathy is directly related to social and emotional competence (Zins & Elias, 2007), and may also be related to student success in academic environments (Zins, 2004). By modeling these skills and building them into curriculum, jazz educators may be able to foster empathy and what Hendricks (2018) described as relational trust among students.

Empathy in Jazz Pedagogy

Jazz musicians often experience feelings of empathy and connectedness while performing with one another (Berliner, 1994) and these feelings can be integrated into jazz improvisation pedagogy. While conducting an inquiry into empathy and compassion in educational contexts, Cain (2019) suggested that educators not only model the outcomes of empathy but also integrate practices into the curriculum, because students "need to see empathy and compassion in practice and know what it is to be the recipients of empathy and compassion" (p. 52). Hendricks (2018) advocated for speaking out loud to describe how teachers are perceiving the needs of others. In musical terms, this might also mean playing out loud and reacting and responding to the music of others. In the context of jazz improvisation, musicians are often playing simultaneously, so the act of responding to another musician does not necessarily manifest in the form of traditional dialogue. Seddon (2005) described this experience of complete unpredictability as highly collaborative and empathetic because it "involves risk-taking in a state of uncertainty where repetition and predictable responses become virtually impossible" (p. 48). While in this vulnerable state, musicians must be able to trust one another and honor the musical abilities of the other performers. In doing so, strong emotional bonds can often be formed. It is often these personal connections that help musicians to achieve the flow state and that are necessary for empathetic attunement to occur (Seddon, 2005).

What might this look like for educators who want to model and demonstrate empathy? Hendricks (2018) valued active listening and consciously keeping kindness at the forefront of one's mind before reacting or responding. It is also important for students to understand what the educator may think or feel regarding a given situation, so expressing those opinions in a non-confrontational way may be quite valuable (Hendricks, 2018). Through maintaining brave spaces such as this, students can develop a sense of safety in knowing that acceptance and trust are paramount, which is a pre-condition for risk-taking (Cain, 2019; Kessler, 2000). This might be particularly important in the jazz classroom because musicians often feel hesitant and do not trust themselves to achieve performance levels of experienced players (Kenny, 2014). In the following section, I explore some ways that jazz educators can model empathy for their students who in turn can begin to implement these strategies in their own learning. These include mentorship, engaging in open-ended dialogue, considering place-based pedagogy, and integrating musical empathy.

Mentorship

Seddon (2005) maintained that the collaborative nature of group jazz improvisation is a practice of empathy. Effective teaching and learning of improvisation skills are predominantly conceptualized through mentorship (Berliner, 1994). During lessons, students develop technical and aural skills, as well as imagination and creativity, all in a situation that requires risk-taking in a brave space. Further, *peer* mentoring may be an effective way to cultivate care and collaboration in the jazz classroom, while allowing students to have flexibility and freedom in the artistic and educational process (Goodrich, 2007). Peer mentoring may help to establish the deep bonds that are necessary for student improvisers to tackle the strategies of perspective-taking, flow, deep listening, and empathetic attunement more easily (see Goodrich, this volume).

Peer mentorship can be implemented in the jazz classroom with a particular focus on developing empathy among students. I recommend having students take turns leading the class in short lessons. When students mentor one another in this way, they may develop a strong emotional understanding of one another (Jones, 2015). Additionally, if students work in pairs to transcribe one another's improvised solos, they may develop an understanding of each other through third-person perspective-taking (Leiberg & Anders, 2006) and they may better understand how other students articulate their artistic voice (Schnabel, 2021).

Open-Ended Dialogue

For students to grow and have opportunities to refine their awareness of empathy, Hendricks (2018) advised engaging students in dialogue with one another. By "providing student voice and choice" (p. 70), students may be more motivated to participate in musical activities. Watts et al. (2020) encouraged using open-ended dialogue to facilitate a caring environment, in which students can deepen their understanding of each other's perspectives. Through open-ended dialogue, students may be more apt to develop deep listening skills; according to Junkin (2017), there seems to be a relationship between deep listening skills (including self-awareness, awareness of others, and awareness of music) and the transformative dialogue skills of self-reflection, self-expression, and responsibility. However, deep listening does not necessarily translate directly into dialogue skills without proper facilitation by an instructor (Junkin, 2017). Facilitation can happen through instructor modeling, role play, and using musical elements as an analogy for the components of dialogue (Junkin, 2017), which I discuss in the section on nonverbal communication later in this chapter.

For teachers to be able to properly listen, students must be allowed to think aloud, both verbally and musically (Watts et al., 2020). When students think aloud in the classroom, they are engaging in the process of forming and reflecting on their own thoughts. This is a similar process to experimenting with sound and improvising jazz music; therefore, students may better integrate these concepts when instructors model thinking aloud (Junkin, 2017). Open-ended dialogue is a conversation in which the participants do not know the end result when they start talking. The same is true with improvised jazz melodies. Open-ended dialogue can instill in students a desire to seek out more information (Noddings, 2005), which may lend itself to the adventurous spirit of risk-taking in a jazz ensemble. Instructors can model caring, open-ended dialogue by asking questions without pre-conceived answers and by actively listening to student responses (Noddings, 2005). Further, students can be encouraged to role play as leader, follower, speaker, and listener in order to more deeply understand the point of view of others while engaging in dialogue (Junkin, 2017).

I now extrapolate various scenarios depicting open-ended dialogue from Watts et al. (2020) for use in the jazz classroom. Open-ended dialogue may occur when students share their thoughts or feelings about the lyrics of a jazz standard, to facilitate greater meaning during performance. Perhaps students might share their experiences regarding their practice and development process on their instruments, to bring about shared understandings among the group. Finally, students might be encouraged to improvise on different instruments (e.g., wind players on rhythm section instruments, or vice versa) in a free jazz setting, to encourage sound exploration without the constraint of technical training. These activities might also foster empathy among students, as they may become aware of the inherent joys and challenges of playing an instrument other than their chosen one, which may help them to better understand one another (Watts et al., 2020).

Place-Based Pedagogy

Place-based pedagogy is "based on the notion that student learning is greatly enhanced when traditional classroom instruction is supplemented by incorporating field experiences that utilize specific localities or places as primary resources" (Strait, 2012, p. 194). Music is a situated art (Saraydarian, 2021): We often associate music with our commute, social events, a concert hall, special occasions, and other places. To help students center their creativity and make it more meaningful, music educators might consider making a "space for place" (Saraydarian, 2021, p. 154), by facilitating opportunities for students to "be in places where certain music is/was created" (p. 154) to help center their creativity and make it more meaningful. Jazz educators can model this place-based pedagogy by reflecting on their own sense of place within an ensemble and a local community. For example, when working with students who live in large metropolitan areas, perhaps while learning the chord changes to "Take the A Train," the students might ride the subway and absorb the environment, listen to the sounds, and engage with other passengers. Or the class might research local musical venues and musicians to discover their backstory, history, and challenges. Then, instructors can create rehearsal and performance opportunities with those musicians or in those venues.

One goal of connecting music-making to place is to illustrate how music reflects an expansive range of cultural, historical, and geographical conditions (Saraydarian, 2021) and to develop a sense of empathy to the music and to other performers by using the place as a grounding connection. Place-based pedagogy allows one to better understand the content from a different perspective and evoke a wisdom that otherwise might not be present. Saraydarian (2021) argued that one of the most important responsibilities of jazz musicians is to "see that awareness, exposure, and opportunities to develop musicality are embedded in the local community" (p. 160). Jazz educators and students can build meaningful, co-created learning spaces that are tied into place and evoke a sense of understanding of the music. The experiences may have a profound impact on the connections between music-makers and their sense of community.

Musical Empathy

Musical empathy is a discrete form of empathy in which the content and structure of music "act as a vehicle through which [performers] can relate empathically" to others

(Ockelford, 2017, p. 39). To better understand the ways that learners engage with music, Ockelford (2017) developed an interactive model of musical empathy, which strengthens the relationship between a composer and an improviser/performer. A composer imparts their feelings in the music by producing content within a particular structure. The improviser/performer enhances the music with their own layer of interpretation, often using expressive devices, such as rubato, timbre, tempo, vibrato, and dynamics to convey that meaning. The result is what Ockelford (2017) called "an aesthetic response" (p. 81), which represents an empathic synthesis of the expressions of both the composer and the improviser/performer. The aesthetic response can be deepened through the interaction of multiple improvisers performing together (Ockelford, 2017). In this situation, the improvisers perceive the structure and content of the music, and this evokes their own thoughts and feelings. These thoughts and feelings are, in turn, influencing the structure and content of the music, resulting in empathic creativity (Ockelford, 2017).

There are several ways that jazz educators might engage students in interactive musical empathy. A major component of integrating care into education is confirmation (Noddings, 2005), which might involve providing words of acknowledgment to help encourage student progress and development. This could take the form of something as simple as letting students know that they correctly interpreted chord changes. Perhaps it is praise for performers who master the composer's written intentions of a musical work, or when students improvise ideas that connect to those of other students. Importantly, educators should encourage students to extend confirmation to one another, as care can be multidirectional (Watts et al., 2020).

The experience of musical empathy might be deepened when students work together on group composition (Laird, 2015). While composing together, students will actively create the structure and content of the music, which may foster a sense of shared understanding and reflection (Laird, 2015), and thereby set up the conditions for musical empathy with one another. Group improvisation is similar to group composition, with the structure and content of music being developed in real time (Berliner, 1994). Improvisation itself is a form of social communication that can develop self-expression, as well as emotional bonds among musicians and with members of an audience (Grant, 2002). To cultivate a caring environment, I suggest that jazz educators encourage all musicians to improvise. This experience of improvisation may be heightened in a jazz combo setting because all performers must constantly improvise in the combo, unlike the jazz big band (Grant, 2002). The jazz combo is inherently a cooperative learning setting, which lends itself well to the development of empathy and care among musicians (Berliner, 1994).

Nonverbal Communication

Ockelford's (2017) empathic creativity is a form of nonverbal communication used by musicians and aligns with research by Cross et al. (2012), who examined the role that

Table 17.1 From Seddon, F. A. (2005). Modes of communication during jazz improvisation. *British Journal of Music Education, 22*(1), p. 53. https://doi.org/10.1017/S0265051704005984

Mode of Communication	Verbal	Nonverbal
Instruction	Musicians are told what and when to play in pre-composed sections (the head)	Musicians learn pre-composed part by ear or read from music notation
Cooperation	Musicians discuss and plan the organization of the piece prior to the performance in order to achieve a cohesive performance	Musicians achieve sympathetic attunement and exchange stocks of musical knowledge, producing cohesive performance employing: body language, facial expression, eye contact, musical cues, and gesticulation
Collaboration	Musicians discuss and evaluate their performance of the music in order to develop the content and/or style of the piece	Musicians achieve empathetic attunement, take creative risks which can result in spontaneous musical utterances. When they do, this signals empathetic creativity

empathy plays in musical interactions, as well as by Seddon (2005), who investigated the ways that student jazz musicians communicated with one another while making music together. The latter author's analysis revealed six modes of communication, divided into two main categories: verbal and nonverbal communication. Each of these contained three distinct methods or modes: instruction, cooperation, and collaboration, which are detailed in the Table 17.1.

The modes of collaboration were the most impactful to students and facilitated higher order thinking. Nonverbal collaboration included the musicians achieving what Seddon (2005) called "empathetic attunement" (p. 53), or a state of being in which the musicians were so absorbed in their activity, that the opportunity for "exploration, risk-taking, and concentration" (p. 48) was rife and deepened. Seddon (2005) proposed that nonverbal collaboration may have specific relevance in how jazz educators assist student musicians with communication and understanding while making music together. The nonverbal modes of communication (Seddon, 2005) were used by professional jazz musicians in performance as a way to practice deep listening. Whereas deep listening has been shown to foster a strong sense of empathy with professional jazz musicians (Davis, 2020), the development of nonverbal communication skills in the jazz classroom may similarly deepen empathy among students. Seddon (2005) described several scenarios that represent the various nonverbal modes of communication, as described below. These may be useful ideas for instructors to implement in jazz education instructional settings.

Implementation

In this final section, I outline some techniques based on Seddon's (2005) nonverbal interactions, which may be valuable to integrate into the jazz classroom. During nonverbal *instruction*, students engage in musical dialogue geared toward one student teaching another student (or group of students) by rote. Students play for each other repeatedly, to allow others to learn a melody by ear. This technique is often referred to as "call and response" and is regularly used in jazz pedagogy (Berliner, 1994). When implementing nonverbal *instruction*, it is important to recognize that students develop empathy with one another when students are the demonstrators, as this type of dialogue helps them better understand the needs of others (Noddings, 2005).

During nonverbal *cooperation*, students attune sympathetically to one another (Seddon, 2005). Evidence of sympathetic attunement among musicians may be in the form of complementary musical responses and a sense of musical cohesion among the group. In Seddon's (2005) research, the call and response format was expanded, so that students did not simply play back what they heard others perform. Musical responses tended to be different from the "call" of the initial player. This musical engagement took on the form of dialogue, so the call and response was more akin to a "question and answer." Students were perceived as "improvising without taking risks or challenging their ... creativity" (p. 54). Despite this lack of challenge, the musicians did engage the use of their body language to facilitate communication. Gestures included making eye contact with one another, giving musical cues, and changing facial expressions. According to Seddon (2005), these nonverbal gestures helped the group to play more cohesively. An instructor might incorporate this into rehearsal by teaching students how to use nonverbal gestures to communicate while performing.

The final nonverbal mode that Seddon (2005) observed was *collaboration*. During nonverbal *collaboration*, students attune empathetically with one another. Communication among the students is "focused on creative exchanges" (p. 54) and conveyed solely through musical interaction. Students who incorporate nonverbal *collaboration* might regularly challenge themselves to engage in risk-taking, such as with musical phrases and altering the time of the music. As mentioned previously, they may also exhibit "spontaneous musical utterances," animated body movements, head nods, and verbal utterances. Instructors might incorporate nonverbal *collaboration* into their pedagogy by demonstrating ways that students can take musical risks in their playing and building in repertoire to extend their knowledge base and musical vocabulary.

Similarly, language can be used as the vehicle for jazz students to better understand how to incorporate deep listening skills. I recommend facilitating this through two methods. First, students can create lyrics to already written melodies. Second, students may use the inflection of their language to influence phrasing in their music. Students might record themselves while telling a story or giving a speech. Upon listening back, students might be instructed to focus on the speech patterns: Where are the inflections? Where does the tone or timbre change? Where are the cadence points? What is the pacing of the speech? All these guiding questions can help frame the work so they can use those same elements (inflection, tone, timbre, cadence points, and pacing) in their musical phrasing. Students are thereby building a routine to help them develop their skill of deep listening. The elements from the routine can help students build knowledge and musical vocabulary. With a stronger knowledge base, students may be more apt to take risks during performance, thereby facilitating nonverbal *collaboration* with their peers and deepening a sense of empathy with one another.

Each of these nonverbal modes of communication—instruction, cooperation, and collaboration—have been found to increase student output, aid in ensemble cohesion, and help students develop empathy with one another (Seddon, 2005). The implementation methods that I described in the previous paragraphs are not new jazz pedagogy techniques. For example, Berliner (1994) described them as strategies that have been used by jazz musicians for decades. However, what has not been previously considered in detail is how to use these techniques specifically to develop empathy among musicians, as opposed to using them simply to improve the technical aspects of a musical performance.

In this chapter I presented some potential strategies to support the musical growth of students through deep listening and empathy. The examples of ways that jazz educators might model empathy for their students through mentorship, engaging in open-ended dialogue, considering place-based pedagogy, and integrating musical empathy are only limited descriptions. Jazz educators may wish to explore these with more depth to facilitate enduring understandings and expand the potential mechanisms for fostering empathy and deep listening among music learners.

References

Batson, C. D., Sager, K., Garst, E., Kang, M., Rubchinsky, K., & Dawson, K. (1997). Is empathy-induced helping due to self-other merging? *Journal of Personality and Social Psychology*, 73(3), 495–509. http://doi.org/10.1037/0022-3514.73.3.495

Berliner, P. F. (1994). *Thinking in jazz: The infinite art of improvisation*. University of Chicago Press.

Cain, M. (2019). "But it wouldn't be me": Exploring empathy and compassion for self and others through creative processes. In G. Barton & S. Garvis (Eds.), *Compassion and empathy in educational contexts* (pp. 39–57). Palgrave Macmillan. https://doi.org/10.1007/978-3-030-18925-9_3

Cross, I., Laurence, F., & Rabinowitch, T.-C. (2012). Empathy and creativity in group musical practices: Towards a concept of empathic creativity. In G. E. McPherson & G. F. Welch (Eds.), *The Oxford handbook of music education* (Vol. 2, pp. 337–353). Oxford University Press. https://doi.org/10.1093/oxfordhb/9780199928019.013.0023

Csíkszentmihályi, M. (1990). *Flow: The psychology of optimal experience*. Harper & Row.

Davis, M. H. (1996). *Empathy: A social psychological approach*. Westview.

Davis, T. E. (2020). *Self-assessment in jazz improvisation: An instrumental case study of professional jazz musicians in a jazz combo setting* (Publication No. 28149451) [Doctoral dissertation, Boston University]. ProQuest Dissertations and Theses Global.

Feshbach, N. D. (1978). Studies of empathic behavior in children. In B. A. Maher (Ed.), *Progress in experimental personality research* (pp. 1–47). Academic Press.

Goleman, D. (2000). *Working with emotional intelligence.* Bantam Books.

Goodrich, A. (2007). Peer mentoring in a high school jazz ensemble. *Journal of Research in Music Education, 55*(2), 94–114. http://doi.org/10.1177/00224294070550020

Grant, C. (2002). Fostering cooperative behavior in jazz performance classroom. *Canadian Music Educator, 43*(3), 13–15.

Hendricks, K. S. (2018). *Compassionate music teaching.* Roman & Littlefield.

Jeddeloh, S. C. (2003). *Chasing transcendence: Experiencing "magic moments" in jazz improvisation* (Publication No. 3103587) [Doctoral dissertation, Fielding Graduate Institute]. ProQuest Dissertations & Theses Global.

Jones, J. L. (2015). *Learning to care: The influence of a peer mentoring program on empathy and moral reasoning in high school student mentors* (Publication No. 3363176) [Doctoral dissertation, The University of Maine]. ProQuest Dissertations & Theses Global.

Junkin, J. S. (2017). *Orchestral-dialogues: Accepting self, accepting others—Translating deep listening skills to transformative dialogue skills* (Publication No. 10636435) [Doctoral dissertation, Drexel University]. ProQuest Dissertations & Theses Global.

Juslin, P. N. (1997). Emotional communication in music performance: A functionalist perspective and some data. *Music Perception, 14,* 383–418. http://doi.org/10.2307/40285731

Kenny, A. (2014). "Collaborative creativity" within a jazz ensemble as a musical and social practice. *Thinking Skills and Creativity, 13,* 1–8. http://doi.org/10.1016/j.tsc.2014.02.002

Kessler, R. (2000). *Soul of education: Helping students find connection, compassion, and character at school.* Association for Supervision & Curriculum Development.

Kossak, M. S. (2007). *Attunement: Embodied transcendent experience explored through sound and rhythmic improvisation* (Publication No. 3295954) [Doctoral dissertation, Union Institute and University]. ProQuest Dissertations & Theses Global.

Laird, L. (2015). Empathy in the classroom: Can music bring us more in tune with one another? *Music Educators Journal, 101*(4), 56–91. https://doi.org/10.1177/0027432115572230

Leiberg, S., & Anders, S. (2006). The multiple facets of empathy: A survey of theory and evidence. *Progress in Brain Research, 156,* 419–440. https://doi.org/10.1016/S0079-6123(06)56023-6

Mazzola, G. B., & Cherlin, P. B. (1998). *Flow, gesture, and spaces in free jazz: Towards a theory of collaboration.* Springer Berlin.

Noddings, N. (2005). *The challenge to care in schools: An alternative approach to education* (2nd ed.). Teachers College Press.

Ockelford, A. (2017). Towards a developmental model of musical empathy using insights from children who are on the autism spectrum or who have learning difficulties. In E. King & C. Waddington (Eds.), *Music and empathy* (pp. 39–88). Routledge.

Sarath, E. W. (2013). *Improvisation, creativity, and consciousness.* SUNY Press.

Saraydarian, G. W. (2021). "Space is the place": Thinking through a place-based pedagogy for jazz improvisation. *Jazz Education in Research and Practice, 2*(1), 154–162. http://doi.org/10.2979/jazzeducrese.2.1.10

Schnabel, B. (2021). *Using solo transcription to develop a personal jazz improvisational style* (Publication No. 28491455) [Doctoral dissertation, George Mason University]. ProQuest Dissertations & Theses Global.

Seddon, F. A. (2005). Modes of communication during jazz improvisation. *British Journal of Music Education, 22,* 47–61. http://doi.org/10.1017/S0265051704005984

Strait, J. (2012). Experiencing blues at the crossroads: A place-based method for teaching the geography of blues culture. *Journal of Geography, 111*(5), 194–209. https://doi.org/10.1080/00221341.2011.637228

Watts, S., Eldreth, J., Grant, T., & Renne, J. (2020). Caring and connectivity: A framework for active caring in the music classroom. *Music Educators Journal, 106*(4), 50–56. https://doi.org/10.1177/0027432120936329

Zins, J. E. (2004). *Building academic success on social and emotional learning: What does the research say?* Teachers College Press.

Zins, J. E., & Elias, M. J. (2007). Social and emotional learning: Promoting the development of all students. *Journal of Educational and Psychological Consultation, 17*(2–3), 233–255. https://doi.org/10.1080/10474410701413152

CHAPTER 18

FACILITATING TRUST AND CONNECTION THROUGH MUSICAL PRESENCING

Case Study of a Conflict Transformation Facilitator

KARIN S. HENDRICKS, DELANEY A. K. FINN,
CHERYL M. FREEZE, AND JESSANDRA KONO

CARE HANDBOOK TOPICS

Co-creating caring relationships

MUSIC education involves multifarious human interactions, and fostering relational trust is essential for those interactions to be authentic and pedagogically effective (Hendricks, 2018). Trust in other people is experiencing a generally downward trend, however—whether concerning trust of those across the world or those nearby in our own political systems and institutions of learning (Tschannen-Moran, 2014). Trust has been defined as the "willingness to be vulnerable to another based on the confidence that the other is benevolent, honest, open, reliable, and competent" (Tschannen-Moran, 2014, p. 20). These facets of trust are defined as follows:

- Vulnerability (willingness to risk, losing control of the decision but remaining responsible for the outcome)
- Confidence (expression of security and poise in face of risk)
- Benevolence (the understanding that the trusted individual will not exploit one's vulnerability and, instead, will protect one's well-being)
- Reliability (stability and regularity in expectations)

- Competence (successful demonstration of a skill: When a person is dependent on another, but some level of skill is involved in fulfilling an expectation, an individual who means well but who is not competent in that skill may not be trusted)
- Honesty (truthfulness, integrity)
- Openness (sincerity with personal vulnerability, willingness to share authentic self) (Hoy & Tschannen-Moran, 1999; Tschannen-Moran & Hoy, 1998, 2000)

Trust in education is often discussed through the lens of power structures, such as in Tschannen-Moran's (2014) *Trust Matters*, which is intended for an audience of school administrators who supervise teaching professionals. In music-learning settings, however, teacher–student power differences can often be a hindrance to trust: Unequal power dynamics in spaces intended for musical expression might place students in situations where they lack a sense of agency over their emotional, physical, and/or spiritual vulnerability (Hendricks et al., 2014)—which could lead to potential trauma (see Bradley & Hess, 2021).

On the other hand, communal music-making can provide a unique space for fostering trust when relationships are reciprocal and individuals are open to the expressive contributions of others (Benson, 2021; Hendricks, 2018). Trust is the foundational element of the compassionate music teaching framework (Hendricks, 2018), and it is considered to pave the way for other qualities of compassion (i.e., empathy, patience, inclusion, community) to culminate in experiences of *authentic connection*—what Hendricks and Boyce-Tillman (2021) have defined as genuine, honest, spiritual/emotional bonding through music.

Authentic connection in music-making encompasses authentic behaviors relevant to trust-building in any setting (e.g., accountability, being "real" rather than performing roles, and avoiding manipulation; Tschannen-Moran & Hoy, 1998). However, it also involves a sense of presence in musical expression:

> [T]he notion of authentic connection extends beyond connection to others, to include connection within oneself (Boyce-Tillman, 2016), as an experience of heart/mind coherence. [It involves] ways in which musickers might look inward and outward with self- and other-awareness, demonstrating a willingness to be vulnerable as their authentic selves are exposed—and challenged—through activities of musical and emotional risk-taking. (Hendricks & Boyce-Tillman, 2021, pp. 4–5)

In music education specifically, instances of authentic connection exist in spaces of "caring with," or shared experiences between individuals who are seen as equals but with unique contributions (Hendricks, 2018, 2021). Authentic connection involves relationships focused on "spiritual communion rather than roles to be performed, and where neither I nor You need be superior nor inferior" (Hendricks, 2021, p. 246; see also Buber, 1970). Given the foundational importance of trust in forging such authentic connections in music-making, as well as the essence of vulnerability and non-domination within these connections, there is a need for greater insight into the ways that trust might be fostered in non-hierarchical music relationships.

PURPOSE AND METHOD

The purpose of this instrumental case study (Stake, 1995) was to explore aspects of trust and connection embodied by Dani (Danielle Carragher, artist name Dani Larkin),[1] a Belfast-based singer-songwriter, folk musician, and peacebuilding activist who works within the field of conflict transformation.[2] She has been involved in an array of international programs working toward change through activism, creative writing, and music. Dani strives to create a warm and safe environment by meeting people where they are emotionally, and connecting to them through humor, music, and storytelling. One member of the research team described her as follows: "She has an incredible ability to be present and has a deep understanding of trust and mutual respect, which she embodies not only in her workshops but also in every aspect of her life."

Dani works in and outside of schools and has experience facilitating workshops in conflict areas in different parts of the world. Her work involves the process of making music with others in a variety of situations, entering each space explicitly without any agenda or goal except to be present. Her background in conflict transformation was of particular interest to our research as she engages in music, presence, and safety in ways that attempt to break down power structures and facilitate authentic human connections.

Procedures

The research team consisted of three music teacher/researchers, one of whom had a professional relationship with Dani prior to the commencement of the research due to an international collaboration through Musicians Without Borders.[3] Dani consented to participate in the research through IRB-approved protocols. Data collection included two 90-minute, semi-structured interviews with Dani, using Zoom, in May 2021; and extensive review of related artifacts (e.g., music videos, website, prior interviews with others) that Dani provided. Data also included notes of researchers' own experiences of authentic connection (Hendricks & Boyce-Tillman, 2021) with Dani prior to, and during, the interviews.

Prior to the interviews, we gave Dani a pre-interview writing prompt to allow her to reflect on questions related to the seven facets of trust. The prompt consisted of two questions: (a) "How do you believe the [listed] seven facets of trust are important in

---

[1] See https://www.danilarkin.com.
[2] Dani described her conflict transformation work as an engagement with music to experience and attune to others. Her goal was not to take sides or attempt to resolve conflict; rather, the goal of the transformation work was to foster human connection and expression.
[3] https://www.musicianswithoutborders.org

your role as a music teacher?" and (b) "Please describe a specific instance in which you practiced or experienced one (or more) of the [facets of trust]." The first interview focused on three topics: (a) lived experiences as a musician and conflict transformation facilitator, (b) the role of trust in that work, and (c) follow-up questions from the pre-interview prompt. The second interview involved a series of follow-up questions from the first interview, which the research team created after discussing particularly relevant and poignant issues that arose.

During the interviews, the researchers took a role of "facilitator, collaborator, and 'travel companion' in the exploration of experience" (Gemignani, 2014, p. 127). By exercising active attentiveness with Dani we had an opportunity to witness, firsthand, the ways she practiced presencing,[4] vulnerability, trust, and connection. Although we jotted down some notes during each interview, we also allowed moments of full engagement in the conversation to run their course without interruption so that we could embody the sense of "presence" that Dani elicited (see Ellingson, 2017). We videorecorded interviews for later transcription and analysis.

Following each interview, we wrote further notes about the ways in which Dani not only facilitated facets of trust and connection in her professional work, but how she modeled them in her interactions with us. We also reviewed artifacts prior to, during, and after our interviews and throughout the analysis. Reviewing artifacts assisted with triangulation (Stake, 1995), helped us frame interview questions, and assisted with data interpretation. Furthermore, the use of data from multiple genres (including text, audio, music, video, and our own art representations, as shown in figures below) allowed for a process of crystallization (Ellingson, 2009, 2017) in which the multifaceted experiences of trust and connection became more evident.

Coding and Analysis

Analysis was in the form of researcher interpretation (Stake, 1995), based on interview notes, review of artifacts, and extant scholarship on trust and authentic connection. We coded interview transcripts and other artifact-related notes according to seven facets of trust. Two researchers first coded both interview transcripts separately. Next, the first three authors met together to discuss interpretation and alignment of codes, and to achieve interpretive convergence (Hendricks & Bucci, 2019). We then went through the document again, organizing pertinent quotes by theme.

We engaged in member checks by sharing our report with Dani, to verify that data are represented accurately and that our interpretations were consistent with her perceptions. Dani returned requested edits to us via email. As a result of the member check, we made necessary clarifications and added further description where necessary. By studying the ways in which Dani facilitates trust through her musical engagements,

---

[4] We define presencing as the act of being fully immersed in the present moment and place, without care for the past or future, and eliciting a state of presence in others. See Berg (this volume) for a complementary conceptualization.

we hope to offer implications for community musicians, classroom teachers, and other individuals working in conflict situations.

Findings

Five particularly relevant themes emerged through the process of data interpretation: (a) the multifaceted and dynamic nature of trust in Dani's work, (b) facilitating a multilayered space of presence to foster trusting connections through music, (c) vulnerability and choice, (d) competence as self-awareness, and (e) trust in the process of music-making. Each of these themes is addressed in the following sections.

The Multifaceted and Dynamic Nature of Trust

Through crystallization (Ellingson, 2009, 2017) we took a holistic view of Dani's work, seeing evidence of the facets of trust both in what she was saying and in what she demonstrated through her interactions with us. It also allowed us to see the interlapping and dynamic nature of the facets of trust from multiple perspectives. For example, we noted five intersecting facets of trust (vulnerability, benevolence, competence, honesty, openness) in Dani's description of the creative process involved in creating a musical album in which she would express aspects of her authentic self to others:

> I am just delighted because that [album] is the truest depiction of myself that I could possibly offer to the world, and yeah, that's terrifying, but that is the only way I want to be, and it's the only way I can be.... It's not so much the album ... the album is perhaps the physical manifestation of that. But it's the process of knowing and learning and hoping and trusting and loving, and you know, seeing what happens.

We also noted an overlap of three facets of trust (i.e., openness, honesty, vulnerability) as she described her reasons for doing conflict transformation facilitation in Palestine and Belfast—her desire to learn for herself about the political and human complexities of these conflicts, her self-checks to avoid white saviorism, and experiencing what she termed "a soul thing" that compelled her to do the work:

> I just didn't want to be a person who only talked about all of the good things that they did and the experiences that they had and thought that was enough.... That's not enough, and that's never enough; it just isn't.

Vulnerability, honesty, and benevolence were evident in her admittance of the political complexities surrounding the Israel/Palestine narrative, when she asserted: "It's easy to see things in black and white and believe that you're right."

The intersections of multiple facets of trust (vulnerability, confidence, honesty, openness) were evident both in Dani's descriptions and demeanor when she discussed the difference between peace and healing in conflict transformation work:

> Healing is the magic that we have. There are so many terms we use, there are so many words that carry their own sense of burden or stability or whatever it is, but healing? Healing. Oh wow.... Healing is the ability to sit with truth, to know that it's going to be painful, but committing to it anyway.

Facilitating a Multilayered Space of Presence

During the first interview it became apparent to us that Dani highly valued "being present" not only in her conflict transformation work, but in every other interaction she had, such as with musicians in her band, with her friends and family, and even with us. When we asked her to define the essence of presencing, she offered to explain by first describing what it isn't: "Being present is . . . it's both nothing—there is nowhere else to be—there is nothing else to do, there is only that moment." She went on to describe a second layer of presence, where there is "nowhere else to be, nothing else to do, [but] we're able to communicate and recognize our feelings, our hearts, our souls, our minds" while also respecting the relative level of vulnerability that others in the same space were willing to experience. Finally, a third layer of presence involved an aspect of expression of those feelings that were recognized and communicated in the previous layer. She added a qualifier:

> It definitely doesn't always work (laughs), you know, sometimes being present is, like, physically being there, and if that's what the person is comfortable doing, and they're not physically being present in other places, but they are comfortably physically present in the facilitation space, then that's incredible.

Dani later described emotional and musical presencing as a process of surrender and improvisation:

> It's that kind of thing, you know, I just get so excited about it, I really do! . . . It's succumbing to fluidity. It's that surrendering to be like "here I am, this is how I am, I recognize that in this space that's going to change. I don't know how that's going to change, that might only change because for the next half an hour, I'm gonna play a blues solo," you know? And then I come out and that's grand, but it's a wonder, being present, to know that utterly means transformation.

The process of crystallization led us to create a three-dimensional figure outlining the layers of presence that Dani explained above and elsewhere in our discussions of trust. As shown in Figure 18.1, these layers build on one another and intersect with the facets of trust to facilitate increasingly deeper layers of presence. The base layer is "physical and mindful being," which according to Dani requires a willingness to risk vulnerability to

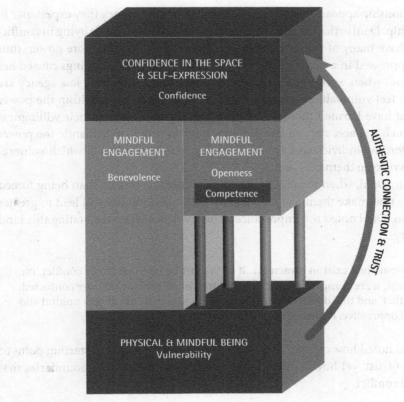

FIGURE 18.1 Layers of presence.

enter the space both physically and emotionally. Vulnerability and openness have their own reciprocal relationship, and both are necessary to experience a state of presence at this foundational layer. However, because physical and mindful being occur within a space of vulnerability, vulnerability is placed as the foundation. The second layer is the recognition of "our feelings, our hearts, our souls, and our minds," which occurs in the space of benevolence to oneself and others, with openness to the feelings surrounding recognition of self and "succumbing to fluidity" in mindful engagement with others. The third layer of presence is confidence in the safety of the space and in one's own competence to express an awareness of those recognitions. These layers happen organically and cannot be forced, but rather emerge through increasing levels of trust, which foster authentic connections, which in turn foster deeper layers of trust.

Vulnerability and Agency

Dani discovered through her conflict transformation work that vulnerability within a relationship—whether a music-making relationship or a relationship of conflict—is not always by choice. Furthermore, she found that the level of vulnerability a person feels in a relationship appears negatively related to the level of agency they experience in that relationship. Dani articulated how, for example, oppressed people living in conflict areas do not have many of the conveniences enjoyed by those with more power, thus placing the oppressed in a more vulnerable position. Such understandings caused her to consider how, when working in a facilitation space, those who have less agency are more likely to feel vulnerable, especially if the facilitator is working within the power structures that have harmed them in the past (thereby diminishing their willingness to trust). In such a space, she can use different tools in order to dismantle the power structures, affording individuals a choice to engage in various ways in which vulnerability feels less risky to them personally.

According to Dani, when people choose to be vulnerable (rather than being forced into situations that make them feel vulnerable), their vulnerability will lead to greater transformation. Dani noted the importance of benevolence when facilitating this kind of vulnerability:

> Conflict doesn't just exist in a vacuum. It didn't just be like, "oh here's conflict, oh, we're humans, we're going to go over to this thing called conflict." We *are* conflicted, we *are* conflict, and that doesn't have to manifest in ways that are deeply unkind and violent and oppressive. It can be transformed.

Similarly, Dani noted how conflict and disagreement can be used as a starting point to build spaces of trust, yet how it might be diminished by overbearing boundaries that limit potential conflict:

> We get stuck in this place of conflict, which isn't always a bad thing, you know. Disagreement has a great capacity to build community, right? Conflict is fine, but when it comes to putting down those [unconstructive] boundaries where there is nowhere to go, then that's different, because it doesn't [foster] trust, it feels more like a power struggle. It feels like you're trying to get people to do something, rather than, you know, having some kind of structure, but trusting that we're all open to wherever it will go.

As a facilitator, therefore, Dani attempted to strike a balance between overbearing boundaries and unstructured chaos. This process required that she, also, choose to be vulnerable, "succumbing to fluidity" herself, as she could not always know how things will turn out from session to session.

Competence as Self-Awareness

Competence in music education is often assumed to focus on particular musical talents or abilities (see Hendricks & McPherson, this volume). However, despite her many musical accomplishments, one kind of competence Dani exemplified most often was

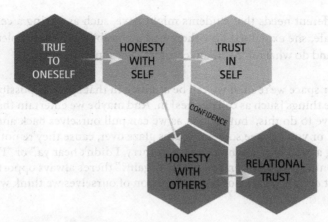

FIGURE 18.2 The process of being true to oneself (musically and otherwise) leading to trust in self and others.

that of self-awareness. On a fundamental level, her self-awareness was evident as she recognized her own virtue of being present: "I think I'm quite a present person, so by virtue of being in a room, when I am there, I am present." She further demonstrated competence as self-awareness through (a) exercising honesty and benevolence, (b) the ability to hold space, and (c) confidence in her own competence.

Exercising Honesty and Benevolence

As shown in Figure 18.2, Dani explained how the process of being true to oneself (musically and otherwise) leads to trust in self and others. Dani exemplified her own priority of self-awareness and self-truth as she explained her decision to turn down a well-funded PhD opportunity and instead engage in conflict transformation work:

> I just fundamentally believed that sitting at a desk was not going to fulfill my needs as a human being, my creative needs as a musician, as a person who wants to share that experience with others and to create change in that way.

Dani explained that, in order to have trust in oneself, one must be honest about one's own needs and fulfill those needs. According to Dani, if one is not honest with oneself in terms of needs, those needs are not likely to be met, which hinders the development of trust in oneself. Furthermore, she articulated how honesty with oneself may facilitate greater honesty with others, which in turn facilitates relational trust. This honest assessment and fulfilling of needs aligns with the four-part nonviolent communication process (Rosenberg, 2003), where one states observations, feelings, needs or values, and requests, without judgment.

Dani viewed both honesty and benevolence as being critical to building trust in conflict transformation work, and she encouraged communication as a means of helping others—as well as herself—work toward increasing levels of trust. For example, when addressing different needs that students might have, such as having a cell phone with them to feel safe, she explained how there was a possibility for benevolence (allowing them to have and do what offered them comfort), without judgment:

> [W]hatever space we're in, if we can be as much in that space as possible, we can bring those things [such as cell phones] in. And maybe we entertain that thought of "oh I have to do this," but so long as we can pull ourselves back and say, "no, I am here," or you can see someone's eyes glaze over, cause they're not listening, but so long as you have a sentence of "I'm sorry, I didn't hear ya," or "I'm sorry, I wasn't listening properly, can you say that again?" there's always opportunities to create trust even if we are not the best version of ourselves we think we possibly can be.

The Ability to Hold Space

Throughout the interviews Dani repeatedly used the phrase "hold space" to refer to the ways in which she engaged in conflict transformation work as well as musical performance. It was clear that doing so was her principal priority—she expressed multiple times in her interviews that she entered a space with no other agenda than to be present with people. Her description of herself "as someone who holds space" revealed how this aspect of her work was a large part of her identity as a musician and conflict transformation facilitator. Yet self-awareness was critical to further strengthening and refining this skill:

> [F]or me the biggest accomplishment has to be being able to recognize where I am at, and know that I'm not always able to be in a space to hold space for other people, and how do I, as a musician, overcome that?

Confidence in Her Own Competence

According to Dani, as a part of the process of presencing, "succumbing to fluidity" entails persisting through moments of trial and error with a confidence that trust will develop—whether in musical performance ("oh, I hit a wrong note, am I going to trust myself again to do that?") or working with youth who are resistant to adult intervention:

> If that trust isn't there [at first], what it comes across is like, "Oh you're another adult telling me what to do," or "you're another person who doesn't believe in me, or believes that just because I'm not interested in what you want me to do, that I'm not valuable in the same way." Trust takes time, right?

Dani explained that the development of trust had been critical to her work for years, and that it involved a self-awareness of competence that every party in a space of presence must develop eventually:

I have practiced creating it on my own, but at some point, the other person or other people have to also come in or also be competent in a way that is either, not necessarily musically, but have that sense of confidence in themselves.

Trust in the Process of Music-Making

Discussions of music-making were sprinkled throughout the interviews, and elements of trust and connection are present in our observations of Dani's music from her albums and website. To her, trust and music are inseparable:

> To put it simply, all music is an exercise in trust. That comes from showing up in the room to learn an instrument. That goes to improvising on stage, playing to a hundred thousand people. It doesn't matter what part of the spectrum you're on or experience, it is all an exercise in trust.

Facets of trust including competence, confidence, and benevolence were evident in her description of the initial steps of music-making, particularly in a facilitation space where she emphasized free improvisation with musical instruments that are shared among the group:

> I think a big thing is having instruments that you can play together. Like, I have the hapi drum, and I can give the beater to another person, and we can move in that space of presence together, because there are no wrong notes, well there are no wrong notes anyways, but whatever note you hit, it's gonna sound nice. So, it's instruments like that that are a gateway to music in ways that people maybe have put barriers in for themselves before.

Dani described how trust develops through the act of listening to one another in a group music-making setting:

> I think it's magic, you know, because essentially you're given a task, an activity to do, right? It's something that everyone can do. And if we start at the starting point, whatever that might be for people, and continue to do that over and over and over again, and have the skills to facilitate that, if we have the skills to show up and be kind and improvise . . . and listen.

From Dani's description of improvisation and presencing we observed an interplay of the seven facets of trust: Individuals show up with whatever skills they have (competence) with an invitation for them to determine what those skills are (honesty), and expectation that the task is something anyone can learn to do (confidence). They improvise together (vulnerability), continue the process repeatedly (reliability), and genuinely listen to one another (openness) with kindness (benevolence).

Through this process of listening, Dani articulated how individuals can forge trusting relationships that promote authentic connections, leading to healing and transformation:

> Listening is class! That's for me, like 90 percent of music! That's what makes music different from other things. It's not only the want to learn another instrument and play an instrument, but it's the listening to other people in it that encourages the building of trust. We use music to relate to each other. It's in relating to each other through music that we can heal.

Discussion

In this intrinsic case study, we observed ways in which Dani, a Belfast-based singer-songwriter, folk musician, and conflict transformation facilitator, exercised seven facets of trust (vulnerability, confidence, benevolence, reliability, competence, honesty, openness) to forge authentic connections with others through music. We were particularly interested in this case because of the way that Dani sought to work outside of power structures such as those more common in music education settings. Our analysis of interview data, artifacts, and reflections of our own interactions with Dani led to the discovery of five themes: (a) the multifaceted and dynamic nature of trust, (b) facilitating a multilayered space of presence to foster trusting connections through music, (c) vulnerability and choice, (d) competence as self-awareness, and (e) trust in the process of music-making.

Our findings on layers of presence resonate with those of Hibbard (2021), who described three aspects of presence in music teaching settings: (a) connection to self, (b) connection to students, and (c) connection to pedagogical content knowledge. However, whereas much of the previous research on trust has centered in educational settings where power structures are assumed, and where competence is viewed within a lens of achievement-based practice, Dani demonstrated a different understanding of competence as self-awareness, to facilitate increasingly deeper layers of presence that can lead to spiritual and/or emotional transformation.

This study of the ways in which Dani exemplified multiple facets of trust simultaneously to facilitate authentic connections, caused us to wonder what music education settings might look like if they focused less on external notions of achievement as a means of success, and instead focused on more global—yet simultaneously more individualized—goals of self-awareness and transformation. Transformation might be viewed as a personal or collective journey (whether musical, physical, emotional, psychological, spiritual, and/or social); whereas self-awareness might be a competency to act as a compass and support along the path toward individual and collective transformation. As Kellum (2021) has articulated, music education has the "power ... to transform and to be transformed by social life" (p. 179). Given more recent calls to boost the priority of creativity and improvisation in music-learning settings (Sarath et al., 2016), and our findings of the potential for improvisation to lead to trust, connection, and transformation, the time may be ripe to explore this possibility.

Acknowledgments

This research was made possible through the Boston University Undergraduate Research Opportunities (UROP) program.

References

Benson, B. E. (2021). Improvisation as spiritual exercise: The improvisational virtues of empathy, humility, and trust. In K. S. Hendricks & J. Boyce-Tillman (Eds.), *Authentic connection: Music, spirituality, and wellbeing* (pp. 33–45). Peter Lang.

Boyce-Tillman, J. (2016). *Experiencing music–restoring the spiritual: Music as well-being.* Peter Lang.

Bradley, D., & Hess, J. (Eds.). (2021). *Trauma and resilience in music education: Haunted melodies.* Routledge.

Buber, M. (1970). *I and Thou* (W. Kaufmann, Trans.). Simon & Schuster. (Original work published 1937)

Ellingson, L. L. (2009). *Engaging crystallization in qualitative research.* Sage.

Ellingson, L. L. (2017). *Embodiment in qualitative research.* Routledge.

Gemignani, M. (2014). Memory, remembering, and oblivion in active narrative interviewing. *Qualitative Inquiry, 20*(2), 127–135. https://doi.org/10.1177/1077800413510271

Hendricks, K. S. (2018). *Compassionate music teaching.* Rowman & Littlefield.

Hendricks, K. S. (2021). Authentic connection in music education: A chiastic essay. In K. S. Hendricks & J. Boyce-Tillman (Eds.), *Authentic connection: Music, spirituality, and wellbeing* (pp. 237–253). Peter Lang.

Hendricks, K. S., & Boyce-Tillman, J. (2021). Music, connection, and authenticity. In K. S. Hendricks & J. Boyce-Tillman (Eds.), *Authentic connection: Music, spirituality, and wellbeing* (pp. 3–15). Peter Lang.

Hendricks, K. S., & Bucci, M. G. (2019). "Everyone is always learning": Case study of a Suzuki-inspired preschool. *International Journal of Music in Early Childhood, 14*(1), 89–109. https://doi.org/10.1386/ijmec.14.1.89_1

Hendricks, K. S., Smith, T. D., & Stanuch, J. (2014). Creating safe spaces for music learning. *Music Educators Journal, 101*(1), 35–40. https://doi.org/10.1177/0027432114540337

Hibbard, S. L. (2021). Disrupting "what we know too well": A relational frame for considering trauma in music education. In D. Bradley & J. Hess (Eds.), *Trauma and resilience in music education* (pp. 35–48). Routledge.

Hoy, W. K., & Tschannen-Moran, M. (1999). Five faces of trust: An empirical confirmation in urban elementary schools. *Journal of School Leadership, 9*(3), 184–208. https://doi.org/10.1177/105268469900900301

Kellum, B. W. (2021). *A phenomenological investigation of access and participation: Music education in El Sistema, Venezuela's system of youth orchestras* [Unpublished doctoral dissertation]. University of Illinois at Urbana-Champaign.

Rosenberg, M. B. (2003). *Life-enriching education: Nonviolent communication helps schools improve performance, reduce conflict, and enhance relationships*. PuddleDancer Press.

Sarath, E. W., Myers, D. E., & Campbell, P. S. (2016). *Redefining music studies in an age of change: Creativity, diversity, and integration*. Routledge.

Stake, R. E. (1995). *The art of case study*. Sage.

Tschannen-Moran, M. (2014). *Trust matters: Leadership for successful schools*. Jossey-Bass.

Tschannen-Moran, M., & Hoy, W. (1998). Trust in schools: A conceptual and empirical analysis. *Journal of Educational Administration, 36*(4), 334–352. https://doi.org/10.1108/09578239810211518

Tschannen-Moran, M., & Hoy, W. K. (2000). A multidisciplinary analysis of the nature, meaning, and measurement of trust. *Review of Educational Research, 70*(4), 547–593. https://doi.org/10.3102/00346543070004547

CHAPTER 19

SOMETIMES I JUST CRAWL UNDER THE COVERS AND HIDE

Caring by, for, and with Community Music Leaders During Crises

FIONA EVISON

CARE HANDBOOK TOPICS

Co-creating caring relationships
Musical development
Philosophical perspectives
Wellbeing and human flourishing

THE years 2020–2022 were extraordinary, dangerous times, bringing powerful resonance to the sentiments of a folk rock ballad describing how one day, we feel dazzled by the beauty of life, but the next day, we wait for the sky to fall (Cockburn, 1984). Humanity's struggle against disease on a global scale wrought drastic changes to our relationships with one another. Compounded by additional political and social concerns, communities experienced great turmoil. Furthermore, communal music-making was suddenly interrupted—even suspended—in many places, depriving music makers of the comfort and connection that these activities normally bring. The recent crisis will eventually wane, but future emergencies may arise involving financial instability, ethical crisis, weather calamity, natural disaster, violence, disease, or even famine and war (Anderson, 2018; George, 2010; McNulty et al., 2019). Such times of turbulence can induce meaningful self-examination in which we, as music educators in communities and classrooms, reflect on and reconsider our practices and relationships.

Music participation's numerous benefits at all life stages and within diverse contexts are well documented and include a sense of connection to others, mutual respect, belonging, and physical and emotional wellbeing (Carr, 2006; Parkinson, 2020). Music educators are keenly aware of these benefits, and often are motivated by love of people and love of music in their commitments to music-making. Subsequently, disruptions to musical activity are deeply felt, and for many, the pandemic brought "chaotic and traumatic life-altering events that overwhelmingly touch every aspect of human life" (Ozin, 2020, para. 3). For music educators, this impact has depended on geography, governance, and instrument. For example, some regions experienced ongoing periodic lockdowns as case numbers spiked, making activity planning a challenge or impossibility. Early widely distributed reports of choral spread of the virus (Williams, 2020) alarmed music directors, but lack of scientific understanding about transmission set educators adrift in seas of uncertainty, often posting on social media to receive or share guidance (e.g., Dialogues on a Safe Return to Choral Singing, n.d.). As aerosol viral spread became understood, implicating vocal, choral, and wind instruments, care normally enacted through music-making suddenly became care that limited or avoided music-making. Consequently, disappointment replaced eager anticipation as classes, rehearsals, gatherings, and concerts were quickly suspended or moved online for what became extended seasons of muted music-making.

In the midst of this turmoil were leaders committed to caring for their musical communities. This chapter focuses on community music (CM) leaders, 12 of whom, through phone and email interviews, shared their perceptions and experiences of maintaining the "community" in their CM groups from March to August 2020. Using care ethics (Noddings, 2010) as a framework, I investigated the influences of extraordinary times on care relations within CM groups. In this chapter, I consider how care might be received and reciprocated when the face-to-face interactions between music leaders and their members are disrupted, and I reflect on broader implications to music education and leadership.

The following inquiry[1] arose out of care for colleagues and a desire for mutual support in March 2020, following the realization that community music was facing unprecedented prohibitions to music-making. Participants—eight male and four female—were invited to share their experiences based on their leadership of Canadian community singing groups, with ten leaders from the same geographical region. Nine lead faith-based groups, and all have amateur adult ensembles (sometimes multiple groups, including two children's choirs, one combined amateur/professional ensemble, and one professional ensemble). All but two participants are remunerated for their leadership. For clarity, I refer to CM colleagues as leaders or participants and to community

---

[1] This ongoing investigation has Western University Research Ethics' Board approval.

music makers as members. Pseudonyms are used to preserve confidentiality, and all participants have approved the following quotes and depictions.

I write as one who navigated crisis alongside these participants, with an insider's perspective as a CM leader for almost 40 years. As the director of both adult and children's CM choirs and the accompanist for a third CM choir, I rode the COVID-19 rollercoaster, attended virtual rehearsal techniques' training and safety webinars, and offered (and asked for) leadership insights. Isolation, disappointment, frustration, and technology challenges are familiar experiences. I have also cared for, received care, and felt absence of care over this time period; therefore, thinking through issues presented here is a meaningful process that helps me to understand the complexities of my own experiences, and to develop a new framework to consider care occurring under crisis within musical contexts.

Care Relations

Although caring for others is a concept found in both religious teachings and secular philosophies, Noddings's (2010) non-religious moral theory of caring is centered in women's relational experiences. Her relational emphasis ensures mutuality in which the cared-for are always active in the relation because their responses are used by carers to develop need-meeting strategies. In Noddings's education work, she proposes that teachers foster caring "climates" (2012, p. 777) where the essence of caring is reflected by the response, "I am here" (2002, p. 444). Other care ethicists have also argued for the centrality of face-to-face encounters in enacting care relations. For instance, Held (2005) states that "human relatedness and the daily reaffirmations of connection" (p. 2) are developed and reinforced through active, ongoing engagement between carers and the cared-for. Over time, positions of care (i.e., the carer and the cared-for) in adult relationships can switch so that the cared-for becomes the carer (Noddings, 2012). Additionally, Noddings argues that even though some care relations are "by their nature, not equal relations, and mutuality cannot be expected" (2012, p. 772; e.g., teachers and students), both parties still have valuable roles in establishing and maintaining the caring relationship.

Face-to-face interactions facilitate the attention required in care relations, enabling dialogue in which both parties speak and listen: The carer listens to and seeks to understand the needs expressed by the cared-for, and the cared-for learns the aims of the carer (Noddings, 2010). This receptive listening (attention) "is at the heart of caring for human others" (Noddings, 2012, p. 776) because it shows trust. If possible and ethical, carers respond to needs, and the cared-for shows that care has been received. No matter how small or indirect, the cared-for recognizing and responding to the needs-based efforts of the carer is a fundamental relational aspect of care relations. Without this response, Noddings (2012) states that there is no care relationship.

Community Music Care Relations

My focus is caring music education in communities where "teachers" are CM leaders using informal or no curriculum (Higgins & Willingham, 2017), and "students" are CM members (though both parties likely do not verbalize their identity in this way). So, how might Noddings's care framework apply to community music? Moreover, how does it apply to crisis contexts where face-to-face encounters of listening and response are severely restricted? CM groups, with their inherent community focus, have great potential to be caring climates such as those described by Noddings (2012), in which caring is practiced and confirmed, and members are guided to extend care relations indirectly to others in society. Care can be a central ethic within community music—especially when values include equality, accessibility, love, service, and humility, and making music might be considered less important than making community (Evison, in press). Long-term social bonds are built with members, and individualism and independence are balanced by relationships (Hendricks, 2018).

Noddings (2012) considers dialogue fundamental to care relations; however, while dialogue plays a role, I propose that music educators also enact caring relations through music-making, especially in communities with less emphasis on formal learning, with leaders who facilitate inclusive music-making. The music-making exists as a form of musical face-to-face encounter involving musical dialogue, listening, and response. Consequently, crises that suddenly disrupt CM activities also disrupt care relationships because not only are normal routes for listening, dialogue, response, and face-to-face encounters in disarray, but so is the music-making itself.

THEMES

How did such chaos affect carers and the cared-for in my findings? Framed through the lens of care ethics, the following themes emerged: *the challenges of novel care; shifting goals; need-based approaches; muted music-making; leaders' heightened care needs; diverse care experiences; outsourcing support;* and *care has a price.* These themes are intertwined with the tensions of increased expenses, responsibility, work, and stress, yet decreased income, resources, interactions, and sense of control.

The Challenges of Novel Care

Stemming from their commitment to caring through continued member engagement, CM leaders experienced many challenges as they found various new ways to maintain their communities, and thus their care relations, in the midst of crisis. All participants halted in-person rehearsals and gatherings, and steep learning curves resulted from drastic alterations to program content and length. For many leaders, new or existing social media accounts were used to facilitate and increase community engagement, often through online music activities requiring additional skill and time (Evison, forthcoming). In some cases, new staff were hired, or volunteers responded or were recruited for related tasks; but often, leaders acquired or adapted technological skills. Pre-recorded activities required additional planning, increased rehearsals, and advanced deadlines to accommodate production, editing, and posting processes, so schedules often changed. Only one participant's organization was already livestreaming, and she felt fortunate to already have equipment and personnel; however, as with other participants, she had to learn new procedures and software. Thus, the almost ubiquitous shift to virtual music-making resulted in stress, difficult new tasks to learn, vastly increased time demands, and frustrations inherent in media production and online operations. As one participant noted,

> It would've been nice to have tried this all a few months ago so that you actually knew what you were doing now in the midst of the crisis, rather than trying to do it for the first time, not really knowing what you're doing. (Sam)

Shifting Goals

Inspired by Internet groups who shared virtual projects, several participants attempted online rehearsals, only to be surprised by the cacophony of latency. (That latency was unexpected indicates the isolation in which CM leaders can operate). After a single rehearsal, one leader switched to hosting social check-ins, but others took Zoom rehearsal training, purchased specialized equipment, then held rehearsals where attendees were muted except for warm-ups and socializing. These directors eventually abandoned the season's repertoire, opting for simple, enjoyable pieces reflecting goals that had shifted from musical learning and performing to uniting their communities and providing "something that's worth tuning into, something to look forward to . . . something that they can think about . . . work on . . . because many people are very at loose ends" (Joe). Out of care for his wider community, Joe also initiated well-attended weekly virtual singalongs. Another participant, John, had his co-leader send out weekly repertoire lists so their choir could sing along at home to the leaders' videos. John felt that this activity, while a new venture for members, was all that could be done within the limitations of his choir. This extra effort was intended to maintain connection with the choristers, who were like a big family: "I just feel like they are there for me and we are there for them."

Need-Based Approaches

Anecdotes like these from Joe and John are no longer novel. They have been echoed in a multitude of contexts since March 2020, and they represent leaders' efforts to maintain various types of face-to-screen engagement. Perhaps more revealing, then, are the notable instances in which committed CM leaders did not provide musical encounters. These scenarios illustrate well the disruptions to caring, leadership, and music-making that a crisis can yield, especially because these leaders are committed to the benefits of participatory music.

The first example is the contrasting decisions of the two leaders with children's choirs. Pam moved online immediately, using Zoom sessions to focus on musical skill development and socialization. Angelica, however, did not offer any musical activity because parents worried about increased screen time required for schooling. Paradoxically, both responses demonstrate musical care relations because they were need-based and were recognized as acts of care by their members.

A second example is Sam's group, who illustrate evolution in care relations from non-musical to musical. They began with no musical engagement plans. Instead, written reflections were sent to members, and leaders maintained verbal connections diligently through a "phone tree" where everyone received (and often made) weekly check-in calls. These acts of care were appreciated and reciprocated. Sam then decided to send the choir emails with listening links about musical "anecdotes and discoveries." His initiative morphed into a daily project of research and writing—eventually 100 emails were sent to maintain connection and provide distanced musical activity. Members reciprocated with feedback, expressing gratitude. A missing—and missed—element, however, was sharing participatory videos. Comments during the weekly calls alerted leaders that members had begun engaging with other communities' videos. To respond to an obvious need, and concerned about disconnection, leaders began producing weekly videos, which Sam organized and filmed. Despite Sam's fears about potential low engagement from older members, feedback was positive, and members eagerly contributed to the mutual goal of maintaining their community. Within three months, the videos had tripled in length and participation, evolving from 15 minutes with two leaders to 45 minutes with five or more members and leaders providing a variety of content. So, although this group's musical response to the crisis was delayed, their care efforts were well received, reciprocal, and became musically and socially balanced.

Muted Music-Making

I have suggested that CM leaders provide care relations through music-making and are highly committed to participatory music, so a potentially surprising theme is the total absence of musical and social activity. One instance involves choristers in a seniors' wellness program in which only one member could use a computer. This example underscores the impact of technological inaccessibility since virtual rehearsals and meet-ups were impossible for this choir. Their leader, Janet, prioritized her choristers' physical safety and canceled all music activities. Members responded with understanding despite missing their normal musical and social engagement, exhibiting the reciprocity inherent in Noddings's (2012) care relations framework.

Leaders' Heightened Care Needs

As noted in the introduction, chaos and trauma can affect all aspects of life. Thus, relationships and support structures become disturbed for leaders as well as members. This impacts leaders' ability to participate in care relations with members and leads to a heightened need for leader care and support. For example, Janet, the leader of the suspended seniors' wellness choir, had no outside support and was disconnected from social media. She felt that "the whole world was in such an uproar that [she] couldn't cope with anything else." Likewise, this chapter's title, "Sometimes I just crawl under the cover and hide," comes from David, a leader whose need for emotional support—fueled by social isolation, program changes, and media reports—resulted in times of anxiety and feeling overwhelmed.

Janet and David are not unique because all participants were keenly aware of their emotions and unanimously described the sudden changes to programing and routines in negative terms like *weird, bizarre, strange, awful, appalling, peculiar, a downer, unsatisfying,* and *struggle*. They felt disappointed, empty, sad, powerless, terrified or mistrustful of technology, concerned for members, afraid for humanity, emotionally fatigued, discouraged, exhausted, overwhelmed, and even traumatized at times. Joan, whose adult CM choir transitioned online (but with less than half of her members engaging), remarked tiredly, "Everything seems to take a lot longer to do and is much more difficult." Leaders' fluctuating anxiety and energy levels conflicted with increased demands requiring peak performance, such as desires and expectations for professional quality virtual music-making. Moreover, factors outside of leaders' CM work that were also impacted by crisis—such as health, family, and financial worries—furthered their emotional burdens. This heavy weight is illustrated in Figure 19.1, which displays participants' interview word choices regarding their experiences.

Diverse Care Experiences

Each participant's story is unique, ranging from those who felt great care to those who felt uncared for. I expected that larger organizations with more staff and resources would provide more support, resulting in higher perceptions of care. This was not always the case. For example, Sam's previously described small, rural group with mostly volunteer leadership developed a flourishing care network. In contrast, a larger group with more staff and resources provides a striking example of muted music-making and disrupted interaction. Paul experienced months without personal communication from his organization, which also did not provide activities for members, but sent them elsewhere for

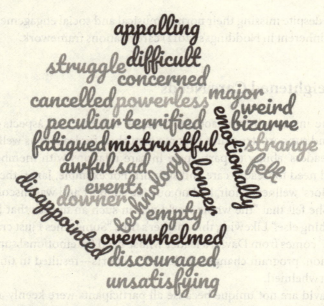

FIGURE 19.1 Participants' emotions varied but were often expressed in negative terms.

virtual engagement. Although Paul initiated email chains containing socially interactive prompts and music links for his choir, this effort stopped after a few months when he interpreted members' reduced responses as lost interest. This is vastly different from Pam's experiences within a large urban organization with abundant support and reciprocal care:

> [Leaders] have been nothing but supportive, also at the same time caring for myself and for everyone. They have been nothing but encouraging in terms of all the ideas that I have had this last little while, but at the same time watching out for us as well.... It brings tears to my eyes even just to spell out how grateful I am.

Senior leaders in Pam's organization visibly demonstrated care for members and staff by attending virtual music events and addressing the choir, as well as leading planning sessions where they cautioned Pam against undertaking too many projects and advised self-care as a prerequisite to caring for others.

Outsourcing Support

Some participants benefited from the support of skilled and supportive co-leaders, but in smaller organizations with only one leader, support, guidance, and training were often found through social media interactions. Organizations occasionally partnered together to draw on leaders' various strengths. Such mergers appear to have to overcome care disruptions, resulting in similar outcomes to what Pam experienced. Additionally, support from board members and other organizations helped many leaders manage the crisis.

Care Has a Price

When thinking of care relations, emotional engagements readily come to mind. There is, however, a practical, financial aspect to care, evidenced by organizational commitments to provide continued income for musicians, and a willingness to secure new resources such as equipment, training, copyright licenses, and dedicated personnel to record or run online sessions or projects. Usually, leaders' work hours increased, but they often did not track the additional time or ask for additional remuneration because many (but not all) organizations had reduced income. Members also recognized the price tag of novel care, and they reciprocated in practical ways, such as loaning or volunteering personal equipment and donating funds. Participants' comments about doing whatever was necessary and loving their community indicates strong CM commitments. In two cases, however, accompanists were laid off without discussion of potential financial impact. The peculiar fact that normally caring participants did not discuss this situation with the affected staff—or in our interviews—seems to indicate extraordinary levels of emotional turmoil and care disruption.

The Tensions of Care Relations During Crisis

As participants recounted their experiences and perceptions over the first six months of the COVID-19 pandemic, it was evident that this crisis had resulted in challenging and novel care, shifting goals, need-based approaches, muted music-making, heightened care needs, diverse care experiences, and support outsourcing, all with financial implications. Mutuality, face-to-face encounters, dialogue, and the presence of a caring educator are key to creating a caring environment (Noddings, 2002, 2010, 2012), but crises can erect barriers to such elements. The results, then, can be tensions surrounding the continuation of care relations, such as not being able to have personal encounters due to lack of support, resources, interest, or ability. If the essence of caring is reflected by the response, "I am here" (Noddings, 2002, p. 444), can care relations exist when leaders are unable to be present? Participants faced these obstacles by being willing to be flexible and experiment with new methods of making music as a community. They also attempted to support at-home music-making, which meant that approaches varied according to leaders' skills and comfort levels, in combination with what community members desired or could accommodate. For example, Joe not only hosted choral Zoom rehearsals for his choirs but also initiated new community singalongs, due to wide community interest and his desire to establish a caring climate that reached out to the wider world (see Noddings, 2012). Virtual face-to-face musicking was not the norm, though, and in some cases, no music-making even occurred. Members' appreciation and responses shaped how care was offered, and by whom, illustrating Noddings's principles of mutuality and reciprocity. For example, Sam's videos would likely not have evolved in the same way had member response and engagement been low.

One particular tension exists between leader support and how care relations were maintained. For example, additional support might have enabled Janet to find ways to overcome the technology barriers within her seniors' wellness choir, or explore alternative avenues for continued care relations. For Paul, who inexplicably received no support and who abandoned his engagement attempts, care and communication from his organization might have changed his interactions and feelings of perplexity, anger, guilt, frustration, and worry.

Paul's situation is also multifaceted when viewed through Noddings's framework. Although halting emails to members might be seen as a needs-based response, mutuality is likely more of a factor because Paul's cessation was caused by members' lack of interaction. From this perspective, Paul's choir did not fulfill their responsibility in maintaining care relations (Noddings, 2012). Thus, tensions can surround the expectations that exist at multiple levels of community music-making.

In contrast, Pam's caring and supportive organization created a care climate that produced a myriad of creative musical and social engagements for members and nurturing care for leaders. Angelica, too, received essential support from the board of her children's choir. Though they were not singing, her choral community initiated socializing, including Angelica in a network of care. This example also illustrates the fluidity of positions in Noddings's (2012) framework since, in a reversal of their pre-pandemic interactions, the leader became the cared-for, and group members became the carers.

Alternate Care Routes: A Model

During unprecedented, prohibited music-making, participants undoubtedly missed musical activities with their communities, but isolation from relationships was often more difficult. This aligns with observations that community music can be more about creating community than making music (Evison, in press). As this chapter illustrates, most CM leaders maintained member connections in practical and creative ways. They recognized the many possibilities for bringing together their community—a point summarized by Pam: "It doesn't have to be whatever everyone is doing.... It all depends on what you have at hand. Make your best out of it, be patient with one another, and support each other." This support could come from multiple sources such as other leaders,

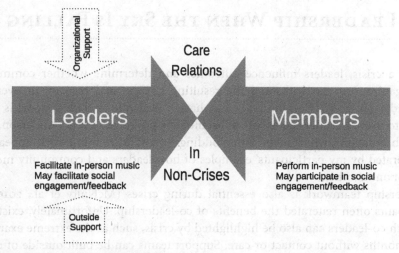

FIGURE 19.2 Routes of care in non-crisis times.

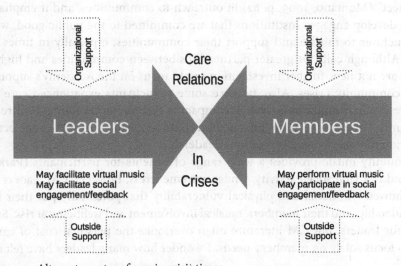

FIGURE 19.3 Alternate routes of care in crisis times.

staff, and/or the community, all seeking to care for each other regardless of whether or not music-making is possible.

I posit that herein is an answer to disrupted care relations: Instead of using preexisting routes of care (see Figure 19.2), multiple routes of care may provide the necessary support. As Figure 19.3 illustrates, if support is not available from within an organization, then it might be outsourced to the wider music world. These care routes existed previously, but they took on greater significance during the crisis:

Leadership When the Sky Is Falling

During a crisis, leaders influence outcomes and determine whether communities and organizations can withstand the resulting stresses and recover, or even benefit (Anderson, 2018). Communities, too, have a vital role as their support is fundamental to helping leaders cope with substantial or prolonged stress (Anderson, 2018). These observations, which align with Noddings's (2012) care framework, appear to be corroborated by my participants' examples of how leaders and community members cared for one another.

Leadership teamwork is also essential during crises (McNulty et al., 2019), and participants often reiterated the benefits of co-leadership. Unfortunately, existing issues with co-leaders can also be highlighted by crisis, such as the extreme example of Paul's months without contact or care. Support teams can be built outside of organizations if needed, and, indeed, social media played a considerable support role for many participants. Surprisingly, participants rarely mentioned support from educational institutions and choral organizations, which reflects existing "disjointedness and disconnect" (Montaño, 2009, p. 62) in outreach to communities, and it emphasizes a need to develop engaged institutions that are committed to the public good, with the infrastructures to initiate and support their communities, especially in times of upheaval. Although calls for greater partnerships between communities and higher education are not new, further investigation might focus on the Academy's support role during community crises. Also, because some participants experienced care breakdown, researchers might investigate the impact of such disruptions on an entire caring community. For example, more information could be gleaned from the perspectives of Paul's choir members and organizational leadership.

Community music provides a wide range of benefits for participants (Parkinson, 2020) and is a vital social activity. Under extreme stress, however, CM leaders in this study showed emotional and physical vulnerability that potentially put their health, their leadership, and their members' musical involvement and wellbeing at risk. Support is vital for leaders, but CM literature often overlooks the personal cost of caring in order to focus solely on members' needs. I wonder how many leaders have felt similar to David:

> I have been doing my best to stay upbeat and positive during the pandemic, but I will admit that sometimes I succumb to the desire to just crawl under the covers and hide.... I guess I would call it surrender or, perhaps, giving up.

The field would certainly benefit from a better understanding of CM leaders' needs. My discussions with CM leaders grew out of care for colleagues and a desire for mutual support, so it is possible that my interpretations are biased by familiarity and positionality. Participants, though, have confirmed my portrayal of their experiences and perceptions, underscoring an awareness of care needs at multiple organizational levels. I have attempted to broaden my discussion beyond the context of a pandemic, but perhaps COVID-19 restrictions and impacts represent an exceptional crisis with limited application to other contexts. Nonetheless, it is important to take this opportunity to consider what has been learned about music-making, music makers, and music leaders. At the risk of sounding trite, the pandemic has shown us how much we need one another, and how much we need music. Creative CM leaders have demonstrated what it is possible to achieve socially and musically under extreme disruption, but they also need caring support systems, which will benefit leaders and members.

I close with David's suggested antidote for anxiety: Do things with the people that you love, and make music. Although challenging when social distancing is mandated, community music offers the opportunity to do both at once. Whether in person, on paper, or online, it offers ways of making music that can be embedded in care for all parties—in times of calm, or in times of crisis.

References

Anderson, L. (2018). Leadership during crisis: Navigating complexity and uncertainty. *Leader to Leader*, *90*, 49–54. https://doi.org/10.1002/ltl.20389

Carr, D. C. (2006). Music, socializing, performance, and the web of social ties. *Activities, Adaptation & Aging*, *30*(3), 1–24. https://doi.org/10.1300/J016v30n03_01

Cockburn, B. (1984). *Lovers in a Dangerous Time [Song]*. On STEALING FIRE. Golden Mountain Music Corp.

Dialogues on a Safe Return to Choral Singing. (n.d.). *Home* [Facebook page]. Facebook. Retrieved February 22, 2022, from https://www.facebook.com/groups/dialoguesonasafereturn

Evison, F. (forthcoming). Musical engagement at any cost? Community music leaders' embrace of technology-enabled music-making during the COVID-19 pandemic. *Journal of Popular Music Education*, *7*(2).

Evison, F. (in press). The place of the composer in community singing. In K. Norton & E. M. Morgan-Ellis (Eds.), *The Oxford handbook of community singing*. Oxford University Press.

George, B. (2010). Leading in crisis. *Leader to Leader*, *55*, 24–29. https://doi.org/10.1002/ltl.398

Held, V. (2005). *The ethics of care: Personal, political, and global*. Oxford University Press. https://doi.org/10.1093/0195180992.001.0001

Hendricks, K. S. (2018). *Compassionate music teaching*. Rowman & Littlefield.

Higgins, L., & Willingham, L. (2017). *Engaging in community music: An introduction*. Routledge. https://doi.org/10.4324/9781315637952

McNulty, E. J., Marcus, L. J., & Henderson, J. M. (2019). Every leader a crisis leader? Prepare to lead when it matters most. *Leader to Leader*, *94*, 33–38. https://doi.org/10.1002/ltl.20470

Montaño, D. R. (2009/2010). Academic citizenship and schools of music in twenty-first-century "engaged" universities dedicated to the public good. *College Music Symposium*, *49/50*, 59–64. https://www.jstor.org/stable/41225231

Noddings, N. (2002). Caring, social policy, and homelessness. *Theoretical Medicine and Bioethics*, *23*, 441–454. https://doi.org/10.1023/a:1021385717732

Noddings, N. (2010). Moral education and caring. *Theory and Research in Education*, 8(2), 145–151. https://doi.org/10.1177/1477878510368617

Noddings, N. (2012). The caring relation in teaching. *Oxford Review of Education*, 38(6), 771–781. https://doi.org/10.1080/03054985.2012.745047

Ozin, G. (2020, March 27). Seeking connection through art in a pandemic. *Advanced Science News*. https://www.advancedsciencenews.com/seeking-connection-through-art-during-a-pandemic/

Parkinson, D. (2020). *A mixed methods study exploring diversity and inclusion in adult amateur singing groups in a multicultural urban setting* (Publication No. 2522320729) [Doctoral dissertation, University College of London]. ProQuest Dissertations & Theses Global.

Williams, D. (2020, May 13). How coronavirus spread from one member to 87% of the singers at a Washington choir practice. *CNN*. https://www.cnn.com/2020/05/13/us/coronavirus-washington-choir-outbreak-trnd/index.html

CHAPTER 20

"THIS GUITAR HURTS!"

Empathy and Caring in Inclusive Ensembles

KIMBERLY A. MCCORD

CARE HANDBOOK TOPICS

Co-creating caring relationships
Identity expressions

C.J. was playing the electric guitar for the first time. He was barring a chord across the adapted guitar with four strings tuned to A, E, A, E with colored stickers that guide musicians to match the color and shape of the notated music to the color and shape of the stickers on their instrument. C.J. understood how to decode the Figurenotes©[1] music, but the feel of the scratchy guitar strings under his finger was very irritating. "This guitar hurts."

His teacher was becoming exasperated and let out a big sigh. He mumbled to the other music teacher, "These kids complain all the time." C.J. once again said, "This guitar hurts! THIS GUITAR HURTS!" C.J. stood up and started to remove the guitar. Mr. Roberts (Mark), his teacher, replied, "You have to build up calluses and that takes a while. Why are you giving up so soon? We just barely got started."

"I SAID, THIS GUITAR HURTS!"

"C'mon C.J., tough it out! We need to learn this song today so next week we can start on a new one. Can you stick with this a little longer, just for me?"

"NO!" He drops the guitar as he struggles to get the strap off his shoulder.

Both appear to lack empathy for each other. Mark could stop the lesson and brainstorm solutions with C.J. His focus is on getting C.J. to comply long enough to learn the song, his way. C.J. just wants to leave. He no longer cares about learning guitar or playing rock music. He wished Mr. Roberts understood that the feeling of the strings

---

[1] Figurenotes© is an adaptive notation that connects to stickers on instruments that are used in rock bands.

under his fingers bothers him. He was excited about playing the guitar until the combination of the loud sound of all the other students playing badly and the strings rubbing on his fingers overwhelmed him. Mark doesn't understand why C.J. is so upset. He can't ignore the entire class while taking care of C.J. every time he has a complaint. He told Sherrie, the special educator that he needed an aide to come with C.J. because he knew it would be difficult for him to accommodate for a kid like C.J. What was he supposed to do now? He can't have C.J. having outbursts in class and he can't have him dropping his instrument.

Hendricks (2018) advises teachers to "provide a safe learning culture where mutual caring and concern is the norm" (p. 70). van Manen (1991) cautions teachers to put aside their needs and consider the child first or to consider, "how does the child *experience* the situation?" (van Manen, 2002, p. 1). Individuals who are sensory defensive can present puzzling behaviors that seem to be an overreaction to typical people (van Manen, 2002). Many people on the autism spectrum experience stimulation to one or more senses as irritating or even painful. Sherrie, C.J.'s special educator, might not have prepared Mark Roberts for C.J.'s sensory needs, or maybe Mark didn't expect a guitar to bother C.J. so much. The first class was missing caring and concern from Mark Roberts, and C.J. did not feel safe playing a guitar.

Blair (2009) explains the importance of the teacher creating a place of safety and belonging for students. Kelly-McHale (2017) further describes the importance of the music teacher to establish a classroom that is a safe space where students can have positive musical and social interactions. Mark might have been unsure how to respond when C.J. became upset. He might have reflected on a teacher in his past that said similar things to Mark. Mark had a difficult time in some ensembles much like C.J., but he can't imagine he was ever this belligerent.

How might this introductory lesson have gone smoother if Mark had been able to not only anticipate C.J.'s needs, but also to prepare himself to make the classroom a safe and accepting place for all students? He probably would not have been able to anticipate C.J.'s reaction to the guitar strings, but he likely would have known that a chaotic, loud classroom would be a difficult place for C.J. to not only stay calm, but also to focus on learning. After all, Mark was also feeling overwhelmed by the chaos and noise of the class. Perhaps Mark and C.J. might have experienced a more positive lesson if it went differently.

The lesson with C.J. was going amazingly well, thought Mark. He picked up how to read the music by matching his finger with the sticker on his guitar. In fact, C.J. seemed to understand Figurenotes© better than Mark! He was glad that teacher from Vermont suggested it in the Facebook group. When C.J. pulled up his finger and frowned at it for a moment Mark asked, "is your finger bothering you?" C.J. nodded his head. Mark asked, "what is making your finger hurt?"

C.J. pointed at the part of his fingers that hurt and put his fingers down close to the strings and said, it hurts my fingers." Mark mirrored what C.J. said and elaborated, "you say the guitar strings are hurting your fingers? That must make it very hard to keep up with the song, plus I bet you want to stop and give your finger a rest too, am I right? I'm going to have to think a bit about how to make the guitar strings feel better for your fingers. While I do that, can you rest your sore fingers and watch and listen to the other musicians playing?" C.J. agrees and lays his guitar in his lap.

"A guitar hurt my finger!" C.J. says looking at Mark. "My fingers hurt!" (C.J. struggles with speech and not only has trouble speaking, but when he does speak, he uses a very loud voice). Mark acknowledges what C.J. says, "I agree, I wouldn't want to play guitar if it hurt my fingers all the time. C.J., I am going to figure out how to fix the guitar, so it won't hurt your fingers." Mark says this while looking at C.J. and smiles. C.J. sits down after carefully picking up the guitar and laying it on his lap. It is a bit difficult to tell but C.J. does seem satisfied. Mark wishes C.J. would thank him for helping to make the guitar comfortable for him to play.

Empathy

Empathy is a necessary skill for individuals to cultivate to maintain a relationship with another person. The American Psychiatric Association (2013) defines empathy as the "comprehension and appreciation of other's experiences" and the "tolerance of differing perspectives" (p. 821). Typical individuals rely on emotional and cognitive forms of empathy to understand individual experiences of another person (Davis, 1996; Hendricks, 2018; Lewis & Brooks-Gunn, 1979; Shamay-Tsoory, 2009). The two components function together when the affective skill is focused on how the other person feels and the cognitive skill focuses on understanding how the other person feels (Zaki & Ochsner, 2012).

C.J.'s special educator discussed his Individual Education Plan (IEP) goals with Mark and explained that, in addition to his speech challenges, C.J. was neurodiverse; he is on the autism spectrum. Individuals with autism often struggle with understanding how another person feels and are often categorized as lacking empathy.

Musical Empathy

Ockelford (2017), among other researchers (Greenberg et al., 2015) identified a form of empathy that does not require recognition of the other person's experiences through speech or nonverbal forms of communication. Instead these researchers describe musical empathy as a way for people with communication challenges to relate empathically with others through music (see Davis, this volume).

Musicians (my preferred term instead of "students") who demonstrate empathy through music can connect with an individual or a group through expressive music that is experienced by others. Ockelford (2017) created a model based on case studies that demonstrates how the *sounds of intent framework* can be used to measure musical empathy in musicians who have severe or profound (dis)abilities. He focuses on the relationship between the composer/performer/improvisor and the listener or co-musicians. He describes how the fusion of structure and content create a blend of thoughts and feelings that produce the *aesthetic response*. This process surmises that the creator and re-creator use music to share thoughts and feelings or an *aesthetic response*.

I notice musical empathy occurring in several musicians with autism who otherwise have strong musical skills on par with typical peers. Even though the musicians I work with are not in the severe or profound range of functioning, I notice musical empathy regularly as they make music with others. Musicians with autism respond to improvised phrases that musically communicate a particular mood. Berliner (1994) describes this practice among jazz masters, "when soloists trade eights or fours and other short, improvised phrases, they sometimes respond to the most general features of each other's phrases" (p. 369). I recognize this call and response type improvisation as musical empathy. General features include tempo, harmony, rhythm, and emotion.

Edith Stein (1964) describes empathy as going beyond the I and you and instead becoming we through becoming members of a community. Many recognize a music ensemble as a community (King & Roussou, 2017; Oliver, 2017; Rahaim, 2017; Waddington, 2017). Donald Rindale, a musicologist with autism, describes the joy of playing with an ensemble:

> I found ensemble performance to be a welcome refuge from the interpersonal engagements that I had to endure in the outside world. The music did not laugh, or judge, or make nasty comments, or quizzical facial expressions and gestures at the sight of some of my unexpected behavioral tendencies. (Bakan, 2018, p. 45)

Rachel[2] describes singing with a group of good musicians as "the only time in my life that I truly feel myself" (personal communication, October 5, 2021).

Ockelford (2017) explains that music has the potential to convey emotion and create a sense of interpersonal connection. Others in the field of music psychology and education (Juslin, 2001, 2009; Juslin & Vastjall, 2008) highlight the ability of people listening to music to perceive the emotional expression conveyed by musicians in performance and then "mimic" this expression internally (Cross et al., 2012; Seddon, 2005). Ockelford (2017) further dissects musical empathy as being a "different route (through abstract patterns of sound rather than words or actions)" (p. 42). Livingstone and Thompson (2009) believe musical empathy is distinct from the two other types of empathy (emotional and cognitive). Is it possible that persons with autism who struggle with empathy can access musical empathy and connect with the emotions of others being conveyed through music?

---

[2] Rachel is a young singer with autism. She has perfect pitch, and the ability to hear six pitches at the same time and the ability to decipher and label each note.

Promoting a Safe Environment

A safe learning environment can become complicated when we welcome students with (dis)abilities. Collaborating with the special educator to understand fully what a safe learning environment might be for each specific student is essential for less-experienced teachers. Recently I interviewed 22 university music education students in a popular music course that included learning to play unfamiliar rock band instruments by ear. Only one person shared being diagnosed with autism; two others had accommodations for their learning (dis)abilities. None of the 19 remaining students had accommodations or shared any further need for accommodations. Several themes emerged from my students' description of a safe learning environment:

- A place where musicians need to feel valued by their bandmates.
- A place where musicians feel safe enough to receive feedback from their bandmates.
- A place where musicians feel supported as soloists by their bandmates.
- Bandmates respond appropriately to others when confronted with differences.
- Musicians feel that they contribute musically in ways that make the band sound good.
- Musicians feel a sense of community through making music with each other

Students with (dis)abilities are often bullied and studies report that many are bullies. Having a (dis)ability was associated with increased "victimization, assisting, and defending behavior" (Malecki et al., 2020, p. 127). Students with emotional disorder are more likely to be involved in bullying behaviors (Malecki et al., 2020). Previous research also supports the claim that students with (dis)abilities have nearly double the rate of bullying than students without (dis)abilities (Bear et al., 2015; Eisenberg et al., 2015; Janssen et al., 2004; Robinson & Espelage, 2012). In addition, students with (dis)abilities are bullied at greater rates than students without (dis)abilities. Students with learning disabilities, autism, and emotional disorders report being bullied more than students with other types of (dis)abilities. (Baumeister et al., 2008; Carter & Spencer, 2006; Rose & Espelage, 2012). Glumbic and Zunic-Pavlovic (2010) found that students with intellectual (dis)abilities were 18% more likely to take part in bullying others or to be bullied themselves.

Young musicians sometimes need coaching on how to function socially and musically as empathic and caring bandmates. Consider the ethical consequences for attempting to develop empathy and caring among students on the autism spectrum. Personality is fairly engrained by the time someone becomes a teenager. Is it ethical to expect individuals with autism to take on something that is exceptionally difficult for many people to change? Consider how much energy it must take for someone with sensory challenges to take in and function in our ensembles and classrooms. Often our ensembles are noisy and chaotic classrooms. Our rehearsal rooms might also include very large groups of students who knowing that only one adult is in the room, take advantage of an opportunity to engage their colleague with autism who might be rocking back and forth in an effort to calm herself. Bakan (2018) describes the person with autism as often being rejected socially because they are devoid of social and communication skills. If he is right, teachers cannot expect empathy and caring to be present in their interactions with others. Imagine C.J. and Mark trying to interact when both have difficulty with empathy and caring. Is it possible for either to change or even recognize that the other struggles with social skills and communicating feelings because their sensory integration disorder takes so much energy that there is nothing left to give the other?

Another example of a situation that came up in a high school choral rehearsal involved Rachel (see footnote 2). In addition, when the band plays, she can hear if a guitarist is playing an F chord versus an F7 chord and is not afraid to yell, "how many times do I have to hear F instead of F7? Just add the Eb PLEASE!!!" The others in the room value her musicianship but fear her when she becomes angry at them. She is creating an unsafe environment, yet the mistakes others make are highly frustrating to her and it is very difficult for her to not become angry. She has little patience for musicians who do not play the music perfectly, even herself. She rarely makes mistakes, and she is quick to point it out. She does not remember to thank the musicians who were playing her music but expects them to want to accompany her when she needs a band. She wants to be a professional singer and she has the prerequisite musical skills needed, but she lacks communication skills required to lead a band at least in a way that encourages band members to continue to want to collaborate with her.

Rachel's previous music teachers have removed her from choir, the musical, orchestra, and general music classes, essentially every school music class in which she was ever enrolled. Her outbursts are not meant to hurt people, but they do. Being removed from music was not only embarrassing, but it was the one class that she felt like her peers respected her and valued her musicianship. Rachel can manage her behavior when the choir is singing their parts well and the director catches and fixes the mistakes. When mistakes occur too frequently without being fixed, she is unable to remain silent. She corrected her high school choral teacher, Mrs. Charles, so often that choir became unsafe for the teacher.

Mrs. Charles began to dread the afternoons the choir rehearsed because she knew Rachel would be there making her look incompetent. It was beginning to impact her command of the group. As soon as Rachel would call her out on a mistake, they would begin arguing about how inappropriate it was for Rachel to behave that way. Meanwhile, the class would either be laughing or talking to each other, and when she tried to regain their attention, it was impossible to gain their focus and continue with a productive rehearsal. She could tell that the students who really wanted to sing were frustrated too.

Mrs. Charles had lost her ability to interact positively with Rachel. Rachel would often mention that she was just trying to help Mrs. Charles because the same singers kept making the same mistakes and Mrs. Charles wasn't addressing the problem. Is it possible that like Mark and C.J., Mrs. Charles and Rachel were also at a point of lack of care for each other? Mrs. Charles was so frustrated with Rachel that she had grown to dislike her and the problems she was causing with the choir. Rachel on the other hand, was so distracted by hearing the choir sing the wrong notes that she felt like she had to speak up or she would start screaming. The choir was no longer a safe place for Rachel, Mrs. Charles, and most of the choir members. Eventually the teacher insisted on having Rachel transferred to an art class. Was the best solution to have Rachel removed?

It is unfortunate that the situation was allowed to escalate to such an unbearable state. How could this ensemble have functioned differently for everyone? Teachers in such a situation might do well to find out about any students registered for a class or ensemble who has adaptations or accommodations to access their curriculum. Often these adaptations or accommodations might look different in a music class. For example, the sound is at times overwhelming to process for both C.J. and Rachel. In these cases, teachers might work with the special educator to find a quieter, safe place where the student can take breaks when they feel overwhelmed. Noise-canceling headphones work wonders, and with the right guitar amplifier, students like C.J. can control the volume and hear themselves over their peers.

It is important for teachers to be consistent and fair. Rachel and Mrs. Charles could benefit from an objective facilitator to work out a compromise. For example: Rachel may not be allowed to argue and interrupt the choir rehearsal, and Mrs. Charles would not remove her from the group. They might work out a subtle sign (e.g., Rachel tugging her ear lobe) when Rachel finds herself trying to hold back her urge to correct the mistakes. If Mrs. Charles doesn't respond to the sign because she isn't noticing Rachel, the prearranged quiet spot is an acceptable place for Rachel to go sit and cool down. Rachel can then return whenever she feels ready.

Exercising empathy through compassionate teaching, as theorized by Hendricks (2018), might mean recognizing the difference between a student truly being unruly to hurt someone, and a student hurting someone in the process of expressing her frustration about a mistake. Creating strategies for returning the choral rehearsal to an ensemble that feels like a community makes it a safe musical environment and an efficient use of everyone's time. Rachel feels cared for because she now has the autonomy to be in the choir rehearsal or not, depending on her tolerance level. Mrs. Charles ends the rehearsal a bit early and goes over the pieces with Rachel and often makes a note of problems based on what Rachel heard. She remembers to thank Rachel for helping and Rachel returns the compliment with "you are welcome!" Both feel that the other values her, and this feeling causes the two to want to try other ways of creating a caring relationship between them. Rachel has an enlarged score for every piece and keeps her notes on this copy. At times Mrs. Charles notices her taking the score with her to the cool-down place. This makes Mrs. Charles feel better about Rachel leaving the class. She is still staying musically engaged.

There is a commonly used instrument that is very accessible for students with physical (dis)abilities. It does not cost much, is adaptable so almost anyone can play it independently, and is easy enough to set up that the student's aide does not need any assistance from the music teacher. It is a Velcro band with jingle bells attached to it. Would you want to play that every day in music class?

How does the music teacher who values mutual caring and concern work with students with severe or profound (dis)abilities when the class plays instruments? Unfortunately, the Velcro jingle bells are not usually selected by the student, and they often do not fit with the other instruments or songs we teach, except at winter holiday time. How do we know if the student wants to play them? Why do we avoid the other instruments in our classroom? Checking in with the student and asking, "Is this the best way for you to learn?" shows caring and empowers the student to have control over their own learning.

Neither Rachel nor C.J. can show empathy for the adults as they work hard to enable the two students to participate and make music in their classrooms. At times this continues to irritate both Mark and Mrs. Charles. Mark gave up a hiking trip with his friends to be prepared to help C.J. C.J. has never thanked him.

Later in the year students in C.J.'s class are offered the chance to play solos. The solos are call and response over a twelve-bar blues. Each musician plays on one chord and the other plays when the chord changes. C.J. agrees to play a solo with another guitarist. He plays first and the other musician plays an answer that complements C.J.'s musical question. C.J. looks at the other guitarist and smiles.

Call and response is an excellent way to access musical empathy (McCord, 2009; Ockelford, 2017). C.J. was able to communicate musically with his peers and his smile was his way of expressing affective empathy. Imagine the joy he must have felt when he recognized his peer answering his musical question. Imagine his big smile when his teacher told him after class that he played one of the best solos he had ever heard and that he was proud of him. Finally, imagine the phone call home that night to C.J.'s parents and Mark relaying the solo moment that occurred that day in class. His parents initially were worried about why Mark was calling; previous calls from teachers were about behavioral or academic complaints. Imagine the celebration at C.J.'s home that night.

Final Thoughts

This chapter has provided vignettes about C.J., Rachel and their teachers, all of whom struggled with empathy and caring, which created an unsafe learning environment. Often former students of mine email me out of frustration when they have students with difficult and often puzzling behaviors. Unfortunately, there never is one answer that works for all situations. I have had success using jazz improvisation to help musicians access musical empathy, but it is always dependent on countless different factors, any one of which could throw off the whole activity.

I remember one rehearsal when Rachel was particularly enjoying the lead guitar players' improvised solos on a blues-based tune she selected. Another musician asked her if she would like to trade fours with him and what occurred was magical. Their improvisations continued for something like a dozen choruses, each one better than the one before. She was enjoying scat singing imitating his solos and then he switched and imitated her. They were both delighted with the entire experience. The guitarist remembers that moment when she shouted at him for being a quarter step sharp. Rachel is working on her professionalism, and although she still forgets to thank the musicians, she has been working on not shouting orders. C.J. only played guitar for one year. It was fun but he prefers the yoga class he is in now. Mark and Mrs. Charles continue to have an occasional perplexing student who gets under their skin from time to time, but goosebumps still occur for their young musicians and their teachers when those musically empathic rehearsals make everyone recall why they love music so much.

References

American Psychiatric Association. (2013). *Diagnostic and Statistical Manual of Mental Disorders* (5th ed.). APA. https://doi.org/10.1176/appi.books.9780890425596

Baumeister, A. L., Storch, E. A., & Geffken, G. R. (2008). Peer victimization in children with learning disabilities. *Child and Adolescent Social Work Journal, 25*, 11–23.

Bear, G. G., Mantz, L. S., Glutting, J. J., Yang, C., & Boyer, D. E. (2015). Differences in bullying victimization between students with and without disabilities. *School Psychology Review, 44*, 98–116. https://doi.org/10.17105/SPR44-1.98-116

Blair, D. V. (2009). Nurturing music learners in Mrs. Miller's "family room": A secondary classroom for students with special needs. *Research Studies in Music Education, 31*(1), 20–36. https://doi.org/10.1177%2F1321103X09103628

Carter, B. B., & Spencer, V. G. (2006). The fear factor: Bullying and students with disabilities. *International Journal of Special Education, 21*, 11–23.

Clark, C. A., & Chadwick, D. M. (1980). *Clinically adapted instruments for the multiply handicapped*. Magnamusic-Baton.

Cross, I., Laurence, F., & Rabinwitch, T. (2012). Empathic creativity in musical group practices. In G. McPherson & G. Welch (Eds.), *The Oxford handbook of music education* (Vol. 2, pp. 337–353). Oxford University Press. https://doi.org/10.1093/oxfordhb/9780199928019.013.0023

Davis, M. (1996). *Empathy*. Westview Press.

Edgar, S. N. (ed.). (2017). *Music education and social emotional learning: The heart of teaching music*. GIA Publications.

Eisenberg, M. E., Gower, A. L., McMorris, B. J., & Bucchianeri, M. M. (2015). Vulnerable bullies: Perception of peer harassment among youths across sexual orientation, weight, and disability status. *American Journal of Public Health, 105*(9), 1784–1791. https://doi.org/10.2105/AJPH.2015.302704

Elliott, B., Macks, P., Dea, A., & Matsko, T. (1982). *Guide to the selection of musical instruments with respect to physical ability and disability*. MMB.

Glumbic, N., & Zunic-Pavlovic, V. (2010). Bullying behavior in children with intellectual disability. *Procedia—Social and Behavioral Sciences, 2*(2), 2784–2788. https://doi.org/10.1016/j.sbspro.2010.03.415

Greenberg, D., Renfrew, P. J., & Baron-Cohen, S. (2015). Can music increase empathy? Interpreting musical experience through the empathizing-systemizing (E-S) theory. *Empirical Musicology Review, 10*(1), 79–94.

Hendricks, K. S. (2018). *Compassionate music teaching*. Rowman & Littlefield.

Janssen, I., Craig, W. M., Boyce, W. F., & Pickett, W. (2004). Associations between overweight and obesity with bullying behaviors in school-aged children. *Pediatrics*, *113*(5), 1187–1194. https://doi.org/10.1542/peds.113.5.1187

Juslin, P. (2001). Communicating emotion in human performance: A review and a theoretical framework. In P. Juslin & J. Sloboda (Eds.), *Music and emotion: Theory and research* (pp. 309–337). Oxford University Press.

Juslin, P., & Vastjall, D. (2008). Emotional responses to music: The need to consider underlying mechanisms. *Behavioral and Brain Sciences*, *31*(5), 559–575. https://doi.org/10.1017/s01405 25x08005293

Juslin, P. N. (2009). Emotion in music performance. In S. S. Hallam, I. Cross, & M. Thaut (Eds.), *Oxford handbook of music psychology* (pp. 377–389). Oxford University Press.

Kelly-McHale, J. (2017). Socialization in the music classroom. In S. N. Edgar (Ed.), *Music education and social emotional learning: The heart of teaching music* (pp. 29–54). GIA Publications.

King, E., & Roussou, E. (2017). The empathic nature of the piano accompanist. In E. King & C. Waddington (Eds.), *Music and empathy* (p. 267–282) Routledge.

Lewis, M., & Brooks-Gunn, J. (1979). *Social cognition and the acquisition of self*. Plenum Press.

Livingstone, R. S., & Thompson, W. F. (2009). The emergence of music from the theory of mind. *Musicae Scientiae*, *13*(2, Suppl.), 83–115. https://doi.org/10.1177%2F1029864909013002061

Malecki, C. K., Demaray, M. K., Smith T. J., & Emmons, J. (2020). Disability, poverty, and other risk factors associated with involvement in bullying behaviors. *Journal of School Psychology*, *78*, 115–132. https://doi.org/10.1016/j.jsp.2020.01.002

McCord, K. (2009). Improvisation as communication: Students with communication disabilities and autism using call and response on instruments. *Australian Journal of Music Education*, *2*, 17–26.

McNeeley, C., Whitlock, J., & Libbey, H. (2010). School connectedness and adolescent well-being. In S. L. Christianson & A. L. Reschly (Eds.), *Handbook of school-family partnerships* (pp. 266–286). Taylor & Francis.

Ockelford, A. (2017). Towards a developmental model of musical empathy using insights from children who are on the autism spectrum or who have learning difficulties. In E. King & C. Waddington (Eds.), *Music and empathy* (pp. 39–88). Routledge.

Oliver, R. (2017). In dub conference: Empathy, groove, and technology in Jamaican popular music. In E. King & C. Waddington (Eds.), *Music and empathy* (pp. 194–208). Routledge.

Rahaim, M. (2017). Otherwise than participation: Unity and alterity in musical encounters. In E. King & C. Waddington (Eds.), *Music and empathy* (pp. 175–193). Routledge.

Bakan, M. B. (2018). Donald Rindale. In M. B. Bakan (Ed.), *Speaking for ourselves: Conversations on life, music, and autism* (pp. 40–67). Oxford University Press.

Robinson, J. P., & Espelage, D. L. (2012). Bullying explains only part of the LGBTQ-heterosexual risk disparities: Implications for policy and practice. *Educational Researcher*, *41*(8), 309–319. https://doi.org/10.3102%2F0013189X12457023

Rose, C. A., & Espelage, D. L. (2012). Risk and protective factors associated with the bullying involvement of students with emotional and behavioral disorders. *Behavioral Disorders*, *37*(3), 133–148.

Seddon, F. (2005). Modes of communication during jazz improvisation. *British Journal of Music Education*, *22*(1), 47–61. https://doi.org/10.1017/S0265051704005984

Shamay-Tsoory, S. G. (2009). Empathic processing: Its cognitive and affective dimensions and neuroanatomical basis. In J. Decety & W. Ickes (Eds.), *The social neuroscience of empathy* (pp. 215–232). MIT Press.

Stein, E. (1964). *On the problem of empathy* (W. Stein, Trans.). Martinus Nijhoff. (Original work published 1917)
van Manen, M. (1991). *The tact of teaching: The meaning of pedagogical thoughtfulness.* Althouse Press.
van Manen, M. (2002). *The tone of teaching: The language of pedagogy.* Althouse Press.
Waddington, C. (2017). When it clicks: Co-performer empathy in ensemble playing. In E. King & C. Waddington (Eds.), *Music and Empathy* (pp. 230–247). Routledge.
Zaki, J., & Ochsner, K. N. (2012). The neuroscience of empathy: Progress, pitfalls, and promise. *Nature Neuroscience, 15,* 675–680. https://doi.org/10.1038/nn.3085

CHAPTER 21

FOSTERING RECIPROCAL AND RESPONSIVE MUSICAL RELATIONSHIPS IN A YOUTH INSTRUMENTAL ENSEMBLE

One Guest Conductor's "Caring With" Approach

ALLEN R. LEGUTKI, KARIN S. HENDRICKS,
TAWNYA D. SMITH, AND KRISTI N. KING

CARE HANDBOOK TOPICS

Co-creating caring relationships
Musical development

MUSIC-MAKING in an ensemble is a means of emotional expression, identity development, and community building for youth (Campbell et al., 2007; Campbell & Wiggins, 2013; O'Neill, 2005). The conducting style and teaching characteristics of ensemble directors can have an impact not only on skill development but also on rapport and social skills of young learners (Bergee, 1992; Duke, 1999; Hamann et al., 1998; Matthews & Kitsantas, 2013; VanWeelden, 2002). In *Compassionate Music Teaching*, Hendricks (2018) describes ways in which music teachers engage with young musicians to forge collective experiences of trust, community, self- and other-connections, and musical expression. She provides multiple case studies of ensemble directors to demonstrate how conductors can nurture a delicate and careful balance between conductor authority and student ownership, and between structure and agency, to challenge students musically while also instilling meaningful connections between students and with the music they make.

Over the past century, secondary school honor ensemble festivals in the United States have provided opportunities for adolescents to advance their musical skills while connecting and expressing with other young musicians (Barnes & McCashin, 2002; Hendricks, 2014; Hendricks & Smith, 2018; Hendricks et al., 2016). Participation in honor ensembles can dramatically influence adolescents' musical futures, even in cases of short-term engagement. For example, nearly one-fourth of surveyed music education majors in the United States attributed their participation in all-district and/or all-state festival ensembles to their decision to become a music teacher (Bergee & Demorest, 2003). Although guest conductors work with students for a relatively limited amount of time, given the intensive nature of some honor festivals, it is possible to have an impact on students' musicianship and sense of musical identity.

Fostering Reciprocal and Responsive Relationships

It is also possible for guest conductors to foster relationships of mutual trust, ownership, and shared leadership with ensemble members in a short time span. For example, a study of 11 guest conductors and 19 professional orchestra musicians revealed three stages of interaction between guest conductors and players (Atik, 1994). First, conductors establish a sense of leadership authority and trust, in which they demonstrate their competence and sense of musicianship (e.g., knowledge of the score, musical sensitivity, ability to communicate) to the ensemble members. Second, as rehearsals continue, conductors and players relax into a working relationship with expected roles and expectations (e.g., conductor leads activities and offers suggestions for improvement or expressive intent; ensemble members practice those suggestions together).

In some cases, a third phase emerged over time, in which the "superior" role of the conductor dissipated and the relationship between conductor and players became more dynamic, mutual, and flexible. In this third phase of interaction, the conductor demonstrated responsiveness to players' ideas and expressions, not only sharing decision-making but also allowing ensemble members' musical creativity to inspire unexpected musical phrasing and flow. This third stage resonates with the notion of co-learning and "caring with" as described in compassionate music teaching, where teachers and students are viewed as equal contributors, each with different strengths and contributions, learning from and inspiring one another (Hendricks, 2018, 2021).

The importance of fostering a responsive and reciprocal relationship may be even more critical when working with student musicians, particularly at a time when youth musical skills, engagement, and identities are still developing. It has been asserted that "engagement in musical activities should be associated with positive or healthy outcomes for all young people" (O'Neill, 2006, p. 463). Whether guest conducting or working with one's own ensemble, a conductor's awareness of student needs and responsiveness to students' musical expressions might help to foster such positive musical experiences.

A "Caring With" Approach: Conductor Mark Russell Smith

In this chapter we describe the ways in which one guest orchestra conductor, Mark Russell Smith,[1] fosters responsive and reciprocal musical relationships with youth as he prepares for and executes high school all-state orchestra festivals. We studied Mark because of his status as a highly regarded conductor who is regularly contracted as an all-state and honor festival orchestra director across the United States, and regularly guest conducts university and professional orchestras. He was particularly fitting for study of a "caring with" or compassionate (Hendricks, 2018, 2021) approach to motivation and engagement, given his prioritization toward modeling and fostering "enthusiastic commitment" with members of his ensemble (Smith, 2020, para 1).

For this intrinsic case study (Stake, 1995) we used multiple forms of data to capture the essence of the festival experience. Data included the following: observations of the conductor in rehearsals of two different all-state orchestra festivals on opposite ends of the United States; a two-hour interview with the conductor following the second event; notes from informal conversations with festival participants; and other artifacts (concert program, rehearsal schedule, printed music scores, emails). We made observation notes, which we discussed with one another following each rehearsal and the concert, to consider multiple perspectives from different locations within the venues. We also made video recordings of rehearsals and audiorecorded the concert from the second all-state orchestra festival, later comparing recordings to the observation notes. The two-hour interview was conducted by one of the researchers and transcribed by a second researcher. We conducted a member check with the orchestra conductor to verify and expand on the interview and observation data.

The interview, observation, and archival data were coded using the constant comparative method (Glasser, 1965) to determine what themes emerged in regard to the conductor's approaches to fostering responsive and reciprocal musical relationships. Field notes were analyzed first, and then additional observations, interviews, and other data were compared throughout the analysis to generate and refine thematic codes. We noted three cornerstones to Mark's approach: (a) musician-oriented rehearsing, (b) building a community of music learners, and (c) modeling expressive musicianship.

---

[1] For more information about Mark Russell Smith, see http://markrussellsmith.net/

Musician-Oriented Rehearsing

Mark used a musician-oriented rehearsal approach, which he demonstrated through literature choice, rehearsal style, conducting, and pacing (as described below). At the most basic level, he suggested, conductors must be "realistic about what's possible," referring to the skill of the performers, technical demands of each instrument, dynamic and color possibilities, amount of rehearsal time, and other performer-specific concerns.

Literature Choice

For Mark, appropriate literature choice was an important first step in guiding students through the process of making beautiful music. While preparing for all-state orchestra experiences, he communicated with festival organizers about whether the students could handle certain literature that would stretch them beyond their current skill level. He explained:

> You choose repertoire where there's always something to be done. You don't want it to be too easy. I think [Prokofiev's *Romeo and Juliet*] is a great all-state piece because it stretches [emotionally and technically], and it's so expressive.... I really carefully choose all-state repertoire because to be in touch with a masterpiece and to live with a masterpiece ... even if it's something that stretches you—*especially* if it's something that stretches you—that's what it's all about.

Rehearsal Style

Once the rehearsals began, listening, analyzing, and responding in each moment was critical for Mark to gain a sense of what outcomes were possible with a specific group. He shared:

> React to what you hear. If you go into an orchestra knowing what you're going to say ... if you say "I'm going to say boom, boom, boom, boom, boom, because it's going to be like this," it's a really wrong approach.... You go in, analyze, and figure out fast who's going to need some help and who's not.

Despite his flexible approach, Mark entered rehearsals with a plan, keeping a big picture in mind.

> Especially in a festival situation, it's all about pacing. It's all about figuring out where you need to be, how much to delve, how deep to dig or what to leave alone. Part of that plan is analyzing which kids can do what I want, what to work on and what not to work on, and pacing-wise, how many times you have to play a certain part. You still need to react to what's going on. You still need to have the capability to be spontaneous and change the plan, but you also have to have the overarching plan.

That plan included having a firm idea about musical ideas and possibilities prior to a rehearsal. According to Mark, these ideas came from "knowing what is possible because you've experienced it or you've heard it, knowing what kind of sound you want," and knowing the idiosyncrasies of each instrument.

Mark also focused on each student's understanding of their musical role in the ensemble. For example, he cited the need for wind players to "have a more soloistic approach in orchestral playing, which some kids are more comfortable with than others." He emphasized the importance of recognizing varying skills and experience of students in an ensemble, because "people start in different places." Having a formative image of musical interpretation prior to the first rehearsal allowed Mark to accomplish the first two of Atik's (1994) stages, establishing trust and developing a working relationship, after which he could later move into more reciprocal and responsive relationships after he spent some time with the ensemble.

Conducting

Mark's conducting approach was musician-centered in the way he communicated with students to improve ensemble cohesion and support individual members. For Mark, the conductor's role was critical to developing the students' listening skills and sense of individual responsibility. His approach was less about controlling the students, and more about communicating the expressive intent of the composer: "I try not to overconduct—even kids—because I conduct the kids just like I do a professional orchestra. . . . When you stop conducting, they start listening."

Pacing

Festival conductors often have limited input into the rehearsal schedule, simply by nature of the event itself. Organizers need to try to fit as much rehearsal time as possible into a limited number of days. Pacing is another way Mark was sensitive to the needs of the individuals in the ensemble. Specifically, his rehearsal style addressed the endurance concerns of high school students, while keeping all students active in the rehearsal whether they were playing their instrument or not. Mark reflected:

> When you look at those schedules, it's punishing. You always have to keep it in mind. In the way I rehearse, I break it apart so much that I know there's a lot of sitting around, but that's intentional. Having the brass section sit there and listen to the strings is good. Or, having the trumpet player listen to the flute player, even though he's not playing that movement, is good. You wouldn't play the big loud movement for an hour straight, over and over again, without stopping to fix things or giving people a rest. These kids don't have the endurance.

The vignette below illustrates how Mark engaged all students in listening and learning while allowing differentiated levels of repetition versus rest.

> "I would like the opinion of the low brass," he said with a thoughtful expression. He called for the cellos to play from measure 42. "Now let's hear the horn and clarinet." The

French horn and clarinet played their parts. He looked back at the low brass, saying, "One of these things is a melody, and one of them is the accompaniment. Trombones, which one would you consider the melody?" The trombones offered their thoughts. "French horn and the clarinet?" A nod confirmed their answer is correct. He then sang the intervallic, non-melodic, oom-pah-pah cello part and smiled, shaking his head, "Not that." With this acknowledgment, he reminded cellos to play softer and reminded the horns and clarinet that they needed to "sing out a little more."

In another moment of the rehearsal, he engaged the full ensemble by asking students to make judgments about the relative dynamics of different sections.

He cut off the orchestra. "You have to guess the dynamic," he said. He called for the first violins to play, and asked the other members of the orchestra what dynamic they thought the violins were playing. He listened to their answers but shook his head in disagreement. With his eyes back on the first violins, he shook his head again, giving them a mildly disappointed look. "I would call that mezzo piano." Again he challenged, "Now you have to guess the dynamic AND the Italian word." The violins played again, this time appropriately loud. "Good, good," he said, pleased with their performance. He nodded at the member that guessed both the dynamic and musical term correctly. He turned his head back to the first violins, nodded, smiled, and said, "Very good, very good."

The above vignettes offer examples of Mark's "caring with" approach, in which he modeled and taught reciprocity and responsiveness among the ensemble. Rather than simply calling out orders and demands from the podium, he took rehearsal time to teach students to listen to one another; asked them for their opinions; sought to understand what they did or didn't understand; and facilitated dialogue between students. Although he maintained his presence as "conductor" on the podium, he nevertheless fostered a spirit of mutual engagement where everyone was expected to listen and contribute to the musical process, even when not playing.

Building a Community of Music Learners

Mark built a sense of ensemble community by first teaching about orchestral traditions, such as rehearsal etiquette and "shuffling" (applauding with feet) for one another. He also built a sense of ensemble community by establishing rapport: "Hopefully, as a conductor, you have good relationships with your players. Not necessarily they're your best friends, but at least so you can talk to them. . . . It's a balance, and it's tricky." He also monitored the students' focus levels, and tried to engage them in appropriate ways when he sensed that he needed to shift the direction of the rehearsal.

> [When they need a break], I talk to them more. I tell them little stories. They need those kind of psychological breaks, and by that time, hopefully you've developed a relationship [so] you can take the time in rehearsals to really talk about stuff, where

you never would [talk like that] in a professional situation.... So maybe you become more educational, or theoretical, or at least talk about [music] more as the day wears on.

Mark also used humor to build community, as shown in the following vignette:

The orchestra was warming up for the afternoon session. Snippets of songs, scales, and other notes filled the air. Without a gesture, the cacophony of sound stopped as the conductor settled behind his music stand. "Good afternoon. How was lunch?" he asked the orchestra members with a playful smile dimpling his face. He listened politely to their varying answers. "The Dairy Queen? Did you get your complimentary cone?" he questioned with a smirk. When the saxophone player said a resounding "no," the conductor questioned him directly: "Well how come the sax player did not get a cone?" His head swung back and forth between the winds and strings sections as they discussed the injustice. "So the violinists get complimentary cones?" Apparently they did. "Were you carrying your case?" he asked the saxophonist, who replied affirmatively. "Maybe that's why." He mimicked a fast food server and said with a negative shake of his hand "No courtesy cones for sax players." Still with a lingering smile and hands outstretched for the downbeat he said, "Okay, let's continue in our journey."

Mark emphasized the importance of community because he recognized that many students were having a new type of orchestral experience, were meeting most of the other ensemble members for the first time, and were being asked to perform challenging music. He stressed that students can sometimes feel intimidated by high-level literature when playing alone, but "when you're surrounded by people who are your peers, it sounds like a million bucks. That's what's cool about orchestra."

Modeling Expressive Musicianship

Mark's approach to rehearsing also centered on the importance of modeling expressive musicianship. He described modeling as a type of "osmosis," in which appropriate models can transfer to a musician's performance. Mark shared stories of his mentors playing with student groups during his own training, reflecting that "we were transformed," and he stressed the importance of being around people who were more advanced than he. His observations of master conductors and hearing hundreds of auditions for orchestras helped to hone his concepts of sound. Mark modeled what he expected through his conducting, through guided listening of performances by certain members of the ensemble, and by performing himself.

Conducting

From the first rehearsal, Mark used conducting as a means of discovery for both the conductor and the ensemble. He acknowledged that the first run-through of a piece was an opportunity for analysis by the conductor, also stressing that "the ensemble can see what I want." He explained:

> Conductors need to have artistic authority, not authority in a ruler kind of sense. You know what you want, and you know how this should be, and somehow in your body and in your presence, you make that inevitable. Conductors need to get to a point where they can say, "I know what I want," and then your body shows it. Hopefully you've developed your technique enough where you just show what you want.

Mark's approach to conducting was to visually give the ensemble what they needed in such a way that "to *not* react to it, is hard." He also modeled emotional engagement through conducting.

> [Cultivating emotional engagement is] being relentless and demanding [such] that the character and the emotion in the music is brought out, and that the full potential of what's there in the music is reached. You use what [the composer] has given you, and you don't allow them to take the easy way out, or to stop concentrating. You just can't allow that, and you don't allow yourself that either. That's why you're on the podium and you're giving all of the time, because if you're doing that . . . if you're into the moment . . . those are the kinds of unspoken things.

Mark highlighted the role of conductors in modeling full engagement, saying:

> You lead by example, you are engaged all of the time, you are demanding of yourself, and you just push. You just don't accept that it's not going to have the full expressive potential that [the composer] intended, or that you as an interpreter intended. It has to be soft. It has to be loud. It has to be sustained. It has to beautiful. You can't give up. Not just for the sake of it, but because it's expressing something. If you just keep underscoring that and you keep living that, then you get excited when it works. Not because it's fake, but because it's really there. . . . It's so powerful.

Mark's descriptions of expressive authority above are reflective of Atik's (1994) first phase of leadership, where the conductor establishes a sense of authority and trust. As Atik (1994) explained, this first phase can shift into a more reciprocal and responsive form of expressive engagement after a conductor and ensemble members become more attuned to one another. Mark facilitated this kind of attunement, in part by guided listening to peers, as described below.

Guided Listening of Peer Performance

Mark occasionally asked members of the ensemble to perform sections as demonstrations of a technique or style. He guided their listening experience throughout the rehearsals to encourage students to listen to soloists or other sections, to analyze what they hear, and to make decisions about how to perform. He used this strategy so students learned to listen, to get them "psychologically on board," and to "get their souls on board with the music," hoping that other students might say, "Wow, it's possible."

Mark took care when implementing peer-modeling approaches with younger musicians, noting when students were "put on the spot" they might get anxious, embarrassed, or not perform well consistently:

> If it's not going to be possible, you have to recognize that as a conductor, too. There were certain players that I knew if we got through it, that would be good enough. You don't push the point to the degree to embarrass someone or to turn them off. There are conductors who do that. There are the screamers and the people who make people cry, but that's so counterproductive. What good is it? You need to do things in a positive way.

In this quote, Mark demonstrated his commitment toward fostering students' holistic wellbeing and maintaining a positive learning environment, which resonates with Hendricks's (2018) argument that expressive engagement requires a climate of trust toward risk-taking.

Performing for the Students

In addition to modeling through gesture and student examples, Mark used his own voice and his cello to communicate expressive musicianship.

> *He cut the orchestra off. Judging by his expression, the horns were not giving him what he desired. "This is a big romantic Russian melody." He sang the melody in a robust, resonant tenor voice, with chest out and arms flowing wide as wings. "The little notes cannot be so little," he said, his eyes scanning the members of the horn section. "It's probably not literally the right rhythm," he continued, seemingly a little unsure of his words but certain of his thoughts. He sang the melody first in strict time and then again, adding weight to the notes modeling the desired rhythm and timbre. "You guys are part of the big expression." He then called for the melody only in the horns.*

Through such an approach, Mark modeled the essence of the expressiveness that he reinforced in his conducting gestures, while also demonstrating his own willingness to take risks and continually improve his own musicianship.

Perhaps a less conventional means of modeling expression was through solo instrumental performance by the conductor. In the last rehearsal of each festival he conducted, Mark enjoyed performing for the students on his cello. We witnessed this tradition in both festivals we observed. In both cases, we noted that his performance of a Bach cello suite from the podium left students transfixed. Mark explained how this cello performance "parting gift" summed up his approach for the entire all-state experience and reinforced the messages he had been working to convey to the students.

> It's really important as a conductor, that you are capable of making sounds. I try to keep my cello up, but I'm not always successful. It's really important for humility and

for understanding how difficult it is to really do what I'm asking. If I'm asking them to play a phrase, then I better be able to do it. So much is about expression, and so I always choose cello pieces that are expressive on purpose, where it's all the things I've been talking about with bow speed, connection, and with using silences. ... It's not that I want to show them that I can play. That's not it at all. It's "here's an example of what I've been talking about the past two days. Here's an example of [how] music can express things that words can't." It's my way of saying thank you. It's my way of saying "we're having a special experience together, and it means something to me." ... These timeless masterpieces can mean something totally different at different times, and that's part of the reason that I do it, because it says something that words can't say.

These cello performances offered a quintessential example of Mark's "caring with" (Hendricks, 2021) and "compassionate" (Hendricks, 2018) approach. At the end of the final rehearsal of each festival, when he put down the baton and sat down at the podium with a cello in his hands, he became, in essence, an "equal" to the other musicians in the group. With each cello performance, he demonstrated a level of vulnerability not typically expected of a conductor. However, he chose to do so at a time when Atik's (1994) stages of leadership had already been established, and the group had developed a sense of trust, community, and reciprocity.

Conclusion

Fostering reciprocal and responsive musical relationships is not only possible with long-term or professional musical ensembles, but—as shown through the case of Mark Russell Smith—is something that can be fostered even in guest conducting situations. We observed how Mark progressed through Atik's (1994) three stages of leadership interaction with the players in his ensemble: First, he established a sense of leadership authority and trust, and then relaxed into roles and expectations (including those that he taught the students along the way). Third, as trusting relationships developed over the course of the festival, Mark used a "caring with" (Hendricks, 2021) approach to balance authority and collective ownership as he (a) opened up moments of dialogue, (b) invited students to listen musically to one another, (c) showed more of his own vulnerabilities, and (d) invited students to share in his joys of the "orchestra world."

Finally, in his interviews, Mark stressed the importance of listening and responding to the ensemble, and emphasized how the conductor-performer interaction is key to the shared musical experience where "everybody is synced" (i.e., making sounds in response to one another and in combination with the conductor's expressive gestures, performing and making music together). Although conductors and instrumentalists are most often beholden to a pre-conceived musical score, the experience of expressive collaboration shares many similarities with the concepts of empathic creativity and shared intentionality as described by Cross et al. (2012). As applied to a compassionate music teaching framework, shared intentionality suggests that "each person is free to completely express themselves while also cooperating with and experiencing the feelings and expressions of others" (Hendricks, 2022).

The case study of Mark Russell Smith offers one example of how a "caring with" approach might be possible even in instances such as instrument ensembles, which have traditionally been some of the most top-down structures within music education. This case has implications for music educators, particularly in the ways that they might nurture increasingly reciprocal and responsive musical relationships over time, beginning by establishing trust, and then working with ensembles to establish expectations and roles, and eventually creating a mutually expressive community with shared intentionality. As Mark noted, "I try to unleash the expressive potential in music. That's what turns kids on, and that's why we do it. That's why we develop technique, so we can express. It's important."

References

Atik, Y. (1994). The conductor and the orchestra: Interactive aspects of the leadership process. *Leadership and Organization Development Journal, 15*(1), 22–28. https://doi.org/10.1108/01437739410050123

Barnes, G. V., & McCashin, R. (2002). All-state orchestras: A survey of practices and procedures. *Update: Applications of Research in Music Education, 20*(2), 16–20. https://doi.org/10.1177/87551233020200205

Bergee, M. J. (1992). A scale assessing music student teachers' rehearsal effectiveness. *Journal of Research in Music Education, 40*(1), 5–13. https://doi.org/10.2307/3345770

Bergee, M. J., & Demorest, S. M. (2003). Developing tomorrow's music teachers today. *Music Educators Journal, 89*(4), 17–20. https://doi.org/10.1177/002242941730572

Campbell, P. S., Connell, C., & Beegle, A. (2007). Adolescents' expressed meanings of music in and out of school. *Journal of Research in Music Education, 55*(3), 220–236. https://doi.org/10.1177/002242940705500304

Campbell, P. S., & Wiggins, T. (Eds.). (2013). *The Oxford handbook of children's musical cultures.* Oxford University Press.

Cross, I., Laurence, F., & Rabinowitch, T.-C. (2012). Empathy and creativity in group musical practices: Towards a concept of empathic creativity. In G. E. McPherson & G. Welch (Eds.), *The Oxford handbook of music education* (pp. 337–353). Oxford University Press.

Duke, R. A. (1999). Measures of instructional effectiveness in music research. *Bulletin of the Council for Research in Music Education,* (143), 1–48. https://doi.org/10.1177/0255761416659509

Glasser, B. G. (1965). The constant comparative method of qualitative analysis. *Social Problems, 12*(4), 436–445. https://doi.org/10.2307/798843

Hamann, D. L., Lineburg, N., & Paul, S. (1998). Teaching effectiveness and social skill development. *Journal of Research in Music Education, 46*(1), 87–101. https://doi.org/10.2307/3345762

Hendricks, K. S. (2014). Changes in self-efficacy beliefs over time: Contextual influences of gender, rank-based placement, and social support in a competitive orchestra environment. *Psychology of Music, 42*(3), 347–365. https://doi.org/10.1177/0305735612471238

Hendricks, K. S. (2018). *Compassionate music teaching.* Rowman and Littlefield.

Hendricks, K. S. (2021). Authentic connection in music education: A chiastic essay. In K. S. Hendricks & J. Boyce-Tillman (Eds.), *Authentic connection: Music, spirituality, and wellbeing* (pp. 237–253). Peter Lang.

Hendricks, K. S. (2022). Contexts and conceptualizations of care in music education. In C. Randles & P. Burnard (Eds.), *The Routledge companion to creativities in music education* (pp. 404–415). Routledge.

Hendricks, K. S., & Smith, T. D. (2018). Eclectic styles and classical performance: Motivation and self-efficacy belief at two summer music camps. *String Research Journal, 8*(1), 33–49. https://doi.org/10.1177/1948499218769632

Hendricks, K. S., Smith, T. D., & Legutki, A. R. (2016). Competitive comparison in music: influences upon self-efficacy belief by gender. *Gender and Education, 28*(7), 918–934. https://doi.org/10.1080/09540253.2015.1107032

Matthews, W. K., & Kitsantas, A. (2013). The role of the conductor's goal orientation and use of shared performance cues on collegiate instrumentalists' motivational beliefs and performance in large musical ensembles. *Psychology of Music, 41*(5), 630–646. https://doi.org/10.1177/0305735612441738

O'Neill, S. A. (2005). Youth music engagement in diverse contexts. In J. L. Mahoney, R. W. Larson, & J. S. Eccles (Eds.), *Organized activities as context of development: Extracurricular activities, after-school, and community programs* (pp. 255–273). Lawrence Erlbaum Associates.

O'Neill, S. A. (2006). Positive youth musical engagement. In G. E. McPherson (Ed.), *The child as musician: A handbook of musical development* (pp. 461–474). Oxford University Press. https://doi.org/10.1093/acprof:oso/9780198744443.001.0001

Smith, M. R. (2020). Mark Russell Smith. http://markrussellsmith.net/

Stake, R. E. (1995). *The art of case study research.* Sage.

VanWeelden, K. (2002). Relationships between perceptions of conducting effectiveness and ensemble performance. *Journal of Research in Music Education, 50*(2), 165–176. https://doi.org/10.2307/3345820.

CHAPTER 22

SINGING AND CARING

ELIZABETH CASSIDY PARKER
AND JENNIFER C. HUTTON

CARE HANDBOOK TOPICS

Co-creating caring relationships
Philosophical perspectives
Wellbeing and human flourishing

HUMANS arrive in the world primed for mutuality and belonging (Dissanayake, 2000). Before birth and in their first months of life, infants attune to their primary caregiver's voice and heartbeat, seeking basic needs and safety (Parncutt, 2016). When a caregiver shares smiles and expressions with infants, who then imitate or respond in their own ways, the basis of mutuality is formed as infants see themselves through another's eyes. Infants age into toddlers, and the home environment becomes a primary basis of sonic experience, shaping one's preferences and ways of interacting (Bannan & Woodward, 2009). Expanding outward from their home environment, children add persons and spaces to their contexts, building additional affiliative relationships with peers and other adults (Erikson, 1950). Even as adolescents take ownership of choices and interactions, they also strive to see themselves reflected in others and experience belonging and solidarity with a group, whether it be through musical preferences or influencers (Hargreaves et al., 2016). When contexts shift, humans continue to look for mutuality from others within interactions that bring encouragement, comfort, recognition, and affection (Reis et al., 2000).

The human voice is one of the earliest experiences of mutuality and belonging. A fetus's first experience of the sonic world includes attunement to their mother's voice and movement (Kisilevsky et al., 2003). After birth, an infant's voice develops in relation to their experiences in the womb as they imitate the pitch behaviors of their caregivers (Welch, 2016). Imitation continues as children and teens emulate their favorite artists and songs, expressing mutuality with a movie character or storyline (Davis, 2016; Parker, 2020). Adolescents use their voices to share who they are becoming as individuals and as tools of self-expression. One's sense of voice therefore, is rooted in interconnections and regular interactions with others.

We propose in this chapter that the human voice—specifically the singing voice, represents an important way for individuals to care for one another in the world, a care desperately needed as discord appears more prevalent than consonance. We begin by describing connections between singing and caring, propose a singing-caring relation, and offer a holistic approach through which we might build singing-caring spaces in school and community music education settings.

Singing-Caring Relations

Reciprocal interactions between the cared-for and the one-caring form caring relations (Noddings, 2013). The one-caring is present and motivated toward the cared-for, seeking to reach and understand the other. When the one-caring reaches the cared-for, they receive them, which makes possible further caring relations. Noddings (2013) said of the one-caring, "I allow my motive energy to be shared; I put it at service of the other" (p. 33).

Many singing interactions can be characterized as singing-caring relations. Singing-caring relations can occur within oneself. Individuals act as the one-caring when they move their attention inward, develop self-understanding, and use singing for emotional regulation and expression, a process that evolves over the lifespan (Thompson, 1991). Children soothe themselves by singing familiar tunes and making up new songs, often while moving (Campbell, 1998). Adolescents sing to express emotions, like 15-year-old Zoe, who said, "Because when I'm sad I can sing a sad song.... I don't have to be limited, and I can just cheer myself up or just speak to my own feeling with music" (Parker, 2020, p. 89). Adults may use music to elaborate on their feelings and recognize emotions, helping them to resolve dilemmas or identify what might work in a given situation (DeNora, 2000).

Merleau-Ponty (2012) proposed that as an individual's body represents a system, similarly, another body might be considered another side of the same phenomenon. Therefore, as individuals learn to care for themselves, they reciprocally learn to care for others (Sweet, this volume). One such context of caring for others exists among singers and listeners. For example, singing-caring relations may be visible when a singer shares a favorite song at a memorial service, which helps others grieve or remember. In this singer-to-listener interaction, the cared-for receives energy from the one-caring. Perhaps the cared-for changes their body posture or attention which signals the one-caring to emphasize the text, to crescendo on a certain phrase, to make eye contact or breathe with another, and to send attention to the cared-for. Through this interaction, the one-caring and cared-for have the potential for deeper connection.

Multidimensional, continuous, and reciprocal singing-caring relation cycles occur when singing with others. For example, a member of the alto section may express that they feel cared for by the basses who are providing a harmonic foundation in a certain song. Within sections, individuals lean on one another for support and act as the one-caring for others when they might not feel well and have less voice to give (Parker, 2011). Although singing-caring relations remain in flux as the one-caring becomes the cared-for on a different day or when singing a different song, the distinctive sound of the unique collection of voices and interdependence built from regular work continually knits the group together (Parker, 2010, 2014). The sum of singing-caring relations cannot be counted or named, but they represent impactful ways for singers to know their world.

Singing-caring relations offer music educators pathways to help singers value additional ways of knowing. Rather than focus on propositional knowledge (Boyce-Tillman, 2020), educators can spotlight connection with others and unity with the universe known in I-Thou more than I-It relationships (Buber, 2000). I-Thou relationships may result in young people choosing to remain connected to themselves and to others during difficult times. Singing-caring relations then inspire teacher-to-singer and singer-to-singer relationships based in compassion, or caring-with, where individuals can act as champions and supporters of each other's dreams and aspirations (Hendricks, 2018). As individuals care-with, they begin to shed prescribed roles and find meaning in their shared becoming (Hendricks, 2021).

Singers use themselves to communicate thoughts, feelings, and self-identity, embodying their experiences (Thurman & Welch, 2000). Developing singing-caring relations therefore necessitates a holistic approach that embraces the whole person. Miller (2019) posits that educators adopt a holistic approach by recognizing the interconnectedness of experience and by bringing greater awareness to physical, intellectual, emotional, and spiritual dimensions of the self. Through foregrounding interconnected experiences, a holistic approach might build a sense of compassion for others and oneself, and wisdom about the world (Miller, 2019). In the remainder of the chapter we use Miller's (2019) anchors of inclusion, balance, and connection to outline a holistic approach with which educators might scaffold singing-caring relations in schools and community spaces. We begin by sharing our United States primary through secondary teaching settings to provide greater context of our recommendations.

Context

Prior to her position at the university level, Jenny taught choir at a public high school just outside of Philadelphia. The choir program enrolls over 100 9th–12th graders in four curricular ensembles. Singers perform in two or more school concerts yearly and frequently sing at school and community events. Many singers also take part in the school's extracurricular show choir, a cappella groups, and/or musical theater productions, and the vocal pedagogy offered reflects techniques specific to these and other genres. Choir members engage in varied musicianship activities, including connecting the music they enjoy to concepts embedded in choral repertoire. Activities in the choral program aim to help singers experience a place of connection in school, develop confidence in using their voice for self-expression, and experience meaningful rewards as singers and musical community members. Jenny worked with this program for 12 years and taught in school music programs for over 20 years.

Elizabeth is a co-artistic director of a Philadelphia-based community choir program that serves approximately 600 children and youth. The mission of the choral program is to transform young people's lives through the power of making music together. Choirs perform a wide repertoire in their own concerts and collaborate frequently with other not-for-profit arts groups and professional artists. Singers range in age from 7 to 18, sing in treble through mixed-voice ensembles, and reflect the racial, ethnic, socioeconomic, and religious diversity of the Greater Philadelphia area. The majority of singers reside in local neighborhoods and adjacent counties, and several come from more remote areas. Elizabeth's primary weekly rehearsals include working with treble singers in three different choirs, age 10–18, who identify as girls, genderfluid, or non-binary. She has been working in youth community choir programs for more than 20 years and with this program for 7 years.

INCLUSION

Inclusion reflects a belief system and commitment to offer every person the opportunity to belong (Falvey & Givner, 2005). Aligning with universal design principles, inclusive educators plan activities and interactions where everyone benefits, especially students who have been historically marginalized. Our definition of inclusion differs from that used more commonly in special education where students with disabilities learn alongside students who are typically developing (Darrow, 1999; Jellison & Draper, 2015). Though some special education inclusion settings may reflect our definition, scholars such as Keefe and Carrington (2007) have challenged special education inclusion settings where educators expect students with disabilities to assimilate into existing structures rather than consider new possibilities for all learners. We choose a definition of inclusion in which an educator's commitment provides new possibilities and where existing structures remain open to revision.

Inclusion means that educators honor students' learning needs and what they bring to the environment, that students can access and express their learning in multiple ways and at different times, and that students have varied opportunities for learning simultaneously (Hammel & Hourigan, 2016). Perhaps most importantly, inclusion reflects a commitment to self-reflection whereby educators unpack how they might care-with students who have been historically marginalized in music education and education, including students from minoritized groups, of low socioeconomic status, who may identify as LGBTQIA+, those with disabilities, and their intersectionalities. Such practices might include introducing dialogue around structures that reinforce perceptions of gendered or voice part associations within ensembles, or limit potential access or full participation because of ensemble requirements.

Educators who adopt inclusion recognize and bring attention to educational structures that perpetuate a "hidden curriculum" (Hendricks, 2018). In choral music settings, systems of vocal pedagogy may conceal messages that elevate some forms of vocal production over others. For example, in predominantly white higher education music programs and PreK–12 schools, the primary mode of vocal instruction for over a century has been the *bel canto* tradition. *Bel canto* is not only a technique, it is "also a prioritization of a specific vocal sound" (Good-Perkins, 2020, p. 162). *Bel canto* pedagogy, therefore, is part of a Eurocentric music education model that categorizes desirable sounds as "clean" and "trained," in contrast to "other" sounds categorized as unrefined, uncivilized, and even physically dangerous (Good-Perkins, 2020; Potter, 1998). Music educators who pass on these values and perpetuate biases can damage, erase, and reject singers' cultural and musical affinities; they also negate or disregard musical forms and vocal approaches created predominantly by persons of color, such as contemporary R&B, mariachi, and gospel music. The result is exclusion of countless singers who do not listen to, relate to, or desire to replicate *bel canto* singing inside or outside the music classroom (Shaw, 2020).

Alternatives to *bel canto* vocal pedagogies can facilitate inclusive, liberating music education that recognizes, affirms, and guides singers' technique in a variety of vocal styles and timbres. Pedagogies including Estill Voice Training®, Complete Vocal Technique, Somatic Voicework™ The LoVetri Method, and various contemporary commercial music pedagogies provide ways to teach transferable and flexible vocal skills. By providing singers guidance and practice using these vocal tools, educators can affirm singers' identities, recognize and respond to musics that singers listen to and identify with (Shaw, 2020), and give singers tools for emotional expression that can deepen their growth as musicians (Hendricks, 2018).

INCLUSION IN PRACTICE

Inclusion is critical to singing-caring relations. As educators, our first step to build singing-caring relations is to affirm each person's voice, the basis of which is vocal timbre. Vocal timbre, which we define here as a combination of physical processes, acoustic characteristics, and listener perceptions that describe vocal sound, reflects one's identity and experiences. Researchers in music education settings have documented important connections between vocal timbre and racial and cultural identities (Shaw, 2016, 2020), and classroom instruction's power to affirm or discourage timbral qualities with which singers identify (Chinn, 1997).

Because vocal quality and timbre are central elements of vocal development and expression, honoring and making space for exploration of varied vocal timbres can create an inclusive space that supports singer development. In teaching high school choral singers, I (Jenny) aimed to explore vocal technique by incorporating singers' musical preferences into instruction and by affirming diverse vocal timbres. Using Estill Voice Training® techniques based on Jo Estill's philosophy that "everyone has a beautiful voice" (Steinhauer & Klimek, 2019), singers in choir classes first engage in physical exploration of sounds, then match that exploration to characteristics they hear in their favorite vocal recordings. After gaining further understanding of vocal anatomy, they apply that understanding to their own physical experience of singing and experiment with physical adjustments that create different timbres in the choral repertoire. Singers have expressed a musical passage's mystery and intimacy using breathy, aspirate onsets; they have used high-larynx, twang timbre for musical theater and for Mongolian folk music; and they have sung in speech-like qualities to enhance text and phrasing in pop, R&B, and jazz. This process has provided space where singers expressed feeling valued, cared for, and respected for the flexible, diverse voices they bring to the group and to the music they enjoy.

In working with younger singers in community choral programs, I (Elizabeth) have learned to embrace their expansive ranges. When I meet a child for the first time, I encourage them to sing a comfortable pitch and we work from their choice rather than from mine. Connected to this idea, I have noticed that bringing the lighter mechanism (commonly known as head voice) into the heavier mechanism (chest voice) through warm ups can exclude singers. To revise this practice, I have begun applying speech as a transition to singing, and using familiar songs or hymns reflecting singers' experiences rather than vocal exercises that may be unfamiliar. I have incorporated individual voice checks a few times each year where I have the opportunity to affirm each singer's voice, to talk with them about their role models, and discuss aims for their singing. I use one-on-one interactions to plan repertoire and structure activities that empower singer capabilities. In rehearsals, I ask singers to model how phrases should be sung for one another, which helps to build additional singing-caring relations.

BALANCE

Using yin and yang as a model, Miller (2019) urges holistic educators to see contrasting elements of education as complementary and interconnected. A holistic approach emphasizes balance between pairings such as knowledge and imagination, or rational and intuitive; such elements are not distinct polar opposites but part of a larger whole, each one needing the other for its existence (Miller, 2019). A holistic approach embodies an opportunity to re-envision what educators might experience as tensions and replace them with interconnections and relationships. In viewing possibilities rather than challenges, educators might bring learning into balance and link to a vision of the whole person (Miller, 2017).

A critical area of need in group music-making involves greater balance between the individual and group. Group is the overriding concept in many music classrooms where large ensemble structures and performance practices emphasize collective identity more than expression of individuality. Common choral practices elevate the group over the individual, such as encouraging a unity of sound, ensemble blend, and uniformity in choir members' performance attire. Though positive group experiences can foster a sense of team and belonging (Parker, 2010, 2014), when educators focus on the group they can lose sight of individuals and treat the group rather than the individual as the cared-for (Parker, 2016). Singers learn from educators to attend to the ensemble more than they attend to one another, which develops an I-It relationship between individuals and the group as they view the ensemble as an object (Buber, 2000; Parker, 2016). In creating a unified sound and viewing each other as one unit, singers lose their connection as individuals and shed their uniquenesses, making I-Thou relationships impossible.

At first glance, bringing the individual and group into greater balance may appear a simple task, but complexities and chaos emerge as educators experiment with smaller groups or attempt individual assessments within the context of large programs. Critical to making change is the uncertainty and unpredictability of the outcome, which may feel more imbalanced than balanced—the choral classroom will be different and, at times, unsteady. But exploring and staying open to the potential chaos means that change is already underway. Fahim and Talabari (2014) recommend that educators come to accept uncertainty as natural to the teaching and learning process. One benefit of uncertainty is it heightens an educator's sense of remaining present and attentive to singers and their needs.

Balance in Practice

Within the school choral ensembles I (Jenny) work with, singers mostly experience full-ensemble singing as predictable and secure. Conversely, small group activities require greater flexibility and attention as the open-endedness of musical tasks and interpersonal interactions make processes less predictable. Work in small groups can provide new opportunities to appreciate singers' unique contributions. For example, after groups of five or six singers arrange short, known songs and perform them for the larger class, listeners customarily offer praise for their peers' musical choices, singing styles, and performance personalities. Small group activities focused on musical interpretation can lead to similar recognition. To help singers explore expression in a musical passage, I sometimes group singers by voice part, offer each group time to explore and come to consensus, and invite them to perform their interpretation for the larger group. By working within their smaller group and hearing each section's distinct interpretation, singers learn how to reconcile differing ideas to balance individual with group needs. Full-group activities that invite individual singers to share can also help singers feel seen and recognized. Simple classroom practices make space for singers to show gratitude for peer contributions to the choir or school, to discover and discuss their personal strengths, and to share everyday experience, entertaining stories, or wisdom gained from recent events. These experiences provide multiple levels of singing-caring relations while helping to balance the notions of individual and group.

The COVID-19 pandemic highlighted the interconnections between group and individual, and injected feelings of chaos and uncertainty in our community choral program. Like many, we held synchronous meetings on Zoom each week. For the first time, I (Elizabeth) attended to each singer's face and facial expressions because of their closeness on the screen. As a group, we prioritized learning about one another because the choral rehearsal could not operate in the same way as it did in person. Though some singers had difficulty with synchronous rehearsal platforms and kept their cameras off, all seemed to rally when they relied on one another to improvise a pattern or pass a musical idea to another singer. Those who described feeling disappointed with the loss of in-person singing still submitted audio recordings when I asked to hear their progress. Through those audio interactions I came to know their voices and strove to meet singers individually where they were.

As we emerged later in the pandemic to begin socially distant, outdoor singing, we worked to become an in-person collective. Because of those individual interactions, the close proximity of faces on Zoom and time we shared, we found ways to weave ourselves together as a group. I had never experienced such interconnectedness between the individual and group in a choral setting. Today, the choir staff plans a better balance of individual and group activities to build singing-caring relations between each singer. Chaos and uncertainty present real challenges, but we have learned to view uncertainty as an opportunity to care for each individual.

Connection

As the world becomes more and more fragmented, Miller (2019) calls for a return to connection. Connection comprises relationships among the world's interwoven elements—relationships that include an individual's connection to the earth, to their community, and to a deeper sense of self, or the soul. Connection also includes commitments to openness, dialogue, and to bringing one's whole self into the space (Hendricks, 2021). In this chapter, we focus on two forms of connection that cultivate singing-caring relations, including beauty (Hart, 2019) and eudaimonia (Boyce-Tillman, 2020; Smith & Silverman, 2020).

Connecting with one's emotions makes beauty possible (Hart, 2019). As humans walk in awareness of their emotions, they become grounded and awaken the soul. Specific to group music-making, educators who find windows into learners' experiences can reinforce relationships among what singers are learning, how they learn, and who they are. Singers then open themselves to attach their learning to a larger connection with the world where they might receive beauty and nourishment. Additionally, interactions that focus on human connection may bring about the potential for eudaimonia, broadly defined as human flourishing (Smith & Silverman, 2020). Individuals experience eudaimonia when they engage actively, when they see their purpose as benefiting the community and grounded in ethical action, when they recognize their experiences as connecting to those that lie beyond themselves, and when they feel a sense of agency to act alone and with others to create meaning.

Singing-caring relations represent generative spaces with which to realize beauty and eudaimonia. Humans develop their voices, literal and metaphorical, through interactions with others. Thus, the voice reflects self-identity and the amalgam of one's experiences. Educators can build singing-caring relations by encouraging singer attunement and connection to the body as the basis of understanding one's relationship with the world. A critical step to help singers embody their life experiences is through self-expression. Selecting materials that speak resonantly and encouraging singers to write text, improvise, and compose brings attunement closer into view. Singers feel personally invested, and what they create together becomes the foundation of shared experience with which educators continue to build. Simultaneously educators might devote time to facilitating interactions that heighten attentional awareness to the self, to others, and to the world as possibilities to realize beauty and eudaimonia.

Connection in Practice

I (Jenny) have noted singing activities that invite focus, quiet attention to sound and silence, and space for musical experiences to "breathe" can help high school singers experience connection through co-creation of beauty. Wordless beginnings within rehearsal act as "an invocation, designed to move us into reverence" for the sound of unified voices (Hart, 2019, p. 25), and starting warmups or group improvisations with soft, collective hums brings voices into connection with one another. Activities involving listening to others' voices, such as building on singer-generated vocal or rhythmic loops, encourage musical experiences to unfold organically while highlighting the group's ability to create meaningful and beautiful music. At the end of a musical experience, purposefully leaving silence and omitting instructional commentary provides space for singers to sense the power of their collective voices.

For some singers, dimming the lights or standing in a circle facilitates a sense of connection, reverence, and attunement, and singers request such adjustments when they sense the group's musical experience is particularly powerful. Singers also build connection by identifying repertoire's emotional essence or its purpose for the community. In one activity, singers in a circle take turns describing the essence of a piece of music with one word. The group gains multiple perspectives on the music's meaning, and singer perspectives often coalesce into deeper understanding of musical expression and awe for the collective musical experience.

As educators who aim to model vulnerability as a strength, we (Elizabeth and Jenny) strive to open ourselves to emotional experiences that occur within and outside of music-making. Singers sense when we feel moved by a song. Synchrony of breath, sound, and text makes space for experience-sharing or for compassion and support derived from shared understanding (Hendricks, 2018). By joining in group improvisations, singing alongside group members, or stepping away from a conductor role, we can facilitate possibilities of greater connection and unity. Sharing our vulnerability as persons builds interdependence and fosters a sense of collective trust as students come to know their teachers as people (Hendricks, 2018).

Working closely with youth during the pandemic brought connection to the forefront. For me (Elizabeth), I dedicated more energy to listening and conversation. I strove to provide opportunities for the types of interactions that singers deemed important. Collaborating with community members, including composers, singers, and other musicians, provided rich opportunities for experience-sharing and dialogue on a song's meaning and importance. In particular, intergenerational collaborations allowed singers to share their worlds with one another and feel seen and heard. We have continued those collaborations today as they served to strengthen our sense of connection, which made beauty and eudaimonia possible.

Conclusion

In writing this chapter, we asked how a holistic approach to singing that embraces inclusion, balance, and connection might help educators build caring relations with students. To address this question, we end where we began: Humans are primed for mutuality and togetherness. Together educators and students comprise an organic whole (Miller, 2019) as another's self-experience represents a second side of the same phenomenon (Merleau-Ponty, 2012). As the one-caring, educators look to be received and understood by the cared-for and as such, all members of the community are included and accepted (Noddings, 2013). As those who must be cared-for, educators deserve high-quality professional development for continual growth and self-care practices that nurture the soul. The singing-caring relations we propose in this chapter invite all to flourish within an interwoven community of voices in which individuals and the group are seen and heard.

References

Bannan, N., & Woodward, S. (2009). Spontaneity in the musicality and music learning of children. In S. Malloch & C. Trevarthen (Eds.), *Communicative musicality: Exploring the basis of human companionship* (pp. 465–494). Oxford University Press.

Boyce-Tillman, J. (2020). An ecology of eudaimonia and its implications for music education. In G. D. Smith & M. Silverman (Eds.), *Eudaimonia: Perspectives for music learning* (pp. 71–89). Routledge.

Buber, M. (2000). *I and thou* (R. G. Smith, Trans.). Scribner. (Original work published 1958)

Campbell, P. S. (1998). *Songs in their heads: Music and its meaning in children's lives.* Oxford University Press.

Chinn, B. (1997). Vocal self-identification, singing style, and singing range in relationship to a measure of cultural mistrust in African-American adolescent females. *Journal of Research in Music Education, 45*(4), 636–649. https://doi.org/10.2307/3345428

Darrow, A. (1999). Music educators' perceptions regarding the inclusion of singers with severe disabilities in music classrooms. *Journal of Music Therapy, 36*(4), 254–273. https://doi.org/10.1093/jmt/36.4.254

Davis, S. G. (2016). Children, popular music, and identity. In G. McPherson (Ed.), *The child as musician: A handbook of musical development* (2nd ed., pp. 265–283). Oxford University Press.

DeNora, T. (2000). *Music in everyday life.* Cambridge University Press.

Dissanayake, E. (2000). *Art and intimacy: How the arts began.* University of Washington Press.

Erikson, E. (1950). *Childhood and society.* W.W. Norton & Company.

Fahim, M., & Talabari, F. A. (2014). Chaos/complexity theory and education. *Journal of English Language Teaching and Learning, 6*(13), 43–56.

Falvey, M. A., & Givner, C. C. (2005). What is an inclusive school? In R. A. Villa & J. S. Thousand (Eds.), *Creating an inclusive school* (2nd ed., pp. 1–11). Association for Supervision and Curriculum Development.

Good-Perkins, E. (2020). Rethinking vocal education as a means to encourage positive identity development in adolescents. In I. M. Yob & E. R. Jorgensen (Eds.), *Humane music education for the common good* (pp. 158–171). Indiana University Press.

Hammel, A. M., Hickox, R. Y., & Hourigan, R. M. (2016). Winding it back: A framework for inclusive music education. In A. M. Hammel, R. Y. Hickox, & R. M. Hourigan (Eds.), *Winding it back: Teaching to individual differences in music classroom & ensemble settings* (pp. 1–15). Oxford University Press. https://doi.org/10.1093/acprof:oso/9780190201616.003.0001

Hargreaves, D. J., North, A. C., & Tarrant, M. (2016). How and why do musical presences change in childhood and adolescence. In G. McPherson (Ed.), *The child as musician: A handbook of musical development* (2nd ed., pp. 303–322). Oxford University Press.

Hart, T. (2019). Beauty and learning. In J. P. Miller, K. Nigh, M. Binder, B. Novak, & S. Crowell (Eds.), *International handbook of holistic education* (pp. 25–32). Routledge.

Hendricks, K. S. (2018). *Compassionate music teaching.* Rowman & Littlefield.

Hendricks, K. S. (2021). Authentic connection in music education. In K. Hendricks & J. Boyce-Tillman (Eds.), *Authentic connection: Music, spirituality, and wellbeing* (pp. 237–253). Peter Lang.

Jellison, J. A., & Draper, E. A. (2015). Music research in inclusive school settings: 1975 to 2013. *Journal of Research in Music Education, 62*(4), 325–331. https://doi.org/10.1177/0022429414554808

Keefe, M., & Carrington, S. (2007). *Schools and diversity.* Pearson.

Kisilevsky, B. S., Hains, S. M., Lee K., Xie, X., Huang, H., Hai, H. Y., Zhang, K., & Wang, Z. (2003). Effects of experience on fetal voice recognition. *Psychological Science, 14*(3), 220–224. https://doi.org/10.1111/1467-9280.02435

Merleau-Ponty, M. (2012). *Phenomenology of perception* (D. A. Landes, Trans.). Routledge. (Original work published 1945)

Miller, J. P. (2017). A holistic vision of teacher education. In J. P. Miller & K. Nigh (Eds.), *Holistic education and embodied learning* (pp. 319–329). Information Age Publishing.

Miller, J. P. (2019). *The holistic curriculum* (3rd ed.). University of Toronto Press.

Noddings, N. (2013). *Caring: A relational approach to ethics and moral education* (2nd ed.). University of California Press.

Parker, E. C. (2010). Exploring singer experiences of belonging within an urban high school choral ensemble: An action research study. *Music Education Research*, 12(4), 339–352. https://doi.org/10.1080/14613808.2010.519379

Parker, E. C. (2011). Uncovering adolescent choral singers' philosophical beliefs about music-making: A qualitative inquiry. *International Journal of Music Education*, 29(4), 305–317. https://doi.org/10.1177/0255761411421092

Parker, E. C. (2014). The process of social identity development in adolescent high school choral singers: A grounded theory. *Journal of Research in Music Education*, 62(1), 18–32. https://doi.org/10.1177/0022429413520009

Parker, E. C. (2016). The experience of creating community: An intrinsic case study of four Midwestern public school choral teachers. *Journal of Research in Music Education*, 64(2), 220–237. https://doi.org/10.1177/0022429416648292

Parker, E. C. (2020). *Adolescents on music: Why music matters to young people in our lives*. Oxford University Press.

Parncutt, R. (2016). Prenatal development. In G. McPherson (Ed.), *The child as musician: A handbook of musical development* (2nd ed., pp. 1–30). Oxford University Press.

Potter, J. (1998). *Vocal authority: Singing style and ideology*. Cambridge University Press.

Reis, H. T., Collins, W. A., & Berscheid, E. (2000). The relationship context of human behavior and development. *Psychological Bulletin*, 126(6), 844–872. https://doi.org/10.1037/0033-2909.126.6.844

Shaw, J. T. (2016). "The music I was meant to sing": Adolescent choral singers' perceptions of culturally responsive pedagogy. *Journal of Research in Music Education*, 64(1), 45–70. https://doi.org/10.1177/0022429415627989

Shaw, J. T. (2020). *Culturally responsive choral music education: What teachers can learn from nine singers' experiences in three choirs*. Routledge.

Smith, G. D., & Silverman, M. (2020). Eudaimonia: Flourishing through music learning. In G. D. Smith & M. Silverman (Eds.), *Eudaimonia: Perspectives for music learning* (pp. 1–13). Routledge.

Steinhauer, K. M., & Klimek, M. M. (2019). Vocal traditions: Estill Voice Training®. *Voice and Speech Review*, 13(3), 354–359. https://doi.org/10.1080/23268263.2019.1605707

Thompson, R. A. (1991). Emotional regulation and emotional development. *Educational Psychology Review*, 3(4), 269–307.

Thurman, L., & Welch, G. F. (2000). *Bodymind and voice: Foundations of voice education*. The VoiceCare Network.

Welch, G. F. (2016). Singing and vocal development. In G. E. McPherson (Ed.), *The child as musician: A handbook of musical development* (2nd ed., pp. 441–461). Oxford University Press. https://doi.org/10.1093/acprof:oso/9780198530329.003.0016

CHAPTER 23

DEVELOPING TRUST AND EMPATHY THROUGH PEER MENTORING IN THE MUSIC CLASSROOM

ANDREW GOODRICH

CARE HANDBOOK TOPICS

Co-creating caring relationships

THE primary format for delivery of instruction in US music education has been an authoritarian model, one that involves the music teacher serving as the sole dispenser of knowledge who decides how learning occurs in the music classroom (e.g., Goodrich, 2021a; Hendricks, 2018). Hendricks (2018) noted the military roots embedded in the authoritarian model and remarked that teaching music was akin to "countless band directors leading from the podium like sergeants" (p. 1). Yet, as the music education profession enters the third decade of the 21st century, "we are witnessing an expansion of what it means to be a music educator" (Hendricks, 2018, p. 2). This expansion involves music teachers devising new ways to deliver instruction, including "stepping off the podium and engaging in music-making with and among their students" (Hendricks, 2018, p. 2).

The primary components of the transition of the music teacher's role from sole dispenser of knowledge to facilitator are compassion and empathy (Hendricks, 2018). Compassion in this context embodies "an understanding between equals, where no one is superior, but in which a person knows how to help another simply because of a shared awareness between them" (Hendricks, 2018, p. 4). This understanding between equals may provide a platform for compassion and empathy between the music teacher and students to contribute to the learning that occurs in the music classroom.

The music teacher initially provides the space for students to share their knowledge and experiences with each other so that neither the music teacher nor the students are considered superior to each other in terms of who is sharing the knowledge. Thus, the music teacher and students share in the authority of who makes decisions regarding what knowledge is shared during learning that ultimately brings about a shared awareness in learning subject matter.

Even though the music teacher is sharing in authority of learning, they still possess a high degree of knowledge about musical concepts and pedagogical techniques (Wiggins, 2015). That is, when the music teacher takes on the role of facilitator they are still the "teacher," and continue to be the ultimate authority in the music classroom. Music teachers can engage in these two roles concurrently, or shift between them as determined by the learning situation at a particular moment (Goodrich, 2021a). The music teacher, then, is ultimately responsible for facilitating opportunities for learning in which they maintain an active role in guiding and monitoring learning in partnership with the students (Goodrich, 2021a; Weidner, 2015). Thus, the music teacher and students maintain different roles in the learning process, "but neither role is viewed as superior or inferior to the other" (Hendricks, 2018, p. 4). Learning, then, is a group effort. It is through this context that a music teacher "is one who feels, understands, and even shares the students' enthusiasm for music and reaches out in ways that support the students' passions" for learning (Hendricks, 2018, p. 5). Compassionate music teaching allows for flexibility in delivering instruction between the music teacher and students. An instructional technique that can serve as a platform for compassionate music teaching is peer mentoring.

Approaching Peer Mentoring

Peer mentoring is a multifaceted instructional practice that involves students sharing their knowledge and experiences (Mullen, 2005) under the guidance of the music teacher (Goodrich, 2018). Researchers have found that students can learn when sharing knowledge (e.g., Goodrich, 2021a; Howe, 2009) and receiving knowledge (Goodrich, 2018). Peer mentoring can help students improve academic achievement (Hebert, 2005), help develop their social skills (Goodrich, 2021a; Odegard, 2019), and improve their attitudes toward learning (Goodrich, 2007). Through peer mentoring, students can participate in high levels of learning (e.g., Darrow et al., 2005; Johnson, 2015).

Peer mentoring embodies hierarchical structures and non-hierarchical structures (Goodrich, 2018). In hierarchical peer mentoring, a more knowledgeable peer (the mentor) shares their knowledge and experiences with a peer considered to have less knowledge (the mentee; Goodrich, 2021a; Taylor, 2016). In non-hierarchical peer mentoring, students who possess similar or equal abilities concurrently engage in the roles of mentor and mentee (Graham, 2020; Johnson, 2017; Topping et al., 2017). The music teacher acts as a facilitator, who plays an important role with creating opportunities for peer mentoring, and continually guiding students through the process of learning from each other (e.g., Scruggs, 2008).

Music teachers can use peer mentoring for a variety of reasons including musical reasons, such as learning key signatures (Darrow et al., 2005), and for non-musical reasons, including classroom management (Goodrich, 2007). Peer mentoring provides opportunities for students to take on an active role in their learning during which they, along with their music teacher, become partners in creating learning goals, and together share their knowledge and experiences to elevate their comprehension of subject matter in the music classroom (e.g., Goodrich, 2021a). Because students engage in sharing their knowledge and experiences during peer mentoring under the guidance of the music teacher, a learning environment developed in shared awareness may create meaningful interactions and learning opportunities.

Philosophical Framework

The writings of John Dewey (1938) and his ideas about students leading the learning in the classroom via sharing their knowledge and experiences guide this exploration into peer mentoring and compassionate music teaching. Dewey (1938) argued that students do possess knowledge and experiences that they can share with their peers to contribute to meaningful learning. Throughout this process students take on more active and engaging roles with leading the learning, during which the music teacher is no longer the sole authority of knowledge. Students find learning more relevant, fun, and meaningful (Dewey, 1938). In the role of facilitator, though, the music teacher still plays an important role in guiding the learning in the music classroom to help ensure the quality of knowledge and experiences shared by the students—what Dewey (1938) referred to as "internal factors" (p. 42). Monitoring these internal factors of learning may also help to create a learning environment that is built on "the organic connection between education and personal experience" (Dewey, 1938, p. 25). Mullen (2005) highlighted the importance of the teacher's role as a facilitator for setting up successful learning experiences.

Creating Opportunities for Peer Mentoring

Because of the natural fit between peer mentoring and compassionate music teaching (e.g., engaging in shared learning experiences between music teacher and students), peer mentoring provides opportunities that promote "six qualities of compassion (trust, empathy, patience, inclusion, community, and authentic connections)"

(Hendricks, 2018, p. 33). Communal *trust* entails membership in a music classroom that can help with establishing a collective identity through "reciprocal exchanges among group members" and "understanding the intentions of others in the group" (Hendricks, 2018, p. 34). With trust established, the music teacher and students can engage in *empathy* that "helps to take on the perspective of another person" (Hendricks, 2018, p. 55). Understanding each other's perspectives is a vital component of trust and empathy that sets the foundation for meaningful learning during peer mentoring.

Throughout these processes, *patience* is of utmost importance, for it helps the music teacher and students with "looking beyond the present moment and considering a long-term trajectory for our students" (Hendricks, 2018, p. 78). This understanding helps music teachers to acknowledge the individual knowledge and experiences possessed by each student, and for students to value each other's knowledge and experiences that they contribute to learning. Whereas trust, empathy, and patience established at the core of the music classroom learning environment, it is of vital importance for the music teacher to facilitate *inclusion* at all times in the music classroom when designing peer mentoring opportunities. Through promoting diversity and inclusion in the music classroom, all student voices, regardless of race, gender, gender identity, sexual identity, and abilities are valued (e.g., Goodrich, 2020, 2022a). Peer mentoring can provide opportunities for racialized students to decenter teacher-led instruction in the music classroom toward sharing authority (e.g., Goodrich, 2022a).

With all of these qualities of compassion in place, the music teacher and students can establish a sense of *community*, in which an atmosphere of belonging is heightened. At the core of this sense of belonging are the social interactions between students, referred to as socializing in the peer mentoring literature (e.g., Darrow et al., 2005; Goodrich, 2007; Madsen, 2011). Socializing helps to create a positive learning environment in which all student contributions are valued (e.g., Karcher, 2008; Riese et al., 2012) that, in turn, can lead to elevated comprehension of subject matter and musical performance skills (e.g., Goodrich, 2007).

Finally, *authentic connection* is "the interplay of heart, brain, and emotion within each of us" (Hendricks, 2018, p. 145). New ways of establishing connections, or what Hendricks (2018) calls resonance, are established, and through reflection, the music teacher and students can "recognize the capacity for our behaviors, actions, and even feelings to influence others" (p. 145). Resonance is an important component of these exchanges between the music teacher and students during peer mentoring, and heightens the abilities to engage in shared authority of learning in the music classroom.

Maintaining Brave Spaces for Learning

For peer mentoring to serve as a conduit for open exchanges between the music teacher and students, it is imperative for students to feel safe in the music classroom

(Goodrich, 2022a). Safe spaces are just that: spaces for learning where students feel safe to contribute their knowledge and engage in music-making with their peers. Yet, safe spaces can also reify institutional norms, such as a learning environment in which students from dominant white populations feel safe, and students who are marginalized due to the color of their skin, sexuality, or gender do not feel safe (Hess, 2019). This creates learning situations in which marginalized students do not want to contribute to learning (hooks, 1994). It is imperative, then, that music teachers and students co-create brave learning spaces so that students can "share their stories of pain and struggle" (Arao & Clemens, 2013, p. 139) and can also help music teachers to "go beyond the surface of understanding and explore the complex nature of learning" (Lind & McKoy, 2016, p. 31). Going beyond this surface allows music teachers and students to co-create learning situations in which students from dominant populations reflect on their privilege and biases and move toward becoming self-reflexive in a brave learning space (e.g., Goodrich, 2022a).

Hendricks et al. (2014) identified five components that music teachers should consider when creating such brave learning spaces. These include (a) the importance of listening and being emotionally present, (b) creating learning opportunities that are ability-appropriate in which students focus on the challenge and not each other, (c) making sure that all stakeholders in the education of the students are involved (e.g., parents), (d) being aware of what is going on in a student's life and how this could impact their music-making, and (e) be willing to engage and use different types of instruction to meet the needs of the individual student.

Creating brave learning spaces may provide opportunities for students to be "more likely to freely express themselves" (Hendricks et al., 2014, p. 38), which is a critical part of a learning environment in which their knowledge and experiences are valued (Goodrich, 2022a). Brave spaces aid with intrinsic motivation and musical engagement (Hendricks et al., 2014), both of which help students to be more open to sharing and receiving knowledge from their peers, a critical component of the peer mentoring process (Goodrich, 2021a). At the core of the brave spaces are the social interactions between students in peer mentoring (e.g., Karcher, 2005; Stanton-Salazar, 2011). Thus, peer mentoring goes beyond being used merely as an instructional practice for heightened musical learning and takes on added dimensions when students develop relationships with each other and their music teacher to aid with generating a sense of belonging to the group (e.g., Goodrich, 2022a; Karcher 2005; Pellowski Wiger, 2016; Thornton, 2018). This feeling of belonging to a group sets up a platform for not only the music teacher and students to engage in two-way exchanges of ideas, but embedded within these exchanges are the complexity of providing opportunities for all students, especially those who are marginalized, to contribute to learning (e.g., Goodrich, 2022a; Hess, 2019). Thus, compassionate music teaching and peer mentoring become a multidimensional endeavor for meaningful learning between the music teacher and students.

Peer Mentoring as a Conduit for a Compassionate Learning Environment

With the many components of peer mentoring in place, including two-way exchanges of sharing knowledge and experiences to co-create brave learning spaces, music teachers and students together can create learning opportunities rich in compassionate music teaching. These opportunities include the music teacher and student co-creating learning spaces, creating shared musical goals, establishing trust between music teacher and students, and making authentic music connections toward establishing a community of learning.

Music Teacher and Student Co-Creating Learning Spaces

As a facilitator, the music teacher can engage with students by co-creating learning spaces (e.g., Gramm, 2021; Hendricks, 2018). As a result, students can share their knowledge with each other, and with the music teacher, to contribute to learning that occurs in the music classroom. With student input under the guidance and support of the music teacher, students' ideas are then valued by their peers (e.g., Goodrich, 2021a). In addition, students continue to value knowledge shared by the music teacher.

Co-creating learning spaces during peer mentoring encompasses a vast array of instructional goals that range from learning specific music fundamentals (e.g., fingerings) to performance expectations (e.g., performing repertoire at a high level). To help achieve learning goals, students can share musical ideas by modeling musical sounds (e.g., nonverbal interactions), and by explaining how to perform (e.g., verbal interactions; Goodrich, 2021a). For example, the music teacher and students can work together to establish expectations for elevating individual performance levels for an upcoming concert. This could include students mentoring each other to more efficiently use air support to aid with sound and intonation, and could include modeling sound and verbally explaining ways to make their breathing more efficient (Goodrich, 2021a). Thus, through co-creating learning spaces the music teacher and students develop co-ownership in the learning process. Research has revealed that this leads to heightened learning for students, for both mentors and mentees learn (e.g., Goodrich, 2018; Goodrich, 2021a) in addition to increased ownership and interest in the music program (e.g., Darrow et al., 2005; Johnson, 2015; Webb, 2015).

Creating Shared Musical Goals

To create shared musical goals, the music teacher might meet with students before, during, and after rehearsals or class sessions (e.g., Goodrich, 2007; Scruggs, 2008).

It is important for the music teacher to make time for creating and setting goals (e.g., Johnson, 2015), and during these meetings it is essential for the music teacher to help students evaluate and assess how to determine if they are meeting these goals or not (e.g., Johnson, 2015). For example, the music teacher can ask students about musical goals, such as what is going well (e.g., dynamics), and what is not going so well (e.g., intonation). Through these interactions, the music teacher can guide students through the process of how to mentor their peers to enact the shared goals.

A side benefit of these meetings is that during these conversations, the music teacher and the students gain insights into musical issues they may not have been aware of (Goodrich, 2023). Creating shared musical goals provides another layer of shared authority in learning between the music teacher and students with regards to an understanding between equals, a seminal part of compassionate music teaching (Hendricks, 2018). In turn, this can help students to gain a greater sense of ownership in the music program where they can ultimately take the lead toward establishing goals for learning (e.g., Goodrich, 2007; Webb, 2015).

Establishing Trust Between Music Teacher and Students

As the music teacher and students engage in an understanding between equals in the music classroom, the students begin to learn which learning experiences and goals are successful, and which are not. This process involves reflection from the students. The reflection can occur in real time during class (reflection-in-action) and involve reflection after rehearsal or class (reflection-on-action; Schön, 1987). For example, the music teacher can ask students to reflect about their learning experiences during class sessions immediately after peer mentoring (Goodrich, 2023). Or, reflection could occur later via interactions with students in digital spaces, such as online journal entries, or prompts created by the music teacher and students such as in Google docs (Goodrich, 2021b). Through the processes of co-creating learning spaces and creating shared musical goals, two essential components of compassionate music teaching—trust and empathy—are established. A synergy is then embedded with/in the process: As students co-create learning opportunities with the music teacher, a solid foundation for trust and empathy is created, which in turn deepens these connections established between the music teacher and students for more meaningful learning.

Establishing a Community of Learning

As a result of engagement with co-creating learning spaces via peer mentoring, a learning community is created (Goodrich, 2023). This community comprises the music teacher and students, and is based in empathy and trust (Hendricks, 2018). In this community, then, the music teacher and students are not afraid to contribute their voices to the learning process. Thus, most importantly, students consider their voices to have value. This sense of community also extends into creating learning opportunities in which all student voices are valued. Ultimately, through co-creating learning spaces the music teacher and students value contributions from everyone involved.

Discussion

Peer mentoring can provide a platform for the music teacher and students to co-create learning spaces that result in developing co-ownership of the learning process and opportunities for authentic connections. Co-ownership leads to enhancing the experience of being in a community of learning, where all voices are valued in the learning process. Despite the benefits of co-creating learning spaces, however, it is important to be aware of potential issues during peer mentoring, as described below.

The first issue stems from the music teacher and students sharing knowledge in learning. Allowing students to play an important role in guiding learning via sharing their knowledge is counter to many practices based in conservative policies that reinforce the notion that the music teacher is the sole deliverer of knowledge in the classroom (Biesta, 2012). That is, the music teacher is the expert who is "there to teach" (Biesta, 2012, p. 35), thus reinforcing the authoritarian model in US music education (Hendricks, 2018). Even while co-creating learning spaces with students, however, the music teacher still retains authority as "the teacher" when guiding the learning that occurs in the music classroom. Students still need guidance from the music teacher to gain an understanding, at least initially, of what knowledge is important (Biesta, 2012) and why they are sharing it with their peers (Goodrich, 2021a). For example, initial guidance from the music teacher may include stressing the importance of music fundamentals (e.g., articulations). In conjunction with identifying *what* knowledge is important, the music teacher can guide students through the process of *how* to share their knowledge during peer mentoring (Goodrich, 2023). As a result, the music teacher can also maintain authority via modeling how to share knowledge during peer mentoring. Modeling can include the music teacher modeling peer mentoring for the students, and guiding student volunteers through the process of modeling how to mentor for the entire class. This initial understanding of what knowledge is important and how to share it *then* creates a foundation for students to begin contributing what knowledge they deem important to learning when co-creating learning spaces with the music teacher. Knowledge that students deem worthy of sharing may come from what they learn from the music teacher, other music teachers both in school and outside of school (e.g., youth symphony conductors), social media (e.g., YouTube), and private teachers (Goodrich, 2023; Webb, 2015). With this foundation of what knowledge to share and how to share it, music teachers can also play an active role in guiding learning by monitoring peer mentoring, including reflection-in-action and reflection-on-action.

When monitoring peer mentoring, music teachers can ensure that knowledge is shared in a constructive manner that avoids issues such as peer pressure and sarcasm (Johnson, 2013). Although these efforts can add a significant amount of time to a music teacher's already busy workload, it pays dividends toward creating a brave space for students to take risks toward learning.

When considering the time needed to invest in peer mentoring, however, it is a flexible instructional technique in that music teachers will not use it all of the time, nor use it in the same manner all the time throughout their music classes (e.g., Goodrich et al., 2018). Ultimately, the foundation of understanding what knowledge is important, and thus worth sharing, is the basis for establishing trust between the music teacher and students. Thus, even in school music programs based in conservative policies where the music teacher is expected to serve as the sole authority of delivering knowledge, learning spaces via peer mentoring can still be co-created with students.

Another issue involves co-creating goals between the music teacher and students and the practice of inclusion. Due to the hierarchical structures of many peer mentoring experiences (e.g., a more knowledgeable mentor sharing knowledge with a less knowledgeable mentee), the potential exists for hierarchies to develop in this process, where a select group of students may end up being the only students who help co-create goals with the teacher. This presents a potential conflict when establishing trust and empathy among all students, for the brave spaces end up reifying institutional norms where students from dominant white populations may control the narrative of learning in the music classroom (Hess, 2019). It is vital for the music teacher to play a highly active role in ensuring that all students engage in peer mentoring and the co-creation of learning goals. Throughout these processes, then, empathy takes on an even bigger role to help instill compassionate music teaching in the music teacher and students toward establishing a community of learning where all students feel welcome in the music classroom.

Concluding Remarks

Despite potential issues when co-creating learning spaces, peer mentoring can provide the foundation for forming caring relationships between students and between the music teacher and students. Caring relationships via peer mentoring provide the structure for meaningful learning to occur, including authentic connections, and help to establish a community of learning. Although the product of peer mentoring is important (e.g., learning a musical task), it is the interactions between peers, and between students and their music teacher, that aid with establishing and maintaining trust and empathy in the music classroom. Ultimately, then, peer mentoring is an instructional practice that can aid music teachers and students with creating a learning environment rich in compassion built on the foundations of trust and empathy.

References

Arao, B., & Clemens, K. (2013). From safe spaces to brave spaces: A new way to frame dialogue around diversity and social justice. In L. M. Landreman (Ed.), *The art of effective facilitation: Reflections from social justice educators* (pp. 135–150). Stylus Publishing.

Biesta, G. J. J. (2012). Giving teaching back to education: Responding to the disappearance of the teacher. *Phenomenology & Practice, 6*(2), 35–49. https://doi.org/10.29173/pandpr19860

Darrow, A. A., Gibbs, P., & Wedel, S. (2005). Use of classwide peer tutoring in the general music classroom. *Update: Applications of Research in Music Education, 24*(1), 15–26. https://doi.org/10.1177%2F8755123305024001013

Dewey, J. (1938). *Experience and education*. Collier.

Goodrich, A. (2007). Peer mentoring in a high school jazz ensemble. *Journal of Research in Music Education, 55*(2), 94–114. https://doi.org/10.1177/002242940705500202

Goodrich, A. (2018). Peer mentoring and peer tutoring among K-12 students: A literature review. *Update: Applications of Research in Music Education, 36*(2), 13–21. https://doi.org/10.1177/8755123317708765

Goodrich, A. (2020). Counterpoint in the music classroom: Creating an environment of resilience with peer mentoring and LGBTQIA+ students. *International Journal of Music Education, 38*(4), 582–592. https://doi.org/10.1177/0255761420949373

Goodrich, A. (2021a). Peer mentoring in an extracurricular music class. *International Journal of Music Education, 39*(4), 410–423. https://doi.org/10.1177/0255761420988922

Goodrich, A. (2021b). Online peer mentoring and remote learning. *Music Education Research, 23*(2), 256–269. https://doi.org/10.1080/14613808.2021.1898575

Goodrich, A. (2022a). Valuing racialized student voices: Transforming learning through peer mentoring. *Action, Criticism, and Theory for Music Education, 21*(1), 142–171. https://doi.org/10.22176/act21.1.142

Goodrich, A. (2023). *Peer mentoring in music education: Developing effective student leadership*. Routledge.

Goodrich, A., Bucura, E., & Stauffer, S. (2018). Peer mentoring in a university music methods class. *Journal of Music Teacher Education, 27*(2), 23–38. https://doi.org/10.1177/1057083717731057

Graham, M. F. (2020). *The effects of peer-assisted learning on rhythmic and sight-reading in a middle school chorus* (Publication No. 27955005) [Doctoral dissertation, Boston University]. ProQuest Dissertations and Theses Global.

Gramm, W. (2021). *Peer mentoring in Modern Band* (Publication No. 28317250) [Doctoral dissertation, Boston University]. ProQuest Dissertations and Theses Global.

Hebert, D. (2005). *Music competition, cooperation, and community: An ethnography of a Japanese school band* (Publication No. 3163382) [Doctoral dissertation, University of Washington]. ProQuest Dissertations and Theses Global.

Hendricks, K. S. (2018). *Compassionate music teaching*. Rowman & Littlefield.

Hendricks, K. S., Smith, T., & Stanuch, J. (2014). Creating safe spaces for music learning. *Music Educators Journal, 101*(1), 35–40. https://doi.org/10.1177%2F0027432114540337

Hess, J. (2019). *Music education for social change: Constructing an activist music education*. Routledge.

hooks, b. 1994. *Teaching to transgress*. Routledge.

Howe, C. (2009). *Peer groups and children's development* (Vol. 14). John Wiley & Sons.

Johnson, E. A. (2013). *The effect of symmetrical and asymmetrical peer-assisted structures on music achievement and learner engagement in the secondary large ensemble* (Publication No. 3561981) [Doctoral dissertation, University of Colorado]. ProQuest Dissertations and Theses database.

Johnson, E. A. (2015). Peer-teaching in the secondary music ensemble. *Journal of Education and Training Studies, 3*(5), 35–42. https://doi.org/10.11114/jets.v3i5.906

Johnson, E. A. (2017). The effect of symmetrical and asymmetrical peer-assisted learning structures on music achievement and learner engagement in seventh-grade band. *Journal of Research in Music Education, 65*(2), 163–178. https://doi.org/10.1177/0022429417712486

Karcher, M. (2005). Cross-age peer mentoring. In D. DuBois & M. Karcher (Eds.), *Handbook of youth mentoring* (pp. 266–285). Sage Publications.

Karcher, M. J. (2008). The cross-age mentoring program: A developmental intervention for promoting students' connectedness across grade levels. *Professional School Counseling, 12*(2), 137–143. https://doi.org/10.1177/2156759X0801200208

Lind, V. R., & McKoy, C. 2016. *Culturally responsive teaching in music education: From understanding to application.* Routledge.

Madsen, C. K. (2011). Music teacher education students as cross-age reading tutors in an after-school setting. *Journal of Music Teacher Education, 20*(2), 40–54. https://doi.org/10.1177/1057083710371441

Mullen, C. A. (2005). *Mentorship primer.* Peter Lang.

Odegard, H. (2019). *Dialectic dialogues: A discourse analysis of everyday talk between adolescent guitarists learning music with a peer outside of school* (Publication No. 13857099) [Doctoral dissertation, Boston University]. ProQuest Dissertations and Theses Global.

Pellowski Wiger, N. 2016. *Social capital, education, and earning: The important role of peer relationships for minority Tanzanian youth* (Publication No. 10141942) [Doctoral dissertation, University of Minnesota]. ProQuest Dissertations and Theses Global.

Riese, H., Samara, A., & Lillejord, S. (2012). Peer relations in peer learning. *International Journal of Qualitative Studies in Education, 25*(5), 601–624. https://doi.org/10.1080/09518398.2011.605078

Schön, D. A. (1987). *Educating the reflective practitioner: Toward a new design for teaching and learning in the professions.* Jossey Bass.

Scruggs, B. B. (2008). *Learning outcomes in two divergent middle school string orchestra classroom environments: A comparison of a learner-centered and a teacher-centered approach* (Publication No. 3371516) [Doctoral dissertation, Georgia State University]. ProQuest Dissertations and Theses Global.

Shields, C. (2001). Music education and mentoring as intervention for at-risk adolescents: Their self-perceptions, opinions, and attitudes. *Journal of Research in Music Education, 49*(3), 273–286. https://doi.org/10.2307/3345712

Stanton-Salazar, R. (2011). A social capital framework for the study of institutional agents and their role in the empowerment of low-status students and youth. *Youth & Society, 43*(3), 1066–1109. https://doi.org/10.1177/0044118X10382877

Taylor, J. (2016). *Peer mentoring within the middle and high school music department of the international school of Kuala Lumpur: A case study* (Publication No. 10135020) [Doctoral dissertation, Boston University]. ProQuest Dissertations and Theses Global.

Thornton, D. (2018). Why just me (or few others) in music education: An autoethnographic point of departure. In B. Talbot (Ed.), *Marginalized voices in music education* (pp. 46–64). Routledge.

Topping, K., Buchs, C., Duran, D., & van Keer, H. (2017). *Effective peer learning from principles to practical implementation*. Routledge.

Webb, R. S. (2015). An exploration of three peer tutoring cases in the school orchestra program. *Bulletin of the Council for Research in Music Education*, (203), 63–80. https://doi.org/10.5406/203.0063

Weidner, B. (2015). Developing musical independence in a high school band. *Bulletin of the Council for Research in Music Education*, (205), 71–86. https://doi.org/10.5406/bulcouresmusedu.205.0071

Wiggins, J. (2015). Constructivism, policy, and arts education: Synthesis and discussion. *Arts Education Policy Review*, 116, 155–159. https://doi.org/10.1080/10632913.2015.1038674

CHAPTER 24

USING THE LENS OF PSYCHOLOGICAL SAFETY TO UNDERSTAND THE EFFECTS OF BULLYING WITHIN THE SCHOOL-BASED MUSIC ENSEMBLE CLASSROOM

JARED R. RAWLINGS

Care Handbook Topics

Co-creating caring relationships

According to the American Psychological Association (APA), "school safety, at a minimum, refers to an absence of crime and violence but also includes a supportive social environment where students feel safe from harassment, bullying, and other acts of incivility or hostility" (Cornell & Huang, 2019). The APA definition of school safety encapsulates two essential components of safety: physical and psychological safety. Since the 1950s, American schools have engaged in safety preparation, including developing and practicing emergency protocols addressing crime and violence (e.g., active shooter drills on a large scale). As suggested by the APA, a supportive social atmosphere, one that is absent of harassment, bullying perpetration, and peer victimization, provides a safe learning environment and will likely benefit student learning. Therefore, it stands to reason that a youth's psychological safety is an important consideration in understanding the effects of bullying and peer victimization.

Perhaps more than any other school safety concern, bullying affects students' sense of security. In 2016, Elpus and Carter reported the risk for male music students experiencing face-to-face bullying was 69% greater than the risk for non-arts students, and male music students were confronted with a 63% greater risk of being cyberbullied than non-arts participants. Moreover, researchers report that youth enrolled in a music ensemble demonstrate stronger prosocial behaviors when compared with their peers not enrolled in a music ensemble and that these prosocial behaviors may, in turn, dampen bullying victimization experiences (Rawlings, 2017; Rawlings & Espelage, 2020; Rawlings & Young, 2020). Scholars in human development demonstrate the multidimensionality of prosocial behaviors and present plausible categories for uncovering the nuance of the developmental nature of these behaviors (Padilla-Walker et al., 2015). From this research, eight types of prosocial behaviors that emerge in adolescence are responsiveness, helping, ability to work with others, caring, compassion, trust, connection to peers, and a sense of belonging (Atallah et al., 2019; Eagly, 2009; Padilla-Walker et al., 2015).

Within this chapter, I present current research on bullying alongside explaining the deleterious impact peer victimization experiences may have youths' mental health. Next, I propose using the lens of trauma to understand the effects of peer victimization and psychological safety as an approach to address matters of music classroom inclusivity. Within each section of the chapter, I present a discussion of the recommendations for how music educators may promote prosocial behaviors as a means of dampening peer victimization in their classroom. Researchers examining trauma-sensitive school cultures report that educators understand that learning requires psychological safety and prosocial behaviors such as trust, connection to peers, and a sense of belonging (Atallah et al., 2019). For the purposes of this chapter, psychological safety refers to "as a shared belief amongst individuals as to whether it is safe to engage in interpersonal risk-taking" (Edmundson, 1999, p. 350). Although psychological safety shares conceptual overlap with trust, psychological safety is unique as it focuses on how group members perceive a group norm, whereas trust focuses on how one person views another.

Research on Bullying and Psychological Safety Within School-Based Music Classrooms

Researchers demonstrate that students need to have a sense of being "seen, safe, and soothed in order to feel secure" (Siegel, 2015, p. 145) and Purvis and her colleagues (2007) clarifies that being safe and feeling safe are not the same idea. Since 1999, the Centers for Disease Control's Division of Adolescence and School Health (CDC/DASH) has measured over four million US high school students on health behaviors that contribute to deleterious physical, emotional, and social risk factors including students' sense of safety. According to data from the Youth Risk Behavior Surveillance System (YBRSS)

2007–2017, 5%–7% of US high school students have reported not attending school because of their safety concerns (Kann et al., 2018). This result was similar to the previous decade of data, remains unchanged today, and is alarming.

Research on school bullying started almost 50 years ago and proliferated greatly in the past decades (Olweus, 1973), but it is only in recent years that empirical research examining bullying within school-based music contexts flourished. According to the CDC, "nearly 30% of American adolescents reported at least moderate bullying experiences as the bully, victim, or both" (Hamburger et al., 2011). Bullying behaviors include direct/overt aggression (e.g., physical and verbal aggression) and/or indirect/covert aggression (e.g., psychological, relational, and reputational aggression) depicted as intentional, repetitive, and imposing a power imbalance (Swearer et al., 2009). Moreover, research has consistently linked bullying with an array of negative outcomes for children and adolescents including depression, delinquency, and criminality as adults, as well as intimate partner violence perpetration and possible unemployment (Ttofi & Farrington, 2012). These injurious effects are alarming for education researchers, and rightly so. Within this section of the chapter, I discuss research reporting issues related to bullying and psychological safety within school-based music classrooms or involving populations enrolled in school-based music classes. Moreover, I will address two foundational questions fundamental to the purpose of this handbook including (a) What social and environmental considerations are important for facilitating spaces of compassion and care?, and (b) What aspects of safety are paramount in music-learning settings?

Prevalence Data of Bullying in the Music Classroom

Bullying is a concern for youth enrolled in music education classrooms and resembles previous research conducted with large populations of youth. In one study, I explored middle school band students' perceptions of bullying behavior (Rawlings, 2016). The volunteer participants ($N = 291$) reported experiencing peer victimization more frequently outside of the band classroom than inside the band classroom, with male youth reporting higher frequencies of physical victimization than females. Moreover, racially minoritized band students reported slightly higher frequencies of social aggression when compared to White band students. I concluded that band students' experiences with bullying behaviors (perpetration or victimization) differ depending on the biological sex and self-reported race.

In another study, Dorothy Espelage and I examined the prevalence of homophobic name-calling and its relationship on indicators of mental health including depression and anxiety (Rawlings & Espelage, 2020). Our analysis of data from a large-scale investigation of middle school youth indicated that experiencing homophobic name-calling significantly predicts an increase in hazardous symptoms representing overall mental health for all youth; however, this prediction is more concerning for youth not enrolled in a music ensemble class than for youth enrolled in a music ensemble (Rawlings & Espelage, 2020). From these studies, the researchers acknowledge that there are many possible motivations for the perpetration of aggression and experiencing peer victimization and it is difficult to unravel the complexities of social network behavior exchanges among youth. Several future directions for research should be highlighted based on both the limitations and findings of this investigation. These results indicate that music ensemble classrooms vary in their prevalence of homophobic name-calling and therefore, may vary in their level of psychological safety. One factor that remains underresearched in music education are the specific motivations for perpetrating homophobic epitaphs. As past research suggests, adolescents enrolled in school-based music ensembles are targets for homophobic epitaphs and particularly for males, there may be more pressure to adhere to a socially constructed range of gender expression specifically associated with music listening taste and preference, risk-taking in performance, and instrument selection. More information about these topics is presented later within this chapter.

In addition to this research examining the prevalence of bullying behaviors, there are investigations that examine the peer group influence of prosocial behaviors with youth enrolled in music ensemble courses. The power of groups can be astonishing and within music ensembles and these groups prove to be important mechanisms for social support and growth (Abril, 2013; Adderley et al., 2003; Morrison, 2001). In one study, I examined the effect of middle school music ensemble participation on the relationship between school connectedness, bullying perpetration, and peer victimization (Rawlings, 2016). Results demonstrated that music ensemble students who reported elevated levels of school connectedness were less likely than their non-ensemble peers to report perpetrating cyberbullying behaviors, suggesting that perceptions of school connectedness matter more for music ensemble participants than they do for non-ensemble participants.

In another study combining the examination of prosocial behaviors and bullying, Young and I examined peer-group influence on perceptions of relational aggression and youth empowerment (Rawlings & Young, 2020). Peer groups were identified using social network analysis and results indicated that participation in marching band significantly impacts on feelings of empowerment reducing self-reported relational victimization, even after controlling for gender, caring behaviors, and positive attitudes toward bullying. In a third study examining peer-group influence on prosocial and bullying behaviors, Young and I examined the music ensemble-level effects on self-reported frequency of relational victimization and perceptions of their willingness to intervene (Rawlings & Young, 2021). Data from this study suggest that instrumental music ensembles may differ, according to peer-group association and strength of connection to peers, in terms of the prevalence of relational victimization experiences and how youth are willing to intervene in bullying episodes.

Discussion and Recommendations

Unique from the traditional examples of school-based bullying, which include physical violence and social isolation, there are additional opportunities that bullying in the music ensemble classroom challenges a student's access to a safe learning space. Specifically, there are unique ways in which bullies, or perpetrators of aggression, can assert their power over other students, thereby making a presumably safe space less so. In considering the first guiding question for this chapter, *What social and environmental considerations are important for facilitating spaces of compassion and care?*, it appears that there is one prominent factor identified in research to consider: peer group influence. Human development research emphasizes the strong role of peer groups in determining youths' inclinations toward antisocial and prosocial behavior and early adolescence is the developmental stage when youth spend a greater proportion of time with peers (Brown & Larson, 2009).

An important process contributing to establishing a friendship is the preference for friends who are similar to oneself. The term for this selective affiliation is "homophily," which is one dimension of social structure (e.g., size, centrality and stability are other characteristics of social networks; Kandel, 1978). For music ensemble classrooms, there are contributing factors to the formation of peer groups that may not be present in other classrooms. For instance, instrument selection is a contributing factor to peer group formation as the students performing on the same instrument have similar aesthetic roles in their recreation of music notation. Within a music ensemble classroom, students performing on similar instruments (e.g., single-reeded instruments, double-reeded instruments) assemble as a cohort and may receive instrument-specific pedagogical experiences that are unique to other instrument cohorts and within these pedagogical experiences there may be additional opportunities for feelings of connection or disjunction with their peers.

Another contributing factor to peer group formation may be gender stereotyping of music instruments (O'Neill & Boulton, 1996; Wych, 2012). For example, if a student's gender-instrument association is atypical (e.g., male flute performers, female percussion performers), there may be localized opportunities, for them, to experience peer victimization. Given these contributing factors to the construction and maintenance of peer groups, it seems that youth influence a variety of prosocial behaviors including compassion and care.

O'Neill (2015) demonstrates that musical engagement that focuses on agentive actions or dialogical experiences should also aim to enhance youths' voices, sense of wellbeing, and musical thriving and for music educators, knowing the classroom environment or peer-level beliefs around compassion and care are essential data to collect and analyze. There are several approaches to go about this; however, I would like to recommend that music educators rely on a combined approach to collecting and analyzing these data. First, I recommend locating an open-access and valid instrument for collecting student perceptions of the music ensemble classroom and school, at large (see Jones, 2015;

Parkes et al., 2017). After administering the instrument as a component of a questionnaire, a researcher might solicit the assistance of an administrator or peer by requesting structured observations of the music ensemble classroom. Combining the results of these data allows for a degree of precision not available with either data point alone. For instance, perhaps the data from structured observations reveal that the music educator is effective at managing peer victimization, but data from the questionnaire show that students hold low perceptions of psychological safety overall. This would seem to suggest that while the music classroom climate is adequate, there may be an urgent need to address other parts of the classroom or perhaps the school.

In addressing the second guiding question for this chapter, *What aspects of safety are paramount in music-learning settings?*, there are two clear categories of safety: physical and psychological. The first category, physical safety refers to the learning conditions that may influence the physiological needs of the student. Abraham Maslow's *hierarchy of needs* is often referred to as a framework relating to safety with the premise that basic human needs must be fulfilled before social, esteem, and self-actualization needs are considered (Maslow, 1943). Physical safety in the music classroom is essential for group-based music-making. For instance, instruments and human bodies must be secure and stable as to avoid injury. While physical safety measures are an important part of all school classrooms, students *feeling* safe in the music classroom is not the same as an adult declaration that a school *is* safe.

The second category, psychological safety, refers to whether it is safe to engage in interpersonal risk-taking. For example, risk-taking in a music ensemble classroom include, but are not limited to: (a) performing a solo during a rehearsal of a piece of music; (b) showcasing a music notation composition or improvisation for peer review; and (c) solo performance, in front of peers, of an etude for an academic grade. Student musicians take interpersonal risks when they engage in group-based music-making. For instance, these interpersonal risks may include encountering uncomfortable feelings of vulnerability during performance. Therefore, when students in music classrooms have power over others, issues of psychological safety rise and lead to matters of inclusivity. As music educators, it is critical to protect each student's access to a safe learning space, understand Jackson and Gardstrom's (2012) concept of emotional safety/comfort, and advocate for how issues of safety are paramount in music-learning settings.

Understanding a Possible Effect of Bullying: Trauma

The relationship between bullying and trauma is multifaceted, and victimization experiences can lead to traumatic stress reactions including post-traumatic stress disorder (PTSD), demonstrated through dysregulation of stress chemistry and increased activation of the sympathetic nervous system (McDaniel-Muldoon, 2019). For instance, researchers have reported that students who experience bullying, 27.6% of boys and 40.5% of girls had PTSD scores within a clinically significant range (Idsoe et al., 2012). For the purposes of this chapter, I am aligning my definition of trauma with Hibbard and Price (this volume) to be framed as what Weathers and Keane (2007) refer to an emotionally painful or shocking experience that might result in lasting impact on individuals involved in the situation. Within this section of the chapter, I discuss the typology of trauma and conclude with addressing a foundational question fundamental to the purpose of this handbook: *What is the role of trauma-sensitive education in music-learning settings?*

Typology of Trauma

Traumatization may affect a victim's sensory experience. Specifically, victims may have reactions that they did not have prior to certain sensory experiences including hearing, seeing or touching. These alterations to sensory stimulation can occur after a single exposure to a traumatic event or after repeated exposure to a series of events.

Children and adolescents seem particularly vulnerable to trauma and repeated exposure to traumatic events such as experiencing psychological or physical abuse and experiencing and/or witnessing school violence, may have long-term effects on mental health and physical wellbeing. Common reactions to traumatic events are categorized into several domains including emotional, physical, cognitive, behavioral, and social. First, emotional reactions to trauma vary and are influenced by a victim's sociocultural history with some victims having difficulty regulating emotions such as anxiety, sadness, and shame (van der Kolk et al., 1993). Second, physical reactions or symptoms to trauma include somatic complaints, sleep disturbances, and challenges with cardiovascular, neurological and dermatological disorders (Centers for Disease Control, 2012). Third, cognitive reactions to trauma appear as thought-process changes including cognitive error (misremembering details of a situation), excessive or inappropriate guilt, idealization (demonstrating inaccurate rationalizations or justifications for the perpetrator's behavior), hallucinations or delusions, or intrusive thoughts that may trigger strong emotional or behavioral reactions (Janoff-Bulman, 2010). Fourth, behavioral reactions reflect how victims manage the post-trauma effects. Victims may choose to behaviorally reduce stress tension through avoidant, compulsive (e.g., shopping, overeating), self-medicating (e.g., binge drinking), and impulsive behaviors. Lastly, social reactions or interpersonal reactions including withdrawal from peer groups and rebellion associated with family units occur with traumatic events (Hamblen, 2001). Trauma is both an individual and collective experience and therefore, a child or adolescent reacts uniquely.

In considering the last guiding question for this chapter, *What is the role of trauma-sensitive education in music-learning settings?*, it appears that there are multiple factors identified in research to consider. First, trauma dampens student success and academic achievement. Researchers examining trauma-sensitive school culture report that educators understand that learning requires safety and prosocial behaviors such as trust, connection to peers, and sense of belonging (Atallah et al., 2019). Given some of the research reported previously in this chapter, it seems that in some music ensemble classrooms, prosocial behaviors may be elevated when compared with their non-music ensemble peers. Future work is needed to determine how music educators foster pillars of trauma-sensitive classrooms within their ensemble classes as a means of strengthening student learning and fostering a sense of belonging. This research has the potential to guide changes in practice and policy, which in turn values the importance of a welcoming and inclusive learning environment.

Second, researchers investigating Adverse Childhood Experiences (ACEs) have found that youth who experience more ACEs are also more likely to perpetrate bullying behavior (Sacks et al., 2014). Given some of the research previously reported in this chapter, music ensemble participants may have coping strategies for resolving stress associated with their ACEs. This association may be because most trauma survivors are highly resilient and develop appropriate coping strategies, including the use of social supports, to deal with the aftermath and effects of trauma. Positive youth development provides an essential framework for considering youth's engagement in musical activities whereas its main premise states that all young people have the potential and capacity for healthy growth and development through musical engagement (O'Neill, 2006). O'Neill (2015) defines the process of musically engaging youth as "providing learning opportunities that engage young people in a process that enables then to *speak back* [author emphasis] to the reality of today's uncertain and unstable world" (p. 390). Moreover, Felicity Laurence (2008) suggested that music ensemble participation offers the potential to "enable, catalyze, and strengthen empathic response, ability, and relationship, and it is this potential capacity which lies at the core of music's function within peacebuilding" (p. 14). Future work needs to be conducted with victims and examine their recovery process and timeline to understand the influence group-based music-making has.

Conclusion

Bullying is a traumatic event and not a rite of passage among school-aged youth. By applying the lens of psychological safety to understand bullying experiences, as traumatic events, new considerations about the role of music ensemble classes in schools were uncovered within this chapter. This information is important because examining prosocial behaviors within music ensemble classes, including compassion and care, and how these behaviors influence youths' coping strategies. For instance, measuring youths' perceptions of resilience, as demonstrated in some school environments, may uncover additional nuance, especially when repeated bullying may damage indicators of mental health (Astor et al., 2004; Astor et al., 2013). Furthermore, McFerran and her colleagues (2016) identify that group music-making activities are associated with feelings of enhanced quality of life including youth's social connectedness and personal wellbeing. This research and the investigations outlined within this chapter indicate that youths selecting to participate in a music ensemble, as an example of their resilience and agency, may be a factor that buffers the effects of bullying traumatic events.

REFERENCES

Abril, C. R. (2013). Perspectives on the school band from hardcore American band kids. In P. S. Campbell & T. Wiggins (Eds.), *The Oxford handbook of children's musical cultures* (pp. 435–448). Oxford University Press.

Adderley, C., Kennedy, M., & Berz, W. (2003). "A home away from home": The world of the high school music classroom. *Journal of Research in Music Education*, 51(3), 190. https://doi.org/10.2307/3345373

Astor R. A., Benbenishty, R., Pitner, R. O., & Meyer, H. A. (2004). Bullying and peer victimization in schools. In P. Allen-Meares & M. W. Fraser (Eds.), *Intervention with children and adolescents: An interdisciplinary perspective* (pp. 417–448). Pearson Education.

Astor, R. A., De Pedro, K. T., Gilreath, T. D., Esqueda, M. C., & Benbenishty, R. (2013). The promotional roles of school and community contexts for military students. *Clinical Child and Family Psychology Review*, 16, 233–244. https://doi.org/10.1007/s10567-013-0139-x

Atallah, D. G., Koslouski, J. B., Perkins, K. N., Marsico, C., & Porche, M. V. (2019). An evaluation of Trauma and Learning Policy Initiative's (TLPI) inquiry-based process: Year three. *Boston University, Wheelock College of Education and Human Development*.

Brown, B. B., & Larson, J. (2009). Peer relationships in adolescents. In R. M. L. Steinberg (Ed.), *Handbook of adolescent psychology, contextual influences on adolescent development* (3rd ed., Vol. 2, pp. 74–103). John Wiley & Sons.

Centers for Disease Control and Prevention. (2018). *Youth risk behavior survey: Data summary & trends report 2007–2017*. https://www.cdc.gov/healthyyouth/data/yrbs/pdf/trendsreport.pdf

Cornell, D., & Huang, F. (2019). Collecting and analyzing local school safety and climate data. In M. J. Mayer & S. R. Jimerson (Eds.), *School safety and violence prevention: Science, practice, policy* (pp. 151–175). American Psychological Association. https://doi.org/10.1037/0000106-007

Eagly, A. H. (2009). The his and hers of prosocial behavior: An examination of the social psychology of gender. *American Psychologist*, 64(8), 644–658. https://doi.org/10.1037/0003-066X.64.8.644

Edmundson, A. (1999). Psychological safety and learning behavior in work teams. *Administrative Science Quarterly*, 22(2), 350–383. https://doi.org/10.2307/2666999

Elpus, K., & Carter, B. A. (2016). Bullying victimization among music ensemble and theater students in the United States. *Journal of Research in Music Education*, 64, 322–343. https://doi.org/10.1177/0022429416658642

Hamblen, J. (2001). PTSD in children and adolescents: A National Center for PTSD fact sheet. http://www.georgiadisaster.info/Schools/fs%207%20school/PTSD%20in%20Children%20&%20Adolescents.pdf

Hamburger, M. E., Basile, K. C., & Vivolo, A. M. (2011). *Measuring bullying victimization, perpetrator, and bystander experiences: A compendium of assessment tools*. Centers for Disease Control and Prevention, National Center for Injury Prevention and Control.

Idsoe, T., Dyregrov, A., & Idsoe, E. C. (2012). Bullying and PTSD symptoms. *Journal of Abnormal Child Psychology, 40*(6), 901–911. https://doi.org/10.1007/s10802-012-9620-0

Jackson, N., & Gardstrom, S. (2012). Undergraduate music therapy students' experiences as clients in short-term group music therapy. *Music Therapy Perspectives, 30*(1), 65–82. https://doi.org/10.1093/mtp/30.1.65

Janoff-Bulman, R. (2010). *Shattered assumptions: Towards a new psychology of trauma.* Free Press.

Jones, B. D. (2015). *User guide for assessing the components of the MUSIC Model of Motivation.* https://www.themusicmodel.com/wp-content/uploads/2019/06/User-Guide-to-Assessing-the-MUSIC-Model-Components-December-2017-2.pdf

Kandel, D. B. (1978). Homophily, selection, and socialization in adolescent friendships. *American Journal of Sociology, 84*(2), 427–436.

Kann, L., McManus, T., Harris, W. A., Shanklin, S. L., Flint, K. H., Queen, B., Lowry, R., Chyen, D., Whittle, L., Thornton, J., Lim, C., Bradford, D., Yamakawa, Y., Leon, M., Brener, N., & Ethier, K. A. (2018). Youth risk behavior surveillance—United States, 2017. *MMWR Surveillance Summaries, 67*(8), 1–114. https://www.cdc.gov/mmwr/volumes/67/ss/ss6708a1.htm

Larkin, H., Shields, J. J., & Anda, R. F. (2012). The health and social consequences of adverse childhood experiences (ACE) across the lifespan: An introduction to prevention and intervention in the community. *Journal of Prevention & Intervention in the Community, 40*(4), 263–270. https://doi.org/10.1080/10852352.2012.707439

Laurence, F. (2008). Music and empathy. In O. Urbain (Ed.), *Music and conflict transformation: Harmonies and dissonances in geopolitics* (pp. 131–125). I. B. Tauris.

Maslow, A. H. (1943). A theory of human motivation. *Psychological Review, 50*(4), 370–396. https://doi.org/10.1037/h0054346

McDaniel-Muldoon, J. (2019). *Using the lens of trauma in understanding bullying* [Conference Workshop]. 2019 World Anti-bullying Forum, Dublin City University, Dublin, Ireland.

McFerran, K. S., Garrido, S., & Saarikallio, S. (2016). A critical interpretive synthesis of the literature linking music and adolescent mental health. *Youth & Society, 48*(4), 521–538. https://journals.sagepub.com/doi/pdf/10.2307/3399738

Morrison, S. J. (2001). The school ensemble: A culture of our own. *Music Educators Journal, 88*(2), 24–28. https://doi.org/10.2307/3399738

Olweus, D. (1973). *Hackkycklingar och översittare: Forskning om skolmobbning* [Victims and Bullies: Research on School Bullying]. Almquist & Wilsell.

O'Neill, S. A. (2006). Positive youth engagement. In G. McPherson (Ed.), *The child as musician: A handbook of musical development* (pp. 461–474). Oxford University Press.

O'Neill, S. A. (2015). Youth empowerment and transformative music engagement. In C. Benedict, P. Schmidt, G. Spruce, & P. Woodford (Eds.), *The Oxford handbook of social justice in music education* (pp. 388–405). Oxford University Press.

O'Neill, S. A., & Boulton, M. J. (1996). Boys' and girls' preferences for musical instruments: A function of gender? *Psychology of Music, 24,* 171–183.

Padilla-Walker, L. M., & Carlo, G. (Eds.). (2015). *Prosocial development: A multidimensional approach.* Oxford University Press.

Parkes, K. A., Jones, B. D., & Wilkins, J. L. M. (2017). Assessing music students' motivation using the MUSIC Model of Academic Motivation Inventory. *Update: Applications of Research in Music Education, 35,* 16–22. https://doi.org/10.1177/8755123315620835

Purvis, K. B., Cross, D. R., & Sunshine, W. L. (2007). Disarming the fear response with felt safety. In K. B. Purvis, D. R. Cross, & W. L. Sunshine (Eds.), *The connected child: Bring hope and healing to your adopted family* (pp. 47–72). McGraw-Hill.

Rawlings, J. R. (2016). Middle school students' perceptions of bullying. *Bulletin of the Council for Research in Music Education*, (209), 7–26. https://doi.org/10.5406/bulcouresmusedu.209.0007

Rawlings, J. R. (2017). The effect of middle school music ensemble participation on the relationship between perceived school connectedness, self-reported bullying behaviors, and peer victimization. *Bulletin of the Council for Research in Music Education*, (213), 53–72. https://doi.org/10.5406/bulcouresmusedu.213.0053

Rawlings, J. R., & Espelage, D. L. (2020). Middle school music ensemble participation, homophobic name-calling, and mental health. *Youth & Society*, 52(7), 1238–1258. https://doi.org/10.1177/0044118X19866071

Rawlings, J. R., & Young, J. (2021). High school band and orchestra musician's willingness to intervene in school-based relational victimization experiences. *Contributions to Music Education*, 46, 207–223.

Rawlings, J. R., & Young, J. (2020). Relational aggression and youth empowerment within a high school instrumental music program. *Psychology of Music*. Advance online publication. https://doi.org/10.1177/0305735620923140

Sacks, V., Murphey, D., & Moore, K. (2014). *Adverse childhood experiences: National and state-level prevalence. Child Trends.* https://www.childtrends.org/wp-content/uploads/2014/07/Brief-adverse-childhood-experiences_FINAL.pdf

Siegel, D. J. (2015). *Brainstorm: The power and purpose of the teenage brain.* Penguin.

Swearer, S. M., Espelage, D. L., & Napolitano, S. A. (2009). *Bullying prevention and intervention: Realistic strategies for schools.* Guilford Press.

Ttofi, M. M., & Farrington, D. P. (2012). Risk and protective factors, longitudinal research, and bullying prevention. *New Directions for Youth Development*, 133, 85–98. https://onlinelibrary.wiley.com/doi/pdf/10.1002/yd.20009

van der Kolk, B. A., Roth, S., Pelcovitz, D., & Mandel, F. (1993). *Complex PTSD: Results of the PTSD field trials for DSM-IV.* American Psychiatric Association.

Weathers, F. W., & Keane, T. M. (2007). The Criterion A problem revisited: Controversies and challenges in defining and measuring psychological trauma. *Journal of Traumatic Stress*, 20(2), 107–121. https://onlinelibrary.wiley.com/doi/pdf/10.1002/jts.20210

Wych, G. M. (2012). Gender and instrument associations, stereotypes, and stratification: A literature review. *Update: Applications of Research in Music Education*, 30(2), 22–31.

FOREWORD TO SECTION 3

CARING FOR WELLBEING AND HUMAN FLOURISHING

SUSAN A. O'NEILL

UNDERSTANDING why caring matters is at the heart of the chapters in this section. Together, the authors make a very generous and special contribution to diverse, relational, practice-based and action-oriented ways in which caring, as a deep form of authentic connection, makes a positive difference in the quality of people's lives. As such, it encompasses notions of both "caring for" and "caring with" as Karin Hendricks (this volume) outlines in her introduction (see also Hendricks, 2021). Against the backdrop of today's complex and turbulent world, the chapters offer valuable ways of envisioning how caring interacts with people's understanding of themselves, others, and the world around them, and how music education through this transformative lens fosters conditions of possibility for enhancing wellbeing and human flourishing.

Concepts of wellbeing and flourishing have been central to the human condition since Aristotle's Nicomachean Ethics in the 4th century BCE. These concepts permeate across disciplinary boundaries from philosophy into politics and political science, psychology, sociology, religion and medicine (Heydon & O'Neill, 2016). Aristotle described wellbeing as an ethical choice reflecting the virtues of the Greek gods, especially living the contemplative life and "striving toward excellence based on one's unique potential" (Ryff & Singer, 2008, p. 14). It is noteworthy that wellbeing was not envisioned as an outcome or end state; rather, it was a *process* of striving toward fulfilment such as self-discovery or the self-knowledge that comes from reflecting on your personal development or the values that you believe are important. It also comes from developing unique potentials and using those potentials to fulfill your goals.

More broadly, the notion of flourishing was taken up in the 1950s with a focus on mental illness that later shifted to a focus on mental health primarily through scholarship in positive psychology (Csikszentmihalyi, 1990; Diener, 2001; Seligman, 2011). Ryff and Singer (2008) consider the dimensions of what makes life good for humans as a blending of mental, physical, and social wellbeing. In connecting the concept of caring within the context of music education, the chapters in this section uncover what it is that people do through meaningful forms of music engagement that creates satisfaction, fulfillment, and a life well lived. This entanglement of caring, wellbeing and flourishing offers a more holistic approach to understanding why caring in music education matters and how it is intertwined in learners' lives through complex authentic and ethical encounters with others that foreground possibilities for wellbeing.

Watson et al. (2012) argue that wellbeing is "contextual and embedded" and enacted and realized through circumstances and constituent "encounters" (p. 7). This means that any concept of wellbeing must emphasize that it is relational. Proposing that wellbeing is relational acknowledges that it is produced between and among people, but it also requires an ethical posturing that encompasses "caring for" and "caring with" where one does not absolutely decide for the other what wellbeing means. Watson et al. (2012) reject a totalizing conceptualization of wellbeing where the alterity of the other is compromised. They recognize that people need to be in co-relation and that this involves a complex ethical encounter with the other which Watson and colleagues identify as being "mediated" by "human flourishing" (p. 227). Wellbeing involves our flourishing together within our communities, thereby emerging in the spaces made between people and music.

We find many examples in the chapters within this section where caring is entangled and enacted in music education in ways that provide opportunities for people to experience authentic connection on a deep and fundamental level with positive impacts on wellbeing and flourishing. The scope of the chapters is ambitious in many respects, as they span numerous contexts and conceptualizations of wellbeing from mental health and music therapy through to vulnerability, self-determination, and self-care. A key theme of many chapters could be described as making a contribution to how caring makes a positive influence on the potential of others. Another theme is how the concept of caring emphasizes the importance of critical educators who are "adaptive, reflective, and sensitive to the motivations and skills of each student" (Hendricks & McPherson, this volume), through an enhanced understanding of the ways that learners, communities, culture, pedagogies, and curriculum are linked to impacts on wellbeing and flourishing. Another overarching theme is how music educators and music learners are always in a lively relationship with the world and not only with each other. As such, our lived experience of "caring for" and "caring with" in relation to ourselves and others takes place within a wider context of music education that is diverse, dynamic, interconnected and inextricably linked with possibilities for wellbeing and human flourishing.

REFERENCES

Csikszentmihalyi, M. (1990). *Flow: The psychology of optimal experience*. Harper & Row.
Diener, E. (2001). Psychology of wellbeing (subjective). In N. J. Smelser & P. B. Baltes (Eds.), *International encyclopedia of the social and behavioral sciences* (pp. 16451–16454). Pergamon.
Hendricks, K. S. (2021). Authentic connection in music education. In K. S. Hendricks & J. Boyce-Tillman (Eds.), *Authentic connection: Music, spirituality, and wellbeing* (pp. 237–253). Peter Lang.
Heydon, R., & O'Neill, S. A. (2016). *Why multimodal literacy matters: (Re)conceptualizing literacy and wellbeing though singing-infused multimodal, intergenerational curricula*. Sense Publications.
Ryff, C. D., & Singer, B. H. (2008). Know thyself and become what you are: A eudaimonic approach to psychological wellbeing. *Journal of Happiness Studies*, 9(1), 13–39. https://doi.org/10.1007/s10902-006-9019-0
Seligman, M. E. P. (2011). *Flourish: A visionary new understanding of happiness and wellbeing*. Free Press.
Watson, D., Emery, C., & Bayliss P. (2012). *Children's social and emotional wellbeing*. The Policy Press.

CHAPTER 25

THE VULNERABILITY IN BEING HEARD

Care in the Supervision of Music Students

TIRI BERGESEN SCHEI

CARE HANDBOOK TOPICS

Philosophical perspectives
Wellbeing and human flourishing

VIGNETTE

A student is performing a song in front of their classmates and teachers during the mandatory weekly performance session in the school hall. Hannah loves being in front of the audience. Her voice is sonorous, and she excels at the complicated passages. There is harmony between what she does and what she achieves. Her charisma has a strong effect on the audience, as the applause after her performance makes very clear. As Hannah leaves the podium, she conveys bodily self-esteem and satisfaction.

Another student, Maria, comes onstage. The audience notices her stiff body gestures as she nervously steps onto the podium, where she stands restlessly and looks uncomfortable. The pianist attempts to make eye contact with her, but she seems preoccupied with her trembling legs. Her pitch is off-key, and suddenly she stops singing. The pianist helps her continue, but she is now in an embarrassing and complicated situation. After the performance, Maria describes the intrusion of automatic thoughts about being a failure. She had noticed some of her classmates raising their eyebrows and looking at each other, and this was enough for her to lose focus on her performance and feel shame.

The singers in the above vignette have been created for this chapter on the basis of my research on voice shame (Schei, 1998; Schei & Schei, 2017) and vocal identities (Schei, 2007, 2009), as well as on 13 years of experience teaching students on a three-year music high school program where students had 15 music lessons per week. Imagine that the students are 17 years old. They have chosen voice as their main instrument and take weekly singing lessons from their voice teacher. They are supposed to perform regularly for an audience, as are all of the students on this program. They have received instruction from skilled voice teachers and have learned how much effort it takes to develop not only one's singing voice but also mature stylistic details in various genres. It seems that the recipients of their songs, the audience, may play a far greater role for them than they had imagined.

There is a caring community of supportive teachers for the students at the school. It is a flourishing, youthful environment characterized by rich musical experiences and personal growth. The students sing in the school choir and participate in various singing groups, where they try out different vocal styles and genres. Teenagers undergo a continuous process of social identity formation, as documented in research (Ellefsen, 2014; Oltedal et al., 2016; Parker, 2010). But here, as in any other social milieu, they confront tacit rules, quality hierarchies, and expectations. Unspoken cultural "truths" about vocal ideals and style seem to structure both the singers and their classmates, pressuring them to perform, and listen, in accordance with reigning norms.

All performance is situated somewhere between success and failure, between feelings of mastery and joy and feelings of shame and self-loathing (Fernholz et al., 2019). The two examples above indicate a little-discussed gray zone. It is not obvious who should talk about it or how. The student who struggles on stage needs care and support, as does the successful singer, but they need different kinds of care and support. Voice teachers function as role models. They know how to teach professional skills and musicianship, but they may struggle when it comes to supporting students in a personally responsive manner (Lewis et al., 2021). Given that they are not therapists, to what extent should teachers see to situations in which multiple layers of feelings need to be managed?

In this chapter, the point of departure is the human voice, with a focus on vulnerable self-expression and what may occur if one is not aware of how susceptible one can be when performing in front of an audience. I outline how self-censorship, unwarranted shame, and fear of shame may creep up on music students, crippling their ability to fully develop their artistic and human potential. I will outline these concepts and discuss how, by way of care, music teachers can find ways to liberate students from the entanglements of misplaced shame and defensive shame avoidance.

Audible Bodies

The voice is an innate and natural part of the lives of all human beings. A newborn child takes its first breath through a scream. The voice is our oral communicative tool, and in early childhood we learn ways of expressing ourselves that become part of our identity, of who we feel that we are. We are shaped by and within cultural environments—emotionally, relationally, and communicatively. This means that the way we use the voice, the words we choose, the tone, the sound, and the rhythm, are continually being influenced by interactions with those around us from early childhood onward. The voice, with its timbre and rich variations of expressive form, is an imprint of the life we have lived and find ourselves in, the experiences we have had, what we have been exposed to, the habits we have acquired, and the feedback from others that has affected us. A teenager who sings with joy has most likely encountered people and environments that have encouraged and facilitated self-exposure. Such approval contributes to a singer's feelings of acceptance and value. It expresses deep acceptance of the person.

Memories associated with the use of one's singing voice may be saturated with many different emotions (Lewis & Hendricks, 2022). Some people had uncomfortable classroom experiences during their early schooldays, when their teacher's focus may have been on singing in key and assessing technical issues in terms of norms and ideals rather than the joy of singing together. Such experiences can lead one to have feelings of not being good enough and may sink into the subconsciousness and remain there (Karraker, 2012). Unfortunately, experiences from early childhood can have a very negative impact. Many people are reluctant to speak or sing in groups because they "know" that they do not sing well. Such feelings may remain vivid throughout one's life. I have met teachers and elderly people who cling to this "truth" about their singing voice and have not dared to sing since their early schooldays.

The voice expresses the audible human being by means of information whose complexity no one fully comprehends but which is crucial to how we respond to each other. Music teachers have an ethical responsibility to sense and be alert to this knowledge, which is not often spoken of but is nonetheless fundamental to students' feelings of acceptance and wellbeing. I suggest considering the voice an *audible body*. This concept

> encompasses not only the sound of the voice, but also the communicative, relational and emotional meanings that inevitably color both production and perception of a human voice, within a complex matrix of social and cultural norms connoting beauty, quality, normalcy, health, and more. By talking about the audible body, not the voice, we want to highlight that when people hear each other, or know they are being heard, they inevitably produce complex, tacit, normative interpretations not only of the sound, but of the person whose sound it is (Schei, 2011), and of the person's presentation of self (Goffman, 1959), given the norms inherent in the concrete context. (Schei et al., 2018, p. 198)

When a voice sounds "natural," there is nothing in the way we communicate with others that catches their attention, and we do not pay particular attention to our own voice or the voices of others. Voice is as natural to us as water is to fish.

When the Voice Becomes a Musical Instrument

When the human voice becomes an instrument, the audible body receives novel attention. The vocal instrument is not limited to the vocal cords (Welch & Preti, 2019). It is the whole body—with its muscles, its breathing patterns, and its technical challenges—that requires attention and care (Sweet & Parker, 2019). The singer's ability to exercise self-control, which implies self-evaluation, is a significant puzzle. Most voice teachers can discern a student's subtle signals through the student's tone quality, breath support, gestures, and ways of interpreting a song.

Because the voice, ever present in our body, is both a communicative tool and an instrument, music teachers may benefit from taking the time to identify what is at stake for a young singer and what kinds of voice and communication knowledge should constitute basic knowledge for all music teachers. Care in music education is very much dependent on how we discharge the responsibility of the teacher mandate, on how we as music teachers think, speak, and act when we guide and teach our students. Music education is, as Bowman (2012) puts it, "a helping profession" (p. 2); and "practical wisdom," the intellectual virtue referred to as *phronesis* by the Greek philosopher Aristotle 2,300 years ago, is highly relevant knowledge (Kemmis, 2012; Kinsella & Pitman, 2012):

> [P]rofessional practice knowledge involves the knowledge that comes to life in the *doing* of the practice, the *craft* of the practice, and is embodied in the relationship of the practitioner to the practice and to others involved in and affected by the practice, that is, a kind of *personal* knowledge. (Kemmis, 2012, p. 147)

Teacher competency consists of more than just the ability to convey memorized knowledge and technical skills to students; it also involves being a practitioner who is flexible and able to improvise and be supportive when in concrete situations with students who need us and where we do not have a clear solution or answer. Young students are vulnerable when they go in front of an audience and ask for its attention. This is true of all of us (Goffman, 1959; Kaleńska-Rodzaj, 2020). There is a remarkable difference between talking and singing in everyday life among family and people we know well and standing on a podium to speak or perform a song before a potentially critical audience. Many singers perform according to expectations yet still feel uncomfortable, whereas others may be far from satisfying adjudicator or audience expectations while not having these uneasy feelings. This difference in students' resilience is important for music teachers to be aware of, even in the classroom (Schei et al., 2018). Voice teachers need insight into this gray zone, where singers try so hard to sing well but again and again feel miserable. Some call it "stage fright" (Kokotsaki & Davidson, 2003) or music performance anxiety (Kaleńska-Rodzaj, 2020; Kenny, 2011; McGrath et al., 2016). At the opposite end of the spectrum, "performing music can be a very positive emotional experience," writes Lamont (2012), who states that "the physical act of singing can increase levels of tense arousal" (p. 576). There is a vulnerability in the intimacy connected to the voice and the owner of the voice when it has the status of a musical instrument (Lewis & Hendricks, 2022). The many hours spent on this relationship sometimes causes a fear of failure.

The Mirror Effect

Most singers work hard on technique, language, and style. Development as a young singer entails a transition point when the singer sees themselves, this singing person, from the outside, so to speak, as a listener and as a viewer. This transition may occur in a school setting, as illustrated in the vignette. To understand what is happening, we may need to enter the practice room and put a magnifying glass to some of the details. Singers depend on the mirror as a controller; they know that they must confront it and tolerate it in order to check whether they have performed an exercise correctly. How their cheeks and posture affect the timbre of their voice, for instance, are essential details for the singer during their daily gaze on their audible body. The singer may spend hours in front of the mirror and use it almost as a substitute for a teacher. If they manage to focus on the instrument as such, all is well, but if they use the mirror to see themselves as they believe others see them—"others" meaning the audience, the reviewers in the newspapers, the teacher, and the classmates—they may become overattentive and self-centered (Goffman, 1959; Scheff, 2005). Singers, as well as musicians in general, subordinate themselves to norms of clothing, hair style, and fitness. They are aware that they are being assessed (Monson, 1996, p. 95). *Professional* singers are not only aware of it, they subordinate themselves to the cultural norms "embedded in vocal ideals, voice genres, educational concerns, conceptions of normality and common sense" (Schei, 2009, p. 227). Being a 17-year-old confronted with the reflection in the mirror is not always easy. Such a self-focus can lead to an attitude of severe self-condemnation that pays attention to performing the *self*, rather than performing the music, through the vocal instrument.

Singers are continually confronted with themselves as a *person* because the voice cannot be separated from the living body, with its self-understanding and continuous identity project and where self-assessment is inextricably linked to self-esteem. To understand what comes into play between us when we sing, be it in the school hall in front of classmates and teachers or as music teachers and lead singers in the classroom, or even when performing professionally, it is essential to understand the behavioral patterns that arise in us the moment we become aware of the audience. It is up to us to decide whether we should let their judgement of our performance influence our self-esteem, but this is not obvious without reflection on the mechanisms. On stage there is nowhere to hide: It is the most exposed platform, the space where singers perform what they have been preparing, where they execute the music and, hopefully, convey meaningful moments to the audience. For singers with integrity and confidence, who act in accordance with what they understand to be mature singing within their genre, this can be the perfect existential moment. But it can also be the opposite—the owner of the voice mistakes the voice as an object for the voice as "I"—a characteristic of me as a person. Being overattentive to one's own voice may indicate that one is interpreting others' perceived assessment, which interferes in one's self-confidence and makes the performer acutely aware of the *how* of the situation (Schei, 2019). If the singer thinks that the audience is silently evaluating their voice quality and the singer as a person against norms for correctness, they may produce normative interpretations of themselves while performing. Why does this happen? And why is it so easy for some to perform and so difficult for others?

The introductory example of the two singers illustrates how the voice is deeply social and always intertwined with thoughts, feelings, and issues of self-confidence. As we become aware that we are the focus of attention, we experience this sudden reminder that we are vulnerable bodies and that our voice is simultaneously an extremely important relational tool and a musical instrument embedded in the person.

Voice Shame

Some singers suppress themselves to avoid being heard as not good enough. *Voice shame* can arise when a person

> becomes aware of an observer's attention and believes the evaluation to be negative. It causes intensive monitoring of one's vocal expression and of other's perception of oneself. The effects of voice shame are largely hidden, since performers will tend to gravitate towards self-staging strategies that comply with conventions, in order to avoid shame. (Schei & Schei, 2017, p. 1)

Feelings of shame can take the form of embarrassment, shyness, feelings of inadequacy, blushing, and a desire to be invisible. Such feelings are common among music performers on stage (McGuiness, 2013, p. 109). Shame is part of our emotional register, one of many emotions that every human being needs in order to socialize and to learn cultural norms. The fear of rejection and defeat is linked to the need to avoid feelings of shame (Dickerson et al., 2004; Scheff, 2014a, 2014b). Shame represents an internal sanction against behavior that violates presumed common norms and leads to the avoidance of such behavior. Human beings adapt to systems and patterns by unconsciously producing audible utterances, bodily unfoldment, and self-staging that fit with what one tacitly assumes to be right and normal.

I use the voice as an example to outline perspectives on shame, but the insights are relevant whatever the instrument or genre. For music teachers, it is vital to know how students hold back and disguise such feelings. Voice shame is a devastating self-punishment in the aftermath of exposure to an audience. Reflective self-care is needed in order to understand and manage the mechanisms that produce fear, self-censorship, voice shame, and destructive disciplinary behavior in our students, as well as in us as teachers at times. How we talk together about our experiences may yield important knowledge about why performances are saturated with emotional content from the continuum between shame and pride.

The Caring Relationship

The concept of *care* encapsulates qualities and actions that are necessary for empowering others. Hendricks (2018) points out that compassionate music teaching is not a unidirectional relationship from teacher to learner where only the learner is expected to be vulnerable, in need of learning, and in need of support. What is referred to as "care" can be misunderstood as disempowering one-way interventions which lead to "false separations between humans and afford those with social privilege a vantage point with which to maintain that privilege" (Hendricks, this volume). Examples of oppressive "care" are legion. A challenge for all potentially caring relationships is that they stem from a power asymmetry, in which one person trusts and depends on another person within a given context, such as a song lesson. Trust creates relational power, but power can always be abused. Power is neither good nor bad; it is a power imbalance that can be a problem. Hendricks (2018) states that as long as there is a power struggle, true learning cannot take place, because "power, authority, embarrassment, oppression, pain, and how to 'win' or 'lose' in a system with particular rules that favor one person or idea over another" will be the student's learning outcome (p. 5). Hendricks argues for an equalized version of care, a relational experience-sharing version characterized by a "shared understanding of feelings, hopes, and/or desires" (p. 5). Her six qualities of compassion—trust, empathy, patience, inclusion, community, and authentic connection—are ways of inviting relational and compassionate communication.

How then, can we as music teachers approach our role wisely and use the inherent power of our role with empathy and care so as to promote learning and strength in the student? We need to acknowledge that we do not always understand what the student's needs are and forgive ourselves for that. Sometimes we do not see that we do not understand, or we do not notice that we are biased. Can we practice critical self-reflection whereby we expose our own fast thinking (Kahneman, 2011)? Can we ask ourselves questions that make it clear to us that we are always partly ignorant, questions such as: Who are these students, really? What do they need? What is the best goal for this lesson? Who am I to them? What will happen to the students if we don't attempt to manifest compassionate care in our teaching? Teachers should be persistently curious and seek to understand how to mitigate power imbalances as individuals embark on a relational sharing of experience.

A caring teacher is a good listener whose curiosity conveys interest and respect, creates collaboration, and acknowledges that the teacher can also learn from the student

(Hendricks, 2018, p. 6). Referring back to the situation in the vignette, one might say that this is also about how we create communities, cultures, and environments where we allow, or disallow, conversations with students about such topics. Care in this context involves demystifying the ways in which structural norms affect our behaviors and drawing attention to the ways in which the realities of the world affect all of us. If teachers share some of their own experience and invite students to reflect on such issues, the effect may be a process of normalization in which students realize that feelings of shame and the fear of exposure are emotions that even their teachers have experienced.

As Hendricks (2018) points out, there is strength in "a more dialogic approach, in which teachers and students talk together, with teachers asking students questions and allowing students to come to their own understandings" (p. 5). Considering ourselves and our role more as dialogue partners for those we care for means that we create a space in which we are co-creators of the learning process, where we have the opportunity to take part and learn in all stages of the process, including the critical phases during which something is at stake and the student often disguises their troubles. We can reflect on what caring teachers think, feel, and do when they act in ways that students experience as caring professionalism, while also encouraging dialogue between students and teachers that allows for deliberation and the sharing of experience. Teachers and students alike can experience such sharing as a process of liberation from taboo and as an empowering path—characterized by listening, partnership, and positive authority—toward professional knowledge. It is also a way of taking care of oneself. Silverman's concern is how the teacher is supported in caring relationships and claims that we should ask, "When do the needs of the teacher get met?" (Silverman, 2012, p. 108).

We may need to reflect more on how we educate for professional practice, and what thoughts and actions involve care. Students and music teachers alike experience complex situations that can potentially stimulate growth and courage. Kemmis (2012) writes, "We want something more than knowledge and technical skill in those we aim to educate into professional practice," and argues for *phronesis* to be developed in professional education: "We do not only want *good* professional practitioners, we want practitioners who will *do good*" (p. 148). Being ethical and acting in ways that are good for the student should always be the central role of the teacher. Noddings (2012) states that responsibility is necessary in caring relationships, in which there is always a caregiver and a cared-for. Small signs, such as a trembling voice, may signal that the young singer needs extra attention. By working on our own growth and relational behavior through self-care, complex adaptive responses may unfold. These can serve as tools that guide us as we aspire for better practice.

Phronesis in professional music teachers manifests itself as advanced self-reflexivity and good practical and ethical judgment in situations of uncertainty. Bowman (2012) writes that acting ethically "involves acting rightly in a situation where rightness cannot be stipulated in advance or fully determined aside from the particulars of the situation at hand" (p. 10). In music education, professional care builds on and generates personal contact, relational power, learning, and growth. Educational ethics, relational ethics, and ethics of care are various ways of conceptualizing the relational responsibility that professional care represents. These are arguments for listening with care, catalyzing students' stories, acknowledging complexity, and realizing that small differences can have huge consequences for the relationship between student and teacher.

Concluding Remarks

In conclusion, one should acknowledge that there is a deep and many-layered complexity inherent in being both the *singer* who mediates the music and the *person* who performs for an audience. The voice is deeply personal, even intimate, and assumes countless varieties of expressive form. As music teachers, we should remind ourselves that it is our responsibility to facilitate the student's ability to develop their audible body within a safe space where bold vocal expression is encouraged and where it is possible to become comfortable with uncertainty. Self-respect is maintained within a relationship with a teacher who cares and who acknowledges the vulnerability in performance. Sartre (1943) holds that we recognize ourselves as the "Other" sees us. The teacher can function as an internalized Other, a friendly and generous mirror who gives the students the security and courage they need to perform with their voice, even while knowing that they are fallible, because they know that everyone is.

References

Bowman, W. (2012). Practices, virtue ethics, and music education. *Action, Criticism, and Theory for Music Education, 11*(2). http://act.maydaygroup.org/articles/Bowman11_2.pdf

Dickerson, S. S., Gruenewald, T. L., & Kemeny, M. E. (2004). When the social self is threatened: Shame, physiology, and health. *Journal of Personality, 72*(6), 1191–1216. https://doi.org/10.1111/j.1467-6494.2004.00295.x

Ellefsen, L. W. (2014). *Negotiating musicianship. The constitution of student subjectivities in and through discursive practices of musicianship in "Musikklinja."* Norges musikkhøgskole.

Fernholz, I., Mumm, J. L., Plag, J., Noeres, K., Rotter, G., Willich, S. N., Ströhle, A., Berghöfer, A., & Schmidt, A. (2019). Performance anxiety in professional musicians: A systematic review on prevalence, risk factors and clinical treatment effects. *Psychological Medicine, 49*(14), 2287–2306. https://doi.org/10.1017/S0033291719001910

Goffman, E. (1959). *The presentation of self in everyday life*. Doubleday.

Hendricks, K. S. (2018). *Compassionate music teaching*. Rowman & Littlefield.

Kahneman, D. (2011). *Thinking fast and slow*. Farrar, Straus & Giroux.

Kaleńska-Rodzaj, J. (2020). Music performance anxiety and pre-performance emotions in the light of psychology of emotion and emotion regulation. *Psychology of Music, 49*(6), 1758–1774. https://doi.org/10.1177/0305735620961154

Karraker, A. (2012). The relationship between social support and self-esteem. *Undergraduate Psychology Research Methods Journal, 1*(14), Article 6.

Kemmis, S. (2012). Phronesis, experience, and the primacy of praxis. In E. A. Kinsella & A. Pitman (Eds.), *Phronesis as professional knowledge* (pp. 147–161). Springer.

Kenny, D. (2011). *The psychology of music performance anxiety*. Oxford University Press.

Kinsella, E. A., & Pitman, A. (2012). Engaging phronesis in professional practice and education. In E. A. Kinsella & A. Pitman (Eds.), *Phronesis as professional knowledge* (pp. 1–11). Springer.

Kokotsaki, D., & Davidson, J. W. (2003). Investigating musical performance anxiety among music college singing students: A quantitative analysis. *Music Education Research*, 5(1), 45–59. https://doi.org/10.1080/14613800307103

Lamont, A. (2012). Emotion, engagement and meaning in strong experiences of music performance. *Psychology of Music*, 40(5), 574–594. https://doi.org/10.1177/0305735612448510

Lewis, M., & Hendricks, K. S. (2022, online first). "It's your body, it's part of who you are!": Influences upon collegiate vocalists' performance self-efficacy beliefs. *International Journal of Music Education*, https://doi.org/10.1177/02557614221074057

Lewis, M., Weight, E., & Hendricks, K. S. (2021, online first). Teaching methods that foster self-efficacy belief: Perceptions of collegiate musicians. *Psychology of Music*, https://doi.org/10.1177/03057356211026744

McGrath, C., Hendricks, K. S., & Smith, T. D. (2016). *Performance anxiety strategies: A musician's guide to managing stage fright*. Rowman & Littlefield.

McGuiness, A. (2013). Self-consciousness in music performance. In M. Clayton, B. Dueck, & L. Leante (Eds.), *Experience and meaning in music performance* (pp. 11–29). Oxford University Press. https://doi.org/10.1093/acprof:oso/9780199811328.003.0006

Monson, I. T. (1996). *Saying something: Jazz improvisation and interaction*. University of Chicago Press.

Noddings, N. (2012). The caring relation in teaching. *Oxford Review of Education*, 38(6), 771–781. https://doi.org/10.1080/03054985.2012.745047

Oltedal, E., Gamlem, S. M., Kleivenes, O. M., Ryslett, K., & Vasset, T. (2016). Teachers' assessment experiences and perceptions in the practical-aesthetic subjects. *Scandinavian Journal of Educational Research*, 60(6), 649–662. https://doi.org/10.1080/00313831.2015.1066431

Parker, E. C. (2010). Exploring student experiences of belonging within an urban high school choral ensemble: An action research study. *Music Education Research*, 12(4), 339–352. https://doi.org/10.1080/14613808.2010.519379

Sartre, J.-P. (1943). *Being and nothingness: An essay on phenomenological ontology*. Taylor & Francis.

Scheff, T. (2014a). Goffman on emotions: The pride-shame system. *Symbolic Interaction*, 37(1), 108–121. https://doi.org/10.1002/symb.86

Scheff, T. (2014b). The ubiquity of hidden shame in modernity. *Cultural Sociology*, 8(2), 129–141. https://doi.org/10.1177/1749975513507244

Scheff, T. J. (2005). Looking-glass self: Goffman as symbolic interactionist. *Symbolic Interaction*, 28(2), 147–166. https://doi.org/10.1525/si.2005.28.2.147

Schei, T. B. (1998). *Stemmeskam: hemmede stemmeuttrykks fenomenologi, arkeologi og potensielle rekonstruksjon gjennom sangpedagogikk* [Master's thesis, Bergen University College].

Schei, T. B. (2007). *Vokal identitet. En diskursteoretisk analyse av profesjonelle sangeres identitetsdannelse* [Doctoral dissertation, University of Bergen]. BORA. https://bora.uib.no/bora-xmlui/handle/1956/2549

Schei, T. B. (2009). "Identitation": Researching identity processes of professional singers from a discourse-theoretical perspective. *Nordic Research in Music Education Yearbook*, 11, 221–236. http://hdl.handle.net/11250/172247

Schei, T. B. (2019). Musical performance and tacit self-censorship. In D. G. Hebert & T. B. Hauge (Eds.), *Advancing music education in Northern Europe* (pp. 64–80). Routledge. https://doi.org/10.4324/9781351045995

Schei, T. B., & Schei, E. (2017). Voice shame: Self-censorship in vocal performance. *The Singing Network, 1*, 1–10.

Schei, T. B., Åvitsland, B. S., & Schei, E. (2018). Forgetting the audible body: Voice awareness in teacher education. *Nordic Research in Music Education Yearbook, 19*, 197–215.

Silverman, M. (2012). Virtue ethics, care ethics, and "the good life of teaching." *Action, Criticism, and Theory for Music Education, 11*(2), 96–122. http://act.maydaygroup.org/articles/Silverman11_2.pdf

Sweet, B., & Parker, E. C. (2019). Female vocal identity development: A phenomenology. *Journal of Research in Music Education, 67*(1), 62–82. https://doi.org/10.1177%2F0022429418809981

Welch, G. F., & Preti, C. (2019). Singing as inter- and intra-personal communication. In G. F. Welch, D. M. Howard, & J. Nix (Eds.), *The Oxford handbook of singing* (pp. 369–391). Oxford University Press. https://doi.org/10.1093/oxfordhb/9780199660773.013.73

CHAPTER 26

STUDENT AND TEACHER MENTAL HEALTH

Nurturing Wellbeing Within a Climate of Trust

RACHEL L. DIRKS

CARE HANDBOOK TOPICS

Co-creating caring relationships
Wellbeing and human flourishing

It was 5th hour on Thursday and my students entered the room dragging as if carrying a weight from the morning. Clearly, everyone was ready for lunch. I always enjoyed this transition time, which gave me the chance to visit with my students as they entered the classroom. I used this time to monitor and support my students as they navigated the stressors of high school. Questions like "How's your day going?" or more specific queries about ball games, dance recitals, or new jobs were commonly heard during these quick exchanges. Today I was on the lookout for Shane.

Shane was a rock star—intelligent, gregarious, and kind, Shane's personality was infectious. Lately, though, I noticed a change in his behavior. At first it was less eye contact, then fewer interactions with me followed by less time spent with friends. Most recently, I noticed the care Shane typically took with his appearance was no longer a priority. As he rounded the corner of the music wing, I recognized the same hoody he had worn every day for the past two weeks and his body language was extremely withdrawn. "How are you today, Shane?" I asked. No answer. As the bell rang to begin class, one of Shane's close classmates approached me and said, "I'm really worried about Shane. Can you check in with him today?" Later that day, I was so glad I did.

STORIES like these were, unfortunately, common during the past 10 years of my teaching career—and resonate with stories of many other music teachers. This chapter is designed to explore how music educators can take a more active role in the mental health and wellbeing of their students as well as themselves. My hope is that we may all feel a bit more empowered to offer care to those around us who sometimes struggle with managing their mental wellness.

ADOLESCENT MENTAL HEALTH TRENDS

Adolescence, with its biological, neurological, and emotional stressors, is a challenging time, often exposing many young people to a higher susceptibility toward anxiety and/or depression (Ellis et al., 2016). Based on these tendencies, researchers have explored the trajectories of adolescent mental health spanning nearly a century. The results of these studies revealed that, although no significant shifts or increases in mental health trajectories had occurred long-term (Costello et al., 2006), adolescent mental health has been dramatically impacted by significant cultural shifts found throughout history (Twenge, 2011). With the increased use of technology and social media in the early 21st century, adolescent anxiety, depression, and suicidal behaviors have been increasing at alarming rates (Burstein et al., 2019; Twenge, 2020). Twenge (2020), for example, revealed that between 2009 and 2017, major depressive episodes in adolescents had increased by over 60%, with a dramatic increase in reported cases beginning in 2011. Unfortunately, these changes in adolescent mental health have impacted not only the current adolescent generational cohort but also the mental wellbeing of those who work with them on a daily basis, including music teachers (Dirks, 2020).

Societal Influences on Adolescent Mental Wellbeing

As researchers and educators examine recent adolescent mental health trends, one often hears the argument that these trends occur due to the increased social discourse and awareness about mental health (Costello et al., 2006). Many researchers have discovered, however, that these trends are a response to specific societal stressors. Twenge (2011) reviewed adolescent mental health trends throughout the past century and revealed how increases in adolescent mental health concerns were triggered by three main categories: (a) dramatic changes in society, including periods of high threat; (b) increased social disconnection; and (c) periods in history when money, image, or fame were of greater societal value than community and connection. Based on these findings, the current societal trends our students are navigating would suggest we are experiencing all three categories of stressors simultaneously.

Within Twenge's 2011 study, high threat situations were identified as times of war or high crime. Following these parameters, one could argue that global concerns about the environment (Smith, 2021a) or the health of humanity due to the COVID-19 pandemic may be generating stressors as impactful as that of war. Moreover, adolescents from marginalized populations have sometimes experienced high threat situations on a more personal level. For example, a growing body of research has revealed the serious impacts of systemic policies and structures that unfairly disadvantage communities of color and how this affects the mental health of adolescents within those communities (Williams & Etkins, 2021). In a study of adolescents from Latinx immigrant families, participants identified mental health and wellbeing as their greatest health concern, mainly due to the stressors associated with navigating the immigration process and Deferred Action for Childhood Arrivals, commonly known as DACA (Siemons et al., 2016). Additionally, adolescents within the LGBTQIA+ community experience a different set of stressors. According to the Trevor Project, these youth are "four times more likely to consider, plan for, and attempt suicide than their non-[LGBTQIA+] peers" (Smith, 2019, para. 7). This same study, however, revealed that just one supportive adult in the lives of these youth, whether parent, teacher, or counselor, reduced the chance of a suicide attempt by 40%.

The social disconnections that have impacted adolescent mental health in the past are also found in our society today as we have become increasingly focused on individualism (Twenge, 2011). Furthermore, the social isolation caused by the increased use of technology (Twenge, 2020), as well as the required physical isolation linked to the COVID-19 pandemic (Chase, 2020), have also contributed to the current trend of social disconnectedness. For example, in 2019, four in ten adolescents experienced feelings of loneliness and isolation (Beresin, 2019)—by 2020, this number had increased to over 6 out of every 10 adolescents (Chase, 2020).

Along with an increased focus on individualism, today's society has also placed a higher value on the acquisition of money, the promotion of image, and the pursuit of fame (Giroux, 2011). These extrinsic societal values are highlighted by how we experience and interact with social media and the 24/7 media culture. Due to this shift in values, adolescents are at a greater risk for mental health concerns due to phenomena such as social comparison via social media (Nesi & Prinstein, 2015) or the use of social media as their primary source of social support (Meshi & Ellithorpe, 2021). When combining the intersection of multiple societal factors, whether from high threats, disconnection, or the importance of extrinsic values, with the natural stressors of adolescence, it appears our society has created a pressure cooker of stress in which today's youth are navigating their lives.

Teacher and Student Mental Wellbeing

When examining the relationships within the music education experience it is important to recognize how these relationships impact both student and teacher mental wellbeing. Research has found that positive relationships in school, including those between students and teachers, are key contributors to the positive mental health of adolescents (Oberle et al., 2018). An additional study (Harding et al., 2019) revealed that teacher wellbeing was associated with lower psychological distress in adolescents, as well as positive student wellbeing. Harding et al. (2019) also revealed, however, that higher levels of depressive symptoms in teachers were associated with poorer student psychological distress and wellbeing. Additional evidence suggests that when students are aware a teacher is suffering from mental challenges, they are more likely impacted (Glassard & Rose, 2019). Ultimately, when teachers continue to work while suffering from poor mental health, teacher–student relationships suffer (Greenberg, 2009).

Although teacher–student relationships have the potential to make both positive and negative impacts on student wellbeing, it is important to note that when teachers work with students who suffer from mental health concerns, they may also suffer negative impacts from these interactions (Dirks, 2020). Teachers who support students with trauma, for example, may be at an increased risk for traumatic symptoms themselves, a condition known as secondary traumatic stress (STS) or vicarious traumatization (Borntrager et al., 2012; Smith, 2021b). In addition to STS, the many stressors of teaching have been found to be similar to those of paramedics, social workers, and police officers (Johnson et al., 2005). These high levels of stress, especially experienced over long periods of time, can lead to burnout, which can compromise a teacher's physical and emotional wellbeing (Koenig et al., 2018). When teachers suffer from burnout, STS, or a combination of both they are susceptible to developing compassion fatigue, which is characterized by mental, physical, and emotional exhaustion (Ollison, 2019; Smith, 2021b), sometimes leading to an emotional disconnection from the needs of one's students. These studies highlight how teacher and student mental health are intertwined and emphasize the importance of addressing both.

Relational Trust as a First Step

Amid the current mental health crisis, it is imperative to focus on creating environments that support and encourage mental wellbeing for both students and teachers. The nurturing of healthy and trusting relationships with students stems from the daily interactions shared in partnership with a collaborative focus on the work students and teachers do in classrooms (McDermott, 1977). Hendricks (2018) approaches trust in the music education experience by focusing first on relational trust. She defines relational trust as a "confidence in group membership that results from (a) shared group identity, (b) reinforcing of community through reciprocal exchanges among group members, and (c) understanding the intentions of others in the group" (p. 34). When teachers build relational trust with students, they are cultivating relationships with each student, which strengthens a "positive climate" (p. 34) within their classes and programs. This trust is forged through shared experiences in the classroom as well as during concerts, festivals, trips, and over the multiple years teachers spend with students (see Carter, 2011; Dirks, 2020; Gregory & Ripski, 2008). As teachers and students strengthen this trust through musical experiences, they can weave a connective tissue between teacher to student as well as student to student that opens opportunities for both relational trust and collective trust, or "trust experienced by the group as a whole" (Hendricks, 2018, p. 34). Establishing these trusting relationships within the music experience, both individually and collectively, provides a foundation for creating an environment in which teachers can nurture and support student wellbeing. Goodrich (this volume) and Hendricks et al. (this volume) offer specific strategies for fostering trust in music-learning settings.

Awareness, Inquiry, and Response: AIR for Music Educators

When faced with situations in which our students are in need of support, like Shane in the vignette above, it is important to take time to examine and reflect on steps taken, especially when teachers are unsure how to respond. Brown (2021) defines this moment in time in the following way:

> The space between the thing that grabs us and how we respond to it is, in my opinion, what differentiates leaders [and teachers]. [Teachers] blow air into that space. They make it bigger. They stay in the quiet.... They stay in the vulnerable and really think through the response.

In 2019 through January of 2020, I had the opportunity to conduct two separate studies that focused on music educators' experiences with adolescent anxiety and depression. From these studies, the data appeared to support Brown's observations, revealing a preliminary framework of how music educators experienced adolescent mental health concerns. This framework included the following core elements: awareness, inquiry, and response—AIR (see Figure 26.1).

Awareness

Awareness begins the moment teachers first meet their students. The care teachers take in daily conversations, observations, and interactions can help to solidify a baseline of information about students' psychological, physical, behavioral, and social selves. As teachers begin to notice subtle or more significant changes in any of these areas, these observations provide the opportunity to be more aware of students' mental wellbeing. Within the opening vignette of this chapter, for example, I had been observing changes in Shane in all four areas of his expression of self: His affect had become more

FIGURE 26.1 AIR—Framework of Music Educators' Experiences with Adolescent Mental Health Concerns (adapted from Dirks's [2020] preliminary framework).

withdrawn, his appearance was more disheveled, he would avoid making eye contact, and he was pulling away from friends, often entering the room by himself. These observations placed me "on alert" and I continued to monitor Shane for more serious behaviors. Fortunately for Shane, his friend was paying attention too.

Inquiry

Once teachers become aware of any changes in students' minds, physical affect, or behaviors, they are then presented with a dilemma—what now? Brown (2021) suggests that teachers "stay in the quiet" and create space for reflection, before determining next steps. Within the AIR framework, inquiry serves as this space as it encompasses a period of questioning and critical reflection, often followed by further observation (Dirks, 2020, p. 89). Inquiring about a student's mental wellbeing could include a series of conversations regarding a particular concern or stressor followed by further observation of that student. Or perhaps inquiry might include conversations about the student with parents, fellow teachers, or the school's mental health team. For example, as I began noticing changes in Shane's affect and behavior, I would follow up with questions like, "Hey Shane, what's been the best part of your day so far?" or "I'd love your opinion on our rehearsal yesterday—how did you think the roll-out of that new piece went?" By asking open-ended questions, as opposed to yes/no or short answer questions, I could further observe Shane's affect and behavior through these inquiries. Because our conversations had been short and very unlike the typical interactions I had experienced with Shane in the past—and because a student had shared their concern—I asked Shane if he could stay after class for a few minutes to chat. I hoped this conversation/inquiry would help me formulate an appropriate response.

Response

By gathering important information about students through the processes of awareness and inquiry, teachers may be better equipped to respond to students' needs when faced with a mental wellness concern. Within the AIR framework, response is defined as the action teachers choose to make as they address the mental wellbeing of their students (Dirks, 2020). The National Alliance on Mental Illness has identified a series of strategies designed to help adults respond to students of concern (Spencer-Thomas, 2019, para. 5–11). I have incorporated these strategies (italicized and in bold below) within the framework of my response to Shane.

Lean in. After class I asked Shane if he would visit with me for a few minutes.

Create a safe space. We held our conversation in my office, where Shane felt comfortable and knew that what we discussed would be private.

Get comfortable feeling uncomfortable. As I dug into the heart of the conversation, there were moments when I felt very uncomfortable and I could tell Shane felt the same. My drive to continue on this path, however, was fueled by my desire to support and care for Shane.

Start with, "I've noticed . . . " I shared some of the differences I had noticed in Shane's appearance and behavior and said that I was concerned about him.

Ask open-ended questions. Questions like "How have you been feeling lately?" were helpful to continue shaping the conversation.

Practice active listening. Throughout the conversation with Shane I would repeat what I had heard him say to make sure I was hearing him correctly and to affirm that I was actively listening to his concerns. I would often follow up some of his statements with prompts like "Tell me more."

If you are concerned for your student's safety, use direct language framed in empathy and compassion. After we had visited for a few minutes, it was clear that Shane was very low and my "red flag" was on alert. Even though I was scared of the answer, I asked Shane if he was considering hurting himself. When he said "yes" I knew I was out of my depth and needed to ask for help.

Know your resources. I was glad that I knew each member of the mental wellness team at our high school. As soon as I had decided to talk with Shane after class, I asked a student to tune the orchestra while I stepped into my office to call a school social worker whom I trusted. I informed her that I would be visiting with a student of concern after class and asked if she could be available in case we needed further support. Once Shane had revealed how serious his situation was, I was able to extend the opportunity to visit with the social worker, a person I trusted, immediately. I offered to go with him until he felt comfortable for me to leave. That afternoon his parents were notified and he was able to receive the support he needed.

Although my response to Shane felt comfortable for my situation, other teachers might not feel like responding in the same way. Different responses could have also included (a) holding a conversation that addressed what I was observing, but did not include the question about self-harm; (b) reporting my concern directly to the mental wellness team at the school with or without the conversation with Shane; or (c) taking time to offer Shane a positive affirmation followed by more observation and/or inquiry. What is important to recognize is that, as trusted adults, teachers have the opportunity to provide support to our students in need of help, and that support can come in myriad ways.

Although I have described the model of AIR in linear terms, students' mental wellbeing and teachers' reactions seldom occur in a prescribed order. Emotions that stem from stress manifest in unique ways for every person. Sometimes teachers' interactions with students may require multiple attempts at connection before they feel receptive enough to respond. And, some of a teacher's most cherished students may not find the connection they need in their classrooms. Although making connections with our students may seem daunting and often mysterious, the AIR framework is a tool that can help teachers identify concerns as well as pathways on the journey toward helping students cope with their feelings.

It should be mentioned that the AIR framework also works for music educators struggling with their own reactions to stress. As teachers grapple with their own mental and physical challenges, they must first be mindful of how they respond to the stressors of teaching by monitoring mind, body, and behaviors (see Berg, this volume; Diaz, this volume). Once teachers understand the impact of these stressors on their health, taking a few deep breaths of "air" can provide time for personal inquiry and reflection that will help determine the next best steps. By doing so teachers can then respond to their personal mental wellness needs through activities that bring peace, rejuvenation, and joy. Not only does an establishment of these habits help teachers cope with their own stressors, but these behaviors also serve as a model for students as they continue to navigate their own responses to stress.

Conclusion

The current trajectories of adolescent and adult mental wellness are in serious peril. Over the coming years, our society will be seeking guidance from those who have successfully navigated these challenges, from mental health professionals to those who work with youth on a daily basis, including teachers. The music education experience offers the opportunity to provide the care that students need to develop a strong and positive wellbeing. By developing trust within music classrooms and programs, opportunities for connection and inclusion are created from teacher to student, student to teacher, and student to student. Once this care and trust are established, classrooms can become a place where teachers and students all find the AIR to navigate stressful moments in their lives—thereby creating a safe environment where all feel welcomed, valued, and supported.

References

Beresin, E. (2019, July 26). Why are teens so lonely, and what can they do about it? *Psychology Today.* https://www.psychologytoday.com/us/blog/inside-out-outside-in/201907/

Brown, B. (Host). (2021, March 8). Brené with Dr. Susan David on the dangers of toxic positivity, part 2 of 2 [Audio podcast episode]. In *Dare to Lead.* Spotify. https://brenebrown.com/transcript/brene-with-dr-susan-david-on-the-dangers-of-toxic-positivity-part-2-of-2/

Borntrager, C., Caringi, J. C., van den Pol, R., Crosby, L., O'Connell, K., Trautman, A., & McDonald, M. (2012). Secondary traumatic stress in school personnel. *Advances in School Mental Health Promotion, 5*(1), 38–50. https://doi.org/10.1080/1754730X.2012.664862

Burstein, B., Agostino, H., & Greenfield, B. (2019). Suicidal attempts and ideation among children and adolescents in US emergency departments, 2007–2015. *JAMA Pediatrics, 173*(6), 598–600. https://doi.org/10.1001/jamapediatrics.2019.0464

Carter, B. A. (2011). A safe education for all: Recognizing and stemming harassment in music classes and ensembles. *Music Educators Journal, 97*(4), 29–32. https://doi.org/10.1177/0027432111405342

Chase, C. (2020, June 17). *New survey finds 7 in 10 teens are struggling with mental health.* 4-h.org. https://4-h.org/about/blog/new-survey-finds-7-in-10-teens-are-struggling-with-mental-health/

Costello, E., Erkanli, A., & Angold, A. (2006). Is there an epidemic of child or adolescent depression? *Journal of Child Psychology and Psychiatry, 47*(12), 1263–1271. https://doi.org/10.1111/j.1469-7610.2006.01682.x

Dirks, R. (2020). *A phenomenological study of adolescent anxiety and depression through the lived experiences of novice and experienced high school music educators.* (Publication No. 27960293) [Doctoral dissertation, University of Kansas]. Proquest Dissertations and Theses Global.

Ellis, R., Seal, M., Simmons, J., Whittle, S., Schwartz, O., Byrne, M., & Allen, N. (2016). Longitudinal trajectories of depression symptoms in adolescence: Psychosocial risk factors and outcomes. *Child Psychiatry Human Development, 48*(4), 554–571. https://doi.org/10.1007/s10578-016-0682-z

Giroux, H. A. (2011). The crisis of public values in the age of the new media. *Critical Studies in Media Communication, 28*(1), 8–29.

Glassard, J., & Rose, A. (2019). The impact of teacher well-being and mental health on pupil progress in primary schools. *Journal of Public Mental Health, 19*(4) 349–357. https://doi.org/10.1108/JPMH-02-2019-0023

Gregory, A., & Ripski, M. (2008). Adolescent trust in teachers: Implications for behavior in the high school classroom. *School Psychology Review, 37*(3), 337–353. https://doi.org/10.1080/02796015.2008.12087881

Harding, S., Morris, R., Gunnell, D., Ford, T., Hollingworth, W., Tilling, K., Evans, R., Bell, S., Grey, J., Brockman, R., Campbell, R., Araya, R., Murphy, S., & Kidger, J. (2019). Is teachers' mental health and wellbeing associated with students' mental health and wellbeing? *Journal of Affective Disorders, 242,* 180–187. https://doi.org/10.1016/j.jad.2018.08.080

Hendricks, K. S. (2018). *Compassionate music teaching.* Rowman & Littlefield.

Jennings, P. A., & Greenberg, M.T. (2009). The prosocial classroom: Teacher social and emotional competence in relation to student and classroom outcomes. *Review of Educational Research, 79*(1), 491–525. https://doi.org/10.3102/0034654308325693

Johnson, S., Cooper, C., Cartwright, S., Donald, I., Taylor, P., & Millet, C. (2005). The experience of work- related stress across occupations. *Journal of Managerial Psychology*, 20(2), 178–187. https://doi-org.unco.idm.oclc.org/10.1108/02683940510579803

Koenig, A., Rodger, S., & Specht, J. (2018). Educator burnout and compassion fatigue: A pilot study. *Canadian Journal of School Psychology*, 33(4), 259–278. https://doi.org/10.1177/08295 73516685017

McDermott, R. P. (1977). Social relations as contexts for learning in school. *Harvard Educational Review*, 47(2), 198–213. https://doi.org/10.17763/haer.47.2.c9umx75267433434

Meshi, D., & Ellithorpe, M. E. (2021). Problematic social media use and social support received in real-life versus on social media: Associations with depression, anxiety, and social isolation. *Addictive Behaviors*, 119. https://doi.org/10.1016/j.addbeh.2021.106949

Nesi, J., & Prinstein, M. (2015). Using social media for social comparison and feedback-seeking: gender and popularity moderate associations with depressive symptoms. *Journal of Abnormal Child Psychology*, 43(8), 1427–1438. https://doi.org/10.1007/s10802-015-0020-0

Oberle, E., Guhn, M., Gadermann, A. M., Thomson, K., & Schonert-Reichl, K. A. (2018). Positive mental health and supportive school environments: A population-level longitudinal study of dispositional optimism and school relationships in early adolescence. *Social Science and Medicine*, 214, 154–161.

Ollison, J. (2019, April 24). *Compassion fatigue: How California can improve teacher retention*. Mindful Schools. https://www.mindfulschools.org/inspiration/compassion-fatigue-how-california-can-improve-teacher-retention/

Siemons, R., Raymond-Flesh, M., Auerswald, C., & Brindis, C. (2016). Coming of age on the margins: Mental health and well-being among Latino immigrant young adults eligible for Deferred Action of Childhood Arrivals (DACA). *Journal of Immigrant Minority Health*, 19, 543–551. https://doi.org/10.1007/s10903-016-0354-x

Smith, G. (2019, July 25). *Just one supportive adult cuts the chance an LGBTQ youth will attempt suicide by 40%*. LGBTQ Nation. https://www.lgbtqnation.com/2019/07/just-one-supportive-adult-cuts-chance-lgbtq-youth-will-attempt-suicide-40/

Smith, T.D. (2021a). Music education for surviving and thriving: Cultivating children's wonder, senses, emotional wellbeing, and wild nature as a means to discover and fulfill their life's purpose. *Frontiers in Education*, 6, Article 648799. https://doi.org/10.3389/feduc.2021.648799

Smith, T. D. (2021b). Teaching through trauma: Compassion fatigue, burnout, or secondary traumatic stress? In D. Bradley & J. Hess (Eds.), *Trauma and resilience in music education* (pp. 49–63). Routledge.

Spencer-Thomas, S. (2019, Sep. 6). *How to ask someone about suicide*. National Alliance on Mental Illness. https://nami.org/Blogs/NAMI-Blog/September-2019/How-to-Ask-Someone-About-Suicide

Twenge, J. (2011). Generational differences in mental health: Are children and adolescents suffering more, or less? *American Journal of Orthopsychiatry*, 81(4), 469–472. https://doi.org/10.1111/j.1939-0025.2011.01115.x

Twenge, J. (2020). Why increases in adolescent depression may be linked to the technological environment. *Current Opinion in Psychology*, 32, 89–94. https://doi.org/10.1016/j.copsyc.2019.06.036

Williams, D. R., & Etkins, O. S. (2021). Racism and mental health. *World Psychiatry*, 20(2), 194–195. https://doi.org/10.1002/wps.20845

CHAPTER 27

MINDFULNESS, SELF-COMPASSION, AND GRATITUDE IN MUSIC TEACHING AND LEARNING

FRANK M. DIAZ

CARE HANDBOOK TOPICS

Wellbeing and human flourishing

IN *The Courage to Teach* (2017), the Quaker writer and activist Parker Palmer writes of teaching as an act of transference, stating that "As I teach, I project the condition of my soul onto my students, my subject, and our way of being together" (p. 2). If we reflect on Parker's usage of the term "soul" as a proxy for our inner life, we might be prompted to reflect on the following questions:

- If what is in my *soul* projects onto my students, do I bear responsibility for cultivating mental habits that might inspire students to flourish?
- When I project onto my students, what do they return to me, and how might we co-create as well as regulate these interactions together? Reflecting on the idea of care as a coordinated act between teachers and students (Hendricks, 2018), how do we learn to care together?
- How might I go about this process of inquiry and engagement? Do practices such as mindfulness, self-compassion, and gratitude contribute positively to collective human flourishing, and how do we contextualize these practices within music teaching and learning?

Emotional Contagion and Coordination

Several years ago, through my work as a mindfulness scholar and teacher, I met a professor, JP, who was concerned about how her anxiety was affecting students: "We do all of this work at the beginning of lessons to reduce tension and anxiety, and to check-in with our bodies and emotions, but I often notice that students are responding more to my nonverbal cues than what I'm teaching them to do, and my nonverbal behaviors are definitely anxious." We followed-up with a discussion about the tensions between our own need for authentic expression and self-care, and our responsibility to our students. Because our conversations were happening within the context of an extended mindfulness and teaching program, we discussed the role that mindfulness might play in helping us work through these tensions, and whether it was indeed possible that our inner life affects our students' lives in ways suggested by Palmer.

The possibility that we affect each other's moods in powerful and often unknown ways is supported by both anecdotes and research. As teachers, we often sense that moods can be contagious, prompting us to actively self-regulate our emotions when working with students. Accordingly, many of us have been told to project a calm, positive, or enthusiastic presence so that students might respond in kind. Some psychologists refer to these instances of affective reciprocity as "emotional contagion" (Hatfield et al., 1992). Scientific evidence suggests that human beings mimic and *coordinate* nonverbal behaviors such as facial expressions, postures, and vocalizations, often without explicit awareness (Barsade, 2002).

In this sense, much of what we believe to be our inner life is quite visible to others, and in music teaching and learning, where so much of what we do is social, imitative, and embodied, it is possible that emotional contagion may be heightened. Moreover, whereas our concerns are often framed around how teachers might affect students, *coordination* implies a process in which teachers and students mutually enact and coregulate activities together. How then, might we explain this reciprocity?

As teachers and learners, we each bring personal histories, habits of mind and movement, patterns of communication, and individual as well as socio-cultural expectations to our shared spaces. In learning to negotiate these spaces, we are both contributors *to* and affected *by* the processes we enact together. In frameworks of cognition derived from the work of Di Paolo et al. (2018), our minds are never solely ours nor are they strictly social. Instead, our minds emerge from the *dance* of personal and collective histories, individual agency, and social expectations present in our encounters with others. Like any dance, what emerges is a dynamic process shaped by the physical space in which we meet, our embodied potentials and limitations, our affective state, our facility with and understanding of the style of dance we are participating in, and our ability to contribute and respond to what is happening in the moment. Whatever we add to this dance will affect our partner(s) and their responses will in turn affect us.

Applied to teaching and learning spaces, when we contribute a particular *affective* dynamic to this dance it will likely be magnified, reciprocated, modified, and/or rejected, but it will never be free of some impact. Therefore, rather than conceptualizing music teaching as an act of transmission that extends exclusively from teacher to student, this perspective highlights the relational and embodied nature of our work and invites us to be mindful of what we bring into these shared spaces. Consistent with notions of care in music education as described by Hendricks (2018), van der Schyff et al. (2016) describes these acts of teaching and learning as consisting of "circular and contingent patterns of action and perception that continuously shape and renew their coupling," and in which teachers and students "reach out to each other and draw themselves together through their mutual care for being and becoming musical" (pp. 91, 94).

Mindfulness

One way to bring awareness to our thoughts, feelings, and behaviors is through the practice of mindfulness. In mindfulness, we bring a state of non-judgmental awareness into the flow of our experiences such that we can examine them without reactivity (Diaz et al., 2020). Musicians who engage in mindfulness are less likely to experience performance anxiety, negative affect, and perfectionism, and are less self-conscious in general (Diaz, 2018; Rodriguez-Carvajal et al., 2017). There are numerous ways to practice mindfulness, but one way that seems both beneficial and accessible to teachers is the practice of STOP (Diaz, 2020). STOP is a mnemonic device that represents a series of steps one can take to enact mindfulness in situations in which a moment of self-inquiry might be helpful. The letters prompt us to:

(S) Stop what we are doing. Because our minds are usually on autopilot, physically pausing helps us to create a space in which we can bring awareness to our feelings, thoughts, and emotions before acting on them in way that may be misaligned with our deepest values and intentions.

(T) Take deep breaths. Deep breathing helps to slow down our physiological and somatic state. For this stage of the process, I usually recommend breathing into your abdomen for four counts, exhaling slowly for eight counts, and then pausing briefly between each cycle to allow your breathing to return to normal. To keep this process grounded in our senses, I usually put my hand on my belly for the added physical sensation.

(O) Observe with curiosity. Before transitioning to your next class, lesson, or rehearsal, scan your mind and body for any thoughts, feelings, or sensations that may be present in that moment. Is your heart racing? Are you feeling tension or physical pain? Can you locate that tension and physical pain? What emotions are you feeling in this moment? What story is your mind creating about the present situation?

Rather than judging any of these experiences as positive or negative, try to notice them with a sense of curiosity or direct some self-compassion at these feelings (see the section on self-compassion later in this chapter). Often, simply enacting a state of non-judgmental awareness is enough to take us out of autopilot and into a more caring state of mind and behavior.

(P) Proceed with intention. Anchor your awareness in your body, assume a kind and dignified presence, and recall the kind of attitude and disposition that you would like to bring into your next interaction. Remember that mindfulness is not about disowning or invalidating our experiences, but about noticing them and when possible, dealing with them in a way that minimizes harm to ourselves and others.

Returning to my conversation with JP, we discussed how STOP might be a useful tool for "checking-in" before or during interactions with students. Usually, we as teachers transition between classes and meetings as well between home and work life in a hurried and habitual state. If we can pause to observe this flow of mental and emotional activity before engaging with others, we may gain some influence over what we choose to "carry" between situations. And, because STOP encourages us to observe our experiences non-judgmentally, we become less likely to fear, repress, or reject aspects of ourselves that may be inconsistent with our desire to be kind, compassionate, or empathetic to ourselves and others. Furthermore, when we approach our own unfruitful dispositions as a normal part of being human, then it may become easier to do this with others, facilitating compassion. Therefore, I believe that STOP should be practiced both individually and collectively. We do it first for ourselves so that we can be present for others, then, by doing it with others, we facilitate our common bonds as human beings who might be vulnerable to suffering. Care then, may emerge through the space of validation and intentional kindness and compassion facilitated by these spaces.

Mindfulness and Self-Compassion

The cognitive and emotional states cultivated through mindfulness practices such as STOP are linked to numerous psychological and behavioral benefits. For instance, in the research literature on self-compassion, Neff (2003) proposes that practices that cultivate self-kindness, a sense of common humanity, and mindfulness over self-identification help promote wellbeing. In STOP, self-kindness may result from observing your experiences through a non-judgmental or neutral perspective. In fact, some iterations of STOP include self-kindness and self-compassion prompts to accompany messages that promote non-judgmental or curious explorations of our thoughts and feelings. Additionally, because STOP encourages mindful awareness rather than rumination on our experiences, our tendency to become fixated or overly identified with a particular thought or emotion is reduced. Finally, engaging empathetically and compassionately with students is something many teachers aspire to. Since STOP includes a "proceed with intention" dimension, the practice provides teachers with an opportunity to recall and enact feelings, thoughts, and behaviors consistent with their values and ethics.

Guided self-compassion practices are abundant and can be accessed through Dr. Kristin Neff's website[1] as well as other resources. Using the principles outlined in Neff's work, I have developed my own version of this practice that I use in both personal and pedagogical settings:

- When I sense some level of distress is arising in my awareness, I take a moment to pause, disengage from any digital, interpersonal, or other tasks I am in engaged in, and breathe deeply into my belly.
- In order to help moderate my physiology, I make my exhalations a little longer than my inhalations, and I pause for a moment in between each breath.
- While acknowledging my experience of distress, I engage in self-talk or prompts such as, "this really hurts right now" or "this is a moment of suffering." The language here purposefully avoids overidentification with whatever you are experiencing (no "I"). This is consistent with the idea that while our feelings are part of who we are, they do not represent WHO we are as a totality.
- To acknowledge our common humanity, I then repeat something such as "we all suffer sometimes," or "I am not the only one that suffers."
- Then, I offer myself some compassion by making statements such as, "May I be patient and strong" or "may I forgive myself." Kristin Neff recommends putting one's hand over the heart or using other gestures of kindness to more fully embody the experience.
- To end the practice, I commit myself to bringing this level of self-kindness and self-compassion to my next interaction if possible.

Although the emphasis of mindful self-compassion is the individual, studies show that it affects interpersonal dynamics as well. In a study that included adults, undergraduate students, and meditators, Neff and Pommier (2012) found that higher self-compassion was associated with greater forgiveness of others, as well as better perspective taking among all groups. Additionally, self-compassion was associated with empathetic concern and altruism among the adults and meditators in the study. Similar associations between self-compassion and prosocial feelings and behaviors have been documented by Yang and colleagues (2019). In their study, the authors found that Chinese adolescents who scored high on self-compassion were more likely to report helping others, being loyal friends, and feeling comfortable being inclusive in social situations.

[1] https://self-compassion.org/category/exercises/

Mindfulness, Oppression, and Gratitude

In the course on mindfulness that I teach at my university, the students and I often talk about systemic oppression as a source of individual and collective suffering in our society, and how mindfulness might help us work constructively with the difficult emotions that may arise when we reflect on these systems. For most of the predominantly white and socioeconomically advantaged students who enroll in my classes, these conversations often end up focusing on the need for social justice and other forms of activism, and on concerns that mindfulness might be used to bypass our responsibility for collective liberation. Though these legitimate concerns will be addressed within another section of this chapter, it is important to note that sometimes, our conversations around justice can devolve into forms of "othering" or into the need to see ourselves as "saviors" whose identities depend on focusing exclusively on an individual's marginalization instead of their strengths (Hess, 2015; Hess et al., 2007).

Recently, a student in my class who identifies as a Latinx and first-generation in college student from abroad, offered the following during one of these discussions:

> Yes, I have problems, yes I've had challenges, but I am not broken. I do not feel like a victim nor do I need anyone's permission to be happy or fulfilled. I am powerful and resilient and have gotten this far despite these challenges, and so I *choose* to feel grateful. Grateful to be here, grateful for those who have been kind and helpful, and grateful for the life I have experienced.

In this case, the student was expressing her frustration over what she perceived to be an *overemphasis* by her classmates on her marginalization, rather than on what she had gained through responding to it. Also, by stating that she "did not feel like a victim," and that she had *chosen* "gratitude," she expressed a very human need for agency and for the right to claim her lived experience as she saw it.

This last point is important, because whatever our opinions about the causes and solutions of suffering, there exists a tension between validating others' difficulties and prescribing a solution to these difficulties that are more reflective of our own perceptions and needs than of those we claim to care for. In these instances, our need to "help" can transform into what Oakley (2013) refer to as *pathological altruism*, described as "behavior in which attempts to promote the welfare of another, or others, results in harm that an external observer would conclude was foreseeable" (p. 10408). As Halifax (2018) explains, these behaviors can emerge from a subconscious compulsion to "fix" others' problems, based partially on our own sense of fear, shame, and guilt, or on the need for social approval (p. 22). However, when our desire to help further diminishes someone else's sense of agency, especially when that individual's agency has already been compromised due to marginalization, we risk acting much like the oppressors we so vehemently denounce. Intentions here, no matter how righteous or noble, might not function how we might imagine they will.

Closer to the context of K-college music teaching and performance, another potential source of focusing on what is disempowering over that which may empower us is musical perfectionism. Among musicians, self-directed and socially prescribed perfectionism have been linked to both depression and anxiety (Diaz, 2018), and may be somewhat exacerbated due to competition (Murayam & Elliott, 2012). As teachers, our own struggles with perfectionism can be projected onto students and create an environment in which expressing gratitude for progress, or for the opportunity to make music with each other, might be hampered or perceived as counterproductive to the aims of musical "excellence." Fortunately, there seems to be some evidence that musicians with more mindful dispositions, and who participate in at least some kind of meditative or contemplative practices at least once a week, experience less performance anxiety than their counterparts (Diaz, 2018).

Returning to mindfulness, it is important to recall that while non-judgmental awareness is the space in which our difficulties and experiences are validated, there is an element of focus and framing that is also needed for these practices to contribute to what we might describe as human flourishing. In STOP as well as mindfulness self-compassion, these dimensions of practice are what happens after validation, in which we are invited to respond to our experiences based on ethical principles and intentions not to harm. Expressing gratitude as a way of focusing on what is good in our lives may be one way of enacting non-harm, in that it reminds of our need for inspiration and self-care in a world in which there will always be some source of difficulty.

With respect to gratitude specifically, research supports the benefits of expressing gratitude, even among individuals struggling with mental health (Wong et al., 2016). In one compelling study, 293 college-aged adults who were seeking counseling for anxiety and depression participated in a study in which they were assigned to one of three groups: one wrote a letter of gratitude to three different people over three weeks, another journaled about their negative experiences, and the last was a control group that did not engage in any specific writing activity. After both 4 and then 12 weeks, the group who wrote the letters of gratitude reported significantly improved mental health compared to members of the other groups. A similar study found that changes due to gratitude practice were indexed not only in participants' self-reports, but in their brains as well (Kini et al., 2016). In this study, participants who had performed the gratitude letter task evidenced greater changes to their medial prefrontal cortex (mPFC) relative to controls three months after their participation in the initial part of the study. The mPFC is associated with various facets of social cognition as well as attention, memory, and decision-making (Grossman, 2013).

As educators, we can create the space for gratitude by expressing it ourselves, or by facilitating both informal as well as formal practices in our classrooms. This process can be as simple as asking students to share their appreciation for something good that may have happened in their day or week, or as complex as a letter writing exercise or appreciation board. In the latter case, dedicating a bulletin board or online forum where students are encouraged to say "thank you" or "I appreciate you" to someone in or outside of class, or just for anything they might be grateful for, may be all that is needed. Furthermore, the coordinated and reciprocal nature of learning and performing music together may provide us with unique opportunities for expressing gratitude, for our fellow musicians, for the music that we play, and for the ways in which we each contribute to the greater whole of a performance. And, consistent with the theme of mindfulness in this chapter, it is important to remember that being mindful is not just about awareness, but about intention and what we choose to focus on within that field of awareness. By focusing on who we are and who our companion musicians are in each moment, we offer grace to one another in the form of a sonic embrace—a musical hug—and that truly is a manifestation of care.

The Shadow Side of Mindfulness

The *Shōbōgenzō* is a collection of works by the influential Zen monk and philosopher Eihei Dogen, who writes, "Unlike things and their reflections in the mirror, and unlike the moon and its reflection in the water, when one side is illumined, the other side is dark" (Tanahashi, 2010, p. 30). Over the last several decades, interest in mindfulness has evolved from being somewhat fringe to almost hyperbolic. Accompanying this expansion of interest has been what some critics describe as an overemphasis on mindfulness as an individualistic practice focused on stress-reduction and personal liberation that can be misapplied to bypass our collective interest in dismantling oppression (Forbes, 2019a). In this chapter, I have focused on the benefits of mindfulness as they relate to care and flourishing in music, but does mindfulness have a shadow side?

Mindfulness, just like any other pedagogical approach, must be subject to the same kind of critical examination that we apply, or *should* apply, to everything we do in music education. This is especially the case when we are working with student who are marginalized, or who may be complicit in marginalization. As Forbes (2019b) explains:

> When mindfulness is taught as an individualized practice, these broader forces are ignored or diminished. Each student and teacher learns to monitor and regulate their own thoughts, feelings and actions, and to "pay more attention" or "focus more effectively," but to what ends? Without a critical awareness of the wider context, self-regulating one's emotions can become a way for people to conform to the dominant values, principles and practices of a power structure that focuses solely on personal responsibility, individualized adjustment and self-blame. (para. 6)

Taking issue with an emphasis on non-judgmental awareness that ends simply in acknowledging our experience as it arises in the present moment, Forbes compels us to go further by identifying thoughts and feelings that are troubling, and then trace them back to their socially conditioned sources. In a process which he describes as "critical social mindfulness," Forbes concludes by encouraging teachers and students to develop self-care strategies that address both the "personal and institutional dimensions of the problems that they face" (para. 17) and to create alternative models that address these issues through collaboration and inclusivity.

Though the problematic practices that Forbes describes are certainly present both in education and corporate mindfulness programs, this approach is not only unnecessary but also inconsistent with what I am proposing in this chapter. Non-judgmental awareness is not where mindfulness *ends*, but rather where it *begins*. Through non-judgmental awareness, we can build the space to look at how our inner and outer lives dance together in ways that either harm ourselves and others or contribute to our liberation. As described in processes such as STOP, mindfulness does not end with seeing, but with acting. Once the landscape of the present moment is discerned with clarity, it is our responsibility to proceed accordingly. Sometimes, this process can mean we give ourselves the space to rest and heal from the forces that oppress us, while at others, it can mean we act collectively to alleviate each other's suffering. Consistent with descriptions of what it means to "care with" others (Hendricks, 2021), mindfulness can provide us with the opportunity to engage as equals in our striving for redemption, embracing each other through mutual regard, vulnerability, and authenticity.

Mindfulness and Care as Invitation

As alluded to in this chapter, musical activities can be mediums for coordinated actions in which we come together to support each other's needs and aspirations for communicating as artistic beings. At their best, these activities serve as vehicles for the kind of human flourishing that results from individual and collective expression, and from the nourishment we receive through social processes based on mutual support. What practices such as mindfulness, self-compassion, and gratitude help provide within these contexts are opportunities for examining and therefore influencing how what we bring might enhance or detract from this collective flourishing. However, it is one thing for teachers to engage in these practices voluntarily, and quite another for the student, who may participate based on feelings of coercion or duress. As in any situation in which the intended benefit of an activity must be weighed against its potential for harm, giving students choices about participating in these practices is of course, paramount. In this sense, care as demonstrated here should be always framed as an invitation—one in which the potential to flourish is a presented as a choice rather than as an imperative.

References

Barsade, S. G. (2002). The ripple effect: Emotional contagion and its influence on group behavior. *Administrative Science Quarterly*, 47(4), 644–675. https://doi.org/10.2307%2F3094912

Di Paolo, E. A., Cuffari, E. C., & De Jaegher, H. (2018). *Linguistic bodies: The continuity between life and language*. MIT Press.

Diaz, F. M. (2018). Relationships among meditation, perfectionism, mindfulness, and performance anxiety among collegiate music students. *Journal of Research in Music Education, 66*, 150–167. https://doi.org/10.1177/0022429418765447

Diaz, F. M. (2020). Using mindfulness as a strategy to improve wellbeing and self-regulation within orchestras. *American String Teacher, 70*(3), 69–71. https://doi.org/10.1177/0003131320940687

Diaz, F. M., Silveira, J. M., & Strand, K. (2020). A neurophenomenological investigation of mindfulness among collegiate musicians. *Journal of Research in Music Education, 68*(3), 351–374. https://doi.org/10.1177%2F0022429420921184

Forbes, D. (2019a). *Mindfulness and its discontents: Education, self, and social transformation.* Fernwood Publishing.

Forbes, D. (2019b, October 20). The need for critical social mindfulness in schools. Open Democracy. https://www.opendemocracy.net/en/transformation/need-critical-social-mindfulness-schools/

Grossmann, T. (2013). The role of medial prefrontal cortex in early social cognition. *Frontiers in Human Neuroscience, 7,* Article 340. https://doi.org/10.3389/fnhum.2013.00340

Halifax, J. (2018). *Standing at the edge: Finding freedom where fear and courage meet.* Flatiron Books.

Hatfield, E., Cacioppo, J. T., & Rapson, R. L. (1992). Primitive emotional contagion. In M. S. Clark (Ed.), *Emotions and social behavior* (pp. 151–177). Sage Publications.

Hendricks, K. S. (2018). *Compassionate music teaching.* Rowman & Littlefield.

Hendricks, K. S. (2021). Authentic connection in music education: A chiastic essay. In K. S. Hendricks & J. Boyce-Tillman (Eds.), *Authentic connection: Music, spirituality, and wellbeing.* Peter Lang.

Hess, J. (2015). Upping the "anti-": The value of an anti-. *Action, Criticism, and Theory for Music Education, 14*(1), 66–92. http://act.maydaygroup.org/articles/Hess14_1.pdf

Hess, D. J., Lanig, H., & Vaughan, W. (2007). Educating for equity and social justice: A conceptual model for cultural engagement. *Multicultural Perspectives, 9*(1), 32–39. https://doi.org/10.1080/15210960701334037

Kini, P., Wong, J., McInnis, S., Gabana, N., & Brown, J. W. (2016). The effects of gratitude expression on neural activity. *NeuroImage, 128,* 1–10. https://doi.org/10.1016/j.neuroimage.2015.12.040

Murayama, K., & Elliot, A. J. (2012). The competition-performance relation: A meta-analytic review and test of the opposing processes model of competition and performance. *Psychological Bulletin, 138*(6), 1035–1070. https://doi.org/10.1037/a0028324

Neff, K. D. (2003). The development and validation of a scale to measure self-compassion. *Self and Identity, 2*(3), 223–250. https://doi.org/10.1080/15298860309027

Neff, K. D., & Pommier, E. (2012). The relationship between self-compassion and other-focused concern among college undergraduates, community adults, and practicing meditators. *Self and Identity, 12*(2), 160–176. https://doi.org/10.1080/15298868.2011.649546

Oakley, B. A. (2013). Concepts and implications of altruism bias and pathological altruism. *Proceedings of the National Academy of Sciences, 110*(Supplement 2), 10408–10415. https://doi.org/10.1073/pnas.1302547110

Palmer, P. J. (2017). *The courage to teach: Exploring the inner landscape of a teacher's life.* John Wiley & Sons.

Rodríguez-Carvajal, R., Lecuona, O., Vilte, L. S., Moreno-Jiménez, J., & de Rivas, S. (2017, August 29). Freeing the performer's mind: A structural exploration of how mindfulness influences music performance anxiety, negative affect and self-consciousness among musicians. https://doi.org/10.31231/osf.io/657n8

Tanahashi, K. (Ed.). (2010). *Treasury of the true dharma eye: Zen master Dogen's Shobo genzo.* Shambala.

Van der Schyff, D., Schiavio, A., & Elliott, D. J. (2016). Critical ontology for an enactive music pedagogy. *Action, Criticism, and Theory for Music Education*, 15(5), 81–121. https://doi.org/10.22176/act15.5.81.

Wong, Y. J., Owen, J., Gabana, N. T., Brown, J. W., McInnis, S., Toth, P., & Gilman, L. (2018). Does gratitude writing improve the mental health of psychotherapy clients? Evidence from a randomized controlled trial. *Psychotherapy Research*, 28(2), 192–202. https://doi.org/10.1080/10503307.2016.1169332

Yang, Y., Guo, Z., Kou, Y., & Liu, B. (2019). Linking self-compassion and prosocial behavior in adolescents: The mediating roles of relatedness and trust. *Child Indicators Research*, 12(6), 2035–2049. https://doi.org/10.1007/s12187-019-9623-2

CHAPTER 28

SELF-CARE AND THE MUSIC EDUCATOR

BRIDGET SWEET

Care Handbook Topics

Wellbeing and human flourishing

Although not classified as a medical condition, the World Health Organization recognized burnout as an "occupational phenomenon" in the 11th Revision of the International Classification of Diseases (World Health Organization, 2021). *Burnout* is generated "by being worn down and feeling depleted due to a chronically over-demanding, threatening and uncertain, or under-stimulating environment" (Gorkin, 2021, para. 6). In music education, teachers work long and hard hours, facilitate large class sizes, and provide public displays of their work. School reform in the era of standardized testing and accountability intensifies stress (Shaw, 2016). Music professionals are increasingly experiencing emotional exhaustion (Bernhard, 2007; Kuebel, 2019) as well as depression and anxiety (Kegelaers et al., 2021; Smith, 2021).

Life became infinitely more complicated and stressful for music educators in 2020 with the initial spread of the COVID-19 virus and the sudden move to online teaching. Pressley (2021) found that COVID-19-related anxiety quickly ranked as a stressor proximal to burnout in Fall 2020 as teachers navigated uncharted teaching demands, parent communication, and administrative support (or lack thereof). Amid continued spread of COVID variants and resulting complications regarding vaccination status, face masks, social distancing, and instrument coverings, music educators were largely expected to return to "business as usual" despite extreme circumstances.

I teach the class *Healthy Music Practices*, a course designed to promote practices of health and wellness for music professionals to support longevity in the profession. The summer 2020 iteration of the course for music education graduate students was offered virtually, as the initial waves of COVID-19 ran rampant around the world. While intentional discussions and strategies of self-care are woven throughout the entire course, this group of students was so deeply entrenched in burnout that any ideas about self-care were almost overwhelming. Discussing her work during the COVID-19 pandemic, music educator Cassidy[1] shared:

> I think I've realized that I need to do more self-care to avoid burnout, but I have also realized that I am solidly *in* burnout. It is affecting my energy levels, I hate going to work, it really feels hard, and I am living for the breaks. And right now, no amount of self-care is going to help with that.

There is a well-known cartoon of a dog sitting at a table drinking coffee in a room that is completely on fire. The dog (while smiling out at the viewer) says calmly, "This is fine." The cartoon is funny because, clearly, all is not fine and the dog is choosing to ignore the severity of the situation. Tiffany, a music educator, compared her work teaching music within the pandemic to this cartoon. In her version, she is the dog, but the table, the mug, the dog, and the fire are also on fire while she calmly states, "This is fine."

Physical and emotional strains of our work as music educators (both during and outside of a pandemic) can be especially heavy for people who intrinsically put the needs of their students before their own. Music educator Emma shared with me that, "It does not come naturally to take care of myself like it comes naturally to take care of others." My own sister, Kate, calls me "a burnt toast eater" meaning that I will eat the metaphorical (or actual) burnt toast so that no one else at the table has to. I will sacrifice my own wellbeing to prevent someone else from experiencing something unpleasant. In my work with teachers, I have found that most music educators try to prevent and/or resolve problems for students (i.e., eat the burnt toast) even if the solutions contribute significantly to their own personal burnout. In her literature review on burnout, Nápoles (2022) writes, "Teachers cannot assume all the responsibility or work harder and harder to solve problems that they have no agency to solve" (p. 24).

I invite you, the reader, to consider your relationship with your work. In caring for students, how do you also care for yourself? In what ways does your approach to teaching contribute to or combat strain? How might new approaches to your practice prevent or reduce symptoms of burn-out?

Changing default behaviors is difficult, even if those changes might be beneficial. Taking stock of one's own wellness and behavioral habits involves vulnerability (Hendricks, 2018; Salvador, 2019), which (especially if perceived as weakness by the self) often thwarts measures of change toward self-care. Holiday (2019) encourages *confidence* as key to inner peace and a clear mind: "Confidence is the freedom to set your own standards and unshackle yourself from the need to prove yourself. A confident person doesn't fear disagreement and doesn't see change as an admission of inferiority" (p. 72).

---

[1] All music educators quoted throughout this chapter gave permission to use their comments.

Developing habits of self-care involves acknowledging the balance of vulnerability and confidence that comes with putting oneself first. We also must understand that habits form over time, and it is best to start small. "Too often, we convince ourselves that massive success requires massive action. . . . The difference a tiny improvement can make over time is astounding" (Clear, 2018, p. 15).

In my own life, I have chipped away on self-care for decades. Sometimes I wonder why self-care does not come more easily to me at this point, but I've realized that caring for myself is not something that I am going to do naturally. It will always take intentional work. What follows here are starting places toward self-care, infused with perspective from practicing music educators. With a little research, it is possible to locate additional resources for specific strategies. My own continued work with a licensed therapist has also been an essential element in learning how to care for myself. I encourage you to speak to your medical professional if such support would assist you in your efforts. But, for now, I invite you to put down that burnt toast and read on.

Self-Care Starting Places

The Health Promotion in Schools of Music (HPSM) Project identified four target areas of wellbeing as crucial for musicians' success and longevity in the music profession: voice care, hearing conservation, musculoskeletal issues, and psychological matters (Chesky et al., 2006). More recently, the Performing Arts Medicine Association (PAMA) and National Association of Schools of Music (NASM) published a series of three collaborations focused on the prevention of health problems in schools of music: Hearing Health, Neuromusculoskeletal and Vocal Health, and Psychological Health (NASM/PAMA, 2011). As both sets of recommendations are focused on the same areas of health and wellness, the ensuing conversation will stay within these parameters too.

Vocal Hygiene

Vocal hygiene is "a set of preventative measures that are actively and consciously undertaken by the voice user to maintain the health, reliability, and consistency of the voice" (Heman-Ackah et al., 2013, p. 27). Both *nonvoiced* and *voiced* factors assist with vocal hygiene. Demands on the voice ebb and flow for music educators during specific stages of teaching, time of school year, or particular activities; all of which can be especially vocally tiring (Brunkan, 2018). Teaching with a limited (or no) voice can foster feelings of frustration and anxiety, exacerbating symptoms of burnout. Although [assigned female at birth] women and choral educators are more likely to report vocal health issues than other music professionals (Brown, 2020), good vocal hygiene is critical for all professional voice users.

Nonvoiced factors do not necessarily involve voice use. Prescription medications, vitamins, recreational drugs, supplements, hormones, and so on involve side effects that may impact vocal tissue. Awareness of side effects provides opportunity to counterbalance effects accordingly, such as increasing fluid consumption or change in diet. A quick Internet search can explain potential risks for the voice from medications and supplements. Additionally, inhaled substances pass between the vocal folds during both inhalation and exhalation (i.e., tobacco, marijuana, vapors, special effect stage smoke) and promote edema (swelling) of vocal fold tissue, fluid retention, and irregular cell production among other problems. Of particular importance: Although lung tissue can self-clean and regenerate, vocal fold tissue cannot. Vocal fold tissue damage is mostly permanent (Heman-Ackah et al., 2013).

Hydration is a nebulous topic because every person requires different amounts of fluid based on body composition, height, activity level, and so forth. Certain foods can increase fluid intake, such as soup or watermelon, whereas alcohol and caffeine are diuretics that pull water from the body and, specifically, from the vocal fold epithelium (Gates et al., 2013). Ultimately "urine color is a good guide to the state of hydration. A pale urine color implies that there is adequate hydration throughout the body" (Heman-Ackah et al., 2013, p. 31). Music educator Zoe spoke of her efforts to not only hydrate herself, but to model good hydration for her students: "Especially as a vocal music educator, what we put into our body really does affect us because our voices are our instrument."

Voiced factors of vocal hygiene are how much and how intensely the voice is used. Acoustics greatly influence voice use and should be closely considered for every space. Technology or acoustical assistance might bring the music room to the teacher, versus the teacher needing to push the voice to fill the room (Doherty, 2011). Teaching, meeting, or performing in naturally noisy spaces may require you to raise the voice to be heard over clamor, contributing to overuse of vocal folds and increased risk of phonotrauma (Rosset i Llobet & Odam, 2007, p. 28).

Vocal rest is crucial, although such opportunities are limited for music educators. A strategy: Think of all voice use as Monopoly money. Each day brings a new, but limited, stack of money representing allotted voice use for that day only. Consider when and where that money is "spent" and where it might be "saved," such as singing along with students, talking over students while they play instruments, singing with the radio in the car, talking through lunch, meetings in noisy locations, or general volume of voice in the music classroom. Ultimately, we each have only one voice and it deserves protection. In their published report, NASM and PAMA encourage people concerned about their personal vocal health to speak with a medical professional (NASM/PAMA, 2011).

Hearing Health

Research has shown that many professional musicians commonly accept hearing loss as inevitable and/or that preventative measures are not worth the fuss (Greasley et al., 2020). Few music educators realize that the National Institute for Occupational Safety and Health (NIOSH), which maintains recommended exposure limits (REL) for hazardous substances and agents, has categorized sound as a hazardous agent:

> Noise-induced Hearing Loss (NIHL) can be caused by sudden exposure to a very loud sound or, most commonly, by prolonged exposure to high intensity noise over many years. NIHL is always irreversible but will cease to progress when the cause is eliminated. It most commonly affects higher frequency hearing. Hearing loss that musicians, instrumentalists, and singers might experience because of noise exposure would be considered NIHL. (Isaac et al., 2017, p. 379.E21)

A decibel (dB) is "a ratio unit of measurement used to express sound intensity levels on a logarithmic scale" (Cook-Cunningham et al., 2012, p. 22). The NIOSH REL for sound exposure is 85 decibels over an eight-hour span of time. So, a music teacher can be in a music classroom or rehearsal registering 85 dB for eight hours before becoming at risk for NIHL. For each 3 dB increase in noise-level beyond 85 dB, the duration of exposure to that sound before becoming at risk for NIHL is cut in half. Consequently, if the exposure level raises to 88 dB, the music teacher will reach their full allotted safe noise dose after only four hours in that classroom. If the exposure level raises to 91 dB in the music classroom, the teacher risks NIHL after only two hours in that space; 94 dB for only 60 minutes of exposure prior to risk of NIHL; 97 dB for only 30 minutes of exposure prior to risk of NIHL; 100 dB for only 15 minutes of exposure prior to risk of NIHL, and so forth.

NIOSH recommends constant monitoring of noise-levels in workspaces, as well as hearing protection for any spaces registering above 85 dB—specifically protective headphones and earplugs. Earplugs are a complicated consideration for musicians, as there are many concerns about them changing the way musical sounds are heard. It is a fair concern, but research indicates that not all earplugs are the same:

> To preserve the integrity of pitch perception, performers and teachers might avoid the use of foam earplugs as a method of hearing protection. Instead, they should opt for musicians' earplugs, with the understanding that they may alter their perception of pitch slightly and incorporate other methods of sound control to protect and preserve hearing. (MacLeod et al., 2021, p. 10)

Music teachers can explore several "hearing loss simulation" tools online to better understand implications of hearing loss. Better yet, exploring these simulations with students may embolden preventative measures in younger musicians before hearing damage occurs. In his graduate project focused on hearing loss, music educator Kevin wrote:

> As music educators, we have a responsibility to model and teach best practices to our students. It important to teach our students how to engage with sound in a healthy manner just as we must teach our students to engage with sound in an effective manner. Imagine a situation where a shop teacher chooses to not teach their students

about the need to wear eye protection or model proper safety habits; it is inconceivable! We must strive for a similar level of expectations towards hearing safety in the music classroom. (Cooley, 2021, p. 16)

It may be helpful for music teachers to consider work spaces and daily decibel level exposure. Several free apps can immediately turn portable devices into sound-level meters and determine decibel levels for the professional and personal spaces they use. Smartwatches are also equipped to cumulatively measure personal sound exposure for a given day. Most importantly, frequent hearing tests provide valuable information and offer calmer "knowns" about one's own hearing health versus frightening "unknowns" and assumptions.

Musculoskeletal Health

Musicians suffer from high rates of musculoskeletal pain largely influenced by a lack of understanding of the body and the resulting ways the body is used (Dora et al., 2019; Leaver et al., 2011; Shafer-Crane, 2006). A music educator's body is exposed to "factors and situations that could weaken you and cause damage if you do not take them into account" (Rosset i Llobet & Odam, 2007, p. 24), such as not adjusting musical tasks to fit individual bodies, caring for musical instruments more than one's own body, or incorrectly holding a body position while using electronic devices. Body awareness can profoundly and positively impact music educators by preventing and combating pain and physical injury that contributes to experiences of burnout.

Somatics is the study of the body in movement, coming from the Greek word *soma* meaning "body of an organism." Similar terms are movement studies, mind-body work, or body work. Body Mapping, Feldenkrais Method, and Alexander Technique are three well-known somatic education techniques designed to promote body awareness of the musculoskeletal system and immerse musicians in mind-body instruction (Buchanan & Hays, 2014; Paparo, 2015, this volume; Westfeldt, 1987). Workshops or classes in one (or all) of these somatic techniques may influence the way one uses the body not only in educational settings but in daily life (Conable, 1995; Malde et al., 2020; Paparo, this volume).

Pain is the body's way of communicating that something is wrong, be it an unsuitable fit between the body and the instrument, the way one holds the body, tension or constriction in places where there should be none, or many other possibilities. Music educators often ignore pain, especially when it strikes at inconvenient times. But according to Rosset i Llobet and Odam (2007), addressing pain is imperative:

> Failing to seek a solution to an injury or problem that lasts more than a week is always a risk, since the longer the problem takes to develop, the more likely it is that treatment will take an equally long time, or even, in the worst-case scenario, that damage is irreversible. (p. 31)

Proactive efforts for preventing and monitoring musculoskeletal issues include regular exercise and stretching (hence the adage, "if you don't use it, you lose it"). Considerations for musculoskeletal movement also include compensating for asymmetric demands of musical instruments to develop full-body wellness and strength.

Forming an exercise habit can feel daunting, but realism and sustainability is key. For example: Ben is a music educator who hates running, so that was not an option for him. Through exploration, he found that he really enjoyed biking, resulting in a regular exercise routine: "I feel like that's probably been the biggest win, just finding habits that are sustainable and that aren't a complete drag." Another teacher, Abbey, also reflected, "Why set a goal for me that is clearly unattainable?" As music educators consider ways to care for the physical body, they might begin with an aim to move every 30 minutes during the day. Even simply standing up from a chair allows a change in position, delivers fresh blood and oxygen around the body, and releases tension from held body parts. However you proceed, it is helpful to be kind to yourself and recognize that everything is a process of self-discovery, especially forming new habits.

Psychological Health

Music educator burnout is fueled by a myriad of distinct, but related, psychological factors encountered at all stages of teacher development. High levels of depression and anxiety are prolific within populations of undergraduate and graduate college music majors (Kegelaers et al., 2020; Koops & Kuebel, 2021). Symptoms of both music performance anxiety and imposter syndrome impair musicians from college-age into older adulthood (Barbeau & Mantie, 2019; Kalenzka-Rodzaj, 2020; Sieger, 2019; Sims & Cassidy, 2020). Professional musicians often equate personal self-worth (or lack thereof) with professional success or the accomplishments of their students (Rosset i Llobet & Odam, 2007).

There is no quick fix when battling psychological matters and sometimes the work lasts a lifetime, as mentioned at the beginning of this chapter. However, cumulative benefits of self-care can ease anxieties as well as encourage self-acceptance. Self-care involves granting permission to feel emotions such as fear, frustration, grief, melancholy, or just be really crabby all day. Music educator Chris believes that accepting all of oneself—the parts that make people laugh as well as the parts that need a counselor and medication—is self-care. Another music teacher, Zoe, spoke of self-advocacy in place of self-sacrifice as a form of self-care:

> I am still working on my complicated relationship with food and am becoming more aware that making my nutrition needs known and advocating for them won't make people like me less—which is something about which I find myself acutely self-conscious. Being an "easy guest/housemate/dinner date" does little to serve me in the long run.

Abbey shared her emotions in a video journal during the COVID-19 pandemic:

> Today I'm having a really awful day. I'm beginning to realize that I'm not going to see my students for the remainder of the school year (*beginning to cry*) and it's a hard pill to swallow. It's hard to be a teacher right now. So I'm worried that my motivation to take care of myself is going to go out the window. I've had really good days, but today is just that one really bad day.

Mindfulness techniques have gained focus in recent years to prevent psychological and emotional burnout. There are many approaches and philosophies surrounding mindfulness, as detailed by Diaz (this volume). Holiday (2019) writes about the importance of stillness in one's life to calm the body and mind, and to be fully present more often: "Being present demands all of us. It's not nothing. It may be the hardest thing in the world" (p. 25).

Looking Forward

Ultimately, self-care comes in all shapes and sizes: relaxation apps, jigsaw puzzles, scented candles, religious study, fancy coffee, stretching, lunch with a friend, sitting in silence, allowing oneself to feel sad or scared or frustrated or mad, increased water intake, deleting emails, unfriending toxic people on social media, purging unused belongings, saying "no" to an invitation, sleep, or, as Jackson described, even caring for one's surroundings: "I have been cleaning. I love the act of working on something and being able to see it being accomplished as you are doing it. I cannot wait until I can start mowing again!"

For many music educators, working at intense, unhealthy levels of stress (often rooting us deep within feelings of burnout) becomes habitual to the point that, when the schedule clears and stress lowers, we feel like something is missing. Because we *can* do more, we refill open spaces in our schedule with more work, rather than fill the spaces with self-care or recovery. As such, scheduling self-care on the calendar–especially following big events—can aid in "refilling the cup" (Emma) and recovering from symptoms of burnout. Zoe emphasized that scheduling is important because "I can't say, 'Oh, I want to be healthier' and expect my life to change without a plan and changes in routine." Overt efforts on our part may also inspire education colleagues to develop healthier habits:

> I have even started a crusade of sorts in my building to convince staff to take their school emails off their phones. I sat in a meeting and listened to a colleague say that she was going to have to start cutting herself off at 8:00 PM at night. *8pm AT NIGHT!* My mind exploded. The ensuing conversation was a good conversation about whether or not my colleague felt like they were doing themselves any good by looking at an email that might ruin their night. I have decided that this kind of

behavior is not for me. I have drawn a clear line in the sand between school and work that I intend to keep. (Jackson, journal entry)

The world in which we live gains intensity with each passing day. Burnout is fueled by promotions of hustle culture (maize, 2020) or toil glamour (Griffith, 2019), which romanticize working both through and beyond stages of burnout. Social media has increasingly provided platforms where "dares" are initiated and spread like wildfire, many of which play out negatively in our school settings—another exhausting force for music educators to battle on top of everything else. More than ever, there is a need to counterbalance the stress and anxiety and overscheduled-ness of our lives.

Although we approach and benefit from methods of self-care individually, such work will be reflected in the larger music education profession. Efforts will lead to increased understanding of self, stronger grounding in work as music educators, healthier people and relationships, increased empathy, stronger connections with students, and amplified enjoyment of most tasks at hand (Hendricks, 2018). We may also be better equipped to battle and counteract burnout, empowered and invigorated to navigate the music education profession more on our own terms by putting aside the burnt toast and continually refilling our own cups along the way.

REFERENCES

Barbeau, A-K., & Mantie, R. (2019). Music performance anxiety and perceived benefits of musical participation among older adults in community bands. *Journal of Research in Music Education*, 66(4), 408–427. https://doi.org/10.1177%2F0022429418799362

Bernhard II, H. C. (2007). A survey of burnout among college music majors. *College Student Journal*, 41(2), 392–401.

Brown, E. P. (2020). Music teacher self-perceived vocal health and job-related stress. *Bulletin of the Council for Research in Music Education*, (224), 46–60. https://doi.org/10.5406/bulcouresmusedu.224.0046

Brunkan, M. C. (2018). Preservice music teacher voice use, vocal health, and voice function before and during student teaching. *Journal of Music Teacher Education*, 27(3), 80–93. https://doi.org/10.1177%2F1057083717741216

Buchanan, H. J., & Hays, T. (2014). The influence of body mapping on student musicians' performance experiences. *International Journal of Education & the Arts*, 15(7), 1–28.

Chesky, K. S., Dawson, W. J., & Manchester, R. (2006). Health promotion in schools of music: Initial recommendations for schools of music. *Medical Problems of Performing Artists*, 21(3), 142–144. https://doi.org/10.21091/mppa.2006.3027

Clear, J. (2018). *Atomic habits*. Avery.

Conable, B. (1995). *How to learn the Alexander Technique* (3rd ed.). GIA Publications.

Cooley, K. (2021). *Noise induced hearing loss [NIHL] prevention in music education* [Unpublished masters capstone paper]. University of Illinois at Urbana-Champaign.

Cook-Cunningham, S. L., Grady, M. L., & Nelson, H. (2012). Hearing dose and perceptions of hearing and singing effort among university choir singers in varied rehearsal and performance settings. *International Journal of Research in Choral Singing*, 4(1), 19–35.

Doherty, M. L. (2011). Making the connection between healthy voice and successful teaching and learning in the music classroom. *Choral Journal*, 51(11), 41–49.

Dora, C., Conforti, S., & Güsewell, A. (2019). Exploring the influence of body awareness on instrumental sound. *International Journal of Music Education*, 37(2), 311–326.

Gates, R., Forrest, A. L., & Obert, K. (2013). *The owner's manual to the voice*. Oxford University Press.

Gorkin, M. (2021, June 16). *Burn-in, burnout, and workplace griefbusting: Part I*. MentalHelp.net. https://www.mentalhelp.net/blogs/burn-in-burnout-and-workplace-griefbusting-part-i/

Greasley, A. E., Fulford, R. J., Pickard, M., & Hamilton, N. (2020). Help musicians UK hearing survey: Musicians' hearing and hearing protection. *Psychology of Music*, 48(4), 529–546. https://doi.org/10.1177%2F0305735618812238

Griffith, E. (2019). Why are young people pretending to love work? *New York Times*. https://www.nytimes.com/2019/01/26/business/against-hustle-culture-rise-and-grind-tgim.html

Heman-Ackah, D. Y., Sataloff, R. T., & Hawkshaw, M. J. (2013). *The voice: A medical guide for achieving and maintaining a healthy voice*. Science & Medicine.

Hendricks, K. S. (2018). *Compassionate music teaching*. Roman & Littlefield.

Holiday, R. (2019). *Stillness is the key*. Portfolio/Penguin.

Isaac, M. J., McBroom, D. H., Nguyen, S. A., & Halstead, L. A. (2017). Prevalence of hearing loss in teachers of singing and voice students. *Journal of Voice*, 31(3), 379.E21–379.E32. https://doi.org/10.1016/j.jvoice.2016.10.003

Kaleńska-Rodzaj, J. (2020). Music performance anxiety and pre-performance emotions in the light of psychology of emotion and emotion regulation. *Psychology of Music*, 49(6), 1758–1774. https://doi.org/10.1177%2F0305735620961154

Kegelaers, J., Schuijer, M., & Oudejans, R. D. (2021). Resilience and mental health issues in classical musicians: A preliminary study. *Psychology of Music*, 49(5), 1273–1284. https://doi.org/10.1177%2F0305735620927789

Koops, L., & Kuebel, C. R. (2021). Self-reported mental health and mental illness among university music students in the United States. *Research Studies in Music Education*, 43(2), 129–143. https://doi.org/10.1177%2F1321103X19863265

Kuebel, C. (2019). Health and wellness for in-service and future music teachers: Developing a self-care plan. *Music Educators Journal*, 105(4), 52–58. https://doi.org/10.1177%2F0027432119846950

Leaver, R., Harris, E. C., & Palmer, K. T. (2011). Musculoskeletal pain in elite professional musicians from British symphony orchestras. *Occupational Medicine*, 61, 549–555. https://doi.org/10.1093%2Foccmed%2Fkqr129

MacLeod, R. B., Geringer, J. M., & Miller, D. S. (2021). The effect of wearing foam and etymotic earplugs on classical musicians' pitch perception. *Journal of Research in Music Education*, 69(4), 444–456. https://doi.org/10.1177%2F0022429421989993

maize. (2020, January 20). *The rise and grind of hustle culture*. https://www.maize.io/magazine/rise-grind-hustle-culture/

Malde, M., Allen, M., Zeller, K.-A. (2020). *What every singer needs to know about the body* (4th ed.). Plural Publishing.

Nápoles, J. (2022). Burnout: A review of the literature. *Update: Applications of Research in Music Education*, 40(2), 19–26. https://doi.org/10.1177%2F87551233211037669

National Association of Schools of Music (NASM)/Performing Arts Medicine Association (PAMA). (2011). *State of the art reviews (stARs)*. https://artsmed.org/resources/pama-nasm-task-force/

Centers for Disease Control and Prevention. (2021). The National Institute for Occupational Safety and Health. https://www.cdc.gov/niosh/index.htm

Paparo, S. A. (2015). Embodying singing in the choral classroom: A somatic approach to teaching and learning. *International Journal of Music Education*, 34(4), 488–498. https://doi.org/10.1177%2F0255761415569366

Pressley, T. (2021). Factors contributing to teacher burnout during COVID-19. *Educational Researcher*, 50(5), 325–327. https://doi.org/10.3102%2F0013189X211004138

Rosset i Llobet, J., & Odam, G. (2007). *The musician's body*. Ashgate.

Salvador, K. (2019). Sustaining the flame: (Re)igniting joy in teaching music. *Music Educators Journal*, 106(2), 28–36. https://doi.org/10.1177%2F0027432119873701

Shafer-Crane, G. A. (2006). Repetitive stress and strain injuries: Preventative exercises for the musician. *Physical Medicine and Rehabilitation Clinics of North America*, 17, 827–842. https://doi.org/10.1016/j.pmr.2006.07.005

Shaw, R. D. (2016). Music teacher stress in the era of accountability. *Arts Education Policy Review*, 117(2), 104–116. https://doi.org/10.1080/10632913.2015.1005325

Sieger, C. (2019). "I do belong here": Identity perceptions of postgraduate music education majors. *Journal of Music Teacher Education*, 29(1), 56–70. https://doi.org/10.1177%2F1057083719865890

Sims, W. L., & Cassidy, J. W. (2020). Imposter feelings of music education graduate students. *Journal of Research in Music Education*, 68(3), 249–263. https://doi.org/10.1177%2F0022429420946899

Smith, T. D. (2021). Teaching through trauma: Compassion fatigue, burnout, or secondary traumatic stress? In D. Bradley & J. Hess (Eds.), *Trauma and resilience in music education* (pp. 49–63). Routledge.

Westfeldt, L. (1987). *F. Matthias Alexander*. Centerline Press.

World Health Organization. (2021, May). *ICD-11 for mortality and morbidity statistics: QD85 burnout*. Retrieved March 20, 2022, from https://icd.who.int/browse11/l-m/en#/http://id.who.int/icd/entity/129180281

CHAPTER 29

SOMATIC SELF-CARE FOR MUSIC EDUCATORS

STEPHEN A. PAPARO

Care Handbook Topics

Wellbeing and human flourishing

GENUINE compassion begins from within. Self-compassion is vital for music teachers who spend much of their time caring for and with their students (Hendricks, 2018). As Hendricks (2018) has written, "The art of genuinely reaching outward requires us first to reach inward.... By first coming to know and show compassion for ourselves, we open up the possibility of showing genuine compassion to others" (p. 33). Teachers who are more in touch with their own needs will be more likely to show compassion for others. In this chapter, I posit that one way to develop inward compassion is through somatic self-care. I draw on the pragmatic philosophical discipline somaesthetics to establish the importance of bodily, lived experience and the inclusion of somatic practice as a means to improve self-function (Shusterman, 2008). The Feldenkrais Method[1] of somatic education offers a unique pedagogy for observing oneself in action and developing sensory acuity that results in enhanced self-awareness and performance (Feldenkrais, 1990). As a Guild Certified Feldenkrais Practitioner, I offer a self-directed Awareness Through Movement lesson as an introduction to this form of somatic learning. Improved somatic awareness and function can provide a reliable and rich source of self-knowledge that is useful for attending to one's own needs (self-compassion) and interacting with students (compassion for others). Moreover, I argue that, through participation in the

---

[1] The following are service or certification marks of the Feldenkrais Guild® of North America in the US: Feldenkrais®, Feldenkrais Method®, Functional Integration®, Awareness Through Movement®, and Guild Certified Feldenkrais Practitioner[(CM)].

Feldenkrais Method, music teachers can learn to cultivate embodied knowledge of trust, empathy, patience, inclusion, community, and authentic connection, and ultimately, more fully realize their potential through compassionate music teaching (Hendricks, 2018). Finally, I offer some recommendations and practical applications of somatic self-care for music teachers and students.

Coming to Our Senses

Music educators are sensing beings. We constantly take in sensory information from our environment throughout the day. We notice the vibe of each class. We attune ourselves to the music we conduct, play, and sing. We watch and listen to our students, anticipating and attending to their needs. As we guide them to become more musical, we often respond to familiar situations without much thought or reflection. Because our attention is almost entirely outwardly focused, we might habitually neglect or ignore our inner experience beyond hunger pangs or the need for a caffeine boost. Turning our attention inward to our lived, bodily experience may seem foreign, unnecessary, or even counterproductive. However, attending to our somatic experience (and helping our students attend to theirs) can renew and sustain our attention and energy as well as help nurture meaningful connections with our students.

Soma refers to "the body perceived from within by first-person perception" (Hanna, 1986, p. 4). It is the internal, lived experience of self. First-person perception allows me to know my internal state and manage my sense of wellbeing. For example, am I tense or do I move with ease? Is my breathing restricted or full? Are my eyes strained or relaxed? Is my abdomen contracted or released? Having awareness of my bodily state tells me about my feelings, emotions, thoughts, and actions. For instance, am I feeling hungry or tired? Am I emotionally content or agitated? Am I thinking clearly or chaotically? Are my actions congruent with my intentions? Am I being productive or do I need to take a break?

Our bodily state can also be a guide for interacting with students and others. For example, what does my gut tell me about my student(s)? What do I say or do in a difficult or stressful situation? How do certain situations or interactions resonate with me? Are my interactions mindful and compassionate? How does my self-understanding help me to appreciate what my student(s) might be experiencing? Answers to each of these questions come from our awareness of ourselves. The more finely tuned we are as teachers the more finely we can attune ourselves to our embodied knowledge to help guide our teaching and interactions with others. The first step of this process is to develop awareness of ourselves through somatic education.

Somatic education is "concerned with the learning process of the living body (the 'soma') as it acquires awareness through movement within the environment" (Joly, 2000, p. 5). Its aim is to develop awareness of self-use through attention to the internal processes of the body (Hanna, 1993). Forms of somatic education include the Alexander

Technique, Body-mind Centering, Clinical Somatic Education (also known as Hanna Somatic Education), and the Feldenkrais Method. Before introducing the Feldenkrais Method below, I first discuss somaesthetics, which provides a foundation for understanding bodily consciousness and the inclusion of somatic practice as a means to improve self-function.

Somaesthetics and Self-Care

Contemporary American philosopher and certified Feldenkrais practitioner Richard Shusterman (b. 1949) defined somaesthetics, a pragmatic philosophical discipline, as "the critical study and meliorative cultivation of the body as the site of sensory appreciation (aesthesis) and creative self-fashioning" (2018, p. 1). In essence, it is the study of the body, both as object and subject, and all the ways to improve its appearance and function.

> A field that seeks to integrate theory and practice, somaesthetics argues that our sensory perceptions (and consequently the feelings and performances based on those perceptions) can be improved by cultivating one's somatic capacities that include both sensorimotor skills and powers of body consciousness. (Shusterman, 2018, p. 1)

In his chapter "Somaesthetics and Care of the Self," Shusterman (2008) asserted the importance of somaesthetics as a means to achieve philosophy's central aims: knowledge, self-knowledge, right action, happiness, and justice. Though Shusterman was concerned with establishing somaesthetics as an interdisciplinary philosophical endeavor, I adapt his rationale to posit the need for somatic self-care for music educators and, subsequently, as a means to more fully realize one's potential for compassionate music teaching.

Because the senses are at the core of music making and teaching, it would be advantageous to improve the actual performance of our senses with somaesthetics in order to heighten our perception of our musicianship and interactions with students. Somaesthetics helps us to become more aware of ourselves, our feelings and emotions, and our actions and habits that undermine or support our wellbeing. Improved somatic efficacy allows us then to act as we intend, such as to skillfully demonstrate a musical phrase or empathetically communicate with a student. With its focus on the body as a source of sensory appreciation, somaesthetics can help us replace the common deficit model that focuses on eliminating pain, stress, and anxiety with a somatic-oriented paradigm that helps to savor the enjoyment and pleasures of music making and teaching (Kenny & Ackermann, 2013; Paparo, 2021a). Somaesthetics allows us to examine and overcome habits of "inscribing social power" as a way of maintaining control and order in and out of the music classroom in favor of creating a community of shared, lived experiences (see Shusterman, 2008, p. 21).

In contrast to purely discursive philosophies, *practical* somaesthetics demands the pursuit of "[self-]care through intelligently disciplined practice aimed at somatic self-improvement" (Shusterman, 2008, p. 29). This distinctive feature calls for actual participation in somatic practice. One such example is the Feldenkrais Method, which is the focus of the next section.

THE FELDENKRAIS METHOD OF SOMATIC EDUCATION

Israeli physicist, engineer, and judo expert Moshe Feldenkrais (1904–1984) developed his method initially in an effort to regain his ability to walk after a knee injury. Born out of Feldenkrais's own bodily, lived experience, the Feldenkrais Method is an approach to learn to recover and create possibilities for sensing, feeling, moving, and thinking to improve quality of life (Feldenkrais, 1990). It is based on the idea that human beings have unlimited potential to improve because of neuroplasticity, the innate capacity of the brain to create new neural pathways as a result of experiences (Doidge, 2015). The Feldenkrais Method comprises two interrelated modalities: Functional Integration (FI), individual lessons in which a practitioner uses touch to guide the Feldenkrais student in a gentle and non-invasive manner; and Awareness Through Movement (ATM), verbally guided group or one-on-one lessons (Feldenkrais Method, n.d.). During FI and ATM, participants make perceptual distinctions while exploring functional movements, such as reaching and turning, so that they can learn to embody more intentional and effective action (Lynn, 2017; Feldenkrais, 1990). Both FI and ATM operationalize the conditions for neuroplasticity to occur (Doidge, 2015). These conditions for learning include moving slowly, reducing effort, doing only what is easy and pleasurable, pausing between each movement, resting frequently, and directing attention while moving (Feldenkrais, 1990).

In order to experience this type of somatic self-care, I invite you, the reader, to take approximately 20 minutes to do the following self-directed ATM lesson.[2] In this lesson that I adapted from *Relaxercise* created by Feldenkrais practitioner trainers David Zemach-Bersin and Mark Reese, you will sense and feel how you move while exploring the movements of turning. Please sit in a chair with a firm, flat surface (as opposed to an office chair with padding and wheels). Read each step of the lesson one at a time, then close your eyes and observe yourself as you move. Repeat for each step until you come to the end of the lesson. Remember to follow the conditions for learning discussed earlier. As a result of doing the lesson, you may notice that you turn your head more smoothly,

---

[2] A free audio recording of this lesson is available at https://drive.google.com/file/d/1xfLzUJqc7yDtHppyBBi9Z4pP39j-YbXo/view?usp=sharing.

sit more erect in your chair, breathe more expansively, and feel calmer and more centered. Whatever you notice will provide useful information about yourself.

1. Sit comfortably toward the front of your chair. Have both feet flat on the floor and spread about hip-width apart so your knees are above your ankles. Rest your hands in your lap. Take a few moments to observe how you are sitting. Observe the contact of your pelvis and buttocks with the chair. Observe all along your spine, feeling the back of your pelvis, lower back, middle and upper back, neck, and head. Observe your shoulders and arms. Finally, observe your breathing. What moves as you inhale and exhale?
2. Slowly turn your upper body, as if to look to the right a very small amount. Then return to facing forward. Repeat this a few times slowly and gently, pausing between each repetition. Exhale as you turn. Make a mental note of exactly how far to the right you can see, without any strain. Stop for a moment.
3. Focus your eyes on an object or spot straight ahead. Keep your eyes still, looking straight ahead, while slowly turning your head and upper body to the right. Then return to facing forward. Exhale as you turn. Repeat this a few times, seeing where you can reduce the effort in your neck, shoulders, chest and legs. Do not stretch or strain. Notice that your upper body does not turn as far to the right because your eyes are not moving. Stop for a moment.
4. Once again, slowly turn your entire upper body to the right, including your eyes. Turn gently and easily. Can you see a little farther to the right? Stop for a moment.
5. Keep your head and eyes facing forward and slowly turn your shoulders and upper body to the right. Exhale as you turn. Repeat this a few times. Relax your jaw, neck, chest, and shoulders. Notice that your right shoulder is moving back and your left shoulder is moving forward. Stop for a moment.
6. Again, slowly turn your entire upper body to the right, including your head and eyes. Then return to the starting position. Is it becoming easier and more comfortable to turn to the right than before? Stop and rest. Feel the difference between your left and right shoulder. Feel how your left side is relaxing.
7. Keeping your left foot still and flat on the floor, move your left knee forward very slightly and return to the starting position. This is a very small movement. Exhale as you move your knee. Repeat this a few times. Relax your left leg and foot as much as possible. Notice that your lower back, shoulders, and head are turning slightly to the right.
8. Simultaneously, move your left knee forward slowly, while turning your entire upper body to the right. Repeat this a few times. Notice that you get a little taller as you turn. Exhale as you turn so your chest can be flexible. Feel how your pelvis moves a little as you turn and how moving your left knee forward improves your ability to turn. Stop and rest. Feel how your left shoulder and left side of your neck and lower back are more relaxed.
9. Repeat steps two through eight, turning to the left. When reading the directions, switch "right" for "left" and "left" for "right." After completing this, continue with the rest of the lesson.

10. Move your left knee forward very slightly, while slowly turning your entire upper body to the right. Then return—go through the starting position—and move your right knee forward, while slowly turning your entire upper body to the left. Exhale as you turn to each side. Repeat this action a few times. Make the movement smooth and continuous. Let your hands slide on your thighs as you turn from side to side. Relax your legs as much as possible. Stop for a moment.
11. Keep your head and eyes still, facing forward, and continue turning the rest of your upper body to the right a little and then to the left a little. Repeat this action a few times. Relax your face, neck, and shoulders. Keep your feet flat on the floor. Breathe freely. Stop for a moment.
12. Turn your entire upper body to the right and then to the left. As you turn to the right, notice that your left shoulder moves forward and your right shoulder moves back. As you turn to the left, notice that your right shoulder moves forward and your left shoulder moves back. Feel how much more easily you can turn. Stop for a moment.
13. Alternately, turn your upper body and pelvis to the right, while turning your head and eyes to the left—and slowly turn your upper body and pelvis to the left, while turning your head and eyes to the right. Repeat this action a few times. Go slowly so the movement is smooth and easy. Do not stretch or strain. Relax your jaw, neck, shoulders, and legs as much as you can. Breathe freely. Stop for a moment.
14. Now move your left knee forward while turning your entire upper body to the right as far as you can, without any strain. Then move your right knee forward while turning your entire upper body to the left as far as you can, without any strain. Notice how easily you are turning and how much farther to the right and left you can see.
15. Now rest. Observe how you are sitting. Are you sitting more comfortably? Is your weight more evenly balanced on your pelvis? Do you feel a slight arch in your lower back? Do you feel taller? What changes do you notice? Do you feel more connected to yourself? Do you feel you are more open to observe and interact with others?
16. Continue to observe any change in yourself throughout the rest of the day. (End of lesson)

Somatic Self-Care and Compassionate Music Teaching

Improved somatic awareness and function can provide self-knowledge that is useful for attending to one's own needs (self-compassion) and interacting with students (compassion for others). Through somatic self-care, music teachers can learn to embody trust, empathy, patience, inclusion, community, and authentic connection—the qualities of compassionate music teaching (Hendricks, 2018). Next, I examine Feldenkrais as somatic self-care in relation to each of these six characteristics.

Trust

Somatic self-care helps us to understand our lived experience by trusting our senses. In the ATM lesson, you may have experienced unnecessary tension or holding that restricted your ability to turn. By the end of the lesson, you likely felt an improvement in turning, which required less effort and was more pleasurable. This improvement could not be taught through anatomical knowledge, for example. Rather, it is the felt experience that guides us in the process of organic learning (Feldenkrais, 1981). Psychologist and therapeutic bodyworker Alan Fogel (2009) explained that the foundation of trust, for oneself and by extension for others, is grounded in the embodied knowledge of "sensing that one's own experiences are trustworthy" (p. 270). Feldenkrais engenders a sense of trust and confidence within ourselves. Furthermore, Fogel (2009) suggested that we must refine our "ability to use positive and negative feelings, comforts and pains, as diagnostic of the current situation and as reliable information on which to learn and to make choices." (p. 270). As previously mentioned, our somatic experience as teachers becomes a source of knowledge when we trust our ability to manage our own wellbeing as well as our interactions with students.

Empathy

Somatic self-care can help develop skills of empathetic teaching. Cognitive empathy involves "being sensitive to verbal, nonverbal, and situational cues" and making "an honest attempt to understand the perspective of our students" (Hendricks, 2018, p. 64). Affective empathy involves being able to physically and emotionally sense what students might be experiencing (Hendricks, 2018). Both are enhanced with greater self-awareness and what Master Somatic Leadership Coach Amanda Blake (2018) refers to as presence.

> Deep presence [of empathy] requires feeling all of your own sensations while also actively "tuning in" to the people around you. This is distinct from focusing all of your attention on someone else while abandoning your own values, vision, and needs. It's also different from focusing all of your attention on yourself at someone else's expense. (p. 167)

Becoming clearer about our own sensations, feelings, and experiences through somatic self-care can build greater capacity for being present with ourselves and our students. The distinction is also important in establishing healthy boundaries and helps us to appreciate that our students' experiences and perspectives are different from our own. The ability to "read" our students can improve when we ourselves are more finely tuned.

Patience

Somatic self-care can help grow our understanding that learning requires patience. In the ATM lesson, you took time to explore various component movements that led to turning with greater ease. This exploratory process is analogous to how babies learn to roll, crawl, sit, stand, and walk. The fact that babies generally learn to walk anywhere between 8 and 18 months clearly illustrates that human beings learn in their own time. Dr. Feldenkrais (1981) explained that people learn in successive approximations toward a goal with the understanding that there is always room for continued improvement. Once we learn how to walk, however, we generally abandon this type of learning unless we encounter difficulties later in life. The Feldenkrais Method can serve as a model for structuring learning experiences as a series of successive approximations, knowing that students face different challenges and benefit from different strategies. As teachers we can also manage our expectations accordingly and adjust instructional goals in conjunction with students' needs and desires. Ultimately, we can recognize that students have unlimited potential for improvement regardless of their current level of achievement.

Inclusion

Somatic self-care can help us know that everyone can learn, no matter who they are. The underlying premise of the Feldenkrais Method that all human beings have the potential to learn at any stage of life is one of inclusion. Dr. Feldenkrais taught concentration camp survivors in Israel to help them to recover and heal from the atrocities of imprisonment. The ultimate purpose of his method is "to restore each person to their human dignity." Each Feldenkrais lesson provides numerous strategies for differentiated instruction. In the ATM lesson, you explored a number of variations or ways to turn. It is likely that certain variations were more engaging and novel than others, which allowed you to discover something unique about your habitual movements. Because everyone has different backgrounds and personal histories that influence their movement patterns, the variety of ways to explore an action enables individualized learning as opposed to a one-size-fits-all outcome. The combination of this philosophical stance and practical application offers a rich model for compassionate music teaching approaches that seek to provide meaningful learning experiences for students in a variety of contexts.

Community

Somatic self-care can help grow our understanding of community. Feldenkrais participants share a common framework and experience of human learning. They view themselves as co-learners who value individual experience. They embrace a non-judgmental environment because the process is non-corrective and non-evaluative. Unlike most forms of exercise or movement training, there are no external models to imitate. Furthermore, the process that creates the conditions for the nervous system to learn provides opportunities to cultivate authenticity, improvisation, risk-taking, and vulnerability.

In the ATM lesson, you focused on your own experience without external evaluation or expectation. You intentionally tried unfamiliar ways of moving, hopefully with an attitude of curiosity and playfulness. Perhaps there was an "aha" moment or two where you discovered something new about yourself. You opened up to internal sensations and feelings, which may have made you feel vulnerable. These aspects are inherent in the Feldenkrais Method and can lead to embodiment of these characteristics. Furthermore, a true sense of community can emerge in which curiosity, playfulness, vulnerability, and authenticity are the norm.

Authentic Connection

Finally, somatic self-care can expand our potential for authentic connection with ourselves and with others. With greater awareness of ourselves, we can act more intentionally by consciously making choices in our interactions with others rather than reacting habitually. In the ATM lesson, you may have experienced an improved ability to turn, but perhaps that allowed you to be more connected to yourself and more available to connect with others. Like empathetic presence, there is both an internal and external aspect of authentic connection. When we experience our true selves through somatic self-care, we can then convey our integrity in our actions. Right action, an aim of philosophy, is the ability to do what we intend, regardless of societal, cultural, or familial expectations or conditioning (Shusterman, 2008). This is at the heart of authentic connection with others (Hendricks, 2018).

RECOMMENDATIONS AND APPLICATIONS

In this final section, I offer some recommendations and applications of somatic self-care. For those interested in learning more about the Feldenkrais Method, there are a number of resources. It is possible to find a Certified Feldenkrais Practitioner for one-on-one or group lessons (either in person or virtually) by searching the Feldenkrais Guild of North America and International Feldenkrais Federation websites. Like musical repertoire, there is a vast range of ATM lessons that can be explored through audio and video recordings. Series of lessons usually relate to a particular theme (e.g., liberating the spine, freeing breathing, improving balance) that might be of interest depending on personal needs and desires. I have included a resource list at the end of this chapter for more information.

Regarding applications to music teaching and learning, I offer the following suggestions:

1. *Observe sensations, feelings, thoughts, and movements.* Shining the spotlight of attention internally can help problem-solve technical and musical challenges. Music teachers can encourage students to focus on their somatic experience (as opposed to anatomical knowledge or musical outcome) to clarify intention and bring greater awareness to the interaction with their instrument.
2. *Explore movements intentionally.* Using physical or imagined movement exploration can expand possibilities for creating sound. Students can do the ATM lesson in this chapter and explore how these movements relate to singing or playing their instrument.
3. *Simplify movement or tasks into small parts.* As with whole-part-whole learning where teachers break down a piece into sections, phrases, measures, and motives before reintegrating the parts into the whole, teachers can simplify movements or tasks for students so they can master the component parts before doing the whole action.
4. *Use variation to generate options.* Like a musical theme and variations, having students play or sing with subtle or not-so-subtle changes can vary the way they experience the music and lead to new possibilities that they might not have otherwise considered. Music teachers might have students play a passage with different rhythms, articulations, tonality (such as from major to minor), and different attitudes (such as joyful, depressed, energized, etc.) to explore a range of options.
5. *Incorporate Feldenkrais lessons in your curriculum.* Invite a guest Feldenkrais practitioner to work with your students or use recordings.
6. *Read and share other Feldenkrais sources.* There are a number of publications regarding Feldenkrais and its applications for musicians, such as Lee (2018) and Paparo (2016, 2021a, 2021b).

In conclusion, without bodily lived experience as knowledge, concepts such as self-care and compassion with students may remain intellectual abstractions. When disconnected from the body, we as music teachers potentially miss the opportunity to foster deep, embodied experiences for ourselves and our students. Somaesthetics provides a compelling rationale for self-care and including bodily experience as a part of music teaching and learning. The Feldenkrais Method of somatic education offers a practical framework to care for self and other. Together, teachers and students can create a community knowing that people have the capacity for continued growth and improvement, which makes everyone more alike than different. This view is congruent philosophically and practically with compassionate music teaching and ultimately provides a new paradigm for all.

REFERENCES

Blake, A. (2018). *Your body is your brain*. Trokay Press.
Doidge, N. (2015). *The brain's way of healing: Remarkable discoveries from the frontiers of neuroplasticity*. Penguin Books.

Feldenkrais, M. (1981). *The elusive obvious*. Meta Publications.
Feldenkrais, M. (1990). *Awareness through movement*. HarperSanFrancisco.
Feldenkrais Method. (n.d.) Retrieved July 1, 2021, from https://feldenkrais.com
Fogel, A. (2009). *Body sense: The science and practice of embodied self-awareness*. W.W. Norton.
Hanna, T. (1986). What is somatics? Part I. *Somatic*, 5(4), 4–8.
Hanna, T. (1993). *The body of life: Creating new pathways for sensory awareness and fluid movement*. Healing Arts Press.
Hendricks, K. S. (2018). *Compassionate music teaching*. Rowman & Littlefield.
Joly, Y. (2000). The experience of being embodied: Qualitative research and somatic education—A perspective based on the Feldenkrais Method. *Feldenkrais Research Journal*, 1. http://iffresearchjournal.org/volume/1/joly
Kenny, D., & Ackermann, B. (2013). Performance-related musculoskeletal pain, depression and music performance anxiety in professional orchestral musicians: A population study. *Psychology of Music*, 43(1), 43–60. https://doi.org/10.1177/0305735613493953
Lee, C. (2018). Musicians as movers: Applying the Feldenkrais Method to music education. *Music Educators Journal*, 104(4), 15–19. https://doi.org/10.1177%2F0027432118766401
Lynn, G. (2017) *Awakening somatic intelligence: Understanding, learning, and practicing the Alexander Technique, Feldenkrais Method® and Hatha Yoga*. Singing Dragon.
Paparo, S. A. (2016) Embodying singing in the choral classroom: A somatic approach to teaching and learning. *International Journal of Music Education*, 34(4) 488–498. https://doi.org/10.1177/0255761415569366
Paparo, S. A. (2021a). Voicing with awareness: An introduction to the Feldenkrais Method. In C. Kapadocha (Ed.), *Somatic voices in performance research and beyond* (pp. 89–97). Routledge.
Paparo, S. A. (2021b). Singing with awareness: A phenomenology of singers' experience with the Feldenkrais Method. *Research Studies in Music Education*. Advance online publication. https://doi.org/10.1177/1321103X211020642
Shusterman, R. (2008). *Body consciousness: A philosophy of mindfulness and somaesthetics*. Cambridge University Press.
Shusterman, R. (2018). Introduction: Aesthetic experience and somaesthetics. In R. Shusterman (Ed.), *Aesthetic experience and somaesthetics* (pp. 1–13). Koninklijke Brill.

Suggested Resources

Feldenkrais, M. (1972). *Awareness through movement*. HarperSanFrancisco.
Nelson, S. H., & Blades, E. L. (2018). *Singing with your whole self: A singer's guide to Feldenkrais awareness through movement*. Rowman & Littlefield.
Wildman, F. (2000). *The busy person's guide to easier movement*. Intelligent Body Press.
Zemach-Bersin, D., Zemach-Bersin, K., & Reese, M. (1990). *Relaxercise: The easy new way to health & fitness*. HarperCollins.

Additional Online Resources

Feldenkrais Access (www.feldenkraisaccess.com)
Feldenkrais Resources (www.feldenkraisresources.com)
Feldenkrais Guild of North America (www.feldenkrais.com)
International Feldenkrais Federation (www.feldenkrais-method.org)

CHAPTER 30

MUSIC'S RELATIONAL IMPERATIVE

Wellbeing, Music-Making, and the Interconnections Between Music Therapy and Music Education

ELIZABETH MITCHELL

CARE HANDBOOK TOPICS

Co-creating caring relationships
Philosophical perspectives
Wellbeing and human flourishing

INTRODUCTION

When I meet a client in music therapy for the first time, I ask if they will tell me about their relationship with music. This prompt almost inevitably leads to rich conversations in which clients, or their caregivers, share the ways in which they have discovered music's ability to help, perhaps in expressing emotions, connecting with others, or coping with stress. Such dialogue allows me to validate individuals' self-awareness and resourcefulness, while introducing music therapy in a way that meets them where they are: *Music therapy is connected to the ways in which you use music in your day-to-day life*. Similarly, when a client experiences music therapy to be helpful in connection to their goals, we explore whether it may be possible to access this helpfulness outside of music therapy, whether through solo music-making, listening, lessons, a community ensemble, jamming with friends, and so on.

One of my guiding principles as a music therapist, and now also as a music therapy educator, is that music therapists do not own music's therapeutic benefits. This is an intuitive message for people who have experienced music's ability to "help" in a wide variety of domains, though the message can bring about some level of discomfort among music therapy students and established music therapists alike.

Historically, music therapists have had to advocate tirelessly for recognition within healthcare and academic settings (Wood & Ansdell, 2018). Over time, as music therapists have conducted research to support music's role in healthcare and established professional standards of practice, they have also often needed to distinguish their work from more familiar musical pursuits, such as music entertainment or education. Any stability the field has achieved has been hard won; certainly, within Canada, the context with which I am the most familiar, employment opportunities still often remain tenuous.

Definitions aside however, music's therapeutic value will always transcend disciplinary context. To say that music therapists do not own music's therapeutic benefits does not imply that the practice of music therapists is not unique or important. Music therapists have an invaluable role to play in healthcare and in any setting in which music's health and wellness benefits are of relevance. Their work also overlaps with others whose practices involve active music-making and human relationships rooted in care, including the vitally important work of music educators. It is these points of overlap that are this chapter's focus.

Rooted in Continuum

The Oxford English Dictionary defines the noun "therapy" as "treatment intended to relieve or heal a disorder" or "the treatment of mental or psychological disorders by psychological means" (Stevenson, 2015a). Music therapists receive specialized training regarding psychological frameworks, the development of treatment plans, the clinical use of musical techniques, elements of the therapeutic relationship, and the safe and effective use of self. Such training poises music therapists to work safely and ethically in healthcare settings. To call one's work "music therapy," one must be certified as a music therapist.

The adjective "therapeutic," however, is defined as "relating to the healing of disease," but also as "having a good effect on the body or mind; contributing to a sense of well-being" (Stevenson, 2015b). If we use this latter notion of "contributing to a sense of well-being," then to limit music's therapeutic value to formal settings of therapy would be simply inaccurate. Human societies have been making music and experiencing its impacts on health and wellbeing for millennia (Aigen, 2014), long before the profession of music therapy was developed and labeled as such.

I, along with other others, have asserted that the fields of music therapy and music education lie on a continuum (Bonde, 2019; Mitchell, 2016; Robertson, 2000). I view music-centered theoretical frameworks from music therapy to be particularly fruitful ground from which to understand the fields' interconnections, and thus to spark transdisciplinary dialogue and collaboration (Mitchell & Benedict, 2020).

At its essence, music-centered music therapy recognizes that "music enriches human life in unique ways" and considers musical enrichment, thus, "to be a legitimate focus of the work of music therapists" (Aigen, 2014, p. 65). Though in some contexts music therapists work exclusively toward health-related goals, and likewise, in some contexts, music educators work exclusively toward music-learning goals, Aigen's notion of lives enriched through music undoubtedly resonates with many practitioners from both disciplines. Conceptualizing our fields as lying on a continuum gives space for educators whose philosophies and practices extend beyond the development of musical skill to the development of the whole person. Such a continuum also validates that music-learning often takes place during therapy, sometimes as a byproduct of musical involvement and sometimes as the medium for therapeutic work (Bruscia, 2014; Jones, 2020; Mitchell, 2016; Tyson, 1982). Furthermore, music-centered perspectives recognize that musical involvement and wellness are often intertwined.

Stige et al. (2010) propose a term—"para-musical"—that is useful in its representation of this interconnected nature of musical experience and its potential affordances. This concept rejects any notion of music as a "stimulus leading to certain outcomes" (p. 299) while taking care not to "artificially separate out music into its own rarefied realm, of 'music for music's sake'" (p. 298). Thinking of music's affordances as *paramusical* implores us to "explore *where* music is performed, perceived, experienced, acted and reflected on in order to understand *how* it helps" (p. 299). This construct can assist both educators and therapists in bypassing the debate between whether access to music should be grounded in music's intrinsic value or extrinsic benefits (Aigen, 2014; Hendricks, 2015; Stige et al., 2010), recognizing that these are inseparable.

Centering one's work in music also necessitates venturing beyond aesthetics to investigate music's contexts, its people, and how these elements dynamically interact within the act of musicking (Small, 1998). Music's communal and relational dimensions may be just as crucial to understanding the artform as its sonic properties are, as demonstrated by ethnomusicological research (Cross, 2012; Dissanayake, 2008). Working in a truly music-centered fashion then implies recognition of the complex and culturally specific nature of music's affordances and rejection of the Eurocentric foundations of music therapy as the only source of truth about music's health benefits. At its best, music-centered practice is also anti-oppressive (Baines, 2013; Hess, 2018), acknowledging the potential therapeutic value in any musical tradition along with the potential for music and therapy to do harm. Abrams and Webb's (2020) observation that "sometimes what we consider to be therapy is really perpetuation of colonial structures" resonates for educators as well (see Hess, 2015).

Music therapy and music education both involve active music-making in the context of human relationship. Even as we recognize legitimate distinctions between our disciplines' goals, focus, training, and relationships (Bruscia, 2014; Mitchell, 2016), our shared relational medium of music implies overlap in our theories and practices, particularly for those educators and therapists invested in practicing relationally and holistically. Additionally, as I will explore in the next section, care, when extended relationally from therapist to client, is fundamental to therapy and even predictive of therapy's success. I propose that this notion holds relevance for educators as well.

Relevant Key Principles from Psychotherapy/Music Therapy

In this section I explore elements of music therapy that are relevant for music educators, drawing on research regarding the therapeutic relationship, along with practices from creative music therapy and community music therapy.

Relationship as a Change Medium

Outside of the musical arena, it is worth considering whether characteristics of therapeutic relationships might be relevant for educators. Though there are facets of therapeutic relationships that are neither pertinent nor ethical for application within education, I propose that some general principles may be of great significance.

The Ontario College of Teachers—the body that certifies and regulates public school teachers in my jurisdiction—requires that its members uphold ethical standards in the areas of care, respect, trust, and integrity (Ontario College of Teachers, 2021). These values must, of course, be enacted in relationship, and such standards are central tenets within therapeutic professions as well (for example, Canadian Association of Music Therapists, 2022). Therapeutic practices generally differ from educational ones, however, in the overt primacy placed on relationship as a foundation to the therapeutic process. For example, Bruscia (2014) defines music therapy as "a reflexive process wherein the therapist helps the client to optimize the client's health, using various facets of music experience *and the relationships formed through them* [emphasis added] as the impetus for change" (p. 36).

The very definition of music therapy includes the central role of relationship. As such, therapy training programs, along with Standards of Practice and Codes of Ethics, typically elucidate in detail the elements that go into establishing, maintaining, and terminating therapeutic relationships while preserving the therapist's safe and effective use of self. Of course, therapists can transgress professional standards of practice, just as teachers can; however, therapists are provided with substantial structural guidance, during training and by their professional and regulatory bodies, in terms of navigating and clinically utilizing the dynamics of these impactful relationships.

Meta-analytic research that examines "common factors" among varied approaches to psychotherapy consistently demonstrates the therapeutic relationship's significant role in facilitating client change. Norcross and Wampold (2011) note that "the therapy relationship accounts for why clients improve (or fail to improve) at least as much as the particular treatment method" (p. 423), and Lambert (2013) states:

> It should come as no surprise that helping others deal with depression, anxiety, confusion, inadequacy, and inner conflicts, as well as helping them form viable relationships and meaningful directions for their lives, can be greatly facilitated in a therapeutic relationship that is characterized by trust, understanding, acceptance, kindness, warmth, and human consideration. (p. 206)

Having a therapist who is trustworthy, kind, and warm—caring, that is—is not a bonus, but rather, is a powerful predictor of a client's success in therapy.

Turning now to education, Lampropolous (2001) suggests that an understanding of relationship's integral and predictive role within psychotherapy might be relevant in identifying the mechanisms that spark positive outcomes within other "change-inducing relationships" (p. 21), including teacher–student relationships. Hendricks (2018), for example, explores and affirms the relevance of relational qualities, such as the teacher's warmth and trustworthiness, in understanding student development in education. Similar to clients in therapy, students too are better able to meet their goals and to thrive when educators skillfully and safely prioritize the student–teacher alliance.

Importantly, in presenting these findings from psychotherapy I am not implying that effective teachers do not already develop strong relationships with students. On the contrary, it is because teachers do exactly this, and because student-teacher relationships are often characterized by significant depth and trust—along with an inevitable power imbalance—that I wonder how teachers might be better supported in navigating the complex and important dynamics of these relationships.

If the quality of the therapeutic relationship is vital to therapy's outcome, regardless of theoretical orientation, I will propose that music therapists hold an advantage over therapists who use words as their therapeutic medium. As described earlier, music is a relational medium, and as practitioners who use this medium, we have an opportunity to facilitate and nurture the types of relationships that will be most growth enhancing for our clients. Undoubtedly, this is significant for educators who work with and through music as well. Relationships developed in music can reinforce hierarchical and patriarchal systems of dominance; however, music-making can also embody reciprocity and mutuality (Boyce-Tillman, 2009; Bylica, 2020; Laurila, 2021). As feminist therapists continue to challenge Western psychology's patriarchal, Eurocentric, and ableist idealization of the so-called autonomous individual (Robb, 2006), relationality is increasingly recognized as a goal for therapy and for a thriving existence. What better way to explore and embody relationality than through music?

Music as a Relational Change Medium

Like many music therapists, I draw on principles from humanism (Maslow, 1970) and client-centered therapy (Rogers, 1951) in my practice. Care, from this perspective, is enacted through what Rogers (1957) terms "unconditional positive regard" and describes as follows:

> It involves as much feeling of acceptance for the client's expression of negative, "bad," painful, fearful, defensive, abnormal feelings as for his expression of "good," positive, mature, confident, social feelings.... It means a caring for the client, but not in a possessive way or in such a way as simply to satisfy the therapist's own needs. It means a caring for the client as a *separate* person, with permission to have his own feelings, his own experiences. (p. 98)

This framework includes a genuine belief in every human being's capacity for development, and the paradoxical guiding assumption that in order to change, people need to be first accepted as they are. Extended to music, this humanistic and caring orientation presumes that every individual has the capacity for musical responsiveness, participation, and development.

Arguably, one limit to humanistic approaches, historically speaking, has been their individualistic focus. As Motschnig-Pitrik and Barrett-Lennard (2010) point out, humans are "inherently social beings who live in a world of connection and relationships and develop their distinctive identity mainly through experiences in relation," and yet belonging and love "fall only in the midrange" of Maslow's hierarchy of needs (p. 375). These authors propose the concept of "co-actualization"—instead of self-actualization—recognizing that "actualization in humans tends particularly to be prompted by being in well-functioning relationships with others" (p. 374). I will explore this notion of developing one's potential in the context of relationship—or, co-actualizing—within two music therapy approaches: creative music therapy and community music therapy.

Relationality and Creative Music Therapy

Creative music therapy is an influential model of music therapy practice developed by composer Paul Nordoff and special educator Clive Robbins. This music-centered approach views "musical processes ... as the medium of therapeutic change" and acknowledges "the power of creative engagement to access clients' capacities for resilience, flexibility, and adaptability" (Guerrero et al., 2016, p. 483). Creative music therapy emphasizes interactive and improvised music-making between therapist and client, grounded in recognition of the "universality of human musical sensitivity" along with the "personal significance of each child's musical responsiveness" (Nordoff & Robbins, 2007, p. 3). These tenets link this model to a humanistic framework.

This approach is also centered in relationship; it embodies and intentionally works with the relational nature of both improvisatory music-making and human development. Creative music therapy's therapeutic potential lies in its facilitation of "increasingly reciprocal communicative interaction" in which therapist and client are "affected by the presence and actions of the other" (Guererro et al., 2016, p. 485). Mutuality is celebrated here, rather than autonomy. Musical and relational development are interwoven, as client and therapist respond to one another's presence and music. As Nordoff and Robbins (2007) write,

> Clinical work aimed at developing musical communicativeness is fundamentally a process of exploration, one that often begins with evoked responses, and moves on to the discovery of a path of communicative experience that is nourished by the realization of particular motives, themes or qualities of musical meaning in coactivity with the therapist. (pp. 395–396)[1]

Creative music therapy exemplifies how music therapists can be "person-relationship-centered" (Motschnig-Pitrik & Barrett-Lennard, 2010, p. 376) through a commitment to improvisatory, flexible music-making. When I begin making music with a client, I listen first, and respond using their tempo, perhaps mirroring or extending their rhythmic or melodic ideas, or simply by matching the quality of their vocalizations or the pulse of their body as it moves in the room. My initial goal is that they hear me hearing them; then, from that place of validation and acceptance, they may hear and respond to the musical ideas I introduce into our space. This flexible music-making may appear to be counter to educationally focused goals such as learning repertoire or developing musical skills. However, as client and therapist work musically toward communicative interaction, musicality is undeniably developed, while mutuality of relationship remains in the foreground. In the next section, the relational significance of performance in music therapy is explored.

Relationality and Community Music Therapy

Another music-centered approach that embodies relationality is community music therapy. Historically, while the field of community music "resisted being institutionalized or professionalized, choosing instead to keep its artistic and ideologic independence in order to pursue a more radical political agenda of cultural democracy" (Wood & Ansdell, 2018, p. 455), music therapy grounded itself in a "predominantly individualistic" medical model that "tended to ignore systematic social and cultural thinking in relation to people, music, and health" (p. 455). Community music therapy balances aspects of both traditions, embracing musicking's ecological, participatory, performative, and activist qualities and demanding from the therapist an understanding of care that includes consideration of and working with the ways in which relational, contextual, and systemic factors impact each individual's health and wellbeing (Stige & Aarø, 2012). This ecological perspective on music and health can, and I would argue must,

---

[1] A compelling example of such relational work in contemporary creative music therapy practice (Nordoff Robbins, 2016) can be found at https://www.youtube.com/watch?v=DSbpoFfqvm8.

exist alongside a humanistic commitment to unconditional positive regard and is relevant to a commitment to care within any musical-relational practice.

Validating that the practices of music therapists, community musicians, and music educators may bear remarkable similarities, Wood (2016) asserts that community music therapy "encompasses within its range of therapeutic activities anything that can be done in music" (p. 51). Performing is one such therapeutic activity that holds its own unique affordances. While working as the music therapist at an adolescent mental health facility, I initiated a biannual coffee house event at which any member of the facility's community—client or staff member—is welcome to perform. For youths who are simultaneously participating in music therapy, preparing to perform, and processing the experience afterward, may become an intentional part of a broader clinical process. Performing in front of an audience, whether an original rap or cover song, or as a member of a rock band or bucket drumming group, is distinct from the dyadic improvisatory dialogue in creative music therapy described earlier; still, both of these settings embody a music-centered philosophy that welcomes participation in music therapy based on a "primary desire to *music*" (Aigen, 2014, p. 33) and views "musical processes" as "the medium of therapeutic change" (Guererro et al., 2016, p. 483).

This notion that musical processes may evoke therapeutic change was evident in research surrounding this coffee house. Many clients noted that performing had provided them with an expanded sense of their own capability, and for some of them, this shift in identity extended beyond music. For example, one youth stated that facing her fear of performing had made her "want to try more things" (Mitchell, 2021, p. 199). The therapeutic benefits experienced by individual performers, however, were intertwined with the relational setting in which the event took place. In particular, the presence of audience members was crucial to the shifts that occurred in youths' identity narratives. As staff members bore witness to clients' performances, they gained a more whole perspective on these youths and their potential and reflected these perspectives back to them. Similarly, as youths witnessed staff members' performances, they saw a vulnerable side of their therapists and teachers not typically seen within this healthcare context. These findings, which resonate with Hendricks's (2018) exploration of the role of teachers' vulnerability and risk-taking within music education, validate that our identities develop relationally (Gergen, 2009) and that musical performance can play a unique role in facilitating such development. Furthermore, the experience of gaining new perspectives on one another fostered mutuality and "embodied nonhierarchical relationships in the moment" (Mitchell, 2021, p. 200).

Though the music therapist's ability to integrate performance into clients' clinical processes and goals is vital, first and foremost, this is an event which focuses on "making music possible" (Stige, 2010, p. 16), providing access to the normative experience of music-making to adolescents who would not otherwise get such an opportunity. One youth compared the coffee house with similar events at her former school, and noted, "If you enjoy singing it's pretty much the same thing everywhere" (Mitchell, 2021, p. 201). The fact that youths can perform at this event simply because they want to, allows the coffee house to exemplify the concept of music's paramusical affordances, discussed earlier. For example, though the client mentioned above performed because she enjoys singing, her teacher understood that the performance held interpersonal significance; she described this youth as an individual who "doesn't get on well with her peers" and noted that performing had allowed her peers to "see a different side" of her (Mitchell, 2021, p. 201). This youth's and teacher's distinct perspectives on the same performance showcase Ansdell's (2014) assertion that "subtle but powerful musical affordances only show up when music retains its wholeness as a phenomenon; when it remains musical" (p. 299). This interweaving of musical experience and its affordances within a community setting is vitally relevant for music therapists and music educators alike.

A Vision for Relational Collaboration

I have drawn attention primarily to the relevance of music therapy practices for music education; however, in the spirit of relationality, I must also acknowledge that such relevance exists in the other direction. Certainly, each chapter in this volume exemplifies that music therapists have much to learn from the discourse of music educators. In highlighting areas of mutual relevance within theory and practice, we challenge convenient but simplistic explanations of the differences between our fields, in which music education is defined solely as "the acquisition of music skills" whereas "goals in music therapy can be physical, emotional, cognitive, or social" (Smith, 2018, p. 183). It is not that such statements are necessarily untrue; however, they are unnecessarily reductive. Music education and music therapy are both complex and nuanced in their navigating of musical and relational dynamics, and within these dynamics exist countless potential points of intersection.

Music-centered music therapists recognize clinical value in "naturalistic" (Aigen, 2014, p. 156) forms of musical engagement. This means that learning to play an instrument or sing, or participating in an ensemble, are legitimate mediums for music therapy. Music therapists using such approaches would be remiss not to draw on research and best practices from music education. Furthermore, celebrating music-learning as a medium through which to facilitate therapeutic growth implies the possibility of such growth within educational settings as well, even as we respect professional and ethical boundaries between the fields. For example, my previous research (Mitchell, 2016) explored students' personal growth as parallel to their musical growth within music lessons.

Importantly, nothing in this discussion implies that music's affordances are automatically positive; the concept of paramusical phenomena demands that we consider all facets of music-making's context to understand its benefits, or its harm. In my clinical practice with adults and older adults, new clients frequently shared their reluctance to participate in music therapy—or any music-making in any context—because they had, as children in music classrooms, received and internalized an explicit or implicit message that they were unmusical. Educators play a crucial role in determining whether students develop musical identities (Lamont, 2017; Welch, 2017), and in turn, whether they ever participate in music again. More broadly, the music we create, whether in therapy or education, can portray and embody hierarchical, power-laden, and harmful relationship dynamics, or our music can embody community, reciprocity, respect, and care.

Music-centered music therapists propose that "as clients develop musically, they are . . . developing their core potentials" (Guerrero et al., 2016, p. 484), an idea likely to resonate for many music educators as well. As we validate the innate musical potential in every person, along with the relational nature of human development and of our musical medium, it follows that there is vast human relevance within the development of musical capacity, whether this takes place within therapy or education. In a society that undervalues artistic experience, and yet also recognizes access to such experience as a human right (United Nations Convention on the Rights of the Child, 1989), our work as music educators and music therapists is invaluable. As we embark on transdisciplinary collaboration with one another, grounded in a shared commitment to furthering access to musical-relational experience despite differences in our training and—sometimes—in our goals, we can in turn bring intentional and caring musical-relational engagement, and its potential affordances, to those we have the privilege of serving.

References

Abrams, B., & Webb, A. (2020, July 7). *Exploring the decolonization of music therapy education: An imaginative dialogue* [Conference presentation]. World Congress of Music Therapy.
Aigen, K. S. (2014). *The study of music therapy: Current issues and concepts*. Routledge.
Ansdell, G. (2014). *How music helps in music therapy and everyday life*. Ashgate.
Baines, S. (2013). Music therapy as an anti-oppressive practice. *Arts in Psychotherapy, 40*(1), 1–5. https://doi.org/10.1016/j.aip.2012.09.003
Bonde, L. O. (2019). Definitions of music therapy. In S. L. Jacobsen, I. N. Pedersen, & L. O. Bonde (Eds.), *A comprehensive guide to music therapy* (2nd ed., pp. 29–39). Jessica Kingsley.
Boyce-Tillman, J. (2009). The transformative qualities of a liminal space created by musicking. *Philosophy of Music Education Review, 17*(2), 184–202.
Bruscia, K. E. (2014). *Defining music therapy* (3rd ed.). Barcelona.
Bylica, K. (2020). Hearing my world: Negotiating borders, porosity, and relationality through cultural production in middle school music classes. *Music Education Research, 22*(3), 331–345. https://doi.org/10.1080/14613808.2020.1759519
Canadian Association of Music Therapists. (2022). *Code of Ethics* (Rev. ed.). CAMT.
Cross, I. (2012). Cognitive science and the cultural nature of music. *Topics in Cognitive Science, 4*(4), 668–677. https://doi.org/10.1111/j.1756-8765.2012.01216.x
Dissanayake, E. (2008). If music is the food of love, what about survival and reproductive success? *Musicae Scientiae, 12*(1 suppl), 169–195. https://doi.org/10.1177/1029864908012001081
Gergen, K. J. (2009). *Relational being*. Oxford University Press.
Guerrero, N., Marcus, D., & Turry, A. (2016). Poised in the creative now: Principles of Nordoff-Robbins music therapy. In J. Edwards (Ed.), *The Oxford handbook of music therapy* (pp. 482–493). Oxford University Press.

Hendricks, K. S. (2015). Music education, character development, and advocacy: The philosophy of Shinichi Suzuki. In P. L. Thomas, P. R. Carr, J. Gorlewksi, & B. Porfilio (Eds.), *Pedagogies of kindness and respect: On the lives and education of children* (pp. 171–184). Peter Lang.

Hendricks, K. S. (2018). *Compassionate music teaching*. Rowman & Littlefield.

Hess, J. (2015). Decolonizing music education: Moving beyond tokenism. *International Journal of Music Education*, 33(3), 336–347. https://doi.org/10.1177/0255761415581283

Hess, J. (2018). Troubling whiteness: Music education and the "messiness" of equity work. *International Journal of Music Education*, 36(2), 128–144. https://doi.org/10.1177/0255761417703781

Jones, C. (2020). The use of therapeutic music training to remediate cognitive impairment following an acquired brain injury: The theoretical basis and a case study. *Healthcare*, 8(3), Article 327. https://doi.org/10.3390/healthcare8030327

Lambert, M. J. (2013). The efficacy and effectiveness of psychotherapy. In M. J. Lambert (Ed.), *Handbook of psychotherapy and behavior change* (6th ed., pp. 169–218). John Wiley & Sons.

Lamont, A. (2017). Musical identity, interest, and involvement. In R. MacDonald, D. J. Hargreaves, & D. Miell (Eds.), *Handbook of musical identities* (pp. 176–196). Oxford University Press.

Lampropoulos, G. K. (2001). Common processes of change in psychotherapy and seven other social interactions. *British Journal of Guidance & Counselling*, 29(1), 21–33. https://doi.org/10.1080/03069880020019356

Laurila, K. (2021). Song as the catalyst that promotes envisioning ethical spaces. In L. Willingham (Ed.), *Community music at the boundaries* (pp. 260–273). Wilfrid Laurier University Press.

Maslow, A. H. (1970). *Motivation and personality* (2nd ed.). Harper & Row.

Mitchell, E. (2016). Therapeutic music education: An emerging model linking philosophies and experiences of music education with music therapy. *Canadian Journal of Music Therapy*, 22(1), 19–41.

Mitchell, E. (2021). Performing identities and performing relationships: Community music therapy and adolescent mental health. *Music Therapy Perspectives*, 39(2), 195–203. https://doi.org/10.1093/mtp/miab004

Mitchell, E., & Benedict, C. (2020). Lives in dialogue: Music therapy and music education. *European Journal of Philosophy in Arts Education*, 5(1), 33–67.

Motschnig-Pitrik, R., & Barrett-Lennard, G. (2010). Co-actualization: A new construct in understanding well-functioning relationships. *Journal of Humanistic Psychology*, 50(3), 374–398. https://doi.org/10.1177/0022167809348017

Norcross, J. C., & Wampold, B. E. (2011). Evidence-based therapy relationships: Research conclusions and clinical practices. In J. C. Norcross (Ed.), *Psychotherapy relationships that work: Evidence-based responsiveness* (pp. 423–430). Oxford University Press.

Nordoff, P., & Robbins, C. (2007). *Creative music therapy: A guide to fostering clinical musicianship* (2nd ed.). Barcelona.

Nordoff Robbins. (2016, October 21). *Mary and Antonia* [Video]. YouTube. https://www.youtube.com/watch?v=DSbpoFfqvm8

Ontario College of Teachers. (2021). *Ethical standards*. https://www.oct.ca/public/professional-standards/ethical-standards

Robb, C. (2006). *This changes everything: The relational revolution in psychology*. Farrar, Straus and Giroux.

Robertson, J. (2000). An educational model for music therapy: The case for a continuum. *British Journal of Music Therapy*, 14(1), 41–46. https://doi.org/10.1177%2F135945750001400105

Rogers, C. R. (1951). *Client-centered therapy: Its current practice, implications, and theory*. Houghton Mifflin.

Rogers, C. R. (1957). The necessary and sufficient conditions of therapeutic personality change. *Journal of Consulting Psychology*, 21(2), 95–103. https://doi.org/10.1037/h0045357

Small, C. (1998). *Musicking*. Wesleyan University Press.

Smith, J. C. (2018). Hidden in plain sight: A music therapist and music educator in a public school district. *International Journal of Music Education*, 36(2), 182–196. https://doi.org/10.1177/0255761417712319

Stevenson, A. (Ed.). (2015a). Therapy. In *Oxford dictionary of English* (3rd ed.). Oxford University Press. https://doi.org/10.1093/acref/9780199571123.001.0001

Stevenson, A. (Ed.). (2015b). Therapeutic. In *Oxford dictionary of English* (3rd ed.). Oxford University Press. https://doi.org/10.1093/acref/9780199571123.001.0001

Stige, B. (2010). Music and health in community. In B. Stige, G. Ansdell, C. Elefant, & M. Pavlicevic (Eds.), *Where music helps: Community music therapy in action and reflection* (pp. 3–16). Ashgate.

Stige, B., Ansdell, G., Elefant, C., & Pavlicevic, M. (2010). When things take shape in relation to music: Towards an ecological perspective on music's help. In B. Stige, G. Ansdell, C. Elefant, & M. Pavlicevic (Eds.), *Where music helps: Community music therapy in action and reflection* (pp. 277–308). Ashgate.

Stige, B., & Aarø, L. E. (2012). *Invitation to community music therapy*. Routledge.

Tyson, F. (1982). Individual singing instruction: An evolutionary framework for psychiatric music therapists. *Music Therapy Perspectives*, 1(1), 5–15. https://doi.org/10.1093/mtp/1.1.5

United Nations Convention on the Rights of the Child. (1989, November 20). https://www.ohchr.org/en/instruments-mechanisms/instruments/convention-rights-child

Welch, G. F. (2017). The identities of singers and their educational environments. In R. Macdonald, D. Miell, & D. Hargreaves (Eds.), *Handbook of musical identities* (pp. 543565). Oxford University Press.

Wood, S. (2016). *A matrix for community music therapy practice*. Barcelona Publishers.

Wood, S., & Ansdell, G. (2018). Community music and music therapy: Jointly and severally. In B.-L. Bartleet & L. Higgins (Eds.), *The Oxford handbook of community music* (pp. 453–476). Oxford University Press.

CHAPTER 31

MUSIC AS A VEHICLE FOR CARING FOR STUDENTS WITH LEARNING DIFFERENCES

RYAN M. HOURIGAN

CARE HANDBOOK TOPICS

Identity expressions
Social activism and critical consciousness
Wellbeing and human flourishing

INCLUSION of students with exceptionalities has evolved as part of the framework for a fundamental education for decades. Some learning communities fully embrace inclusive practices while others are still developing. The term "inclusive excellence" has been embraced and adopted by many communities to describe the inclusion of all marginalized groups within a given society. However, for the purposes of this chapter, I will examine inclusion practices that encourage the acceptance and access for those with learning differences. With that said, the music classroom can serve as a model for sensitivity, empathy, caring, and socially supportive practice. This chapter will include how the essence of care should be applied to the music-learning community for differently abled members and those with learning differences in order to provide a safe and caring learning environment.

The aim of this chapter is to provide strategies to care and support for differently abled students in music education from all stakeholders. The framework provided at the end of the chapter will be couched in emerging disability studies that advocate for treating individuals not as people with special needs but people who should be celebrated as part of a diverse and vibrant culture. Examples of successful practices will be included along with policy suggestions for music programs along with teacher stories and vignettes to provide context. The names of the real-life story contributors will remain anonymous due to the nature of the vignettes provided and the privacy of the students who are mentioned.

A Brief Historical Context

Much has been written on the foundations of inclusion. For the purposes of this chapter, I will examine why the concept of caring can be challenging when societal change is at hand. The foundation of including differently abled students into public school (free/non-private) settings started with concern and empathy by education experts and advocates for the desegregation of certain populations including those with exceptionalities. Up until 1975, many states denied students an equal chance at a free and appropriate education (Martin et al., 1996).

It was not until the civil rights movement that advocates for children with disabilities began to seek federal protection for students resulting in the Individuals with Disabilities Education Act of 1975.[1] I was three years old at this time. I was right in the middle of the implementation of this law. In reflecting on my own biases, I remember that none of "those students" were in a single class with me in public school. There was a school near my elementary school that was a segregated place for students with learning differences. I remember as a child that the playground equipment at that school was much nicer than that of our "regular" school. However, because we were not ever together with students of different abilities, as children, we made judgments and assumptions about the students who attended the school such as that the students in that school "weird" or "strange." Looking back, I often think about what would have happened if the students at this school were integrated into our classrooms and our teachers taught more about caring for all students in our community. The school was literally across the street. This would have been easily accomplished.

Just like with the implementation of the Civic Rights Act of 1960, many communities, educators and lawmakers were opposed to Public Law 94-142. To this day, the quality of education, services, access to the arts, and poverty are directly related to each other (Whelchel, 2010). In fact, often school district, in order to save money, centralize special education efforts (Kerr, 2015). It is not uncommon for students with exceptionalities to attend schools that are outside of their own neighborhood. In fact, it is also not uncommon for the same students to attend a school in a different town or community altogether, further segregating them from society. This is much like what happened during the bussing era of the civil rights movement in the United States.

---

[1] Similar legislation has been passed in other countries such as the Special Educational Needs and Disability Act in the United Kingdom.

> **BOX 31.1 Adam: An example of Segregation for a Student with Exceptionalities**
>
> *Adam is challenged with cognitive disabilities and autism. He has now "graduated" high school and is attempting to enter community living. When he began his public education in 2006 in our current community, No Child left Behind legislation required that all schools meet a standard called "Adequate Yearly Progress." Therefore, anytime a school in our community did not score well on an annual standardized test, the students with exceptionalities were moved to a different school in order to help raise test scores. Adam, in his 16 years in the community, attended seven different schools. For a student who already struggles with being accepted, this was a challenge and affected his mental health. To this day, Adam has a very hard time with change. He never had the opportunity to make lasting connections to his peers, who in turn, did not learn to have empathy for him. This cycle manifests itself over and over in our community.*
>
> Parent somewhere in the Midwestern United States

This issue raises the following questions: How do educators celebrate neurological and physical diversity when segregation is still an underlying practice? How should educators embrace federal law without teaching caring and empathy from lawmakers all the way to students in the classroom?

INCLUSIVE EDUCATION AND CARING: A PHILOSOPHICAL PERSPECTIVE

For the purposes of clarity in this chapter, it is important to offer some definitions. Empathy refers to identification of the thoughts and feelings of another person (Hendricks, 2018). Caring is acting to affect changed based on empathy (Noddings, 2013). To be socially supportive is to be part of a network to turn to when needing help.

One other aspect that should be examined when applying these principles is what some qualitative researchers describe as the epoche. The epoche is when a person comes to grips with their own biases (Patton, 2002). As teachers, recognizing and reflecting on our own biases will help us navigate our musical and instructional decisions.

Before music educators examine caring regarding inclusion practice, we must examine caring as it relates to persons with exceptionalities. Nel Noddings (2013) describes that caring for living things (in this case, our music students with learning differences) requires a larger investment from ourselves. She states, "When my caring is directed at living things, I must consider their natures, ways of life, needs, and desires" (p. 14). In other words, what are the needs and desires of students who are included in music programs? How does their way of life (e.g., family dynamic, school day, activities, and therapies outside of class, etc.) affect their ability to participate in and make music? This

> **BOX 31.2 Adam: An example of Segregation for a Student with Exceptionalities (continued)**
>
> *Adam is challenged with cognitive disabilities and autism. He has now "graduated" high school and is attempting to enter community living. When he began his public education in 2006 in our current community, No Child Left Behind legislation required that all school meet a standard called "Adequate Yearly Progress." Therefore, anytime a school in our community did not score well on an annual standardized test, the students with exceptionalities were moved to a different school in order to help raise test scores. Adam, in his 16 years in the community, attended seven different schools. For a student who already struggles with being accepted, this was a challenge and affected his mental health. To this day, Adam has a very hard time with change. He never had the opportunity to make lasting connections to his peers, who in turn, did not learn to have empathy for him. This cycle manifests itself over and over in our community.*
>
> Parent somewhere in the Midwestern United States

is truly the essence and the beginning of not only caring but celebrating diverse learning needs in our music classrooms.

Nature and Ways of Life

In order to examine the "natures and ways of life" of another person, especially those who face challenges, the family dynamic must also be included in the discussion (Hourigan, 2018). To have true empathy for a person with exceptionalities and to provide them with true access to music, a socially supportive network is a part of how we show that we care. Just merely providing access in the classroom may not be enough. For example, many students with exceptionalities may not participate in the arts because of financial, geographical (e.g., transportation to an event), medical (e.g., medication) needs, or other challenges related to their condition. Often public schools use non-core-academic time (e.g., music, physical education, visual art) as a time to pull a student out for services (e.g., speech therapy). Family members may work and are not able to attend meetings to advocate for their child. Furthermore, there might be a family dynamic where a student is in charge of or caring for a sibling and cannot participate (Hourigan, 2018). If we as music educators truly care about all our students, the family dynamics must also be considered. Concrete strategies will be provided under the suggested framework below.

Needs and Desires Through Self-Determination

Let us examine the next part of Nel Noddings's description of caring for living things, "needs and desires." In the disabilities literature, a term emerged in the 1990s to describe the ability of a person to control their own destiny and advocate for themselves. "Self-determination" is defined as "determination of one's fate or course of action without compulsion" (Wehmeyer, 2005, p. 114). Deci and Ryan (2008) have been developing and revising this theory since 1975. They state: "The theory focuses on types, rather than just amount, of motivation, paying particular attention to autonomous motivation, controlled motivation, and amotivation as predictors of performance, relational, and well-being outcomes" (p. 182). The three main areas of self-determination are autonomy, competence, and relatedness. The more these basic psychological needs are met, the more motivated a person will become (Hendricks & McPherson, this volume).

Often music educators do not consider the needs and desires of an individual who has difficulty advocating for themselves. However, as a person matures in both cognition and communication, music teachers should continue to circle back and attempt to provide opportunity all the way into adulthood. Yes, there are challenges with self-determination with certain students. For example, a student who has communication obstacles cannot always advocate for themselves. The idea is that we should make our best effort, even in small steps, to provide this type of agency for our students.

Encouraging Self-Identity as Part of Caring

As all people become self-determined, they also begin to become self-aware and start to make choices about what makes them who they are. Identity development without compulsion is an important part of caring for a person with exceptionalities. How a student may present themselves may be much different than other students. They may have unique interests or forms of expression. This individuality should be celebrated at all levels as part of our society.

Recently, this topic has become part of the discussion when working with college-aged students (Fink, 2021). For years people have been encouraged to use person-first language when referring to a person with exceptionalities. In other words, "person with autism" rather than "autistic person." This has been a worldwide practice. Recently, however, feedback from the disability community has forced the discussion about disability as part of one's identity (Baker, this volume). The next vignette is from a university college professor who was faced with this challenge.

Student Safety as a Necessary Component of Caring

Much has been examined around harassment and bullying among school-aged children. Full inclusion requires educators to embrace the idea that all students can be both victims and aggressors of behavior and other practices that contribute to either a safe

BOX 31.3 Teacher Story Centered Around Self-Determination and Children with Disabilities

I introduce the ukulele in my 5th grade general music classes. Two students with visual impairment that included no functional vision attended one of my 5th grade classes this past school year. During the day, these students received paraprofessional support, but not during specials (music, visual art, and physical education). Knowing that these students were about to begin the ukulele without assistance, I purchased two adaptive tools for the ukuleles in the event that these students struggled with finger position. These tools attached to the ukulele at the nut of the fretboard and had single buttons for the students to press to form a chord. As we began, I guided these students on where to place their finger(s) for each chord and how to strum with the other hand using hand over hand guidance. Once my 5th graders were playing more than one chord, I could tell that my students with visual impairment were determined to play the ukulele without additional support. As soon as ukuleles were passed out to the students during each music class, they immediately began to familiarize themselves with the layout of the instrument (distance between frets, location of the four strings, and which part of the instrument to strum) by moving their hands and fingers over the instrument. They would lean close to the fretboard to better hear their sounds, and they would adjust their fingers if the sound wasn't correct. Chord changes became easier, and they seemed to enjoy making music on their ukuleles. If we had any down time in which the class as a whole was not playing their ukuleles, these students would immediately practice on their ukuleles so they could better hear their chords and practice chord changes. While I had the adaptive tools to make playing the ukulele chords easier, I didn't want to get in the way of what these students were capable of doing on their own.

Elementary General Music Specialist in the Southeast United States

BOX 31.4 Anna: An Example of Identity Preference

I teach a portion of a methods class for junior music majors on teaching music to students with special needs. It has long been a practice of using person-first language when to referring to students with exceptionalities. This past semester we were discussing this practice. One of my students, Anna, who presents herself as being autistic, was not happy with the idea of person-first language. In fact, she preferred that her disability be part of her identity. This was surprising to me in that it has always been assumed that people with exceptionalities did not want to be known by their diagnosis or label. I have since learned that it is may be appropriate to ask the person for their preference, similar to when individuals declare their pronoun preference. This will be part of my practice moving forward.

Music Education Faculty Member at a Midwest United States University

or unsafe school environment (Rose & Gage, 2017). Students with exceptionalities are more likely to experience bullying and victimization than other students. Because of this, students with disabilities may lack a sense of safety while at school. Rawlings (this volume) states, "Perhaps more than any other school safety concern, bullying affects students' sense of security" (p. 1). Rose and Gage (2017) report that although students with certain types of disabilities can also have a higher rate of perpetration of such bullying when isolated, research shows the students with exceptionalities experience a much higher rate of victimization over time.

What can we do as music educators to curb victimization among those students who have learning differences? The one advantage we have as compared to teachers of other subjects is that we tend to teach our music students for multiple years. Prolonged engagement allows us to forge a deeper relationship with our students. It may also permit us to establish a safe place for a student to report such acts and also allow us to look for a change in behavior of the victim. Most important, the act of harassment or bullying should be something that is talked about and explored in our classes. The good news is that music can provide a vehicle for such discussions. For example, Jay Thomas, a middle school choral music teacher, wrote a series of anti-bullying choral music. One particular piece, "It Shouldn't Bother Me," was written about a 7th-grade student who committed suicide. Thomas writes in his composer notes:

> I began writing the lyrics of this song about three months after the tragic death by suicide of a seventh grader at our middle school. It was learned after her passing that she had been the target of relentless cyber-bullying. It was my wish to create a choral piece that addressed bullying issues faced by both perpetrator and victim with the hopes of helping to foster some understanding of what had happened. (Charter for Compassion, n.d.)

As the above quote suggests, such compositions can provide a safe space for exploring such topics. Because most music educators are usually not trained counselors, including a school counselor is highly recommended to ensure that the appropriate expertise is used when unpacking and discussing such sensitive subjects.

Conclusion: A Suggested Framework for Inclusive Caring

Below, I suggest a basic framework to improve the quality of caring among all music students. This is by no means a rigid set of ideas that are not malleable. Instead, it is a broader set of ideas to frame the learning environment in the music classroom.

Step One: Coming to Terms with Our Own Biases

Research has suggested that bias is related to System 1 associations in the brain. System 1 of the brain processes reactions to stimuli that are automatic and unconscious. Reactions may include incomplete information and circumstances that compromise our cognitive control (Staats, 2016). Therefore, when music teachers make a judgement about a student, family, colleague, or administrator, we must be reminded of the characteristics of implicit bias that might not be intentional and based on accumulated unconscious data. For example, research has shown that attitudes toward certain groups can affect disciplinary decisions unconsciously (Staats, 2016). We tend to label confident behaviors as "aggressive," "disruptive," or "disrespectful" from one group of students (e.g., female students) and not other groups. This could also be true for those students who have behavioral disorders as a comorbid diagnosis. For example, many students who are on the autism spectrum have difficulty with managing behavior. Identifying behaviors as "bad" or "disruptive" can be a detriment to their self-esteem.

As mentioned earlier in the article, self-reflecting on these decisions is a must. Leaning on colleagues that come from different backgrounds or have a different perspective can be helpful. Parents can also assist in understanding the intent of a student. Music teachers might again think about Nel Noddings (2013) and her quote, "When my caring is directed at living things, I must consider their natures, ways of life, needs, and desires" (p. 14). Thinking about our own disposition as teachers through this lens can allow us to strengthen relationships with our students by identifying preconceptions and shelving them in order to focus on the needs and desires of the students. The goal is to help ensure equitable treatment of all students who are in our care.

Step Two: Exploring and Understanding Family and Support System Perspectives

The family dynamic and support structure around a student is important, especially the deeper a student is involved with music. Whether it is arranging a ride to practice or understanding ways to communicate our goals as a teacher to caregivers, encouraging a supportive network is crucial to the success of our students. When a students' support structure weakens, they become less likely to continue to participate in the arts (Hourigan, 2018). This is especially true for those who face learning differences.

A simple questionnaire sent home either on paper or electronically may assist music teachers in providing a caring structure for all of their students. For example, a music teacher could ask questions such as "Are there any transportation challenges that we assist with?" or "Do you have other children involved in other activities that we should know about?" The survey could be voluntary; the aim is to gain some perspective on the lived experiences of the students in your classroom.

After collecting the information that the teachers need, where appropriate, the teachers can initiate conversations with other stakeholders such as other teachers, parent groups (e.g., booster/volunteer groups) and student leadership to attempt to do their best to solve the challenges that students face. Anonymity may be appropriate in certain circumstances. The aim is to not let finances, transportation, overstretched parents, disability, or other non-musical challenges affect a students' ability to access a music education. Stakeholders may not know that such challenges exist. Solutions may be a simple as a ride share plan or an emergency fund provided by fundraising organizations.

Step Three: Teaching Empathy and Emotion as Part of the Curriculum

Music allows for the exploration of empathy through multiple pre-planned conduits. Whether it is a theme, lyrics, or tonality, music provides us with many vehicles to include empathy as part of the music curriculum. Teaching students about their emotions is a close cousin of empathy (Egermann and McAdams, 2013). Research has shown that merely listening to music can help us ignite, recognize, and predict our emotions (p. 142). By recognizing our own emotions, it is hoped that students will learn to care about the emotions of their peers. One could assume that performing music includes listening and therefore performing music can also provide the same context for understanding our emotions and feeling empathy.

At the macro level, music should be a part of a standard curriculum for all students. Where else can students learn about emotion and feeling? This includes the connections students make with each other through making music together. At the micro level, music educators can ensure that exploring the emotional content and empathy be central to music education at all levels. This exploration includes students who may have learning differences. As Reimer (2003) stated: "Creating music as musicians, and listening to music creatively, do precisely and exactly for feeling what writing and reading do for reasoning" (p. 93).

Step Four Celebrating Identity Through Self-Determination

As examined above, it is important for all students to have a path to mold their own identity. Some students with learning differences have unique interests, ideas, behaviors, figures of speech, or other personality traits that may be different than their peers. Curbing these traits can lead to issues with self-esteem and a student's sense of belonging to the music-learning community. In addition, students with communication disorders may be drowned out from their peers when attempting to express themselves (e.g., answering questions, sharing experiences, etc.). It will be helpful to give these students as much agency to participate as possible. It is also important for the teacher to be open to the many ways of learning and demonstrating understanding and a student's choice should be valued. For example, providing questions that might be asked in class in-advance for the student to consider and pre-planning a chance for the student to respond in front of their peers.

It is important to allow all students into the learning environment methodically. For example, when asking questions or sharing experiences, it might be helpful to keep track of what students have not contributed. If they are anxious or unable to share in front of a class, teachers might provide another pathway such as writing or to share at another time. This approach may feel more welcoming and safe to students, as addressed below.

Step Five: Safety

As mentioned above, students with exceptionalities are more likely than their peers to face bullying and other forms of violence at school. Limiting the opportunity for such incidents is important. For example, unsupervised hallways and locker rooms are fertile ground for violent activity. In addition, students might be encouraged to report things that they see in confidence for their own safety. Social emotional learning is also an important consideration (Edgar et al., this volume).

It is hoped that this chapter provided the necessary first steps in including caring strategies for students with learning differences. It is important for music educators to take risks when implementing strategies (Hendricks, 2018). Trying is also caring.

References

Charter for Compassion. (n.d.). *Music as healer for bullying and changing the world*. Retrieved June 23, 2021, from https://charterforcompassion.org/introduction-to-the-third-edition-the-performing-arts-as-educator-and-healer/music-as-healer-for-bullying-and-changing-the-world

Deci, E. L., & Ryan, R. M. (2008). Self-determination theory: A macrotheory of human motivation, development, and health. *Canadian Psychology/Psychologie Canadienne, 49*(3), 182–185. https://doi.org/10.1037/a0012801

Egermann, H., & McAdams, S. (2013). Empathy and emotional contagion as a link between recognized and felt emotions in music listening. *Music Perception: An Interdisciplinary Journal, 31*(2), 139–156. https://doi.org/10.1525/mp.2013.31.2.139

Flink, P. (2021). Person-first & identity-first language: Supporting students with disabilities on campus. *Community College Journal of Research and Practice, 45*(2), 79–85. https://doi.org/10.1080/10668926.2019.1640147

Hourigan, R. M. (2018). Family perspectives on access to arts education for students with disabilities. In J. B. Crockett & S. M. Malley (Eds.), *Handbook of arts education and special education: Policy, research, and practices* (pp. 267–277). Routledge.

Hendricks, K. S. (2018). *Compassionate music teaching*. Rowman & Littlefield.

Kerr, K. (2015). *Why is our public school trying to get rid of my child?* GreatSchools.org. Retrieved May 27, 2021, from https://www.greatschools.org/gk/articles/why-is-our-public-school-trying-to-get-rid-of-my-child

Martin, E. W., Martin, R., & Terman, D. (1996). The legislative and litigation history of special education. *The Future of Children, 6*(1), 25–39. https://doi.org/10.2307/1602492

Noddings, N. (2013). *Caring: A relational approach to ethics and moral education*. University of California Press.

Patton, M. Q. (2002). *Qualitative research and evaluation methods* (2nd ed.). Sage Publications.

Reimer, B. (2003). *A philosophy of music education: Advancing the vision*. Prentice Hall.

Rose, C. A., & Gage, N. A. (2017). Exploring the involvement of bullying among students with disabilities over time. *Exceptional Children, 83*(3), 298–314. https://doi.org/10.1177%2F0014402916667587

Sautner, B. S. (2008). Inclusive, safe and caring schools: Connecting factors. *Developmental Disabilities Bulletin, 36*(1/2), 135–167.

Staats, C. (2016). Understanding implicit bias: What educators should know. *American Educator, 4*, 29–43.

Straus, J. (2016). Autism and postwar serialism as neurodiverse forms of cultural modernism. In B. Howe, S. Jensen-Moulton, N. Lerner, & J. Straus (Eds.), *The Oxford handbook of music and disability studies*. Oxford University Press.

Wehmeyer, M. L. (2005). Self-determination and individuals with severe disabilities: Re-examining meanings and misinterpretations. *Research and Practice for Persons with Severe Disabilities, 30*(3), 113–120. https://doi.org/10.2511%2Frpsd.30.3.113

Whelchel, R. (2010). What's in a name? Minority access to precollege art education. *Arts Education Policy Review, 102*(1), 32–36.

CHAPTER 32

TRAUMA

A Compassionate Lens for Music Teaching

SHANNAN HIBBARD AND ERIN PRICE

CARE HANDBOOK TOPICS

Wellbeing and human flourishing

RATIONALE

Music teachers routinely encounter unexpected reactions from students in the music classroom. Although preservice teachers are provided with special education content in their coursework, many teachers report feeling ill-prepared to navigate relationships with students whose behavior may fall outside expected "norms" (Colwell & Thompson, 2000). A history of trauma might yield behavior that is a threat to student safety or is disruptive to instruction and requires specialized strategies. However, when equipped with special education strategies alone, music teachers may continue to struggle to create conditions where students are empowered in the music classroom, in part due to difficulties in discerning between children with trauma histories and those with other behavior diagnoses. The *Diagnostical and Statistical Manual* (DSM-5) does not include criteria for developmental trauma disorder caused by chronic abuse and neglect (van der Kolk, 2014). As a result, it is likely that many children who have experienced traumas in their lives have been misdiagnosed with a behavioral disorder. The fixation on the difficult behaviors arising from this misdiagnosis might impede teachers in the process of helping students transcend their trauma.

In this chapter, we draw on trauma literature to describe trauma's potential to impact the lives of students and their experiences in school. We describe how teachers' perceptions of students' trauma responses and even misguided attempts to "help" can lead to power struggles, unjust treatment, and marginalization. Through a universal approach of understanding trauma as a lens to end harm rather than a label, we explore ways that music teachers may work toward compassionate, healing environments with the potential to empower students.

Trauma Literature: "What Happened to You?"

I slump forward in my desk chair, my head in my hands. It's only lunchtime and I feel like a complete failure. Jamie, a student in whom I have been investing a lot of energy, had another blow-up in class this morning. Despite my efforts to put boundaries in place with a behavior chart, consequences, phone calls home, and an assigned seat in the front of the general music class, his explosive behavior always seems to come out of nowhere. And this time, he ran. Thankfully the assistant principal was in the hall to help diffuse the situation, but it only worsens my feelings of shame and incompetence.

I don't know how I can face Jamie again with a smile. As I go above and beyond to fix it, his outbursts and disruptive behavior only heighten. My frustration is at its peak, and even worse, I feel resentful and angry toward him—a child just seven years old. I sigh a breath of hopelessness. I just don't know what to do anymore.

Traumatic events or prolonged trauma include environments or events that are life-threatening, stressful, or dangerous, and can be experienced individually or collectively. Although not all individuals develop a trauma response from encountering stressful events, the impact of trauma "can be intense, pervasive, and disruptive, affecting both the mind and body" (Venet, 2021, p. 6). Myriad trauma reactions occur outside of the small number examined in the diagnosis of PTSD (Scaer, 2005) and teachers must be prepared to respond to these reactions. Trauma reactions manifest as visceral emotional responses, and are triggered by unique stimuli (Briere & Scott, 2006) that activate memories associated with current interactions, physical space, or activities with previous traumatic events (Craig, 2008). Practices rooted in trauma-informed care (The Institute on Trauma and Trauma-Informed Care, 2021) can be successfully used in the music classroom to increase student feelings of safety and belongingness.

Student Considerations

Jamie enters the general music room in line with his second-grade classmates. Teasing and conversations that began in the hallway get louder and more animated as students transition to their assigned seats in the front of the whiteboard. Jamie finds his spot right in front, just to the left of where his music teacher will eventually sit. He much preferred his old spot at the back and hates to sit here. He fidgets with his pant legs, crossing and uncrossing his legs. He nervously looks behind him and around the room.

As the music teacher tries to gain the attention of the students and quiet the room, a student playfully fiddles with a djembe in the corner, causing it to tip over. The drum falls into a shelf of hand percussion instruments, sending triangles and cymbals crashing. A half dozen cylindrical wood blocks roll in various directions across the floor. The intense sound of the mishap is met with the roar of giggles and shouts, several students rocking on their backs in response. The teacher raises her voice in exasperation, and several students scramble across the floor to help gather instruments. As Jamie's heart races in response to the chaos, the teacher's angry glare meets his eyes from above. In less than a second, he crawls up and toward the door, pushing students and kicking woodblocks from his path. He is gone from sight.

In trauma-informed care, thinking is switched from "what is wrong with you" to "what has happened to you" (Farragher & Yanosy, 2005, p. 5). This approach is used on a universal level recognizing that any individual within the community might have a history of trauma. Often, teachers may not be aware of student trauma due to unreported abuse histories owing to lack of victim memory (Loftus et al., 1994); lengthy periods between traumatic events and symptom onset (Pitman, 1989); and delayed disclosure due to shame, coercion, or lack or resources (Frattaroli, 2006). Importantly, teachers might not be able to identify students needing supports for trauma responses because trauma impacts individuals at varying levels. Variables including environment, support system, duration, recurrence, and relationship to the perpetrator can impact the severity of the trauma response (Scaer, 2005). Not all children who encounter traumatic events will be traumatized.

Trauma responses are varied in their presentation and impact on student functioning. Some students might experience hyperarousal, where emotional baselines are heightened and environments are perceived as threatening (Jennings, 2019). This state serves to prepare the student to physically respond to perceived threats (Levine, 1997). In this state, attention is shifted from the rehearsal, lecture, or performance at hand, and devoted solely to the threat, preventing students from attending to information intended to improve social skills (see Herman, 1997) or musical tasks (Swart, 2013; Swart & van Niekerk, 2010). Due to permanently elevated stress hormones (Pitman, 1989), students "feel chronically unsafe inside their bodies" (van der Kolk, 2014, p. 98), which is a barrier to student feelings of safety in the music classroom. Increased sensitivity impairs perception of and responses to changing stimulation (Levine, 1997). Students experiencing hyperarousal might display hypersensitivity to minor boundary violations, exaggerated startle responses, a need for routine (Levine, 1997) or impaired perceptions of safety (Briere & Scott, 2006).

Exposure to traumatic events can shape brain development (Scaer, 2005) yielding deficits in attention, memory, reasoning, language development, planning (Jennings,

2019), and impulse control (Herman & van der Kolk, 1987). As students struggle with self-regulation, aggressive, explosive, or withdrawn behaviors may lead to behavioral support needs (Cloitre et al., 2009). Students exposed to trauma (particularly physical abuse) struggle with hostile attributional bias, where benign interactions are often misinterpreted as hostile (Pollak et al., 2000), increasing the likelihood of aggressive or fleeing responses. Being in a position of power, the teacher can be perceived as dangerous to the student (Briere & Scott, 2006). The constant surveying of adult moods, a behavior students may have developed as a necessary survival mechanism in the face of trauma, might supersede learning and relationship building (Herman, 1997). For students with trauma histories, facial expressions or benign images may generate fear or reactivity (van der Kolk, 2014), further exacerbated by impairments to facial signal recognition (Fries & Pollak, 2004). Coupled with a distorted self-view in children with trauma histories (D'Andrea et al., 2012), these impairments to perceptions of safety may contribute to unsafe responses and damage student/teacher relationships.

Teacher Considerations

I dart after Jamie, leaving the rest of the class unattended. He runs past the gym corridor, turning down a long hall that ends in an emergency exit. "Please, not the exit door today," I plead in my thoughts. Ten paces behind him, I round the corner to find the assistant principal standing in front of the exit door, one hand on the shoulder of a sweating, panicked Jamie. Relieved yet still furious and winded, I lay into Jamie, expressing anger and frustration with the choice he has made. Doesn't he understand that his choices affect his peers—who are now in the room alone? Why would he run like this, especially after we've discussed how unsafe this behavior is? What was he thinking? He looks at the floor in silence.

For teachers, unsafe behavior can be triggering. Although engaging in difficult behaviors is beyond the students' control, feelings of music teacher frustration and inadequacy (Hammel, 2001) and personalization of difficult behaviors may impair teacher openness. Students might engage in testing behaviors and boundary violations to evaluate reliability of the teacher or recreate traumatic relationships (Craig, 1992; Stewart & Stewart, 2002). These moments might trigger teachers with personal trauma histories (Alisic, 2012; Jennings, 2019; Smith, 2021) or ignite the teacher's stress response. Jennings (2019) noticed that when teachers' stress response was triggered, they were likely to abandon strategies and engage in punitive behavior. This generates a cyclical effect within the teacher–student relationship.

Teachers who can adequately de-escalate themselves in the face of triggering stimuli can be powerful partners for students with trauma histories. Additionally, teachers can extend emotional support to students after traumatic experiences (Alisic et al., 2012). Being attuned to the needs of students (Siegel, 2003), responding positively (Cummings et al., 2017), patiently, and flexibly (Farragher & Yanosy, 2005) while focusing on building relationships are all viable strategies for teachers.

Shifting the Lens: "What Is Right with You?"

The potential for traumatic experiences to impact students' lives can be an overwhelming consideration for educators. Nearly half of all school-aged children encounter traumatic events (Bethell et al., 2017), which can negatively impact learning and behavior (Shonkoff et al., 2012). Students' experiences are usually hidden or unknown, and trauma responses are often misinterpreted by teachers as "bad behavior," with blame placed on children themselves. Isolation, exclusion, and other humiliating responses to student "misbehavior" are viewed as inevitable means of control over students within the expectation of good classroom management (Shalaby, 2017). In response to unexpected behaviors, "we turn a gaze of pathology on children," (Shalaby, 2017, p. xxvii) as early as preschool, with widely accepted discipline (mal)practices firmly rooted in the school-to-prison pipeline (Love, 2019; Shalaby, 2017). In this way children who have faced some of the greatest hardships can become our schools' greatest "problems."

Challenging Deficit and Salvation Narratives

As music educators consider the pervasiveness of trauma and are made privy to specific instances of hardship in the lives of our students, we are charged with considering more compassionate responses that may disrupt cycles of harm. But the desire to "help" can inform a deficit view of students, bringing to the forefront all they are lacking (Dutro, 2019; Venet, 2021). This misguided view of compassion is also characterized by pity, or a looking down to lift others from above (Hendricks, 2018, p. 3). The unequal footing of pity combined with deficit beliefs can contribute to a savior mentality, which impedes our ability to see students beyond their trauma (Ginwright, 2015; Venet, 2021). Narratives of salvation, while appealing to teachers' desire to help, are also implicated in the need to possess and control power (Hendricks, 2018, p. 4; 2021; Vaugeois, 2007, p. 166). Yet the power of a teacher can trigger fear, aggression, withdrawal, and signal danger in students with trauma histories, and can activate protective survival mechanisms (Briere & Scott, 2006; Pollak et al., 2000; van der Kolk, 2014). Put another way, if an educator's effort to respond to trauma is rooted in the desire to control power or "save" students, it is likely that students' trauma responses will continue, thus perpetuating the cycle of harm.

Considerations of Justice—Trauma as a Lens

Deficit narratives place blame on children, families, communities, and their perceived cultures for trauma and hardship rather than the systems of racism, sexism, homophobia, and poverty that are often the source. Further, "it is far too easy for attention to trauma to be wrapped in already existing assumptions of some children's lives as traumatized" while the baked-in assumptions of the educational system privilege "White, economically secure, heterosexual, English-speaking ways of being" as normal and ideal (Dutro, 2019, p. 34). Thus, our questions of trauma cannot be separated from considerations of justice (Ginwright, 2015; Love, 2019; Venet, 2021; Zembylas, 2020). The identification of "trauma children" is a harmful process that creates further marginalization, thus there is no need to parse out students with trauma histories or be a "trauma detective" (Venet, 2021). As a constant and insidious background noise in society, trauma has the potential to affect the lives of all (Brown, 1995; Zembylas, 2020), therefore approaches that consider trauma can benefit all. From this consideration "trauma" becomes a lens through which teachers may consider their practice rather than a label to place on individuals (Venet, 2021).

As a lens, "trauma" invites educators to seek compassionate approaches for all students while recognizing and ending harm in classrooms. Seeing through a lens of trauma invites educators to consider how harm occurs both inside and outside schools, urging us to also work toward just and equitable solutions to oppression in schools and society (Venet, 2021). This lens also invites educators to open awareness to the strengths, beauties, and joys of students and their cultures and communities (Ginwright, 2015; Love, 2019; Shalaby, 2017). This lens moves the question of trauma histories from "what happened to you?" to "what is right with you?" (Ginwright, 2015).

Relational Work

After sleeping on it, I recognize Jamie needs a new approach. His behavior seems out of both of our control, and his palpable shame isn't motivating him to change. I ask for a meeting with him at lunch, a time I usually observe him smiling and laughing with friends. It is a time when I am also at ease. Head and eyes to the floor, he enters the music room, taking quick, tentative glances up at me. I ask where he would like to sit. After a long silence, he points to the two cozy chairs in the corner. There our eyes can meet on a level plane, but Jamie eyes a puppet I use for Kindergarten classes. As I offer him the stuffed dog, I ask him if he has any pets. He perks up as he snuggles the puppet, sharing the details of his family cat, one his Mom began feeding as a stray. I feel surprised by his expressions of compassion.

Suddenly and with urgency, I interject an apology for what happened in the music room—the loud accident, my yelling, and the way I interrogated him. "I was angry and frustrated," I said, "but I shouldn't have acted like that. I bet you must have felt really awful." Jamie silently nodded at me, his countenance more curious, but still reluctant. I explain that I called him in so we could discuss strategies together that might help him have a better experience in music class. I express concern that he is missing out on music-making. Without blame, I also express concern for his safety. "I'm worried about you, Jamie—what can I do to help?" He returns the question with a shrug. "Would you like some suggestions?" I ask. After a long pause, he meets my eyes and nods. "Well, let's start with your seat—do you feel you can do your best work there?" He furrows his brow and shakes his head. "I want a new spot."

As we talk through several more strategies and changes to allow Jamie a better experience in music class, I feel him softening. He doesn't offer many solutions but provides clear opinions when I give him suggestions. He appears more relaxed than I've ever seen, and even though he is still very quiet, I feel good about the way I am able to speak with him. I am taking lessons from this peaceful moment that I hope will shape our class. I am hopeful.

In order to see students beyond their difficult histories or challenging trauma responses, teachers must create the conditions in which we may work in a relationship with them. Pedagogies that are considered healing, reparative, or buffering to trauma require reciprocity and mutuality (Dutro, 2019; Ginwright, 2015; Hibbard, 2021; Love, 2019; Venet, 2021; Zembylas, 2020). Mutuality can be experienced in moments of connection through teacher, student, and music (Hibbard, 2017), with the health of each member of the triad symbiotically connected (Hawkins, 1974; Stieha & Raider-Roth, 2012). For example, if a teacher and student are in conflict, the musical learning process in which they engage together will mirror the strain. Equitable relationships can disrupt triggering trauma response cycles (for both students and teachers), but more importantly, can offer a buffer from trauma through moments of shared joy, musical expression, and even activism. While we cannot heal students or unpack their trauma directly for them, teachers can work to foster a "healing environment" in which "students are validated, affirmed, and cared for, one in which students feel a sense of agency and the ability to make positive changes in the world" (Venet, 2021, p. 180). A healing environment allows students to "master the skills required by freedom" (Shalaby, 2017, xvi) and feel valued as important, loved members of a classroom community.

Compassionate Music Teaching

Hendricks (2018) described how compassion, or "a shared human experience between equals" shapes music teachers' understanding of students and allows for mutual exchange and support (p. 5). The six qualities of compassionate music teaching: trust, empathy, patience, inclusion, community, and authentic connection (Hendricks, 2018) are helpful guides for music educators who seek a trauma lens. The qualities of compassionate music teaching overlap considerably with principles of trauma-informed care: safety, choice, collaboration, trustworthiness, and empowerment (The Institute on Trauma and Trauma-Informed Care, 2021). The considerable overlap points to the qualities of compassionate music teaching as powerful exemplars for teachers who wish to adopt a trauma lens.

Although seemingly simple or "feel good" elements of pedagogy, the qualities of compassionate music teaching challenge long-held notions of what music teaching should look like, and that may be extremely difficult to sustain in moments where student trauma-responses trigger teachers' authoritative or punitive tendencies. Compassion requires intense relational work that may at times supersede musical goals:

> It also requires that we set our egos aside. If, for example, a teaching approach that has always worked before suddenly or unexpectedly doesn't, we (a) pause, (b) exchange a reactive stance for a reflective one, (c) consider where the students got lost in the translation, and (d) step back to meet them there. (Hendricks, 2018, p. 6)

Conclusion

Standing near the back of the line, Jamie enters the room with his classmates. With a quiet smile and elbow bump from his teacher, he goes to the sensory drawer and chooses a small fidget toy. As peaceful music plays in the room and students take their seats, they create body percussion patterns and read the agenda on the board—some silently, some sounding the words aloud. "Say hello! And how are you?"

The music teacher sings as she fades the soft music. Most students join her in singing, clapping in the rests. Jamie has chosen a chair from a stack in the corner and placed it behind the last row of students. He is content there, listening and popping his fidget in and out. He listens to the singing, rocking gently and swinging his legs back and forth. "Maybe today we will play that game where the eliminated players get to play the pattern on the xylophone?," he thinks to himself. He is hopeful.

Creating safety and choice for the most vulnerable students may be only the first step in a music educator's shift toward a trauma lens. To see through the lens of trauma is to recognize how profoundly adverse experiences can impact student behavior and learning. Appropriate for all students, a trauma lens acknowledges the potential for harm to exist in the lives of all children, both in schools and communities. A trauma lens challenges music teachers to work toward ending harm by centering classroom relationships and creating mutuality that opens space for joy and musical expression. The qualities of compassionate music teaching (Hendricks, 2018) may serve to empower music educators who wish to adopt a trauma lens. In this view, the importance of compassion shifts beyond a nicety, to a force that may open the possibility of musical expression to the most vulnerable students. Compassion, when understood within a trauma lens, can be a powerful conduit for students' fundamental safety, justice, and hope.

References

Alisic, E. (2012). Teachers' perspectives on providing support to children after trauma: A qualitative study. *School Psychology Quarterly*, 27(1), 51–59. https://doi.org/10.1037/a0028590

Alisic, E., Bus, M., Dulack, W., Pennings, L., & Splinter, J. (2012). Teachers' experience supporting children after traumatic exposure. *Journal of Traumatic Stress*, 25, 98–101. https://doi.org/10.1002/jts.20709

Bethell, C. D., Davis, M. B., Gombojav, N., Stumbo, S., & Powers, K. (2017). *Issue brief: Adverse childhood experiences among US children*. Child and Adolescent Health Measurement Initiative. https://www.cahmi.org/docs/default-source/resources/issue-brief-adverse-childhood-experiences-among-us-children-(2017).pdf

Briere, J., & Scott, C. (2006). *Principles of trauma therapy: A guide to symptoms, evaluation, and treatment*. Sage Publications.

Brown, L. (1995). Not outside the range: One feminist perspective on psychic trauma. In C. Caruth (Ed.), *Trauma: Explorations in memory* (pp. 100–112). Johns Hopkins University Press.

Cloitre, M., Stolbach, B. C., Herman, J. L., van der Kolk, B., Pynoos, R., Wang, J., & Petkova, E. (2009). A developmental approach to complex PTSD: Childhood and adult cumulative trauma as predictors of symptom complexity. *Journal of Traumatic Stress*, 22, 399–408. https://doi.org/10.1002/jts.20444

Colwell, C. M., & Thompson, L. K. (2000). "Inclusion" of information on mainstreaming in undergraduate music education curricula. *Journal of Music Therapy*, 37(3), 205–221. https://academic.oup.com/jmt/article-abstract/37/3/205/898467

Craig, S. E. (1992). The educational needs of children living with violence. *Phi Delta Kappan*, 74(1), 67–71.

Craig, S. E. (2008). *Reaching and teaching children who hurt: Strategies for your classroom*. Paul H. Brookes Publishing.

Cummings, K. P., Addante, S., Swindell, J., & Meadan, H. (2017). Creating supportive environments for children who have had exposure to traumatic events. *Journal of Child and Family Studies*, 26, 2729–2741. https://doi.org/10.1007/s10826-017-0774-9

D'Andrea, W., Ford, J., Stolbach, B., Spinazzola, J., & van der Kolk, B. A. (2012). Understanding interpersonal trauma in children: Why we need a developmentally appropriate trauma diagnosis. *American Journal of Orthopsychiatry*, 82, 187–200. https://doi.org/10.1111/j.1939-0025.2012.01154.x

Dutro, E. (2019). *The vulnerable heart of literacy: Centering trauma as powerful pedagogy*. Teachers College Press.

Farragher, B., & Yanosy, S. (2005). Creating a trauma-sensitive culture in residential treatment. *Therapeutic Community: The International Journal for Therapeutic and Supportive Organizations*, 26(1), 97–113. https://www.researchgate.net/publication/237112781_Creating_a_Trauma-Sensitive_Culture_in_Residential_Treatment

Frattaroli, J. (2006). Experimental disclosure and its moderators: A meta analysis. *Psychological Bulletin*, 132, 823–865. https://doi.org/10.1037/0033-2909.132.6.823

Fries, A. B. W., & Pollak, S. D. (2004). Emotion understanding in postinstitutionalized eastern European children. *Development and Psychopathology*, 16, 355–369. https://doi.org/10.1017/S0954579404044554

Ginwright, S. (2015). *Hope and healing in urban education: How urban activists and teachers are reclaiming matters of the heart*. Routledge.

Hammel, A. M. (2001). Preparation for teaching special learners: Twenty years of practice. *Journal of Music Teacher Education*, 11(1), 5–11. https://doi.org/10.1177/10570837010110103

Hawkins, D. (1974). *The informed vision: Essays on learning and human nature*. Algora Publishing.

Hendricks, K. S. (2018). *Compassionate music teaching*. Rowman & Littlefield.
Hendricks, K. S. (2021). Authentic connection in music education: A chiastic essay. In K. S. Hendricks & J. Boyce-Tillman (Eds.), *Authentic connection: Music, spirituality, and wellbeing* (pp. 237–253). Peter Lang.
Herman, J. (1997). *Trauma and recovery: The aftermath of violence—from domestic abuse to political terror* (2nd ed.). Basic Books.
Herman, J. L., & van der Kolk, B. A. (1987). Traumatic antecedents of borderline personality disorder. In B. A. van der Kolk (Ed.), *Psychological trauma* (pp. 111–126). American Psychiatric Press.
Hibbard, S. L. (2021). Disrupting "What we know too well:" A relational frame for considering trauma in music education. In D. Bradley & J. Hess (Eds.), *Trauma and resilience in music education: Haunted melodies* (pp. 35–48). Routledge Publications.
Hibbard, S. L. (2017). *Music teacher presence: Toward a relational understanding* [Doctoral dissertation, University of Michigan].
The Institute on Trauma and Trauma-Informed Care. (2021). *What is trauma-informed care?* http://socialwork.buffalo.edu/social-research/institutes-centers/institute-on-trauma-and-trauma-informed-care/what-is-trauma-informed-care.html
Jennings, P. A. (2019). *The trauma-sensitive classroom: Building resilience with compassionate teaching*. W. W. Norton & Company.
Levine, P. A. (1997). *Waking the tiger: Healing trauma*. North Atlantic Books.
Loftus, E. F., Polonsky, S., & Fullilove, M. T. (1994). Memories of childhood sexual abuse: Remembering and repressing. *Psychology of Women Quarterly*, 8(1), 67–84. https://www.doi.org/10.1111/j.1471-6402.1994.tb00297.x
Love, B. L. (2019). *We want to do more than survive: Abolitionist teaching and the pursuit of educational freedom*. Beacon Press.
Pitman, R. K. (1989). Post-traumatic stress disorder, hormones, and memory. *Society of Biological Psychiatry*, 26, 221–223. https://doi.org/10.1016/0006-3223(89)90033-4
Pollak, S. D., Cicchetti, D., Hornung, K., & Reed, A. (2000). Recognizing emotion in faces: Developmental effects of child abuse and neglect. *Developmental Psychology*, 36(5), 679–688. https://doi.org/10.1037//0012-1649.36.5.679
Scaer, R. (2005). *The trauma spectrum: Hidden wounds and human resiliency*. W. W. Norton & Company.
Shalaby, C. (2017). *Troublemakers: Lessons in freedom from young children at school*. New Press.
Shonkoff, J. P., Garner, A. S., Siegel, B. S., Dobbins, M. I., Earls, M. F., Garner, A. S., McGuinn, L., Pascoe, J., & Wood, D. L. (2012). The lifelong effects of early childhood adversity and toxic stress. *Pediatrics*, 129, 232–246. https://doi.org/10.1542/peds.2011-2663
Siegel, D. J. (2003). An interpersonal neurobiology of psychotherapy: The developing mind and the resolution of trauma. In M. F. Solomon & D. J. Siegel (Eds.), *Healing trauma: Attachment, mind, body, and brain* (pp. 1–56). W. W. Norton & Company.
Smith, T. (2021). Teaching through trauma: Compassion fatigue, burnout, or secondary traumatic stress? In D. Bradley & J. Hesse (Eds.), *Trauma and resilience in music education: Haunted melodies* (pp. 49–63). Routledge.
Stewart, R. W., & Stewart, D. (2002). See me, hear me, play with me: Working with the trauma of early abandonment and deprivation in psychodynamic music therapy. In J. P. Sutton (Ed.), *Music, music therapy and trauma* (pp. 133–152). Jessica Kingsley.
Stieha, V., & Raider-Roth, M. (2012). Presence in context: Teachers' negotiations with the relational environment of school. *Journal of Educational Change*, 13(4), 511–534. https://doi.org/10.1007/s10833-012-9188-z

Swart, I. (2013). South African music learners and psychological trauma: Educational solutions to a societal dilemma. *Journal for Transdisciplinary Research in Southern Africa*, 9(1), Article 221. https://doi.org/10.4102/td.v9i1.221

Swart, I., & van Niekerk, C. (2010). Trauma-related dissociation as a factor affecting musicians' memory for music: Some possible solutions. *Australian Journal of Music Education*, 2, 117–134. https://files.eric.ed.gov/fulltext/EJ916795.pdf

van der Kolk, B. A. (2014). *The body keeps the score: Brain, mind, and body in the healing of trauma*. Penguin Publishing Group.

Venet, A. S. (2021). *Equity-centered trauma-informed education*. W. W. Norton and Company.

Zembylas, M. (2020). Emotions, affects, and trauma in classrooms: Moving beyond the representational genre. *Research in Education*, 106(1), 59–76. https://doi.org/10.1177/0034523719890367

CHAPTER 33

CARING CONNECTION, MUSIC PARTICIPATION, AND QUALITY OF LIFE OF OLDER ADULTS

LISA J. LEHMBERG AND C. VICTOR FUNG

CARE HANDBOOK TOPICS

Wellbeing and human flourishing

Music seems to have co-existed with humans since the earliest recorded history, and it is an essential part of life. Regardless of how music is defined and what music is preferred, music allows humans to make connections among themselves or with beings or phenomena beyond themselves. Evidence suggests that engaging in music contributes to the quality of life of humans across various life stages (e.g., Gembris, 2006, 2012; Gembris & Heye, 2014; McQueen & Varvarigou, 2010; Pitts, 2012). In this chapter, we focus on the reciprocal relationship between music participation of older adults and caring connections as a way of improving quality of life. We begin our exploration of this topic by clarifying the key concepts of *older adulthood*, *connection*, *caring*, *caring connection*, *music participation*, and *quality of life*.

Older Adulthood

The criterion most frequently used to define older adulthood is chronological age; however, there is lack of agreement as to the specific age at which older adulthood commences. The United Nations (UN) defines an older adult as "a person who is over 60 years of age" (UN Refugee Agency, 2021, para 1). Nonetheless, many countries consider individuals to be older adults when they reach age 65 (Sabharwal et al., 2015). This marker is increasingly disputed because of improving life expectancy, physical and psychological functioning, and quality of life around the globe (Sanderson & Scherbov, 2008). In the United States alone, the disagreement looms large. For example, the minimum ages of 50, 60, 65, and 67 years are set as thresholds for "retired persons" (American Association of Retired Persons, 2021), "older adults" (Centers for Disease Control and Prevention Fact Sheet, 2016), government-supported health benefit recipients (US Department of Health & Human Services, n.d.), and government-supported retirement benefit recipients (Social Security Administration, n.d.) respectively. In this chapter, we take a global perspective to adopt the UN demarcation of age 60 as the commencement of older adulthood. At the same time, we acknowledge other definitions that use a psychological, sociological, or a life-stage approach, such as retirement, relying on pension income, and a slower and freer lifestyle, rather than a strict chronological age approach.

Psychological Development of Older Adults

Because older adulthood can be a time of transition and instability, it is important to consider the psychological phases individuals may pass through. Erik and Joan Erikson's (1982/1997) psychological stage theory includes nine stages of development, from birth to old age. Successful navigation of these stages supports the development of cultural values such as hope, wisdom, and love. Older adulthood extends across the final three stages of (a) adulthood (age 40–64), (b) old age (65 and older), and (c) gerotranscendence (age 80 and older).

In the adulthood stage, individuals feel the need to create or nurture things that will outlast them, leading to feelings of usefulness, accomplishment, and being a part of the bigger picture. Finding a way to contribute at this stage helps individuals develop the value of care. The old age stage approaches ego integrity, or the acceptance of the reality of one's life cycle, to develop wisdom and a sense of coherence and wholeness. Successfully navigating this stage enables a person to look back on their life with a sense of closure and completeness. The ninth and final stage is based on Tornstam's (1994) theory of gerotranscendence, a natural process toward maturation and wisdom that comprises the three dimensions of cosmic (sense of time and place), self (perception of self and body), and social and personal relationships (selectivity in social interactions). Gerotranscendence encompasses "a shift in meta-perspective, from a materialistic and rational vision to a more cosmic and transcendent one, normally followed by an increase in life satisfaction" (p. 203). Although an age range is suggested for each of the Eriksons' stages, each stage is fluid and may be compressed, extended, or even skipped, depending on an individual's circumstances, culture, ethnicity, gender, abilities, and socioeconomic strata (Jorgensen, 2021).

Connection

Connection is relational and mutual in nature, assuming the presence of two or more individuals. Romance novels and movies have long alluded to "magnetism" that connects the hearts and minds of compatible humans. Similar phenomena have been chronicled in medical research. Human connection has been explained as "an exchange of electromagnetic energy" in which one person's electrocardiogram signal is registered in another person's electroencephalogram and elsewhere on the body (McCraty et al., 1998). "While this signal is strongest when people are in contact, it is still detectable when subjects are in proximity without contact" (p. 359). Connection with others is important to physiological health and psychological wellbeing (Williams & Galliher, 2006), with loneliness linked to higher rates of cardiovascular disease (CVD) and "early mortality from CVD" (Paul et al., 2021, p. 23). Furthermore, connection is a prerequisite for both caring and caring connection (Ablog et al., 2014).

Caring

Caring is widely thought of as "feeling or showing concern for or kindness to others" (Merriam-Webster, n.d.), and can involve shared feelings of affection between two people or within a group of friends or associates. According to Ablog and colleagues (2014), caring is "the intentional action that conveys physical and emotional security and genuine connectedness with another individual or any group of people" (p. 202). Scholars have identified caring as a universal human need (Edgar, 2014), as well as a human capacity and mutual, reciprocal responsibility (Noddings, 2013). It is ethical to care for others (Noddings, 2005, 2013). Additionally, it is critical that caring "extend beyond sentiment into action" (Nourse, 2003, p. 59). In other words, "care is both value and practice" (Held, 2006).

Noddings (2013) took a bilateral approach to the act of caring, identifying two parties involved in caring as the "one-caring" (or carer, the person doing the caring) and the "cared-for" (p. 4). Tronto (1998) in a similar approach, broke down the concept of caring further, into four phases: (1) *caring about*: awareness of and attention to the need for caring, requires awareness of articulated and unspoken needs; (2) *caring for*: assuming responsibility to meet an identified care need; (3) *caregiving*: performing caring tasks; and (4) *care receiving*: response of the individual receiving the caring.

Tronto (1998) cautioned that caring needs of older adults should not be thought of as separate from the general population because everyone has caring needs. Older adults care for others (families, friends, community members) but also receive care from others. The diversity of caring for their needs is "as great as the diversity of caring for people of other ages" (p. 19). Thus, it is important not to stereotype older adults as needing more care. However, some older adults may be more vulnerable than in younger years, due to physical and mental incapacities developed during the aging process (Tronto, 1998) and due to feelings of instability that may accompany retirement (Hays, 2005).

Caring Connection

The penultimate result of connection interwoven with caring is *caring connection*, with connection as the essential element and caring as the central element. When a connection "forms between the one cared for and the one caring," both individuals benefit from the interaction and it enables them to achieve common goals (Ablog et al., 2014, p. 201). Schwerin (2004) described caring connection as "an empowering dialogue and exchange of the human spirit" (p. 265). It has special significance in today's fast-paced, changing, and often overwhelming world whose atmosphere can lead to "feelings of isolation, abandonment, and frustration" (p. 266). Caring connection helps individuals connect to life around them and thus supports wellbeing and quality of life. In the context of a large public nursing home in Finland, Martela (2012) defined caring connections as "caregiving encounters in which both participants—the carer and the cared-for—are both present in the situation, recognizing the uniqueness of the other and opening up towards the other, and in which affections, care and gratitude are able to flow with ease in the systemic dyad formed between them" (p. 17). He also identified six essential elements of caring connections:

(1) mutual validation of the distinctive worth of the other,
(2) being present in the now-moment,
(3) opening up to each other and the sharing of oneself in a deep way,
(4) establishing a shared space into which participants can bring their thoughts and emotions and feel that they are shared,
(5) heightened flow of affectivity and the moments being affectively highly charged, and
(6) acts of caregiving from the care provider, which are returned by displays of gratitude from the care receiver. (p. 18)

Like other definitions, Martela's clearly emphasizes the relational, mutual, and empathetic interactions between the carer and the cared-for. In other words, for caring connection to occur, both the carer and the cared-for must be open for mutual caring exchange. All of these seem to align well in the context of music participation.

Music Participation

Music participation can take many forms in older adulthood, for example, a relaxing and enjoyable diversion (Lee et al., 2018) or a serious and stimulating leisure pursuit that requires perseverance (Joseph & Human, 2020). Some equate music participation solely with music-making; however, we define the term more broadly, to include making, composing, and producing music, and also active listening to music, which can be a stand-alone activity (e.g., attending a concert) or in tandem with purposeful and deliberate movement to music (e.g., dancing to music). Additionally, we stretch the definition of music production to include not only creating, mixing, syncing, and producing recordings but also processes that support music-making (e.g., managing sound technology for synchronous or asynchronous concerts).

Quality of Life

Like music, quality of life is a universal desire, but there are different preferences for how it is defined. Since the first appearance of the English term "quality of life" in the mid-20th century, it is often associated with, but not the same as, a variety of concepts such as happiness or wellbeing, and even life-satisfaction or eudaimonia. Defining quality of life is daunting and complex as revealed in two editions of the *Encyclopedia of Quality of Life and Well-Being Research* (Maggino, 2020; Michalos, 2014), a gamut of measurement tools developed by numerous researchers and well-trusted organizations such as the World Health Organization (The WHOQOL Group, 1998), and via the huge and still expanding body of research literature. These publications may address quality of life as one overarching construct or state found in a specific individual (e.g., child, student, and adult), condition (e.g., physical, psychological, and social), or aspects of life (e.g., the arts, family, and the service industry). Though the evolution of the meanings of quality of life from the 1950s to the early 2000s is presented elsewhere (Fung & Lehmberg, 2016), its meanings are still evolving in the advent of everlasting economic, social, and scientific developments. Furthermore, individual ideals for quality of life could change as one enters different life stages or as life circumstances shift. The multifaceted nature and evolving definition of quality of life, along with individual predilections, warrant considerations for a broad spectrum of options in services and activities, so everyone can have a chance to achieve a high quality of life throughout the entire lifespan. Because older adults' quality of life through music participation and caring connections is our focus, we explore this conceptualization in the remainder of this chapter. We respectfully acknowledge the many other ways of achieving it in other populations and other areas not addressed here.

CARING CONNECTION AND OLDER ADULT MUSIC PARTICIPATION

Our book *Music for Life* (Fung & Lehmberg, 2016) contains an extensive, interdisciplinary review of scholarly literature from 1985 to 2015 illuminating the benefits of music participation for older adults. These benefits can be categorized arbitrarily as physical, psychological, or social, with much overlap. Though the body of research on this topic has broadened in recent years, findings generally identify similar benefits in a greater variety of contexts.

It is important to note that caring connection relates closely to *psychological* and *social* benefits of music participation, and involves many elements found in shared musical experiences of older adults, such as relationships, friendships, and interactions with others characterized by reciprocal feelings of caring and understanding. Though multiple benefits of music participation are evident (Lehmberg & Fung, 2010), Table 33.1

Table 33.1 Benefits of Music Participation Relating to Caring Connection in Older Adults (Post-2015 Publications)

Caring Connection Benefits	Post-2015 Studies
Cognitive function	Bugos & Kochar, 2017; Hudak et al., 2019
Community engagement	Fung & Lehmberg, 2016; Joseph & Southcott, 2018; Lee et al, 2016; Southcott & Li, 2018
Connection with others	Barbeau & Cossette, 2019; Joseph, 2021; Joseph & Human, 2020; Joseph & Southcott, 2018; Lee et al., 2016
Enjoyment	Barbeau & Cossette, 2019; Barbeau & Mantie, 2019; Lee et al., 2016; Roulston et al., 2015
Heightened sense of wellbeing	Barbeau & Cossette, 2019; Joseph, 2020, 2021; Joseph & Human, 2020; Joseph & Southcott, 2018
Increased self-confidence	Southcott & Li, 2018
Increased musical self-efficacy	Balsnes, 2017; Joseph & Human, 2020; Lee et al., 2016; Woody et al., 2019
Lessening of isolation and loneliness	Fung & Lehmberg, 2016; Southcott & Li, 2018; Joseph & Southcott, 2018
Opportunity to "give back" to community by sharing music	Joseph, 2021; Joseph & Human, 2020; Southcott & Li, 2018; Joseph & Southcott, 2018
Overcome limitations caused by aging	Lee et al., 2016
Positive effect on moods	Joseph & Human, 2020; Lee et al., 2016
Sense of accomplishment	Joseph, 2021; Joseph & Human, 2020; Southcott & Li, 2018
Sense of belonging	Balsnes, 2017; Barbeau & Cossette, 2019; Glen, 2018; Joseph, 2021; Joseph & Southcott, 2018
Sense of identity	Barbeau & Cossette, 2019
Sense of purpose	Balsnes, 2017; Barbeau & Cossette, 2019; Glen, 2018; Joseph & Human, 2020; Lee et al., 2016
Sense of resilience	Joseph & Southcott, 2018
Spiritual fulfillment	Fung & Lehmberg, 2016; Lee et al., 2016; Southcott & Li, 2018

provides more recent examples from the field of music, post 2015, that relate directly to caring connection in older adults.

Our research has shown that "connection has been a main thread that appears to be essential in making the musical experience meaningful" (Fung & Lehmberg, 2016, p. 223). We determined that connection via music participation could be categorized as *social* (connection with self and others) or *temporal* (connection across time: past, present, and future). The concepts of *social caring connection* and *temporal caring connection* expand on our original perspectives by emphasizing the critical importance of caring in meaningful connection.

Social Caring Connection

Congruent with findings from medical research, musical experiences have been shown to elicit feelings of social connectedness that contribute to wellbeing in older adults (Hays & Minchiello, 2005). Connection with others via shared musical experiences helps older adults to develop their musical selves through a sense of community and belonging (Joseph, 2021) within which caring is subsumed, leading to "validation as a valued and worthwhile member of a social network" (Creech et al., 2014, p. 33). As Hendricks (2018) stated, "The need to belong is satisfied through the combination of two experiences: positive interactions with an intimate group and a stable relationship of mutual support and concern that endures over time" (p. 125). Furthermore, shared musical experiences via caring connection allow older adults to find personal joy and contribute to the happiness of others (Baker & Ballantyne, 2012).

Older adults have a strong need to connect to their inner selves. Self-knowledge helps individuals to develop the capacity to care for others (Noddings, 2005). As Hendricks (2018) pointed out, "It is hard to authentically connect with others when you do not truly know yourself" (p. 148). Music participation can provide an avenue by which older adults can access and develop their "possible musical selves" (Creech et al., 2014, p. 33), enabling them to further develop the capacity to care for (Noddings, 2013) and care with others while allowing space for individual characteristics and aspirations (Hendricks, 2018). By accessing their own identities (composed of their rich pool of life experiences, feelings, and wisdom), older adults become better able to express their inner selves to others, which can bring deep satisfaction. Music participation can also provide a means for older adults to connect their inner selves with broader society, in that the musical process and product are always related to life within the current culture and society, regardless of whether the music reflects material culture, the political environment, or emotional sentiments of the time (Fung & Lehmberg, 2016).

Returning to the Eriksons' (1982/1997) stages of psychological development, social caring connection via music participation supports the adulthood stage (ages 50–64) in that caring connections with others via community music activities and organizations lead to feelings of usefulness, accomplishment, and being a part of the bigger picture; thus, allowing older adults to further develop the value of care. Congruent with the old age stage (ages 65 and older), self-expression through musical activities allows older adults to connect with their inner selves and others via caring connections, leading to the development of wisdom through acceptance of and satisfaction with the reality of their lives.

Social caring connection also relates to older adults in the gerotranscendence stage (aged 80 and older), encompassing the dimensions of self and social and personal relationships. Congruent with the *self* dimension, knowledge of the inner self developed through music-making and self-expression allows older adults to redefine themselves musically and personally. Perseverance in musical activities despite age-related physical and psychological issues also allows them to transcend body and self. Congruent with the *social and personal relationships* dimension, as older adults become selective in their social interactions and involvement (Tornstam, 2011), music remains as a popular choice because it aids in developing and maintaining deep and meaningful connections (Baker & Ballantyne, 2012; Fung & Lehmberg, 2016; Hays & Minchiello, 2005). Connections made via music participation in this stage of life lead to a sense of social and self-affirmation, which is an important dimension of quality of life.

Temporal Caring Connection

Because life is a journey through time, older adult music participants have a strong need to connect their musical experiences with the past, present, and future. Based on continuity theory (Atchley, 1999), which suggests that one could maintain a consistent sense of self in later life by making adaptive choices, Breheny and Griffiths (2017) viewed connection as "an attempt to preserve continuity of attitudes, dispositions, preferences, and behaviours which have been accumulated throughout their life" (p. 41). Congruent with the gerotranscending stage of psychological development, connecting musical experiences with the past, present, and future in older adulthood leads to satisfaction upon reflection on one's musical life.

Musically, connections with the past include individuals' musical histories, such as the music they preferred to listen to, performed, composed, or produced at various stages of life. Research shows a strong connection between music participation in youth and music participation in older adulthood (Maruszewski et al., 2017; Yeung et al., 2014), with many older adults participating in the same types of musical groups as during their younger years (Helton, 2020). Connection with the past can also be viewed within a lifespan context, from childhood on. Many older adults are extremely fond of the music of their younger years. It helps them reflect on the events and memories of their lives; thus, creating a timeline of their lives organized by the music in their lives. This reflection supports the older adulthood and gerotranscendence stages of psychological development (Erikson & Erikson, 1982/1997) as individuals develop a sense of coherence, wholeness, and wisdom; and look back on their life with a sense of closure and completeness.

As seen in studies listed in Table 33.1, musical experiences in the present are also critical in expanding older adults' capacity to nurture and develop their musical identities. The popularity of shared musical experiences attests to the deep and meaningful connections made therein. Older adults enjoy contributing musically to the environment in which they live by sharing their music with others. This, in turn, increases self-caring and sense of purpose in life, reaffirming self-worth and the meaning of their existence (Fung & Lehmberg, 2016; Southcott & Li, 2018) and is congruent with the Eriksons' adulthood stage of psychological development.

Older adult music participants have a deep desire for their descendants and younger generations to be involved in musical activities and strive to ensure the future continuation of these opportunities to enhance quality of life. They promote and maintain family music-making traditions by passing on familiar, much-loved songs. They support music-making activities of their descendants and younger generations through positive reinforcement, attendance of performances, and help in obtaining musical instruments. They also believe that music education should be available to all students throughout the schooling years (Fung & Lehmberg, 2016). This reinforcement of family and school music participation relates to the Eriksons' adulthood stage of psychological development in that ensuring opportunities for descendants and younger generations to participate in music in the future satisfies the need to create or nurture things that will outlast them.

Contributions to Quality of Life

Research converges to illuminate caring connection as an integral, critical element of older adult music participation that contributes to quality of life. Older adults benefit from caring connection in ways that are congruent with their psychological development and lead to an enhanced sense of wellbeing. Their quality of life is improved by the availability of the activities of their choice while sustaining caring connection. Music is among many older adults' choices for engagement due to the diverse nature of its activities, from listening to creating to actively moving, with a wide range of musical styles from classical to vernacular. A gamut of instruments is easily accessible, from the singing voice to all sorts of acoustic and digital instruments. Furthermore, musical groups organized for older adults often welcome participants of any competency level.

Empowering dialogue and meaningful human interaction accessed through musical activities allow older adults to reflect on their life's journey, situate themselves in their present life, connect to and express their inner selves (including their musical selves), feel a sense of belonging and purpose, care about and with others, and make meaningful contributions to the future. Caring connection through music is often extended beyond music participants to the community at large. As volunteer musicians, music participants show their care for the community and contribute through their musical expressions, which satisfies many older adults' desire to "give back" to society (Fung & Lehmberg, 2016, p. 215). Without a doubt, caring connection via music participation contributes to a better quality of life in many ways as revealed in theories and data analyses found in the literature.

IMPLICATIONS

Based on extant literature, we suggest that older adults and service providers consider including musical activities in their regular schedules. These activities could include listening to preferred music with the option to engage at different levels, such as moving along, singing or playing along, or even composing, depending on the background, interest, and readiness of the individuals. Appropriate space, equipment, and personnel should be accessible to older adults. Musical activities can be held in conjunction with other projects, such as creating personal musical history scrapbooks or a focus group sharing of musical memories. These and many more music participatory activities should be used to establish and cultivate caring connections to support an overall sense of wellbeing. Music is regarded as a highly meaningful activity, so it should be utilized if the interest is present, regardless of an individual's previous musical experience. If music-making is not an interest, other music-related activities could be as meaningful in supporting caring connections (e.g., sharing or discussion group on musical topics). The key is to connect meaningfully and regularly with others, via musical activities that are of interest and enjoyable.

Service providers for older adults (including community and senior centers, assisted living facilities, etc.) could prioritize regularly offering a variety of musical activities that support caring connection and within which older adults come together to participate. Music tends to draw people together. Given the diversity of musical styles, genres, and types of activities, there ought to be one that serves each specific individual or group, considering their background, attitude, and state of readiness. It is important to provide a wide range of opportunities, so all older adults can join with a good fit, again, regardless of previous music experience or physical, social, or psychological condition.

Music educators could consider ways to incorporate musical experiences that encourage caring connection at all levels, in schools and communities, from early childhood through older adulthood. The focus could be on scaffolding and spiraling shared musical experiences that support lifelong music-learning and engagement. We encourage music educators to design their curricula based on lifelong goals rather than merely focusing on short- and medium-term goals for the semester and the schooling years. Caring connection through music participation most certainly contributes to the quality of life of older adults; however, it can be extended to all age groups.

REFERENCES

Ablog, J., Anquillano, F., & Nero, F. D. (2014). Caring connection: The essentiality of nursing in the human health experience. *Research Journal of Social Science & Management*, 4(3), 201–208.

American Association of Retired Persons. (2021). *AARP Membership FAQs*. Retrieved July 8, 2021, from https://www.aarp.org/membership/faqs/

Atchley, R. C. (1999). Continuity theory, self, and social structure. In C. D. Ryff & V. W. Marshall (Eds.), *The self and society in aging processes* (pp. 94–121). Springer.

Baker, F. A., & Ballantyne, J. (2012). "You've got to accentuate the positive": Group songwriting to promote a life of enjoyment, engagement, and meaning in aging Australians. *Nordic Journal of Music Therapy*, 22(1), 7–24. https://doi.org/10.1080/08098131.2012.678372

Balsnes, A. H. (2017). The Silver Voices: A possible model for senior singing. *International Journal of Community Music*, 10(1), 59–69. https://doi.org/10.1386/ijcm.10.1.59_1

Barbeau, A.-K., & Cossette, I. (2019). The effects of participating in a community concert band on senior citizens' quality of life, mental and physical health. *International Journal of Community Music, 12*(2), 269–288. https://doi.org/10.1386/ijcm.12.2.269_1

Barbeau, A.-K., & Mantie, R. (2019). Music performance anxiety and perceived benefits of music participation among older adults in community bands. *Journal of Research in Music Education, 66*(4), 408–427. https://doi.org/10.1177/0022429418799362

Breheny, M., & Griffiths, Z. (2017). "I had a good time when I was young": Interpreting descriptions of continuity among older people. *Journal of Aging Studies, 41*, 36–43. https://doi.org/10.1016/j.jaging.2017.03.003

Bugos, J., & Kochar, S. (2017). Efficacy of a short-term intense piano training program for cognitive aging: A pilot study. *Musicae Scientiae, 21*(2), 137–150. https://doi.org/10.1016/j.jaging.2017.03.003

Center for Disease Control and Prevention. (2016). *Understanding elder abuse: Fact sheet.* Retrieved July 6, 2021, from https://www.cdc.gov/violenceprevention/pdf/em-factsheet-a.pdf

Creech, A., Hallam, S., Varvarigou, M., Gaunt, H., McQueen, H., & Pincas, A. (2014). The role of musical possible selves in supporting subjective well-being in later life. *Music Education Research, 16*(1), 32–49. http://dx.doi.org/10.1080/14613808.2013.788143

Edgar, S. N. (2014). An ethic of care in high school instrumental music. *Action, Criticism, and Theory for Music Education, 13*(2), 111–137. http://act.maydaygroup.org/articles/Edgar13_2.pdf

Erikson, E. H., & Erikson, J. M. (1982/1997). *The life cycle completed: Extended version with new chapters on the ninth stage of development.* W. W. Norton & Company.

Fung, C. V., & Lehmberg, L. J. (2016). *Music for life: Music participation and quality of life of senior citizens.* Oxford University Press. https://doi.org/10.1093/acprof:oso/9780199371686.001.0001

Gembris, H. (Ed.). (2006). *Musical development from a lifespan perspective.* Peter Lang.

Gembris, H. (2012). Music-making as a lifelong development and resource for health. In R. MacDonald, G. Kreutz, & L. Mitchell (Eds.), *Music, health, & wellbeing* (pp. 367–382). Oxford University Press. https://doi.org/10.1093/acprof:oso/9780199586974.001.0001

Gembris, H., & Heye, A. (2014). Growing older in a symphony orchestra: The development of the age-related self-concept and the self-estimated performance of professional musicians in a lifespan perspective. *Musicae Scientiae, 18*(4), 371–391. https://doi.org/10.1177/1029864914548912

Glen, N. L. (2018). Music in a new key: The sociocultural impact of the New Horizons Band programme and its relationship to Baltes' Selective Optimization with Compensation model. *International Journal of Community Music, 11*(2), 199–212. https://doi.org/10.1386/ijcm.11.2.199_1

Hays, T. (2005). Well-being in later life through music. *Australasian Journal on Aging, 24*(1), 28–32. https://doi.org/10.1111/j.1741-6612.2005.00059.x

Hays, T., & Minchiello, V. (2005). The contribution of music to quality of life in older people: An Australian qualitative study. *Aging & Society, 25*, 261–278. https://doi.org/10.1017/S0144686X04002946

Held, V. (2006). *The ethics of care.* Oxford University Press. https://doi.org/10.1093/0195180992.001.0001

Helton, B. C. (2020). The phenomenon of adults relearning instrumental music in an American wind band. *International Journal of Music Education, 38*(1), 66–78. https://doi.org/10.1177/0255761419869137

Hendricks, K. S. (2018). *Compassionate music teaching.* Rowman & Littlefield.

Hudak, E. M., Bugos, J., Andel, R., Lister, J. J., Ji, M., & Edwards, J. D. (2019). Keys to staying sharp: A randomized clinical trial of piano training among older adults with and without mild cognitive impairment. *Contemporary Clinical Trials*, *84*, Article 105789. https://doi.org/10.1016/j.cct.2019.06.003

Jorgensen, E. R. (2021). On values and life's journey through music: Reflections on the Eriksons' life stages and music education. In K. S. Hendricks & J. Boyce-Tillman (Eds.), *Authentic connection: Music, spirituality, and wellbeing* (pp. 67–80). Peter Lang.

Joseph, D. (2021). "The Potted Palms is bigger than each of us individually": Older musicians playing as community and for community. *Creative Industries Journal*. Advance online publication. https://doi.org/10.1080/17510694.2021.1890378

Joseph, D., & Human, R. (2020). "It is more than just about music": Lifelong learning, social interaction and connection. *Muziki: Journal of Music Research in Africa*, *17*(1), 72–93. https://doi.org/10.1080/18125980.2020.1855082

Joseph, D., & Southcott, J. (2018). Music participation for older people: Five choirs in Victoria. *Research Studies in Music Education*, *40*(2), 176–190. https://doi.org/10.1177/1321103X18773096

Lee, J., Davidson, J. W., & Krause, A. (2016). Older people's motivations for participating in community singing in Australia. *International Journal of Community Music*, *9*(2), 191–207. https://doi.org/10.1386/ijcm.9.2.191_1

Lee, P., Stewart, D., & Clift, S. (2018). Group singing and quality of life. In B.-L. Bartleet & L. Higgins (Eds.), *The Oxford handbook of community music*, pp. 503–523. Oxford University Press. https://doi.org/10.1093/oxfordhb/9780190219505.001.0001

Maggino, F. (Ed.). (2020). *Encyclopedia of quality of life and well-being research* (2nd ed.). Springer Reference.

Lehmberg, L. J., & Fung, C. V. (2010). Benefits of music participation for senior citizens: A review of the literature. *Music Education Research International*, *4*, 19–30. http://cmer.arts.usf.edu/content/articlefiles/3122-MERI04pp.19-30.pdf

Martela, F. (2012). *Caring connections—Compassionate mutuality in the organizational life of a nursing home* [Doctoral dissertation, Aalto University]. Aalto University Publication Series. http://urn.fi/URN:ISBN:978-952-60-4848-2

Maruszewski, T., Bonk, E., Karcz, B., & Retowski, S. (2017). Elderly people's preferences regarding reminiscence material. *Educational Gerontology*, *43*(11), 531–539. https://doi.org/10.1080/03601277.2017.1283931

McCraty, R., Atkinson, M., Tomasino, D., & Tiller, W. A. (1998). The electricity of touch: Detection and measurement of cardiac energy exchange between people. In K. H. Pribram (Ed.), *Brain and values: Is a biological science of values possible?* (pp. 359–379). Lawrence Erlbaum Associates.

McQueen, H., & Varvarigou, M. (2010). Learning through life. In S. Hallam & A. Creech (Eds.), *Music education in the 21st century in the United Kingdom: Achievements, analysis, and aspirations* (pp. 159–175). Institute of Education, University of London. https://doi.org/10.1080/14613808.2012.667942

Merriam-Webster. (n.d.). Caring. In *Merriam-Webster.com* dictionary. Retrieved June 24, 2021, from https://www.merriam-webster.com/dictionary/caring

Michalos, A. C. (Ed.). (2014). *Encyclopedia of quality of life and well-being research*. Springer Reference. https://doi.org/10.1007/978-94-007-0753-5

Noddings, N. (2005). *The challenge to care in schools: An alternative approach to education* (2nd ed.). Teacher's College Press.

Noddings, N. (2013). *Caring: A relational approach to ethics and moral education* (2nd ed.). University of California Press.

Nourse, N. (2003). The ethics of care and the private woodwind lesson. *Journal of Aesthetic Education*, 37(3), 58–77. https://doi.org/ 10.1353/jae.2003.0024

Paul, E., Feifei, B., & Fancourt, D. (2021). Loneliness and risk for cardiovascular disease: Mechanisms and future directions. *Current Cardiology Reports*, 23, Article 68. https://doi.org/10.1007/s11886-021-01495-2

Pitts, S. (2012). *Chances and choices: Exploring the impact of music education*. Oxford University Press. https://doi.org/10.1093/acprof:oso/9780199838752.001.0001

Roulston, K., Jutras, P., & Kim, S. (2015). Adult perspectives of learning musical instruments. *International Journal of Music Education*, 33(3), 325–335. https://doi.org/10.1177/0255761415584291

Sabharwal, S., Wilson, H., Reilly, P., & Gupte, C. M. (2015). Heterogeneity of the definition of elderly age in current orthopaedic research. *SpringerPlus*, 4, Article 516. https://doi.org/10.1186/s40064-015-1307-x

Sanderson, W., & Scherbov, S. (2008). Rethinking age and aging. *Population Bulletin*, 63(4).

Schwerin, J. (2004). The timeless caring connection. *Nursing Administration Quarterly*, 28, 265–70. https://doi.org/10.1097/00006216-200410000-00007

Social Security Administration. (n.d.). *Retirement benefits*. Retrieved July 8, 2021, from https://www.ssa.gov/benefits/retirement/planner/agereduction.html

Southcott, J., & Li, S. (2018). "Something to live for": Weekly singing classes at a Chinese university for retirees. *International Journal of Music Education*, 36(2), 283–296. https://doi.org/10.1177/0255761417729548

The WHOQOL Group. (1998). The World Health Organization Quality of Life assessment (WHOQOL): Development and general psychometric properties. *Social Science Medicine*, 46(12), 1569–1585. https://doi.org/10.1016/S0277-9536(98)00009-4

Tornstam, L. (1994). Gerotranscendence: A developmental theory of positive aging. In L. E. Thomas & S. A. Eisenhandler (Eds.), *Aging and the religious dimension* (pp. 203–225). Greenwood Publishing Group. https://doi.org/10.1097/00019442-199503040-00013

Tornstam, L. (2011). Maturing into gerotranscendence. *Journal of Transpersonal Psychology*, 43(2), 166–180.

Tronto, J. C. (1998). An ethic of care. *Generations*, 22(3), 15–20.

United Nations Refugee Agency. (n.d.). *Older persons*. UNHCR Emergency Handbook. Retrieved July 6, 2021, from https://emergency.unhcr.org/entry/43935/older-persons

U. S. Department of Health & Human Services. (n.d.). *Answers: Medicare & Medicaid: Who is eligible for Medicare?* Retrieved July 6, 2021, from https://www.hhs.gov/answers/medicare-and-medicaid/who-is-elibible-for-medicare/index.html

Williams, K. L., & Galliher, R. V. (2006). Predicting depression and self-esteem from social connectedness, support, and competence. *Journal of Social and Clinical Psychology*, 25(8), 855–874. https://doi.org/10.1521/jscp.2006.25.8.855

Woody, R. H., Fraser, A., Nannen, B., & Yukevich, P. (2019). Musical identities of older adults are not easily changed: An exploratory study. *Music Education Research*, (21)3, 315–330. https://doi.org/10.1080/14613808.2019.1598346

Yeung, H. C., Baker, F., & Shoemark, H. (2014). Song preferences of Chinese older adults living in Australia. *Australian Journal of Music Therapy*, 25, 103–121.

CHAPTER 34

RECONSIDERING MUSICAL ABILITY DEVELOPMENT THROUGH THE LENS OF DIVERSITY AND BIAS

KARIN S. HENDRICKS AND GARY E. MCPHERSON

CARE HANDBOOK TOPICS

Identity expressions
Musical development
Social activism and critical consciousness
Wellbeing and human flourishing

SOCIAL narratives shape the ways that people perceive musicianship—what it means to be musical, as well as what kinds of musical abilities are considered valuable (Hendricks, 2018, 2021a). They also shape our understandings of how individuals develop the skills requisite to become experts in their chosen field. Although music teachers nearly universally emphasize the importance of hard work and practice, the appeal of commercially successful artists and so-called prodigies who seemingly produce the most effortlessly and extraordinary examples of music often overshadows the much more common, and much more routine narrative of proximal musical development (see Ericsson, 2014; Ericsson et al., 1993; Gagné & McPherson, 2016; McPherson & Williamon, 2016). The "10,000 hour" rule proposed by Gladwell (2008) is often cited without a clear understanding of the importance of deliberate practice and individual commitment, potentially leading to an inaccurate assumption that all practice is equal or that practice alone will always result in improvement (Gagné & McPherson, 2016; McPherson, 2001).

A similarly harmful social narrative is the myth of meritocracy, which downplays the role of environmental catalysts and/or systemic barriers that boost the musical access and achievement of some learners while impeding the growth of others (Hendricks, 2018; Gagné & McPherson, 2016). In some cases, the meritocracy myth is invoked in ways that rationalize and reinforce the marginalization of underrepresented groups (López-Íñiguez & Westerlund, this volume; Smith & Hendricks, 2022; Wright, 2015). Given the oversimplified and potentially misleading that exists regarding how musicians learn and grow, it is important for music teachers to understand the complexities of ability development to support students with compassion and care.

In this chapter we describe some of the social, environmental, and interpersonal factors that play a role in the development of musical abilities. We first provide definitions for "giftedness" and "talent," and explain the complex and individualized developmental pathway from the former to the latter. We then draw on psychological constructs related to self-determination theory, to detail the ways in which students' basic psychological needs (relatedness, autonomy and competence) might be supported with care in music-learning settings. We use these psychological principles to offer suggestions for promoting student motivation and engagement.

In the final section, we address care by introducing the concept of implicit bias, describing potential unconscious beliefs and perceptions that well-meaning music teachers might hold about students' backgrounds, abilities, and/or stated interests. We explain how unchecked habits of mind might affect the ways in which teachers interact with, and respond to, different students in their care, in some cases reinforcing inequities among students even when teachers maintain explicit goals to help all students to achieve musically. We share recent research about how implicit biases can be confronted and addressed, including through debiasing interventions and the adoption of mindframes that focus teachers' attention on the types of actions that can make a profound difference to the musical development of the students they teach. Inherent in this latter role is the critical role of evaluating the effect teachers have on their students, such that learning is seen as a journey by both the teacher and the student, and development seen as a particular point that has been reached along that journey (Hattie & Zierer, 2018; McPherson & Hattie, 2022). As we discuss these research-based interventions, we offer suggestions for reflecting on pedagogical practices to address individual student needs in ways that foster greater equity in music-learning settings.

Understanding Music Ability Development

Conceptions of musical giftedness and talent are often misunderstood, not only in their complexity, but also in how they differ from one another (McPherson et al., 2022). Indeed, because conceptions of these two constructs are socially constructed there is no single theoretical explanation that all researchers can agree on (Borland, 2021). Of even greater concern is how researchers and teachers react to students who demonstrate exceptional levels of ability that far exceeds their peers. Rather than focusing their attention on the types of curricula and instructional techniques that will maximize their potential to thrive, all too often the focus is centered on whether the student is gifted and the extent of their giftedness; what Borland (2021) describes as turning our attention "away from what the student *needs* to what the student *is*, away from the educational and toward the existential" (p. 86). This is partly why a number of recent, prominent explanations have turned from emphasizing how to measure giftedness and talent, to devising general talent development frameworks (such as TAD, the Talent Development in Achievement Domains) that can be used as a tool in the education of learners with high potential in music or other fields (Müllensiefen et al., 2022).

Explaining Giftedness

Within Gagné's (2013) differentiated model of giftedness and talent, *giftedness* is defined as "the possession and use of untrained and spontaneously expressed outstanding natural abilities," while *talent* reflects the "mastery of systematically developed competencies" (Gagné & McPherson, 2016, p. 5). Stated differently, giftedness refers to a range of mental (intellectual, creative, social, perceptual) and physical (muscular, motor control) abilities that are not innate but which can develop in the early years of life, even though they are partially controlled by the individual's genetics (Glasser & McPherson, in press). Talent, on the other hand, is something that can be demonstrated after natural abilities and a range of intrapersonal, environmental, and developmental forces have all exerted their influence, and the person is able, for example, to demonstrate their talent in some tangible way such as by playing or composing music.

The range of natural ability in the DMGT model does not simple refer to being "innate" or "God-given," as some social narratives might suggest. Instead, natural abilities represent the potential for musical development, provided that conditions are such to support musical growth. Our adaption of Gagné's model (see Figure 34.1) outlines the types of mental and physical natural abilities that work in combination with a host of intrapersonal, environmental, and developmental processes to blossom into specific talents, such as the music-oriented examples listed in the right-hand side of the figure.

Environmental catalysts might include certain social supports and provisions, the latter of which are not equally accessible across the population of music learners (see Smith & Hendricks, 2022; Talbot, 2018). Social structures may also privilege some music learners and marginalize others depending on how their backgrounds and interests align with the beliefs and values of those who hold power and influence (Hess, 2018). In addition, access and opportunities to engage in a range of developmental processes (various activities, investments, and stages of progress) also influence a student's long-range musical trajectory. Importantly, therefore, Figure 34.1 makes it clear that each student has a different path—as well as a different destination—for their own individual musical development journey.

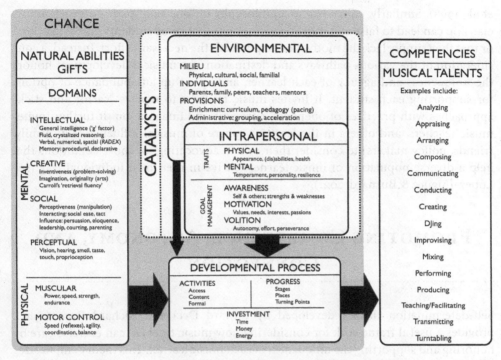

FIGURE 34.1 Differentiated Model of Giftedness and Talent (adapted from Gagne, 2009, p. 64).

This model offers a way to understand musical development that is potentially more empowering for music learners as well as teachers. First, if musical abilities are exclusively a product of "nature" then the educational rationale for teaching music in public schools would be on shaky ground, and the necessity of employing music teachers could be seriously questioned. And given that learning in music draws on many of the same conceptual, intellectual, and skill-based activities we see in other subject areas, this same way of thinking would be equally valid in other areas of the curriculum as well. In contrast, this model implies that there are multifarious ways in which teachers might respond to their students' dispositions toward certain musical competencies—not to mention certain musics—as they negotiate with them about how to fulfill their own individual goals.

Second, an understanding of the complexity of musical talent development recognizes that music-learning is not a "one size fits all." This helps to dispel any notions of "innate talent"[1] that can lead to discrimination and/or marginalization of students who do not appear responsive to certain pedagogical approaches (see Howe

---

[1] Francoy Gagné has published widely on the common—but inappropriate—use of the term "innate talent" (see Gagné & McPherson, 2016). His work attempts to understand and explain the delicate interplay between nature and nurture.

et al., 1998). Similarly, adherence to a philosophy of "one right path" to expert musicianship can lead to false and hurtful assumptions that some students just "don't care," or that they simply lack the motivation to put forth the necessary effort. Instead, a consideration of the various pathways and destinations for musical development honors the uniqueness and agency of each learner, and opens up an abundance of options for supporting each student. It invites music teachers to replace "carrot and stick" approaches with practices of openness, curiosity, and imagination. It further invites music teachers, and others in the learner's sphere of musical influence (e.g., family, friends, policy makers) to consider their role in advocating for those conditions that help a diverse population of music learners thrive in their own individual way (see López-Íñiguez & Burnard, 2021).

Promoting Competence, Autonomy, and Connection

Self-determination theory, developed by Edward Deci and Richard Ryan (1985), provides a useful framework for considering how music teachers can exercise care by honoring and supporting the uniqueness of each music learner. This theory emphasizes the role of agency and intrinsic motivation as an individual strives toward certain performance outcomes. It is unique in its emphasis not on quantity of motivation, but quality, particularly as it relates to one's sense of self (Evans, 2015). Self-determination theory has two primary and interrelated features that apply to music education (Evans, 2015). First, students can flourish musically when learning conditions support their basic psychological needs of competence, autonomy, and relatedness. Second, music-learning may be more personally fulfilling and more likely to foster a sense of wellbeing when external sources of motivation align with a student's internal motivations and sense of self. An understanding of self-determination theory may be helpful to music teachers as they practice "caring with" students (e.g., fostering reciprocal and mutually supportive relationships; Hendricks, 2021b) and support them in becoming independent and self-fulfilled music-makers (Hendricks, 2018).

According to self-determination theory, students are motivated by reinforcements of their *competence* through tangible demonstrations of achievement and by overcoming challenges. A sense of competence is related to self-efficacy belief, or an individual's awareness of their ability to accomplish certain tasks (Bandura, 1997; McPherson & McCormick, 2006); and collective efficacy, which refers to a group's shared belief of their task-based competence (Bandura, 1997; Ray & Hendricks, 2019). Music teachers can enhance students' sense of competence by (a) providing them with ability-appropriate, proximal steps toward mutually shared goals; (b) avoiding unhealthy social comparisons and encouraging them to view peer and adult models as examples of what they can potentially accomplish themselves; (c) offering timely, specific, and constructive advice, support and words of encouragement; and (d) providing strategies to support their physical and emotional wellbeing (Hendricks, 2016).

Autonomy refers to a student's sense of independence and self-regulation as they accomplish musical achievements, exercise ownership of their own music-learning, and have opportunities to make decisions for themselves. In contrast to structure-free environments (which can be frustrating and lead to a sense of incompetence) or controlling environments (where students have no sense of self in the music-making process), music teachers support autonomy by balancing structure and agency—providing sufficient support and task-specific feedback while also engaging *with* students in music-making decisions (Evans, 2015; Hendricks, 2018; Legutki, 2010).

Relatedness is strengthened whenever music learners form positive relationships with others. It is associated with feelings of belonging and authentic connection (Hendricks, 2018, 2021; Hendricks & Boyce-Tillman, 2021). The quality and experiences of relatedness have been shown to change over the course of a student's musical development: Students may need warm and fun interactions during early stages of music-learning; relatively high standards and skill development support during middle stages; and a relationship primarily focused on task-based mastery in later stages (Bloom, 1985; Evans, 2015). Experiences of relatedness may follow a different trajectory with adult amateur learners whose reasons for learning music may vary substantially (Leahy & Smith, 2021). It is critical, therefore, for teachers to recognize the dynamic and developing needs of students in terms of their musical relationships with others, noting—again—that students' needs are not "one size fits all."

Longitudinal research has shown that individuals' decisions to continue formal musical instruction, or not, are likely associated with their feelings of competence, autonomy, and relatedness (Evans et al., 2013). Importantly, learners who have ceased musical instruction cite reasons associated with these basic psychological needs being suppressed. Citing a number of commonly-used practices in music education that misalign with the support of basic psychological needs, Evans (2015) cautioned:

> [E]nticing children to practise by using rewards and punishments, encouraging ego-involvement through the use of excessive praise or ego-avoidance through the imposition of guilt or shame, teaching in a controlling and prescriptive way, and encouraging damaging levels of competitiveness may be at best ineffective strategies, and at worst, deeply harmful to their music motivation and their wellbeing. (p. 78)

Competition is nearly ubiquitous in music education, and is often overused or misused as a form of short-term, external motivation. An overemphasis on socially comparative performance events can not only steer students' attention away from a sense of competence, autonomy, and/or relatedness but also reinforce social inequities in cases where school music programs with less resources are pitted against programs with an abundance of provisions for success (Hendricks, 2018). In addition to selecting competitive experiences with caution and care, music teachers may engage with students to (a) reframe competitive events as informing rather than controlling; (b) emphasize expressive goals and personal improvements rather than winning over others; and (c) focus attention on feedback received as a means toward improvement (Legutki, 2010). By focusing on alignment with internal motivations and promoting a sense of autonomy, competence, and relatedness, music teachers can help to redirect the focus away from fear of judgment, toward freedom of expression.

Recognizing Implicit Biases

Everything thus far in this chapter has worked within an assumption that teachers are able to discern students' needs and internal motivations, and to respond without bias or interference from their own values or worldviews. This assumption is reflective of what Noddings (1984) refers to as a "displacement of interest" (p. 34) when caring for another. Unfortunately, however, human interactions—particularly in instances of caring *with*, where needs and values are in continual negotiation toward the creation of equal and authentic relationships (Hendricks, 2021b)—are not that simple. Teachers can only support student ability development to the extent that they understand their own biases, and the ways in which their assumptions about students might influence a student's musical development and/or sense of self. Unchecked habits of mind might affect the ways in which teachers interact with, and respond to, different students, in some cases reinforcing inequities among students even when teachers maintain explicit goals to help all students to achieve musically. For this reason, it is important to address issues of implicit bias to bring awareness to the complexities of a music teacher's contribution to the learning process, and to provide suggestions for fostering self-awareness among music teachers.[2]

Implicit bias is associated with the unconscious beliefs and/or associations that individuals might hold about others (Johnson, 2020). It is common for people to hold unconscious associations that are in opposition to their explicit, or conscious, beliefs—such as when people who have an explicit desire to promote equity nevertheless make "snap judgments" about others from different backgrounds (e.g., race, class, sexual orientation, religion). Scholars from a variety of disciplines have recently amplified the argument that biases and stereotypes are a part of the human condition, and that acknowledging these biases (rather than, for example, claiming to be "color blind," or viewing racism, sexism, homophobia as someone else's evil) is a healthful first

---

[2] One of the most common contemporary critiques of behavioral psychology is that a sole focus on the individual—most often a focus on the white, educated, industrialized, rich, and democratic (WEIRD) individual (Henrick et al., 2010)—does not account for institutional and structural causes of injustice. However, it is also possible that focusing only on systems and structures shifts the responsibility for action away from individual efforts. Issues of equity must be considered from a psychological (individual, cognitive) perspective in addition to a sociological (structural, systems) perspective for multi-leveled change to take place (see Beeghly & Madva, 2020).

step toward tangible change (Beeghly & Madva, 2020; Hendricks, 2021a; Kendi, 2019). Project Implicit (n.d.) is a not-for-profit research network dedicated to promoting awareness about individual and group biases, and providing education and resources about bias mitigation. They have administered tens of millions of Implicit Association Tests that have advanced research in this area, while also helping individuals who take the test recognize their own implicit biases.[3]

Implicit bias exists in the mind and the body, extending to habits and sociality (Leboeuf, 2020). Perceptual habits involve the automaticity with which we have learned to interact with our environment, which is influenced by the social world around us. Just as musical ability is developed through a complex process of repetition and practice that is influenced by environmental and interpersonal catalysts, so are habits of mind and body (Leboeuf, 2020). Yet these habits are not restricted to individuals, but are a part of our social worlds, developed through patterns of social interaction that have developed over time (Bourdieu, 1980/1990). Stated differently, implicit bias might be considered as a product of habit, developed as an interaction of mind, body, and sociality, "as shaped by and shaping of the social world" (Leboeuf, 2020, p. 52). An awareness of the structural complexity of biases can help in efforts to untangle them from our everyday lives and ways of being. Such disentanglement involves, however, a careful and courageous look at the practical payoffs that one receives from maintaining the status quo (see Bell, 1992).

Biases are also informed by stereotypes, which stem from the human propensity toward categorization (Beeghly, 2020). Although the practice of labeling and organizing information is routinely helpful and often necessary, stereotypes are not always reliable, and can be hurtful. In the field of Western classical musical performance, for example, discriminatory stereotypes against women, lower-classed persons, people of color, and/or disabled individuals have led to the marginalization of many individuals who may otherwise have had successful performance careers (Smith & Hendricks, 2022). Furthermore, stereotypes that are deeply ingrained in the social habitus may lead individuals to doubt themselves or underperform because of the ways in which their identity relates to those stereotypes—a phenomenon known as stereotype threat (Greene, 2020)—or to experience a "double consciousness" of identity (Robinson & Hendricks, 2018).

Given the compounding complexity by which implicit biases are developed, it may not be easy—even for music teachers committed to inclusivity—to confront and overcome them. However, it is necessary work for those seeking to promote a more equitable system of music education. Just as habits of bias are developed over time, so can we strive to develop habits of epistemic responsibility, open-mindedness, humility, and a desire to learn about, from, and with others (see Dominguez, 2020).

Fortunately, debiasing intervention strategies exist (Madva, 2020a) and might be applied to care in music education by:

---

[3] The Implicit Association Test is available at https://implicit.harvard.edu/implicit/takeatest.html

- *Viewing action as an imperative for both individuals and communities.* Simply put, it takes all of us—individually and collectively—to make change.
- *Recognizing the multifaceted nature of stereotypes and biases.* Rather than pointing fingers at someone else—or, conversely, taking on the burden of responsibility alone—we might consider the complex array of habits of mind, body, and sociality that are at play, and begin, step by step, to change what we have the power to change.
- *Adopting epistemic humility.* Music education has a history of viewing the teacher as the "maestro" or "master," a perspective that unfairly disallows a teacher from being able to admit mistakes, let alone make them. Moving from a "deficit" to a "strengths" perspective, and engaging with what students bring rather than judging how they fit (or not) within a particular pedagogy, requires teachers to remain open to vulnerability, and learning along with their students (Hendricks, 2018).
- *Encouraging perspective-taking through humility, toward action.* Music teachers can practice empathy for, and with, their students to overcome biases and foster more inclusive classrooms where students can thrive in a number of different ways. Learning to see the perspective of another can lead to "questioning, wondering, dialogue, authentic allyship, and collaborative action toward social change" (Hendricks, 2021a, p. 59)—so long as the process involves humility. Mature or authentic empathy "requires letting go of superiority or 'hero' narratives and exercising compassion not as a badge of morality, but as a way of recognizing common humanity" (Hendricks, 2021a, p. 76; see also Smith, this volume).
- *Exercising an experimental mindset.* Earlier in this chapter we challenged the notion of "innate talent" (which presumes a mindset that talent is fixed) to suggest that ability development involved a complex system of processes, whereby student ability could grow in any number of ways (see also Dweck, 2008). Applying Madva's (2020b) concept of experimental mindset for implicit bias intervention to music education, music teachers may better serve a variety of student needs and dispositions by practicing curiosity and imagination, with a willingness to try new things and a disposition to let go of what does not work.
- *Practicing diversified experimentalism* (Madva, 2020b). In the stock market, diversification involves having an array of investments so that one does not go bankrupt from putting too much money into a bad investment. Applied to social justice work, one might "explore a bunch of different individual and social experiments and interventions to see which ones stick and which ones stink" (Madva, 2020a, p. 241). Applied to music education, teachers and students might be open to a number of different approaches for inclusive pedagogy, recognizing that not everything will be successful, but that different approaches will work better in certain contexts or at different times.

Conclusion

Caring for, about, and with music students involves not only understanding their various abilities, backgrounds, and interests, but also attending to the multifarious ways in which they might manifest musical potential. It is not enough to simply respond to perceived students' needs in any given moment. Teachers may benefit from a type of "student literacy" (Hendricks, 2018, p. 65) that allows them to determine where their students are on a longer trajectory toward a particular goal, and how they are perceiving and receiving feedback related to that goal. This literacy involves collaborative questioning and may develop as teachers exercise empathy as well as self-awareness, and as they foster relational and collective trust with students (Hendricks, 2018).

Engaging with students in this way may require a mindframe that McPherson and Hattie (2022) describe as a willingness to constantly reflect on the impact of their teaching on their students' learning (i.e., the mindframe "I am an evaluator of my impact on student learning"). Feedback that provides information back to an educator about the success of their teaching is of more consequence to a student's learning than other forms of feedback focused on what students have just done or achieved. It involves making appraisals about the teaching approaches they choose and engaging in a collaborative inquiry with their students about those approaches.

This type of mindframe also enables the teacher to avoid thinking about whether their students are capable of achieving a learning goal because they lack sufficient ability or commitment to the task. Instead, it reorients their thinking to diagnose what the student brings to their lesson, their motivation for learning, and their willingness to actively learn. It also encourages teachers to (a) apply more varied interventions or change directions when their approach doesn't work, (b) not blame students when they cannot meet the challenge, (c) use multiple methods for tackling learning tasks, and (d) work with students collaboratively so that they are jointly involved in the act of teaching.

Similar to the dispositions of compassionate music teaching (Hendricks, 2018), this type of mindframe ensures that students help co-construct learning within an environment where teaching is celebrated for being adaptable, reflective, and sensitive to the motivations and skills of each student (see McPherson & Hattie, 2022). Music teachers' willingness to reflect on and evaluate their impact on student learning may be enhanced by an awareness of the many ways in which musical ability can be developed. Furthermore, a commitment to self-reflection about personal and cultural biases, and the adoption of an experimental mindset (Madva, 2020b) might elicit an openness to exploration, curiosity, and imagination for teachers and students alike.

References

Bandura, A. (1997). *Self-efficacy: The exercise of control*. Freeman.
Beeghly, E. (2020). Bias and knowledge: Two metaphors. In E. Beeghly & A. Madva (Eds.), *An introduction to implicit bias: Knowledge, justice, and the social mind* (pp. 77–98). Routledge.
Beeghly, E., & Madva, A. (2020). Introducing implicit bias. In E. Beeghly & A. Madva (Eds.), *An introduction to implicit bias: Knowledge, justice, and the social mind* (pp. 1–19). Routledge.
Bell, D. (1992). *Faces at the bottom of the well: The permanence of racism*. Basic Books.
Bloom, B. S. (Ed.). (1985). *Developing talent in young people*. Ballantine.
Borland, J. H. (2021). The trouble with conceptions of giftedness. In R. J. Sternberg & D. Ambrose (Eds.), *Conceptions of giftedness and talent* (pp. 81–94). Palgrave Macmillan.
Bourdieu, P. (1980/1990). *The logic of practice*. Stanford University Press.

Deci, E. L., & Ryan, R. M. (1985). *Intrinsic motivation and self-determination in human behavior*. Plenum Press.

Dominguez, N. (2020). Moral responsibility for implicit biases: Examining our options. In E. Beeghly & A. Madva (Eds.), *An introduction to implicit bias: Knowledge, justice, and the social mind* (pp. 153–173). Routledge.

Dweck, C. S. (2008). *Mindset: The new psychology of success*. Random House.

Ericsson, K. A. (2014). Why expert performance is special and cannot be extrapolated from studies of performance in the general population: A response to criticisms. *Intelligence, 45*, 81–103. https://doi.org/10.1016/j.intell.2013.12.001

Ericsson, K. A., Krampe, R. T., & Tesch-Römer, C. (1993). The role of deliberate practice in the acquisition of expert performance. *Psychological Review, 100*, 363–406. https://doi.org/10.1037/0033-295X.100.3.363

Evans, P. (2015). Self-determination theory: An approach to motivation in music education. *Musicae Scientiae, 19*(1), 65–83. https://doi.org/10.1177/1029864914568044

Evans, P., McPherson, G. E., & Davidson, J. W. (2013). The role of psychological needs in ceasing music and music learning activities. *Psychology of Music, 41*, 600–619. https://doi.org/10.1177%2F0305735612441736

Gagné, F. (2009). Building gifts into talents: Detailed overview of the DMGT 2.0. In B. MacFarlane & T. Stambaught (Eds.), *Leading change in gifted education: The festschrift of Dr. Joyce VanTassel-Baska* (pp. 61–80). Prufrock Press.

Gagné, F. (2013). The DMGT: Changes within, beneath, and beyond. *Talent Development and Excellence, 5*, 5–19.

Gagné, F., & McPherson, G. E. (2016). Analyzing musical prodigiousness using Gagné's Integrative Model of Talent Development. In G. E McPherson (Ed.), *Music prodigies: Interpretations from psychology, education, musicology and ethnomusicology* (pp. 3–114). Oxford University Press.

Leboeuf, C. (2020). The embodied biased mind. In E. Beeghly & A. Madva (Eds.), *An introduction to implicit bias: Knowledge, justice, and the social mind* (pp. 41–56). Routledge.

Gladwell, M. (2008). *Outliers: The story of success*. Little, Brown and Company.

Glasser, S., & McPherson, G. E. (in press). The role of natural abilities in early childhood musical development. In M. Barrett & G. Welch (Eds.), *Oxford handbook of early childhood music learning and development*. Oxford University Press.

Greene, N. (2020). Stereotype threat, identity, and the disruption of habit. In E. Beeghly & A. Madva (Eds.), *An introduction to implicit bias: Knowledge, justice, and the social mind* (pp. 134–152). Routledge.

Hattie, J. A. C., & Zierer, K. (2018). *10 mindframes for visible learning: Teaching for success*. Routledge.

Henrick, J., Heine, S. J., & Norenzayan, A. (2010). *The weirdest people in the world?* (RatSWD Working Paper Series, 139). Rat für Sozial- und Wirtschaftsdaten (RatSWD). http://hdl.handle.net/10419/43616

Hendricks, K. S. (2016). The sources of self-efficacy: Educational research and implications for music. *Update: Applications of Research in Music Education, 35*(1), 32–38. https://doi.org/10.1177%2F8755123315576535

Hendricks, K. S. (2018). *Compassionate music teaching*. Rowman & Littlefield.

Hendricks, K. S. (2021a). Counternarratives: Troubling majoritarian certainty. *Action, Criticism, & Theory for Music Education, 20*(4), 58–78. http://act.maydaygroup.org/articles/Hendricks20_4.pdf

Hendricks, K. S. (2021b). Authentic connection in music education: A chiastic essay. In K. S. Hendricks & J. Boyce-Tillman (Eds.), *Authentic connection: Music, spirituality, and wellbeing* (pp. 237–253). Peter Lang.

Hendricks, K. S., & Boyce-Tillman, J. (2021). Music, connection, and authenticity. In K. S. Hendricks & J. Boyce-Tillman (Eds.), *Authentic connection: Music, spirituality, and wellbeing* (pp. 3–15). Peter Lang.

Hess, J. (2018). Musicking marginalization: Periphractic practices in music education. In A. M. Kraehe, R. Gaztambide-Fernández, & B. S. Carpenter II (Eds.), *The Palgrave handbook of race and the arts in education* (pp. 325–346). Palgrave Macmillan.

Howe, M. J., Davidson, J. W., & Sloboda, J. A. (1998). Innate talents: Reality or myth? *Behavioral and Brain Sciences*, 21(3), 399–407. https://doi.org/10.1017/S0140525X9800123X

Johnson, G. M. (2020). The psychology of bias: From data to theory. In E. Beeghly & A. Madva (Eds.), *An introduction to implicit bias: Knowledge, justice, and the social mind* (pp. 20–40). Routledge.

Kendi, I. X. (2019). *How to be an anti-racist*. One World.

Leahy, K., & Smith, T. D. (2021). The self-directed learning of adult music students: A comparison of teacher approaches and student needs. *International Journal of Music Education*, 39(3), 289–300. https://www.doi.org/10.1177/0255761421991596

Leboeuf, C. (2020). The embodied biased mind. In E. Beeghly & A. Madva (Eds.), *An introduction to implicit bias: Knowledge, justice, and the social mind* (pp. 41–56). Routledge.

Legutki, A. R. (2010). *Self-determined music participation: The role of psychological needs satisfaction, intrinsic motivation, and self-regulation in the high school band experience* (Publication No. 3452091) [Doctoral dissertation, University of Illinois at Urbana-Champaign]. ProQuest Dissertations Publishing.

López-Íñiguez, G., & Burnard, P. (2021). Toward a nuanced understanding of musicians' professional learning pathways: What does critical reflection contribute? *Research Studies in Music Education*. Advance online publication. https://doi.org/10.1177/1321103X211025850

Madva, A. (2020a). Individual and structural interventions. In E. Beeghly & A. Madva (Eds.), *An introduction to implicit bias: Knowledge, justice, and the social mind* (pp. 233–270). Routledge.

Madva, A. (2020b). Integration, community, and the medical model of social injustice. *Journal of Applied Philosophy*, 37(2), 211–232. https://doi.org/10.1111/japp.12356

McPherson, G. E. (2001). Commitment and practice: Key ingredients for achievement during the early stages of learning a musical instrument. *Bulletin of the Council for Research in Music Education*, (147), 122–127.

McPherson, G. E., Blackwell, J., & Hallam, S. (2022). Musical potential, giftedness and talent development. In G. E. McPherson (Ed.), *The Oxford handbook of music performance* (Vol. 1, pp. 31–55). Oxford University Press.

McPherson, G. E., & Hattie, J. (2022). High impact teaching mindframes. In G. E. McPherson (Ed.), *The Oxford handbook of music performance* (Vol. 1, pp. 123–152). Oxford University Press.

McPherson, G. E., & McCormick, J. (2006). Self-efficacy and music performance. *Psychology of Music*, 34, 322–336. https://doi.org/10.1177/0305735606064841

McPherson, G. E., & Williamon, A. (2016). Building gifts into musical talents In G. E. McPherson (Ed.), *The child as musician: A handbook of musical development* (2nd ed., pp. 340–360). Oxford University Press.

Müllensiefen, D., Kozbelt, A., Olszewski-Kubilius, P., Subotnik, R., Worrell, F., & Preckel, F. (2022). Talent development in music. In G. E. McPherson (Ed.), *The Oxford handbook of music performance* (Vol. 1, pp. 84–105). Oxford University Press.

Noddings, N. (1984). *Caring: A feminine approach to ethics and moral education*. University of California Press.

Project Implicit. (n.d.). https://www.projectimplicit.net/

Ray, J., & Hendricks, K. S. (2019). Collective efficacy belief, within-group agreement, and performance quality among instrumental chamber ensembles. *Journal of Research in Music Education*, 66(4), 449–464. https://doi.org/10.1177/0022429418805090

Robinson, D., & Hendricks, K. S. (2018). Black keys on a white piano: A Negro narrative of double-consciousness in American music education. In B. C. Talbot (Ed.), *Marginalized voices in music education* (pp. 28–45). Routledge.

Ryan, R. M., & Deci, E. L. (2000). Self-determination theory and the facilitation of intrinsic motivation, social development, and well-being. *American Psychologist*, 55(1), 68–78. https://doi.org/10.1037/0003-066X.55.1.68

Smith, T. D., & Hendricks, K. S. (2022). Diversity, inclusion, and access. In G. E. McPherson (Ed.), *The Oxford handbook of music performance* (Vol. 1, pp. 528–549). Oxford University Press.

Talbot, B. C. (Ed.). (2018). *Marginalized voices in music education*. Routledge.

Wright, R. (2015). Music education and social reproduction: Breaking cycles of injustice. In C. Benedict, P. Schmidt, G. Spruce, & P. Woodford (Eds.), *The Oxford handbook of social justice in music education* (pp. 340–371). Oxford University Press.

CHAPTER 35

CONVEYING PUPIL ACCESS TO WELLBEING THROUGH RELATIONAL CARE IN MUSIC EDUCATION

KARI HOLDHUS

CARE HANDBOOK TOPICS

Wellbeing and human flourishing

INTRODUCTION

In this theoretical chapter, my main claim is that teachers' pedagogical facilitation of aesthetic, pedagogic transitional rooms for their pupils is deeply connected with care. To explore and justify this claim, I discuss music teachers' relational values and approaches of care for and with pupils. My argument is that the aesthetic, when performed relationally and rooted in an educational context, is especially suited to convey wellbeing and human flourishing, and that working to enhance pupils' musical life-worlds[1] can therefore be described as teacher acts of care.

My formulated chapter question is: Why should, and how can, music teachers nurture musical flourishing and enhance pupils' musical wellbeing as acts of care?

---

[1] Life-world: The world as immediately or directly experienced in the subjectivity of everyday life. The life-world includes individual, social, perceptual and practical experiences (Life-World, Encyclopedia Britannica).

The multifaceted, theoretical answer comprises pedagogical stances of relational and reciprocal equity, acceptance of teacher vulnerability, the concept of "eudaimonia" (understood as wellbeing through citizenship) and a view on pedagogy's transitional rooms as aesthetic and vice versa.

Throughout the text, I provide practical snapshots of classroom situations in general school where music is a subject, in order to connect the text to real-life situations. Vignettes and citations stem from either of the eight public schools participating in the innovation research project "*School and concert—from transmission to dialogue*" (DiSko)[2], more precisely from observations and interviews related to the project's main activities of developing dialogic musician-teacher partnerships (Holdhus, 2019; Holdhus et al., 2021). In my fieldwork, I observed many of the project's participating teachers as preoccupied by pupils' wellbeing through musicking, in class and in general. Teachers seemed to care about pupils' personal and social relations with music, on short and long-term basis. To be engaged in their work rests in any teacher's backbone; however, as I argue, aesthetic enterprises have some special properties that connect to compassion and reciprocal care. In the following, I thus explore care as contribution to underlying theories of a relational aesthetic education.

> *The class is busy creating a text for a verse about technology and cars to a melody from a pop song, theme and melody suggested by pupils during a prior lesson. Many of them sing, and some pupils improvise movements. The teacher, Asta, wants to work on another song. She starts singing a verse about baking. Listening to the text, the Baker starts to giggle. The others look at him, smiling. "Anyone here like to bake?," the teacher asks. The class shouts the Baker's name, pointing enthusiastically at him, all smiles. They then start negotiating more verses to his song, line by line.*
>
> (Researcher's note, DiSko project, October, 2018)

The above depicts a 4th grade music classroom situation[3] following an invitation to the pupils to bring their musics to school. While working with songs, the small class of 16 pupils and their teacher decided to create new texts mirroring the pupils' interests. Thanks to the teacher's practical, student-centered approach (Blair, 2009; Coss, 2019), both teacher and researcher learned a lot about the pupils, such as the fact that many were interested in cars and motorcycles, that several pupils liked to do dance and parkour and that one pupil in particular dreamed of becoming a baker.

The teacher, Asta, from Disko project school 2, can represent many of the teachers through her focus on pupil care in music teaching. During an interview, Asta pointed out the explicit goals of many of her classroom music activities:

---

[2] The innovation project "School and concert—from transmission to dialogue" (DiSko) was undertaken in the years 2017–2021 and financed by the Norwegian Research Council, project number 260390. Consent and ethical considerations were attended to in accordance with Norwegian Centre for Research Data regulations.

[3] In Norway, 96.5% of the population attend public school grades 1–10. Music is a compulsory school subject allotted one or two hours a week per grade.

"When we do music in class, I want to strengthen my pupils' self-esteem and to facilitate their reflection on themselves and others in joint musicking."[4]

Asta's aim is to model and facilitate communal diversity as something acceptable and desirable in the music classroom and beyond. Enhancing the ability to incorporate music into the pupils' lives is a common music teacher goal (Stige, 2021). The deeper intention of the teachers may be to "forward the experience of the learning self by linking inner thoughts, feelings, memories, fears, desires and ideas to external others, events, history, culture and socially constructed ideas" (Ellsworth, 2005, p. 44). During my empirical work at schools, Ellsworth's precise intentional educational formulation was hardly explicit among the teachers. However, I experienced the aims Ellsworth purports modeled in practical ways.

The situation described above could not have taken place without profound teacher understanding of the pupils' personal and group interests, as well as musical skills. In applying knowledge derived from pupil and group mapping, the teacher also was able to "meddle in the middle" (Craft et al., 2012), which can be described as progressively providing the pupils with relevant materials and questions to keep the educational, creative, collaborative and aesthetic wheel spinning.

This chapter opens with a discussion on facilitation of "musical asylums" (DeNora, 2016) and liminal rooms, two important vehicles in aesthetic experience and learning important for human flourishing and wellbeing. It is my argument that many music teachers' work on establishing musical asylums or liminal rooms in class is grounded in reciprocal care and vulnerability. This both implies caring for pupils and, as member of school and society: Caring about the music and the meaningfulness of being a relational music teacher. The second part of the chapter is dedicated to the relationality in educational situations I claim are grounded in care and compassion.

Human Flourishing and Aesthetic Rooms

In their teaching, many teachers in the research project DiSko worked explicitly with aesthetic educational approaches. There are many reasons for doing so that connect with care, because the aesthetic is often seen as a vehicle for tackling life, emotionally and socially. The aesthetic as a phenomenon has an array of characteristics. It is, among else, simultaneously bodily, subjective, emotional, sensual, ambiguous, empathic, contextual, culturally embedded, cognitive, intersubjective, and passing (Lehmann, 2013). These characteristics correspond to the characteristics of music as a source of wellbeing, as presented by MacDonald et al. (2012) in the book *Music, Health, and Wellbeing*. These writers claim music to be ubiquitous, emotional, engaging, distracting, physical,

---

[4] Citations originate from DiSko interviews and are translated from Norwegian.

ambiguous, social and communicative, and they further point at how it affects behavior, identities, and life skills. The properties of the aesthetic and of music can be seen as possibilities for human flourishing. Such flourishing, however, is not only personal; it has to relate to society. Thus, there is a need for an understanding of music as something practical and communal. Translating the noun "music" into the verb "musicking," Christopher Small (1998) provides this understanding by directing his gaze explicitly toward the human relationship:

> The act of musicking establishes in the place where it is happening a set of relationships, and it is in those relationships that the meaning of the act lies. They are to be found not only between those organized sounds which are conventionally thought of as being the stuff of musical meaning but also between the people who are taking part, in whatever capacity, in the performance. (p. 9)

Small's definition of musical relationships refers to any affiliation with music as musicking. Musicking manifests musicality in a myriad of participation, creation, and appreciation. A teacher who takes this seriously cares about the establishment of musicking as an important component of every pupil's personal life-world. Choosing such an approach can be viewed as a moral stance and should be complemented by engaging with closeness, empathy, understanding and compassion toward individual and group life-worlds (Hendricks, 2018; Noddings, 2013). Musicking thus legitimizes a view on musicality as a general human and societal trait, expanding narrower notions of musicking for a selected few.

Aesthetic experiences are difficult to pin down in words, as they are tacit or unspeakable (Polanyi, 1958). Consequently, they also reflect embodiment (Merleau-Ponty, 1962) and prelinguistic knowledge (Trevarthen, 1979). This taciturnity offers an important opportunity to deal with personal or societal taboos (Bale, 2009) and problematic life issues, which brings us to an interesting aspect of the aesthetic, namely the sublime. It is through the sublime (Burke, 2013) that we deal with horror, fear, pain, sorrow and danger, and the sublime relates to "negative experiences, chocks, blockings, a hint towards death" (Bale, 2009, p. 89).[5]

Dealing with music thus offers possibilities to process both the joyful and problematic sides of one's personal and social life. This does not necessarily point toward individualism, as being and acting in the world are always relational (Gergen, 2009). However, it is not possible to share our personal perception of an experience in full range. Herein lies a freedom, a space or a so-called room of one's own, often referred to as "liminal" (Gennep, 1960) or "liminoid" (Turner, 1969), to point out the possibility of withdrawal, contemplation and resurrection. The notion *liminality* stems from anthropology, describing rites of passage, i.e., when a person changes status, such as from girl to woman or from unmarried to married.

"Liminoidity" is a sort of liminality executed by (post)modern (Western) humans:

---

[5] Translated from Norwegian.

Liminoidity possesses the characteristics of a liminal experience, but it is optional and does not necessarily involve the resolution of a personal crisis or cultural rite. A graduation ceremony may be regarded as liminal, while a rock concert may be understood as liminoid, resulting in reconfiguration. In liminality, this reconfiguration will be new statuses, rights and duties. In liminoidity, this will primarily be different behaviour, revitalization, reflections and possible changes in social collaborations, morals, traditions, and customs. (Fagerheim, 2010, p.151)[6]

Both modalities contain a recombination of cultural and symbolic materials in which the liminoid appears different from liminality through voluntary, experimentation, play, and games. It should be noted that any withdrawal, not only artistic or aesthetic (such as attending a football match or going to the beach) can be labeled as liminoid. However, I would argue that aesthetic experiences and actions are inherently liminoid. The anthropological theory of the liminal can reflect art's deep cultural roots of a psychological transitive room linked to learning, creativity, change, and the exploration of the self and its relations as transitive. Young people's identities as such are at stake and interchangeable (O'Neill, 2015); and access to liminoid aesthetic rooms can be of great importance for their wellbeing and flourishing. DeNora (2016), who introduces the notion of "musical asylums," however, points out the lack of productivity in only visiting a musical shelter (p. 55) without possibilities for transformation. DeNora labels such a shelter as a "removal." To her, it represents a "timeout from social spaces where one needs to perform/act" (p. 55). This need for withdrawal is recognizable to many of us. We may rest in it and return to social life refreshed. However, an aesthetic removal entails potential risks for permanent social withdrawal without problem-solving. To provide relief, DeNora claims that the "asylum" (or liminoid room) needs to offer possibilities to "refurnish" the room for the better. A transformative musical asylum thus takes place in participatory art/social activities like classes, choirs and bands, or when attending a concert, leading to a better capacity for action in a social space together with others (p. 56).

Maya: We invented a lot and when we disagreed, we had to find the fastest way to figure things out because there was little time . . .
Clara: . . . . and then we often had three persons trying to decide . . .
Sarah: . . . but everyone couldn't do what we wanted; not all of us could do the splits . . .
Maya: . . . so we had to come up with something else . . .
    (Group interview, 4th grade pupils, creative dance lesson, Disko school 4)

This small group of creative dancers are finishing each others' sentences; their creativity and collaboration seems without inhibitions. Together, they are in a relational "bubble" when creating and rehearsing their choreography. This situation can be an example of DeNora's transformative asylum. However, facilitating transformative liminal

---

[6] Translated from Norwegian.

situations in a group or class demands good-enough facilitation and maintenance by teachers. This implies creating an environment that is trustful enough to dare to show vulnerability, and to expose shortcomings, failures and unusual ideas in the group (Hendricks, 2018). Profound group trust may emerge in any group (Brookfield, 2015), and in music education, the teacher's compassionate facilitation seems fundamental (Holdhus, 2019).

In terms of music education, Smith & Silverman (2020) discuss the ancient Greek notion of *eudaimonia*, which has often been translated as "happiness," suggesting a hedonistic concept. However, eudaimonia, they claim, cannot represent the good life without connecting to others and as part of society. They also claim that this is the case with music and music education. To be truly meaningful, music must be part of and interwoven in societal situations and challenges; and a relationally-oriented, caring teacher will aim at providing possibilities where pupils can experience music as connective in these ways. DeNora's (2016) refurnishing, as well as Smith and Silverman's (2020) interpretation of eudaimonia, describe the aesthetic as transformative. Least but not least, the aesthetic room corresponds to a pedagogical potential room (Winnicott, 1991), because transformation also lies at the heart of education (Ellsworth, 2005; Biesta, 2015).

Relation, Care and Compassion for Human Flourishing

Buber (2012) views relation as the ontological grounding for human enterprise. Human care cannot be otherwise than a relation. This applies whether care is performed to keep someone safe and happy, or whether care is understood as working meticulously or acting with caution. However, relations are not inherently good (Bingham & Sidorkin, 2004), and therefore a moral aspect and stance has to be at play in educational relations as well as in aesthetics and arts. Further, care and morals seem inherent, because immoral care comes forth as an oxymoron. When discussing music education, care, education and aesthetics should be treated as profoundly relational, deeply interwoven elements (Thompson, 2015). Other interwoven aspects dealing with care is whether one cares for someone or cares about something (Hendricks, this volume; Silverman, this volume). The relational explanation would be that to care for something or someone, one has to care about them. Explicitly, this means that the carer's moral motivation must be present within caring *for* (Cronquist et al., 2004).

Noddings (2013) has constructed the notions of *one-caring* and *cared-for* to explain the functions of a caring relationship. *One-caring*, according to Noddings (2013), denotes the caregiver, and *cared-for* refers to the one receiving the care (p. 28). In this respect, in a teacher–pupil relationship, the teacher will therefore act as *one-caring* and the pupil will consistently be labeled as *cared-for*. However, in Noddings's writings, I perceive a resolution of these two roles, as the role of the one-caring cannot only be of moral duty or obligation (pp. 62–63). Care, Noddings claims, cannot thrive if it is grounded in mere duty because care is reciprocal and entangled: "Each of us is dependent upon the other in moral relationships" (p. 73).

I find it difficult to label teachers as ones-caring and pupils as cared-for. This is because the wellbeing and companionship of pupils imply not only the binary one-caring and cared-for, but also contributes to a much more complicated web of relations, especially in classes and groups. Could it be more relevant to apply the notion of "compassion" (Hendricks, 2018)? Compassion, Hendricks writes, is more of an equalizer than an uneven relationship. Hendricks understands compassion as a "relationship of experience-sharing in which one might offer support to another based on a shared understanding of feelings, hopes and/or desires" (p. 5). This means that the one cared-for can contribute to the development and character of the other's ways of caring, and vice versa. Pupils, then, will demand and shape the specific character of their teacher's care and vice versa (Cekaite & Bergnehr, 2018).

This way of viewing the teaching relation also was displayed in music teacher reflections during Disko project interviews, here exemplified by teacher Ole's statement below:

As a teacher, you need synergy between your own musical knowledge and the pupils and their contributions or the pupils will not find participation meaningful. (Teacher Ole, school 1)

To achieve synergy between teacher and pupils, teacher knowledge of, and empathy toward, pupils is essential. Conversely, without proper familiarity, teacher engagement can be imposing and based on assumptions: the one-caring (teacher) believes that engaging with a certain kind of music in a certain way will enrich and improve the life-world of the cared-for (pupil). This approach can be viewed as a counterfactor to the main definition of a caring relation, which builds on relationship and empathy, placing the emphasis not on what the teacher thinks should happen, but rather on an analysis of the pupils' situation in time and context (Noddings, 2013).

The relationship between teacher and pupil, however, is not bound to be asymmetric. In his writings, Biesta (2004) suggests overcoming the teacher's power dilemma by proposing that educational activities are undertaken in *the gap* or in the relationship between teacher and pupil. To Biesta, a teaching obligation therefore does not necessarily produce uneven relations if the relationship is grounded in equity. Explicitly, this means that an 11-year-old pupil and a 40-year-old teacher's contributions to a relationship must be perceived as of equal worth, yet profoundly different. In terms of care and compassion, such an approach corresponds to Hendricks's (2018) definition of compassion as "one of shared human experience with another," a process of relating to others through acknowledging diversity (p. 5). This, ideally, points at a shared need for care in both teacher and pupil, as well as a shared urge to perform care. However, caring teachers also must pursue their duty to teach, that is, to offer their expertise and to execute professionally elaborated teaching activities aiming at enhancing pupils' knowledge and skills (Biesta, 2012).

In a DiSko interview, teacher Eva (school 7) pointed out a resembling teaching quest in music:

"I think, as music teachers, we try to provide pupils with room for their imagination and creation and help them undergo a kind of creative skill development."

Classroom life is imprinted by such pupil contexts as location, age, local culture and contemporary challenges. Pupils are influenced by their sociocultural and socioeconomical origins, surroundings and interests outside of school, and teachers therefore must approach music teaching as something shared yet individual. Encountering other pupils of different origins can offer the possibility to address how to contend with, treat, and respect the conflicting views and ways of others (Stengel, 2004).

The *manifesto of relational pedagogy* (Bingham & Sidorkin, 2004, pp. 5–7) points out that relations are difficult, and this also includes care and compassion as relational elements in experiencing, teaching and learning. One of relational pedagogy's primary aims is to provide pupils with tools to overcome the unfamiliar and conflicting in productive ways. Working with pupils' musics in safe liminal rooms can simulate how to handle more profound societal issues and conflicts than musical taste and personal wellbeing. This adds dimensions to the notions of wellbeing and flourishing that go beyond musical asylums as personal refurnishing. Rather, it can be described by the notion of eudaimonia in its full and deep meaning, as eudaimonian human flourishing entails living and acting for "the betterment of oneself and one's community" (Smith & Silverman, 2020, p. 13). Applying a Smallian approach to musicking, educating "through" music means addressing a wider concept that confirms music teaching's societal functions as elements of flourishing through music. For a teacher, these are aims based on values (Bowman, 2016) deciding techniques and ways of approaching pupils, classes and musics.

Compassionate music teachers live through and comply with a relational form of educational philosophy (Bingham & Sidorkin, 2004). From practical life, I find such a relational involvement strategy exemplified in teacher Ole's statement from a Disko interview, where he points at the importance of balancing teaching aims and pupil interests:

"A musical project must never become more important than the pupils. Managing a balance demands profound dialogue." (Teacher Ole, school 1)

Reflecting Ole's stance of putting the pupils first, compassionate music teaching thus "requires that we listen, that we empathize, that we truly put ourselves in students' shoes and consider what learning looks like from the students' perspective" (Hendricks, 2018, p. 5). Thus, teachers "move toward shared music-making with others whom, despite their usually younger age and lesser experience in certain areas, we recognize to be equal to us in the collective place we call humanity" (Hendricks, 2018, p. 16).

Ljungblad (2019) proposes the concept of pedagogical, relational teachership (PeRT), which demands "pedagogical tact and stance" from teachers. Teacher tactfulness, Ljungblad suggests, provides pupils with opportunities to act, whereas a caring, listening and empathetic pedagogical stance creates "possibilities for the students to influence their own participation even in dilemma situations" (p. 6).

What I draw from this is that compassionate teachers must relate to profound ethics of equity. However, in everyday life situations, things are complicated. Undoubtedly, there will be mistakes and regrettable situations for all participants. Thus, a trustful class and school environment is pivotal to strive toward because there must be opportunities for failure and regret for children and teachers alike. In a relational approach, teacher vulnerability is therefore visible and acknowledged (Hendricks, 2018). To Pijanowsky (2004), it is even a positive thing: the teacher should strive neither for constant positive relations nor to be perfect, because few people are; and collaboration, companionship and responsibility grow from this joint state of imperfection. Pijanowsky grounds this view in Winnicott's (1991) concept of the good-enough mother, who leaves/must leave parts of problem-solving and exploration to the child, as opposed to a "curling parent," who smoothes out every bump in the road in front of the child. Good-enough teachers are the ones who dare to display and even use their vulnerability in teaching situations (Romney & Holland, 2020). Good-enough teachers thus are able to bring their vulnerability, engagement, and investment in care to the table, however imperfect:

> "In a way, it affects all of us to have a joint musical warm-up. Doing these exercises together ... softens me and the pupils and prepares us to give it a try. I think they have a unifying effect." (Teacher Hans, Disko school 2)

This statement from Hans displays an example of togetherness in class that also reveals the teacher's feeling of—need for—belonging in the educational relationship.

Relational teaching can, at its best, result in a rewarding, good life of teaching, or perhaps flourishing, here exemplified by Marissa Silverman's (2012) teaching of "musical appreciation" in a large and diverse New York secondary school. "In the end," she writes, "we had grown together in acknowledging, welcoming, and understanding new musics. I was not the only teacher in the room: my students, my young colleagues, were continuously excited and proud to teach me 'their musics'" (p. 113).

Conclusion

In this chapter I have approached the question *Why should and how can music teachers nurture human flourishing and enhance pupils' musical wellbeing as acts of care?*

Aesthetic experiences can be seen as personal shelters and models for handling feelings, sensations and taboos, and such experiences are contextual, communal, and educational. Thus, musical and aesthetical experiences are important for pupils' wellbeing and flourishing. Many music teachers aim at such wellbeing in pupils and groups of pupils. This begs an understanding of wellbeing and human flourishing as hinging on societal contribution or eudaimonia for pupils as well as teachers.

I have argued the aesthetic to be a profound vehicle for relational human flourishing and as such implicit in a caring approach to music teaching. Teachers' moral stance and motivation, or caring *about* grounds in which ways they care *for* pupils when teaching music.

The educational gap (Biesta, 2004) and transitional space (Winnicott, 1990) correspond to aesthetic shelters and liminal rooms. To activate reciprocal care, music teachers should work toward furnishing such gap rooms as safe spaces, within which aesthetic enterprises can be orchestrated skillfully and in a trustful environment. This as well relates to the teacher's own need for belonging, contribution and meaningfulness. Teacher's care for and exposure to pupils and musics then comes forth as an investment to belong and be a part of the music, the class and the school, seen as communal and societal entities. Thus, teacher caring for pupil's musicking in and through liminal room is profoundly reciprocal.

References

Bale, K. (2009). *Estetikk: En innføring* [Aesthetics: An orientation]. Pax.
Biesta, G. J. J. (2004). "Mind the Gap!" Communication and the educational relation. In C. Bingham & A. M. Sidorkin (Eds.), *No education without relation* (p. 11–22). Peter Lang.
Biesta, G. J. J. (2012). Giving teaching back to education: Responding to the disappearance of the teacher. *Phenomenology & Practice, 6*(2), 35–49. https://doi.org/10.29173/pandpr19860
Biesta, G. J. (2015). *Beautiful risk of education*. Routledge.
Bingham, C., & Sidorkin, A. M. (2004). *No education without relation*. Peter Lang.
Blair, D. V. (2009). Stepping aside: Teaching in a student-centered music classroom. *Music Educators Journal, 95*(3), 42–45. https://doi.org/10.1177%2F0027432108330760
Bowman, W. (2016). Artistry, ethics, and citizenship. In D. Elliott, M. Silverman, & W. Bowman (Eds.), *Artistic citizenship: Artistry, social responsibility, and ethical praxis* (pp. 59–80). Oxford University Press.
Brookfield, S. D. (2015). *The skillful teacher: On technique, trust, and responsiveness in the classroom*. John Wiley & Sons.
Buber, M. (2012). *I and Thou* (W. Kaufmann, Trans.) [eBook]. eBookit.com. (Original work published 1937)
Burke, E. (2013). *A philosophical inquiry into the origin of our ideas of the sublime and beautiful: With an introductory discourse concerning taste*. Gegensatz Press. (Original work published 1823)
Cekaite, A., & Bergnehr, D. (2018). Affectionate touch and care: Embodied intimacy, compassion and control in early childhood education. *European Early Childhood Education Research Journal, 26*(6), 940–955. https://doi.org/10.1080/1350293X.2018.1533710

Coss, R. G. (2019). Creative thinking in music: Student-centered strategies for implementing exploration into the music classroom. *General Music Today*, *33*(1), 29–37. https://doi.org/10.1177%2F1048371319840654

Craft, A., Chappell, K., Rolfe, L., & Jobbins, V. (2012). Reflective creative partnerships as "meddling in the middle": Developing practice. *Reflective Practice*, *13*(4), 579–595. https://doi.org/10.1080/14623943.2012.670624

Cronqvist, A., Theorell, T., Burns, T., & Lützén, K. (2004). Caring about-caring for: Moral obligations and work responsibilities in intensive care nursing. *Nursing Ethics*, *11*(1), 63–76.

DeNora, T. (2016). *Music asylums: Wellbeing through music in everyday life*. Routledge.

Ellsworth, E. (2005). *Places of learning: Media, architecture, pedagogy*. Routledge.

Fagerheim, P. (2010). *Nordnorsk faenskap: produksjon, ritualisering og identifikasjon i rap* [North-Norwegian devilry: Production, ritualisation and identification in rap]. Norwegian University of Science and Technology.

Gennep, A. V. (1960). *The rites of passage*. Routledge & Kegan Paul.

Gergen, K. J. (2009). *Relational Being*. Oxford University Press.

Hendricks, K. S. (2018). *Compassionate music teaching*. Rowman & Littlefield.

Holdhus, K. (2019). The polyphony of musician–teacher partnerships: Towards real dialogues? *Thinking Skills and Creativity*, *31*, 243–251. https://doi.org/10.1016/j.tsc.2019.01.001

Holdhus, K., Romme, J. C., & Espeland, M. (2021). *Skole og konsert—fra formidling til dialog: Sluttrapport fra et innovasjonsprosjekt* [School and concert—from transmission to dialogue: Final report from an innovation project]. Western Norway University of Applied Sciences.

Lehmann, N. O. (2013). En mangfoldighed af andethedserfaringer: Om æstetik på flere måder [A plurality of otherness-experiences: About the many ways of the aesthetic]. *Tidsskrift for Børne- Og Ungdomskultur*, *57*, 25–36.

Ljungblad, A. L. (2019). Pedagogical relational teachership (PeRT): A multi-relational perspective. *International Journal of Inclusive Education*, *25*(7), 860–876. https://doi.org/10.1080/13603116.2019.1581280

Merleau-Ponty, M. (1962). *Phenomenology of perception*. Routledge.

Noddings, N. (2013). *Caring: A relational approach to ethics and moral education*. University of California Press.

O'Neill, S. A. (2015). Youth empowerment and transformative music engagement. In C. Benedict, P. Schmidt, G. Spruce, & P. Woodford (Eds.). *The Oxford handbook of social justice in music education* (pp. 388–405). Oxford University Press.

Pijanowski, C. M. (2004). Education for democracy demands "good-enough" teachers. *Counterpoints*, *259*, 103–119.

Polanyi, M. (1958). *Personal knowledge*. University of Chicago.

Romney, A. C., & Holland, D. V. (2020). The vulnerability paradox: Strengthening trust in the classroom. *Management Teaching Review*. Advance online publication. https://doi.org/10.1177%2F2379298120978362

Silverman, M. (2012). Virtue ethics, care ethics, and "the good life of teaching." *Action, Criticism, and Theory for Music Education*, *2*, 96–122. http://act.maydaygroup.org/articles/Silverman11_2.pdf

Small, C. (1998). *Musicking: The meanings of performing and listening*. Wesleyan University Press.

Smith, G. D., & Silverman, M. (Eds.). (2020). *Eudaimonia: Perspectives for music learning*. Routledge.

Stengel, B. (2004). Knowing is response-able relation. *Counterpoints*, *259*, 139–152.

Stige, B. (2021). Artistic citizenship and the crafting of mutual musical care. In K. Holdhus, R. Murphy, & M. Espeland (Eds), *Music education as craft: Reframing theories and practices* (pp. 89–105). Springer.

Thompson, J. (2015). Towards an aesthetics of care. *Research in Drama Education: Journal of Applied Theatre and Performance*, 20(4), 430–441.

Turner, V. W. (1969). *The ritual process: Structure and anti-structure*. Routledge.

Trevarthen, C. (1979). Communication and cooperation in early infancy. In M. Bullowa (Ed.). *Before speech: The beginning of interpersonal communication* (pp. 321–347). Cambridge University Press.

Winnicott, D. W. (1991). *Playing and reality*. Psychology Press.

CHAPTER 36

FOSTERING CARE THROUGH CORE REFLECTION

MARGARET H. BERG

CARE HANDBOOK TOPICS

Wellbeing and human flourishing

IN the midst of a teacher's busy life, there seems to be little time to identify our unique characteristics and motivations for teaching. However, as Kate, a fourth year teacher in a study by Adams et al. (2013) reminds us: "We teach who we *are* and if we aren't being us, if we're not being true to ourselves, and what we believe, then we're sunk" (p. 67).

Consider this fictitious, although typical post-rehearsal reflection by an experienced teacher:

> "The first violins still aren't quite together on their eighth-note entrances in the first measure of Eine Kleine!," Ms. Smith says to herself as she collapses into her office desk chair at the end of rehearsal. "I could go back to basics tomorrow, having them clap the rhythm while chanting the eighth-note subdivisions. Maybe I should have them play the measure individually to make the point that they need to practice outside of rehearsal?!" An image of Sam and Katy (who sit in the last stand of the first violin section) flashes across Ms. Smith's mind. Sam and Katy joined the orchestra program in 5th grade. They continue to participate in high school orchestra with limited practice outside of rehearsals and neither student takes private lessons, either by choice or due to family finances. Ms. Smith dismisses the image, returning to her reflection on the rehearsal. "I never liked it when my high school orchestra teacher had us play individually in front of the whole orchestra, but we've got to get Eine Kleine to the next level since district festival is only one month away!" Ms. Smith quickly decides to first use the "back-to-basics" approach, and if that doesn't fix the issue, she will then use the "playing individually" approach.

This post-rehearsal reflection is example of "action-oriented reflection" (Korthagen, 2015), based on Dewey's (1910) reflective thinking model. The reflection takes little time as she notices a problem, hypothesizes potential causes, devises solutions by drawing on strategies used in previous rehearsals, and chooses a solution that she will then evaluate for its impact in a subsequent rehearsal. At the same time, Ms. Smith does not attend to felt aspects of the situation (e.g., tiredness at the end of the rehearsal, frustration with student behaviors, and underlying anxiety about the number of remaining rehearsals before district festival) or consider the conflict between the use of "playing individually" and her past experience of, along with her current students' potential response to, this strategy. Moreover, her underlying motivations are unclear, given her fleeting awareness of particular students and mention of the upcoming district orchestra festival.

Music teachers are socialized into a profession where social comparison is a norm (Hendricks, 2018). For many, social comparison begins during middle school or high school with ensemble chair placements or section leader assignments, progressing to extracurricular community-based ensemble auditions, followed by college entrance auditions and subsequent ensemble auditions, studio performance classes, juries, and recitals. Comparison to others can continue throughout a music teacher's career through enrollment numbers, variety of ensemble or course offerings, ensemble festival ratings and peer selection to perform at professional conferences. This comparison can result in self-doubt or fear about being exposed as an underqualified musician or teacher, which is referred to as "imposter phenomenon" (Clance, 1985; Shaw, 2017).

Comparisons between our teaching and/or other programs and teachers often stimulates reflection, although this comparison often exists below the surface of our awareness. On a constant basis, teachers make decisions that are informed by their musical knowledge, students, available resources, and contextual factors. Whereas Dewey's (1910) reflective thinking approach can inform decision-making, it originates from a problem: something that is lacking and needs correction. It also does not take into account the person doing the reflection and how the situation relates to and impacts the teacher and students.

What Is Core Reflection?

Core reflection was developed by Fred Korthagen, professor emeritus of Utrecht University, and associates, to deepen teacher reflection by considering not only "professional" aspects of the teacher (e.g., behaviors and competencies) but also the "personal" (e.g., beliefs, identity, mission/ideal/motive, and core qualities). Core reflection has been characterized as an "inside-out" (King & Lau-Smith, 2013) or "learning from within" (Korthagen & Nuitjen, 2021) approach, designed to promote "meaning-based" (Korthagen, 2015) reflection. Core reflection has been used in various settings including preservice teacher coaching (Meijer et al., 2013), in-service teacher coaching (Hoekstra & Korthagen, 2011), school district elementary teacher professional development

(Attema-Noordewier et al., 2013), university teacher education programs (Adams et al., 2013; King & Lau-Smith, 2013; Wilder et al., 2013) and with other populations including elementary students (Ruit & Korthagen, 2013), university student procrastinators (Ossebaard et al., 2013), and teacher educators (Kim & Greene, 2013).

Core reflection is informed by positive psychology, which is focused on potential rather than deficiency and finding a cure (Korthagen, 2013a). From the perspective of positive psychology, "treatment is not just fixing what is broken; it is nurturing what is best" (Seligman & Csikszentmihalyi, 2000, p. 7). For each person, "what is best" are their core qualities that are often connected to a broad-based teaching and learning mission, ideals, or motives that crystalize over time. Core qualities, which are sometimes referred to as character strengths or innate qualities, include creativity, curiosity, sense of justice, precision, openness, persistence, decisiveness, flexibility, patience, enthusiasm, courage, caring, sensitivity, and humor, to name a few.

Core qualities can be compared to the facets of a diamond (Evelein & Korthagen, 2015), which, when taken together, are a collection of characteristics unique to each person and result in a sense of fulfillment when used (Korthagen & Vasalos, 2005; Seligman & Peterson, 2003). They can initially be identified by naming the characteristics of an inspiring person (e.g., "this person is..."). Then, the teacher can consider prior teaching experiences when they have had energy and enjoyed teaching, pointing to character strengths used in this situation (e.g., humor, creativity, or enthusiasm). Core qualities can also be identified by reflecting on experiences that had a positive impact on the teacher and students, then noticing what character strengths used by the teacher contributed to the positive impact (Evelein & Korthagen, 2015).

Core reflection principles are incorporated into the five-phase core reflection model. The five phases include:

1. Describing a concrete situation or problem;
2. Reflection on the ideal (in a situation) and core qualities;
3. Reflection on an obstacle (e.g., how do you limit or block yourself);
4. Using the core potential; and
5. Trying a new approach. (Evelein & Korthagen, 2015)

The ideal in a situation is deeper than a learning objective like wanting students to play correct rhythms. Rather, ideals are linked to a teacher's basic psychological needs for competence, autonomy, and/or relatedness (Deci & Ryan, 2000). Because core qualities and ideals are connected, a teacher who, for example, identifies "patience" as a core quality may have relating to students as an ideal or underlying motivation in their work. In the opening post-rehearsal reflection, the obstacle originates from Ms. Smith's limiting belief (e.g., "my success as a teacher is primarily evident in our district festival performance") and a conflict between her core qualities, her ideal/mission, and actions. In phase 4, the teacher realizes the potential of their core qualities by noticing the tension or discontinuity between their core qualities and prior actions. This reflection then leads to phase five, where they design a different approach to the situation (Evelein &

Korthagen, 2015; Korthagen & Nuijten, 2017). It is important to realize that core reflection was not designed to alleviate obstacles, but rather to help the teacher recognize a different approach to perceived challenges (Evelein & Korthagen, 2015). Focusing on one's strengths broadens the "thought-action repertoire," thus helping to promote the use of creative and flexible strategies that can lead to finding new approaches (Hoekstra & Korthagen, 2013).

While engaged in core reflection, the teacher is aware of and cycles through one's thoughts, feelings (which can include bodily responses and emotions), and motivations, which are characterized as "information channels" (Evelein & Korthagen, 2015). The analogy of an elevator is used to remind the teacher to move between each floor (e.g., thoughts, feelings, and motivations) during core reflection. The awareness of thoughts, feelings, and motivations is referred to as "presencing," which is the combination of two words: "present" and "sensing" (Senge et al., 2004; see also Hendricks et al., this volume).

Core reflection necessitates being present in the here-and-now, rather than "downloading" (Evelein & Korthagen, 2015) or having an automatic response that usually originates from merely thinking about an issue. The concept of "presence" is akin to mindfulness-based ideas including "full awareness" (Mingyur Rinpoche, 2007) and "wide-awakeness" (Greene, 1973). "Presencing" indicates the senses and body awareness can be reference points as a teacher probes for what they are feeling and also stays with a feeling (Meijer et al., 2013) as a means for tapping into motivations and ideals in a situation. Furthermore, "presencing" is aligned with a holistic view of the teacher who uses not only their skills and knowledge but also their beliefs, identity, mission/ideals/motives, and core qualities to engage in more effective and more fulfilling professional behavior (Rodgers & Raider-Roth, 2006).

POST-REHEARSAL CORE REFLECTION

Let's return to the post-rehearsal reflection from the beginning of this chapter, which has been expanded via additional emboldened text to illustrate a teacher using core reflection. Core reflection concepts have been added in brackets.

"The first violins still aren't quite together on their eighth-note entrances in the first measure of Eine Kleine!" [core reflection model-phase 1] *Ms. Smith said to herself as she collapses into her office desk chair at the end of rehearsal, the last period of the day.* **Ms. Smith takes three deep breaths, followed by a body scan from her feet to her head. During the body scan, she notices tension at the nape of her neck.** [presencing] **Ms. Smith then asks herself a series of questions, each followed with a response. "What am I thinking right now? Clearly I'm thinking about the first violin entrance in the first measure! What am I feeling? I'm feeling tension and frustration. What do I want in this situation? Well, obviously, I'd love uniform entrances from the first violins in the first measure!"** [information channels] **Instead of thinking about various**

rehearsal strategies used in previous rehearsals [downloading], she next takes a few deep breaths [presencing], pausing to think about what went well in today's rehearsal. "It was really great to see the looks in their eyes, especially from the students in the back of the sections, when they heard for the first time how it sounds and feels to have everyone begin together, playing softly at the tip of the bow. It took several tries, but they hung in there with each other, as did I with them, for us to sound like 'one big violin.'" Ms. Smith says to herself, "That's what I want." [ideal; core reflection model-phase 2] "I'm patient and persistent, and I have a gift for building community in my orchestra classes." [core qualities; core reflection model-phase 2] Ms. Smith then returns to thinking about the first violin eighth-note entrances in the first measure. "I could go back to basics tomorrow, having them clap the rhythm while chanting the eighth-note subdivisions. Maybe I should have them play the measure individually to make the point that they need to practice their orchestra music outside of rehearsal?!" Ms. Smith feels a shiver run down her spine as her eyes tear up. [presencing] "Is this the kind of teacher I want to be, embarrassing some of the students as a way to get them to practice more?" [core reflection model-phase 3] An image of Sam and Katy (who sit in the last stand of the first violin section) flashes across Ms. Smith's mind. Sam and Katy joined the orchestra program in 5th grade. They continue to participate in high school orchestra—with limited practice outside of rehearsal—and neither student takes private lessons, either by choice or due to family finances. Ms. Smith continues to focus on this image, smiling as she thinks about how Sam and Katy have grown to be good kids who are fun to chat with after rehearsals, despite their lack of consistent home practice. [presencing] "I never liked it when my high school orchestra teacher did this (playing individually), but we've got to get Eine Kleine to the next level since district festival is only 1 month away!" Ms. Smith pauses her thinking, noticing that her shoulders raised as she started thinking about district festival. [presencing] "Hmm. It seems like I might be getting focused on our rating. Perhaps my ego and misguided belief that a rating less than a '1' will lead my colleagues to question my competence and musicianship are getting me off track." [core reflection model-phase 3] Ms. Smith returns to thinking about her strengths as a teacher [core qualities], and what she experienced today during rehearsal, with she and the students focused, working toward a common goal, and having a meaningful musical experience. She also thinks about Sam and Katy, and how her focus on the district festival rating, and her subsequent use of the "playing individually" strategy could create some distance between herself and these students, perhaps leading them to quit orchestra. [core reflection model-phase 3] Ms. Smith ponders these questions as she imagines the feeling in her body as draws on her strengths during rehearsals. [core reflection model-phase 4] "The 'back-to-basics' and 'playing individually' approaches could be modified" she says to herself. "Tomorrow I'll begin rehearsal by talking honestly with the first violins about why I was frustrated with them today. I will tell them I realized, after reflecting, that I needed to take a step back to think about what was most important—our district festival rating or their improvement and experience as an ensemble and as individuals. I'll also remind them that one of the judges will clinic with us for a few minutes after we perform as way to keep all of us focused on festival as a learning experience. I'll then talk to them about continuing to improve during the next few weeks while experiencing moments of 'brain meltdown' focus and 'orchestra family' support for each other during rehearsals. When we rehearse measure 1, I'll start with the back-to-basics approach, and if this doesn't fix the problem with the first violins, I'll have them play this measure one stand rather than one person at a time. I'll also be sure to engage the rest of the orchestra in 'finding a smile (something their peers did well) and a question (asking a question about something you noticed that could be improved).'" - [core reflection model-phase 5] Ms. Smith's shoulders lower as a smile comes across her face, accompanied by a twinkle in her eye. "Looking forward to seeing how rehearsal goes tomorrow!" she says to herself as she continues to plan for tomorrow's rehearsal.

The five core reflection phases are evident in this expanded post-rehearsal reflection. The teacher began with noticing a problem (first violins' lack of unified entrances following eighth note rests). For the next few minutes, rather than initially thinking about possible rehearsal strategies, the felt experience of tension led her to consider deeper motivations beyond improved performance (phase 2). As she recalled past instances of student improvement and her connection with students, she named her core qualities (patience, persistence, building community) (phase 2), then realized how her focus on their district festival rating and likely her comparison with other orchestra teachers created an obstacle to the use of her core qualities of patience and building community during rehearsal (phase 3). With core qualities in mind (phase 4), she planned to talk to students at the beginning of the next rehearsal about her frustration as a result of a misguided focus on their festival rating. The use of modified rehearsal strategies would engage students, keep them focused, and create a more positive atmosphere during rehearsals (phase 5). At the same time, Ms. Smith's teaching would be aligned with her core qualities.

Note that "presencing" was one of the first core reflection concepts identified in the second reflection, and was used throughout the reflection. Also, notice how Ms. Smith was aware of both positive (a feeling of ensemble connection) and less comfortable (indicated by her eyes tearing up) emotions. Attending to this range of feelings helped her throughout the reflection to not only identify teaching ideals ("That's what I want!") and the obstacle, but also create modified rehearsal strategies.

In summary, rather than reflecting on problems, the past, and the situation using a cognitive orientation, core reflection is focused on positive meaning making, the present and the future through the use of personal strengths and awareness of one's thinking, feeling, and motivations (Korthagen, 2013b). Initial attention given to one's strengths can be unsettling since in "education, (we are) so used to looking at problems, not at strengths and opportunities" (Hoekstra & Korthagen, 2013, p. 100). However, core reflection can be life-changing for teachers and their students.

CORE REFLECTION AND CARE

Core reflection might be considered a type of self-care (Hendricks, 2018) given the attention to and incorporation of a person's emotions and motivations in the approach. However, this form of self-care goes beyond attending to immediate emotional and physical needs as it fosters integration of a teacher's mission—or inspiration that provides meaning and significance to the teacher's work (Korthagen & Nuijten, 2017), identity, and beliefs, along with particular musical passions and interests. Core reflection can result in a teacher feeling less pressure or responsibility to meet external demands because actions and decisions originate from, and are better aligned with, the purpose of their work. Naming one's core qualities and engaging in core reflection fosters wellbeing through continued learning and development. Core reflection has been identified for its potential positive impact on teacher attrition and teacher burnout (Korthagen, 2015), given the transformative learning that can occur in the way teachers adjust their view of themselves and their surroundings (Mirriam et al., 2007).

At the same time, identification of a teacher's strengths, needs, and mission fosters self-knowledge. Teacher self-knowledge is necessary for the creation of authentic connection between a teacher, their students, and music (Palmer, 1998). A teacher who is aware of their passion and enthusiasm for music, for teaching, and for contributing to others' lives by using their distinct combination of core qualities is positioned to foster enthusiasm in their students, which may lead to building relationships and community with and among students. Through teacher modeling of core reflection, their students may, in turn, foster compassion for and connection with others through music experience.

Moreover, core reflection is aligned with a broader definition of effective teaching that includes competence, character, and caring (Obermiller et al., 2012). Teachers "care for" themselves, which, in contrast to "caring about," is action-oriented (Hendricks, 2018, this volume). Core reflection begins with taking the time to be present as one considers various environmental (e.g., school culture, district or state content standards, resources); professional (teacher skills and knowledge); and personal (teacher beliefs, identity, motives, and core qualities) factors. Rather than quickly moving from problem identification to solution as Ms. Smith did in the first post-rehearsal reflection, environmental, professional, and personal layers of reflection (Korthagen, 2015)—along with obstacles experienced as a result of these factor(s) not being initially considered—are taken into account prior to choosing a solution. As evident in the second post-rehearsal reflection, core reflection contributed to Ms. Smith "caring for" herself when she named her core qualities, considered her ideal rehearsal atmosphere, noting the discontinuity between the two. Her flourishing as a professional and human, evident toward the end of the reflection as she looked forward to tomorrow's rehearsal, was promoted as she "cared for" or took into account the self when considering the personal levels of reflection.

At the same time, Ms. Smith's core reflection led to "caring for" her students as she modeled lifelong learning, in this case, her learning about teaching, the situation and the self. Moreover, Ms. Smith's core reflection—where she identified an obstacle that resulted from a discontinuity between her core qualities and a limiting belief about the function of orchestra festivals—resulted in different rehearsal strategies being proposed. These rehearsal strategies might lead to increased teacher–student rapport and continued teacher–student and student–student relationship development. Core reflection promotes self-care and extends to care of others—as trust, empathy, patience, and authentic connection are developed in music-learning spaces (Hendricks, 2018).

Many veteran music teachers seem to engage in core reflection as they display caring for students via their ability to be present to students, and to remain calm as they consider the "bigger picture" for students' long-term learning from music experiences (Chua & Welch, 2021; Conway, 2021; Robinson, 2020). This bigger picture is linked to a broader goal of creating meaningful lives which "emerges in the intersubjective interactions of shared and fulfilling activities" (Silverman, 2013, p. 36). A teacher who is aware of their core qualities and mission—which are often integrally linked to their particular musical passions—cares for the music being learned, and this care is manifested in enthusiasm shared with students (Hendricks, 2018).

Indeed, core reflection promotes care in the music classroom, and by extension, in the world as the teacher and student adopt mindful approaches to challenges, approaches that emerge from the teacher's unique strengths.

Core Reflection Resources

Core reflection can be used in a variety of settings on an individual basis or with others via peer coaching, professional development workshops, or age-appropriate programs. Several resources exist for implementing core reflection including the book *Practicing Core Reflection: Activities and Lessons for Teaching and Learning from Within* (Evelein & Korthagen, 2015). The activities and accompanying text help the teacher first recognize their core qualities, destructive (limiting) and constructive beliefs, identity/roles, and mission linked to their passions and core qualities. Teachers also learn how to apply the five-phase core reflection model to daily situations. In my experience facilitating core reflection workshops with in-service music teachers,[1] these activities foster self-understanding, which might encourage a teacher to seek out additional professional leadership opportunities or a different teaching position.

Another resource on core reflection, which includes several case studies, is *Teaching and Learning from Within: A Core Reflection Approach to Quality and Inspiration in Education* (Korthagen et al., 2013). Information on recent research studies and core reflection workshops, including videos, are available on Korthagen's website.[2] Particularly useful core reflection coaching resources include the Guidelines for Coaching Core Reflection/Table 9.1 (Evelein & Korthagen, 2015, p. 158) and the Relations Between States in the Teacher's Development, Key Principles of the Core Reflection Approach, and the Coaching Interventions/Table 6.1 (Meijer et al., 2013, p. 90).

---

[1] For more information, see https://www.colorado.edu/music/summer-college-music/summer-master-music-education

[2] https://korthagen.nl/en/

Returning to the opening statement of this chapter, recast in the positive, regular core reflection promotes the development of teachers who "teach who we *are* and if we *are* being us, if we're being true to ourselves, and what we believe, then we *float*." This recasting is aligned with Miller's (2013) characterization of core reflection which "is truly an inside-out approach to change. It is only when our deepest values are viewed within a positive frame that we can hope to have an education that is truly inspiring and life affirming" (p. ix). Certainly, core reflection promotes human flourishing as we attend to our—and by extension each other's—thinking, emotions, and motivations. The potential ripple effect as individuals, dyads, music classes, schools, and teacher education program personnel engage in this important and challenging work gives all of us hope as teachers and students care for and about each other via the use of core reflection in the present, and hopefully, over a lifetime.

References

Adams, R., Kim, Y. M., & Greene, W. L. (2013). Actualizing core strength in new teacher development. In F. A. J. Korthagen, Y. M. Kim, & W. L. Greene (Eds.), *Teaching and learning from within: A core reflection approach to quality and inspiration in education* (pp. 61–75). Routledge.

Attema-Noordewier, S., Korthagen, F. A. J., & Zwart, A. C. (2013). A new approach to educational innovation. In F. A. J. Korthagen, Y. M. Kim, & W. L. Greene (Eds.), *Teaching and learning from within: A core reflection approach to quality and inspiration in education* (pp. 111–130). Routledge.

Boniwell, I. (2012). *Positive psychology in a nutshell: The science of happiness*. Open University Press.

Chua, S. L., & Welch, G. F. (2021). A lifelong perspective for growing music teacher identity. *Research Studies in Music Education*, 43(3), 329–346. https://doi.org/10.1177/1321103X19875080

Clance P. R. (1985). *The impostor phenomenon: Overcoming the fear that haunts your success*. Peachtree.

Conway. C. (2021, April 9). *Profiles of veteran teachers* [Paper presentation]. American Research Association Annual Conference, online.

Deci, E. L., & Ryan, R. M. (2000). The "what" and "why" of goal pursuits: Human needs and the self-determination of behavior. *Psychological Inquiry*, 11(4), 227–268. https://doi.org/10.1207/S15327965PLI1104_01

Dewey, J. (1910). *How we think*. D. C. Heath & Co.

Evelein, F. G., & Korthagen, F. A. J. (2015). *Practicing core reflection: Activities and lessons for teaching and learning from within*. Routledge.

Greene, M. (1973). *Teacher as stranger*. Wadsworth.

Hendricks, K. S. (2018). *Compassionate music teaching*. Rowman & Littlefield.

Hoekstra, A., & Korthagen, F. A. J. (2013). Coaching based on core reflection makes a difference. In F. A. J. Korthagen, Y. M. Kim, & W. L. Greene (Eds.), *Teaching and learning from within: A core reflection approach to quality and inspiration in education* (pp. 93–107). Routledge.

Hoekstra, A., & Korthagen, F. A. J. (2011). Teacher learning in a context of educational change: Informal learning versus systematic support. *Journal of Teacher Education*, 62(1), 76–92. https://doi.org/10.1177/0022487110382917

Kim, Y. M., & Greene, W. L. (2013). Aligning professional and personal identities: Applying core reflection in teacher education practice. In F. A. J. Korthagen, Y. M. Kim, & W. L. Greene (Eds.), *Teaching and learning from within: A core reflection approach to quality and inspiration in education* (pp. 165–178). Routledge.

King, J. T., & Lau-Smith, J. (2013). Teaching from the inside out: Discovering and developing the self-that-teaches. In F. A. J. Korthagen, Y. M. Kim, & W. L. Greene (Eds.), *Teaching and learning from within: A core reflection approach to quality and inspiration in education* (pp. 45–60). Routledge.

Korthagen, F. A. J. (2015). *Core reflection approach* [Keynote lecture]. University of Cologne. Korthagen Professional Development. https://korthagen.nl/en/focus-areas/core-reflection-multi-level-learning/

Korthagen, F. A. J. (2013a). A focus on the human potential. In F. A. J. Korthagen, Y. M. Kim, & W. L. Greene (Eds.), *Teaching and learning from within: A core reflection approach to quality and inspiration in education* (pp. 12–23). Routledge.

Korthagen, F. A. J. (2013b). The core reflection approach. In F. A. J. Korthagen, Y. M. Kim, & W. L. Greene (Eds.), *Teaching and learning from within: A core reflection approach to quality and inspiration in education* (pp. 24–42). Routledge.

Korthagen, F. A. J., Kim, Y. M., & Greene, W. L. (Eds.). (2013). *Teaching and learning from within: A core reflection approach to quality and inspiration in education*. Routledge.

Korthagen, F. A. J., & Nuijten, E. E. (2017). Core reflection approach in teacher education. *Oxford Research Encyclopedia of Education*. https://doi.org/10.1093/acrefore/9780190264093.013.268

Korthagen, F. A. J., & Vasalos, A. (2005). Levels in reflection: Core reflection as a means to enhance professional development. *Teachers and Teaching: Theory and Practice, 11*(1), 47–71. https://doi.org/10.1080/1354060042000337093

Meijer, P. C., Korthagen, F. A. J., & Vasalos, A. (2013). *Teaching and learning from within: A core reflection approach to quality and inspiration in education.* Routledge.

Miller, J. P. (2013). Foreword. In F. A. J. Korthagen, Y. M. Kim, & W. L. Greene (Eds.), *Teaching and learning from within: A core reflection approach to quality and inspiration in education* (pp. ix–x). Routledge.

Mingyur Rinpoche, Y. (2007). *The joy of living: Unlocking the secret & science of happiness*. Harmony Books.

Mirriam, S. B., Caffarella, R. S., & Baumgartner, L. S. (2007). *Learning in adulthood: A comprehensive guide*. Jossey-Bass.

Obermiller, C., Ruppert, B., & Atwood, A. (2012). Instructor credibility across disciplines: Identifying students' differentiated expectations of instructor behaviors. *Business Communication Quarterly, 75*(2), 153–165. https://doi.org/10.1177/1080569911434826

Ossebaard, M. E., Korthagen, F. A. J., Oost, H., Stavenga-De Jong, J., & Vasalos, A. (2013). A core reflection approach to reducing study procrastination. In F. A. J. Korthagen, Y. M. Kim, & W. L. Greene (Eds.), *Teaching and learning from within: A core reflection approach to quality and inspiration in education* (pp. 148–162). Routledge.

Palmer, P. J. (1998). *The courage to teach: Exploring the inner landscape of a teacher's life*. Jossey-Bass.

Robinson, J. (2020). Australian super veteran secondary school music teachers: Motivated and valuable. *International Journal of Music Education, 38*(2), 226–239. https://doi.org/10.1177/0255761420902870

Rodgers, C. R., & Raider-Roth, M. B. (2006). Presence in teaching. *Teachers and Teaching: Theory and Practice, 12*(3), 265–287. https://doi.org/10.1080/13450600500467548

Ruit, P., & Korthagen, F. A. J. (2013). Developing core qualities in young students. In F. A. J. Korthagen, Y. M. Kim, & W. L. Greene (Eds.), *Teaching and learning from within: A core reflection approach to quality and inspiration in education* (pp. 131–147). Routledge.

Seligman, M. E. P., & Csikszentmihalyi, M. (2000). Positive psychology: An introduction. *American Psychologist, 55*(1), 5–14. https://doi.org/10.1037/0003-066X.55.1.5

Seligman, M. E. P., & Peterson, C. (2003). Positive clinical psychology. In L. G. Aspinwall & U. M. Staudinger (Eds.), *A psychology of human strengths: Fundamental questions and future directions for a positive psychology*. American Psychological Association.

Senge, P., Scharmer, C. O., Jaworski, J., & Flowers, B. S. (2004). *Presence: Exploring profound change in people, organizations and society*. Nicolas Brealey.

Shaw, J. T. (2017). Creating artistry: Pathways to teacher growth in a professional development short course. *Bulletin of the Council for Research in Music Education*, (213), 27–52. https://doi.org/10.5406/bulcouresmusedu.213.0027

Silverman, M. (2013). A conception of "meaningfulness" in/for life and music education. *Action, Criticism, and Theory for Music Education, 12*(2), 20–40. http://act.maydaygroup.org/articles/Silverman12_2.pdf

Wilder, E. M., Greene, W. L., & Kim, Y. M. (2013). Core reflection as a catalyst for change in teacher education. In F. A. J. Korthagen, Y. M. Kim, & W. L. Greene (Eds.), *Teaching and learning from within: A core reflection approach to quality and inspiration in education* (pp. 179–192). Routledge.

FOREWORD TO SECTION 4

CARE, SOCIAL ACTIVISM, AND CRITICAL CONSCIOUSNESS

CATHY BENEDICT

For years I have been interested in the ways in which the language we use with our students shapes the possibilities of the educative process, or in other words, the broader purpose of education. This is an overarching purpose that I believe transcends the purpose of music education, and yet at the same time provides a path forward for the possibilities of an education in and through music. This purpose is inextricably bound to the everyday language we use with our students in contexts from primary to university to studio encounters. Equally as bound to the process and purpose, then, is the human, the other, with whom we daily engage in those contexts. Che Guevara (2003) writes:

> One must have a large dose of humanity, a large dose of a sense of justice and truth in order to avoid dogmatic extremes, cold scholasticism, or an isolation from the masses. We must strive every day so that this love of living humanity is transformed into actual deeds, into acts that serve as examples, as a moving force. (p. 226)

While not connected to musicking, nor even education, purpose resides in what it means to *be* human. For Paulo Freire (1970/1993) this was made manifest in his lives project: the struggle for humanization amid the historical forces that seek to dehumanize. As we move further into this century this purpose feels rather lost. Perhaps not "simply" lost, but purposefully decimated by acts of extremisms that are "designed to dissuade the people from critical intervention in reality" (p. 34). Spaces that once existed for dialogue with the other are now persistently orchestrated for purposeful division; taking sides is rewarded, "agreeing to disagree" the best we can hope for.

Hope. Again, attention to language calls us to think through this particular construction of hope as one that is paralyzing, one that makes it "impossible to muster the strength we absolutely need for a fierce struggle that will re-create the world" (Freire, 1994, p. 8). Hope thus constructed is unanchored in practice, it is a hoped-for state of being framed by hegemonic forces propagating inaction, immobilism (Freire, 1994). However, rather than settle for or depend on "raw hope" (p. 9), which is void of action, or transformative meetings, our engagements with the other must be grounded in conscious decisions that manifest what Freire would call "critical hope" (p. 8) for the common good.

I would argue that words such as "care" and "empowerment" can also be used in service of the oppressor, toward systemic forces that seek to destroy foundations of love for this world and the other. Too often we are told to believe that we can be empowered by authorities external to our own subjectivity. We can be empowered to buy, to take on, to be something else, contributing, then, to the "homogenizing influence of mainstream culture" (Hicks, 1990, p. 44). Too often we are called to care for ourselves without understanding that our selves do not exist without the other. Too seldom, then, are we taught the strategies that will allow us to both interrogate and "assess this language and make explicit both the ways in which it facilitates ... domination ... and the ways in which it may be reappropriated for liberatory purposes" (Hicks, 1990, p. 36).

Throughout this book, and in particular this section, each author pushes us toward liberatory purposes by uncovering systemic mechanisms of oppression. They provide concrete manifestations of care and compelling examples of lives lived in critical hope with others and by doing so "unveil opportunities for hope, no matter what the obstacles may be" (Freire, 1994, p. 9). This is not to say that within this section there is a wholesale acceptance of words such as "care," "hope," and "love." Many of the authors nuance these terms from varied critical perspectives, asking us to think through that which constitutes the presentations of each of these. They also take care with language, again modeling, to each of us readers, the importance of examining the concepts we use to describe our engagements with the world, underscoring that there is no generic method that will "magically work" (Bartolome, 1994, p. 174). While, in some instances, we are offered particular contexts and relationships to think through the caring relation, each author reminds us that the questions we formulate based on our understandings of societal transformation are those that will sustain us as we pursue the dismantling of oppressive systems.

These authors help us to understand that without developing our own critical consciousness grounded in reflexive processes, social activism has the potential of floundering in either ideological reflection or reaction bereft of critical thought. "Action," as Freire (1970/1993) warns, "is human only when it is . . . not dichotomized from reflection" (p. 35) and directed at "the structures to be transformed" (p. 33). These structures—whether they be taken for granted practices embedded in, for instance, popular music, the incarceration system, curriculum, Jewish and Arab relations, deficit views of deafness—should be seen, then, not as closed systems, but rather as "limiting situations" (Freire, 1970/1993, p. 31) that can be transformed through, in this context, conceptions of care.

Be clear, there is great risk involved in the caring frameworks they offer us. To care for, about, and with the other entails coming to know oneself. And as we come to know ourselves in our engagements with the other, we confront our strengths as well as our inabilities and limitations in ways we perhaps had not wanted to confront. However, if a path of social justice is one we desire to walk, we must choose risk. How beautiful, then, are the words of Lanas and Zemblylas (2014):

> We can choose to love or we can choose not to love, but unless we choose to love, love does not exist. And even when we choose to love, it is a decision that must be constantly reaffirmed. (p. 36)

I am thankful that the authors in this section have chosen these paths they walk. Their constant reaffirmation reminds us that we must choose to care, no matter the risk of Self, no matter the seemingly closed systems surrounding us. This risk, this struggle, is that which keeps critical hope alive, this *is* the "love of living humanity" (Guevara, 2003, p. 225).

REFERENCES

Bartolome, L. I. (1994). Beyond the methods fetish: Toward a humanizing pedagogy. *Harvard Educational Review, 64*(2), 173–194. https://doi.org/10.17763/haer.64.2.58q5m5744t325730

Freire, P. (1970/1993). *Pedagogy of the oppressed: New revised 20th-anniversary edition.* Continuum.

Freire, P. (1994). *Pedagogy of hope: Reliving pedagogy of the oppressed* (R. R. Barr, Trans.). Continuum.

Guevara, E. C. (2003). Socialism and man in Cuba. In D. Deutschmann (Ed.), *Che Guevara reader* (2nd ed., pp. 212–230). Ocean Press.

Hicks, L. (1990). A feminist analysis of empowerment and community in art education. *Studies in Art Education*, 32(1), 36–46. https://doi.org/10.2307/1320398

Lanas, M., & Zembylas, M. (2014). Towards a transformational political concept of love in critical education. *Studies in Philosophy and Education*, 34(1), 31–44. https://doi.org/10.1007/s11217-014-9424-5

CHAPTER 37

THE SOUNDS OF HOPE

Music Homeplaces and Compassionate, Abolitionist Music Teaching

EMILY GOOD-PERKINS

CARE HANDBOOK TOPICS

Identity expressions
Social activism and critical consciousness

THE United States' tumultuous and turbulent history of racial oppression and systemic racism is at the forefront of contemporary American discourse as advocates for racial justice shed light on police brutality and systemic inequity. Though the fight for racial justice is not a new one, technology and social media—and the bravery of those who are harnessing their power—have allowed injustices to be revealed, people to be assembled, historical myths to be questioned, and the call for equity to be an immediate, indisputable reckoning with American racism.

This reckoning has been the driving force behind educational initiatives at the Mississippi Civil Rights Museum,[1] the Alabama Legacy Museum and the National Memorial for Peace and Justice, among others.[2] The National Memorial for Peace and Justice, for example, tells the name and story of more than 4,000 women, men and children who were brutally lynched from 1877 to 1950; without this project their stories would have never been heard (Equal Justice Initiative, n.d.). Though these initiatives aim to educate the public about the atrocities of slavery and the subsequent racial terror

---

[1] https://mcrm.mdah.ms.gov
[2] https://museumandmemorial.eji.org/memorial

killings, their mission is rooted in the belief that change and racial justice are only possible when society reckons with the past.

To communicate hope amid the horrific reality of the past, museum attendees are flooded with the sounds of gospel music and light emanating from a 40-foot light sculpture. These sounds of hope have provided sustenance and connection for generations of African Americans. This music—according to Wesley Morris (2019) in the third episode of the *New York Times's* audio series, "1619"—is the sound of "possibility [and] struggle"—the "sound of a people who, for decades and centuries, have been denied freedom." It is because of that struggle that, in Morris' words,

> Black music is the ultimate expression of a belief in that freedom, the belief that the struggle is worth it, that the pain begets joy, and that that joy you're experiencing is not only contagious, it's necessary and urgent and irresistible. (32:46)

The transformative and profound ways in which music carries, connects and sustains communities is irrefutable. Music as a vehicle for hope and joy is even more necessary today as Black and Brown Americans are disproportionately at risk of being incarcerated or killed by police, and systemic racism continues to permeate all aspects of the American criminal justice system (Edwards et al., 2019; Sawyer, 2020). The disproportionate rate at which Black men and women are incarcerated is particularly harmful for their children, the most vulnerable victims of an inherently racist judicial system. It is they who society must empower, nurture, and protect.

As we[3] reckon with the atrocities of the past and hope for a better future, we must invest in the futures of children. This investment must reach far beyond basic human needs to account for children's joys, hopes and dreams.

In her discussion about abolitionist teaching and educational freedom, Love (2019) considers music and arts education to be vital and necessary for Black and Brown children especially within school settings, which are oftentimes hostile environments and places of what Love calls "dark suffering" (p. 15). Music and art classrooms, therefore, can be spaces in which students find their cultural centeredness and the courage to persist in the face of hostility.

> Art education in schools is so important because, for many dark children, art is more than classes or a mode of expression; it is how dark children make sense of this unjust world and a way to sustain who they are, as they recall and (re)member in the mist of chaos what it means to thrive. For many dark folx, art is a homeplace; art is where they find a voice that feels authentic and rooted in participatory democracy. (Love, 2019, p. 100)

How can our music classrooms be a "homeplace" (Love, 2019, p. 100) for all that enter? Much like Love, Hendricks (2018), in her discussion about compassionate music

---

[3] "We" and "us" throughout this chapter refer to society at large.

teaching, recognizes the ways in which music classrooms can be spaces in which students feel at home—where students feel that they belong (p. 125). These music homeplaces are enacted with compassion and care by teachers who actively and intentionally aspire to know their students and their students' musical ways-of-being. Music homeplaces, therefore, are each uniquely built on the musical cultures of their students.

In their current forms, do our music teaching practices celebrate the musical-cultural wealth of *all* students? If not, how might we expand our boundaries to recognize and empower those who have traditionally been forgotten? Discussions with two African American university music majors; results from a study that investigated university voice faculty's attitudes about diversity; and the National Association for Music Education's (NAfME) recent diversity initiative shed light on current practice and in doing so, the work that must be done to reckon with and abolish systemic inequities and equitize music teaching practices. This work is part of an abolitionist and compassionate paradigm shift in which children's needs are valued over the preservation of methods, standards and traditions.

Counterstories and Musical Equity

Using counterstories and the assertion "that the experiential knowledge of people of color is legitimate, appropriate, and critical to understanding, analyzing and teaching about racial subordination" (Solórzano & Yosso, 2002, p. 26), the purpose of this study was to "[tell] the stories of those people whose experiences are not often told" (Solórzano & Yosso, 2002, p. 32). Semi-structured, open-ended interviews were conducted with two African American university music education majors at predominately white universities.[4]

Davion

Home and School Musical Cultures

Davion described a sharp contrast between the university music culture and his own musical culture, which began in the Black church.

> The gospel stuff is different. It's solely based upon emotion. I mean there's all the soft palate lifting and all that stuff, but you know, mother so-and-so who sits in the front

---

[4] Prior to conducting interviews, IRB permission was secured. Interviews were audio recorded and transcribed. Member checks were conducted with both participants following transcription, and the interviews were coded using Creswell and Poth's "data-analysis spiral" (2018, pp. 185–187). Pseudonyms are used.

> pew with her hat turned to the side, she don't know nothing about soft palate this. But she knows to sing, you know, "I love the Lord. He heard my cry."
>
> You have to be very careful with the repertoire that I do here [university].
>
> It's more strict. You want to make it make poetic sense as well as musical sense, while with the gospel stuff it's, you know, how you're feeling. You can ad lib here, you know, you can choose your . . . the words don't have to specifically be right here, you know. You can kind of change that while, you know, the kind of music we do [at the university], it has some strict rules.

Despite the cultural incongruences between Davion's home musical life and his university musical life, he manages to navigate both worlds. His description is reminiscent of DuBois's (1903) discussion about a "double-consciousness" (p. 3).

> My music has split in two to a sense. So, in the one half I'm going to school to learn the, you know, the "bel canto" style, and you know, I need to buckle down and really get into that. While I still have the gospel stuff that I do with my choir, with my little church choir on Tuesday night. But that's my safe haven.

When discussing the cultural implications of a homogenized music environment, Davion expressed his beliefs inclusively and collectively.

> I think it affects or it should affect all of us. Uh, you know as students, you should want to be a part of an environment where everybody feels welcome and everybody feels safe to, um, you know, express their culture and their traditions.

Musical diversity and equality among all musical cultures is extremely important for Davion. His personal experience of being from a cultural and musical background that is not recognized or understood by the music faculty makes his call for recognition even more poignant.

> You have to know that everybody is not coming from the same cultural background. Everybody is not coming from the same artistic background. Everybody is not coming from any of the same backgrounds but you have to, as a successful teacher, you should work to try to meet their needs so they can become successful.

Kesha

My Music Doesn't Matter

Much like Davion, Kesha described the ways in which music education both at the university level and within primary school settings prioritizes the Western classical music tradition at the expense of other musical traditions—so much so, she concluded, that children come to believe that their musical cultures are inferior or inconsequential.

> And that's my issue, that all music is not really taught equally. It's not respected equally and that's why you're going to continue to have groups of people that feel

like they're better than others or groups of people that continue to be oppressed because they're taught endlessly that the things of their culture don't matter. They're taught endlessly that what they like or what they enjoy isn't real or isn't supposed to be respected at the same level of classical music. And it frustrates me that music education is now tailored to Eurocentric music because yeah that's music, but that's not all music.

Kesha suggested that the delineation between academic and nonacademic music perpetuates a hierarchy and communicates musical elitism.

And you can't say that what is being done in Africa is not music. You cannot say that what is being done in African American communities is not music. It's just not the music that you are willing to teach academically and I really don't understand where that came from. Why all of a sudden music has to be Eurocentric or it's not music. Or it has to be classical or it's not real music or not music that's worthy of being taught at the academic level. I don't understand where that comes from especially when I'm a part of a culture where music is literally ingrained in our DNA. I don't think that there is such a thing as academic music and then music that you listen to on a regular basis. All music should be academic and I feel like that's the purpose of music education.

Meaningful Music Education

As a music education major, Kesha articulated the ways in which music education could be particularly meaningful for African American children.

I particularly feel strongly about music education in urban communities and predominately African American communities because music is in our blood, it's in our DNA, it's in our culture. Everywhere in Africa, music is utilized because it's so deeply ingrained in African culture. In the African Diaspora, and in African American culture, it's ingrained in everything we know and everything we do.

Both Davion and Kesha's perceptions of music education in the United States provide insight into the ways in which current music teaching practices alienate students. In addition to recognizing the limitations, they both shed light on the ways in which music education has the potential to be transformative and meaningful for children from minoritized communities.

The Paradox of Musical Equity

Whereas Davion and Kesha provide student perspectives, a study investigating the perceptions of 62 university voice faculty at universities accredited by the National Association of Schools of Music from 30 states representative of the different geographical areas of the United States sheds light on faculty's attitudes about diversity and the ways in which diversity is addressed in university music programs.[5]

The findings from this study indicate that a majority of voice faculty members who participated in this study value programmatic and structural diversity. They support curricular and pedagogical approaches that would allow for a more equitable approach to music teaching and they recognize, structurally, the need for diverse faculty to support students. However, their responses indicated that they expected programmatic and structural diversity could be addressed within the same in situ climate with which they are familiar. That is, the same audition criteria, namely Western classical art song in Italian, German, and French sung with Western classical vocal technique; the same musical standards, in which accurate timbre, pitch, and music listening are tied to Western classical musical ideals of comportment and sound; and the same musical traditions deeply rooted in elitist Europe and musical colonialism.

The following statement is one example of faculty responses in this study and indicative of the ways in which discourses of Western classical musical superiority and universality are normalized in schools of music.

> While each style has its own value, a university does not have the resources to specialize in all of those styles. And there is some question whether all those styles will be of enduring import over hundreds of years. Universities don't have unlimited funds to hire enough faculty to teach all the different styles, nor is there a lengthy enough tradition to justify the lasting nature of such topics. I am not qualified to teach all styles of music and am unable to master so many types personally. I feel like we are able to give students vocal tools to use in the future on the music of their choice. We do that through classical Western singing. Classical Western singing is a solid technique to preserve and optimize the voice and can be used as the underpinning for healthy singing in all styles.

In situ diversity relates to the ways in which diversity is addressed in the school's climate, social interactions, and the nuanced and unquantifiable perceptions of those who experience that educational environment. In situ diversity can be difficult to recognize and therefore even harder to change, but it is in the in situ aspects of diversity that schools of music continue to exclude students of color (Good-Perkins, 2021). A more equitable approach to music education, particularly at the university level, is not possible without an expansion of the ways in which "standards" and "foundation" are defined as well as a reckoning with the ways in which students' cultural, financial and

---

[5] The attitude scale used in this study was adapted from an initial pilot study in which it was developed and tested (Henerson et al., 1987). Five categories of statements were developed to address different aspects of the attitude: (a) musical diversity in pedagogy and repertoire, (b) value of diversity, (c) faculty and student diversity, (d) vocal questions, and (e) access and audition issues. In addition, some participants provided additional qualitative data to be considered with their survey. The mean and discrimination index of each item were found as well as the standard deviation and variance of the discriminating items.

social capital impact their access to university music schools. The paradox of musical equity is that valuing diversity is not enough to ensure that university music schools adequately address the diverse needs of diverse students. Rather, a paradigm shift is necessary, one in which the *in situ* aspects of diversity within schools of music, which are typically enigmatic, are fully recognized and reconsidered to allow students from all backgrounds the opportunity to study university music in ways that are meaningful and relevant for them.

NATIONAL ASSOCIATION FOR MUSIC EDUCATION AND EQUITY

The need for a paradigm shift in the United States was addressed by Mackie Spradley, the current president of the National Association for Music Education (NAfME), in an October 2020 statement in which she addressed racism in music education publicly: "Given the history of our country, systemic racism is embedded in all facets of our life including education. NAfME, with its 113-year history, is no exception to the impact of racism" (p. 1). Spradley then revealed that in 2019, NAfME hired an external organization—which specializes in the assessment of institutional unconscious bias—to conduct an assessment of NAfME. The Cook Ross firm produced a *Diversity, Equity, Inclusion, and Access Current State Study* (2019) and determined that NAfME's "foundational structure is in fact a barrier to progress in the areas of equity, diversity, inclusion, and access" (Spradley, p. 1). Spradley then called for music educators to recognize "the urgency to respond . . . [to] the outcry for equity, diversity, inclusion, and access" (p. 2).

The *Current State Study* provided an assessment of NAfME's institutional culture, organization and leadership and the ways in which they supported or hindered "diversity, equity, inclusion and access" (Cook Ross, 2019, p. 2). The study reported that the prioritization of Western classical musical traditions has created what participants described as "an elite culture and worldview that is resistant to change" (p. 5). Music education "traditions" were reported to be a hindrance to diversity and equity. In addition, participants described "historical systems of oppression" within the field of music education that "have prevented diverse musicians, educators and composers from gaining visibility" (p. 5). These systems of exclusion, like "music auditions and competitions" that were described in the report as "inherently biased and exclusionary" (p. 5), have inhibited NAfME's ability to adequately address diversity and equity.

The benefit of having an outside organization well-versed in unconscious, and perhaps, conscious bias, conduct an assessment of an organization deeply steeped in institutional racism and elitism is obvious. Those within the organization who are aware of systemic inequity may have found it hard to articulate or convince others within this organization of these problems. The outside assessment, however, is only beneficial in its analysis of that which *is* and not that which *could be*. The entrenched beliefs—the normalized assumptions of Western classical music and the hierarchy of musical styles, singing styles, and ensembles—are deeply ingrained and invisible to those unfamiliar with music education culture. In fact, it is their presumed universality that makes them invisible even to those within the music education field.

Though the *Current State Study* provided official documentation of that which is problematic within music education, the changes needed to equitize and diversify the field of music education are far more complex and nuanced than can be represented in a neat, quantifiable report. At the end of her address, Spradley (2020) poses the question, "What can we do to eradicate systemic racism and center equity?" (p. 2). Her leadership is providing the impetus for institutional change; however, changing an organization and educational field whose identity is rooted in the preservation of white supremacism will require a complete overhaul of all that has been presumed and assumed to be true.

Abolitionist Pedagogy and Compassionate Empathy

Love's (2019) framework for abolitionist teaching is centered on just that—a complete overhaul. She argues that educational initiatives claiming to equitize education, if enacted within the same educational structures, will continue to perpetuate inequity. Instead, educators must challenge and dismantle racist structures and practices. Within the field of music education, the seemingly innocent emphasis on standards, musical literacy, and the elements of music, among other things have provided a neoliberal glossing over of the ways in which these goals and their Eurocentric origins allow for perpetuated racism (Good-Perkins, 2021). Of course, musical standards are good. Why would a teacher or music teacher education program say otherwise? Why shouldn't we emphasize the elements of music and musical literacy? The inherent problem with this discourse is that it implicitly prioritizes the Western classical music knowledge system over children themselves. According to Hendricks (2018),

> This is where compassion comes in. By making space for diverse musics, learning styles, and pedagogical approaches, we shift our attention away from exacting external standards and move toward shared music-making with others whom, despite their usually younger age and lesser experience in certain areas, we recognize to be equal to us in the collective place we call humanity. (p. 3)

Compassionate music teaching prioritizes children and their cultural ways of being above standards and traditions. Teachers who actively harness compassion and caring in their teaching do so because they are able to empathize with their students. This form of "compassionate empathy," according to Hendricks, is not a passive stance but rather an active and intentional "moral choice" in which a teacher "feels for (and with) others" and "also feels compelled to make things better" (Hendricks, 2018, p. 57). Compassionate music teaching, therefore, like abolitionist teaching, *actively* harnesses the arts for social justice. According to Love, "art is freedom dreams turned into action" and "is a vital part of abolitionist teaching because it is a freeing space of creativity, which is essential to abolishing injustice" (Love, 2019, p. 100). Music homeplaces in which students can create, imagine, and express their musical selves are vital to abolitionist teaching, particularly for Black, Indigenous, Children of Color because as Love puts it, "their art makes them visible and makes clear their intentions for love, peace, liberation, and joy" (p. 101). In defiance of standards, testing, and deficit language like "achievement gap" and "grit," compassionate, abolitionist music teaching is a brave stance in musical solidarity with all children where all children's musical cultures are sustained and made visible in the music classroom.

Critical Inquiry and Analysis of Current Practices

To enact a compassionate, abolitionist music pedagogy, we must first reckon with and abolish the practices, assumptions, and pedagogies that have allowed for perpetuated exclusion within the field of music education. A necessary part of this process is recognizing our own worldview and our assumptions about music teaching and learning that are framed within it. By shedding light on our beliefs, we can begin to interrogate and rethink that which we have come to believe is incontestable. The following practical exercise provides a means for music educators and teachers to question their own beliefs and practices (Good-Perkins, 2021).

I. Music Teacher's Credo—What Are My Beliefs and Assumptions?

Consider your beliefs about music teaching and learning—that which you have come to believe as universally applicable. Use the following guiding questions to devise statements about your beliefs.

Overarching
- What methods and beliefs inform my teaching?
- How do students respond to my teaching?

Discipline/Classroom Management
- What do I believe is appropriate or inappropriate behavior in the music classroom?
- How do students respond to my classroom rules?

Vocality (Singing and Speaking)
- What singing styles have I been taught to "correct"?

- How do students respond to my singing and speaking voice?
- Do my students sing freely in the classroom or do they feel inhibited or nervous about singing?

Movement
- What body movements have I been taught to "correct"?
- What do I believe is appropriate musical embodiment in the music classroom?

Methods
- What do I believe about musical standards and musical literacy?

Listening/Music Engagement
- What do I believe is appropriate music listening behavior in the music classroom?
- What musical forms or ways of making and experiencing music do I discourage?

Repertoire
- What do I believe is appropriate repertoire for music teaching?
- How do students respond to the repertoire I choose?

Caring/Knowing My Students
- What are my assumptions about my students and their musical backgrounds?
- How do I get to know my students?

Interactions/Engaging My Students
- How do students respond to my body language?
- How do I interact with my students?
- How do I know if my students are engaged?

II. Music Teacher's Workshop—How Might I Interrogate That Which I Believe?

Now, consider the ways in which your beliefs impact your teaching and students. How do we come to believe what we believe? Use the following questions to guide your inquiry and interrogation of that which you had assumed to be irrefutable.

Overarching
- What will happen if I allow musical sounds, musical movement, and musical behavior that I believe are incorrect or inappropriate to take place in the classroom?
- In what ways might my teaching be alienating students?

- In what ways is my teaching impacted by my definition of musical success?
- Do I employ methods without careful consideration of their impact?

Vocality (Singing and Speaking)

- Do I believe that I must achieve a unified vocal sound? If so, why?
- Do I discourage certain ways of speaking and singing? If so, why?

Methods

- Why do I value certain music teaching methods?
- In what ways do my teaching methods inform my beliefs about teaching and music-making?
- How do my students respond to my methods?
- Do I discourage certain musical activities and behaviors? If so, why?

Repertoire

- Do I believe that certain repertoire is more appropriate than other repertoire? If so, why?

Caring/Knowing My Students

- Do I feel cautious about getting to know my students? If so, why?
- Is it hard for me to understand my students and their behavior?

III. Music Teacher's Epistemic Expansion—How Might I Rethink My Practice and Assumptions?

With the following guiding questions, consider the ways in which you might expand your practice to incorporate a multi-centric approach to music teaching.

Overarching

- How might I rethink my beliefs about what is musically incorrect or correct?
- How might I approach all aspects of my music teaching from multiple musical vantage points?
- How might I discover new ways of making and *knowing* music?
- How might I incorporate a wide range of musical epistemologies into my teaching?

Discipline/Classroom Management

- How might I rethink the ways in which I consider discipline?
- How might I discover the underlying reasons of student disengagement?

Vocality (Singing and Speaking)
- In what ways can I make my singing and speaking in the classroom be familiar for students?

Movement
- In what ways can I allow my students to have freedom of movement and expression in the classroom?

Methods
- How do I find ways to implement my students' musical cultures into my teaching?
- How might I broaden my understanding of the elements of music and musical literacy?
- How might I demonstrate the value of oral musical traditions?

Listening
- How can I challenge Western classical assumptions about music listening?
- Can I allow my students to freely dance while listening? Make sound? Sing along?

Repertoire
- How might my repertoire choices reflect the cultures of my students?
- In what ways can the repertoire I choose deepen my students' understanding of diverse musical epistemologies?

Caring/Knowing My Students
- How do I get to know my students?
- How do I care for my students?
- How do I create a musical homeplace in which my students feel able to express themselves freely?

Interactions/Engaging My students
- How might I interact with my students in meaningful ways?
- How might I incorporate their ways of communication into my teaching?

Student Empowerment
- How do I empower and motivate my students?
- How can I celebrate my students' musical-cultural identities in the classroom?

Student Choice/Agency
- How do my students experience music outside of school?
- How would my students like to experience music in the classroom?
- In what ways can I allow my students to make curricular and musical choices in the classroom?

Creativity

- How might I incorporate more opportunities for my students to create and be creative agents of their own musical expression and entrainment?
- How might I incorporate musical creativity and composition in ways that differ from the way they are conceived within a Western classical epistemology?

Moving Forward

To criticize and reflect on the ways in which our own music teaching practices might perpetuate inequity is a highly vulnerable task. It may, in Hendricks's (2018) words "require that we ourselves transform in some way, which may be the scariest part of all," but she goes on to say, "only by taking these kinds of risks can we experience the greatest rewards" (p. 33). To be compassionate, abolitionist music teachers who prioritize the care and wellbeing of all students, regardless of their cultural backgrounds, takes bravery and humility. It takes empathy, imagination, and a willingness to actively fight for educational justice. Compassionate, abolitionist music teachers nurture musical homeplaces for their students. They do so by knowing, incorporating, and celebrating their students' musical cultures and musical ways-of-being in the classroom. They are able to do so because they have taken the time to actively care for, about, and with their students (Hendricks, 2018). While a global pandemic, racial violence, and economic disparities continue to wreak havoc on our world, musical homeplaces in which children can dream, create, imagine, hope, and musically express themselves in meaningful ways are even more crucial today. After all, it is children's hope—their sounds of hope—that will carry us into a more just future.

References

Cook Ross. (2019, October). *Diversity, equity, inclusion, & access current state study: Findings & recommendations report.* National Association for Music Education. https://nafme.org/wp-content/uploads/2020/01/NAfME_DEIA_Executive-Summary_2019.pdf

Creswell, J. W., & Poth, C. (2018). *Qualitative inquiry & research resign* (4th ed.). Sage Publications.

Du Bois, W. E. B. (1903). *The souls of Black folk.* Blue Heron Press.

Edwards, F., Lee, H., & Esposito, M. (2019). Risk of being killed by police use of force in the United States by age, race–ethnicity, and sex. *Proceedings of the National Academy of Sciences, 116*(34), 16793–16798. https://doi.org/10.1073/pnas.1821204116

Equal Justice Initiative. (n.d.). *The National Memorial for Peace and Justice.* https://museumandmemorial.eji.org/memorial

Good-Perkins, E. (2021). Culturally sustaining music education and epistemic travel. *Philosophy of Music Education Review, 29*(1), 47–66. https://doi.org/10.2979/philmusieducrevi.29.1.04

Good-Perkins, E. (2021). *Culturally sustaining pedagogies in music education: Expanding culturally responsive teaching to sustain diverse musical cultures and identities.* Routledge.

Hendricks, K. S. (2018). *Compassionate music teaching.* Rowman & Littlefield.

Henerson, M. E., Morris, L. L., & Fitz-Gibbon, C. T. (1987). *How to measure attitudes.* Sage Publications.

Love, B. L. (2019). *We want to do more than survive: Abolitionist teaching and the pursuit of educational freedom.* Beacon Press.

Morris, W. (2019, September 6). Episode 3: The birth of American music [Audio podcast episode]. In *1619*. New York Times. https://www.nytimes.com/2019/09/06/podcasts/1619-black-american-music-appropriation.html

Sawyer, W. (2020, July 27). *Visualizing the racial disparities in mass incarceration.* Prison Policy Initiative. https://www.prisonpolicy.org/blog/2020/07/27/disparities/?gclid=CjwKCAjw55-HBhAHEiwARMCszi7ir_wS2XUE7bvhh4UCNUuc66AkJeUZH6vKFORr2_sRozcJWe9NsxoC1iEQAvD_BwE

Solórzano, D. G., & Yosso, T. J. (2002). Critical race methodology: Counter-storytelling as an analytical framework for education research. *Qualitative inquiry, 8*(1), 23–44. https://doi.org/10.1177%2F107780040200800103

Spradley, M. V. (2020, October 8). *Statement on upcoming national town hall meetings.* National Organization for Music Education. https://nafme.org/wp-content/uploads/2020/10/NAfME-Town-Hall-invitation-FINAL.pdf

CHAPTER 38

CRITICAL RACE THEORY AND CARE IN MUSIC EDUCATION

AMY LEWIS

CARE HANDBOOK TOPICS

Co-creating caring relationships
Identity expressions
Social activism and critical consciousness

INTRODUCTION

In this chapter, I discuss how an understanding of race and racism is essential to creating an environment that centers care in the music classroom. Critical race theory (CRT) founding scholar, Derrick Bell, discusses how the United States of America experiences racism in a way where it is endemic and seen as a normal, accepted part of reality (Bell, 1995). Racism manifests in music education in multiple ways such as incorporating racist minstrel folk songs (McHale, 2018); limiting music-making experiences to white, Eurocentric, classical music (Fiorentino, 2019; Hess, 2018); and maintaining audition practices that privilege White students (Koza, 2008). In this chapter I discuss how music educators can extend care by understanding what perpetuates harm. Abolitionist practices in education focus on the source, structures, and practices that produce harm in order to identify how students can thrive (Love, 2019). These practices additionally emphasize importance of recognizing how individual actions can either perpetuate systemic harms or challenge those harms. By being able to recognize racism and other forms of oppression, through a critical race theory lens, music educators can intentionally embrace characteristics of care in a way to challenge systemic barriers.

I begin this chapter by describing critical race theory and contextualizing how music education scholars use critical race theory as a way to understand racism and systemic oppression. I then detail how four music educators experienced learning about critical race theory through a professional learning development. I then discuss how their experiences connect to concept of care and compassion. I conclude this chapter by providing reflective questions for the reader to consider how an understanding of race and racism can influence how they provide care in the music classroom.

Understanding Systemic Racism and Critical Race Theory

I lean on Taylor's (2016) definition of structural racism to contextualize how I choose to use racism and structural oppression in this chapter. Taylor (2016) states, "Institutional racism, or structural racism, can be defined as the policies, programs, and practices of public and private institutions that result in greater rates of poverty, dispossession, criminalization, illness, and ultimately mortality of African Americans" (p. 8). This definition describes structural barriers as the policies, programs, and practices of institutions and individuals that result in greater rates of dispossession, marginalization, and exclusion. With a thorough understanding of music education policies, programs, and practices through a CRT lens, music educators can make intentional choices that challenge institutionalized racism.

Scholars use critical race theory to further understand how racism manifests in the context of the United States. CRT emerged from critical legal studies as a way to analyze and explore how racism exists in law (Bell, 1995). Throughout the 1990s and 2000s CRT expanded into multiple disciplines including education, disability studies, and much more. Although CRT has existed and evolved over decades, Dixson and Rousseau (2018) discuss and the amount of work that still needs to be completed in order to address racism in education.

Dixson and Rousseau (2018) also discuss the importance of creating boundaries for CRT in education as a way to maintain a clear understanding of how CRT scholarship aligns with education. The following five tenets resonate in education and music education research:

- ordinariness,
- whiteness as property,
- counternarratives,
- interest convergence, and
- intersectionality.

Ordinariness involves the understanding that racism is an ordinary facet of society (Delgado & Stefancic, 2017; Ladson-Billings, 1998). Counternarratives establish the importance of highlighting voices and stories that challenge dominant, stereotypical narratives (Hendricks, 2021a; Solorzano & Yosso, 2002). Whiteness as property furthers the concept of White privilege by comparing the rights of property ownership to the economic and social rights afforded to White people (Harris, 1995). Intersectionality recognizes the deep intersections of many identity points such as low-income, queer, or racialized individuals (Collins, 2000; Crenshaw, 1996; Delgado & Stefancic, 2017). Intersectionality additionally focuses on the unique political needs of Black women when analyzing both feminist and anti-racist politics.

The final feature, identified as interest convergence, suggests that dominant, White society only fights for racial equality when it benefits from the object of the fight (Delgado & Stefancic, 2017). For example, in Bell's (1995) monumental work, he describes how the *Brown versus Board of Education* decision to desegregate schools benefited White people and those in power by establishing humanitarian credibility for the United States among developing countries as well as the potential of creating economic growth in the southern part of the United States. Over 25 years after the *Brown* decision, Bell (1995) notes the lack of positive transformation for Black individuals with "millions of Black children who have not experienced the decision's promise of equal educational opportunity" (p. 20). These CRT tenets drive CRT scholarship and can influence educational practices in ways that will be further mentioned in this chapter. In the next section I detail a particular research project focused on the experience of how four public school music educators embraced CRT.

Experiencing Critical Race Theory in Music Education

CRT's expansion into music education highlights the importance of explicitly recognizing race and racism, and challenging the harmful barriers and systems that exist. Harmful structures and practices in music education include bias against teachers and students of color, biased audition requirements, or narrow options of creating music at the collegiate level. For example, Wahl (2018) describes her experience of interacting with adjudicators who maintained harmful biases toward her and her students. Adjudicators placed assumptions on her as a racialized, Black individual where they assumed her and her students to be more capable or successful by singing music from the continent of Africa as opposed to singing European classical music. Wahl's experience and writings exemplify a counternarrative used to absolve and challenge majoritarian stories and stereotypes. An understanding of CRT can provide a lens for music educators to examine critically their own practices and assumptions as teachers, and to consider what equitable teaching practices might look like in their classroom. Music education scholars could use CRT as a way to better understand race and racism and as a way to combat and challenge racism in the music education classroom. Scholars and music educators can gain a deeper awareness of power, oppression, and racism in order to transform our profession toward a more caring-centered profession.

Lewis (2021, 2022) explored how four music educators experienced learning about CRT in a professional learning community (PLC) and examined how an understanding of CRT influenced their teaching. Each participant engaged in an eight-session, in-person learning community where they discussed readings centered on CRT, asked questions, and created ideas to apply their learning into their classrooms. All four participants identified as White. Two participants identified as cisgender women, and the other participants identified as cisgender men. Lewis, who identifies as a Black cisgender woman, created and facilitated each session. All participants taught in a small town in the southeast part of the United States. Three of the participants taught in a racially and ethnically diverse district and one participant taught in a homogeneous White and low socioeconomic status district. The data Lewis collected included three interviews with each participant throughout the course of the PLC, recordings of each session, written journal reflections, and written activities that took place during the PLC sessions. This research project provides an example of the potential impact of learning about system racism through the lens of CRT.

The PLC closely explored five CRT tenets related to education mentioned above: ordinariness, counternarratives, whiteness as property, intersectionality, and interest convergence. The participants grappled with the meaning of racism and how it manifests in the music classroom. After learning about whiteness as property, one of the participants wrote in their journal post, "Am I racist or are my actions racist?" (Lewis, 2021, p. 140). Lewis discussed the importance of both questions by stating,

> Here, [the participant] has thought deeply about the weight of his actions as an educator. He distinguished between the questions, "am I racist?" and "are my actions racist?" Both questions are important in order to address racist systems and racist actions. [The participant] acknowledged the deep, personal feelings attached to considering himself as racist and attempted to embrace that discomfort. (p. 141)

Lewis shared the importance of being able to use self-reflection to recognize racist actions and highlights the journey it takes to be able to not only acknowledge racist actions, but to think about how to challenge to actions.

Discovering how their actions could be considered racist created a sense of tension for each of the participants. These moments provided an opportunity for the participants to reflect on the cause of the tension and for them to process their tension by embracing vulnerability. By being able to acknowledge racist behavior, the participants were able to think about how they might alter or modify different actions in the classroom.

One participant, an after-school beat-making educator, reflected on how he intends to create a learning environment that centers vulnerability. He models his vulnerability as the educator as a way to encourage students to embrace their vulnerability as high school students in search of learning about themselves. According to Lewis (2021), "in discussing race, racism, and equity, the PLC provided an opportunity for participants to share their stories, personal reflections, and to embrace vulnerability on a sensitive topic, in order to be able to recognize and challenge racism and racist practices" (p. 25). As the participants expanded their understanding of oppression, they made connections to practices of care, compassion, and vulnerability, as important attributes to their classroom.

Care in Music Education

Compassion and vulnerability in music education provide direction for music educators to consider racist structures and practices in their classrooms, and to consider other practices that comprise care. With an understanding of systemic racism, music educators and music teacher educators can gain a deeper awareness of power, oppression, and racism. This awareness can transform our profession to embrace a more thorough understanding of compassion and vulnerability leading to a more caring centered profession. Hendricks (2018) describes the experience of vulnerability that can take place as teachers exercise qualities of compassion (e.g., trust, empathy, patience, inclusion, community, authentic connection) with their students:

> By bringing our awareness to these ... qualities, we are inviting ourselves to walk into a vulnerable state of being: We may open ourselves up to new feelings and new experiences that may challenge us, our beliefs, our convictions, and our pedagogical practices. Encountering this state of newness may require that we ourselves transform in some way, which may be the scariest part of all. Yet only by taking these kinds of risks can we experience the greatest rewards. . . . [T]rust is critical when confronting our vulnerabilities. (p. 33)

Hendricks (2018, 2021b) emphasizes the importance of compassionate teaching where typical student-teacher power dynamics are challenged and care is shifted to be "with" students as opposed to for students. She furthers this concept by describing how music teachers can embrace more of a facilitator role, continue to learn along with their students, and decenter competition as a top priority in the music classroom. Similarly, the findings from Lewis (2021) suggest that after gaining an understanding of CRT, the music educators believe that embracing more of a facilitator role and centering exploration as opposed to competition would be beneficial in creating a more racially conscious music classroom.

Similar to Hendricks (2018), Palmer (2018) discusses how care requires vulnerability, integrity, authenticity, and trust; and he emphasizes how authentic teachers continue to learn with and from their students. The music educators in Lewis's (2021) study describe how an understanding of systemic racism by learning about CRT helped them to better understand issues regarding racism and the importance of embracing vulnerability as a music educator. In learning about CRT, the participants expanded their understanding of providing care by embracing vulnerability and they exhibited moments of vulnerability through constant self-reflection and group discussions. This type of emotional vulnerability includes being open and honest about what they did not know regarding race and racism. Additionally, they recognized the fear of potentially identifying their teaching practices as being considered racist. As participants grappled with considering if and how their practices in the classrooms might be considered racist, they made intentional choices to be vulnerable in order to embrace a transformative experience.

A Moment of Reflection

Music educators have the opportunity to expand the way they provide care in their classrooms with a thorough understanding of how racism and systems of oppression operates. Although learning about oppression may feel uncomfortable and politically charged for some people, bell hooks (2014) reminds us that "no teaching is politically neutral" (p. 37). With an understanding of how race and racism operate in the classroom, music educators can expand the way they embrace and provide care. An understanding of systemic racism and barriers provides a pathway for music educators to better understand how racism and oppression manifest in the classroom. Educators can gain this understanding by embracing vulnerability, practicing self-reflection, and immersing themselves in an opportunity to learn about these concepts.

Tsui et al. (this volume) describe elements of anti-racist self-reflection in music education including: (a) centering student voices, (b) self-awareness, (c) naming and questioning, (d) action, and (e) student expression. These elements occur over time as students and teachers learn together about themselves and about racist structures, decenter supremacist practices, amplify student voices, and celebrate student expressions. Although not directed to anti-racist work specifically, Berg (this volume) describes how core reflection can involve affirmative approaches to embracing vulnerability, where teachers focus on their strengths rather than deficits to help them see positive ways to address challenges. According to Berg (this volume), core reflection "involves five phases: (a) describing a concrete situation or problem, (b) reflection on the ideal (in a situation) and core qualities, (c) reflection on an obstacle, (d) using the core potential, and (e) trying a new approach."

I invite you to use the following questions to help contextualize how an understanding of racism can influence how you establish care in your classroom:

1. How can an understanding of systemic racism challenge your assumptions of how racism operates in education?
2. How can an understanding of systemic racism influence the way you provide care in your classroom?

3. What challenges or barriers exist in order for you to embrace an understanding of systemic racism? In what ways can you challenge those barriers?

An understanding of systemic racism provides an opportunity for music educators to think critically and explicitly about race and racism in the classroom. Recognizing and addressing systemic oppression can expand the ability to provide care by embracing vulnerability and critical self-reflection. Gloria Ladson Billings (1998) states, "If we are serious about solving these problems [race, racism, and social injustice] in schools and classrooms, we have to be serious about intense study and careful rethinking of race and education" (p. 22). This knowledge can create an opportunity for music educators to ground their practices of care in a way that challenges oppressive and harmful systems. As teachers engage in establishing a foundation of care that explicitly challenges systemic racism and oppression, they might be better positioned to support students in their care.

References

Bell, D. B. V. (1995). Board of education and the interest-convergence dilemma. In K. Crenshaw, N. Gotanda, G. Peller, & K. Thomas (Eds.), *Critical race theory: The key writings that formed the movement* (pp. 20–29). New Press.

Bradley, D. (2017). Standing in the shadows of Mozart: Music education, world music, and curricular change. In R. D. Moore (Ed.), *College music curricula for a new century* (pp. 205–222). Oxford University Press. https://doi.org/10.1093/acprof:oso/9780190658397.003.0011

Collins, P. H. (1990/2000). *Black feminist thought: Knowledge, consciousness, and the politics of empowerment*. Routledge.

Crenshaw, K. (1996). Mapping the margins: Intersectionality, identity politics, and violence against women of color. In K. Crenshaw, N. Gotanda, G. Peller, & K. Thomas (Eds.), *Critical race theory: The key writings that formed the movement* (pp. 357–384). The New Press.

Delgado, R., & Stefancic, J. (2017). *Critical race theory: An introduction*. New York University Press.

Dixson, A. D., & Rousseau Anderson, C. (2018). Where are we? Critical race theory in education 20 years later. *Peabody Journal of Education*, 93(1), 121–131. https://doi.org/10.1080/0161956X.2017.1403194

Fiorentino, M. C. (2019). Considering antiracism in student teacher placement. *Journal of Music Teacher Education*, 28(3), 58–71. https://doi.org/10.1177%2F1057083718820713

Harris, C. I. (1995). Whiteness as property. In K. Crenshaw, N. Gotanda, G. Peller, & K. Thomas (Eds.), *Critical race theory: The key writings that formed the movement* (pp. 276–291). The New Press.

Hendricks, K. S. (2018) *Compassionate music teaching*. Rowman & Littlefield.

Hendricks, K. S. (2021a). Counternarratives: Troubling majoritarian certainty. *Action, Criticism, and Theory for Music Education*, 20(4), 57–78. http://act.maydaygroup.org/counternarratives-troubling-majoritarian-certainty/

Hendricks, K. S. (2021b). Authentic connection in music education: A chiastic essay. In K. S. Hendricks & J. Boyce-Tillman (Eds.), *Authentic connection: Music, spirituality, and wellbeing* (pp. 237–253). Peter Lang.

Hess, J. (2018). Detroit youth speak back: Rewriting deficit perspectives through songwriting. *Bulletin of the Council for Research in Music Education*, (216), 7–30. https://doi.org/10.5406/bulcouresmusedu.216.0007

hooks, b. (2014). *Teaching to transgress*. Routledge.

Kaba, M., & Meiners, E. R. (2021). Arresting the carceral state. In M. Kaba (Ed.), *We do this 'til we free us: Abolitionist organizing and transforming justice* (pp. 76–82). Haymarket Books.

Kelly-McHale, J. (2018). Equity in music education: Exclusionary practices in music education. *Music Educators Journal*, 104(3), 60–62.

Kelley, R. D. (2002). *Freedom dreams: The black radical imagination*. Beacon Press.

Koza, J. E. (2008). Listening for whiteness: Hearing racial politics in undergraduate school. *Philosophy of Music Education Review*, 16(2), 145–155.

Ladson-Billings, G. (1998). Just what is critical race theory and what's it doing in a nice field like education? *International Journal of Qualitative Studies in Education*, 11(1), 7–24. https://doi.org/10.1080/095183998236863

Lewis, A. (2021). *Am I racist or are my actions racist?: The experiences of four music educators who learn about critical race theory* (Publication No. 8322304) [Doctoral dissertation, Michigan State University]. ProQuest Dissertation Publishing.

Lewis, A. (2022). Dreaming out loud: Four music educators dream for the future of music education. *Bulletin of the Council for Research in Music Education*.

Love, B. L. (2019). *We want to do more than survive: Abolitionist teaching and the pursuit of educational freedom*. Beacon Press.

Palmer, E. S. (2018). Literature review of social justice in music education: Acknowledging oppression and privilege. *Update: Applications of Research in Music Education*, 36(2), 22–31.

Solórzano, D. G., & Yosso, T. J. (2002). Critical race methodology: Counter-storytelling as an analytical framework for education research. *Qualitative inquiry*, 8(1), 23–44. https://doi.org/10.1177%2F107780040200800103

Taylor, K. Y. (2016). *From #BlackLivesMatter to Black liberation*. Haymarket Books

Wahl, C. P. (2018). A choral "Magical Negro": A lived experience of conducting choirs in Canada. In A. Kraehe, R. Gaztambide-Fernandez, & B. S. Carpenter, II (Eds.) *The Palgrave handbook of race and the arts in education* (pp. 503–514). Palgrave.

CHAPTER 39

CALL ME BY MY NAME
Knowing Our Students' Names as Intercultural Sensitivity

KÍNH T. VŨ

CARE HANDBOOK TOPICS

Identity expressions
Social activism and critical consciousness

Mary Ann Shelly (2017), a special education teacher, mother, and author, wrote a memoir about her late daughter Sara, who suffered from a rare disease. Mary Ann shared a letter written by her son Joe (Sara's brother), to Joe's son Jordan, expressing the importance of his name: "We wanted your name to bear significance. We had chosen the name, Isaiah Lee, but we did not have a significant reason for the name Isaiah" (Shelly, 2017, p. 199). Joe further described a simultaneous moment in which his 27-year-old sister, Sara, was dying; this event prompted Joe and his wife to immediately change their son's birth certificate before leaving the birth center:

> It [was] clear that we had to make a new birth certificate with the name Jordan Lee. The water birth, the emotional river that had to be crossed, and the possible passing of your aunt from this life to the next made our choice clear and the story unique to your life's beginning. (p. 200)

Much of my professional life I have asked these two questions: Do I teach music or do I teach people? To say that I have doubted my impact in the lives of young musicians is an understatement. My intention is not to cast aspersions on my younger self, but in truth, I did not considered myself as "successful" a band director as other band directors in neighboring towns (see Berg, this volume). I never fully came into my own personhood when I taught public school music, and I now wonder if this sort of self-doubt stemmed from an experience of badly balancing the demands of being a white-named and white-educated teacher with a smudge of shame living inside an Asian body. It was far easier to focus on subject matter knowledge than it was to know my students as whole people rather than sonic tools meant to produce concerts that would ultimately elevate me in the opinion of peer band directors. What if I had known my students, really known them rather than feigning intimate knowledge of them? Noddings (1984) expressed this powerfully in her text *Caring*:

> The teacher ... is necessarily one-caring if she [sic] is to be a teacher and not simply a textbooklike [sic] source from which the student may or may not learn. Hence, when we look at "pedagogical caring" we shall begin not with pedagogy but with caring. (p. 70)

My point here is to underscore an important tenet of music education. I contend that knowing music and knowing people are not entirely the same thing. Where musical skill development and performance outcomes (e.g., concerts) may be useful if measurement and evaluation are highly valued in the field, they may be rendered wholly unimportant when/if the music-makers are relegated to first and second fiddle, assigned folder numbers, or worse yet, are subservient to the wishes of their music directors *under* whom they serve.

This chapter is an exploration of two white music teachers' experiences of knowing their Asian and Asian American students' names; it is also about knowing my own name. Knowing in the context of this exploration refers to director's professional relationships with band students, particularly concerning knowing and pronouncing their names. I used Bennett's (1986, 2013) developmental model of intercultural sensitivity (DMIS) as a lens through which to learn how teachers developed intercultural sensitivity in their own teaching lives.

Intercultural Sensitivity

Bennett's (1986, 2013) DMIS delineates stages of cultural self-awareness. Intercultural sensitivity is "the ability to discriminate cultural differences and to experience those differences in communication across cultures" (Bennett, 2013, p. 12). Intercultural sensitivity emerged from Bennett's studies of sympathy, empathy, and ethnorelativism. Bennett (1986) noted that "[i]ntercultural sensitivity demands attention to the subjective experience of the learner" (p. 179). In this chapter, making space to explore how participant band directors moved between recognition of their own life experiences (e.g., ethnocentrism), and that of possibly empathizing with the experiences of their Asian and/or Asian American students (e.g., ethnorelativism) was facilitated by using Bennett's theory about learners' subjective experiences relative to that of teachers.

It is important to note that people's encounters with any of Bennett's six DMIS stages will most likely not be limited to the experience of one stage at a time. There is a possibility that teachers, for example, might exhibit traits of more than one stage simultaneously and in varying degrees of conformity to Bennett's definitions. Mellizo (2018) suggested that the indicators are not necessarily linear, beginning on the left (see Figure 39.1), but may be experienced starting in any one (or more) of the stages. The six stages are grouped into two categories: ethnocentric and enthorelative. A brief description of the stages follows:

Ethnocentric Stages

- *Denial* occurs when one group has not encountered another or refuses to recognize differences between groups of peoples.
- *Defense* takes place when one tries to "counter perceived threat to the centrality of one's [own] world view" (Bennett, 1986, p. 183).
- *Minimization* is the stage in which "cultural difference is overtly acknowledged and is not negatively evaluated" (Bennett, 1986, p. 183).

Ethnorelative Stages

- *Acceptance* represents the shift from ethnocentrism to ethnorelativism; it is the moment when differences are recognized and respected.
- *Adaptation*, according to Bennett, commonly manifests as empathy. In empathy, one might see from another's point of view. Resultant worldviews may be characterized as bi- or multicultural.
- *Integration* is how people apply "ethnorelativism to one's own identity" and Bennett (1986) considers this stage a "culmination of intercultural sensitivity [as] an essential and joyful aspect of all life" (p. 186).

Intercultural sensitivity has been examined in fields such as media studies (Coffey et al., 2013, 2017) and music education (e.g., Mellizo, 2018). Of Mellizo's many studies on intercultural sensitivity in music settings, most closely related to this chapter is a 2018 study in which the DMIS framework was applied to music teacher educators and

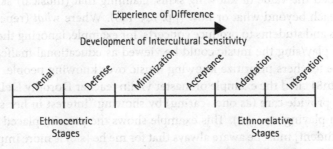

FIGURE 39.1 Developmental Model of Intercultural Sensitivity (DMIS) (Bennett, 1986, p. 182).

preservice teachers as a guide toward developing greater levels of cultural sensitivity as teachers. This is a notable study, because Mellizo did not simply discuss diversifying music curriculum (e.g., Mellizo, 2020); rather, the idea is that teachers themselves are the progenitors of music educational change. Using the DMIS to track one's personal traits as a pre-/in-service teacher or teacher educator might assist in a potential sea change toward a realization of student-centered, culture(s)- and community-specific music practice(s) (e.g., curriculum) in schools.

Intercultural sensitivity is also closely related to other concepts such as intercultural competence (e.g., Bankul & Bukhnieva, 2019; Khasanova, 2020; Miettinen, 2020), intercultural learning (e.g., Antão & Moreira, 2015; Kallio & Westerlund, 2020), and intercultural literacy (Heyward, 2002). Of the myriad related terms, intercultural education is the most widely used in the field of music education and music teacher education (e.g., Miettinen et al., 2020; Westerlund et al., 2020). Although intercultural education might have served this chapter sufficiently, Bennett's DMIS helped to illuminate intersecting concepts of intercultural sensitivity and care in the teaching lives of participant band directors. The following segments are about how teachers know their students, and why knowing them beyond musical participation in band is a vital aspect of a process in which teachers move, theoretically, across the DMIS from left to right.

Knowing What, Knowing Who

To know and be known is key in relationship making. Noddings (1984, p. 64) used "confirmation" of cared-fors to describe the completion of a bi-mutual relationship in which the one-caring sees or makes visible the people in their classroom. There must be some degree of fulfillment of a human pledge between ones-caring and their cared-fors. When I was a novice teacher, I did not think this way. "To know" meant making relationships with repertoire; the more songs I knew, the more I would be respected by my colleagues from other high schools. Epistemologically speaking, how I *knew music* was a priority task in my development as a music teacher. Hence, I invested in developing skills that ultimately spiraled upward to *knowing music*.

However, the process of knowing "what" (music) is not the same as knowing "who" (people). These two kinds of knowing are not analogous with each other. Noddings (1984) described the value of knowing skills, claiming that (musical) skills can assist students to reach beyond what or how (pp. 145–146). Where *what* (repertoire) might serve teachers and students to produce concerts, for example, ignoring the personhood of those who play/sing the music could be viewed as educational malfeasance to the extent that we teachers prioritize knowing music over knowing people. For instance, Hendricks (2018) cited the example of master violin teacher Dorothy DeLay to explain how teachers provide care (as ones-caring) by showing "interest in her students' lives beyond violin playing" (p. 124). This example shows the priority placed on who over what: "[The student] must be aware always that for me he [sic] is more important, more valuable, than the subject" (Noddings, 1984, p. 174).

Knowing Me

I have two positionalities to share. My first position is one of being a Vietnamese American whose childhood was fraught with tensions of being a yellow body adopted into a white world.[1] Growing up as an adoptee who was brought to the United States at the end of the war in Việt Nam was confusing. Living among white people, I thought I was white.

Stemming from the first position, the second is one that I did not anticipate having to disclose in this chapter; however, interview data generated by participants requires me to discuss the complexity of my name. When I was adopted by white parents, my Vietnamese name was replaced with an American name.[2] I never related to it and always asked people to address me with only my first initial, or first and second initial, or first initial and middle name. Teachers rarely knew what to do with my American name even though it was easy to pronounce. To some of my friends, even into adulthood, my American name gave way to nicknames like Seth, Depeche, and Sam (Secret Asian Man). When I finally reclaimed my Vietnamese name, it too became a series of complexities that included knowing the order of names (i.e., last, middle, first), pronunciation of seemingly impossible vowel combinations, and having to explain my "name change" to scores of friends and colleagues. How could I know me if I did not know my name?

Get to Know Mr. Martin and Dr. Brewer

I have known both teachers for several years. When I first met Mr. Martin,[3] he was a high school senior (percussionist and drum major) where I taught in the New England region of the United States. Mr. Martin earned bachelors and master's degrees in music education and became a full-time music teacher in Massachusetts. When I talked to Mr. Martin for this chapter, he had just completed his eighth year teaching at a racially mixed high school where approximately 40 percent of the band students lived in Vietnamese households.

Dr. Brewer and I met in 2014, when he was enrolled at Boston University as a doctoral student. Aside from course content, we spent time commiserating about being euphonium players. In spring 2022, Dr. Brewer marked his 18th year teaching in the same high school where he had been a student teacher. His band program boasts 450 students, of whom 25 to 40 percent of the students are Korean or Korean American.

---

[1] See my blog "From White to Yellow: A Different Point of Vu" at https://www.kinhtvu.com/blog/from-white-to-yellow-a-different-point-of-vu

[2] Misca (2014) discussed criticisms of intercountry adoption noting that "adopted children's identities are lost and replaced by a new name and a new nationality when they are assimilated to their adoptive country" (paraphrasing Abernathy, 2010).

[3] All names of people and places are pseudonyms.

Both Mr. Martin and Dr. Brewer identify as white, cisgender males. They teach in suburban communities approximately 20 miles from large international airports, world-class symphony orchestras, and major league sports teams. Martin and Brewer shared that school bands and other music organizations (e.g., chorus, chamber groups) play a significant role in their communities, especially during school sporting events, music festivals, and townwide events such as parades and special concerts.

In separate conversations with Mr. Martin and Dr. Brewer, as well as in a group interview, the teachers focused much of their discussion on repertoire selection and how choosing music for concert or marching bands might be an act of care for their students. Both music educators want to provide an array of musical selections for their students to perform. They were somewhat appalled by their past notions of "Asian" music in the context of band education, each citing John Barnes Chance's (1967) *Variations on a Korean Folk Song* as the work they associated with meeting their Asian students where they are as well as fulfilling multicultural music standards.[4]

The conversations about repertoire were robust; however, when the subject of Korean and Vietnamese students' cultural, familial, and social experiences was broached, Mr. Martin and Dr. Brewer became very animated, even agitated. One topic that particularly stirred them was the issue of pronouncing students' names. This exchange serves as the point of departure for exploring issues of intercultural sensitivity in relation to knowing our students' names. In the script below, I have displayed an uninterrupted portion of the transcript to showcase the dynamic exchange of stories and ideas between the three of us.

Knowing Students' Names

Mr. Martin and Dr. Brewer discussed the significance of knowing students' names. A particular challenge is pronouncing learners' names that are unlike ones such as Lily, Andrew, or Clara. Brewer, for instance, lamented how his younger self might have glossed over a Korean student's name. The following transcript is a dialogue between Brewer, Martin, and me as we discussed the importance of names.

v: Dr. Brewer, I want to go back to something you talked about in your interview, and I think it has to do with a sort of care: pronouncing student's names.
b: Care and respect, I think about the way that a person's identity is shaped, especially at an early age. Are they immediately learning on the first day of school to be ashamed of themselves, to be ashamed of their heritage? Or is it the running joke

---

[4] An exploration of "Asian" band music is outside the scope of this chapter. It is worth mentioning instances of wind band repertoire that have extended the range of Asian-influenced musics beyond Chance's *Variations*. Examples include Soichi Konagaya's *Japanese Tune* (Molenaar Edition, 1987), Michael Sweeney's *Year of the Dragon* (Hal Leonard, 2000), and Philip Sparke's *The Year of the Dragon* (Studio Music, 1984).

with their friends like, "uh-oh it's coming up to his name and then, oh, the teacher's not gonna be able to pronounce it." For some teachers, they're gonna go, "I'm gonna call you Tom, is that good? We're good, alright, moving on."

M: My blood pressure, just like spiked.

V: I'm about to break into tears because of the whole name thing and how my Vietnamese name was taken away. I really struggled with the American name I was given and now struggle a bit with the Vietnamese name that I have reclaimed.

B: And [difficulty with names] is not particular to the Asian American students. [At my school], it's a very diverse population, and so having basic . . . pronunciation skills for names that are in Spanish or Japanese versus Korean versus Filipino, they're going to have different inflection and where two vowels go together, and they mean different things, or they sound differently in different contexts. I'm not an expert in that, by any means, but I want the student to feel like they matter enough to have their name said properly. And yeah, I had a kid [who] said, "My teachers for 10 years have called me Abhi."[5] And he [said], "At a certain point, you know, you like, you're worn down." He had no desire to correct anybody anymore, and it was genuinely a shock to him when I said it right. [Abhinav said], "You're the only teacher that pronounces it right." That's not an "attaboy" for me; it's just to say that that's really basic. That's a real small effort to make that person feel a bit of value and dignity in the classroom.

M: That's also not okay that he went 10 years and had to forgo his identity. That's called whitewashing, isn't it?

At this point in the conversation, Mr. Martin became very animated, even agitated. He explained his own challenges as a teacher whose Vietnamese band students' names are not always easy to pronounce.

M: Vũ, do you remember T. E.? Yeah, so when she was a freshman, I said if I can't pronounce it, I don't, I don't try. I say, "Hey, how do I pronounce your name?" She pointed to her skin and then pointed to her eye (as a mnemonic device), and I was like, "Okay, but how do I really pronounce it?" and she wouldn't tell me. She wouldn't tell me until her senior year. But again, that's what she went through for those eight or nine years . . . and that's what she was used to. I just don't think that that's okay. . . . I want [students] to feel comfortable being who they are, and the fact that they can't do that because they've had to assimilate for the past number of years. It's just not okay.

B: I think it probably is a source of embarrassment [for teachers], like if I don't know enough to say your name properly. I'm going to gloss over it, or we're gonna come to an understanding that I say "this," and that means you.

M: It's infuriating . . . it breaks my heart. Because [students] say their names, and you know they're saying it in an [American] way so that you can say it. Which is fine, but like, I don't think it's their responsibility to have to change the pronunciation of their name, just so yet another white person can say it. I would rather have some basic inflection skills to be able to say who they are.

---

[5] Pseudonym.

"To be able to say who they are" is critical information. Mr. Martin's idea that someone's name is more than just a word is vital—that it is an embodiment of a living, breathing human being whose presence in music class is a precious gift. Perhaps Noddings (1984) might say to teachers that as ones-caring, it is out of an abundance of deep consideration for the persons we claim to teach that we make every attempt to learn the students' lives: "[The] main interest here is the attitude of the one-caring and how it affects the cared-for" (p. 64). Noddings again: "[t]he one-caring sees the best self in the cared-for and works with him [sic] to actualize that self" (p. 64).

Where intercultural sensitivity enters is Bennett's emphasis on how people come to know other people's cultural viewpoints. Dr. Brewer and Mr. Martin were keenly aware of their students only after several years of glossing over the pronunciations of their names. A shift from minimization (ethnocentrism) to a combination of acceptance and adaptation (ethnorelativism) appears to have occurred for these teachers as their awareness of students' names helped to showcase individual identities.

Music teachers' consternation regarding the pronunciation of students' names was a surprising discovery. I noted in the Knowing Me section that I was unprepared to "come out" with a reckoning of my own name/naming as a point of connection to participants' stories. The robust and feeling-filled conversation between Dr. Brewer, Mr. Martin, and me raised the idea that music teachers must try to know their student musicians in an effort to foster, maintain, and grow community; to make welcome actions (not mere gestures); and recognize the significance of names—significance of who—as part and parcel of a music ensemble experience.

For the band directors in this study, saying a difficult-to-pronounce name is an experience of difference between the teachers' lives and that of their students. Recognition of that difference might be situated simultaneously within and between two stages of Bennett's (1986, 2013) DMIS: acceptance and adaptation. The acceptance stage is where people shift from knowing only oneself to knowing others, and the adaptation stage is when focus is placed on empathetic behaviors, particularly growth behaviors. In a theoretical sense, movement across the DMIS may have been an ancillary benefit for Mr. Martin and Dr. Brewer who wish to provide special care for their student musicians (see Figure 39.2). In this movement, an expansion of one's world (and world view) might be possible.

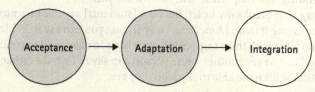

FIGURE 39.2 Ethnorelative stages from Developmental Model of Intercultural Sensitivity (DMIS).

Who They Are Matters

At the outset of this chapter, I noted that knowing music and knowing people are not the same thing. When the subject of pronouncing students' names arose in my discussions with Dr. Brewer and Mr. Martin, what surfaced was uneasiness and deep concern for personal past habits of ignoring or glossing over students' names. Names (who) might be tied to teachers' demonstrations of intercultural sensitivity, particularly where the adaptation stage is concerned. Engaging with course content such as music must never supplant caring for and engaging with, or "caring with" (Hendricks, this volume) our student musicians.

This exploration was a promising way to begin my foray into the teaching lives of music educators and their relationship to Asian and Asian American students. It is just the beginning of a longer story involving the lived (and living) experiences of teachers and students who, in a deeply connected world, might play in parallel and contrary motions throughout their musical lives. Of particular interest to me is how Asian identity, specifically Vietnamese identity, and adoption are related to music teaching and learning. I realize that there are different ideas regarding the extent to which Asianness is highlighted in the arts such as John Cho's or Lulu Wang's somewhat opposing opinions expressed in the *Los Angeles Times*'s "Asian Enough" podcast series.[6] What is unexplored, however, is how those of us yellow-bodied peoples adopted into white worlds manifest our art(s) and how mysteries of an adopted self unfold because of and despite our music education lives, especially in the United States (Vũ, 2020). Related to intercultural sensitivity, how do the experiences of teachers who are transracial adoptees track theoretically along the DMIS, particularly as they may or not personally identify with an Asian culture?

I realize that *what* and *who* are simultaneously different yet related entities. The music we program in ensembles and general music classes must be sounded by people who may (or not) resonate with our repertoire choices. Oftentimes I cannot listen through the music to see the people who breathe life into the very music I purportedly teach because the what and the who are inextricably linked as a multidimensional and continually changing entity. The intersection of intercultural sensitivity and care, as intimated by the band directors in this study, is one place where we teachers might begin to establish long-lasting, deep pedagogical relationships with all our student musicians.

Each of us—students and teachers—is a gift of one to another: Interpersonal interactions and sonic celebrations are amplified when we confirm each other. Noddings (1984) suggests that when we ask questions in class, students answer. But it is not the answer so much that matters as the student themself. In fact, we receive the student as a sort of gift who joins our lives each day. In a sonic sense, the sounds (what) produced by musicians (who) are received within the contexts of ensembles and general music

---

[6] Listen to two seasons of *Asian Enough* at https://podcasts.apple.com/us/podcast/asian-enough/id1501446978

classes, but it is imperative that we know the human beings who we receive into our community of artists first. "What he [sic] says matters" (Noddings, 1984, p. 176). In light of the discussion presented in this chapter, I suggest an amendment to this quote: "Who they are matters." Receiving a student, or anyone for that matter, is a special gift. To receive our students is to receive a feeling-filled, artistic, musical, and beautiful human being into our teacher lives (Palmer, 2007) and our personal lives as well.

Returning to the opening reference: As Isaiah Lee Shelly was received into the world and his Aunt Sara graduated to the next realm simultaneously,[7] Joe and his wife Kelly made an important, life-altering choice to change their son's name to Jordan Lee. This decision may seem fickle to some people; however, delving into the meaning of my own name(s), I have developed heightened awareness about other people's experiences with names, naming, renaming, reclaiming names—and for many of us, moments or lifetimes of namelessness. Although this story is focused on teachers' interactions with Asian and Asian American students, all students will benefit from our thoughtful care of their names, which stand as totems to the living, breathing, and immense humanity within them *and* us.

REFERENCES

Abernathy, S. (2010). Intercountry kinship adoptions: Limits to the Hague Convention on the Protection of Children and Intercountry Adoption. *Kotuitui: New Zealand Journal of Social Sciences*, 5(1), 26–40. https://doi.org/10.1080/1177083X.2010.495050

Antão, G., & Moreira, D. (2015). Intercultural musical learning in the era of technology. *Third 21st Century Academic Forum Conference at Harvard*, 6(1), 55–65. 21st Century Academic Forum.

Bankul, L., & Bukhnieva, O. (2019). Validation of the requirements for intercultural competence forming for future teachers of music art on the Danube territories. *Journal of Danubian Studies and Research*, 9(1), 342–348.

Bennett, M. J. (1986). A developmental approach to training for intercultural sensitivity. *International Journal of Intercultural Relations*, 10(2), 179–196. https://doi.org/10.1016/0147-1767(86)90005-2

Bennett, M. J. (2013). *Basic concepts of intercultural communication: Paradigms, principles, and practices* (2nd ed.). Intercultural Press.

Chance, J. B. (1967). *Variations on a Korean folk song*. Boosey and Hawkes.

Coffey, A. J., Kamhawi, R., Fishwick, P., & Henderson, J. (2013). New media environments' comparative effects upon intercultural sensitivity: A five-dimensional analysis. *International Journal of Intercultural Relations*, 37(5), 605–627. https://doi.org/10.1016/j.ijintrel.2013.06.006

Coffey, A. J., Kamhawi, R., Fishwick, P., & Henderson, J. (2017). The efficacy of an immersive 3D virtual versus 2D web environment in intercultural sensitivity acquisition. *Educational*

---

[7] The phrase "graduated to the next realm" refers to one's passing from this life into the next. For more context, see Maria Kramer's blog at https://awakenpeaceandlove.com/2018/11/05/awakening-oneness/amp/.

Technology Research and Development, 65(2), 455–479. https://doi.org/10.1007/s11423-017-9510-9

Hendricks, K. S. (2018). *Compassionate music teaching: A framework for motivation and engagement in the 21st century*. Rowman and Littlefield.

Heyward, M. (2002). From international to intercultural: Redefining the international school for a globalized world. *Journal of Research in International Education*, 1(1), 9–32. https://doi.org/10.1177/147524090211002

Kallio, A. A., & Westerlund, H. (2020). The discomfort of intercultural learning in music teacher education. In H. Westerlund, S. Karlsen, & H. Partti (Eds.), *Visions for intercultural music teacher education* (pp. 47–61). Springer Nature.

Khasanova, N. (2020). The role of music lessons in the formation of national and intercultural competence in students. *Mental Enlightenment Scientific-Methodological Journal*, 2020(2), 130–139.

Mellizo, J. M. (2018). Applications of the developmental model of intercultural sensitivity (DMIS) in music education. *Topics for Music Education Praxis*, 2018(2), 46–67. http://topics.maydaygroup.org/2018/Mellizo18.pdf

Mellizo, J. M. (2020). Music education, curriculum design, and assessment: Imagining a more equitable approach. *Music Educators Journal*, 106(4), 57–65. https://doi.org/10.1177/0027432120917188

Miettinen, L. (2020). Towards relational music teacher professionalism: Exploring intercultural competence through the experiences of two music teacher educators in Finland and Israel. *Research Studies in Music Education*, 43(2), 226–238. https://doi.org/10.1177/1321103X20936399

Miettinen, L., Westerlund, H., & Gluschankof, C. (2020). Narrating change, voicing values, and co-constructing visions for intercultural music teacher education. In H. Westerlund, S. Karlsen, & H. Partti (Eds.), *Visions for intercultural music teacher education* (pp. 177–193). Springer Nature.

Misca, G. (2014). The "quiet migration": Is intercountry adoption a successful intervention in the lives of vulnerable children? *Family Court Review*, 52, 60–68. https://doi.org/10.1111/fcre.12070

Noddings, N. (1984). *Caring: A feminine approach to ethics and moral education*. University of California Press.

Palmer, P. J. (2007). *The courage to teach: Exploring the inner landscape of a teacher's life*. Jossey-Bass.

Shelly, M. A. (2017). *Sara*. Masthof Press.

Vũ, K. T. (2020). My body was left on the street: Making pathways toward home. In K. T. Vũ & A. de Quadros (Eds.), *My body was left on the street: Music education and displacement* (pp. 239–247). Brill. https://doi.org/10.1163/9789004430464_023

Westerlund, H., Karlsen, S., & Partti, H. (2020). *Visions for intercultural music teacher education*. Springer Nature.

CHAPTER 40

CRITICAL LISTENING AND AUTHORIAL AGENCY AS RADICAL PRACTICES OF CARE

KELLY BYLICA

CARE HANDBOOK TOPICS

Musical development
Social activism and critical consciousness

INTRODUCTION

Listening is a complex process, one that is central to the ways in which individuals experience music and communicate with the world. Yet listening can be undervalued in the music classroom, addressed only when the focus is on understanding a concept, paying attention to a speaker, or seeking to label a musical characteristic. Indeed, individuals' minds are so attuned to quickly and efficiently making meaning from the things they hear, that the multiple possible interpretations of a sound, comment, or musical encounter can be missed. In a rush to respond or react, one may only engage with a singular dominating interpretation, often failing to reflect on how it may be informed by one's own experiences, assumptions, and social realities.

This rush to react can be particularly true in North American music education settings. Despite continued calls for change, linear and functional narratives that privilege singular understandings often still pervade interactions in school music (Gould,

2009). Furthermore, though opportunities for critical and creative musical engagements have continued to grow, the performance-based structure in the United States has often left such engagements as an addendum to rather than a foundational part of the curriculum (Hess, 2015).

In the pluralistic society in which we live, finding ways to explore and engage with diverse ideas and understandings, especially in classroom settings, can be challenging. This is particularly true when such ideas and understandings challenge individuals to consider different perspectives, some of which are drastically different from one's own. As educators, we are used to speaking, listening, and acting in particular ways, and often find comfort in patterns and routines. To choose not to engage with diverse ways of knowing, however, is to deny the reality that "multiple musical, educational, and cultural values are always in play" in the music classroom (Kallio, 2021, p. 163). Listening, particularly when deliberately practiced critically as an act of care, may be one way to encourage and navigate the multiple narratives that arise through musical and dialogical interaction.

The aim of this chapter is to examine how musical engagements and dialogical encounters that promote critical listening practices can be conceived of as acts of care. As I employ here, critical listening involves actively exploring that which we hear to help us consider musical works or encounters from multiple perspectives (Lipari, 2014). In particular, critical listening diminishes the focus on analyzing or understanding, allowing instead for the emergence of multiplicity. I argue that critical listening then becomes a *radical* act of care when it allows for authorial agency to develop, wherein individuals author their own subjectivities as they listen to others and the world. Such practices have the potential to reframe how the purpose of music education is both understood and enacted through everyday interactions.

Critical Listening

Communications scholar Lisbeth Lipari (2014) notes that in current North American culture, listening is often "done primarily with the aim of conquest and control" (p. 2). The goal of listening is often to persuade someone to join one's own point of view. Although such practices may be grounded in noble efforts to encourage compromise or collaboration, this form of listening may unintentionally lead toward a false or masqueraded form of agency wherein one's individual goals are shaped to become those of another. In educational contexts, Matusov and colleagues (2016) refer to this as "effortful agency," wherein listening becomes code for encouraging students to "want what the teachers want them to want" (p. 429).

Listening may also be used to master a skill or as a tool to help us efficiently analyze and understand a concept in an attempt to uncover the "right" or "best" answer. In music education, developing listening skills is often for the purpose of identifying musical characteristics such as melodic patterns or instrumental timbres (Kratus, 2017).

Such listening can lead toward "instrumental agency," wherein individuals develop skills to complete a particular task that has been predefined in advance (Matusov et al., 2016). Although beneficial, this kind of listening can also be stationary and result in unproblematized norms and singular narratives (Schmidt, 2012).

Lipari (2014) makes a case for listening as something more complex, and indeed more challenging, than transferring information, understanding content, or persuading others. Drawing from the work of Buber (1958) and Levinas (1989), she explores listening as central to the ethical obligation of being human. Too often, she suggests, human beings neglect listening in favor of a focus on utterance, speech production, and visual interactions. Listening is left by the wayside, banished to "the silent subservience of dialogue's other" (Lipari, 2014, p. 188). In response, Lipari argues that listening be thought of not as an instrument, object, or tool, but as a process that makes the ethical response possible. In doing so, one is able to "receive the otherness of the other" (p. 178), thus deliberately recognizing and "receiving" an individual's subjectivity.

As one listens, Lipari (2014) argues, the focus should not necessarily be on trying to understand or persuade, wherein one might impose one's own experiences on that of another. Rather, engaging in a process of critical listening might be an opportunity to set aside one's own desire or need to analyze in order to embrace alterity and "honor the other *as* other" (Lipari, 2014, p. 179). Such practices align with Hendricks's (2018) framework of compassion and care, as these practices require the listener to be vulnerable, open, and present in and with the world. Both Hendricks and Lipari agree that compassion in this context is not meant to be understood as sentimental, nor as paternalistic, guilt-ridden, or weak. However, whereas Hendricks (2018) suggests that compassion, and more precisely compassionate empathy, occurs when "a person . . . understands and feels for (and with) others" (p. 57), Lipari (2014) suggests that understanding need not necessarily be intertwined with compassion. Indeed, Lipari notes that the relationship between compassion and alterity requires an awareness that "I may not, in fact, be *able* to understand," reminding us that "understanding without misunderstanding does not exist" (p. 183). Compassion requires us to recognize the vulnerability and subjectivity in all beings, without insisting that this vulnerability be rationally understood.

As an act of care for the otherness and subjectivity of the other, Lipari (2014) notes that compassion is "the very ground from which listening . . . may spring" (p. 183). Listening, then, can be a means to "inquire more deeply into . . . differences, and to question our own already well-formed understandings of the world" (p. 8). It can be an opportunity to take seriously words and ideas that are shared, to consider the world through various frames, and engage in a particular form of "caring with" (Hendricks, 2018) wherein one is attuned to another's values, needs, and feelings by listening *with* another without the precursor of understanding.

Although listening in order to *be with* another through words or music can be conceived of as an act of care, I argue that care becomes *radical* when listening creates opportunity for authorial agency, wherein individuals not only listen with openness, but also, through listening, become the unique authors of their own subjectivities (Matusov et al., 2016). Unlike instrumental agency (to gain a skill) or effortful agency (to work toward a predetermined end), authorial agency emphasizes the unpredictability of relational engagements and defines the purpose of educational endeavors as the "critical examination of the self, the life, and the world in critical dialogue" (p. 162). The goal in such encounters is to transcend the "givens" of an experience, aiming to engage with the surpluses of, for example, a musical or dialogical interaction in order to investigate personal desires and ideas while developing new questions and inquiries (Matusov et al., 2016). These surpluses, that is "all that is generated by actions, interactions, or texts, but is nevertheless absent from their 'central points'." (Schmidt, 2012, p. 9), serve as opportunities to consider the narrative of cultural, civic/political, social, economic, and interpersonal structures that underpin all relational experiences. For individuals, this personal awareness can help one unpack the complexities inherent in how they make meaning from listening experiences. Structurally, placing listening encounters that create opportunities for authorial agency shifts the purpose of music education from skills-oriented practices to relational engagements that take into account personal experience intertwined with the complex realities of others and the world.

Critical Listening in the Context of Music Education

Critical listening in the music classroom can be "an active, creative, and political engagement that foregrounds relationality, connectedness, and an ethic of care" (Kallio, 2021, p. 164). Such processes can allow for "the recognition of each individual's complex personhood in ways that do not seek consensus but work towards new democratic visions of understanding and solidarity" (Kallio, 2021, p. 164). Stauffer (2017) notes, however, that "to listen radically takes effort" and requires a willingness to "step into and learn in a place of discomfort" (pp. 8–9), as allowing oneself to remain vulnerably open and present can be challenging. As such, practices in critical listening may be absent or undervalued in the music classroom, passed over or left untaught in favor of more cleanly delineated outcomes wherein the purpose of an educational encounter is to acquire knowledge or skills. Although there are, at times, benefits to such practices in music education, more recently scholars have begun to explore how practices of critical listening might also operate within the music classroom (e.g., Benedict, 2021; Kallio, 2021). The following sections focus on two such spaces within music education: critical listening in/through musical risk-taking and critical listening in/through dialogue.

Critical Listening in/Through Musical Risk-Taking

Music education is rife with opportunities to engage in critical listening. Individuals listen as they create, remix, perform, compose, and experience music. And yet, in North American music education, the focus is often on accurate representation of a text, producing a sound or blend that is perceived as appealing, or pointing out key themes or phrases that arise as listening takes place. Although this form of listening is important, there is also benefit in listening for the "what else" in a musical work; that is, the various ways in which, as unique individual listeners and/or performers, we might experience and contribute to a musical work. Schmidt (2012) calls this "mis-listening," noting that to engage in mis-listening is "to understand that any interpretation, any practice, any text, any musical interaction produces a surplus and ramifications of meaning and sound, a multiplicity of on-looks and outlooks upon which one can and should enter, contribute, and extend" (pp. 13–14). Instead of aiming for a singular goal, mis-listening allows us to enter a musical work in multiple ways.

In practice, critical and mis-listening might occur in a variety of manners in music education. As musical listeners, these practices require a recognition that artistic work is inherently subjective. Musical works are laden with multiple possible narratives, each of which is made and remade as they collide with listeners' experiences and identities. Critical listening involves an awareness of and engagement with such narratives, imploring the consideration of how one's personal experiences impact, amplify, or even foreclose certain interpretive possibilities.

As an example, consider the song "96,000" from the musical *In the Heights*. The song is an ensemble tour-de-force wherein characters from the musical consider what they would do if they had the winning lottery ticket for a $96,000 jackpot that was sold in a neighborhood bodega. Musically, one might consider the driving beat, ensemble excitement, and clever turns that make the song memorable. Analytically, one might consider how the song illuminates the inner workings of various characters as they explore their personal ambitions. If one were to listen critically in the music classroom, these ideas might be discussed, but students might also be encouraged to consider their own entry points into the work. What do they think of as they are listening? What might that say about our own experiences? How can we think more deeply about ambition, money, structural inequities, and the individual identities we each possess? Critical listening, then, requires not only recognizing the multiple dimensions of a musical work, but also the ways in which those works are imbued with historically and culturally accumulated meanings as well as how those meanings are impacted by the conditions of one's life.

As performers, critical listening practices can be witnessed, for example, in acts of improvisation. As one musical performer listens to another, a multitude of possibilities and musical entrances may materialize. Individuals might draw on their own experiences and engage in practices of listening that seek not to pull the other toward one's own musical trajectory, but to build an improvisatory dialogue that is both personal and communal. This requires an understanding of improvisation that is not based on predetermined patterns, but one that embraces complexity, exploration, and co-creation. Listening becomes central in such interactions, not for the purpose of interpreting or reacting, but for considering the multiple ways in which one might artistically participate in a musical moment.

Students might also engage in critical or mis-listening as they develop their own music. Hickey (2012) notes the importance of creating spaces for students to engage in critical listening as a part of the compositional process, arguing that it can help students add to a "subconscious repertoire of tools for their own composing" (p. 43). More than building a toolbox to pull from, however, critical listening can also involve encouraging student composers to experience sounds and musical works through the lens of creation, considering how one might borrow, remix, or amplify sounds from the world to create new meanings in one's own work. An example of how critical listening might manifest through composition is offered later in this chapter.

Inviting critical or mis-listening through music can be an act of care between teacher and students. Rather than "caring about" a focus on "rightness" when engaging musically, educators who encourage critical or mis-listening embrace an attitude of "caring for" as they deliberately invite multiple entry points into a musical experience (Hendricks, 2018). When musical works are seen not as objects of which to make sense, but as opportunities to explore musical imaginings inquisitively in an ongoing manner, students may come to recognize that their own experiences inform how they engage as listeners, performers, and creators. That care then moves from "caring for" to "caring with" (Hendricks, this volume) and, I argue, becomes radical when individuals' personal contributions to a musical experience are held up by both educators and students as moments of authorship wherein one both recognizes the impact they may have on a musical moment and utilizes that impact to develop new inquiries and musical ideas creatively. Such practices challenge a conception of music education as primarily an opportunity to solve musical problems or reach consensus, instead opting for a "collective sense of purpose" (Hendricks, this volume) that is based in relational interactions that embrace vulnerability, trust, and multiple ways of knowing and experiencing the world.

Promoting critical listening through music as educators can be challenging, and encouraging students to recognize and consider multiple manners of exploring what they are hearing may be antithetical to listening experiences they are having elsewhere in their educational life. It may feel risky to create, perform, or respond to music in a way that does not fit tidily into a pre-determined box. The idea of listening as a practice of sitting with a musical experience, as opposed to analyzing or solving it, therefore, requires both modeling and practice. Educators might begin by exploring, with students, the potential problematics of seeking a singular "right" answer when engaging with something as subjective as music. Students might then be encouraged to move beyond trying "figure out" what a musical work is "about." Rather, students might be encouraged to embrace multiplicity by exploring ideas generated within and because of a musical experience as they draw connections to personal and social experiences. Educators might model engaging in multiple entry points as performers, creators, and listeners, playing with music from a variety of angles. Over time this modeling may encourage creative engagements wherein risk is understood as a welcome element of the musical experience.

Listening Critically in/Through Dialogue

In addition to musical exploration, critical listening can also take place through dialogue. Scholars have noted that there are multiple ways to conceptualize dialogue.[1] Dialogue can be narrowly focused on consensus and amicability without leaving

---

[1] See Burbules (2000) for a thorough review.

space for dissensus, debate, and disagreement. This type of dialogue often focuses on coercion, exclusion, and a strengthening of unequal power relations, potentially producing banal conversations that reinforce singular interpretations (Gould, 2008). Dialogue that has a prescribed end goal can result in teaching that is "hectoring, manipulative, and tacitly authoritarian" even when intentions are otherwise (Burbules, 2006, p. 108).

Dialogue, however, can also be used to challenge and confront, promoting positive dissensus and a multitude of ideas, knowledges, and understandings. Positive dissensus can be achieved when students consider and engage with competing views, multiple explanations, and differing opinions without aiming for an end agreement. Whereas consensus may lead toward acceptance, positive dissensus can lead toward an "ethic that goes beyond tolerance" (Schmidt, 2012, p. 16). Such practices can encourage students to listen in a manner that helps them "explore ways of resisting the unifying forces of 'official' discourse" (Lu, 1994, p. 453) in order to avoid "anodyne conversations" and "see real dialogue and possible conflict as a constructive, engaged, and politically charged practice" (Schmidt, 2007, p. 167).

Critical listening in and through dialogue can also create possibilities for authorial agency to emerge. As individuals listen critically and participate in dialogue that embraces positive dissensus, ideas and notions can be reconfigured and reframed, thus resulting in the creation of something new. Just as in musical endeavors, there can be risk inherent in dialogical processes wherein consensus is not necessarily an end goal, and the tidiness of linear thinking is not revered. This may be particularly true for educators who fear that "things might get out of control" within the classroom (Matusov et al., 2016, p. 439). Care in these moments can be grounded in a belief that part of one's role as an educator is to help students develop a critical consciousness that is turned toward possibility as one deliberately seeks to engage with difference.

Engaging in spaces of positive dissensus can be especially challenging when ethical or moral conflicts arise. Kallio (2021) notes that in these moments, "the silencing of such expressions risk[s] exacerbating the politics of disempowerment by impeding the communicative ethics that are essential for thick democracy" (p. 163). As an alternative, she suggests that listening with an ethic of care, though difficult, "may better foster critical analyses of the conditions underlying such expressions" (p. 164). Such listening is both active and creative, aiming not for consensus nor tolerance, but for increasing understanding of self, other, and the socio-historic processes and framings that underlie expressions that may challenge ethical or moral expectations. As an act of care, this form of listening can help individuals gain personal awareness and work toward seeing one another as human beings bound up in their own socio-historic framings that make each expression possible.

It takes both modeling and practice to help students enter and engage in dialogical interactions wherein risk-taking and positive dissensus are both possible. Practically, this may mean designing curricular experiences that are flexible and responsive. Educators might begin by using open questions that have multiple possible answers and actively challenging students to consider what it is they think they know and how they came to know (Benedict, 2021). Furthermore, it is helpful to deliberately and explicitly discuss what it might mean to listen with care and to practice interactions that move beyond agree/disagree rhetoric and away from pre-determined outcomes or comparisons. This form of listening through dialogue can take time, especially if students have not experienced such interactions in their educational experiences.

Critical Listening Entanglements: A Case in Point

As music-making and dialogue are often entangled in the music classroom, I offer the experiences of Emma[2] as an example to help concretize how these practices can be considered critically in an intertwined manner. Emma and her classmates participated in a project wherein they developed and shared compositions as part of their middle school (ages 12–14) general music class in the United States. The purpose of this project was to explore how the development and implementation of a music composition project in two socioeconomically diverse middle school general music classes in the United States might disrupt top-down instruction and singular approaches to music education in this setting.

In particular, we sought to consider in what ways, if any, this project created opportunities for border crossing (Giroux, 2005) and multiple ways of knowing in the music classroom. Co-designed by the researcher and two participating educators, the four-week composition project consisted of musical listening activities that explored stereotypes and assumptions, as well as the creation of digitally designed student compositions that served as representations of students' lives and experiences. Throughout the project, students, educators, and researcher engaged in ongoing critical reflection wherein they were encouraged to enter contact zones (Pratt, 1991) where existing patterns of thought were questioned and juxtaposed with different ways of being in the world. These opportunities for reflection then went on to inform students' creative practices as they negotiated how they saw themselves and their world.

Emma's composition was an amalgamation of recorded sounds, digitally generated loops, and personal musical improvisations. As part of her composition, she sampled Tchaikovsky's "Dance of the Sugarplum Fairy," playing with dynamics and recasting the melody in juxtaposition with two musical vignettes. In the first, the sound of a ballet pointe shoe hitting the floor and dancers moving across a stage can be heard. The second highlights the loud cacophony of a basketball game, complete with cheers, dribbling basketballs, and buzzers. As one vignette fades, the other responds, and occasionally the two worlds seem to co-exist musically as they become entangled with one another. Tchaikovsky's melody plays throughout, but fades away at the end, without coming to its expected conclusion.

---

[2] Emma is a pseudonym and the example presented here is part of a larger study that can be found in Bylica (2020).

Emma's intention with the composition was to place what she saw as two distinct life experiences (basketball and ballet) in parallel as a way of critically considering her own identity. As a compositional device, Emma reframed a series of recognizable sounds and musical excerpts, purposefully manipulating them to create a new artistic artifact that expanded on the meaning generated by each vignette or piece when listened to separately. In the process, she generated a musical assemblage that disrupts linear thinking and prompts questioning, wonderment, and curiosity as she invites listeners into a space where seemingly incongruent musical ideas are woven together, challenging conceptions of various social spaces and personal identities.

Emma then shared her composition with her classmates. The class had both discussed and practiced critical listening prior to experiencing Emma's composition. They were excited to begin with questions rather than pronouncements and explored how they might move beyond appreciation in the "I liked it and here's why" sense to a way of engaging that encouraged an ongoing and cumulative process of reflection. This preparation led them to move beyond discussions on what Emma's composition was "about" and toward those that considered what her composition made possible within this context with this group of listeners. They began by offering ideas and images that Emma's composition made them think of, parsing out and exploring multiple, sometimes contradictory, ways of entering Emma's composition. They shared stories, asked "why" questions that prompted one another to elaborate and expand on ideas, considered their own identities, and followed their inquiries down various pathways. Their conversations eventually led to a debate surrounding issues of social expectations in various spaces, including at sporting events and arts-based performances, during which they grappled with issues of social class, race, and cultural norms.

In this example, Emma began by hearing a familiar musical piece within the established boundaries of her own experience and expectation. When she moved to transcend those boundaries by mis-listening and considering multiple meanings and reframings, she engaged in authorial agency, eventually producing a cultural artifact through her composition. This artistic rendering was then listened to and experienced anew. When her classmates listened to the piece, they also called on their own experiences, engaging this time not in artistic actualization, but in dialogue as a cultural product. Listening, then, became a creative act, creating opportunities for larger stories that extend beyond a singular interpretation to be explored. What may have been framed as an end product (the composition) was now reframed as a beginning, and, as a result, both the creator and the listeners entered a space wherein they were "in conversation with past, present, and future speakers and listeners" (Lipari, 2014, p. 117). Understanding, in this context, was framed as *always* partial and incomplete, and always mixed in with misunderstanding and mis-listening, building not to an end goal, but to new ways of seeing, hearing, and engaging with the world.

Given the above, Emma's composition might be seen as co-authored, both created and listened to, suggesting that a multitude of interpretations of a piece of music must be recognized, honored, and explored if care is to be made manifest in classrooms.

Rather than an understanding that must be either/or, pedagogically this means helping students think about musical experiences as both/and. In the process of creating and responding, an additional level of meaning is produced through the process of listening. This requires moving beyond an understanding of what a piece is about in order to consider how a composition can create an opportunity for listeners to think divergently about and contribute to discourses of identity, experience, and social struggles both local and global in scope.

Furthermore, in this example, the authorial agency of the student-composer was honored, as well as that of the listening audience. The intent and engagement of the composer's process was not lost or ignored but built on. As Matusov and colleagues (2016) note, it is not a matter of choosing what is "given" or what is new and innovative, but how one uses the given to continuously build and layer as "new goals, new definitions of quality, new motivations, new wills, new desires, new commitments, new skills, new knowledges, and new relationships" emerge (p. 435). In this way, students were enacting radical care. In honoring the voice and ideas present in Emma's composition, they were acknowledging Emma's subjectivity, thus caring *for* her (Hendricks, 2018) by being present with her through her musical work. Equally important, they were afforded space to also author their own subjectivities, as they brought something new into existence. This can be understood as a process of caring *with* (Hendricks, this volume), wherein the experiences, worldviews, and needs of all individuals build toward new collective knowledges and relationships.

Negotiating Authorial Agency as Educators

Educators can face challenges in terms of how they negotiate their own personal authorial agency when engaging with critical listening within the classroom. If there is a desire to encourage authorial agency but educators are unaware of the ways in which their own interpretations are influencing or limiting students' understandings, they may inadvertently promote effortful agency (Matusov et al., 2016), as students seek to match their understandings with that of the teacher. The teacher's authorial agency becomes the dominant narrative, and students may not feel as though alternative understandings are possible.

To be clear, I am not advocating for educators to step back from engaging with students, modeling critical practices, asking provocative questions, or actively partaking in dialogue. To abstain from these pedagogical engagements in the classroom would be to abdicate one's responsibility as an educator. Rather, educators might also engage in their own practices of critical listening, questioning and reflecting alongside students, with an added awareness of the influence carried by our words and actions. This reflexive work is necessary if one hopes to be a true dialogical partner with students. Further, such actions can help educators grow in awareness of the impact they potentially have on the ways in which care is made manifest in musical spaces.

Concluding Thoughts

Lipari (2014) argues that, as human beings in the world, we have lost the ability to *not* understand. There is a security, she notes, in making something known to ourselves through whatever manner possible. Educators are often ingrained with a desire, and indeed a purpose, to help students understand and make meaning in the pursuit of an end goal. Care, however, is not necessarily predicated on understanding and meaning. Rather, care may be found in listening critically to a musical encounter or a dialogical utterance without feeling a need to understand, know, relate, or fix. As a practice of care, critical listening may be a practice of "caring with" (Hendricks, 2018) wherein hierarchical relationships are replaced with an opportunity to simply *be with* something or someone, allowing that which is other to remain other "without having to fit it into some tidy box of 'understanding'" (Lipari, 2014, p. 136). As part of a process of being and becoming, critical listening opens possibility for individuals to develop their own authorial agency, enacting radical care for self and other as the potential for individuals to continually author their own subjectivities is identified, encouraged, honored, and supported.

References

Benedict, C. (2021). *Music and social justice: A guide for elementary educators.* Oxford University Press.

Buber, M. (1958). *I and thou* (R. G. Smith, trans.). Scribner. (Original work published 1923)

Burbules, N. (2000). The limits of dialogue as a critical pedagogy. In P. Trifonas (Ed.), *Revolutionary pedagogies* (pp. 251–273). Routledge.

Burbules, N. (2006). Rethinking dialogue in networked spaces. *Cultural Studies, Critical Methodologies, 6*(1), 107–122. https://doi.org/10.1177/1532708605282817

Bylica, K. (2020). *Critical border crossing: Exploring positionalities through soundscape composition and critical reflection* [Doctoral Dissertation, University of Western Ontario]. Electronic Thesis and Dissertation Repository. https://ir.lib.uwo.ca/etd/7000

Giroux, H. (2005). *Border crossings: Cultural workers and the politics of education* (2nd ed.). Routledge.

Gould, E. (2008). Devouring the other: Democracy in music education. *Action, Criticism, and Theory for Music Education, 7*(1), 29–44. http://act.maydaygroup.org/articles/Gould7_1.pdf

Gould, E. (2009). Music education desire(ing): Language, literacy, and lieder. *Philosophy of Music Education Review, 17*(1), 41–55. https://doi.org/10.2979/PME.2009.17.1.41

Hendricks, K. S. (2018). *Compassionate music teaching: A framework for motivation and engagement in the 21st century.* Oxford University Press.

Hess, J. (2015). Upping the "anti-": The value of an anti-. *Action, Criticism & Theory for Music Education, 14*(1), 66–92. http://act.maydaygroup.org/articles/Hess14_1.pdf

Hickey, M. (2012). *Music outside the lines: Ideas for composing in K-12 music classrooms.* Oxford University Press.

Kallio, A. (2021). Towards solidarity through conflict: Listening for the morally irreconcilable in music education. In A. A. Kallio (Ed.), *Difference and division in music education* (pp. 163–176). Routledge.

Kratus, J. (2017). Music listening is creative. *Music Educators Journal, 103*(3), 46–51. https://doi.org/10.1177/0027432116686843

Levinas, E. (1989). *Entre nous: On thinking-of-the-other.* Columbia University Press.

Lipari, L. (2014). *Listening, thinking, being: Towards an ethics of attunement.* Pennsylvania State University Press.

Lu, M. Z. (1994). Professing multiculturalism: The politics of style in the contact zone. *College Composition and Communication, 45*(4), 442–458. https://doi.org/10.2307/358759

Matusov, E., von Duyke, K., & Kayumova, S. (2016). Mapping concepts of agency. *Integrative Psychological and Behavioral Science, 50,* 420–446. https://doi.org/10.1007/s12124-015-9336-0

Pratt, M. L. (1991). Arts of the contact zone. *Profession,* 33–40.

Schmidt, P. (2007). In search of a reality-based community: Illusion and tolerance in music education and society. *Philosophy of Music Education Review, 15*(2), 160–167. https://doi.org/10.2979/pme.2007.15.2.160

Schmidt, P. (2012). What we hear is meaning too: Deconstruction, dialogue, and music. *Philosophy of Music Education Review, 20*(1), 3–24. https://doi.org/10.2979/philmusieducrevi.20.1.3

Stauffer, S. (2017, September). *Whose imaginings? Whose futures?* [Closing Keynote Address]. Society for Music Teacher Education Symposium, Minneapolis, MN, USA. https://smte.us/wp-content/uploads/2020/04/SMTE2017StaufferKeynote.pdf

CHAPTER 41

LOVE, CARE, REVOLUTION, AND JUSTICE

Loving Oneself and Loving One's Students

GARETH DYLAN SMITH, BRANDI WALLER-PACE, MARTIN URBACH, AND BRYAN POWELL

CARE HANDBOOK TOPICS

Identity expressions
Social activism and critical consciousness

THE four authors of this chapter met several times to talk about ways in which we could draw on our respective and collective experience to add to the discussion about care. Below, we present some of our responses to the Handbook topic questions as they developed from our discussion and reading. We approached writing this chapter using Sawyer & Norris's (2013) "dialogic research methodology," duoethnography, wherein "two or more researchers work in tandem to dialogically critique and question the meanings they give to social issues and epistemological constructs" (p. 2). Care is a social issue, as well as being an epistemological construct and an ontological concern; in this chapter we share representative portions of our discussions with one another, based on our experiences as scholars and educators. Duoethnography was especially appropriate for capturing our collegial conversation, as it is a method "grounded in social justice" (p. 3). We have attempted to share our voices in dialogue below, and occasionally segments may seem disjunct, since we recognize, per Norris and Sawyer (2013, p. 3), that juxtaposition is also an important characteristic of duoethnography. We acknowledge Sawyer and Norris's (2013) point that as duoethnographers engaging in reflexive dialogue we "cannot solve social injustice" (p. 7), but we hope that through this chapter and in subsequent conversations among ourselves and with other colleagues, we might be able to advance it a little.

MARTIN

> To truly love we must learn to mix various ingredients— care, affection, recognition, respect, commitment, and trust, as well as honest and open communication. (hooks, 2001, p. 5)

This authorial team wrote this chapter during the second spring and summer of the COVID-19 pandemic, in 2021. Arundhati Roy (2020) reminded me that COVID-19 "highlighted systemic failings ... as well as offered us a possibility to re-imagine our future." I cannot talk about love, and/or the lack thereof, without acknowledging ourselves as social, political, and historical beings, who as educators must name the world as well as the word (Freire, 2018).

In naming the word, I have to say that prior to COVID-19, the music students in my "Soundtrack of a Revolution" course put their books down, put phones away (most of the time!), and picked up their axes (instruments) to hone their craft including scales, vocal warmups, drum fills, and synth parts. They did this to have fun while connecting with their peers, playing both covers of popular songs and writing revolutionary #BlackLivesMatter songs. Upon transplanting teaching and learning online, however, my students went from using music-making in community as the practice of liberation and the music room as the site for it, to feeling trapped by the neoliberal, bright-lighted tentacles of free web apps that not only stifled their creativity but also collected their personal data and even surveyed their lives. Students who were once slaying A minor pentatonic scales and Freddie Mercury piano parts reported not being in the mood or even able to complete a simple assignment like "curate a playlist of songs" because school music had become a chore. I constantly asked myself what it meant to support students and to love them regardless of their productivity, and to remember not to equate their lack of project output to my level of love input.

In naming the world I have to recognize that COVID-19 affected my Black, Dis/abled,[1] queer, poor, and working-class students at disproportionately higher rates than my white, able, and more affluent ones. I need to name that the system of which Roy (2020) spoke is not necessarily failing, but rather working exactly as it was set up to, so what I am seeing is not students not engaging in music homework, but experiencing the trappings of the systemic oppression they used to perhaps be able to escape for 45 minutes a

---

[1] We have insufficient room in this chapter to do discuss conceptions and understandings of dis/ability as much as the term warrants. For a nuanced exploration of concepts of ability and disability, see David Baker's chapter, "Disability, Lifelong Musical Engagement and Care," in this volume.

day while they were jammed in that Pepto Bismol pink, leaky classroom of ours. I would need to name that teaching music in a school system that has been defunded to the bone over the last 50-plus years, where the school-to-prison pipeline has spirit murdered my Black and Brown students (Love, 2019), and where the vast majority of their music teachers (>80%) are white (Elpus, 2015), is teaching music in a system of white supremacist denial about the United States' systemically racist foundation and societal structure (Baldwin, 1963; Hendricks, 2021; Kendi, 2016).

Brandi

Systemic racism in the United States is manifest in part as colorblindness; people saying they "don't see color." In my work I encounter many educators who claim to adhere to colorblind ideology, yet claim also to love and care for their students. Color does not mean the same to all students, but as a construct in our society it has an impact through the external racialization they experience, their senses of self, and their identity development. Erasing color through colorblind ideology erases parts of students' identities and stories. As rapper Tobe Nwigwe urged in his ode to blackness, "Shine" (2019): "Don't let them make you colorblind, and not adore your skin." hooks wrote of loving blackness as an act of resistance, diametrically opposed to the idea that love only manifests in feelings of warmth and comfort, as our society is swimming in anti-blackness which, when confronted, often results in reactions such as avoidance, discomfort, or outright rage. It is important to note here that anti-blackness is enacted more broadly than against those racialized as Black—it impacts to some degree, as Love (2019) reminds us, the full range of darker skinned, racially minoritized people. She wrote, "We also need to recognize the specific nuances of different types of dark oppression, recognizing that not all injustices are the same," arguing that, "It is important for educators to know how deeply unjust systems affect people and their communities in unique ways" (Love, 2019, pp. 54–55).

In their writing on Black educators' protection of Black children, McKinney de Royston et al. explained critiques of some prevailing theories of care:

> Scholars have challenged color-evasive (i.e., perspectives that minimize or ignore issues of race and/or racism) theories that focus on ethics of care and caring relations with little or no attention to inequalities and power dynamics in schools, especially those experienced by racially minoritized children ... theories of care and caring cannot exist apart from historical and structural analyses of how schools are set up and how educators view their students and the world (Patterson et al., 2008). Indeed, scholars drawing upon Black feminist thought challenge the political and racial neutrality of education, pedagogy, and theories of care and instead acknowledge systemic forces as ongoing sources of everyday societal inequity and oppression (Collins, 2002). (McKinney de Royston et al., 2021, p. 74)

In response, McKinney de Royston et al. developed a framework called "politicized care," containing four domains: political clarity, communal bonds, potential affirming, and developmental appropriateness. Political clarity necessitates the understanding of power dynamics and the sociohistorical foundations of schooling in the United States, in which race plays a central role. This dimension highlights the need to eschew colorblindness and understand "the categorical nature of racial stereotypes and the complicated connections between interpersonal and structural forms of racism that limit the opportunities for Black children to survive and thrive educationally, emotionally, psychologically, and physically" (p. 75). As individual educators reject colorblind ideology to fully serve students, so must theories of care.

BRYAN

An ethic of care in music education provides a pathway for eudaimonia, or human flourishing and, thereby, wellbeing for both music educators and their students (Powell, 2021). This flourishing "can be achieved when one lives for the betterment of oneself and one's community" (Smith & Silverman, 2020, p. 2). Through caring for others, we enrich ourselves. When students are viewed as individuals, with individual goals, aspirations, and music identities, music educators can facilitate opportunities for personal and collective care in the music classroom. This collective group responsibility is integral to the incorporation of a pedagogy of care as students are empowered to see themselves as individual contributors to the musical experience, simultaneously responsible for the collective wellbeing of others. Through this pedagogy of care in music education, "the welfare and growth of one individual is seen as intertwined with the flourishing of others" (Pettersen, 2011, p. 370).

Martin Buber (1958) discussed the nature of interaction between humans as being either *I-It* or *I-Thou*. An *I-It* approach to human interaction regards others as providing a service, experience, or something to be gained. These interactions provide services and experiences and, while practical, the "I" views the "other" as simply an object from which to gain these services or experiences; a relationship devoid of care. An *I-Thou* interaction, conversely, recognizes individuals' uniqueness and humanity, allowing for reciprocal exchange. In an *I-Thou* exchange, individuals are brought into community with one another. Buber (1958) described this in terms of a loving relationship, whereby "love does not cling to the I in such a way as to have the Thou only for its 'content,' its object; but love is between I and Thou. . . . Love is responsibility of an I for a Thou" (pp. 14–15). Hendricks (2021) described Buber's thesis as articulating "a kind of unification of two souls when one (the 'I') comes to truly see and honor another (the 'You')" (p. 244). An *I-Thou* approach positions music educator and student as equals, in dialogue with each other about what each might desire out of musical experience. Buber describes accepting others' whole potentiality by "confirming the other"—loving them, caring with them.

Gareth

If care is a prerequisite for teaching well (Noddings, 1995), and for fostering liminal environments conducive to nurture and growth in others (Hendricks, 2018), it is essential for music teachers to engage in acts of love, both love of others and of self. Encouraging self-love might sound like rallying readers to embrace narcissism. Indeed, I have often struggled to think that I love or should love and care for myself. This is not to say I have lived a life of pure altruism! I engage in plenty of activities with motivations that seem entirely selfish. Perhaps it is the culture of Protestant guilt in which I was raised—where the prevailing orthodoxy seemed to be to be largely self-centered in one's life but then to feel bad about it later and apologize for it each Sunday in church so it seemed less hypocritical and bad—but I have tended to think of things I do for me, not in the positive light of self-love, but through the negative frames of selfishness or narcissism. But this is not what self-love means.

Narcissism is perhaps most often understood as obsessive self-admiration and seeking attention and praise from others in order to affirm one's need to be perceived as excellent or superior (Pincus & Lukowitsky, 2010). A narcissist's posturing, self-aggrandizement, and greed come necessarily at the expense not only of one's own healthy growth and sense of self, but also in one's treatment of others (Freire, 2018). It is essential that we understand love as active, as action. bell hooks (2001) emphasizes how we "must move beyond the realm of feeling to actualize love . . . to see love as practice" (p. 165). Erich Fromm (1956) described the mutuality of loving self and others, and Marianne Williamson (2017) underlined this symbiosis when she noted that, "we can't give to the world what we have not achieved within ourselves, and we can't keep for ourselves what we have not yet given to the world" (p. 13). Without adequate and active *self*-love, then, one is unable to love others. Without the inclination or will to love others, we cannot care for them (Fromm, 1956).

By loving our students, through caring with them, "compassionate music teachers can make a tremendous difference" in the world through our work (Hendricks, 2018, p. 11). In this pursuit, we must center anti-racism (Kendi, 2019) and the contexts of our specific students' lives (Madda, 2019) so that we do not recreate what Simmons called "White Supremacy with a hug" (Madda, 2019, para. 11). We acknowledge that this work is necessarily always a process and never finished. Perhaps we begin with close "attunement to others' feelings as well as their values and goals" (Hendricks et al., 2021, p. 2). In this "caring *with* . . . , relational experiences become mutually reinforcing" (Hendricks et al., 2021, p. 2, emphasis in original). As Greene (1995) underlined, we are "forever on the way" (p. 1).

Brandi

Among K-12 music educators there is much talk about the care and love one has for one's students. "I love my students" often rolls easily off the tongue, and the idea that a teacher would not easily and genuinely love their students can be met with disdain. Discussed much less often is what it actually means to love one's students. In *All About Love*, hooks (2001) described the mistaken conflation of care and love among parents toward their children, and a lack of understanding of what it means to love that passes down to the next generation "a way of thinking about love that makes it difficult for children to acquire a deeper emotional understanding" (p. 19). Just as children are "raised in homes where they are given some degree of care," but where "love may not be sustained or even present" (p. 19), students are in classrooms with teachers who are providing their idea of care with very little or no love. Though scholars have theorized about love and care in education, I assert that the average grade school music educator conceptualizes love as something akin to hooks's description of parental care. It is one thing to quote theory; another thing entirely to live the operational/functional uses of these concepts in the classroom.

hooks (2001) asserts that parents caring for children often confuse a more superficial version of care with love. She writes of genuine love as "a combination of care, commitment, trust, knowledge, responsibility, and respect" (hooks, 2001, p. 7). Teachers, as adult caregivers of children, may also fall prey to assuming that because they provide this version of "care" for their students, they are providing love. In contrast to theoretical ideas of an "ethic of care," inservice educators may see care as the maintenance of and contribution to the physical classroom space, supplying material objects to students, instilling of technical skills, discipline and critique based on their concept of how students should be, and perhaps a dash of fluffy, misguided attempts at socioemotional learning (SEL) that perpetuate white supremacist oppression and erasure of students of varying racial identities, gender identities, and abilities.

hooks connects love to both respect and basic human rights for children—rights that are frequently ignored in ways that would not be tolerated by adults. "Caring for" and "caring with" require us to honor the full humanity of children and "let go of our obsession with power and domination" (hooks, 2001, p. 87). We cannot truly care for students from the position of a kind dictator, "nicely" enacting an autocracy that denies their agency and humanity, and prohibits authentic connections and trust.

As educators aim for "the unity between theory and practice" (Freire, 1997, p. 382), we acknowledge that the jargon developed and shared within academic circles does not necessarily denote the same meanings for those who work and converse primarily within grade school teaching and professional development spaces. As such, music educators must ask themselves what love truly is, and whether or not it is present in their relationships with their students. When we tell our students we love them without embedding in our practices a deep ethic of love that includes justice, we are simply perpetuating a surface-level understanding of what love is.

How can we cultivate the kind of love that contributes to a deeper emotional understanding? Some teachers claim they say "I love you" to students daily because the students do not hear it anywhere else. Without the substance to back up that declaration, though, one could perpetuate the idea that love is about words and affection, "mostly something given to them" (hooks, 2001, p. 18). Without a true ethic of love in practice, such ideas exhibit a deep paternalism rooted in a deficit view of students. Hendricks

(2018) identified this type of care as lacking compassion; being a more superficial "caring about" than deeper, reciprocal "caring *for*," or "caring *with*" (Hendricks et al., 2021, p. 2) that teachers ought to model; enabling what Austina Lee and Gareth Dylan Smith (2023) described as "the potency of caring relationships and approaching others with love" (p. 6). This work requires what Hendricks (2018) described as "making genuine connections with others" (p. 147), in order to do which, music teachers need to live and to demonstrate "connection with our true selves, as well as the integrity we display in our interactions with others" (p. 148). This helps to establish a deep, "authentic connection" with students (Hendricks, 2018, p. 143)—loving students by caring *with* them.

Martin

I have wondered and tried to stay true to my convictions as a student of Black feminist and abolitionist theory and praxis. From Angela Davis's "Abolition Democracy" (2005) call to dream up institutions that are life affirming as well as destroying death affirming ones, to adrienne maree brown's (2017) emergent strategies about trusting the people so they become trustworthy and moving at the speed of trust. To this end of building trust, Hendricks (2018) advocated that music teachers "reach out with a sincere desire to understand what others might be experiencing (including their values and criteria for trust) and work from there" (p. 48). I argue that due to my privilege as a white, cisgender man, I cannot possibly begin to understand most of the oppression(s) that the students I serve might be experiencing, thus I have to go beyond "a sincere desire to understand," and toward getting to truly know them, to break bread with them, to be in community with them as a catalyst to loving them. As Bettina Love (2019) reminds us, we cannot possibly love students whom we do not know.

When I hear a white educator profusely confessing how much they love their Black, Brown, Indigenous, Asian, Queer, and/or disabled students, I wonder if we use the word "love" as an act of charity, much how Freire (2000) referred to the differences between humanitarian versus humanistic education. I do not wish to imply that those words or feelings might not be genuine; I am problematizing the use of such words as "care" and "love" when used without an explicit unpacking of the complex racial contexts and or the inherent power dynamics in student/teacher relationships. Mariame Kaba (2021) called us to remember that love and abolition require us to work toward putting systems in place for people to have what they need; food, shelter, clothing, education, art, beauty, musical instruments, role models who look like them, and teachers who do not shame or silence them.

Rooted in bell hooks' (2014) concept of homeplace—where Black folks, and thus all folks can be subjects and not objects, and can feel safe to rejoice and resist as they need, want or please—I invite us music educators to build homes in our music rooms where our hopes for a brand new world are possible. There, we might realize our dreams of transforming the spaces we inhabit, and in turn transform ourselves, because all that we touch, we change (Butler, 1993). I see myself as an abolitionist, anti-racist white music educator on the journey to become a more caring, loving, compassionate, patient, committed, and trustworthy educator today than I was yesterday. bell hooks (2014) reminded us that love is something we can and must learn; after all, we are teachers. The transformative power of education lies in the symbiotic relationship between teacher and learner, and those labels apply to all in the relationship. We are to learn how to love, and we are to teach how to love. I ask myself this question constantly: How can I learn how to love my students deeper, wider, louder, and quieter?

I say "love deeper" because we might have students who are easy to love, and thus strengthening those relationships as a foundation for an education, combats oppression, and points toward liberation. I say "love wider" because we might have students who at the first sight of a loving interaction, push us away and just like we show students a new raga, ragtime or rock song to "expand" their worldview, we must try a little harder to care, communicate, and commit to those students as well—learning how to love wider because "a justice seeking movement in schools insists that no children are throwaways" (Winn, 2018, p. 39). I say "love louder" because love is as love does, merging intention with action and outcomes (hooks, 1999) and letting students know we are there for them, through thick or thin, as comrades and not allies, as adults who will put something on the line to center, cherish, and care with them.

Finally, I say I must learn how to love quieter because trust and care need space, time, and privacy; gentle and patient interactions do not draw attention to oneself; think opposite of "I love my children, I'd do anything for them." Maybe it is a private message on Zoom, checking in sans prying about a student's week; perhaps it is a piece of constructive and critical feedback that is not "You did so well, *but* . . . ." Loving quieter involves non-transactional relationship building, aimed toward musical collaboration, composition, performance, and analysis, but most importantly for the sake of getting to know each other in the Freirean way, which requires vulnerability and honesty with others if we are going to learn, not from but alongside, and with, one another.

References

Baldwin, J. (1963). *The fire next time*. Dial Press.
Barrett, M. S. (2011). *Towards a cultural psychology of music education*. Oxford University Press.
Boyce-Tillman, J. (2020). An ecology of eudaimonia and its implications for music education. In G. D. Smith & M. Silverman (Eds.), *Eudaimonia: Perspectives for music learning* (pp. 71–89). Routledge.
brown, a. m. (2017). *Emergent strategy: Shaping change, changing worlds*. AK Press.
Brown, B. (2012). *Daring greatly. How the courage to be vulnerable transforms the way we love, love, parent, and lead*. Avery.
Buber, M. (1958). *I and thou* (R. G. Smith, trans.). Charles Scribner's Sons.
Butler, J. (1993). Review: Poststructuralism and postmarxism. *Diacritics, 23*(4), 2–11.
Collins, P. H. (2002). *Black feminist thought: Knowledge, consciousness, and the politics of empowerment*. Routledge.

Davis, A. Y. (2005). *Abolition democracy: Beyond empire, prisons, and torture*. Seven Stories Press.
Derrida, J. (1999). Hospitality, justice and responsibility: A dialogue with Jacques Derrida. In R. Kearney & M. Dooley (Eds.), *Questioning ethics: Contemporary debates in philosophy* (pp. 65–83). Routledge.
Durrant, C. (2003). *Choral conducting: Philosophy and practice*. Routledge.
Elpus, K. (2015). Music teacher licensure candidates in the United States: A demographic profile and analysis of licensure examination scores. *Journal of Research in Music Education, 63*(3), 314–335. https://doi.org/10.1177%2F0022429415602470
Frankfurt, H. G. (2004). *The reasons of love*. Princeton University Press.
Freire, P. (1997). *Pedagogy of the heart*. Continuum.
Freire, P. (2000). *Pedagogy of the oppressed* (30th anniversary ed.). Continuum.
Freire, P. (2018). *Pedagogy of the oppressed* (M. B. Ramos, Trans.; 50th anniversary ed.). Continuum. (Original work published 1970)
Fromm, E. (1956). *The art of loving*. Harper Perennial.
Gallagher, D. M. (1999). Thomas Aquinas on self-love as the basis for love of others. *Acta Philosophica, 8*, 23–44.
Greene, M. (1995). *Releasing the imagination: Essays on education, the arts, and social change*. Jossey-Bass.
Hendricks, K. S. (2018). *Compassionate music teaching*. Rowman & Littlefield.
Hendricks, K. S. (2021). Authentic connection in music education: A chiastic essay. In K. S. Hendricks & J. Boyce-Tillman (Eds.), *Authentic connection: Music, spirituality, and wellbeing* (pp. 237–253). Peter Lang.
Hendricks, K. S., Einarson, K. M., Mitchell, N., Guerriero, E. M., & D'Ercole, P. (2021). Caring for, about, and with: Exploring musical meaningfulness among Suzuki students and parents. *Frontiers in Psychology, 6*, Article 648776. https://doi.org/10.3389/feduc.2021.648776
hooks, b. (1999). Embracing freedom: Spirituality and liberation. In H. Smith & S. Glazer (Eds.), *The heart of learning* (pp. 61–76). Penguin.
hooks, b. (2001). *All about love: New visions*. William Morrow.
hooks, b. (2014). *Teaching to transgress*. Routledge.
Kaba, M. (2021). *We do this 'til we free us: Abolitionist organizing and transforming justice*. Haymarket Books.
Kendi, I. X. (2016). *Stamped from the beginning: The definitive history of racist ideas in America*. Nation Books.
Kendi, I. X. (2019). *How to be an antiracist*. One World.
Lee, A.F., & Smith, G.D. (2023). *Where is the love, y'all? Punk pedagogy in high school choir* (pp. 1–16). Research in Education. https:// doi.org/10.1177/00345237231152605
Love, B. L. (2019). *We want to do more than survive: Abolitionist teaching and the pursuit of educational freedom*. Beacon Press.
Madda, J. M. (2019). *Dena Simmons: Without context, social-emotional learning can backfire*. EdSurge. https://www.edsurge.com/news/2019-05-15-dena-simmons-without-context-social-emotional-learning-can-backfire
Mbiti, J. S. (1971). *African traditional religions and philosophy*. Doubleday.
McKinney de Royston, M., Madkins, T. C., Givens, J. R., & Nasir, N. S. (2021). "I'm a teacher, I'm gonna always protect you": Understanding Black educators' protection of Black children. *American Educational Research Journal, 58*(1), 68–106. https://doi.org/10.3102/00028 31220921119

Noddings, N. (1995). *The challenge to care in schools: An alternative approach to education.* Teachers College Press.

Nwigwe, T. (featuring Madeline Edwards). (2019). Shine [Song]. On *THREE ORIGINALS*. Tobe Nwigwe LLC.

Pettersen, T. (2011). Conceptions of care: Altruism, feminism, and mature care. *Hypatia, 27*(2), 366–389. https://doi.org/10.1111/j.1527-2001.2011.01197.x

Pincus, A. L., & Lukowitsky, M. R. (2010). Pathological narcissism and narcissistic personality disorder. *Annual Review of Clinical Psychology, 6*, 421–446. https://www-annualreviews-org.ezproxy.bu.edu/doi/10.1146/annurev.clinpsy.121208.131215

Powell, B. (2021). Community music interventions, popular music education and eudaimonia. *International Journal of Community Music.* Advance online publication. https://doi.org/10.1386/ijcm_00031_1

Roy, A. (2020, April 3). Arundhati Roy: "The pandemic is a portal." *Financial Times.* https://www.ft.com/content/10d8f5e8-74eb-11ea-95fe-fcd274e920ca

Sawyer, R. D., & Norris, J. (2013). *Duoethnography.* Oxford University Press.

Seligman, M. E. P. (2011). *Flourish: A visionary new understanding of happiness and well-being.* Simon and Schuster.

Silverman, M. (2020). Sense-making, meaningfulness, and instrumental music education. *Frontiers in Psychology, 11*, Article 837. https://doi.org/10.3389/fpsyg.2020.00837

Smith, B. L. N., & Hewitt, R. (2020). Conclusion: Teaching (and learning) through despair with philosophy and love as hope. In B. L. N. Smith & R. Hewitt (Eds.), *Love in education and the art of living* (pp. 187–199). Information Age Publishing.

Smith, G. D., & Silverman, M. (2020). Eudaimonia: Flourishing through music learning. In G. D. Smith & M. Silverman (Eds.), *Eudaimonia: Perspectives for music learning* (pp. 1–13). Routledge.

Williamson, M. (2017). *Healing the soul of America* (20th anniversary ed.). Simon & Schuster.

Winn, M. T. (2018). *Justice on both sides: Transforming education through restorative justice.* Harvard Education Press.

CHAPTER 42

"I JUST WANNA LIVE MY LIFE LIKE IT'S GOLD"

Prioritizing Anti-Racist Music Education

ALICE A. TSUI, JULIET HESS, AND
KARIN S. HENDRICKS

Care Handbook Topics

Social activism and critical consciousness

Over the course of the COVID-19 pandemic, the media, workplaces, and the general population have continually used the word "unprecedented" to describe the events of this period. Indeed, a global pandemic seemed unimaginable prior to December 2019. In the United States, the pandemic has brought issues of racism and white supremacy to the forefront in a way that white people can no longer ignore. Racism and white supremacy are hardly unprecedented; rather, they have changed form over time, while maintaining their lethal and violent qualities.

Race is a social construct, an "evolving social idea" carefully crafted and reshaped over centuries by white people in order to maintain their power and dominant group status (DiAngelo, 2018, p. 17). Kendi (2019) describes how racism and capitalism have worked together throughout history, normalizing a false narrative of white racial superiority to make inequities and oppressions appear justifiable. For example, Europeans relied on theories of ethnic and racial superiority as early as the 15th century to catalyze acts of colonization and expansion (Kendi, 2016). Harmful notions of white supremacy accompanied European colonizers to the United States, where theories were reified into violent practices such as enslavement and displacement and genocide of Indigenous groups (DiAngelo, 2018; Ramsey, 2007).

White supremacy and racism are highly adaptable and maintain many of their lethal and violent qualities as they evolve through what legal scholar Reva Siegel (1997) calls "preservation through transformation" (p. 1113). Enslavement was replaced by Jim Crow segregation in the Southern United States[1] only to give way to the prison industrial complex (Davis, 2000) or what Alexander (2012) calls "The New Jim Crow"--a system in the United States that disproportionately incarcerates Black people. These shifts in the law have changed form over time but maintained their brutal, violent, and segregationist qualities. Moreover, police brutality, specifically against Black communities, has been extremely consistent across time.[2] Public (white) consciousness, however, has increased with the advent of technology to publicly document these murders. George Floyd's murder on May 25, 2020, by police officer Derek Chauvin prompted national and international protests against police violence and in support of the #BlackLivesMatter movement and police abolition--a movement that supports divesting police funding toward social services to better serve communities.

Following the murders of Ahmaud Arbery, George Floyd, and Breonna Taylor in 2020, many white people in the United States became more aware of racism and white supremacy and sought an education about these matters. Kendi's (2019) *How to Be an Antiracist* and DiAngelo's (2018) *White Fragility: Why It's so Hard for White People to Talk About Racism* topped the *New York Times*' bestseller list. The nationwide protests in summer 2020 prompted some moves toward defunding the police and diverting public safety funds to social services.[3] Against this backdrop of police violence, racism and white supremacy have wreaked havoc on minoritized and multiply minoritized populations[4] during the pandemic. Black, Latinx, and Indigenous communities experienced disproportionately high numbers of infections and deaths, while the brutal discourse from Trump about the virus's Chinese origin has prompted a significant rise in anti-Asian hate crimes (APM Research Lab Staff, 2020; Ellerbeck, 2020; McQuaid & Fishbein, 2020; Mineo, 2020; Yam, 2021).

Music Education

Schools are situated within the larger context outlined above. White supremacy has profoundly shaped and influenced education and schools participate in what Bettina Love (2019) calls the "spirit murdering" of Black and Brown children and youth (p. 34). Music education has not been immune to the effects of this dominant power structure. In fact,

---

[1] Jim Crow laws enforced legal segregation in the southern United States. The segregation extended to all public spaces and included schools.
[2] See https://mappingpoliceviolence.org for recent numbers and geography.
[3] See Andrew, 2020; McEvoy, 2020 for example.
[4] We use the term "minoritized" as opposed to "minority" or "marginalized" to avoid potential stigmatization and/or numerical inaccuracies, and to indicate the power relation at play in the social oppression of certain groups (see McCarty, 2002, p. xv).

music education, and therefore music educators, participate readily in white supremacy (Gustafson, 2009; Hess, 2018). Moreover, white populations are overrepresented in school music (Elpus & Abril, 2011; Gustafson, 2009; Thornton, 2018). Some elitist practices in music education are also reflective of the broader societal narrative of supremacy and/or superiority, such as privileging certain musical accomplishments, skills, and/or musics over others; encouraging students to rank themselves against one another; or even the expectation that ensemble members will show devotion to the "maestro" on the podium, without equal opportunity for musical choice or voice.

Although schools have readily enabled white supremacy,[5] they have profound potential to offer something different. Anti-racist music education disrupts supremacist narratives and traditions, recognizes the various contributions that students bring, and decenters the teacher as "expert," thereby affording the teacher space to continue to learn and grow along with other music learners. This view of teachers as co-learners also reflects the concept of compassionate music teaching (Hendricks, 2018), where teachers and students are free to release notions of superiority and/or inferiority and instead see themselves as co-musickers who learn from one another—both musically and toward humanitarian aims.

Compassionate music teaching resists notions of compassion as "pity" or "helping," instead emphasizing shared experience between equals who bring unique strengths and perspectives to the music-learning space (Hendricks, 2018, 2021). In this context, the problematic narrative of "teacher as hero"—which Hendricks (2018) argues is harmful to students and teachers alike—is replaced with practices of curiosity and wonder. Here, music educators move beyond caring "about" or "for" students, to an experience of caring "with" them, promoting authentic connections and relationships that are mutually reinforcing (Hendricks, 2021; this volume).

Anti-racist music education extends beyond "caring with," toward action and social change. Music has played a key role in social activism and resistance to oppressive structures and regimes throughout history (Hess, 2019). Music education presents an opportunity to create spaces within a larger context of oppression and white supremacy, where minoritized students can learn that they are valued, and where white students can learn about their privilege and how to stand up against oppression that others face.

Anti-Racism

Kendi (2019) argues that actions and policies are either racist or anti-racist. For Kendi, there is no neutral stance. Actions and policies either perpetuate white supremacy and racism, or they actively work against these power structures. That also means that

---

[5] See Castagno (2014) for a nuanced discussion of ways that whiteness operates in schools. See also Love (2019).

individuals can be racist or anti-racist at different times, as determined by their actions. In the context of education, for Dei (2000), anti-racism is

> an action-oriented educational strategy for institutional, systemic change to address racism and interlocking systems of social oppression.... Anti-racism explicitly names the issues of race and social difference as issues of power and equity, rather than as matters of cultural and ethnic variety. (p. 27)

Anti-racism requires accounting for one's own positionality in order to understand how it operates in relation to privilege and oppression (Dei, 2000). Anti-racist education refuses a colorblind stance, instead recognizing and valuing the "community cultural wealth" (Yosso, 2005) and the strengths and assets demonstrated across minoritized individuals and groups that may be partially rooted in their racial identities. Moreover, anti-racism requires both critique and interrogation of whiteness, white supremacy, and all of their manifestations. Anti-racism centers race in analysis, while also examining intersecting oppressions (Dei, 2000). Importantly in the context of schooling, an anti-racist stance involves questioning the practice of pathologizing minoritized children and youth and blaming them for their circumstances (Dei, 2000). Instead, anti-racist education encourages educators to look at minoritized youth's contributions while analyzing the systems and structures that shape their conditions.

In a world with a prevailing dominant ideology of global white supremacy (Mills, 1997), which is routinely lethal for minoritized populations, one ethical path forward for schools at this time is to choose anti-racism and to foster it in all facets of education. Doing so involves effecting change at the policy level, in pedagogy, and in curriculum. Anti-racist education requires an integrated approach that explicitly addresses all facets of education that ultimately affect the classroom. Anti-racist curriculum and pedagogy present an important opportunity for minoritized children and youth to understand their value, as well as name and understand the oppressive ideologies that operate to impact their lives. It also provides a mechanism to name and analyze these conditions and actively work against them.

Music classrooms have great potential as anti-racist spaces. Lind and McKoy (2016) have elaborated ways that music spaces can be culturally responsive. Cultural responsiveness provides an important starting point for anti-racist praxis. It involves careful consideration of what students bring to the learning space and requires a deep valuing of their experiences and realities. What an anti-racist approach adds to cultural responsiveness is a profound analysis of the systems and structures of oppression, coupled with a drive to resist and dismantle them. Music, both historically and presently, has always offered a soundtrack of resistance to dominant structures and injustice.[6] Music classroom "spaces" then become "places" (Hendricks, 2018) that can build solidarity between

---

[6] See, for example, Redmond (2014) for a discussion of anthems that have emerged from Black communities.

different groups, communicate children's and youth's profound value and humanity, and center students' experiences in important ways in the curriculum.

The rest of this chapter offers a description of anti-racist pedagogy and programming at New Bridges Elementary in Brooklyn, New York.[7] At this school, students are each empowered to learn and grow into their best self, intellectually, creatively, socially, and emotionally. We highlight specific ways in which anti-racist music and arts experiences at New Bridges Elementary (in-person, remote, and hybrid) promote compassionate and caring practices.

ANTI-RACIST MUSIC EDUCATION AT NEW BRIDGES ELEMENTARY

Music at New Bridges Elementary, an arts-integrated public school in New York City, cultivates the individual and collaborative voice of children. Since its founding in 2013, all students have taken part in music education experiences, and the goal as a school community has always been one of amplifying each child's voice as students learn to express themselves. Every day in the music classroom, students share a community code: "On our team, we want to feel supported, respected, valued, collaborative, safe, and confident."

New Bridges students begin each day with Bright Start, a 10-minute musical, affirmational community meeting where students and faculty musically welcome and unify with "This Day's for Us":

> "Hear our voices together,
> We shine bright together . . .
> For you, and me, and all of us"

Students collectively sing a "Song of the Day," which changes daily based on school theme and connected to what students are learning in music, and share affirmations:

> "I am Excellent.
> I am ME.
> My best me is what I strive to be.
> Showing excellence in every way,
> I am Excellent today and everyday!"
> "A Bright Start for you and me, can help us be all that we can be."[8]

---

[7] The first author of this chapter is the founding music educator and arts coordinator at New Bridges Elementary.

[8] "I Am Excellent" is an affirmation shared at the end of every Bright Start. See https://youtu.be/I_08 yplyG5A for the affirmation in action with Fourth Grade students.

Anti-Racist Programming

The music program at New Bridges was founded in 2013; however, the idea and affirmation of "Our Voices Have Power" were born in the heat of July and August 2016 as a result of the continued violence perpetrated against unarmed Black people across the country. The acknowledgment of and response to the continued harm Black people faced occurred through artistic expression in the New Bridges music classrooms such that students were able to affirm for themselves that they matter. This direct work to not only acknowledge racism against Black people but speak against it is the anti-racist, non-neutral action that can occur in the music classroom. As Kendi (2019) stated:

> The only way to undo racism is to consistently identify and describe it—and then dismantle it. The attempt to turn this usefully descriptive term into an almost unusable slur is, of course, designed to do the opposite: to freeze us into inaction. (p. 9)

"Powerful"

The work toward justice began to shape the lyrical discussions prompted by "Powerful," a song the entire school community, including students, teachers, and families, learned to sing together. Students across all grades participated in discussions on systemic racism, police brutality against Black people, and the power of unified voices. In addition, the faculty at New Bridges Elementary, families of students, and community members who attended the performance learned to sing the chorus of "Powerful" and were encouraged to join in singing with the students in the finale. This activity continues to be a way for the New Bridges community of students, teachers, and families to raise their voices together in unity and solidarity with one another such that the "fourth wall"[9] is broken.

From the song "Powerful," the lyrics "I matter, you matter, we matter" became an affirmation that students started sharing aloud daily beyond the initial performance of this song, and continue to this day. Affirmations are a key part of anti-racist praxis, and according to hooks (2006), "Beloved community is formed not by the eradication of difference but by its affirmation, by each of us claiming the identities and cultural legacies that shape who we are and how we live in the world" (pp. 263–265). Although song lyrics can serve as entry points into discussions on race and racism, teaching or learning to sing songs that contextualize racism in America lyrically do not alone suffice.

---

[9] Imaginary wall separating the audience and the performer.

Self-Reflection

Kendi (2019) describes the heartbeat of anti-racism as self-reflection. The onus of anti-racist music education is continuously renewed by music educators who engage in this work (Lewis, this volume). Simmons (2019) outlines the following actions for teaching for an anti-racist future:

1. Engage in vigilant self-awareness
2. Acknowledge racism and the ideology of white supremacy
3. Study and teach representative history
4. Talk about race with students
5. When you see racism, do something.

Over time, New Bridges educators and students have intentionally connected active self-reflection with anti-racist thoughts, speech, and action. Statements such as "everyone is equal" and "I do not see color" have been eradicated over time, and classroom discussions have become radically honest spaces for racial truths as experienced by teachers and students. According to Bonilla-Silva (2014), colorblind racism cannot be the "racial music" that educators and students continue to uphold, particularly if conversations about race in the classroom are erased, silenced, or do not occur. Affirmation of racial identity in the music classroom is clearly named and stated at New Bridges.

Centering Student Voices

Anti-racist curricula center student voices in the classroom. In discussions of race, students have shared affirmations that include "I'm Black and I'm proud" and "Black Lives Matter." One student shared why they say that Black Lives Matter: "[U]ntil Black Lives Matter and are protected, then all lives can't matter." Discussions about personal meanings behind these affirmations align with a compassionate music-teaching approach (Hendricks, 2018) in that students are encouraged to listen to each other's truths and build on each other's thoughts, feelings, and ideas as they, not the educator, deem necessary.

Self-Awareness

In 2019, equity team educators at New Bridges Elementary began the work of developing lessons for Speaking Proactively About Race with Kids (S.P.A.R.K.). In exploring the Culturally Responsive Sustaining Education (CRSE) framework alongside Kendi's ideas on anti-racism, each equity team educator's structural implementation of this work included time in whole school professional development for individual reflection on race as it affected each educator's life. The objective for educators was and is to acknowledge and become more aware of their own identity and their own implicit biases, and an understanding of how to interrupt any negative impact the biases have on their teaching and their interactions (see Hendricks & McPherson, this volume).

Naming and Questioning

Lessons and discussions began with skin color, introduced by educators to students across all grades, Pre-K through Fifth, in "All the Colors We Are." The intentional introduction and development of common language for all educators at New Bridges was critical for discussions across the school between students, and continued in the music ensembles that were composed of students from varying grades. For Fourth and Fifth Grade musicians, discussions involved students naming and questioning differences between skin color, a biological result, versus race, a social construct. Creating brave spaces in the music classroom for students to speak, react, and process—where students are not expected to output their lives in musical playing or creation—was considered essential for New Bridges Elementary's anti-racist work. As described by Good-Perkins (this volume) and Lewis (this volume), brave spaces where students can speak their truths must be co-cultivated and co-built upon over time between educators and students.

Action

Such discussions prompted a reflection on what was represented and was not visible in the classroom, including in decor. In the first few years of the music program, posters in the music classroom featured primarily traditional Western music notation, Curwen hand signs with white hands, and a painting of Beethoven in the front and center of the class. Over the years, the music classroom at New Bridges began including images of non-white musicians and, specifically, portraits of New Bridges students making music in action. Amplifier Art[10] featuring portraits of activists fighting for justice in different fields started to be front and center as well, and on the door to enter the classroom. The white hands of the Curwen hand signs were replaced with hands of different skin tones to more accurately represent the students in the classroom. Beethoven as a role model was ultimately replaced by Alicia Keys.

Student Expression

Immediately after the murders of George Floyd, Breonna Taylor, Tony McDade, and many more Black people in America in May 2020, students entered the music classroom on Zoom sharing the following sentiments in the chat box without any prompting:

"Being Black is not a crime!!!"
"This is sad, frustrating."
"Stop killing Black people for no reason!"
"I want racism to stop affecting the community."
"Stop thinking people with different skin are a threat."
"Sometimes I wonder do white people even think we are human beings just like them."

---

[10] Amplifier Art is a non-profit design lab that builds free and open source art to amplify activists and movements. See more at https://amplifier.org/

While student reactions to the news flooded the Zoom chat box, it was necessary to also give students the option of what they wanted to do in this moment of racial crisis. Some students opted to play on their instruments and rehearse together, some wanted muted time off-camera, and some wanted to continue sharing thoughts in the chatbox or out loud. A music classroom can be anti-oppressive when adaptable to the needs of students in any given moment, and particularly, in response to national tragedies due to systemic racism.

Lessons Through the Arts

At New Bridges, the work speaking directly to racism and oppression was amplified and continued through an Arts Festival with music, visual art, and dance where students and alumni shared openly their responses to what "Black Lives Matter" means to them:

> "Black Lives Matter because we are human and we should be treated like humans."
> "Black Lives are brightly illuminated."
> "Black Lives Matter because Black lives are beautiful . . . shine on."

Immigration

In addition to speaking and amplifying "Black Lives Matter," students started to learn and unlearn histories of immigrants in America and spoke to issues of border crossing, undocumented people, and stereotypes that the students themselves have faced thus far. Students explored these issues through "Immigrants (We Get the Job Done)" by K'naan (Trooko et al., 2016) and included discussions on immigration and stereotypes of immigrants, freedom in United States history and as it currently stands for Black Americans, and the representation versus reality of the so-called American dream.

Race and Identity

Students also discussed that the black and white binary prevalent in discussions of race is not inclusive enough, particularly when considering where immigrants fall within societal definitions of race. Through anti-racist work at New Bridges Elementary, educators must move beyond tackling white supremacy from a binary stance. Expansive and inclusive anti-racist work needs to improve, proactively, the students represented in each classroom and reckon with BBIA[11] people who are facing harm as a result of oppression but who may not be necessarily reflected in the students' identities in one's specific classroom.

---

[11] BBIA refers to Black, Brown, Indigenous, Asian people, to center and specify the minoritized groups we are discussing, as coined by Lorelei Batislaong of Decolonizing the Music Room. See "BBIP-BBIA: Evolution of Terminology" at https://youtu.be/nMrlgoYmLUo.

Stereotypes

Students were also inspired by "Stereotypes," originally by Black Violin, to share their own in writing, portrayed visually while playing their instruments:

> "People have judged me as a Latina because we would 'always' have a sassy or bad attitude."
> "People judge my family because we all have different shades of skin colors."
> "People judge me based on my belief, gender, and culture."
> "People think Caribbean people have trouble talking because of their accent."

"Freedom Dreams"

Anti-racist music education at New Bridges was expanded through freestyle rap, written rap, and music production. In response to the racial protests and inequities further highlighted by the COVID-19 pandemic, students created "freedom dreams" through music, working toward liberation, affirming their identities, and doing the real work, which Love (2019) breaks down as personal, emotional, spiritual, and communal. In the students' words:

> "I don't want to live in a world where people say I can't do nothing because of my skin.
> I wanna live where in a world, we'll be great
> I wanna live in a world, won't be alone
> I don't want nothing to do with my skin, I don't want anything to happen to me
> I just wanna live my life like it is
> I just wanna live my life like it's gold."

> "I was going to think of a time
> When whites don't hurt Black lives
> A thought came in me today
> It wasn't going the right way
> We stayed at home due to the crisis,
> We figured out, it was a virus
> And today, we had an envelope
> It had one word, and it was 'hope'
> Don't go down the slope."[12]

Centering Joy Within Each Learner's Identity

The community cultural wealth that Yosso (2005) discusses is created by students' individual and collaborative music productions. These self-expressions are integral in anti-oppressive music education at New Bridges Elementary, in that their creations and

---

[12] Fourth Graders wrote and freestyled freedom dream raps as part of the song "Believe." See https://youtu.be/NTU-l7ENrGk for both written and freestyled verses.

identities can be affirmed musically, and not compared or held against an unfair hierarchy of what specific musics or musicians are deemed most important or successful. Music creation and centering of joy within each learner's identity is especially important when speaking authentically to race and racism.

Microaffirmations

Music education can be a medium through which compassionate affirmation of identity continues to occur and is renewed. Hess (2016) describes how schools can be wrought with microaggressions toward individuals who embody difference, including the exhausting experience of having continually to "translate" dominant language and structures to fit with one's own identity. Hendricks (2018) suggests that a compassionate approach to music education might, instead, utilize "microaffirmations," where teachers and other co-learners engage in small acts of identity recognition (e.g., using a genderqueer person's preferred pronouns) to disrupt hurtful and/or insensitive practices and discourse.

Affirming One Another

Affirmation of identity is a cornerstone of the philosophy and arts programming at New Bridges Elementary. In 2021, alumni and current students wrote "Be the Light," inspired by Amanda Gorman and her poem from the presidential inauguration, "The Hill We Climb" (Gorman, 2021). In "Be the Light," students envision our future through being the light for each other in our communities and our world. Through standing up and speaking up for each student, students continue to celebrate themselves, fight for justice, and shine bright:

> "Be The Light" (written by New Bridges Elementary students and alumni)
> Rap
> ...[W]e see the power in each other
> So why don't we help one another...
> We will not be undermined, we'll stand together
> Raise our hands and our signs, through any weather...
> Be true to yourself cause our joy is revolutionary...
> Be the light
> Stand strong with all of your might...
> Follow your heart to do what's right[13]

REFERENCES

Alexander, M. (2012). *The new Jim Crow: Mass incarceration in the age of colorblindness.* New Press.

Andrew, S. (2020, June 17). *There's a growing call to defund the police: Here's what it means.* CNN. https://www.cnn.com/2020/06/06/us/what-is-defund-police-trnd/index.html

---

[13] "Be the Light" is an original song produced by the Class of 2020 and Class of 2021 of New Bridges Elementary. See https://youtu.be/p1OSZVCnDJI for the song that includes footage of the songwriters and producers, as well as the entire New Bridges community through the pandemic.

APM Research Lab Staff. (2020, May 20). *The color of Coronavirus: COVID-19 deaths by race and ethnicity in the U.S.* APM Research Lab. https://www.apmresearchlab.org/covid/deaths-by-race?fbclid=IwAR2Y4IrKTkTzD_qsG5VC5_ckwhY8rPRkP2LKikOYBvXknBaOSg4VF7dRtPU

Black Violin. (2015, August 31). *Black Violin—Stereotypes* [Video]. YouTube. https://www.youtube.com/watch?v=WYerKidQGcc&feature=youtu.be

Bonilla-Silva, E. (2014). *Racism without racists: Color-blind racism and the persistence of racial inequality in America* (4th ed.). Rowman & Littlefield.

Castagno, A. E. (2014). *Educated in whiteness: Good intentions and diversity in schools.* University of Minnesota Press.

Davis, A. Y. (2000). *The prison industrial complex.* AK Press.

Decolonizing the Music Room. (2021). *Decolonizing the music room—Our mission.* https://decolonizingthemusicroom.com/mission

Dei, G. J. S. (2000). Towards an anti-racism discursive framework. In G. J. S. Dei & A. Calliste (Eds.), *Power, knowledge and anti-racism education* (pp. 23–40). Fernwood Publishing.

DiAngelo, R. (2018). *White fragility: Why it's so hard for White people to talk about racism.* Beacon Press.

Decolonizing the Music Room [decolonizingthemusicroom]. (2020, July 21). *BBIP— BBIA: Evolution of Terminology | A Conversation with Lorelei Batislaong and Alice Tsui* [Video]. YouTube. https://www.youtube.com/watch?v=nMrlgoYmLUo&feature=youtu.be

Ellerbeck, A. (2020, April 28). *Over 30 percent of Americans have witnessed COVID-19 bias against Asians, poll says.* NBC News. https://www.nbcnews.com/news/asian-america/over-30-americans-have-witnessed-covid-19-bias-against-asians-n1193901

Elpus, K., & Abril, C. R. (2011). High school music ensemble students in the United States: A demographic profile. *Journal of Research in Music Education, 59*(2), 128–145. https://doi.org/10.1177/0022429411405207

Eskeerdo Smollett, J., Riley, T., & Rotem, J. R. (2015). *Powerful* [Lyrics]. Retrieved from https://genius.com/Empire-cast-powerful-lyrics

Gorman, A. (2021). *The hill we climb: An inaugural poem for the country.* Viking.

Gustafson, R. I. (2009). *Race and curriculum: Music in childhood education.* Palgrave Macmillan.

Hendricks, K. S. (2018). *Compassionate music teaching.* Rowman & Littlefield.

Hendricks, K. S. (2021). Authentic connection in music education. In K. S. Hendricks & J. Boyce-Tillman (Eds.), *Authentic connection: Music, spirituality, and wellbeing* (pp. 237–253). Peter Lang.

Hess, J. (2016). "How does that apply to me?" The gross injustice of having to translate. *Bulletin of the Council for Research in Music Education,* (207–208), 81–100. https://doi.org/10.5406/bulcouresmusedu.207-208.0081

Hess, J. (2018). Musicking marginalization: Periphractic practices in music education. In A. M. Kraehe, R. Gaztambide-Fernández, & B. S. Carpenter II (Eds.), *The Palgrave handbook of race and the arts in education* (pp. 325–346). Palgrave Macmillan.

Hess, J. (2019). *Music education for social change: Constructing an activist music education.* Routledge.

hooks, b. (2006). *Killing rage: Ending racism.* Henry Holt and Company.

Kendi, I. X. (2016). *Stamped from the beginning: The definitive history of racist ideas in America.* Bold Type Books.

Kendi, I. X. (2019). *How to be an anti-racist.* One World.

Lind, V. L., & McKoy, C. L. (2016). *Culturally responsive teaching in music education: From understanding to application*. Routledge.

Love, B. L. (2019). *We want to do more than survive: Abolitionist teaching and the pursuit of educational freedom*. Beacon Press.

McCarty, T. L. (2002). *A place to be Navajo: Rough Rock and the struggle for self-determination in Indigenous schooling*. Routledge.

McEvoy, J. (2020, August 13). *At least 13 cities are defunding their police departments*. Forbes. https://www.forbes.com/sites/jemimamcevoy/2020/08/13/at-least-13-cities-are-defunding-their-police-departments/#29affbc129e3

McQuaid, G., & Fishbein, D. (2020, May 7). *COVID-19's distinctive footprint on immigrants in the United States*. The Hill. https://thehill.com/opinion/immigration/496414-covid-19s-distinctive-footprint-on-immigrants-in-the-united-states

Mills, C. (1997). *The racial contract*. New York University Press.

Mineo, L. (2020, May 11). *The impact of COVID-19 on Native American communities*. Phys.org. https://phys.org/news/2020-05-impact-covid-native-american.html

PS 532 New Bridges Elementary [ps532newbridges]. (2020, June 12). *Alumni Orchestra Performs "Stereotypes"* [Video]. YouTube. https://www.youtube.com/watch?v=RiPNfLESJmo

PS 532 New Bridges Elementary [ps532newbridges]. (2021a, March 17). *Bright Start 3.18.21* [Video]. YouTube. https://www.youtube.com/watch?v=I_08yplyG5A

PS 532 New Bridges Elementary [ps532newbridges]. (2021b, May 27). *"Believe"* [Video]. YouTube. https://www.youtube.com/watch?v=NTU-l7ENrGk

PS 532 New Bridges Elementary [ps532newbridges]. (2021c, May 27). *"Be the Light"* [Video]. YouTube. https://www.youtube.com/watch?v=p1OSZVCnDJI

Ramsey, G. P., Jr. (2007). Secrets, lies and transcriptions: Revisions on race, black music and culture. In J. Brown (Ed.), *Western music and race* (pp. 24–36). Cambridge University Press.

Redmond, S. L. (2014). *Anthem: Social movements and the sound of solidarity in the African diaspora*. New York University Press.

Siegel, R. (1997). Why equal protection no longer protects: The evolving forms of status-enforcing action. *Stanford Law Review, 49*(5), 1111–1148.

Simmons, D. (2019). *How to be an anti-racist educator*. ASCD Education Update. http://www.ascd.org/publications/newsletters/education-update/oct19/vol61/num10/How-to-Be-an-Anti-racist-Educator.aspx

Thornton, D. (2018). Why just me (or few others) in music education: An autoethnographic point of departure. In B. C. Talbot (Ed.), *Marginalized voices in music education* (pp. 46–64). Routledge.

Trooko, Residente, Snow Tha Product, Ahmed, R., K'naan, Miranda, L. (2016). *Immigrants (We Get the Job Done)* [Lyrics]. Retrieved from https://genius.com/Knaan-immigrants-we-get-the-job-done-lyrics

Wang, J. (2016). Classical music: A norm of "common" culture embedded in cultural consumption and cultural diversity. *International Review of the Aesthetics and Sociology of Music*, 195–205. https://www.jstor.org/stable/44234969

Yam, K. (2021). *There were 3,800 anti-Asian racist incidents, mostly against women, in past year*. NBC News. https://www.nbcnews.com/news/asian-america/there-were-3-800-anti-asian-racist-incidents-mostly-against-n1261257

Yosso, T. J. (2005). Whose culture has capital? A critical race theory discussion of community cultural wealth. *Race, Ethnicity, and Education, 8*(1), 69–91. https://doi.org/10.1080/1361332052000341006

CHAPTER 43

MUSIC-MAKING IN PRISONS AND SCHOOLS

Dismantling Carceral Logics

REBECCA D. SWANSON AND MARY L. COHEN

Care Handbook Topics

Social activism and critical consciousness
Wellbeing and human flourishing

WORDS regularly attributed to the Dalai Lama suggest that "compassion is the radicalism of our time." Despite the national ideology about the equality of all people, settler colonialism and racism played a direct role in establishing the United States. The colonialization of Native American populations, the enslavement of Africans, the subsequent creation of a racial caste system (Wilkerson, 2020), and the multiple outcomes of heteronormative and racist behaviors and attitudes have created harmful inequities in society. We consider these inequities in the parallels between prisons and schools.

"Carceral logics" refers to ways of thinking, even by those who are not explicitly connected to prisons, that are shaped by practices and ideas of imprisonment (Coyle & Nagel, 2022). For example, assumptions that police and prisons are solutions to complex social problems such as poverty, addiction, and mental health is an expression of carceral logics. Scholars and activists have argued that carceral logics occur in schools through inequitable punishment practices (Gopalan & Nelson, 2019) and deficit-based instruction and assessment (Love, 2019).

Punishment in schools reflects punishment in prisons. In criminal legal systems, a variety of practices such as plea bargaining, mandatory minimum sentences, and lack of restorative conferencing options may result in non-personalized outcomes for both crime survivors and perpetrators without consideration of their backgrounds, situations, and needs. Similarly, when teachers and administrators use pre-determined disciplinary actions for student offenses without attempting to understand the students' stories and individual needs, their responses conform to carceral logics instead of common sense and fairness (Kajs, 2006).

People of color, especially Black people, are disproportionately punished in schools (Welsh & Little, 2018) and incarcerated in US prisons compared to white people (Smolkowski et al., 2016). Implicit bias of teachers (Staats, 2014) and law enforcement professionals (Glaser, 2014) contribute to these inequities. One consequence of this web of racism and colonialism is the school to prison nexus. Students, disproportionately students of color, who receive punitive disciplinary action in schools, even for one act of misconduct, experience suspension, expulsion, isolation, and even youth sentencing (Petrosina et al., 2010).

Specific pedagogical approaches such as standardized testing may be considered extensions of carceral logics. Wayne Au (2019) describes how standardized tests were originally used over 100 years ago to "prove" intelligent superiority of whites in comparison to non-whites. Standardized tests, Au notes, miss most experiences, processes, and relationships central to teaching and learning. They also suppress student creativity, individuality, and empowerment in learning. To a lesser extent, such conditions reflect more extreme depersonalization that occurs in prisons, where incarcerated individuals are stripped of their personhood, many times referred to by their last names and ID numbers, and perform mundane tasks with few opportunities for creativity, individuality, and personal choice.

For substantial and meaningful change to occur within structures deeply webbed with racism and oppression, abolitionist thinking—the de-epistemology and re-imagining of current oppressive constructs—must take place (Ben-Moshe, 2018). Abolitionist thinking leads to the deconstruction of harmful systems and the construction of communities of caring based on needs. Prison abolitionists such as Angela Davis (2003), Mariame Kaba (2021), and creator of the Abolitionist Teaching Network, Bettina Love (2019), work to re-conceptualize society without prisons or the carceral structures of schools. They insist that instead of simply reforming old inequitable structures that prioritize power, punishment, and control, leaders such as school administrators, wardens, and legal professionals must implement new structures that promote growth, restoration, individuality, and flourishing in individuals and communities. This type of top-down approach, they maintain, is essential to change.

Social change can also be multi-directional. Bottom-up change occurs through grassroots efforts by workers and volunteers who are not making policy decisions yet challenge the status quo on local levels. Social change can also occur from the inside-out through individuals within oppressive systems who perceive themselves with self-compassion and who imagine problem-solving processes rooted in caring social and personal responsibility. Multi-directional abolition enables people oppressed by institutional systems to acquire mental and emotional tools needed to resist power imbalances. This internal resistance is essential to breaking down systems that use power and control to diminish one's sense of interior strength and freedom.

Interior strength and freedom can be cultivated through the development of self-compassion. Kristin Neff (2003) defines the three basic components of self-compassion as: (a) extending kindness and understanding to oneself rather than harsh self-criticism and judgment, (b) seeing one's experiences as part of the larger human experience rather than as separating and isolating, and (c) holding one's painful thoughts and feelings in balanced awareness rather than over-identifying with them. Rogers (2015) describes self-compassion as "the secret to interior freedom and personal restoration" (p. 33). Individuals within oppressive systems can engage in one of the smallest components of abolition, self-compassion, because no one can take away one's individual inner strength and freedom. Self-compassion is an element of compassion-based activism (Rogers, 2018). The development of self-compassion sets the groundwork for the abolition of carceral frameworks in institutions such as the criminal legal system and schools.

Our experiences in a prison-based music program have convinced us that effective pedagogical practices in music-learning environments provide opportunities for learners and teachers to cultivate compassionate spaces and develop self-compassion, creating inside-out steps toward transformative justice. As such, music-making can equip individuals to resist carceral systems and make strides toward social change.

Relationships Among Self-Compassion, Compassion, and Music-Making

Neff (2021) describes the need to balance "tender self-compassion" or nurturing and caring for oneself with "fierce self-compassion" or asserting healthy boundaries and standing up for one's rights. When a system operates under the premise that there is something inherently wrong with the people in it, those individuals may internalize a sense of being unworthy of success, thus falling complicit to this deficit approach to operating the system. Sometimes in schools and prisons, power structures limit individuals' ability to stand up for themselves, but if those experiencing oppression practice kindness and understanding toward themselves, they build resilience against punitive forces that benefit from any lack of self-compassion.

Self-compassion entails perceiving one's experiences as a part of a larger human experience, but it does not imply that the oppressed should accept oppression and justify the barriers they experience. Their awareness that others experience similar harm can diminish their sense of isolation and over-identification with negative thoughts and feelings, thus enabling them to practice self-compassion collectively with an intention of solidarity.

Rogers (2018) positions self-compassion as a gateway to compassion toward others: "We can only treat another with dignity when we know our own dignity. We can only extend compassion to others when compassion has been extended to us" (p. 37). When people within oppressive spaces have not healed from past or present trauma, it is difficult to build compassion for themselves and others (see Hibbard & Price, this volume).

Rogers's (2015) "compassion practice" (p. 19) includes the steps of getting grounded, cultivating self-compassion, cultivating compassion for others, and discerning compassionate action. Clinical psychology research suggests the following foundational elements of compassion: recognizing suffering, understanding the universality of suffering, feeling for the sufferer, toleration of distressing feelings, and motivation to alleviate suffering (Strauss et al., 2016). In this chapter, we focus on toleration of distressing feelings and understanding of human suffering as they relate closely to the creation of compassionate spaces within prisons and schools.

"Distress tolerance" (Zvolensky et al., 2010) means enduring troublesome emotions within oneself without feeling overwhelmed. The Dalai Lama (2002) takes this further when he notes that enemies provide teaching opportunities for us to practice tolerance, patience, and compassion. In the context of prisons, correctional staff and volunteers must tolerate their awareness that incarcerated people and their victims have suffered greatly. They must resist the inclination to frame incarcerated people as the enemy because their past actions conflict with prevailing moral codes. School teachers may witness hurtful behaviors such as bullying in their classrooms and need to find care for the perpetrator. Compassion in prisons and schools cannot take place without working through these conflicting feelings.

Understanding the universality of suffering distinguishes between pity and compassion. Because pity involves an implicit feeling of superiority over those who are suffering, the alleviation of suffering motivated by pity can be paternalistic (Hendricks, 2018, 2021), such as when helpers believe the "subordinate group" lacks knowledge, money, or skills to act in their own best interests. An understanding of universal suffering, however, subverts this feeling of superiority because it is a reminder of one's own inherent vulnerability to suffering.

The interrelatedness of self-compassion, compassion, and activism is captured in Rogers's (2018) compass of compassion-based activism. As Figure 43.1 shows, Rogers envisions the eight qualities of CBA as moral imperatives in balanced tension around an essential self. The eight imperatives on Rogers's compass include "universal inclusivity," "nonreactive presence," "curious openness to another's truth," "empowered personal dignity," "love for one's adversary," "strategic focus on systemic violence," "imaginative social problem solving." The final imperative, "firm limits on violations," raises questions of what those limits might look like, who should enact and enforce them, and by what means limits should be made firm (pp. 39–40). Rogers asserts that our core self is wise and compassionate but can be disrupted by violence and violation. Until restored and re-grounded, the self cannot respond with compassion and love. Stopping offensive behavior is not the single goal of CBA; it also seeks to set adversaries into right relationships by finding connections, listening to the other's concerns, and believing in their humanity.

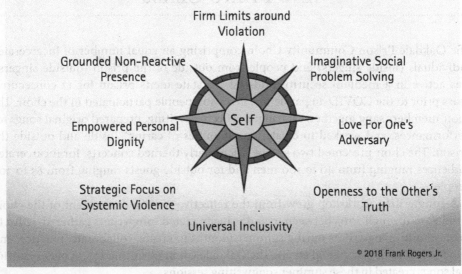

FIGURE 43.1 Compass of Compassion-Based Activism, copyright 2018, Frank Rogers Jr., Center for Engaged Compassion.

Music educators have rich opportunities to incorporate CBA into their teaching, cultivate compassion and self-compassion for themselves and their students, and advance abolitionist thinking. Researchers suggest a relationship between group music-making and the development of empathy, a key component of compassion (Rabinowitch et al., 2013). Hendricks (2018) notes that our increased sensitivity to sound "can transfer to myriad other ways in which we cultivate sensitivity to other people" (p. 63) and recommends using musical learning spaces to encourage sensitivity, kindness, and connection (p. 62). Juliet Hess (2020) adds that self-affirming and regulated feedback in music classrooms can support self-compassion among students, deepening their capacity to recognize and accept complex aspects of identity.

As music educators in a prison program, we have seen that the natural relationship-building and mindful qualities of music-making, combined with purposeful implementation of compassion and self-compassion practices, can pave the way for music students and teachers to gain self-acceptance, building a sense of internal care and compassion for others. This three-part case study describes development of compassion and self-compassion among incarcerated men and community volunteers through music-making in a prison. In this environment of punishment, control, and coercive power, we examine how building relationships among incarcerated and non-incarcerated musicians through musical learning nurtured our capacities for compassion and abolitionist thinking.

Case Study: The Oakdale Community Choir, Summer Songwriting Workshop, and Piano Class

The Oakdale Prison Community Choir, comprising an equal number of incarcerated individuals (inside singers) and people from outside of the prison (outside singers), was active in a medium security Midwest US state men's prison for 12 consecutive years prior to the COVID-19 pandemic. Over 300 people participated in the choir. The choir members sang together, exchanged reflective writing, prepared original songs for performances, and worked to create "communities of caring" inside and outside the prison. The choir presented two sets of twice-yearly themed concerts, for incarcerated audiences ranging from 40 to 100 men and for outside guests ranging from 85 to 300 people.

A songwriting workshop grew from the reflective writing component of the choir. From 2010 through 2019, between 10 and 15 incarcerated songwriters gathered with 2 to 5 community songwriters during summer months to create, collaborate, practice, and provide feedback on original songs. The Oakdale Choir performed 75 of over 150 original songs created in these summer songwriting sessions.

In late 2015, an outside singer, Marilyn Knight, began a group piano class that met weekly in the prison. Several instructors throughout the years, including co-author Rebecca Swanson, taught from 3 to 10 incarcerated students. Each class began with a group lesson on general musical skills such as keeping the beat or reading traditional notation. Then, volunteers worked with individuals or small groups at several keyboards around the room on piano-specific skills.

The Oakdale Community Choir

Choir practices began in mixed formation, giving members an opportunity to meet new people and reconnect with members they already knew. We warmed up physically and vocally, and occasionally changed seats during practice to facilitate interactions among singers. Eventually, musicians in the group took turns leading warm-ups and directing the choir. Rehearsals ended in a large standing circle singing "May You Walk in Beauty." Some members walked along the inside of the circle giving high fives or fist bumps to people in the outer circle. However, it was not until the choir stopped due to COVID-19 that I (Cohen) sought to learn more about the roots of our closing song for a podcast interview. Once I discovered the Navajo Nation's Dineh concept of "Walking in Beauty" or traveling through life by living in right relationships with the elements of the four cardinal directions, I realized that I neglected to align the deeper meanings of this song with our overarching goals of building communities of caring. When the outside members met in a park in the summer of 2021, I explained this concept, apologized, and encouraged us to be curious about another's truth, in this case the deep wisdom of the Navajo Nations and the concept of "walking in beauty."

In the choir, singing together was a straightforward way to gather as one communal voice, despite the disparate backgrounds and current life situations of the members. Listening to the group blindfolded, one could not distinguish which voices would leave the facility at rehearsal's end and which would stay. In this way, the communal voice created in choral singing was both an embodiment and a symbol of universal inclusivity. Weekly rehearsals, preparations for concerts, and performances all created spaces where members extended compassion and care for one another. Inside singers who had not previously talked with one another built new relationships; inside and outside singers used a weekly reflective writing exchange as an opportunity for self-reflection and relationship-building across the carceral divide (Cohen, 2012). In these and other ways, the choir created a process for participants to open up to one another's truths. When inside singers' family members attended concerts, outside singers could meet them, deepening their sense of universal inclusivity.

Singing original songs written by inside singers contributed to a compassionate environment as well. When the choir rehearsed original songs by members, the group expressed musically what was important to the songwriters. Many inside singers wrote songs for family members about their own childhood and family interactions. Each time choir members brought an original song to life the group members became more open to the individual songwriter's truth. This humanizing effect extended to audience members, who developed compassion for the songwriters when they listened to these songs in concerts. One incarcerated singer wrote and sang "Four Times Bonita," a love song to his wife, who sat in the front row of the concert with their two grown daughters. The song expressed a deep love and longing, and the tears in his family's eyes revealed to choir members how difficult imprisonment was for them. Singing this song in front of over 200 people required a great deal of personal dignity.

The location of the choir inside a medium security adult prison enabled outside singers and audience members to develop non-reactive presence. Audience guests in the prison typically did not know how the men came to be incarcerated. Each rehearsal and some concerts started with a brief meditation to allow people to fully enter the choral experience, release unnecessary tension, breathe deeply, and set intentions for the rehearsal or performance. Concerts included invitations for all to sing together, giving audience members, too, a chance to feel musically embodied and grounded in the community.

Participation in the choir inspired some incarcerated individuals to join other prison programs including a writers' workshop, yoga class, dog training program, running club, and Braille program. Many enrolled in college courses through a new University of Iowa Liberal Arts Beyond Bars program. For outside singers, participation in the choir increased awareness of human rights issues in criminal law and justice systems, leading many to become involved in advocacy and social justice groups devoted to eliminating systemic violence. These included Alternatives to Violence, which held weekend workshops in the prison and the Inside Out Reentry Community, which supports people returning to society from prisons.

A peacebuilding class that Cohen designed in conjunction with the choir engaged students in imaginative social problem-solving through reading and conversing about restorative justice, exploring cases that align music-making practices with peacebuilding goals, and designing two peacebuilding projects—one focused on personal inner peace and a second geared toward building peace with someone else. They presented summaries of their work on posters at concerts, and during the COVID-19 pandemic, for one another in class and for outside and former inside singers on Zoom. One inside singer/student in the Peacebuilding class discussed restorative justice with a state representative who came into the prison for an educational event.

Songwriting

The Songwriting Workshops at the prison provided opportunities for participants to practice self-compassion by learning to honor the process of writing songs and reflecting on their content. As Hendricks (2018) notes, "songwriting provides artistic experiences for perspective taking" (pp. 69–70). In a prison context, original songs written by men in custody gave outside volunteers and audience members opportunities to open themselves to others' truths and recognize others' suffering while tolerating their own distress or discomfort at hearing personal stories inside a prison.

We used the four-step Liz Lerman Critical Response Process (Borstel & Lerman, 2003) to provide strength-based feedback, giving workshop participants opportunities to practice compassion and self-compassion simultaneously. The process of giving and receiving supportive feedback offered practice in developing non-reactive presence and personal dignity. After the songwriter shared an original song or lyrics, respondents provided affirming comments that recognized meanings and acknowledged strengths of the work in progress. Next, the songwriter asked questions about their composition. Then, the respondents asked neutral questions, seeking information about the work without offering a direct or hidden opinion. This third step required a sense of mindfulness and groundedness in both responder and songwriter. Responders needed to consider how to phrase their questions effectively; in some instances, they rephrased their questions after re-thinking, to avoid expressing potentially harmful opinions. In the last step, after meaningful interactions occurred between the group and the songwriter, the songwriter could choose whether to hear group members' opinions about the original composition. This process offered many opportunities for participants to regulate their emotions, to ground themselves in a non-reactive presence, to open themselves to others' truths, and build personal dignity while giving and receiving critiques.

Prominent themes of Oakdale songs and concerts were making a positive impact on the world, practicing forgiveness, accepting who we are, and finding gratitude—all components of compassion and self-compassion. For example, Michael Blackwell's inspiration for collaboratively writing "Remember: Be Love," was his desire to change relationships grounded in hatred to relationships grounded in love. The lyrics of the chorus are as follows:

> Life was not designed for us to hate,
> But a masterpiece birthed from above
> Evil will not be what seals our fate
> Forget complaining, remember . . . Be Love, be Love, be Love.
> Every life needs a heart to live
> Every soul wants peace like a dove
> Every wrong is the reason to forgive
> Forget revenge, remember . . . Be Love, be Love, be Love.

Songwriting can be a tool for imaginative social problem solving and strategic focus on systemic violence. One incarcerated choir member, Perry Miller, wrote "Grain of Sand" as an allegory of the prison experience of incarcerated individuals. In this song, a machine represents the prison system, as the wheels of a vindictive, unjust system grind slowly away, creating painful and negative experiences for those incarcerated. The lyrics assert that individual efforts to resist the system are like grains of sand that can eventually break a large machine and bring it to a halt:

> Behold man's mightiest machine with surface cold, metallic gleam
> And giant parts with power strong; the toughest thing man's ever seen.
> But then a grain of sand slips in beneath machine's protective skin
> And travels quickly toward its core, creating an enormous din
> Some massive gears begin to creak swiftly flowing fluids leak;
> Then warning lights come brightly on as power drops from strong to weak.
> The great machine cries out in pain and struggles to run on in vain,
> Its awesome power come to naught disrupted by one tiny grain.

In discussing his lyrics, Miller noted great value in small acts such as volunteers offering hope through programming, letters, and visits, or a correctional officer complimenting an incarcerated person for a job well done. Such acts can help stop the grinding.

Piano Class

Piano class instructors sought to promote self-compassion by leveling the instructor-student power dynamics. One means of accomplishing this was to build personal relationships on musical interests. Throughout the class, students and instructors discussed childhoods, interests, aspirations, and daily experiences. Some students and I (Swanson) exchanged favorite songs to play on the piano and explained how these songs had affected us. Despite clear differences in life experiences and incarceration status, we deliberately highlighted our commonalities, increasing a sense of universal inclusivity.

Our most direct commonality was our shared identity as musicians learning to play the piano.

Instructors, even those who were professional pianists or studying in a doctoral piano program, shared their personal struggles in learning to play the piano. I (Swanson) tried to recognize and apologize for my pedagogical mistakes and let students know that piano class was a learning experience for me as well as for them. Admitting our struggles increased our mutual openness to vulnerability by disrupting a pedagogical façade of expertise and superiority (Hendricks, 2021). Diminishing our perceived power in a place that often reinforces power and control differential offered incarcerated students more freedom to explore their personal dignity and exercise some of their own power in the classroom.

Several students mentioned during lessons that they had been told from a young age, mostly by their music teachers, that they were not musically talented. They felt discouraged from participating in musical activities until deciding to try music programs while incarcerated. Showing up to piano class demonstrated empowered personal dignity with fierce and tender self-compassion, as they worked through these past judgments and extended kindness and understanding to themselves in order to take up the challenge of learning to play piano.

In piano class, we often talked about "honoring where we are in the process," or accepting our current ability at a task or skill, even if it is far from where we would like to be. Students practiced non-reactive presence when we prompted them to identify, without self-judgment, the aspects of their playing that needed improvement. Their neutral identification of their deficits encouraged student-led goal setting and deepened student motivation. When students grew frustrated, we modeled compassionate self-talk and took breaks to shake out our bodies and refocus. Sharing our struggles as a group not only improved our sense of community, but also prevented students from feeling isolated in their frustration, encouraging a collective commitment to self-compassion.

When I (Swanson) first started teaching, I mistakenly pushed students to learn arrangements of Western classical music and traditional American folk songs—music that was central to my personal musical education but unfamiliar to most of the students. Confused by their reluctance to learn these pieces, some students explained that they would prefer to play rap, pop, and hip-hop songs. Thanks to their brave communication, I admitted my mistake of assuming only Eurocentric music was appropriate for a piano class and changed our repertoire to songs that more closely aligned with students' musical interests and experiences. Omitting these popular, contemporary genres operates as a "colonizing discourse" (Bradley, 2012, p. 415), especially to students of color, who see that their music is unworthy of study. Providing musical learning experiences that are more culturally connected to students' lives was a small-scale form of strategic focus against systemic violence, a step toward de-colonizing the classroom. Attendance for piano class nearly tripled after the inclusion of students' musical preferences. When there were miscommunications with staff about who was allowed to use the keyboard between class sessions, students advocated for themselves and worked together for permission to practice, developing firm limits around violation. Because playing piano brought them joy, confidence, and fulfillment, they did not want to lose these opportunities.

APPLICATIONS FOR MUSIC EDUCATORS

Our experiences in this prison program have convinced us that development of compassion and self-compassion through music-making in prison settings can also occur in music classrooms outside of prisons. Admittedly, the need to meet musical standards while preparing students for performances can easily supersede a teacher's focus on relationship-building and cultivation of students' wellbeing. But classroom community grounded in compassion for self and others seeks to blend musical engagement with personal and social growth. Rogers's compassion-based activism is a framework that can guide music teachers toward such balance.

When music students learn new skills, feel overwhelmed in a competition, or worry about their musical competency, they need instruction on how to work through frustration to build grounded, non-reactive presence and empowered personal dignity. Teachers who collaborate with learners to co-create individualized goals that match their interests can more effectively empower students' sense of personal dignity than those who measure students according to an established standard of musical achievement. Activities such as affirmation-based improvisation can help students learn to be vulnerable when making music with others, creating more comfortable social relationships in the classroom that enable students to open themselves to one another's truth.

To dismantle carceral logics and transform punitive systems, teachers must first recognize their own contributions to systemic racism, xenophobia, sexism, homophobia, transphobia, and ableism, even unintentionally. A first step in this process is admitting to ourselves, students, parents, and administrators when we do something wrong; then we need to practice self-compassion and commit to imagining new ways of thinking and doing.

When teachers and students alike practice self-compassion, transformative change can occur on micro levels. Students can find opportunities to develop empowered personal dignity through musical composition, through leadership roles such as helping choose repertoire, and through their work with relatable and honest teachers who design learning experiences to promote learners' sense of control. Once learners have connected ideas of self-compassion with self-affirmation, they can build on group strengths (Hess, 2020, p. 63; see also Berg, this volume). Hess (2020) advises teachers to practice and instruct students in the skills of self-affirmation and self-kindness rather than self-judgment. From such small changes in classroom practices, teachers may further cultivate change on macro levels through such practices as discussing with students the intersections of music and human rights and encouraging students to imagine how music-making skills (including the skills of compassion and self-compassion) can shape social responses to the most pressing local and global needs.

Conclusion and Reflection Questions

Through practicing compassion and self-compassion, individuals on both sides of the prison wall can begin to imagine positive realities by experiencing healthy relationships and self-growth. This development allows individuals to participate in small acts of opposition against systems of oppression by rejecting power and control-centered relationships, and instead building personal resources and the ability to engage in compassion-based activism.

Music educators must think about the oppressive systems that may block relationship-building in classrooms and consider how music-making can oppose them. Adopting abolitionist thinking and compassion-based activism as desirable instructional practices and educational outcomes, we pose the following questions for music educators to consider for their own classrooms:

1. What practices in your music classroom originate from and continue to perpetuate carceral logics, systemic racism, and other forms of oppression?
2. What currently makes relationship-building difficult among students, educators, and the school community in music classes and ensembles? What classroom activities contribute to meaningful relationship building?
3. What creative, music-based approaches allow students and educators to develop skillsets to respond to themselves with self-compassion and others with compassion?

References

Au, W. (2019). Racial justice is not a choice: White supremacy, high-stakes testing, and the punishment of Black and Brown children. *Rethinking Schools*, 33(4).

Ben-Moshe, L. (2018). Dis-epistemologies of abolition. *Critical Criminology*, 26, 341–355. https://doi.org/10.1007/s10612-018-9403-1

Borstel, J., & Lerman, L. (2003). *Liz Lerman's Critical Response Process: A method for getting useful feedback on anything you make, from dance to dessert.* Dance Exchange.

Bradley, D. (2012). Good for what, good for whom? Decolonizing music education philosophies. In W. Bowman & A. L. Frega (Eds.), *The Oxford handbook of philosophy in music education* (pp. 409–434). Oxford University Press. https://doi.org/10.1093/oxfordhb/9780195394733.013.0022

Cohen, M. L. (2012). Writing between rehearsals: A tool for assessment and building camaraderie. *Music Educators Journal*, 98(3), 43–48. https://doi.org/10.1177%2F0027432111434743

Coyle, M. J., & Nagle, M. (Eds.). (2022). *Contesting carceral logic: Towards abolitionist futures.* Routledge.

Davis, A. Y. (2003). *Are prisons obsolete?* Seven Stories Press.

Glaser, J. (2014). *Suspect race: Causes and consequences of racial profiling.* Oxford University Press.

Gopalan, M., & Nelson, A. A. (2019). Understanding the racial discipline gap in schools. *AERA Open*, 5(2), 1–26. https://doi.org/10.1177%2F2332858419844613

Hendricks, K. S. (2021). Authentic connection in music education: A chiastic essay. In K. S. Hendricks & J. Boyce-Tillman (Eds.), *Authentic connection: Music, spirituality, and wellbeing* (pp. 237–253). Peter Lang.

Hendricks, K. S. (2018). *Compassionate music teaching*. Rowman & Littlefield.

Hess, J. (2020). Towards a (self-)compassionate music education: Affirmative politics, self-compassion, and anti-oppression. *Philosophy of Music Education Review*, 28(1), 47–68. https://doi.org/10.2979/philmusieducrevi.28.1.04

Kaba, M. (2021). *We do this 'til we free us: Abolitionist organizing and transforming justice*. Haymarket Books.

Kajs, L. T. (2006). Reforming the discipline management process in schools: An alternative approach to zero tolerance. *Education Research Quarterly*, 29(4), 16–28.

Lama, D. (2002). *How to practice: The way to a meaningful life*. Pocket Books.

Love, B. L. (2019). *We want to do more than survive: Abolitionist teaching and the pursuit of educational freedom*. Beacon Press.

Neff, K. D. (2003). Self-compassion: An alternative conceptualization of a healthy attitude toward oneself. *Self and Identity*, 2(2), 85–101. https://doi.org/10.1080/15298860309032

Neff, K. D. (2021). *Fierce self-compassion: How women can harness kindness to speak up, claim their power, and thrive*. HarperCollins Publishers.

Peterosina, A., Turpin-Petrosina, C., & Guckenburg, S. (2010). Formal system processing of juveniles: Effects on delinquency. *Campbell Systematic Reviews*, 6(1), 1–88. https://doi.org/10.4073/csr.2010.1

Rabinowitch, T., Cross, I., & Burnard, P. (2013). Long-term musical group interaction has a positive influence on empathy in children. *Psychology of Music*, 41(4), 484–498. https://doi.org/10.1177%2F0305735612440609

Rogers, F. (2015). *Practicing compassion*. Fresh Air Books.

Rogers, F. (2018). Warriors of compassion: Coordinates on the compass of compassion-based activism. In J. Baldwin (Ed.), *Taking it to the streets: Public theologies of activism and resistance* (pp. 25–42). Roman & Littlefield.

Smolkowski, K., Girvan, E. J., McIntosh, K., Nese, R., & Homer, R. H. (2016). Vulnerable decision points for disproportionate office discipline referrals: Comparisons of discipline for African American and White elementary school students. *Behavioral Disorders*, 41(4), 178–195. https://doi.org/10.17988%2Fbedi-41-04-178-195.1

Staats, C. (2014). *Implicit racial bias and school discipline disparities: Exploring the connection* [Kirwan Institute Special Report]. Retrieved December 20, 2021, from http://kirwaninstitute.osu.edu/wp-content/uploads/2014/05/ki-ib-argument-piece03.pdf

Strauss, C., Lever T. B., Gu, J., Kuyken, W., Baer, R., Jones, F., & Cavanagh, K. (2016). What is compassion and how can we measure it? A review of definitions and measures. *Clinical Psychology Review*, 47, 15–27. https://doi.org/10.1016/j.cpr.2016.05.004

Welsh, R. O., & Little, S. (2018). The school discipline dilemma: A comprehensive review of disparities and alternative approaches. *Review of Educational Research*, 88(5), 752–794. https://doi.org/10.3102%2F0034654318791582

Wilkerson, I. (2020). *Caste: The origins of our discontents*. Random House.

Zvolensky, M. J., Vujanovic, A. A., Bernstein, A., & Leyro, T. (2010). Distress tolerance: Theory, measurement, and relations to psychopathology. *Current Directions in Psychological Science*, 19(6), 406–410. https://doi.org/10.1177%2F0963721410388642

Chapter 44

Popular Music Education, Aesthetic Judgment, and Gender Relations in Hungary

Emília Barna

Care Handbook Topics

Social activism and critical consciousness

Introduction

This chapter addresses the topic of music education and sociocultural reproduction with a focus on gender relations in a Hungarian context. I focus predominantly on popular music education in formalized settings, that is, taking place in music schools. My analysis concerns the perspective of learners, that is, musicians who have gone through such processes of music socialization, and highlights the experiences of women in line with feminist empiricism (Lykke, 2010). As Bourdieu's sociology has made it widely known, formal education does not provide a straight path to social mobility or emancipation, on the contrary: the school functions as a "conservative force" (Bourdieu, 1974) reproducing existing social relations and perpetuating social inequalities along class, gender, or race and ethnicity. Bourdieu (1984) also famously highlighted the role of musical taste and judgment in the social processes of distinction and classification, bringing attention to the deep relationship between social position and musical aesthetic knowledge and practice. Of social relations, the present chapter focuses on gender in particular, and how socialization into popular music worlds through music education perpetuates, rather than facilitating the challenging of, the patriarchal order.

Looking at the experience of Hungarian musicians active and pursuing professional careers—with varying degree of popularity and economic success—in jazz, alternative rock, and pop, of engaging in formal music education, I ask, specifically, how the relationship between genre conventions and the musical education experiences of girls and women can be described.[1] How is a patriarchal order maintained, reproduced, and reinforced through these conventions? And finally, what practices of care and (female) solidarity can be identified, if any, that respond to, or even question, the patriarchal structure of music worlds? In order to answer these questions, I first propose a framework of analysis drawing on Bourdieu's cultural sociology and his theoretical approach to education, in particular the notions of *habitus* and *symbolic violence*. I draw on previous studies employing these notions with the aim of understanding power relations, and in particular gender relations, in music education and culture, as well as studies that are not explicitly based on a Bourdieusian framework, but are nevertheless compatible with his approach.

In the following section, based on my own semi-structured interviews with Hungarian female musicians, I shed light on the ways in which symbolic violence is used in Hungarian popular music education to keep women in a subordinate position, and highlight the connection between acts of symbolic violence and locally embedded genre conventions. I also argue that even well-meaning acts of care may contribute to the reinforcing of the gender order. In the final section, I conclude with a discussion of coping strategies, partly individualistic, and partly collective and solidarity-based. I argue that it is only the latter that may offer a challenge to the male-dominated world of the Hungarian popular music profession.

GENDER AND POWER RELATIONS IN MUSIC CULTURE AND EDUCATION

The cultural sociology of Bourdieu (e.g., Bourdieu, 1984, 1993) and his theoretical approach to education and pedagogy (e.g., Bourdieu 1974; Bourdieu & Passeron 1977/ 1991) is a logical starting point from which to address the complex set of relations between social structure, power relations, education, and modes of cultural expression and engagement. According to Bourdieu, pedagogical practice can be considered as *symbolic violence* insofar as it involves the imposition of a "cultural arbitrary" (in the formal education system, typically the culture of the dominant class) which is presented

---

[1] Genre conventions are understood as locally embedded but also globally shaped practices and discourses.

as legitimate, while "concealing the power relations which are the basis of its force" (Bourdieu & Passeron 1977/1991, p. 4). This imposition takes place through the inculcation, through pedagogical practice, of a *habitus*, which is "the internalization of the principles of a cultural arbitrary capable of perpetuating itself after [pedagogic action] has ceased" (Bourdieu & Passeron 1977/1991, p. 31). Bourdieu's notions of the habitus—as "socially constituted cognitive capacity" (Bourdieu, 1986, p. 27), *cultural capital* (Bourdieu, 1986), and his theorization of the sociology of taste (Bourdieu, 1984) have generated a multitude of insightful studies of how power relations operate in cultural production (e.g., Prior, 2008; Fournet, 2010), in cultural scenes and subcultures (e.g., Thornton, 1996), or in the consumption of culture (e.g., Rimmer, 2012). Rimmer (2012) developed the concept of *musical habitus* as "a means of explaining how individuals' relationships to music and their associated embodiment of cultural capital . . . enduringly connect to factors associated with their socialization and social locations" (p. 306).

Following Bourdieu's focus on the "bodily schemas" and "operations" of the habitus, the concept of the musical habitus enables an understanding of the ways in which sonic structures or musical affordances (DeNora, 2000)—"music's material qualities"—incorporate the social, and resonate with social subjects (Rimmer, 2012, p. 308). The musical habitus also "incorporates into its understanding of conceptualization of actors' relationships with music the (associated) embodied nature of cultural capital and its expression through embodied practices" (Rimmer, 2012, p. 308). Rimmer describes the processes whereby the musical habitus is formed as both primary—referring, predominantly, to the space of the home—and secondary musical socialization, which can include multiple contexts and relations, including formal education, but also the media, friends, and so forth (pp. 308–309). Havas (2020) employs the concept of musical habitus in a Hungarian context to point to and analyse symbolic distinctions in the Hungarian jazz field. He demonstrates how social divisions—class and ethnicity in particular—find their expression in the discursive divisions (mainstream vs. free jazz) of the field, and through this, also brings attention to intragenre variability, as opposed to a unified ideology or discourse (see Green, 2003).

Bourdieu's theories have also informed critical enquiries into music education and practice from a gender perspective, including Fournet's (2010) study of female rock instrumentalists in Florida. Fournet argues that having a male body in itself functions as a dominant form of embodied cultural capital in the field of rock music, and that women lack not only this embodied capital, but also the "right" musical habitus that would ensure their seamless entry to, and participation in, the field.

Looking at the field of classical music, Bull (2019) similarly asks how "musical institutions, practices, and aesthetics [are] shaped by wider conditions of economic inequality, and in what ways might music enable and entrench such inequalities or work against them" (p. xxvi). Although her prime concern is with the reproduction of class, her nuanced analysis of practice, aesthetics, roles, and other conventions as embodied memories of social hierarchies can also be applied to the reproduction of gender relations. Bull herself demonstrates how gender is reproduced through the interaction between the male conductor and female members of the choir, arguing along similar lines as Fournet for the "pre-existing affordances of the privileged male body," which makes it easier for middle- and upper-class men to inhabit the role of the conductor than others (Bull, 2019, p. 130).

Green (1997) also argues that the school music classroom can illuminate processes of the construction of individual gendered identity through the musical experience (p. 17). She explores, through rich empirical detail, what she terms the affirmation and interruption of femininity in the music classroom—affirmation, for instance, through singing and playing classical instruments, and interruption through playing popular music—which, Green argues, contrasts the dominant "family values" and code of sexual conduct represented by the school.

Lastly, Almqvist (2016), while not explicitly relying on Bourdieu, demonstrates the ways in which strong musical values based on a "patriarchal agreement regarding musical qualities"—a favoring of "jazz licks and technical brilliance"—dominated the ensemble playing setting of upper secondary musical education in Sweden, which contributed to female students, who had been socialized into more "feminine" styles and modes of playing, taking on less visible roles, and thereby reproducing an unequal gender order (para. 26).[2]

Gender inequality and gender segregation—in terms of genre, style or professional role (singer or instrumentalist, musician or behind-the-scenes worker, and so forth)—in the music industries are also indicative of dominant conceptions about femininity and masculinity which also shape education, and how these translate into ideologies and discourses about music and musical practice. In their classic study, Frith and McRobbie (1978) explored rock as an ideological and cultural form, pointing to the relation between the rock aesthetic and male-defined sexuality, arguing that this aesthetic prevents, or significantly curtails and constrains the participation of women in the making of rock music. This dominant aesthetic is reproduced not only through recordings or performances, but also the broader, collective male culture of rock, including the predominantly male readership of rock magazines or the predominantly male pursuit of record collecting.

In the following, I look at the relationship between genre conventions and gender through the experience of women in formal popular music education in Hungary. In addition to revealing ways in which symbolic violence is aimed at female students and experienced by them in these educational settings, I also reflect on practices of care and solidarity emerging from the narratives of the musicians. I, however, argue that these instances of care and support at least partly remain within the hegemonic gender order and thus ultimately also serve to reproduce this order.

---

[2] There is no space here for a more detailed overview of the literature on gender and music education, but see also Björck, 2011; de Boise 2018; Strong & Raine, 2019.

Gender and Symbolic Violence in Popular Music Education in Hungary

The presented analysis relies on qualitative research conducted in Hungary in 2018–2020 on the work of musicians in various music genres, but predominantly pop, rock, and jazz.[3] Whereas in the study we explored various questions besides gender and education (creative labor and working conditions, the relation to digital technology, social relations within their music scene or industry environment, and further issues), the present analysis focuses on music education and women's early careers. Here I make no attempt to provide a complete analysis of the interview data; rather, I primarily draw on the experience of four women, who have all participated in formal popular music education. Formal popular music education in Hungary takes place primarily at private music schools in the form of vocational training.[4] These vocational institutions typically offer programs in jazz and rock, with some combining the two under popular music tuition. There are also musical theater schools, where singers can be trained, and more recently, producer schools have also been established, important especially for songwriter- or composer-artists.

The experiences of the female musicians of formal popular music education in the study were structured according to their roles—being singers, instrumentalists, and/or writers. The status of singing as a legitimate role for women in popular music is evident from many previous studies (including Frith & McRobbie, 1978, and the abovementioned Green, 1997). Studying jazz in France, Buscatto (2007) observed that more than 90% of jazz musicians were men, yet about 65% of singers were women. Moreover, she shows how gender-based conceptions underlie sophisticated symbolic distinctions and judgment within jazz, which in their turn help to reinforce the unequal gendered order:

> Male instrumentalists and female singers are distinguished by gender-specific conceptions of music. Singers want to produce a melodic, textual interpretation of songs, often standards composed by others; instrumentalists dream of composing their own songs and associate women singers with commercial jazz, which they denigrate. (p. 47)

Simply put, there is a paved route through popular music schooling and beyond for women as long as they are singers, although, as the experience of the interviewed

---

[3] The interviews were conducted as part of the research project "Creative labour in the Hungarian music industry," supported by the Hungarian National Research, Development and Innovation Office under Grant FK-128669. I was assisted by Ágnes Blaskó and Andrea Rajkó (Budapest University of Technology and Economics) in the data collection.

[4] State music schools primarily offer classical music education from primary to university level, and university-level jazz education is also available.

Hungarian musicians also confirm, by no means is this route easy or unquestioned. As an indication of the force pushing women toward the singer role, one of the interviewed artists narrated how she had been pressured into leaving playing an instrument behind by her instructors on entering a popular music vocational school: "That was when I gave up playing the guitar, because the job of a female singer is to sing, she shouldn't strive for more, she shouldn't try and learn other things" (female singer-songwriter, 31).[5] The possibility to pursue a degree as an instrumentalist is of course also open to women; however, according to the interviewed artists, studying an instrument is made even more difficult than a singing degree.

Female singers experienced, during their formal education, various forms of disadvantage, discrimination, and symbolic violence aimed at highlighting their specific position as women, as opposed to addressing them as young music enthusiasts who are there to learn. These contribute ultimately to securing their subordinate position in the gender order, and thus the reproduction of patriarchal gender relations. The forms of symbolic violence included frequent references by male teachers to female musicians' looks—clothes, makeup, typically evaluative remarks regarding whether they looked good or not—in class, before or after an exam situation, or in between classes. At times even including unwanted touching, such actions positioned female students as objects of the male gaze: "There were remarks such as, 'wow, you're looking really good,' when I happened to have put makeup on, 'because at other times, you don't look remarkable at all'" (female singer-songwriter, 31). Although Almqvist's (2016) above-mentioned account demonstrates how gendered musical roles are reproduced by students in an informal music ensemble learning setting that lacks active control and interference by teachers, in this case, the mentioned remarks and actions constitute active controlling intervention on the part of teachers in order to highlight female's students' position as women and maintain male dominance.

On occasions, such remarks were directly linked to the questioning of competence and the degrading of female musicians: "There was a pianist girl who left her exam crying because they told her it was really crap, 'you're lucky because you are pretty, so you get a four [B]'" (female jazz singer, 24). The remarks were also aimed at the regulation of the appearance of the women to conform to feminine standards from a heteronormative patriarchal perspective, punishing those that deviate from this norm. The following quote, which details a former students' experience that involves not only controlling male instructors, but also the supportive intervention of a female one, is simultaneously a story of controlling behavior and an instance of care in the school environment. It also indicates, however, that the intervening female instructor is also in a dominated position within the school—from the musicians' narration, she appears terrified on behalf of her student, fearing the reactions of her male colleagues—and her suggested solution completely leaves the power relations unchallenged:

---

[5] The interviews were conducted in Hungarian and are quoted in my own English translations. I have used pseudonyms for the interview participants where necessary, otherwise they and the institutions in question are anonymized.

> [Before my exam] we rehearsed my song one more time and suddenly [my singing teacher] came running up to the room, tearing her sandals from her own feet, saying, "Vera, put these shoes on immediately!" I asked her why. [She says] because the entire faculty [mentions names of male instructors] is talking about how pretty I am but I need high heels, because I was wearing a pair of boots. And I was just looking at her like this is a joke, I'm not going to put on those sandals, I'm really happy in my boots. (female jazz singer, 24)

In this case, it took active defiance on the part of the student to resist the symbolic violence committed on her, in which the female teacher was unwillingly complicit. The exhibited concern on the part of the teacher may, in a certain sense, be interpreted as an act of care—she was meaning to protect the student from the criticism that indeed came after her performance ("and then I of course got [these remarks] in private [...] 'it would have been good to wear heels with the mini skirt'" [female jazz singer, 24]). At the same time, being in a subordinate position herself, the teacher merely acted as a mediator of the symbolic violence, as opposed to forming a bond of resistance with the student. Such a bond would have necessitated a relation of "caring with" as opposed to "caring for," which, instead of solidarity, is rather based on "pity" or "helping" (Hendricks, 2018). In other words, it would have meant shifting the inferior–superior teacher–student relationship toward a relationship of equals, in order to promote authentic connections and mutually reinforcing relationships (Hendricks, 2021, this volume).

The asserting of power through personal charisma on the part of male instructors, which Bull (2019, pp. 112–131) also observes in the relation between conductors and choir, became evident in the account of female musicians. In addition to their position as men in a patriarchal system along with the inherent "superiority–inferiority" relationship of teaching (Hendricks, 2018), the power of leading male instructors also stemmed from their status and prestige as jazz and rock "legends" in the Hungarian popular music field: their decades-long careers and possession of multiple awards—institutionalized cultural capital—in some cases combined with symbolic power arising from their association with powerful political actors. Hendricks (2018) argues for the harmfulness of the "teacher as hero" narrative, and indeed such positions empowered these male teachers to degrade students, especially female ones. Three out of the four interview subjects that had participated in formal popular music education mentioned a general experience of losing their self-confidence during the years of their education and having to rebuild themselves—their musician identities—after the school, having endured, in some cases, traumatic experiences and psychosomatic illness ("I had never been ill that many times before attending the school.... It wasn't even inflamed vocal cords, some other throat problem, which prevented me from singing—I made it impossible for myself" [female singer-songwriter, 31]).

They also told me that many students leave before finishing, some giving up the idea of pursuing a musical career altogether: "There are so many people, not only girls, whose lives change so much. They go there with so much enthusiasm, they want to become musicians, and then they are completely disappointed, not only in doing this, but music itself" (female jazz singer, 24). In the words of another artist: "Then I was accepted at [a popular music school] for a singing degree, where I managed to come to hate music. . . . I practically stopped even listening to music, everything stopped" (female singer-songwriter, 31). Or: "At [music school], my self-confidence really deteriorated. . . . The phase of learning is a very sensitive period . . . and the exams, the constant evaluating and judging . . . that is not constructive in nature" (female singer-songwriter, 33).

It is important to understand how the mentioned acts of symbolic violence are connected to music genre discourses and ideologies—how, in other words, power is enacted through the articulation of aesthetic judgment and the evaluation of performance along adherence to genre conventions. The (undeclared) rock-centeredness of instructors in leading positions in one of the schools illustrates this process. One of the interviewed singers, whose declared familiar music world, chosen for herself during her secondary school years, was jazz, told me about how she had been repeatedly humiliated in the school for her taste and denied the option of playing songs of her own choice during band practice or exams. She felt she was forced to perform rock classics corresponding to the taste world of her instructors: "I, for instance, always wanted to sing jazz during band classes, and I was always told, no way, we will play Led Zeppelin now, and [jazz] doesn't fit the curriculum" (female jazz singer, 24).

The seriousness of the way in which the conforming, or not, to a rock aesthetic and taste world, became intertwined in the school setting with the young musician's self-confidence, talent, and value, is indicated by her later experiences of being triggered by hearing classic rock: "There were times when I heard a Led Zeppelin song and broke down in tears. I just felt I didn't want to hear this. Because it triggers feelings and memories that I just don't want" (female jazz singer, 24). Another singer recalled a similar experience when talking about her own, and one of her fellow singer's, preference for French chanson: "There is a particular set of values [characterizing] the school, in terms of genre as well. The fact that I was singing in French, and Gabi too, that was something totally disparaged. They were, like, what *is* this?!" (female singer-songwriter, 33).

The above examples indicate that in institutions of popular music education, the disciplining of female singers through taste and style took place simultaneously with gestures highlighting their position as women (e.g., remarks on their looks)— *situating* them as women, as Almqvist (2016) puts it based on de Beauvoir's (1953) theory—and the dominance of a hegemonic masculine perspective. The masculine aesthetic and ethos of rock in particular, not only in a general sense as a global music genre (Frith & McRobbie, 1978), but also its particular hegemonic status in Hungarian popular music culture[6] ensured that it served as a natural expression of the dominance of male instructors. The hostility expressed toward (mainstream) jazz or French chanson, which may be perceived as more legitimate routes for female singers—in Green's terms, styles that enable the affirmation of femininity—can be interpreted as violent assertion of "the place" of women who entered the dominantly masculine

---

[6] See, for example, Szemere (2001) for the [post]socialist legacy of rock in Hungary.

space of the "rock school": They are allowed to be there on the premises that they "do as the boys do" and express themselves through a masculine musical language—adhere to, in Almqvist's (2016) words, the "patriarchal agreement regarding musical qualities" (para. 26). When they try, however, they often fail in the eyes of their instructors, which leads to further derision and a self-fulfilling prophecy—that they never belonged here anyway.

Strategies of Care and (Female) Solidarity

I want to conclude with a reflection on the strategies of care and solidarity employed by female—but also male—musicians to counteract the symbolic violence and exclusion detailed above, and challenge the reproduction of hierarchical gender relations through music genre conventions, aesthetics, and practice. On the one hand, strategies of taking control are to a significant extent individual ones, which do not, ultimately, question the social order. The interviewed musicians, according to their own narratives, built up resilience and in retrospect, often—although not in all cases—spoke of their negative experiences in schools as a kind of *rite de passage*, something they had to go through to build up the strength required for pursuing a career in music. After finishing school, strategies of continuing their education in a more effective and fulfilling manner included finding private tutors—which, of course, requires material resources—or, more typically, continuing their music socialization through musical collaborations, with writing partners and in bands. Female musicians would typically persist in the industry by asserting their professional identity through such rigorous, hard work that their position becomes unquestionable—a strategy of outperforming male colleagues in order to secure their position. A different strategy is represented by so-called bedroom musicians, who make music in the space of their own homes to circumvent masculine spaces of the music industries (detailed in Barna, 2017; see also Wolfe, 2019). One of the interviewed musicians "returned" to the bedroom after finishing the music school and took time—three years—to perfect her songwriting in a safe environment before debuting as a solo artist.

Nevertheless, collective strategies based on female solidarity and care were also present. A reflection on gender relations within the scene, and in society more generally, was more characteristic of the underground sphere, where some female musicians actively worked on organizing events and establishing networks based on feminist principles. These included events with all-female line-ups, facilitating female collaboration and collective female spaces of education (e.g., songwriting workshops), such as Ladyfest Budapest; the Sisters Voice Music collective, who organize female-only open-mic nights, jam sessions and talks; the Fuck the Roles feminist collective, focusing on underground electronic music; and most recently, from 2021, the *Lányok a popszakmában* ("Girls in the pop business") group, connecting female music industry workers. Such initiatives, however, with the exception of the last example, tended to remain in the relatively autonomous sphere of the underground. In contrast, the majority of professional artists, who operate in a harshly competitive environment, tended to cope predominantly on their own.

A notable instance was narrated by one of the female artists who embarked on a solo career a few years after finishing a popular music school. She contrasted her experience in the school, where her self-confidence had severely declined, she had (as mentioned above) suffered from psychosomatic symptoms and felt unable to fully develop her multifaceted musical skills, to her membership in a community choir:

> This is a really big community, and the important thing is that everyone is really positive [based on a philosophy of] "it doesn't matter if you can't sing, you still can!"—and there is a really great level of acceptance as well as creativity. Somehow the entire climate is very positive and very humane and everyone [contributes to] an atmosphere of "let's stick together and help each other"—it was a supportive environment which helped me a lot. (female singer-songwriter, 31)

The community was not only supportive in a spiritual and moral sense, but also enabled the artist to organize her debut show, and, ultimately, to launch her career, in a material sense, through crowdfunding the costs. In an industry that is greatly unequal, individualistic and competitive, such collective effort—an economic as well as moral take on solidarity—makes a crucial difference. In Hungarian and other Eastern European societies, as Barna et al. (2019) argue based on Szelényi (2011), the middle classes are rarely capable of securing their own social position through merely market-oriented activities. This leads to an increase in value of cultural embeddedness and cultural capital becoming a primary resource in career building. In the struggle for resources, the assertion of cultural capital through the instances of symbolic violence shown above serves the preservation of the symbolic order. Communities and economies built around care and solidarity may well mean the only possible systemic challenge to this order.

REFERENCES

Almqvist, C. F. (2016). Becoming a guitar playing woman—the risk of unequal gender role conservation in non-formal ensemble music education. In R. Wright, B. A. Younker, & C. Beynon (Eds.), *21st century music education: Informal learning and non-formal teaching approaches in school and community contexts* [Ebook]. Canadian Music Educators' Association.

Barna, E. (2017). A translocal music room of one's own: Female musicians within the Budapest lo-fi music scene. In E. Barna & T. Tofalvy (Eds.), *Made in Hungary* (pp. 59–70). Routledge.

Barna, E., Madár, M., Nagy, K., & Szarvas, M. (2019). Dinamikus hatalom: Kulturális termelés és politika Magyarországon 2010 után [Dynamic power: Cultural production and policy in Hungary after 2010]. *Fordulat, 26*, 225–251.

De Beauvoir, S. (1953). *The second sex* (H. M. Parshley, Trans.). Alfred A. Knopf. (Original work published in 1949)

Björck, C. (2011). *Claiming space: Discourses on gender, popular music, and social change*. University of Gothenburg.

De Boise, S. (2018). Gender inequalities and higher music education: Comparing the UK and Sweden. *British Journal of Music Education*, 35(1), 23–41.

Bourdieu, P. (1974). The school as a conservative force: Scholastic and cultural inequalities (J. C. Whitehouse, Trans.). In J. Eggleston (Ed.), *Contemporary research in the sociology of education* (pp. 32–46). Routledge.

Bourdieu, P. (1984). *Distinction: A social critique of the judgement of taste*. Routledge and Kegan Paul.

Bourdieu, P. (1986). The forms of capital. In J. Richardson (Ed.), *Handbook of theory and research for the sociology of education* (pp. 241–258). Greenwood.

Bourdieu, P. (1993). *The field of cultural production*. Columbia University Press.

Bourdieu, P., & Passeron, J.-C. (1977/1991). *Reproduction in education, society and culture* (R. Nice, Trans.). Sage. (Original work published 1970)

Bull, A. (2019). *Class, control, and classical music*. Oxford University Press.

Buscatto, M. (2007). Contributions of ethnography to gendered sociology: The French jazz world. *Qualitative Sociology Review*, 3(3), 46–58. https://doi.org/10.18778/1733-8077.3.3.04

DeNora, T. (2000). *Music in everyday life*. Cambridge University Press.

Finnegan, R. (1989). *The hidden musicians: Music-making in an English town*. Cambridge University Press.

Fournet, A. K. (2010). Women rockers and the strategies of a minority position. *Music and Arts in Action*, 3(1), 20–47.

Frith, S., & McRobbie, A. (1978). Rock and sexuality. *Screen Education*, 29, 3–19.

Green, L. (1997). *Music, gender, education*. Cambridge University Press.

Green, L. (2003). Why "ideology" is still relevant for critical thinking in music education. *Action, Criticism, and Theory for Music Education*, 2(2), 2–20. http://act.maydaygroup.org/articles/Green2_2.pdf

Havas, Á. (2020). The logic of distinctions in the Hungarian jazz field: A case study. *Popular Music*, 39(3–4), 619–635. https://doi.org/10.1017/S0261143020000537

Hendricks, K. S. (2018). *Compassionate music teaching*. Rowman & Littlefield.

Hendricks, K. S. (2021). Authentic connection in music education. In K. S. Hendricks & J. Boyce-Tillman (Eds.), *Authentic connection: Music, spirituality, and wellbeing* (pp. 237–253). Peter Lang.

Lykke, N. (2010). *Feminist studies: A guide to intersectional theory, methodology and writing*. Routledge.

Prior, N. (2008). Putting a glitch in the field: Bourdieu, actor network theory and contemporary music. *Cultural Sociology*, 2(3), 301–319.

Rimmer, M. (2012). Beyond omnivores and univores: The promise of a concept of musical habitus. *Cultural Sociology*, 6(3), 299–318. https://doi.org/10.1177%2F1749975511401278

Strong, C., & Raine, S. (2019). *Towards gender equality in the music industry: Education, practice and strategies for change*. Bloomsbury.

Scharff, C. (2017). *Gender, subjectivity, and cultural work: The classical music profession*. Routledge.

Szelényi, I. (2011). The rise and the fall of the second Bildungsbürgertum. In P. H. Reill & B. A. Szelényi (Eds.), *Cores, peripheries and globalization* (pp. 165–182). CEU Press.

Szemere, A. (2001). *Up from the underground: The culture of rock music in postsocialist Hungary*. Pennsylvania State University Press.

Thornton, S. (1996). *Club cultures: Music, media, and subcultural capital*. Wesleyan University Press.

Wolfe, P. (2019). *Women in the studio: Creativity, control and gender in popular music production*. Routledge.

CHAPTER 45

CARING ABOUT DEAF MUSIC IN CULTURALLY RESPONSIVE MUSIC EDUCATION

WARREN N. CHURCHILL AND CLARE HALL

Care Handbook Topics

Identity expressions
Social activism and critical consciousness

Caring for Deaf Students in Music?

It is the late 1980s and I (Warren) am a preservice teacher completing a teaching internship in upstate New York. At this public school I'm working with a quiet second grade student with a hearing impairment in a general music setting. Each week, Amari (a pseudonym) and their classmates excitedly scrambled to their assigned seats in the music room. Entering right behind, Amari's sign language interpreter greets my supervising teacher and gives them a microphone and FM transmitter set to wear during the lesson. Amari wears a corresponding pendant-like receiver that is connected to their hearing aids. The interpreter then sits in a chair directly facing Amari so they can see the interpreter signing clearly.

I understand that these accommodations are intended to facilitate Amari's access to spoken language, which are stipulated as part of their Individualized Education Program (IEP). I imagine that Amari's hearing aids give them some access to what is happening in our predominantly sound-based learning environment. However, my care for Amari's music education does not extend to informing myself to what extent musical sounds are made perceptual by the accommodations that allow access to spoken language. Therefore, I do not make any kind of music-specific accommodations for Amari. Nor was this modeled for me. Nonetheless, I suspect that my sponsor teacher has been grappling with these issues, albeit not so obviously. I suspect this because during the weeks leading up to the annual December concert, the entire second grade performed "I'd Like to Teach the World to Sing" using sign language while-singing.

Although I appreciate the inclusive efforts, what these students learned about the Deaf[1] community was likely minimal, given the limited rehearsal time and the rote approach to teaching the signed lyrics. Furthermore, I believe that this was a one-time collaboration to see whether a sign language–enhanced choral performance could be successfully undertaken. Given these factors, I doubt whether students had the opportunity to meaningfully engage with sign language or to learn about the signing community in culturally responsive ways. As such, I wonder to what extent my supervising teacher and I had really enacted care for the Deaf community?

Teaching situations such as the one shared above present complex issues of care. The idea of *teaching the world to sing* mentioned in the title of the song compels us to consider how care manifests in different ways in educational settings, especially through music teaching. For instance, thinking back to Amari's experience in the music classroom, the educational accommodations provided addressed both sensory and communicative needs..Providing these accommodations might be described as caring, given the overarching goal of facilitating Amari's access to the mainstream curriculum. However, it is worth noting how this approach aligns with medical model thinking in two key ways (Goodley, 2017). First, the medical view assumes that disability resides within the individual. In line with this, special education is premised on identifying students who have some kind of condition that impedes their academic and/or social development. Second, the usual response to disability is to cure or minimize it as much as possible. As such, caring educational professionals and other stakeholders usually seek out effective methods to alleviate recognized deficits. However, what is often overlooked in this is the power differential, which might lead educators to discount the disabled person's experience toward determining the best accommodative route.

To be clear, we are not claiming that students who need educational support should be denied it. Nor are medicalized approaches without merit in certain circumstances. Rather, we write this chapter to expand thinking on what care might look like in music education for students who are deaf or hard of hearing. In terms of resources for music educators, Hammel and Hourigan (2017) provide links to several deaf-related sites, including a few that take a sociolinguistic approach to deafness.[2] We find these

---

[1] James Woodward (1975) originated the distinction between big "D" Deaf, which refers to people who use sign language as their primary language, as opposed to small "d" deaf, which refers to the condition of being unable to hear, or those who have lost their hearing but are not affiliated with the signing community.

[2] These include the web pages for the National Association of the Deaf (NAD) and Mark Drolsbaugh's "Deaf Culture Online."

recommended resources encouraging, because deficit approaches to education tend to privilege certain kinds of normative musical practices and musical learners. Teaching the world to sing is often premised on the idea that music is primarily an aural activity, and deafness seemingly troubles this pedagogical foundation of music education. Recognizing this tension, we are led to imagine other possibilities for the musical performance described in the vignette above.

Before we can discuss these possibilities, we must first consider how music educators might come to care about such a student's needs and personal worldview. For instance, in the vignette above, the supervising teacher seemingly cared *about* Amari giving thought to American Sign Language (ASL) and took adequate care *of* Amari by taking action to incorporate ASL into the December performance. This suggests that Amari was also cared *for* in the way their views and interests are addressed, although there are limitations to the depth of dialogue between the one-caring and the cared-for. We draw distinctions between these different kinds of caring inspired by Noddings's (2013) observation that to care has multiple definitions characterized by different degrees of reciprocity. She points out one can demonstrate care in the sense they are "charged with the protection, welfare, or maintenance of someone or something" (p. 9), a charge common to educators. However, caring about someone can be performed in a "perfunctory or grudging" way and, therefore, may not be caring at all from the point of view of the one cared-for.

The process of caring in musical contexts is mediated through our various subjectivities that underpin our constructions of ability. For instance, we tend to associate certain sound-related abilities as essential attributes of *musicians*. And for this reason, music educators might regard "signed-singing" (Churchill & Hall, 2022) as a communicative compensation rather than a legitimate form of vocality and artistic expression in its own right (Holmes, 2016). Leigh (2001) observes that "(c)urriculum decisions, such as decisions about objectives, will be influenced by the particular social construction of deafness that is adopted" (p. 156). In other words, as educators, our assumptions about our students influence how we enact care in the music classroom. Leigh further notes that the hearing world tends to view deafness as "a condition to be either avoided or ameliorated by either (or some combination of) medical or educational/therapeutic interventions" (p. 156). And more often, the mainstream does not recognize that deaf and hard of hearing people sometimes cohere as a particular social and cultural group within the community.

Reflecting back on my (Warren's) student teaching internship, I realize our responses to Amari's difference in hearing deferred to the medical framework. In effect, this student was cared for by their legally mandated hearing devices and a single interpreter in an environment designed for people with normal hearing and communication abilities. As a result, Amari could be present within this educational paradigm without the need for further curricular accommodations. In addition, there was very little in the way of deaf musician role models to guide our teaching in the 1980s, and the idea of Deaf culture was only beginning to emerge in the mainstream. Yet, in the present day, we see a proliferation of Deaf musicians achieving success in the music industry on their own terms.[3] Many of these deaf/Deaf artists use sign language and signed-singing as a creative art form that reflects the diversity of these sociolinguistic minority groups (Churchill & Hall, 2022). Taking into account the present-day proliferation of Deaf music that some people are learning outside of educational institutions, we reflect on the missed opportunity to help Amari participate more fully in music.

We suggest that little has changed from a formal music education point of view for deaf students to the present day. A significant obstacle in this is that music educators are largely unaware of Deaf communities and how these people engage with music. Dominant discourses tend to focus on deafness as a medical problem. Yet, there can be limitations with such institutionalized forms of care that are enmeshed with medicalized responses to hearing impairment.[4] As such, the idea of "teaching the world to sing" highlights the need to promote a pedagogical praxis that is culturally responsive to the diversity of Deaf music and culture. To advance this aim we ask, "How might we be more critically reflexive about an ethics of care between music educators and Deaf people in educational contexts?"

THEORETICAL ASSEMBLAGE

The majority of music educators only consider Deaf music when presented with the "problem" of teaching a hearing-impaired student, and then the challenge of learning how best to respond to the student's needs ensues. The cultural dimension of the communities in which our Deaf students inhabit is often an overlooked aspect of responding to their learning needs with the focus being on remedying audiological deficit to support normative musical practices. Stewart (2001) suggests, however, that to become ethically responsible educators for Deaf students, teachers look "instead at who it is that they are teaching this year and what it is that each of these deaf children really need from the teacher?" (p. 166). Although this standpoint may seem simplistic, the positioning of the educator as one who responds to the learner by questioning their teaching as opposed to enacting a particular unexamined philosophical belief, as Stewart suggests, is fundamental to our reflection on how hearing music educators go about the inclusion of Deaf students.

---

[3] Successful Deaf musicians include Signmark, https://en.wikipedia.org/wiki/Signmark; Sean Forbes, https://en.wikipedia.org/wiki/Sean_Forbes; and T. L. Forsberg, https://en.wikipedia.org/wiki/TL_Forsberg.

[4] Testing hearing and dispensing hearing aids is a form of medicalized care that has a well-documented history. For example, see Hui et al. (2020). Also see the documentary *Sophie's choice: Li family*, about how Mao's Last Dancer, Li Cunxin's deaf daughter makes a decision to participate in both the Deaf and hearing world and the family's negotiation of medical interventions for hearing (Clark, 2021).

This kind of questioning of positionality draws us to the philosophical vision of Noddings's (1984) feminist ethics of care in education, whereby theorizing the nature of reciprocity is at the heart of remedying inequalities in teacher–student relationships. The continued relevance of Noddings's (2013) work exists in the unceasing salience of what it means to care and to be cared for. This is despite the somewhat outmoded gender binary evoked in her definition of a "feminine" approach to caring as one primarily "rooted in receptivity, relatedness, and responsiveness" (p. 2), as opposed to the "masculine" approach that is wedded to moral principle and logic.

What might a feminist approach to caring look like in practice? Noddings (1984) explains, in relation to the one-caring that "my caring must be somehow completed in the other if the relation is to be described as caring" (p. 4). To this end,

> we are dependent on each other even in the quest for personal goodness. How good I can be is partly a function of how you—the other—receive and respond to me. Whatever virtue I exercise is completed, fulfilled, in you. The primary aim of all education must be nurturance of the ethical ideal. (Noddings, 1984, p. 6)

Noddings's emphasis on the way in which reciprocity is enacted encourages us to reflect on the ways in which we meet the deaf or hearing-impaired learning morally. For instance, when a mainstream choir engages in signed-singing the performance is usually seen as "caring" for its display of empathy and heartrending inspiration. We also suspect that the signing is assessed more for its choreographic effect rather than its communicative precision. However, when Deaf musicians include phonated singing in their performances, they risk drawing unwanted critiques of their speech and singing abilities. This reversal illustrates a disparity that must be acknowledged while considering how a caring reciprocity might be enacted between hearing and Deaf communities.

Being inclusive of Deaf music and responsive to the learning needs of Deaf students in music draws us as educational researchers toward discourses about culturally responsive pedagogies. This field of research and practice has, to date, been preoccupied with culture as synonymous with race and ethnicity because of its roots in multicultural education (Lind & McKoy, 2016). However, we call for a timely expansion of music education research to consider the specific cultural strengths and assets that Deaf students and musicians around the world possess as members of diverse sociolinguistic minority groups.

Moore and Mertens (2015) highlight the importance of the Deaf community in fostering the resilience of Deaf youth, especially for minority youth. These authors report that "Deaf people of color also foreground culturally-salient strengths" when dealing with adversity (p. 149). And because Deaf culture exists at the intersections of ethnicity, race, age, and geography, it is important not to overlook the Deaf community, to avoid double-disadvantaging students who might otherwise be rendered intersectionally invisible.[5]

---

[5] See Purdie-Vaughn and Eibach (2008) for theorizing on intersectional invisibility.

Although defining "culture" is a slippery task, Lind and McKoy (2016) observe that most cultures "share a common focus on the behaviors or custom, beliefs, and values of groups of human beings" (p. 21), following Hidalgo's (1993) description of three levels of culture. The overlapping levels are: *concrete* being the material dimensions of culture such as music, *behavioral* being the social dimensions such as language, and *symbolic* being the beliefs and value systems that underpin the other dimensions. Lane (1992/1999) similarly asserts that Deaf people comprise a linguistic minority or a cultural group centered around the use of sign language. Many members of this community share *concrete* expressions of culture such as Deaf poetry and visual arts.[6] In addition to understanding the signed language system, members of the Deaf community also understand the *behavioral* rules for communicating as a Deaf person in certain contexts. Attending to the concrete and behavioral characteristics that emerge from this community is a prerequisite for understanding the more abstract *symbolic* basis of community values and beliefs that can inform educational practice.

Hess (2021) makes the acquisition of cultural competence analogous to colonization, in a metaphorical sense, as the means to raise ethical concerns about music educators' culturally responsive teaching through multicultural music-learning. She argues, "efforts to include multiple musics in the curriculum can be seen as an effort to conquer more territory" and in this way "teachers, then, serve as cartographers as they expand classroom material to include racialized musics" (p. 13). Hess (2021) also raises the dilemma around the inclusion of some minoritized musics in the classroom, which is commonly assumed as better than none. However, inevitably simplified, partial, or unknowingly disrespectful inclusions can do more to reinforce stereotypes and reinscribe unequal power relations between dominant and subordinated cultural groups than to be culturally responsive.

Furthermore, Hess (2021) advocates for music educators to interrogate their own identities in the classroom as a step toward diminishing imbalances of power that might have colonizing effects on marginalized students and communities. Countering this potential paternalism, Hess reminds that "culturally responsive teaching centers the student and takes a strengths-based approach to pedagogy that acknowledges the strengths and assets students bring" (p. 15). Rather than promote a list of how-to best practices that lead to notions of mastery over fixed skills, acknowledging the fluid cultural dimensions of communities to which Deaf and hard of hearing students belong might inspire inclusive pedagogical practices that are more ethically aligned with Noddings's (2013) ideal of educational caring.

That is to say, pedagogical choices carry potential moral consequences in terms of who might be included or excluded from the learning community. Characterizing a feminist approach toward navigating moral dilemmas, Noddings (2013) writes, "(i)

---

[6] For an example of Deaf poetry, see Douglas Ridloff's video "Spoken Without Words: Poetry with ASL SLAM" https://www.youtube.com/watch?v=dmsqXwnqIw4. There is also the De'VIA or Deaf View/Image Art movement which approaches visual arts from a Deaf sociolinguistic perspective https://www.museumofdeaf.org/de-via.

deally, we need to talk to the participants, to see their eyes and facial expressions, to receive what they are feeling" (p. 2). This affective acknowledgment of the cared-for is a seeming prerequisite for what Hendricks (2018) identifies as compassionate music education, which is inherently connected with affirming diversity and fostering inclusion (p. 105). Educators working within this paradigm resist notions of "pity" or "helping," seeking to move beyond caring "about" or "for" students toward a more dialogical experience of caring "with" (Hendricks, 2021).

Deaf Film Camp and Caring with Community

In this section, we draw on our previously outlined theoretical assemblage and apply this to an analysis of an evocative video of a Deaf film camp performance. Given our positionality as hearing (Clare) and hard of hearing (Warren) researchers, we are not naively interpreting this video ethnographically as fully realistic representations of camp as lived by this group of people. Nonetheless, it can provide an opportunity for music educators to see what kinds of artistic and musical practices take place within the Deaf community and how care is enacted within this community. The particular video is a collaborative cover of Philip Philips's song "Home," which was produced by the participants of Camp Mark Seven Foundation in the summer of 2015. This film camp program is based in the Adirondacks in upstate New York. According to the organization's mission statement, it "offers an array of recreational, educational, leadership and spiritual programs for deaf, hard of hearing, and hearing individuals of all ages."[7]

The organization's name is inspired by the New Testament biblical story, Mark 7:34, in which Jesus restores the speech and hearing of a deaf-mute man. This miracle cure or divine act of love exemplifies the moral or religious model of disability (Goodley, 2017). However, the young participants who attend this camp are not seeking to regain their hearing and speech miraculously. Instead, we suspect that they may be engaging their voices and learning to be Deaf in the company of others like themselves, rather than contending with being deaf in the hearing world. These camp participants have likely encountered many social barriers connected to difficulty accessing sound-based language. Because of the need to communicate in sign language, the Deaf community offers an interesting counterpoint to mainstream ideas about educational inclusion. Van Cleve and Crouch (1989) offer an historical retrospective on the formation of the Deaf community in the United States during the 19th century, highlighting the importance of linguistic freedom and having the agency to create "a place of their own." Reflecting back on our opening vignette, Amari was the only deaf child in a mainstream school

---

[7] https://www.campmark7.org/about

and depended on their interpreter to connect with their hearing teachers and peers. For this reason, we have purposefully selected this Deaf camp video because of this contextual difference. One outcome of this is a collaborative video that documents the experience of Deaf camp through signed-singing. In the following section, Warren provides an overview and analysis of this video[8] based on his understanding of ASL.

The video begins with upbeat folk-style guitar playing. As I watch the opening, I have the sense of traveling in a vehicle that is going across a bridge. A white railing seems to undulate in time with the rhythm of the guitar, creating for the impression of a multisensory duet. I am reminded of the musical line art produced by a well-known Deaf artist named Christine Sun Kim,[9] who experiences moving lines as a kind of visual music. A short while later, a woman appears in the frame. The camera moves alongside her, and it becomes clear that she is walking down a footpath that leads to a lakeside beach. I recognize that this is Rosa Lee Timm, a Deaf musical performer who is known for her signed-singing covers of mainstream popular songs. When Phillips sings "hold on to me as we go," Timm looks directly at the viewer and uses the sign for TRAVEL, as if two people were embarking on a long journey together. She follows this with the sign for SOON, and finishes the idea with a sign that I understand to mean APPROACH. She repeatedly draws this last sign out, which gives me a sense of anticipation, as if waiting for a musical cadence to resolve. However, her hands do not make contact in a way that would signal a definite arrival. Given the context, I read this to mean that this Deaf camp is not a destination, but rather, a space where participants are continuously moving together toward new relationships. Deaf camp is a space of becoming with one another.

Timm's signed-singing is not a word-for-word English translation of Phillips's lyrics. Rather, she conveys these ideas in line with the visual-based grammar of ASL. For example, further into the video, when Phillips sings "I'm gonna make this place your home," Timm renders this as HERE-COME-CONNECT. Given the context of arriving at Deaf camp, I suggest that the idea of *connection* is the key to creating a sense of wellbeing or *home* for the campers.

There is perhaps a sacred quality to this space in that the Deaf campers' signed voices are momentarily liberated away from the hearing mainstream. Having this linguistic freedom makes it possible to participate in this unique cultural space that they are learning to belong to. More immediately apparent is the portrayal of caring adult members of this community, the "ones-caring," who work actively to facilitate connections and create a space for the campers, or the "cared-for." They encouragingly facilitate the activities and empathetically provide emotional support to anxious campers.

These actions at the behavioral level of culture may not appear as something so dissimilar to the everyday actions of caring music educators in wide ranging contexts, like in the opening vignette. The difference in the relationship between adult and

---

[8] https://www.youtube.com/watch?v=CxHMO4mH16k
[9] See Christine Sun Kim's line art http://christinesunkim.com/work/available-spaces-for-composers/.

child at Deaf camp is the recognition by the students of the educators' virtues as care. To echo Noddings's (1984) ethical ideal mentioned above, the caring is "completed" in the cared-for because of the shared cultural location with the ones-caring as signers within a Deaf community. Without deeper insights at the symbolic level of Deaf culture, such behaviors enacted by hearing educators may well be received by Deaf youth as patronizing or disingenuous at worst, and impotent at best.

Drawing on Hidalgo's (1993) third level of culture, it is through sign language's symbolism, like all languages, that beliefs and values are reflected, which underpins the other dimensions of culture. Subtly different messages are communicated through signed-singing. This is not because deaf sign languages lack the precision to communicate word-for-word spoken concepts. Rather, sign languages derive their communicative nuance through a unique visually based grammar system.[10] Although this music video, at the concrete text level, is actually a hybrid cultural production in the sense that it is signed-singing primarily for a hearing audience, this is not to suggest that Deaf communities do not have their own culturally inspired musical practices. This might be one explanation for the bi-cultural musical production that also supports the diverse audience needs of Deaf communities with people of varying capacities to hear. In addition, given that this is a promotional video to showcase the agency of Deaf youth, the sponsors and production team might have seen it advantageous to enlist music with inspirational messaging that would appeal to hearing audiences. However, to address Hidalgo's (1993) behavioral level of culture (language), the signed-singing that derives from Phillip's lyrics is not subservient to English semantics. Rather, the signing performers express related sentiments in a way that maintains and affirms an autonomous linguistic space.

For instance, the video narrative shifts to the newly arriving camp attendees coming off a yellow school bus. The camera focuses on a high school-aged girl who appears anxious. "Settle down, it'll all be clear," Phillips sings. A youthful female camp counselor empathetically connects with this girl, perhaps sensing that she is trying to find her equilibrium amid the exuberant adolescent energy around her. Phillips' subsequent lyrics, "The trouble, it might drag you down," are interpreted by the newly arrived camper as WORRIES BECOME SADNESS. At this point, two girls put their arms around her shoulders in a show of support. Here care is not just enacted hierarchically from adult to youth, but depending on the situation, campers have the agency to be the ones-caring as well. As I continue to watch the video, I am struck by how the empathetic camp counselor interprets Phillips' lyrics, "if you get lost, you can always be found." She uses three distinct signs: DISCONNECT, RECONNECT, and then, she offers a hopeful gesture to the FUTURE. Given the context, I understand this to mean that if you become disconnected from the community, there is always the possibility of reconnecting at some point in the future.

---

[10] For example, see Cohen (1995), *Train go sorry: Inside a deaf world*. One might assume TRAIN-GO-SORRY means that a toy train is saying the word "sorry" (p. 188). However, Cohen explains that for Deaf people, this signed phrase means to miss an opportunity or a connection.

We might also consider how the children are the ones-caring, not just of their peers, but of the adults. In this video, care for the adults is evidenced by the campers' willful participation and trust they have for the adults who motivate them to move past their fears of expressing themselves in front of fellow campers. For instance, I observe that midway through the video, a young man is summoned to the stage. Clearly apprehensive, he accepts the challenge. Phillips's lyrics support a motivating signed musical dialogue between the young man and camp co-leader Azora Telford. "If you're lost, you can always be found." Telford conveys this idea using the sign for SUPPORT. In due course, the young man and Telford appear on stage facing one-another, and there is an affecting moment where they smile at one another as seeming equals. Thereafter Telford uses the sign for CONNECT to propel him into performing for his peers in a moment of reciprocal care between adults and youth.

The caring we observe happening at this Deaf film camp is radically different from the mandated kind of educational care provided to Amari in the opening vignette. Although the care at the Deaf camp is constituted through creating a mutually accessible space, Amari did not appear to have access to such a community in school. However, in the Deaf camp video there was a child artist who was depicted as being disconnected from the group. A fellow camper seemed concerned to see him alone. On noticing his drawings, she alerted the others to his impressive work. And in this way, this community shows care for one of its own by gathering around him to celebrate what he has to offer artistically.

Conclusion

The Deaf camp video offers music educators a model of what care can look like in the Deaf community. Although there is considerable fluidity in the roles of "one caring" and "cared for," the important distinction that emerges is the idea of caring *with* community. This is something that music educators may miss because they may not be aware that there *is* a cultural dimension to Deafness to consider in the first place. Present well-intended educational discourses tend to promote a paradigm of care based on identifying and remedying perceived deficits. As such, students labeled as having special needs tend not to be viewed as resourceful agents or partners in the educational relationship. Rather, they become positioned as objects of care (Beattie, 2001).

As we (Warren and Clare) reflect back on Amari from our opening vignette, we recognize that the mandated approach of providing an interpreter privileged a concrete dimension of the Deaf community, namely, sign language. And in the educational setting, this served as a compensatory adjunct to spoken English rather than a way of creating connection with the Deaf community. In the interest of working toward a more ethical relationship with students who are Deaf and hard of hearing, we suggest it is time to move beyond the concrete fascination with signed-singing. In other words, this should not be taught to hearing singers as though it were choreography. As a language, (behavioral level) signed-singing has a richness that one cannot truly apprehend without speaking that language and sharing the culture. Written and spoken translations can help non-signers to grasp the symbolic meanings to a degree, but even symbols are a proxy for the lived experience of culture.

We come back to the question leading our inquiry, "how might we be more critically reflexive about an ethic of care between music educators and Deaf people in educational contexts?" Based on our analysis of the video we assert that a sociocultural practice of becoming Deaf is taking place. For the participants, this experience is likely viewed as a position of empowerment and flourishing. Furthermore, the relationships of care that we read from the video challenge the assumption that only the empowered can care *for* others. The potential flip side of this is that when these camp participants return to hearing world contexts, they may still be faced with barriers and regarded as disabled. However, having a community that one can reconnect with as needed is presumably hugely empowering for these campers. Music educators can promote such flourishment by caring "with" their Deaf students and the rich culture within their communities.

References

Beattie, R. G. (Ed.). (2001). *Ethics in deaf education: The first six years*. Academic Press.

Churchill, W., & Hall, C. (2022). Toward "little victories" in music education: Troubling ableism through signed-singing and d/Deaf musicking. In C. Frierson-Campbell, C. Hall, S. Powell, & G. Rosabal-Coto (Eds.), *Sociological thinking in music education: International intersections* (pp. 72–85). Oxford University Press.

Clark, M. (Producer). (2021, April 12). *Sophie's choice: Li family* [Documentary]. ABC. https://www.abc.net.au/austory/sophies-choice/13293706

Cohen, L. H. (1995). *Train go sorry: Inside a deaf world*. Vintage.

Goodley, D. (2017). *Disability studies: An interdisciplinary introduction*. Sage.

Hammel, A. M., & Hourigan, R. M. (2017). *Teaching music to students with special needs: A label-free approach*. Oxford University Press.

Hendricks, K. S. (2018). *Compassionate music teaching*. Rowman & Littlefield.

Hendricks, K. S. (2021). Authentic connection in music education. In K. S. Hendricks & J. Boyce-Tillman (Eds.), *Authentic connection: Music, spirituality, and wellbeing* (pp. 237–253). Peter Lang.

Hess, J. (2021). Cultural competence or the mapping of racialized space: Cartographies of music education. *Bulletin of the Council for Research in Music Education*, (227), 7–28. https://doi.org/10.5406/bulcouresmusedu.227.0007

Hidalgo, N. (1993). Multicultural teacher introspection. In T. Perry & J. Fraser (Eds.), *Freedom's plow: Teaching in the multicultural classroom* (pp. 99–106). Routledge.

Holmes, J. A. (2016). Singing beyond hearing. *Journal of the American Musicological Society*, 69(2), 542–548. https://doi.org/10.1525/jams.2016.69.2.525

Hui, A., Mills, M., & Tkaczyk, V. (Eds.). (2020). *Testing hearing: The making of modern aurality*. Oxford University Press.

Lane, H. (1992/1999). *The mask of benevolence: Disabling the deaf community*. Dawn Sign Press.

Leigh, G. R. (2001). Curriculum considerations. In R. G. Beattie (Ed.), *Ethics in deaf education: The first six years* (pp. 143–166). Academic Press.

Lind, V., & McKoy, C. L. (2016). *Culturally responsive teaching in music education: From understanding to application*. Routledge.

Moore, E. A., & Mertens, D. M. (2015). Deaf culture and youth resilience in diverse American communities. In L. Theron, L. Liebenberg, & M. Ungar (Eds.), *Youth resilience and culture: Commonalities and complexities* (pp. 143–155). Springer.

Noddings, N. (1984). *Caring: A feminine approach to ethics and moral education*. University of California Press.

Noddings, N. (2013). *Caring: A relational approach to ethics and moral education*. University of California Press.

Purdie-Vaughn, V., & Eibach, R. (2008). Intersectional invisibility: The distinctive advantages and disadvantages of multiple subordinate-group identities. *Sex Roles*, 59(5–6), 377–391. https://doi.org/10.1007/s11199-008-9424-4

Stewart, D. A. (2001). Ethics and the preparation of teachers of the deaf. In R. G. Beattie (Ed.), *Ethics in deaf education: The first six years* (pp. 167–184). Academic Press.

Woodward, J. (1982). *How you gonna get to heaven if you can't talk with Jesus? The educational establishment vs. the deaf community*. T. J. Publishers.

Van Cleve, J. V., & Crouch, B. A. (1989). *A place of their own: Creating the deaf community in America*. Gallaudet University Press.

CHAPTER 46

IN SEARCH OF MEANING, JOY, AND JUSTICE IN MUSIC EDUCATION

Teachers Matter

GRAÇA MOTA

CARE HANDBOOK TOPICS

Co-creating caring relationships
Identity expressions
Social activism and critical consciousness

SETTING THE STAGE—EDUCATION MATTERS

In 2020 the British film director Steve McQueen produced *Small Axe* (McQueen et al., 2020), an anthology of five films that tell the stories of the lives of the West Indian immigrants in London from the 1960s to the 1980s. The title comes from an African proverb that became popular through Bob Marley's 1973 song with the same name, which features the lyrics, "If you are the big tree, we are the small axe." It means essentially that even the mighty can be brought down through small, however sustained, action. From those five films, two called my attention as they deal with key issues I address in this first section: *Alex Wheatle* and *Education* (McQueen et al., 2020). Both set the tone on the importance of education and how it matters in people's lives.

In *Alex Wheatle*, McQueen tells the story of a Black award-winning successful writer whose childhood was deeply painful, having ended up in prison during the 1981 Brixton uprising. Simeon, an older Rastafari who is his prison cell mate strongly believes in the power of education, and talks him into confronting his past and find a path to another life:

s: Free yourself from that negativity, Alex, man. They have been lying to your people . . . You have to supplement what them teach you by teaching yourself.
a: Teaching how, then, man?
s: You have to unlearn what you have learn. And you can start by reading . . . That will turn your life around.
Education, Alex. Education is the key! Hear me now? Alex! You see, if you don't know your past . . . you won't know your future.[1] (McQueen et al., 2020)

In *Education* we witness the life of 12-year-old Kingsley as a science-fascinated boy despite having strong difficulties in reading, and being brutally yelled at by his teachers at school. The film describes how in the 1970s some London councils unofficially transferred Black children from mainstream education to schools for the so-called educationally subnormal. Due to the engaged intervention of mothers from the neighborhood, some of those children were able to leave those institutions and get back on track to have access to a proper education. Young Kingsley learned quickly to read and write and could realize his love for science and mathematics.

These two examples represent strong views on the power of education, and how it may transform lives and empower young people to find their own path, and thrive in contexts of injustice, inequality and violence. However, learning and education can operate at the level of "the reproduction of the existing socio-political order and thus on the adjustment of individuals to the existing order" or "highlight the importance of processes and practices that challenge the status quo in the name of democracy and democratization" (Biesta, 2011, p. 2). Borrowing from the ideas of Hanna Arendt in *The Human Condition*, the educational philosopher Gert Biesta (2016) reminds us of the danger of reducing all education to matters of learning, while he questions

> whether in our schools, colleges and universities children and young people still have opportunities of encountering the reality of being called into question, for practicing what it might mean to reconcile oneself to reality and, through this, sincerely try to be at home in the world, that is, in this "eccentric" state of being that is the "truly human life." (pp. 190–191)

In this chapter I begin by presenting an understanding of education in the sense of Gert Biesta and his pedagogy of interruption, enabling the appearance of uniqueness, and not allowing that our children and students may become immune to what might "affect, interrupt and trouble them" (Biesta, 2010, p. 90).

---

[1] https://scrapsfromtheloft.com/2020/12/07/small-axe-alex-wheatle-transcript/

Compassion, Humanity, Hospitality, Love, Care

Compassion, humanity, hospitality, love, and care are cherished concepts throughout this chapter. Coming from a Catholic country I grew up with a view of *compassion* as "feeling sorry for someone's suffering." However, in his homily at the Santa Marta Chapel in Vatican, Pope Francisco affirmed that *compassion* is not a feeling of pity but rather getting involved, taking risks, being on the other side of indifference (comshalom, 2019). Such a view is completely attuned with Hendricks (2018), who defines compassion as "shared enthusiasm" and writes that "those who exercise compassion have a sense of the feeling and needs of another and are motivated by that understanding to reach out and support one another" (p. 5).

Humanity is central to education, to music education (Jorgensen, 2020). In times of great inhumanity, Yob takes the wide-angle view to tell us that "there is no Other." "The way forward is by recognizing and validating the Other, the individual who is different from us, and at the same time, fully appreciating the commonalities and the wholeness of humankind as if there is no Other" (Yob, 2020, p. 26).

Hospitality follows almost seamlessly after the previous lines. Borrowing from Derrida's concept of unconditional hospitality, the one that envisions a cosmopolitan democracy where one welcomes the other with no preconditions (Bal & Vries, 2000), I embrace Lee Higgins's usage of the concept within the context of community music. This is also based on "unconditionality such as a welcome without reservation, without previous calculation, and, in the context of community music, an unlimited display of reception toward a potential music participant" (Higgins, 2012, p. 139).

Love is reclaimed by Silverman (2012) in the context of social justice, and I am attuned with the idea that "the ethic of love is essential in any concept of care and, therefore in education and social justice." As a neglected concept in academic renderings, love is here conceived as action, and "as people caring for people" (Silverman, 2012, p. 158).

I believe that all these concepts are contained in, and reversibly defined through *Care*, while accounting for our belief that care is essential in education, in music education. However, care does not exist independently of its understanding in the broad context of society. Together with Karin Hendricks, I believe that "mere focus on competence without character and caring leaves music education dry and vacuous, like an empty container without soul" (Hendricks, 2018, p. 36).

From a wide point of view, the concept goes historically hand in hand with social reproduction and has been mainly performed by women. Nancy Fraser points out: "Comprising both affective and material labor, and often performed without pay, it is indispensable to society. Without it there could be no culture, no economy, no political organization" (Fraser, 2016, p. 99). As an expression of the social-reproductive contradictions of financialized capitalism, Fraser identifies a "crisis of care." Going back to Marx and Engels' dream of imagining capitalism as entering its terminal crisis, she points out the reverse: "Over time, capitalist societies found resources for managing this contradiction [economic production *vs* social reproduction]—in part by creating 'the family' in its modern restricted form; by inventing new, intensified meanings of gender difference; and by modernizing male domination" (Fraser, 2016, p. 105).

Nothing of what has been said is indifferent to education. On the contrary, I believe that music educators ought to be part of a wide movement of social activism and critical consciousness in the sense of topic questions 1 and 3[2] from the three listed on the top of this chapter.

Music Education Matters— "Interruption, Suspension, Sustenance"

Between 2010 and 2013 Simon et al. produced a drama television series beginning three months after Hurricane Katrina hit the neighborhood of Treme in New Orleans. It features the residents, including musicians, chefs, Mardi Gras Indians,[3] and other New Orleanians, trying to reconstruct their lives, their homes, and their unique culture while facing the consequences of the 2005 hurricane and the subsequent severe flooding of the city. In one particular moment, Antoine Batiste (a community trombonist) talks to his young and promising band student Jennifer, who is failing classes, not showing around as she is taking care of her younger siblings while parents are away:

J: I'm tired.
AB: I see. I don't want you to give up on this music thing, you got potential . . .
J: My sister had potential . . . had high marks on the exams . . . never finished high school. Coacher said my brother had potential. He could get a scholarship if he persists. . . . Everyone I know got potential." (Simon et al., 2013)

Antoine Batiste cares for his student, knows how she loves to be part of the band project; however, he does not know how to react to Jenifer's response. The fact that every child has potential, musical potential that so often remains undeveloped in face of an unfair educational system that marginalizes rather than includes, ought to be a concern of us all. As a number of authors have been pointing out (Biesta, 2011; Hendricks, 2018; Jorgensen, 2020; Mota & Figueiredo, 2018; Mota & Teixeira Lopes, 2017; Wright, 2015, 2019), the capitalist society has been systematically acting in the sense

---

[2] 1. How can caring relationships be co-created in music-learning spaces, in relation to trust and/or empathy between music learners and teachers? 3. How might care in music education promote social activism and/or critical consciousness, in relation to efforts toward diversity, equity, inclusion, and anti-oppressive practice?

[3] "The Mardi Gras Indians named themselves after native Indians to pay them respect for their assistance in escaping the tyranny of slavery. It was often local Indians who accepted slaves into their society when they made a break for freedom. They have never forgotten this support." https://www.mardigrasneworleans.com/history/mardi-gras-indians/

of social reproducing a cultural *status quo* that privileges those that are already privileged. Therefore, and in connection with Antoine Batiste's helplessness in responding to Jennifer, it is significant to attend to Ruth Wright's words:

> If we agree that we are *all* musical, that we have a *need* for music, and we have a *right* to an education that develops all of our talents and abilities, then I believe that diverse, personally and culturally relevant music educations that develop the *musical* talents and abilities of *all* young people should be a human right, and that access to rewarding music learning throughout the life course should be one measure of a socially just society. (Wright, 2019, p. 218)

I would like to close this section by adopting for music education Biesta's new parameters for arts education. Trying to respond to what he defines as a double crisis in the domain, he starts by suggesting that "if education takes its existential orientation seriously, it has to center on the world—rather than on the curriculum or the child—because it is only there, in the world, with others, that we can actually live our lives" (Biesta, 2019, p. 10). He makes a strong argument for education as existential and world-centered, highlighting three of its specific components: interruption, suspension, and sustenance. I will come back to his proposal in the next section on music teacher education; however, the following words set the tone for what Biesta (2019) calls a genuine "home" for world-centered education:

> Art, after all, *interrupts*, not in order to destroy but in order to pull us towards the world, to bring us into dialogue with what and who we are not. Art slows down [*suspends*]; art provides the time and many forms in which we can meet our desires, work through them, invent ways of being in and with the world. And art can provide *sustenance*, can provide support and nourishment for staying in the middle ground. Art, in this sense, is not just the support for world-centered education, art is world-centered education. (p. 16, emphasis added)

Music Teacher Education—Creating the Space for Democratic Meaning Making

That teachers are crucial in the process of change in music education has been recurrently recognized and object of many and sometimes controversial discussions. These also entail the acknowledgment that music in the university needs to take new pathways if we want to be able, among other significant issues, to continue justifying the presence of music in the school curriculum and respond to the big challenges of the world (Christopherson, 2021; Madrid, 2017; Philipott & Spruce, 2012; Robin, 2017).

It was in the light of the aforementioned recognition that the *Manifesto for Progressive Change in the Undergraduate Preparation of Music Majors* was launched (Campbell et al., 2014). Although the *manifesto*'s content might appear as predominantly applicable to the context of the United States, its breath and scope are completely attuned with the

European context of music in higher education. In particular in acknowledging that "the academy has remained isolated, resistant to change, and too frequently regressive rather than progressive in its approach to undergraduate education" (Campbell et al., 2014, p. 2).

While I resonate with the three recommended pillars in the rethinking of the curriculum for music majors—creativity, diversity and integration—(and even more in the following elaboration of Ed Sarath by "placing creativity at the center of the change conversation" (Sarath, 2018, p. 3), I go back to Gert Biesta and his systematic questioning of both the child-centered and the curriculum-centered approach (see previous section). His encompassing argument includes the "What if?" question, and how democracy may enter the context of arts education if great significance is placed in the expression of young people's own voice: "What if the voice that is expressed is racist? What if the creativity that emerges is destructive? What if the identity that is revealed is entirely ego-centric?" (Biesta, 2019, p. 12). From his point of view we face here an impossibility to justify at all costs expressiveness in arts education, but rather to acknowledge that the educational task has to go beyond letting anything to emerge except "to constantly ask the question whether and in what ways what emerges is going to help children and young people in leading their lives well in the world, or whether what emerges is going to hinder" (Biesta, 2019, p. 12). Arts education not for its own sake, but to contribute for an understanding of the multiple ways in which we can be in the world through an ongoing existential dialogue.

Against the backdrop of these ideas I will briefly discuss a possible framework for music teacher education based on a curriculum rationale that enables (a) the construction of objects of experience beyond mere learning strategies and outcomes, and (b) the approach to existential meaning through moral responsibility.

The Project Based Curriculum—Constructing Objects of Experience

In 2005–2006 my institution started a revision of its undergraduate curriculum in music education in the context of the creation of a common European educational system. This process involved the whole community of teachers and students in fruitful and highly participated discussions, and I was particularly interested in moving away from an atomistic view of the curriculum as a collage of multiple subject areas "towards allowing students to find greater coherence in the domain of multiple meanings made possible in the construction of an object of experience" (Mota, 2014, p. 222).

As one of the results of the whole process,[4] our colleagues from the visual arts department collaborated in devising an integrated arts project to be implemented in the second semester of the first (Project I) and second years (Project II) of our undergraduate curricula in music education (ME) and visual arts (VA). Later these projects

[4] Unfortunately, traditional courses in music history sequence and music theory sequence prevailed over another, more flexible way of curriculum organization.

incorporated not only the specific art domains of music and visual arts but also other subjects of the students' general curriculum: literature and drama. Beyond that, we acknowledged the need to include, in the first semester of the first year, a visual arts workshop for the ME students and a music workshop for the VA students.

An agreed-on format for the whole process (Projects I and II) was established. From commencement of the second semester, all teachers (music, visual arts, literature, and drama) met once a week for two hours with all students (approximately 20 each from ME and VA) for about 10 weeks. The first two sessions were usually used for the identification of the concept, theme, author, in a process during which teachers suggested a few proposals that were discussed among all of the involved actors. In the next one or two sessions, the literature teacher took over, to set the whole context of the chosen theme, discuss the script and/or scripts, and decide the groups of students that would be working together on this task. From this point onward, the time management was decided from session to session, according to the tasks of the groups concerning the scenarios, costumes, mise-en-scène, music, and the overall production. In the 11th week, all classes were canceled to enable the whole schedule to be organized around rehearsals and intensive work toward a final presentation. All teachers involved in the project were present in the different spaces where action took place, ideas were interchanged, modified, redefined.

In Project I, the final presentation took the form of several small performances and happenings in different spaces in and outside of the college. Project II differed significantly in that it lead to a staged performance (Mota, 2014).

Although this is not the space to elaborate on the results of the almost 15 years of implementation of the model,[5] I still believe that moving away from the predominant subject matters based curriculum toward a project-based one is the closest I have come to Biesta's notion of "being at home in the world," and establishing new parameters for music teacher education. Further, it was in the course of constructing together such objects of experience that concepts of democracy, cultural ethnocentrism, genderism, social justice, were suddenly on the table as something that could not be overlooked.

The Project-Based Curriculum—Addressing Moral Responsibility and Care

> *The music class is about to start. The music teacher welcomes 24 children from a fifth-grade classroom, 10–11 years old, 13 girls and 11 boys: eight from Portugal, four from Angola, three from Cabo Verde, three from Pakistan, three from the Roma community, two from Morocco, and one from Romania. The teacher announces: "Today we will learn an African song."*

---

[5] I have elsewhere reflected on these challenging times and its academic consequences (Mota, 2014).

Although this is a fictitious situation, it is a good example of what classrooms look like today in many schools in European countries. By presenting what the teacher defines as an African song, it may trigger a sort of perplexity among her students especially among those from the west sub-Saharan part of Africa, and the two from Morocco, the northern part of the African continent. Culturally, they hardly share music that may be simply classified as "African."

Music teacher education should encompass and discuss how to create spaces for dialogue that courageously face difficult and burning issues that impact on how music is delivered in schools and society. In view of a music classroom like the one above, music teachers must be prepared to promote among their students a strong feeling of hospitality, care, and joy for their diverse musics, and cultural practices (Hendricks, 2018). This has also a strong social and political implication. Bearing in mind today's massive migration tragedies, there is the strong need to counter the idea, primarily within the school environment, that "'The other' is no longer a brother or sister to be loved, but simply someone who disturbs my life and my comfort" (Vatican, 2013).

In the same line of thought, Zygmunt Bauman in one of his very last books strongly criticizes the policy of "securitization" and reminds that

> once they have been cast in public opinion in the category of would-be-terrorists, migrants find themselves beyond the realm of, and off limits to, moral responsibility—and, above all, outside the space of compassion and of the impulse of care. (Bauman, 2016, p. 35)

Though music can serve very dark purposes it can also "evoke solidarity, inclusion, peace, hope, love, courage, and joy. The very ambiguity requires musician-teachers to deliberately weigh them, choose specific repertoire, and balance the multiplicity of ends that music serves" (Jorgensen, 2020, p. 8).

I return to Gert Biesta (2012), who states that teacher education is primarily about the *formation of the person* and placing "the ability for educational judgements at the very centre of the 'art' of teaching" (p. 18). Although his whole argument on this matter is far too elaborated to be fully displayed in the context of this chapter, I argue that my proposal of a project-based curriculum represents the possibility of putting forward the kind of discussions and controversies that may strengthen students cultural, social and political beliefs. And by so doing to assume moral responsibility and care about the most candent issues they will face in the profession, also in the context of school music, and in the sense of the second topic question listed at the top of this chapter.[6]

---

[6] 2. How might music educators support students' identity expressions with care, in relation to students of various races/ethnicities, cultures, genders, sexual orientations, religions, economic backgrounds, ages, and beyond standard school settings?

The Role of Research—"Embracing a Fundamental Human Intrigue with Music"

In a keynote on the issue of relevance as a context for research in music education, David Myers characterized it as "embracing a fundamental intrigue with music" (Myers, 2008, p. 1). He went on by urging the music education community to have the courage to ask "the difficult questions about music education's real-world relevance" (p. 3).

In the last part of this chapter I adopt Myers' (2008, p. 9) four challenges as part of a desirable research agenda to be included in the curriculum for music teacher education, and toward the search for relevance while embracing "human intrigue with music":

- Seeking versus finding
- Understanding versus proving
- Dynamic versus static
- Status quo versus new horizons

Later, Myers (2018) elaborated: "Music education research, like music itself, must have an artistic bent. Researchers must adopt attitudes of openness, flexibility, and improvisatory adjustments as data unfold and questions arise, particularly during the course of studies" (pp. 113–114). In the same line of thought, the fulfillment of the above suggested agenda calls for the adoption of a pluralistic research, where the place of methodological choice should not be neglected. Having said that, I will briefly outline three methodological approaches that I propose should be included in a research course for future music teachers.

Narrative Inquiry

Narrative inquiry approaches the study of human lives as a way of honoring lived experience and as a source of important knowledge and comprehension. It is about people's experience, but it calls for an understanding of the "social, cultural, familial, linguistic, and institutional narratives that shape, and are shaped by, the individual" (Clandinin, 2013, p. 33).

Sociological Portraits

Complementary to narrative inquiry, sociological portraits is a methodology that allow us to "pull out" the different strings that produce individuals socially. It unveils the origins and development of any project's participant dispositions, as well as the plural forms in which those dispositions intersect with each other. This is a means to construct the biographies of social actors without conceptualizing them as mere fractioned identities unaffected by any sort of social structuring (Lahire, 2002, 2003, 2010). In particular, it strives to give space to the lived experiences, ideas, opinions, and trajectories of those who are the targets of music projects aiming to promote social action through music.

Participatory Action Research

Participatory Action Research, as conceived by Orlando Fals Borda (2013), redefines "action-research and participatory learning as a base of another worldview, as necessary experiences to achieve progress and democracy" (p. 162). It also constitutes a philosophy of life, proposing immersion in communities mostly living in severe political situations.

Concluding Thoughts

In this chapter I have started by taking inspiration from episodes from two TV series in order to attempt to situate access to education, and music education in the broad picture of inequalities and social justice. Concepts of compassion, humanity, hospitality, love, and care formed the backdrop of my assertion that it is not possible to claim for democracy and justice without assuming a critical and engaged position within the profession. I hope to have made clear my strong resonation with Karin Hendricks's (2018) work on these matters.

I proposed an organization of the curriculum for music teacher education that privileges the collective construction of objects of experience while addressing moral responsibility and care. I believe that this is a possible way to construct meaning, joy, and artistic/musical knowledge through an utmost democratic and world-centered arts education process (Biesta, 2019).

Finally, I addressed research as central to music teacher education, while outlining three methodologies that draw on lived experience in the recognition that ideas are often generated or take root there. Adopting David Myers's research agenda, critical exchange is encouraged through a significant space for thought.

I conclude by reminding that it cannot be overlooked that the recent educational situation created by the COVID-19 pandemic uncovered consequences that are catastrophic for children and young people from underserved families, as opposed to those that have access to cultural and artistic means capable of having them thrive while away from the school environment. Together with Ruth Wright (2015), I believe that if we keep the hope that music education may have even a small role to play in the construction of a more just and democratic society, there must be a space for thought that encourages social and political engagement toward bringing about change in view of such tremendous educational inequalities.

References

Bal, M., & de Vries, H. (Eds.). (2000). *Of hospitality: Anne Dufourmantelle invites Jacques Derrida to respond* (R. Bowlby, Trans.). Stanford University Press. (Original published 1997)

Bauman, Z. (2016). *Strangers at our door*. Polity.

Biesta, G. J. J. (2010). *Good education in an age of measurement: Ethics, politics, democracy*. Routledge.

Biesta, G. J. J. (2011). *Learning democracy in school and society: Education, lifelong learning, and the politics of citizenship*. Sense Publishers.

Biesta, G. J. J. (2012). The future of teacher education: Evidence, competence or wisdom? *Research on Steiner Education*, 12(1), 8–21.

Biesta, G. J. J. (2016). Reconciling ourselves to reality: Arendt, education and the challenge of being at home in the world. *Journal of Educational Administration and History*, 48(2), 183–192. https://doi.org/10.1080/00220620.2016.1144580

Biesta, G. J. J. (2019). Trying to be at home in the world: New parameters for art education. *Artlink*, 39(3), 10–17.

Campbell, P. S., Myers, D., & Sarath, E. (2014). *Transforming music study from its foundations: A manifesto for progressive change in the undergraduate preparation of music majors*. The College Music Society.

Christopherson, C. (2021). Educating music teachers for the future: The crafts of change. In K. Holdhus, R. Murphy, & M. I. Espeland (Eds.), *Music education as craft* (pp. 63–74). Springer.

Clandinin, D. J. (2013). *Engaging in narrative inquiry*. Routledge.

comshalom. (2019, September 17). *Papa Francisco: A compaixão "não é um sentimento de pena"* ["Compassion is not a feeling of pity"]. https://comshalom.org/papa-francisco-a-compaixao-nao-e-um-sentimento-de-pena/

Fals Borda, O. (2013). Action research in the convergence of disciplines. *International Journal of Action Research*, 9(2), 155–167.

Fraser, N. (2016). Contradictions of capital and care. *New Left Review*, 100, 98–117.

Hendricks, K. (2018). *Compassionate music teaching*. Rowman & Littlefield.

Higgins, L. (2012). *Community music: In theory and in practice*. Oxford University Press.

Jorgensen, E. R. (2020). *Some challenges for music education: What are music teachers to do?* https://cipem.ese.ipp.pt/en/2021/06/25/some-challenges-for-music-education-what-are-music-teachers-to-do-by-estelle-r-jorgensen/

Lahire, B. (2002). *Portraits sociologiques: Dispositions et variations individuelles* [Sociological portraits: Dispositions and individual variations]. Nathan.

Lahire, B. (2003). From the habitus to an individual heritage of dispositions: Towards a sociology at the level of the individual. *Poetics*, 31, 329–355. https://doi.org/10.1016/j.poetic.2003.08.002

Lahire, B. (2001/2010). *The plural actor*. Polity Press.

Madrid, A. L. (2017). Diversity, tokenism, non-canonical musics, and the crisis of the humanities in U.S. academia. *Journal of Music History Pedagogy*, 7(2), 124–130.

McQueen, S., Scoffield, T., Tanner, D., Richer, L., & Garnett, R. (Executive Producers). (2020). *The Small Axe* [TV series]. BBC.

McQueen, S. (Writer), Siddons, A. (Writer), & McQueen, S. (Director). (2020, December 11). Alex Wheatle (Episode 4) [TV series episode]. In S. McQueen, T. Scoffield, D. Tanner, L. Richer, & R. Garnett (Executive Producers), *The Small Axe*. BBC.

McQueen, S. (Writer), Siddons, A. (Writer), & McQueen, S. (Director). (2020, December 18). Education (Episode 5) [TV series episode]. In S. McQueen, T. Scoffield, D. Tanner, L. Richer, & R. Garnett (Executive Producers), *The Small Axe*. BBC.

Myers, D. E. (2008). Lifespan engagement and the question of relevance: Challenges for music education research in the twenty-first century. *Music Education Research, 10*(1), 1–14. https://doi.org/10.1080/14613800701871330

Myers, D. E. (2018). Research realities: Embracing the complexity of expressive-creative learning and teaching. In D. R. Dansereau & J. Dorfman (Eds.). *Pluralism in American music education research* (pp. 99–121). Springer.

Mota, G. (2014). Thorns and joys in creative collaboration: A project with music education and visual arts students. In M. S. Barrett (Ed.), *Collaborative creative thought and practice in music* (pp. 221–238). Ashgate.

Mota, G., & Teixeira Lopes, J. (Eds.). (2017). *Growing while playing in Orquestra Geração: Contributions towards understanding the relationship between music and social inclusion.* Edições Politema.

Mota, G., & Figueiredo, S. (2018). Initiating music programs in new contexts: In search of a democratic music education. In G. McPherson & G. Welch (Eds.), *The Oxford handbook of music education* (Vol. 1, pp. 187–205). Oxford University Press.

Philpott, C., & Spruce, G. (Eds.). (2012). *Debates in music teaching*. Routledge.

Robin, W. (2017). *What controversial changes at Harvard means for music in the university*. National Sawdust. https://nationalsawdust.org/thelog/2017/04/25/what-controversial-changes-at-harvard-means-for-music-in-the-university/

Sarath, E. (2018). *Black music matters: Jazz and the transformation of music studies*. Rowman & Littlefield.

Silverman, M. (2012). Community music and social justice: Reclaiming love. In G. E. McPherson and G. F. Welch (Eds.), *The Oxford handbook of music education* (Vol. 2, 155–167). Oxford University Press.

Simon, D., Overmyer, E., Pelecanos, G., Noble, N. K., Strauss, C., & Incaprera, J. (Executive Producers). (2010–2013). *Treme* [TV Series]. HBO Entertainment.

Simon, D. (Writer), Overmyer, E. (Writer), Yoshimura, J. (Writer), Mills, D. (Writer), Elie, L. E. (Writer), & Holland, A. (Director). (2013, December 1). Careless love (Season 4, Episode 4) [TV series episode]. In D. Simon, E. Overmyer, G. Pelecanos, N. K. Noble, C. Strauss, & J. Incaprera (Executive Producers). *Treme*. HBO Entertainment.

Vatican. (2013, July 8). *Visit to Lampedusa*. Homily of the Holy Father Francis. https://www.vatican.va/content/francesco/en/homilies/2013/documents/papa-francesco_20130708_omelia-lampedusa.html.

Wright, R. (2015). Music education and social reproduction: Breaking the cycle. In C. Benedict, P. Schmidt, G. Spruce, & P. Woodford (Eds.), *The Oxford handbook of social justice in music education* (pp. 340–356). Oxford University Press.

Wright, R. (2019) Envisioning real utopias in music education: Prospects, possibilities and impediments. *Music Education Research, 21*(3), 217–227. https://doi.org/10.1080/14613808.2018.1484439

Yob, I. M. (2020). There is no Other. In I. M. Yob & E. R. Jorgensen (Eds.), *Humane music education for the common good* (pp. 17–28). Indiana University Press.

CHAPTER 47

CULTURAL HUMILITY AND ETHICS OF CARING IN MULTICULTURAL SETTINGS OF MUSIC TEACHER EDUCATION

AMIRA EHRLICH

Care Handbook Topics

Identity expressions
Social activism and critical consciousness

Introduction: QIAN: The Virtue of Cultural Humility

This chapter explores the possible contribution of Chang et al. (2012) conceptualization of cultural humility to an ethic and practice of authentic care in multicultural contexts of music education. Translating Chinese philosophy into a plan of action, Chang et al. described a "curriculum of humbleness" using the Chinese acronym of the word QIAN (which literally means humbleness), to describe four main attributes that their notion of humility entails:

Q: self-Questioning
I: bidirectional cultural Immersion
A: mutually Active listening
N: flexibility of Negotiation

In this chapter I explore the ways in which these four attributes can be applied to the music classroom, and why this is important: How and why music teachers can become models of self-questioning, in addition to being authorities of knowledge; how and why repertoires and pedagogies can be mutually shared by students and teachers of diverse cultural backgrounds as an invitation and opportunity to immerse ourselves in each other's cultural worlds; how and why active deep listening to music and to each other can cultivate caring relationships in the classroom; and how and why all such practices turn the music classroom into a safe space for exploration and on-going negotiation of complex social identities and realities.

The QIAN model of cultural humility is grounded on a specific cultural construct of humility grounded in Chinese Daoism and Confucianism (Yaohuai & Deyuanc, 2008). In these traditions, humility (also translated sometimes as humbleness) is an esteemed virtue through which it is believed that true knowledge can be achieved: the openness of professionals, and of elders, to learn from every interaction, from every person, child, student and/or patient. As I engage with these notions in Chinese philosophy, my own cultural heritage echoes with the words of an ancient Jewish Rabbi who wrote: "Who is wise? The one who learns from every person." (Pirkei Avot—[the Ethics of the Fathers], 4:1).

Chang et al. (2012) presented what they called "The QIAN curriculum" as a practice set to "enhance the exploration, comprehension and appreciation of the cultural orientations between healthcare professionals and patients" (p. 269). In this chapter I present the relevance of the QIAN model to the music classroom, to the cultivation of an ethic of care between music teachers and students.

NAVIGATING QIAN: CHAPTER ORIENTATION

I begin with a brief description of the need for diversification in music classrooms as an act of social responsibility, as a rationale for why the QIAN model might be of interest for music educators. Next, I explore how challenges of multiculturism translate into notions of care. In doing so, I reinforce my interest in the QIAN model, through the resonance with notions from Jewish philosophy, and exploring social implications through additional frameworks of diversity and "otherness." In an attempt to enact the ideas that I present, I offer background and data collected from my own practice of Israeli music teacher education. I organized this material to outline and manifest the four attributes of QIAN:

For Q: Self-questioning: I share sociological information about the society in which I live and work, alongside autoethnographic narratives and illustrations.

For I: Immersion: I offer a multimodal experience of my practice, inviting readers to immerse themselves in three scenes described in words, illustrations, and audio recordings.

For A: Active listening: I reflect on further insights moving beyond appearances within the context of the examples offered above.

For N: Negotiation: I present a series of written vignettes that represent classroom interactions that exemplify musical acts of ongoing negotiation to show how simple but meaningful such moments can be.

Finally, in summary, I offer an equation in which humility combined with validation create an ethic of care. Having shown how this might work in the music classroom in the data presented above, I end the chapter in thoughts about broader social impacts that such a practice may emanate.

Cultural Humility for Diversification and Social Responsibility in the Music Classroom

Music education, as a field of practice, has been slow in its response to challenges of diversity. Benedict et al. (2015) summarized the status quo of formal music education as a "deficit model of education ... often epitomized by an overly narrow definition of what counts as legitimate musical knowledge, which intimidates children who lack the appropriate cultural capital while allowing teachers to ignore much of the wealth of music that exists in the world" (p. xii). When a student or a group of students do not encounter samples of music from their lived experience in the classroom, they miss out on a core experience of feeling validated in that classroom, and risk the danger of going out into a society in which their lives, histories, and lived experiences are not deemed as valuable.

Education, as a core social asset, prepares younger populations to take part in the social fabric of their communities and society at large. McCarthy (2015) described public education as "a critical site for changing reality and for engaging individuals as 'agents for social change in a participatory democracy'" (p. 30). Roberts and Campbell (2015) described the goal of multicultural education "to develop experiences that lead to the validation and empowerment of students from every community" (p. 274), which finally contribute to "the socially responsible citizens they will become" (p. 284). Music education, as an integral part of the enterprise of education, and of educational institutions, entails a social responsibility.

Without the systematic commitment of music teachers to incorporate diverse musical experiences and diverse sets of musical knowledge in their classrooms, music education as a practice is in danger of contributing to the constitution and enforcement of a monoculture. Such an approach is an endorsement of ethnocentrism that can in no way be considered a socially responsible education anywhere in the world of the 2020s.

While the practice of the QIAN acronym as a working model of cultural humility was introduced in the context of medical education, it can be easily applied in all dyad and group interactions, especially in multicultural settings. Humility, as conceptualized by Chang et al. (2012), acts as framework for taking responsibility in unequal care dyads and diversity groups—something that music classrooms around the world should be striving to do better.

Multiculturalism, "Otherness," and Care

My interest in the QIAN model relates to my own practice of music teacher education in Israel. As a Jewish Orthodox woman teaching students from diverse Jewish and Arab socioreligious sectors in Israel, I found myself fascinated by the relevance of cultural humility to my ongoing questioning and negation of my positionality within the social context of my work.

This Israeli context is explored throughout this chapter as an example of conflictual multiculturalism that may be similar to—and different from—other international settings. In contemplating the Chinese notion of QIAN, I rely on philosophical underpinnings from my own Jewish cultural background—recognizing and playing on the ways in which ideas of the Jewish philosophers Emanuel Levinas (1969) and Rabbi Lord Jonathan Sacks (2007, 2020) are similar, and different, from the conceptualizations inspired by Chinese language and culture. Such intercultural engagement framed by an ebb and flow of similarity and difference emerges as an important theme in the pursuit of cultural humility and is therefore an important notion to keep in mind as you engage with this chapter.

Multiculturalism has become one of the major challenges of 21st century societies around the world. Rabbi Lord Jonathan Sacks—who was chief rabbi of the United Hebrew Congregations of the Commonwealth from 1991 to 2013—has become a leading voice in rethinking general theology, Judaism, and multiculturalism in the global post-secular realities of the 21st century. Sacks (2007, 2020) has noted characteristics of conflictual contexts—places where different cultural groups are in competition and struggle over the same limited public resources in a way that does not allow them to simply exist side by side for mutual enrichment. Within such contexts, if one side wins, the other loses: it is a zero-sum game. Multiculturalism, in such areas, according to Sacks, can end up being counterproductive rather than instrumental in cultivating overall social coherence and individual personal wellbeing.

In the academic world, and in the field of music education, scholars have been exploring practical implications of conceptualizations such as "(inter)cultural sensitivity" (e.g., Bennett, 2017); "(inter-)cultural competence" (e.g., Deardorff, 2006); culturally relevant pedagogy (e.g., Ladson-Billings, 1995); and "cultural diversity" (e.g., Banks, 2016).[1] My choice, in this chapter, is to focus on ways through which Chang et al. (2012) model of cultural humility can shed new shades of light on this richly diverse discourse—not because it is any better or superior to any of the other concepts mentioned above; but precisely because it is both different and similar to the core elements shared by each of the similar and diverse approaches that have developed.

I believe that humility is a gateway to a new paradigm of multiculturalism—a model termed by Sacks (2007) as "integrative diversity." This model entails a commitment to diversity that celebrates and validates difference in ways that resonate deeply with Levinas's (1969) ideas of ethical "otherness." Emmanuel Levinas—the Jewish French philosopher who fought in the French army in World War II, and survived his imprisonment in the Jewish barracks of a German war camp—dedicated much of his philosophic writings to the experience and the notion of "otherness." Unknowing, and not-knowing, are core constituents of Levinas's ideas about all interpersonal encounters, not only intercultural interactions. Recognizing that we do not and cannot "know" the "other" can lead to more meaningful conversations that both Levinas and Sacks envision as a crucial factor of personal wellbeing, of social coherence, and of solidarity.

Finally, the construct of cultural humility resonates deeply with paradigms of care and compassion. Bates (2004) and Noddings (2005) conceptualized care as a function and product of relationship that emanates empathy. Silverman (2012) described care in pedagogy as an act of cultivating civic and democratic agency and encouraged music teachers to explore inequalities in teacher–student relationships. Hendricks (2018) suggested a framework focused on compassion that moves beyond empathy in its commitment to action, and in doing so may work to deconstruct inequalities in classroom relationships.

The combination of acts of Questioning, Immersion, Active-Listening, and Negotiation in the QIAN model work to legitimize a basic mindset of unknowing. In doing so, risks are taken, unspoken and unexpressed needs can emerge. Care becomes daring and committed—perhaps as an opposite of compliance or apathy; perhaps an enactment of Valenzuela's (1999) distinction between *authentic* care verses *aesthetic* care: Acts of care that emerge from the smallest human interactions, that entail emotions, and are centered on the wellbeing of the people involved rather than on institutional or social norms and expectations. The focus is shifted from learning goals, benchmarks, and achievements, to learning relationships.

---

[1] For a detailed discussion of the spectrums of such concepts and their application in music education discourse, see Westerlund et al. (2021).

In order to understand exactly what may be at stake in the cultivation of such relationships, an acute awareness of social context is required. As an enactment of the first of the four QIAN attributes (self-questioning) I now present some key aspects of my specific social context, in a tone of open contemplation.

Q: Self-Questioning: Or, Why Secular Israeli Women Refuse to Wear Dresses

In 2015, Israeli President Rivlin described the "new social order" beginning to emerge from the country's demographics as a partnership between four rival socioreligious "tribes": (a) Jewish Secular, (b) Jewish Orthodox, (c) Jewish Ultraorthodox, and (d) Arab Populations.[2] Journalist Ari Shavit (2021) coined the phrase "the war of the tribes" to depict the contemporary social climate of escalation that he hoped to cure. Micro-intricacies of socioreligious tensions in Israeli society[3] play themselves out in concrete ways in everyday life, most evidently in the very clothes we wear.

The idea that fashion is a central function of Israeli sociology was most beautifully expressed in 2011 by *Haaretz* journalist Gili Izikovitch in her analysis of television fashionistas "Trinny and Susannah's" special Israeli episode[4] Izikovitch quoted the fashion hosts' surprise at secular Israeli women's hesitation to wear dresses and skirts—no doubt from fear of being identified as religious women, noting that "in Tel Aviv they looked all day for a woman in a dress and couldn't find one."

Israelis use their outer appearances as socioreligious signifiers. This tendency intensifies discourses of identity politics and can promote a judgmental mindset that may limit moments of mutual humility. My own personal experiences—and the variety of clothes in my closet—resonate with this reality.[5] As a religiously observant Orthodox Jewish Israeli woman, I have often felt how easily people in Israel are too quick to identify me with my apparent socioreligious "tribe," leading them to categorize me mentally: judging by my clothes, they think they know very much about me, my life, my home, my political stance, and my thoughts and beliefs.

Fourteen years ago, when I turned 30, I actually chose to remove all of my religious signifiers, opting for what in Israel is perceived as a secular dress code (see Figure 47.1).[6] Although many women in my religious community today have made this fashion

---

[2] A video with simultaneous English translation of this speech is available at: https://www.youtube.com/watch?v=hmRDrH5VcNY. Further details on the ramification of this speech can be found here: https://www.idc.ac.il/en/research/ips/pages/4tribes.aspx
[3] For a more detailed discussion of micro-intricacies that move beyond the "four tribe" model, see Ehrlich (2018).
[4] https://www.haaretz.com/1.5137683
[5] See Ehrlich (2018).
[6] Illustrations by my sister, Chaviva Billauer, drawn for Ehrlich (2018). Used with permission.

FIGURE 47.1 Self-portraits.

transition, often in encounters *outside* my community some people are visibly unsettled and confused when I reveal my religious affiliation—it shakes the presumptions that we Israelis are so used to making about each other, based on our clothes; it opens up a space of unknowing, that I believe to be crucial to emanating interpersonal moments of authentic care.

I have had many opportunities for self-questioning this decision of mine. One prime example occurred during an academic visit to the United States—to a location not far from the US state where I was born and raised. Twice during this visit I was referred to by local colleagues as a "person of color." When, under this premise, I was invited to take part in a panel discussion on race and racism I became very uncomfortable. I politely declined this offer, explaining that judging by appearances and much of my biography, I am very much a White American-born woman. My conscious decision to deny any outward socioreligious signifiers is not a viable option for many people of color. Another lesson in humility.

I: Immersion

Negotiating the balance between my own socioreligious camouflage and Israeli sociological norms is a central feature of my music teacher education practice. Although primary and secondary education in Israel take place mostly in socioculturally segregated institutions, higher education is a rare meeting-ground where members of diverse sectors study together in integrative institutions. What then can be expected when students and teachers from various sociocultural groups and subgroups are grouped together in the context of music teacher education? What kind of ethical approach can guide a Jewish Orthodox lecturer (as myself) who is teaching a mix of Jewish secular, Muslim, Druze, and Christian students? How can the dangers of a segregated approach to multiculturalism be avoided or transformed?

Teaching classes of mixed socioreligious populations, I find myself fascinated at the iconography often present in the classroom. Socioreligious signifiers of students' personal dress codes often emanate powerfully imagery in the Israeli context. Seeking a way to share this sentiment ethically without violating privacy, I asked my sister, a professional illustrator, to recreate some characteristic scenes from my practice.[7] In an attempt to evoke a sense of the QIAN notion of Immersion, I attach QR code links to some field recordings that can help bring these drawings to life (see Figures 47.2–4).

FIGURE 47.2 A student group of three (secular woman of Russian descent; Christian-Arab woman; and Jewish Orthodox woman) teach the class a Jewish Ethiopian prayer chant: *Salam Licha Ir* ("Hello [Holy] City").

---

[7] Original illustrations by Chaviva Billauer. Used with permission.

FIGURE 47.3 A secular Jewish student leads the class in an improvised folk dance to a traditional tune being shared by a Muslim student on the piano.

FIGURE 47.4 A student ensemble including a Muslim man on piano, a secular Jewish man on electric guitar, an Ultraorthodox Jewish woman on darbuka drum, and a Muslim woman on oud. The illustrative recording depicts a similar ensemble playing Mosh Ben Ari's Israeli pop song *Salam* ("Bring Peace upon Us").

A: Active Listening: Beyond Appearances

Anyone engaged in Israeli politics can be easily moved by such depictions of interreligious and intercultural musical sharing. Nevertheless, stopping at this stage of enthusiasm can belittle what is actually going on, and opens up a danger of perpetuating focus on external signifiers and group identity presumptions. Sacks (2002, 2007, 2020) acknowledges how identity politics have served an important role in the history of social justice. At the same time, Sacks is brave enough to highlight the dangers of focusing on group identities at the expense of two other crucial sociological factors: personal particularity, and social cohesion.

Cultural humility demands moments of active unknowing: of deconstructing any presumptions we may have about the person we encounter. Integrating humility into my curriculum within my context first and foremost is about moving beyond the iconography of interreligious and intercultural interaction. It is about challenging the Israeli norm of automatic socioreligious categorizations—but doing so without asking anyone in the room to change the way they dress.

Within the framework of this challenge I recall a story that I heard in high school about a Modern Orthodox Jew who decided to remove his religious head covering (his *kipa*). Traveling on a train, he sat behind an Ultraorthodox Jew who wore traditional garments and head covering. A woman who got on at the next station spotted only two empty seats left. She looked at both men and decided to sit next to the man who appeared to be secular; out of respect for the Ultraorthodox conceptions of modesty she assumed her sitting next to him would make him uncomfortable. The bareheaded man politely turned to the woman and asked her why she chose to sit next to him, revealing that he is actually religiously observant. Trying to explain himself to her, he told her: "I am happy you chose to sit here. It is fine with me even though I am religious. You see," he said, smiling, "I am like a secret agent." In my practice I sometimes function as such a secret agent—a catalyst for arousing some element of cognitive dissonance and questioning—creating a space where dialogue can begin.

N: Negotiation

Scene 1: "How Do You Say 'Music' in Arabic?"

An inner dialogue from my teacher-researcher journal:

> How do you say "music" in Arabic?
> This is how I began an undergraduate introduction to music education research in Tel-Aviv, Israel in 2015. There I was: a young religiously observant Jewish-Israeli lecturer, facing a classroom of students from the diverse Muslim, Christian, and Druze populations of Northern Israel.
> "What can I teach them?" I wondered.
> "How should I teach them?" I worried.
> "How can I get them to teach me?" I thought in almost desperation. It was clear to me that any efforts made to teach this course to this group must address the cultural gap

between me and the students. It was also clear to me that this encounter could turn out to be life changing for all sides. Moreover, I was fascinated by the possibilities that such a semester could contribute towards a mutual knowledge production process that might reshape what I and they each previously thought of as music education.

My instincts urged me to get the students to tell me something I don't know. In doing so I was placing myself as unknowing, and opening up my own vulnerability through the language gap. Often during group work in class I encouraged students to talk among themselves in whatever language they felt most comfortable in—meaning that I would not necessarily be able to understand what they are saying and discussing. I allow myself spaces and times to be unknowing; I validate their choice of language, I create spaces where their chosen language is welcome. I trust them. Sometimes they translate each other for me. They help me try to understand them.

Scene 2: You Call That Music?

Teacher–Student dialogue recorded and transcribed from my music teacher education class:

T: *What kinds of music do the kids in your class listen to at home?*
S: *"I'm not sure I'd call it music."*
T: *"Try me! ... When you were a teenager or if you were a teenager now in your home village, would you listen to this too?"*
S: *"Yeah! [playing an Arabic Hip-hop selection on YouTube] This is what they think is cool ... but here in college I'm not sure we'd call that music. ... Isn't my job as a music teacher to teach them that?"*
T: *"To teach them that the music that they love isn't music? ... hmm ... is that what music teachers do?"*

As a teacher educator, I am working to challenge and expand definitions of what qualifies as music in an academic context; Modeling acts of validation, and encouraging them to validate musics that students bring to their classrooms.

Scene 3: What's Your Music?

Class discussion recorded and transcribed from my music teacher education class:

T: *Have you chosen a piece of music you would like to perform at our concert?*
S1: *"People from my hometown always expect me to sing in Arabic. Actually ... I prefer Anglo Pop music, and I would really like to sing in English. Do you think that is OK?"*
S2: *"And I have been working on a 'Song Without Words' by Mendelssohn on the piano. Can I play that?"*
S3: *"We want to perform as a group! We are working on a medley that combines Um Kaltum with Adele. We are really not sure it'll work but we'd like to try!"*

I am creating an open space by formulating an open question: when I ask what *your* music is, we work against any prior expectations. We embrace humility—I do not know what music you feel is your own; you may perhaps not know yourself. We can search together. We can work to validate your choices.

Scene 4: What's in a Scale?

Class discussion and inner dialogue documented in retrospect in my teacher-researcher journal:

T: *"The Arabic term for musical scale is Maqam."*
Or is it?
Working on translations of musical terminologies to Arabic with a group of Arabic-speaking undergraduates leads us on a wonderful journey of musical exploration.
I ask the students to try and break-down their knowledge of scales verses Maqamat:

T: *"The Western scales of Major and Minor indicate a fixed progression of whole tones and half-tones that can be applied to any given note. Shifting a musical piece from C major to D major is generally considered to have no underlying consequences."*
Are you sure about that? Which Western composers and theoreticians would debate this claim?
Is a Maqam the same?

S1: *"Even though they too are structured on a fixed pattern of intervals, Maqamat are usually affiliated with a fixed tone."*

S2: *"Maqamat include stricter rules regarding phrase beginnings and endings, and so they actually entail specific mini-musical motifs that should always be included."*
Do scales include such motifs? What about the Medieval modes? Or Indian Ragas? Or Jewish Steigers?
How many gateways have we now opened to realms of musical knowledge that often remain way beyond the formal music classroom and even the informal music workshop? Which of these gateways will each of us choose to pursue, and who and what will assist us in our journeys?

Students and I are exploring language gaps together. Using language gaps as gateways to expand the realms of musical knowledge in the academic music classroom. Opening up spaces for cross-cultural comparison that functions to broaden perspectives rather than oversimplify for the sake of commonalities.

Discussion: Humility × Validation = Care

Cultural validation (Benet-Martínez, 2012) can be a crucial aspect of creating a sense of belonging. Sacks (2002, 2007, 2020) insisted that validating cultural identities must be a first step in building a common narrative. Indeed, Levinas (1969) describes the ethics of encountering "the other" as an insistence on maintaining a keen sense of difference, and even strangeness, that he conceptualized as an integral part of the deepest interpersonal respect. Levinas's writing is critical of encounters that focus on bridging gaps between people by stressing similarities. Sacks's theory of bridge-building and peacemaking similarly does not stop at similarities, and even criticizes overall attempts at universalism.

Recognizing what we do not and perhaps cannot know about the "others" that we encounter opens up spaces for safe, humble, deliberation. Chang et al.'s (2012) QIAN model of Questioning, Immersion, Active-Listening, and Negotiation can push us to celebrate and validate each other's particularities and can allow us to engage in difficult conversations while maintaining emotional safety.

Humility that incorporates validation emanates care. This is the equation that emerged from my self-research. I studied my practice from the standpoint of the four QIAN principles and discovered just how crucial and how potent such a mindset can be when enacted in the music classroom.

From the Classroom to Society: Integrative Diversity

Even on his deathbed, what troubled Rabbi Lord Sacks (2020) more than anything was the danger of the segregating forces of multiculturalism and the loss of a common narrative—which he conceptualizes as the loss of social cohesion, and perhaps of the moral commitment to a common good. Sacks argues that without a sense of common good, personal wellbeing was inevitably impossible. Instead of multiculturalism, Sacks calls for integrative diversity: a social model that celebrates diversity through validation; and incorporates patterns of care and compassion that open up spaces for sharing and collaboration. An integrative diverse society is a society that emanates a deep ethic of care by inspiring mutual compassion—the kind that Sacks posits can be achieved best by building something together.

The uses of cultural humility described and demonstrated in this chapter work toward such a goal. Sharing my experience and analysis helps me learn more about myself, about the students who I am lucky to work with, and about the socioreligious challenges of the context in which we live. Small acts of sharing can resonate deeply and trigger new ripples of thought and of action. This chapter hopes to be such a ripple.

References

Banks, J. A. (2016). *Cultural diversity and education: Foundations, curriculum, and teaching* (6th ed.). Routledge. https://doi.org/10.4324/9781315622255

Bates, V. C. (2004). Where should we start? Indications of a nurturant ethic for music education. *Action, Criticism, and Theory for Music Education, 3*(3). http://act.maydaygroup.org/articles/Bates3_3.pdf

Benedict, C., Schmidt, P., Spruce, G., & Woodford, P. (Eds.). (2015). *The Oxford handbook of social justice in music education.* Oxford University Press.

Benet-Martínez, V. (2012). Multiculturalism: Cultural, social, and personality processes. In K. Deaux & M. Snyder (Eds.), *Oxford handbook of personality and social psychology* (pp. 623–648). Oxford University Press.

Bennett, M. J. (2017). Development model of intercultural sensitivity. In Y. Kim (Ed.), *International encyclopedia of intercultural communication.* John Wiley & Sons.

Chang, E. S., Simon, M., & Dong, X. (2012). Integrating cultural humility into health care professional education and training. *Advances in Health Sciences Education: Theory and Practice, 17*(2), 269–278. https://doi.org/10.1007/s10459-010-9264-1

Deardorff, D. K. (2006). The identification and assessment of intercultural competence as a student outcome of internationalization. *Journal of Studies in International Education, 10*(3), 241–266. https://doi.org/10.1177%2F1028315306287002

Ehrlich, A. (2018). *Pray, play, teach: Conversations with three Jewish Israeli music educators* [Unpublished doctoral dissertation]. Boston University.

Hendricks, K. S. (2018). *Compassionate music teaching.* Rowman & Littlefield.

Ladson-Billings, G. (1995). Toward a theory of culturally relevant pedagogy. *American Educational Research Journal, 32*(3), 465–491. https://doi.org/10.3102%2F00028312032003465

Levinas, E. (1969). *Totality and infinity: An essay on exteriority.* Duquesne University Press.

McCarthy, M. (2015). Understanding social justice from the perspective of music education history. In C. Benedict, P. Schmidt, G. Spruce, & P. Woodford (Eds.), *The Oxford handbook of social justice in music education* (pp. 29–46). Oxford University Press

Noddings, N. (2005). *The challenge to care in schools* (2nd ed.). Teachers College Press.

Roberts, J., & Campbell, P. (2015). Multiculturalism and social justice: complementary movements for education in and through music. In C. Benedict, P. Schmidt, G. Spruce, & P. Woodford (Eds.), *The Oxford handbook of social justice in music education* (pp. 272–286). Oxford University Press.

Sacks, J. (2002). *The dignity of difference: How to avoid the clash of civilizations.* Continuum.

Sacks, J. (2007). *The home we build together: Recreating society.* Continuum.

Sacks, J. (2020). *Morality: Restoring the common good in divided times.* Basic Books.

Shavit, A. (2021). *Bayit shlishi* [Third home]. Yediot.

Silverman, M. (2012). Virtue ethics, care ethics, and "the good life of teaching." *Action, Criticism, and Theory for Music Education, 11*(2). http://act.maydaygroup.org/articles/Silverman11_2.pdf

Valenzuela, A. (1999). *Subtractive schooling: U.S.-Mexican youth and the politics of caring.* State University of New York Press.

Westerlund, H., Karlsen, S., & Kallio, A. A., Treacy, D. S., Miettinen, L., Timonen, V., Gluschankof, C., Ehrlich, A., & Shah, I. B. (2021). Visions for intercultural music teacher education in complex societies. *Research Studies in Music Education.* Advance online publication. https://doi.org/10.1177%2F1321103X211032490

Yaohuai, L., & Deyuan, H. (2008). The tradition of the virtue of Qian and its contemporary fate. *Frontiers of Philosophy in China, 3*(4), 558–576. http://www.jstor.org/stable/40343898

CHAPTER 48

POLICY PRACTICE AS CITIZENSHIP BUILDING

From Duty to Care to Solidarity in Music Education

PATRICK SCHMIDT

CARE HANDBOOK TOPICS

Social activism and critical consciousness

INTRODUCTION

The year 2020 will serve as a historical inflexion point in social and racial relations, with implications striated onto all aspects of life, including education. The manner in which the multiple disruptions and crises that emerged out of this sociohistorical moment are mobilized in permanent or at least sustainable manner, are yet to be fully understood. At the time of this writing, meaningful change seems dependent on the strategic, deliberate, recurrent, and structural ways social actors—in their own professional spaces—come to harness and operationalize the space created by such significant disruption. Will the initial reactive and compensatory actions established in response to the pandemic be translated into a reconfiguring of traditional music and educational practices? Will the consciousness raising around racial justice lead to a sustained and serious re-imaging of curricula? Will the reckoning with systemic othering lead to collective re-valuing of the educational care, relationality, and solidarity?[1]

---

[1] Although I write primarily based on the experiences of my professional practices in North America, as I engage with colleagues and music educators in South America (where I grew up) and in Europe

In this chapter I argue that discursive change in the music education field of action would benefit from a thoughtfully aligned re-capturing of interest in the impact of policy practice, functioning as a central tool/praxis in efforts to actualize and structurally embed the renewal of music educational practice. If the 2020 pandemic has indeed provided lessons about the fragility of institutions, relations, and social norms, it must also have alerted many to the possibilities—awaiting mobilization—of a redirection and amplification of educational aims; specifically in higher education and public schooling, but also in community settings.

In these terms, today more than ever, policy practice can be more widely approached as a personal and local practice. There is ample space and reason to re-route normative—and often econometric—understandings that place policy as that which is deliberately distant and at the service of managerial sorting. Drawing from my ongoing work on policy (Schmidt, 2009, 2015, 2017, 2020), I argue for the increased presence of policy knowhow as formative to any professional community of care, drawing connections between solidarity and governance as essential elements of sustainable change. Policy practice, in such a view, functions as a critical contributor and conduit for professional, organizational, and pedagogical activism essential to the realization of more socially just and equity directed practice within music programs. Though philosophical/ideological articulations of such visions have been provided by many and in many forms, the profession has only partially, and still reluctantly, acknowledged that this kind of professional citizenship building is depended on grassroots, systematic, and well-informed policy practice—by music educators, for music educators, and their communities of care.

REFRAMING POLICY PRACTICE

I believe it is important to say that when I speak of policy, I am *not* simply referring to policy texts, rules or distant legislative action. Nor am I simply advocating for educators to become "consumers" of policy information, developing a form of functional policy literacy as advocated by neoliberal politics. I want to make that clear, because my aim is precisely to diminish the normative "elsewhereness" such conceptions of policy suggest. Why? Because, as I see it, when what counts as policy is significantly delimited by external directives and demands, we risk naturalizing as *not policy* any discursive, curricular, pedagogical, governance and personal action *by* teachers (see Bylica & Schmidt, 2021).

Key here is that decentering our existing *convenient professional knowledges* (see Schmidt & Edwards, in press), that is, all the highly familiar, the assumptive, all we hide behind, requires more than establishing a managerial understanding of the status quo

(where I hold close ties), I see similar questions and challenges emerging in a significant cross section of music education, internationally.

and taking advantage of it. In other words, policy practice is more than enacting administrative savvy.

Educational leaders working in school environments, such as the scholar-practitioner Eric Shieh, embody this kind of position toward policy and teacher leadership in consequential ways, highlighting that this is feasible, while testifying to the challenges therein and what is at stake:

> I face the difficulty of working against institutional inertia—particularly thinking about what's expected from music teachers in schools, depending on where you're working. The number of times I've had visitors in my school say "Oh—I could never do that in my school," before giving me a litany of reasonable-but-not-insurmountable-rationales for not changing. (Conway et al., 2019, p. 909)

Who Is the Subject in Policy?

Over the last decade, I have been concerned with the fact that regardless of the pervasiveness of policy and the evidence on the scarcity of local stakeholder voice in educational policy discussions, music education, and music teacher education have only marginally engaged with policy, its practices, and its potential role in teacher voice, curricular change and educational governance (Ball, 2003; Coburn & Russell, 2008; Hinnant-Crawford, 2016). Policy practice, as I have argued, can be understood as a form of governance; personal, sustained, and situated in contradistinction to the *managerialism* education has experienced under neoliberal politics. Important to educators, such a view of policy practice places the possibility of school culture change as indelibly connected to giving priority and sustained support (for instance through teacher preparation) to teacher political empowerment—how we better and more fully embed ourselves in the micropolitics of schools—and teacher pedagogical empowerment—how we cope with the discomfort of regularly adapting practice (Schmidt, 2020).

Pragmatically, I have argued that understanding policy practice as teacher practice could (a) better prepare music educators to engage as active players in the larger ecology of decision-making within and beyond the school community and (b) help them navigate the complex social, economic, curricular, and political tensions lived in schools (see Bylica & Schmidt, 2021). All this, however, also has implications to an understanding of *policy practice as professional solidarity* (explored later) and to Hendricks's (2018) call to extend the field of music education's thinking and practice beyond caring for and about students, to an experience of caring with one another. I believe that efforts to re-frame policy practice as a personal, meaningful, and solidary practice capable of significant (perhaps essential) contributions toward changing school and other organizational learning environments are indispensable to sustained and sustainable equity and decolonial efforts on the march today. Further, I argue alongside Bert Biesta (2013) that efforts to move education practice beyond its current obsessions with "qualification" and "socialization" requires labor toward subjectification, that is, that we are able to recognize ourselves and others as subjects of our own educational endeavors—and that means policy and governance as well. Lastly, I suggest that these aims are fully aligned with the goals articulated by/in this handbook, in particular the notion of care/ing moving "toward connection and empowerment" and how it may "inspire music teachers to practice persistent curiosity, and to be fiercely demanding of the things that truly matter to music students and within shared musical communities" (Hendricks, this volume).

Policy Practice in a Nutshell

Alongside a significant and growing literature, I try to think of *policy practice as a form of teacher practice*, re-situating the rather normative and often misunderstood concept back within the realm of grassroot influence—with all the practice implications we can see in this image. Differently from 20 years ago when I started in higher education, I have come to realize that insightfully constructed rationales (the philosophical why) and thoughtfully considered practice (the pedagogical how) are routinely insufficient toward sustainable change without equal consideration to enactment processes (the policy "by which means"). Putting this in slightly different terms, what I have suggested is that *the distance between teacher's work and policy practice is constitutional to the realities of school micropolitics, and that this gap is a strong contributor to deficits surrounding professional and pedagogical adaptability, responsivity, and autonomy* (Schmidt, 2017).

Bringing this to teacher education, the question becomes if and to what extent the absence of policy practice and knowhow as a form of legitimate professional practice has enabled, or at least safeguarded, the non-systemic and non-sustainable ways in which educators have been located within their own school/work environs. And finally, vis-à-vis the purpose of this handbook, one cannot but ask if silences regarding teachers as policy practitioners (rightly engaged in governance) must be broken if sustainable care/ing practice is to be brought to the center of the educational enterprise.

At the same time, it is also necessary to acknowledge that whenever one speaks of social and educational change, there is often a failure to recognize and provide space to address the costs of said activism, individually and collectively. This is necessary work, as these costs are not hypothetical nor abstract: They are the cost to changing self-identity and impostor syndrome fears; the cost of creating the space for failure in front of students, peers and administration as new practices are attempted; the cost of shedding ingrained ideological beliefs; the cost of time expenditure and its impact on a teacher's private life; the cost of conscientization; the cost of saying no.

Culturally-Sustaining Practices in the Milieu of Governance

In order to illustrate in more concrete terms what I have argued above, I suggest that we consider how governance and policy practice are often relegated to second order efforts toward change; losing out to ideological, discursive and pedagogical priorities. My point is that opportunity for advancement or failure of sustainable change is connected to a kind of comprehensive or ecological standpoint, whereby (appropriate) focus on changing curriculum and music practice toward equity, decolonialization and other socially-oriented (and necessary) change, should be paired with similarly careful discourse toward governance, and a recognition that policy design can account (and historically has) for much of the failure in school culture change. A quick look at educational multiculturalism might help to clarify what I mean.

Although multiculturalism has lost its impact and pre-eminence as an educational theory, multiculturalism remains an important parameter for discussion regarding efforts to manage, contain, and or promote cultural difference and diversity. If one looks at James Banks's (1995) model and how it arguably remains one of the most, if not the foundational effort to shape this educational arena, one is reminded that the model identified five dimensions of multicultural education: (a) curriculum integration; (b) the knowledge construction process; (c) prejudice reduction; (d) an equity pedagogy; and, significant to my point, (e) an empowering school culture and social structure. Multicultural education researchers and practitioners, while extensively researching and arguing for the first four have, however, largely neglected the last. Lauri Johnson (2003) argues that the failures of multicultural efforts are importantly connected to this last and least emphasized element (empowering school culture and social structure). I see that as failure in/of policy practice and governance, which is another way of saying a failure to integrate teacher pedagogical and content knowhow with policy knowhow. Critical is the consideration that perhaps a failure of establishing policy practice culture and structures and relations designed to create and sustain a disposition toward adaptation, re-engaging with pedagogical challenges, was critically absent, just as multiculturality continued to change requiring adaptation and re-contextualization. As the current (and absurd) backlash against critical race theory makes painfully evident,[2] caring and critical commitment toward educational equity, diversity, and social justice cannot survive without similarly critical and conscious policy practice and governance.

I am not arguing that the manner in which multiculturalism failed (particularly in the United States) was simply a problem of policy practice silence at the ground-level of schooling. But it is reasonable, and rather plain, that managerial governance and the

---

[2] See, for example, the remarkable number of gag order legislations proposed in multiple US states, by early 2022. https://pen.org/educational-gag-orders-target-speech-about-lgbtq-identities-with-new-prohibitions-and-punishments/

absence of teacher led policy practice contributed to how multiculturalism ended up enforcing "outmoded conceptions of culture that require individuals to embrace narrowly essentialized identifications that have significant—and often negative—political consequences" (Gaztambide-Fernandez, 2012, p. 44). It is also true that multiculturalism experienced developments (consider *critical multiculturalism*) that attempted to design and engage in the enactment of "a purposely elastic collection of characteristics, rather than a fixed and static definition, that addresses the varying contexts of communities and the changing process of education" (Nieto et al., 2008, p. 179). The challenge, as Gaztambide-Fernandez (2012) asks, is how to re-center "difference through a focus on the particularities of human interdependency rather than the generalities of human universality" (p. 45) and how to bring such conceptions and practices within school governance and curricular policy commitments.

Sustainable Policy Subjectivity

Biesta (2013) argues that perhaps *the* educational question "is about what it is that we want to give authority to; it is about deciding what it is that we want to have authority in our lives" (p. 55); that is, what is of value to us, which includes why/when we "give authority to the teaching we receive" (p. 55). Coming to understand how/when/why to make such decisions is a form of cultivation, Biesta argues, which has at its center the process of subjectification. Contrary to qualification and socialization (both critical to teacher preparation and linked to content and pedagogical knowhow), subjectification is not about how individuals become part of existing orders but how they can be "independent, some would say autonomous, subjects of action and responsibility" (p. 64). This is a critical understanding because policy can demonstrate the ways in which we can be subjects in the lives of schools or communities. In those terms, educating future educators toward policy practice is to express a joint commitment toward their subjectification and toward a kind of school citizenry where "independent" action and responsibility can function in a dynamic collective environ. If complex social and cultural issues are to have a meaningful life within schools (and if schools are to represent and address such social and cultural entanglements meaningfully) then governance and policy practice cannot be relegated to mere management. Just as important, young educators cannot be left to learning and engaging with such challenges through trial and error alone.

I am particularly fond of the work of Stephen Ball, specifically in his articulation that the way in which policies are spoken and spoken about, their vocabularies, are part of the creation of their conditions of acceptance and enactment. This is how they construct what is perceived to be inevitable and necessary (Ball, 2009). If music educators speak as subjects, as policy practitioners, as full citizens within their own labor environments, isn't it likely that they may see the "inevitable and necessary" differently? Ball is not alone, as a convincing and growing literature articulates the impact of policy practice of and on school members and how powerfully they can shape and influence teaching and learning, but also relationships, governance, reform efforts, and indeed the nature and character of what could be called school citizenship (Blase & Blase, 2002; Malen & Cochran, 2008; Malen & Ogawa, 1988).

Perhaps as significant, these concerns are not just academic, but represented in myriad examples and sites of learning and practice where educators take on policy practice and engage in governance. We see this evidenced in a resurgence of the role of Unions, the growth of case-based work done by organizations such as Teach Plus,[3] as well as in arts organizations. In the US, even the National Association for Music Education has taken policy more seriously. In the last year or so, this work has also been lifted by dozens of not-for-profits and think tanks working toward multiple social policy environments, all aimed at questions of diversity, equity and decolonization. The Banff Center is doing remarkable work on indigenous music leadership, for example.[4] Emerging are explorations on notions that vary from the need to theory, to policy as a form of critical pedagogy, to the cultivation of dispositions toward policy practice.

Solidarity and Personal Policy Practice

Writ large and in the face of challenging political division, it is not difficult to understand that manipulation of policy texts and policy practices can enable social justice just as easily as structural racism; cultural plurality just as promptly as consumerism; consultative practice just as much as power-driven hierarchy. Today, knowing that polarization is openly manipulated through policy and discourse, and made stronger by the growing valuing of vocality (in social media and in politics, see Schmidt, 2021), a focus on solidarity and how it may positively impact relations and governance (a broad definition of policy practice, to which I subscribe and briefly address below) seems rather timely. In these terms, and considering how to contribute to such environment, any educational professional—be it at the individual or collective/organizational levels—is faced with mounting pressure to ask themselves:

- What is my role in influencing policy framing, decision-making, and enactment within my own working environment?
- Is it possible to enact solidarity and name myself part of a community of care, while staying outside policy practices that shape discourse and action, particularly when they contribute to exclusion and inequity, or ensconce spaces for meaningful, open, and critically oriented engagement?

[3] https://teachplus.org
[4] https://www.banffcentre.ca/leadership

- Can practices of care find new space and oxygen between conscious sociocultural identarian critique and policy practice or governance inflected toward solidarity?

Solidarity as Pathway

Personal and organizational practices toward care, that is, toward the subjectivization of the social actor (in our case the music educator), and all that has been articulated thus far, brings us to the notion of care as a manifestation of solidarity, and policy practice as an expression of professional solidarity.

The way Bayertz (1999) describes and critiques the notion of solidarity is a helpful place to start, as he presents an understanding that aligns with the potential of policy practice, particularly as an ambient for agency development within schools:

> "Solidarity" is now comprehended as a mutual attachment between individuals, encompassing two levels: a *factual* level of actual common ground between the individuals and a *normative* level of mutual obligations to aid each other, as and when should be necessary. (p. 2)

Gaztambide-Fernandez (2012), interpreting Bayertz's view, argues that the "two aims of the concept are intimately related, as those who use the concept of solidarity in a descriptive mode do so in search of patterns that might yield prescriptive norms in order to address social or political problems" (p. 47). Such a view goes to the center of the relational principle guiding policy practice enacted by school community members as I have argued (Schmidt 2002, 2015), exemplifying the struggle and cyclical tensions embedded in work that aims toward ethics, equity and inclusion. This is particularly significant when educators work to build *relations*, to enact *recognition* of others and of diversity, to strive toward pedagogical and ideological *adaptation*, and to facilitate the *enactment* of governance and curricular change.

As I noted above, any enterprise (such as policy) and any notion/guiding principle serving as parameters for action in the social world, are subject to manipulation and thus to constructive as well as deleterious operationalization. Gaztambide-Fernandez (2012) does not shy from such clarification and highlights extensively the limitations of notions of solidarity:

> Bayertz astutely demonstrates ... that human solidarity is based on an idealized human moral community that does not properly account for "anti-solidary feelings and actions" between humans (p. 7). Civic solidarity, as a characteristic of the welfare state, while based on the moral principle of shared responsibility for collective wellbeing, also operates through a form of institutionalized coercion. What Bayertz's analysis reveals are the ways in which notions of solidarity are caught within conceptions of humanity, citizenship, social belonging, and moral obligation. These are the same concepts around which colonization and other dynamics of oppression

also operate, pointing to how solidarity always operates in tension with logics of domination. (p. 47)

Regardless of such ambivalences, I argue that there can be no care without solidarity, and that any care-filled structures and relations are only sustainable within spaces where solidarity is part of pedagogical and operational ethos of school-level policy practice. Care relations that are unattuned to solidarity "as the basis for relationships among diverse communities [where] diversity and difference are central values" (Mohanty, 2003, p. 7) will eventually devolve to tokenism, or cynicism, or worse.

Care and Solidarity

Following Biesta (2013) and Ball (2003), I see policy practice as a form of pedagogy, where pedagogy is that which "takes place in an encounter between subjects, who are also made—and therefore transformed—in and through the encounter as subjects" (Gaztambide-Fernandez, 2012, p. 51). As a form of pedagogy, policy practice at the level of the community (including school community) demands an engagement with solidarity in order to be equitable and inclusive—that is, in order to operate in and through care relations that are renewable, adaptable, and respectful of nuance and change.

These processes are replete with challenges, dissensus, and, at times, violence. Thus, it is critical to recognize that care and solidarity are not conforming practices, neither formulaic nor always peaceful. As with any educational endeavor that aims to be inclusive, equity oriented and even transformational, practices of solidarity (and indeed care) often carry with them (or must employ) a disruptive kind of ethics, the "difficult inheritance" that is embedded in decolonial work, and a reckoning with the fact that it "is bound up with the ethical problem of learning how to imaginatively account for the forms of life it leaves in ruins" (Tarc, 2011, p. 16). This should not be a deterrent to, but rather the impetus to consider solidarity relationally within and outside the classroom. Such willingness may lead to engagements where questions such as these shape our practice: "how am I being made by others? What are the consequences of my being on others? What kinds of sacrifices are implied in the mythology of myself as being and my insistence in my individual freedom?" (Gaztambide-Fernandez, 2012, p. 52).

Central to solidary education or governance/policy practice is that it ought to foster "action that also affects or modifies the one who acts" (Gaztambide-Fernandez, 2012, p. 53). And this kind of action brings us back to the subjectivity that Biesta speaks of, where a sense of self-consciousness comes into play without a simplistic sense of self-empowerment—essential in policy practice that is decolonizing and equity-oriented and not simply identity-affirming. A sense of solidarity then creates the conditions (or highlights them) whereby Freirian (1970) conscientization can be materialized without self-aggrandizing, zealotry, virtue-signaling—or worse—false consciousness.

This is a transitivity kind of solidarity that Gaztambide-Fernandez argues for, which demands a praxis, where "deploying an action that re-creates the agent even as the agent is creating the action—in an ongoing, chiasmic loop of transformation" (Sandoval, 2000, p. 157).

Solidarity and Music Education on the Ground

The work of Gabriela Ocadiz (2020) provides another concrete linkage here as she articulates work with student refugees in schools and community centers highlighting solidarity by seeing students not just as "vulnerable populations'" but as highly adaptable. This kind of framing invites educators to consider how solidarity to students might begin by enacting a pedagogy of discomfort. Ocadiz's experiences developing music engagements with refugee youth follows the work of Zembylas (2019; see also Zembylas & Papamichael, 2017). It demonstrates how public spaces of learning, supported by policy practice at the local level guided by solidarity, can establish programs with a pedagogy based on critical forms of care, focusing on "ethical encounters that rearrange structural conditions, including both the symbolic and material dimensions that produce the encounter" (Gaztambide-Fernandez, 2012, p. 57). Porto and Zembylas (2020) argue that particularly when engaging in what Britzman (1998) has called difficult knowledge, "discomfort is not only unavoidable in relation to difficult issues but may also be necessary, as long as discomfort is handled not only critically but also strategically" (p. 359).

Education that engages care in a critical manner then, must face the challenges of developing pedagogical practices based on "affective-political contingency that demands the practice of a strategic approach which minimizes ethical violence and maximizes the potential of ethical and emotional transformation that breaks complicity with social injustice and human rights abuse" (Zembylas, 2020, p. 360). I believe this is also foundational in terms of policy practice, given that doing this kind of critical work within the classroom, without engaging in coterminous dialogue, collaboration, and general governance within the school/district environment, seems a recipe for unsustainable work (Schmidt, 2017).

Ocadiz (2020) shows how music practitioners can engage in multimodal forms of critical pedagogy that both establish care/ing relations based on solidarity, while also fostering expression around areas of "discomfort" involving racial, ethnic, gender as well as mobility and forced dislocation. Her work exemplifies what Thomas and Stornaiuolo (2016) have called "*bending*," a form of *restoring* or "a process by which people reshape narratives to represent a diversity of perspectives and experiences that are often missing or silenced in mainstream texts, media, and popular discourse" (p. 313).

While writing in the context of immigration and youth, Ocadiz follows Clark (2002) pointing out that "*vulnerable*, as an adjective, is a label 'that designates groups of people assumed to share characteristics of physical weakness, emotional instability and economic dependence'" (p. 285). Central in this process of solidarity is the effort to affirm potential. In the case of Ocadiz's students, this is done by showing how their struggles with mobility, re-settlement, as well as discrimination, does not reduce them to a "vulnerable minority." Pedagogical and policy solidarity emerge in acknowledging them as vulnerable but also, and primarily, as "highly adaptable" youth, whom, given a space of care, are perfectly able to tackle music making/composing/creating that is fully in touch with, and critical of, social, cultural and identity challenges impacting their lives and impeding their growth.

I see Ocadiz's (2020) engagement with and creation of the Youth Music Program as imbued by acts of care framed in terms of solidarity, not only to the students themselves and their identities, but to the "multiplicities and implications of previous life experiences" deeming them "crucial to who and what students are and can be" (p. 153). Ocadiz argues that their absence, that is, failing to acknowledge and engage with the challenging experiences of mobility lived by these "newcomer" (refugee) students, would have "hindered the opportunities for a music education that responded to social change" and social challenges (p. 154).

Final Thoughts

Central to the arguments articulated in this chapter is the notion that care/ing/filled experiences in education, though dependent on intersubjective relations, are also sustained and function through environs and their systems. Caring relations and practices, thus require environmental conditions for flourishing. And in spaces such as schools or other learning organization, such flourishing is impacted by, if not dependent on policy and governance practice.

I have argued here that policy practice can be seen as "circuits of solidarities" demanding "work in which cultural recognition, economic equality, and meaningful representation operate not in lockstep but in tandem, in a dance" (Su, 2019, p. 4). Such efforts require an understanding of policy that diverges from the normative and the managerial, particularly those that defund teacher agency. And this, in turn, invites consideration as to how framing care within music education may require further and more careful articulations of how teacher practice is embedded and at times dependent on policy practice, particularly those framed by professional solidarity.

Systemic change requires, by definition, radicality. Solidary and care might provide new tools to enact it, and in the process foster a rethinking of what is privileged in the music education profession, how teacher preparation is structured and to what ends, while providing further entry into much needed action toward equity, inclusion, decolonization. The jury is out, but the path is promising.

References

Ball, S. J. (2003). The teacher's soul and the terrors of performativity. *Journal of Educational Policy*, 18(2), 215–228. https://doi.org/10.1080/0268093022000043065

Ball, S. J. (2009). *The education debate*. Policy Press.

Ball, S., Maguire, M., & Braun, A. (2012). *How schools do policy: Policy enactments in secondary schools*. Routledge.

Bayertz, K. (1999). Four uses of "solidarity." In K. Bayertz (Ed.), *Solidarity* (pp. 3–28). Kluwer Academic Publishers.

Biesta, G. (2013). *The beautiful risk of education*. University of Colorado Press.

Blase, J., & Blase, J. (2002). The micropolitics of instructional supervision: A call for research. *Educational Administration Quarterly*, 38(1), 6–44. https://doi.org/10.1177%2F0013161X02381002

Britzman, D. P. (1998). *Lost subjects, contested objects: Toward a psychoanalytic inquiry of learning*. State University of New York Press.

Buber, M. (1970). *I and thou* (W. Kaufmann, Trans.). Simon & Schuster. (Original work published 1937)

Bylica, K., & Schmidt, P. (2021). Crossing borders and taking risks: Supporting the music educator as policy practitioner. *Arts Education Policy Review*. Advance online publication. https://doi.org/10.1080/10632913.2021.1955424

Coburn, C. E., & Russell, J. L. (2008). District policy and teachers' social networks. *Educational Evaluation and Policy Analysis*, 30(3), 203–235. https://doi.org/10.3102%2F0162373708321829

Conway, C., Pellegrino, K., Stanley, A. M., & West, C. (2019). Setting an agenda for music teacher education practice, research, and policy. In C. Conway, K. Pellegrino, A. M. Stanley, & C. West (Eds.), *The Oxford handbook of preservice music teacher education in the United States* (pp. 905–916). Oxford University Press.

Clark, C. R. (2007). Understanding vulnerability: From categories to experiences of young Congolese people in Uganda. *Children and Society*, 21(4), 284–296. https://doi.org/10.1111/j.1099-0860.2007.00100.x

Freire, P. (1970/2005). *Pedagogy of the oppressed*. Continuum.

Gaztambide-Fernández, R. A. (2012). Decolonization and the pedagogy of solidarity. *Decolonization: Indigeneity, Education & Society*, 1(1), 41–67.

Hendricks, K. S. (2018). *Compassionate music teaching*. Rowman & Littlefield.

Hinnant-Crawford, B. (2016). Education policy influence efficacy: Teacher beliefs in their ability to change education policy. *International Journal of Teacher Leadership*, 1(2), 1–27.

Johnson, L. (2003). Multicultural policy as social activism: Redefining who "counts" in multicultural education. *Race, Ethnicity and Education*, 6(2), 107–121. https://doi.org/10.1080/13613320308201

Malen, B., & Cochran, M. V. (2008). Beyond pluralistic patterns of power: Research on the micropolitics of schools. In B. S. Cooper, J. G. Cibulka, & L. D. Fusarelli (Eds.), *Handbook of education politics and policy* (pp. 148–178).

Malen, B., & Ogawa, R. T. (1988). Professional-patron influence on site-based governance councils: A confounding case study. *Educational Evaluation and Policy Analysis*, 10(4), 251–270. https://doi.org/10.3102%2F01623737010004251

Mohanty, C. T. (2003). *Feminism without borders: Decolonizing theory, practicing solidarity*. Duke University Press.

Nieto, S., Bode, P., Kang, E., & Raible, J. (2008). Identity, community, and diversity: Retheorizing multicultural curriculum for the postmodern era. In F. M. Connelly, M. F. He, & J. Phillion (Eds.), *The handbook of curriculum and instruction* (pp. 176–197). Sage.

Nieto, S., & Bode, P. (2012). *Affirming diversity: The sociopolitical context of multicultural education* (6th ed.). Pearson.

Ocadiz, G. (2022). Coping with discomfort: Understanding pedagogical decision-making as coping with social change. *Action, Criticism and Theory Journal, 21*(1), 80–109. https://doi.org/10.22176/act21.1.80

Ocadiz, G. (2020). *Music education in a liquid social world: The nuances of teaching with students of immigrant and refugee backgrounds* (Publication No. 6824) [Doctoral dissertation, Western University]. Western Libraries Electronic Thesis and Dissertation Repository. https://ir.lib.uwo.ca/etd/6824

Porto, M., & Zembylas, M. (2020). Pedagogies of discomfort in foreign language education: cultivating empathy and solidarity using art and literature, *Language and Intercultural Communication, 20*(4), 356–374. https://doi.org/10.1080/14708477.2020.1740244

Sandoval, C. (2000). *Methodology of the oppressed*. University of Minnesota Press.

Schmidt, P. (2021). Diluting democracy: Arts education, indigenous policy and the paradoxes of participation. *Action and Theory in Music Education Journal, 20*(2), 30–59. https://doi:10.22176/act20.2.30

Schmidt, P. (2020). *Policy as concept and practice: A guide to music educators.* Oxford University Press.

Schmidt, P. (2017). Why policy matters: Developing a policy vocabulary in music education. In P. Schmidt & R. Colwell (Eds.), *Policy and the political life of music education* (pp. 1–10). Oxford University Press.

Schmidt, P. (2015). The ethics of policy: Why a social justice vision of music education requires a commitment to policy thought. In C. Benedict, P. Schmidt, G. Spruce, & P. Woodford (Eds.), *The Oxford handbook of social justice in music education* (pp. 47–61). Oxford University Press.

Schmidt, P. (2009). Reinventing from within: Thinking spherically as a policy imperative in music education. *Arts Education Policy Review, 110*(4), 39–47. https://doi.org/10.3200/AEPR.110.4.39-47

Schmidt, P., & Edwards, J. (in press). Composition, policy and the formation of agency: Pathways in teacher education and K-16 practice. In M. Kashub (Ed.), *The Oxford handbook of composition in music education.* Oxford University Press.

Su, C. (2019). Research, action, activism: Critical solidarities & multi-scalar powers. *Education Policy Analysis Archives, 27*(57). http://dx.doi.org/10.14507/epaa.27.4450

Tarc, A. M. (2011). Curriculum as difficult inheritance. *Journal of Curriculum & Pedagogy, 8*(1), 17–19. https://doi.org/10.1080/15505170.2011.572478

Thomas, E., & Stornaiuolo, A. (2016). Restorying the self: Bending toward textual justice. *Harvard Educational Review, 86*(3), 313–338. https://doi.org/10.17763/1943-5045-86.3.313

Zembylas, M. (2019). From the ethic of hospitality to affective hospitality: Ethical, political and pedagogical implications of theorizing hospitality through the lens of affect theory. *Studies in Philosophy and Education, 39*, 37–50. https://doi.org/10.1007/s11217-019-09666-z.

Zembylas, M., & Papamichael, E. (2017). Pedagogies of discomfort and empathy in multicultural teacher education. *Intercultural Education, 28*(1), 1–19. https://doi.org/10.1080/14675986.2017.1288448

INDEX

For the benefit of digital users, indexed terms that span two pages (e.g., 52–53) may, on occasion, appear on only one of those pages.

Tables, figures, and boxes are indicated by t, f, and b following the page number

ableism, 61–62, 95–96, 99, 115–16, 117–19, 121–22, 124, 126, 365
Abolition Democracy (Davis), 500
abolitionist pedagogy, 17, 456–57
abolitionist teaching, 450, 456–57.
    See also hope for racial justice in music education
about care, defined, 32, 35–36.
    See also caring about
academic learning loss, 193
acceleration programs, 116–18
acceptance stage, 473
accessibility in social emotional learning, 201–2
accompaniment in LGBTQIA+ music education, 179–80, 182–89
action-oriented reflection, 434
adaptation stage, 473
Adverse Childhood Experiences (ACEs), 299
aesthetical caring, 138
aesthetic care, 570
aesthetic educational approaches, 423–26, 429–30
aesthetic response, 210–11, 247–48
affective empathy, 16, 36–37, 252, 356
AIR. *See* awareness, inquiry, and response
Alabama Legacy Museum, 449–50
Alexander Technique, 344, 351–52
Alex Wheatle (2020), 554–55
All About Love (bell hooks), 498–99
Alternatives to Violence, 523–24
American Jobs Plan, 60–61
American Psychiatric Association, 247

American Psychological Association (APA), 292
American Sign Language (ASL), 544, 548–49
anthropocentrism, 69–70, 142, 144, 150
anti-environment, 57, 64–67
antiracist music education
    action, 511
    centering student voices, 510
    defined, 506–7
    freedom dreams, 513
    identity affirmations, 514
    identity and, 512
    immigration and, 512
    introduction to, 17, 504–8
    joy in learner identity, 513–14
    lessons through arts, 512–13
    microaffirmations, 514
    naming and questioning, 511
    in New Bridges Elementary in Brooklyn, 508–9, 512–13, 514
    overview of, 505–8
    self-awareness, 510
    self-reflection and, 510–12
    stereotypes and, 513
    student expression, 511–12
Arbery, Ahmaud, 505
Arendt, Hannah, 555
Aristotle, 79–80, 304
artistic process, 58, 192–93
ArtsEdSEL Framework, 192–93
assistive device development, 95
atmosphere of caring, 75
authentic care, 170, 566, 570, 571–72

594 INDEX

authentic connection
    in peer mentoring, 283
    in somatic self-care, 358
    trust in music education, 218, 219, 220,
        222–23, 223f, 228–29
authenticity in practice, 1–2
authorial agency of educators, 491
autistic *vs.* person with autism, 197–98, 377
awareness
    gender awareness, 160–61
    in mental health, 322–23, 323f
    non-judgmental awareness, 330–31,
        334, 335–36
    self-awareness, 160, 162, 193, 194–95, 209,
        221, 224–27, 228–29, 350–51, 361, 377, 414,
        416–17, 468, 472, 510
    social awareness, 193, 194–95
awareness, inquiry, and response (AIR), 322–25
Awareness Through Movement (ATM), 353

Bakhtin, Mikhail M., 105–7
be careful, 168–70
behavioral culture, 547
Bell, Derrick, 463–64
bell hooks, 498–99, 500–1
belonging, 34, 84, 194–96, 197–200, 202, 232,
    246, 268–69, 274, 283, 284, 292–93, 298–
    99, 366, 381, 385, 400t, 401, 403, 413, 429,
    430, 577–78, 587–88
benevolence
    care as, 7
    in Confucianism, 133–34
    trust in music education, 217, 221, 222–26,
        227, 228
benign neglect, 97–98
Biden, Joe, 58, 60–61
Biesta, Gert, 555, 559, 561, 582–83
Billings, Gloria Ladson, 469
biological ecosystem, 145–47
Black Lives Matter, 495, 505, 510, 512, 513
Blind Boys of Alabama, 93–94
Body Mapping, 344
Body-Mind Centering, 351–52
brave spaces, 17, 181, 208, 283–84, 288, 511
Buber, Martin, 3, 9, 12, 13, 15, 26n.7, 38n.15, 71,
    82, 105, 110–11, 130, 131, 137–38, 270, 274,
    426, 484, 497

bullying
    distress tolerance and, 520
    LGBTQIA+ issues surrounding, 179, 188
    student safety and, 377–79, 382
    of students with disabilities, 249
bullying in classroom ensembles
    discussion and recommendations, 296–97
    harassment, 292–93, 377–79
    homophily, 296
    homophobia, 294–95
    introduction to, 8, 154–55, 292–93
    peer victimization, 292–93, 294–95, 296–97
    prevalence data, 294–95
    psychological safety, 292–97, 299–300
    research on, 293–97
    school safety, 292–93, 377–79
    trauma and, 293, 297–99
burnout, 321, 339–40, 341, 344, 345, 346–47,
    438–39

call and response, 213, 248, 252
Camp Mark Seven Foundation, 548–51
carceral logics
    compassion-based activism, 520–21,
        521f, 528
    defined, 517
    introduction to, 17, 517–19
    music educators and, 527
    Oakdale Prison Community Choir case
        study, 522–27
    piano class and, 525–27
    reflections on, 528
    self-compassion and, 519–21
    songwriting and, 524–25
cardiovascular disease (CVD), 396–97
care and compassion. *See also* compassion
    co-creating caring relationships, 8–9, 14–15
    conceptualizations of, 7–8
    critical consciousness, 5, 8–9, 16–17
    essence of, 8–9
    ethics of vulnerability, 2–3
    human flourishing, 5
    humanity and, 25–26n.6
    introduction to, 1–3, 5–7
    musical meaningfulness and, 12–14
    relational approach to, 9n.4, 22n.2, 429
    social activism, 5, 8–9, 16–17

in social emotional learning, 196–202
troubled times and, 22–28
wellbeing and, 5, 15–16
care/caring. See also *convivencia* of care; self-care by music educators; singing-caring relations
  aesthetical caring, 138
  atmosphere of, 75
  authentic care, 170, 566, 570, 571–72
  as benevolence, 7
  circular caring, 75–76
  co-creating caring relationships, 8–9, 14–15, 153–55, 170–74
  core reflection and, 438–40
  COVID-19 pandemic impact on, 38–39, 202, 239–40, 495–96
  critical race theory and, 467–68
  Deaf music education, 542–45
  defined, 33
  disabled people in music, 96–99
  feminist moral theory of, 32n.3
  gifted children's musical education, 121–22
  meaning in music education, 556–57
  mindfulness and, 336
  moral theory of, 233
  multiculturalism and, 569–71
  othering/otherness and, 15, 63, 72, 82, 86, 87–88, 103, 105–6, 107–8, 333, 484, 567, 569–71, 580
  philosophical perspectives on, 8–14
  politics of, 2–3, 117–18, 120–21, 122–26
  as prerequisite for teaching, 498
  problematizing idealization of, 71–73
  quality-of-life in older music participants, 397
  sense of, 3, 33, 73, 109, 205
  singing-caring relations, 275
  social caring connection, 400, 401–2
  societal gender roles and, 12n.5
  solidarity and, 586–89
  student safety as, 377–79, 382
  vulnerability in relationships, 313–15
cared for *vs.* one-caring, 14, 70–71, 76, 269–70, 277, 397, 426–27, 472, 474, 478, 544, 546
care ethics
  caring about caring, 32–34
  co-creating caring relationships, 153–55
  educational ethics, 314–15
  in gifted children's musical education, 118–26
  love and, 497, 498–500
  overview of, 9–12
  vulnerability and, 314–15
caregiving, 12, 37, 38, 397–98
care-receiving, 37, 38
caring about, 12–13, 32, 35–36, 97–98, 397, 487
caring about caring
  care ethics, 32–34
  caring about, 32, 35–36
  caring for, 32, 36–37, 40
  caring through, 32, 34
  caring with, 32, 34–35
  empathy and, 37–38
  introduction to, 31
  love and identity-making, 38–41
  preliminary considerations, 31–37
caring connection, 12, 397, 399–403
caring for
  in caring about caring, 32, 36–37, 40
  in compassionate care, 12–13
  gifted children's musical education, 121–22
  love and, 499–500
  one-caring *vs.*, 14, 70–71, 76, 269–70, 277, 397, 426–27, 472, 474, 478, 544, 546
  quality-of-life in older music participants, 397
  social activism and, 141–42
  in wellbeing and human flourishing, 303–5
caring through, 32, 34
caring with
  as compassionate care, 12–13
  love and, 499–500
  musical action and, 3
  in music education, 32, 34–35
  social activism and, 141–43, 145–50
  in wellbeing and human flourishing, 303–5
  as youth instrument ensemble approach, 258–66
Carson, Rachel, 73
Centers for Disease Control's Division of Adolescence and School Health (CDC/DASH), 293–94
Chauvin, Derek, 505
Chicanx artivista, 74

children and wonder, 83–84
circle of care. *See* musical circle of care
circular caring, 75–76
citizenship building through policy practice
    as culturally sustaining, 584–86
    introduction to, 17, 580–81
    music education and, 589–90
    overview of, 583
    personal policy practice and, 586–90
    professional solidarity, 582–83, 587, 590
    reframing of, 581–82
    solidarity and, 586–90
    stakeholder voice in, 582–83
    sustainable policy subjectivity, 585–86
Civic Rights Act (1960), 374
civil rights movement, 374
client-centered therapy, 366
Clinical Somatic Education, 351–52
coactualization, 18, 366
co-creating caring relationships, 8–9, 14–15, 153–55, 170–74
co-creating learning spaces, 285
co-creating shared musical goals, 285–86
cognitive empathy, 36–37, 206, 356
collective thriving, 18
communal diversity, 423
community and somatic self-care, 357–58
community choral programs, 273, 275
community music (CM)
    authoring and, 106–7
    Bakhtin, Mikhail M. and, 105–7
    care and compassion within, 103–4
    Christian worship and, 109–11
    heteroglossia in, 106, 108
    music education dialogue within, 104–7
    music-making experiences in, 108–9
    othering/otherness, 103, 105–6, 107–8
community music (CM) leaders during crises
    alternate route to care, 240–41, 241*f*
    care relations, 233–34
    diverse care experiences, 237–38, 238*f*
    financial cost of care, 239
    heightened care needs, 237
    impact of leadership, 242–43
    introduction to, 231–33
    muted music-making, 236–37
    needs-based approaches, 235–37
    novel care challenges, 234–35
    outsourcing support, 238–39
    shifting goals, 235
    tensions surrounding, 239–40
    themes of, 234–39
community music therapy, 367–69. *See also* music therapy
community of learning, 286–87
community social emotional learning, 199–200
compassion. *See also* self-compassion
    Buddhist understandings of, 13
    carceral logics and, 519–21
    critical race theory and, 467–68
    hope for racial justice in music education, 456–57
    in learning through peer mentoring, 285–87
    meaning in music education, 556–57
    relational care and, 426–29
    social emotional learning and, 194–202
    somatic self-care in music teaching, 355–58
    in teaching students with trauma, 390–91
Compassionate Music Teaching (Hendricks), 5, 9, 12–13, 50–51, 52, 54, 56, 87, 103–4, 154–55, 174, 193–94, 195, 197, 201, 218, 251, 256, 257, 265–66, 280–81, 286, 288, 350–51, 352, 355–58, 359, 390–91, 417, 428–29, 456–57, 461, 467, 498, 506, 510
compassion-based activism (CBA), 520–21, 521*f*, 528
compassion in early childhood musical engagement
    adults as interveners, 57–58
    adults as managers, 60–61
    adults as musical interveners, 58–59
    adults as musical managers, 61
    adults as musical protectors, 60
    adults as protectors, 59–60
    anti-environment and, 57, 64–67
    child-adult interactors, 64–65
    child-adult interventions, 57–60
    child-adult musical interactors, 65–67
    children as labor threats, 60–61
    commonalities in teaching, 61–62
    impediments to, 57–63
    introduction to, 56
    problematic conceptualizations of, 62–63

competence in music education, 218, 221, 222–23, 224–28
concrete culture, 547
confidence in music education, 217, 222–23, 223f, 224–25, 226–28
confirmation, defined, 14
Confucianism
  benevolence in, 133–34
  care through, 132–34
  exemplary personhood in, 134
  introduction to, 130–32
  kindness in, 133
  in music education, 137–39
  sincerity in, 132–33
connection. *See also* authentic connection
  caring connection, 12, 397, 399–403
  in musical ability development, 412–14
  in singing-caring relations, 275–77
  social caring connection, 400, 401–2
  temporal caring connection, 400, 402–3
construction, in music curricula, 86–87
convivencia of care
  circular caring and, 75–76
  eco-literate music, 73
  environmentalism and, 73
  fandango music, 69, 74–75
  historical problems related to gender, 72–73
  introduction to, 69–70
  problematizing idealization of caring act, 71–73
  son jarocho music, 69, 74, 75
  study of, 70–71
Cooke, Sam, 36–37
coordination process, 329–30
core reflection
  action-oriented reflection, 434
  care/caring and, 438–40
  defined, 434–36
  information channels and, 436–38
  introduction to, 433–34
  postrehearsal reflection, 433–34, 436–38, 439
  reflective thinking model, 434
  resources for, 440–41
The Courage to Teach (Palmer), 14, 328
COVID-19 pandemic. *See also* community music (CM) leaders during crises
  abolitionist music teachers and, 461
  community choral programs and, 275
  impact of isolation during, 5–6, 23–24n.5, 24
  impact on caring, 38–39, 202, 239–40, 495–96
  impact on music education, 563–64
  marginalized people and, 131
  mental health and, 320
  racism and, 504
  teacher burnout and, 339–40, 346
  virtual performance logistics, 47–48
creative music therapy, 366–67. *See also* music therapy
Crenshaw, Kimberlé, 168–69
critical consciousness, 5, 8–9, 16–17, 445–47
criticality in practice, 1–2
critical listening
  authorial agency of educators, 491
  case study on, 489–91
  instrumental agency, 483–85
  in/through dialogue, 487–89
  introduction to, 482–83
  LGBTQIA+ students and, 186–87
  musical risk-taking and, 485–87
  music education and, 485–89
  overview of, 483–91
critical race theory (CRT)
  care in music education, 467–68
  counternarratives, 464, 465–66
  experiencing in music education, 465–67
  interest convergence, 464, 465, 466
  intersectionality and, 464–65, 466
  introduction to, 463–64
  ordinariness and, 464, 465, 466
  reflection on, 468–69
  systemic racism and, 464–65
  whiteness as property, 464, 465, 466
critical thinking, 9–14
cultural capital, 170, 531–32, 536, 539, 568
cultural diversity, 570
cultural ecosystem, 145–47
cultural humility. *See* QIAN (Questioning, Immersion, Active-Listening, and Negotiation) model
culturally relevant/responsive/sustaining practices, 8, 146, 170, 194, 200, 202, 507–8, 510, 545–48, 584–86

culture bearers, 147–49
culture-makers/making, 2–3, 147–49
curiosity, 13–14, 149–50, 313–14, 330–31, 358, 389–90, 411–12, 416, 417, 435, 490, 506, 520, 522–23, 582–83

Dalai Lama, 517, 520
Daoism
 care through, 135–37
 equality (*qiwu*) in, 135–36
 flexibility (*rou*) in, 136–37
 introduction to, 130–32
 in music education, 137–39
 nonegoistic action (*wuwei*) in, 135
 observation (*guan*) in, 135–36
 wuwei in, 135
Davis, Angela, 500, 518
Deaf music education
 caring for students, 542–45
 cultural dimension of, 545–48
deep listening, 145–46, 205–6, 207, 208, 209, 212, 213–14, 567. *See also* empathy and deep listening in jazz improvisation
deescalation, 162
defense stage, 473
denial stage, 473
developmental model of intercultural sensitivity (DMIS), 472–74, 473f, 478, 478f, 479
developmental psychology, 59, 70
Diagnostical and Statistical Manual (DSM-5), 384
dialogic research methodology, 494–95
Differentiating Model of Giftedness and Talent (DMGT), 115n.1, 123–24, 410, 411f
differently abled students. *See also* disabled people and lifelong musical engagement; inclusive ensembles
 biases and, 379–80
 family and support systems, 380–81
 historical context, 374–75
 inclusive education and caregiving, 375–76, 379–82
 introduction to, 373–74
 natures and ways of life, 376
 needs and desires, 376–77
 segregation case study, 375b–76b

 self-determination and, 376–77, 378b, 381–82
 self-identity and, 377, 378b
 student safety and, 377–79, 382
 teaching empathy and emotion, 381
digital audio workstation (DAW), 48
Disabilities Education Act (1975), 374
disability ensembles, 95
disabled people and lifelong musical engagement. *See also* differently abled students; inclusive ensembles
 accessible and inclusive practice, 96–97
 care and, 96–99
 caring about, 97–98
 distributive justice, 98–99
 historical traditions, 92–93
 introduction to, 91–93
 medical model of, 94–96
 musical empathy and, 245–47
 reciprocal relationships, 98
 religious model of, 93–94
 social model of, 96
 understanding disability, 92–93
dissent in care, 9–14
distress tolerance, 520
distributive justice, 98–99
diversification, 568–69
Diversity, Equity, Inclusion, and Access Current State Study (2019), 455–56
Dogen, Eihei, 335
Dowland, John, 80–81
drug-related deaths, 6
duoethnography, 494–95
Dzodan, Flavia, 169

ecology/ecosystem/eco-literacy/eco-justice, 17, 28n.10, 69–70, 73, 76, 125, 137, 138, 145–47, 149–50, 161, 367–68, 582–83, 584
Education (2020), 554, 555
educational ethics, 314–15
educational freedom, 450
elitism, 115–16, 117–19, 121–22, 124, 126, 453, 454, 455–56, 505–6
emotional contagion and coordination, 329–30
empathetic attunement, 14–15, 205, 207–8, 212

empathy
    accompaniment and, 180
    affective empathy, 14–15, 16, 36–37, 252, 356
    caring about caring and, 37–38
    cognitive empathy, 14–15, 36–37, 206, 356
    compassionate empathy, 14–15, 456–57
    defined, 14–15, 247
    in Feldenkrais Method, 356
    in gifted children's musical education, 117–18, 119–21, 123
    in inclusive ensembles, 247–48
    intersectionality and, 174
    in jazz improvisation, 206–14
    kinesthetic empathy, 163–64
    mature empathy, 14–15, 135–36, 180
    musical empathy, 14–15, 210–11, 247–48
    somatic empathy, 36–37
    somatic self-care and, 356
    teaching disabled students, 381
Encyclopedia of Quality of Life and Well-Being Research (Maggino, Michalos), 399
engrossment, 9, 15, 70–71, 130–31
ensembles, 46–50, 95, 249–52. *See also* bullying in classroom ensembles; inclusive ensembles; youth instrument ensemble
epistemic humility, 119, 416
epistemic respect, 117–18, 119–20, 123
equality *(qiwu)* in Daoism, 136
equity, 172–73, 193
Eric Whitacre Virtual Choir, 46
Erikson, Erik, 396, 401
Erikson, Joan, 396, 401
Esteva, Gustavo, 69–70
ethics. *See also* care ethics
    educational ethics, 314–15
    feminism/feminine approach to, 22–23, 32–33
    feminist ethics, 9, 32n.3, 38n.15, 546
    Nicomachean Ethics, 304
    relational ethics, 9, 314–15
    of vulnerability, 2–3
ethics of care. *See* care ethics
ethnocentrism, 472–73, 473f, 569
ethnorelativism, 472–73, 473f, 478
eudaimonia, 275, 422, 426
executive functions, 197
exemplary personhood in Confucianism, 134

exercise habits, 345
experience-sharing, 50, 110, 277, 313, 427
experimental mindset, 416, 417
expressive musicianship
    conducting, 262–63
    guided listening of peer performance, 263–64
    performing for students, 264–65
    Smith, Mark Russell, 262–65

face-to-face (vs. virtual) music education, 24–25, 26, 232, 233–34, 239–40
fandango music, 69, 74–75
Feldenkrais, Moshe, 353
Feldenkrais Method, 344, 350–52, 353–55, 356, 357–59
female solidarity, 538–39
femininity, 9–12, 159, 533, 537–38
feminism/feminine approach
    to care, 130–31
    to ethics, 22–23, 32–33
    to experience, 139
    intersectionality in, 168–70
    music therapy and, 365
feminist ethics, 9, 32n.3, 38n.15, 546
feminist moral theory of caring, 32n.3
Figurenotes music, 245
Fisher, Bernice, 33
Fitzgerald, Ella, 36–37
flexibility *(rou)* in Daoism, 136–37
flow state, 207
Floyd, George, 505, 511
Fraser, Nancy, 556–57
Freire, Paulo, 446, 447
Functional Integration (FI), 353

Gagné, F., 123–24, 410, 411f
gender awareness, 160–61
gender differences, 12n.5, 72–73
gender-instrument association, 296
gender relations in Hungary
    female solidarity, 538–39
    introduction to, 530–31
    musical habitus, 531–32
    music culture and education, 531–33
    popular music education, 534–38
    symbolic violence, 531–32, 533, 534–38, 539
gerotranscendence, 396, 401–2

gifted children's musical education
   ableism and, 115–16, 117–19, 121–22, 124, 126
   acceleration programs, 116–18
   care ethics in, 118–26
   caring for, 121–22
   differentiated model of giftedness and talent, 123–24, 410, 411f
   elitism and, 115–16, 117–19, 121–22, 124, 126
   empathy in, 117–18, 119–21, 123
   epistemic respect, 117–18, 119–20, 123
   introduction to, 115–18
   meritocracy and, 115–16, 122–23
   morality of, 118–19
   in musical ability development, 409–12, 411f
   politics of care, 122–24
   relational expertise, 119–20
   systems reflexivity, 117–18, 125–26
Gilligan, Carol, 32–33
Glennie, Evelyn, 85
Gorman, Amanda, 514
grace in music education, 183–84
Graceland (Simon), 84
"Grain of Sand" (Miller), 525
gratitude and mindfulness, 333–35
guided listening of peer performance, 263–64

Hadjidakis, Manos, 1–2
haptification, 95
harassment, 8, 179, 292–93, 377–79
heal/health/healing, 7, 12n.5, 15–16, 18, 28, 35, 60, 74, 80–81, 83, 84, 92, 93, 94–95, 96–97, 157, 158, 159, 163–64, 184, 222, 228, 237, 242, 257–58, 293–94, 299, 309, 336, 339–40, 343–44, 346, 347, 357, 362, 363, 364, 367–68, 384–85, 390, 395–97, 412–13, 414–15, 423–24, 498. *See also* hearing health; mental health; musculoskeletal health; psychological health; vocal hygiene
healing and relationship building through musicing, 157–65
health of biological, social, and musical ecosystems, 141–50
healthcare, 93, 96, 172, 362, 368, 567
Health Promotion in Schools of Music (HPSM) Project, 341
healthy boundaries/relationships, 7–8, 14–15, 16, 356, 519, 528
hearing health, 342–44
hero narrative (upending), 13, 72, 75, 142–44, 416, 536
heteroglossia, 106, 108
hierarchy of needs, 171, 297, 366
holding space, 226
Holiday, Billie, 36–37
holistic acceptance, 17, 175
homeplace, 450–51, 456–57, 460, 461, 500–1
homines curans, 155
homophily, 296
homophobia. *See* LGBTQIA+ issues in music education
honesty, 14, 218, 221–22, 224–26, 227, 228, 501
hope for racial justice in music education
   abolitionist teaching, 450, 456–57
   compassionate empathy, 456–57
   counterstories and, 451–53
   current practices, 457–61
   educational freedom, 450
   future of, 461
   introduction to, 449–51
   as meaningful, 453
   methods and beliefs impacting, 458–59
   methods and beliefs informing, 457–58
   musical equity paradox, 453–55
   music cultures, home *vs.* school, 451–52
   music cultures, importance of, 452–53
   NAfME and, 455–56
   rethinking practice and assumptions, 459–61
hospitality and meaning in music education, 556–57
How to Be an Antiracist (Kendi), 505
human flourishing. *See* wellbeing and human flourishing
humanity and meaning in music education, 556–57
human rights, 188, 370, 499, 523–24, 527, 558, 589
humble/humbleness/humility, 17, 81, 119, 141–42, 147, 149–50, 234, 264–65, 415, 416, 461, 566. *See also* QIAN (Questioning, Immersion, Active-Listening, and Negotiation) model.
humor in community-building, 262
Hungary. *See* gender relations in Hungary

Ich und Du. See Buber, Martin
identity/identity-making
   in antiracist music education, 512, 513–14
   in caring about caring, 38–41
   identity affirmations, 514
   introduction to, 8
   joy in learner identity, 513–14
   in SEL, 195
   self-identity, 270, 276, 377, 378*b*, 583
   social identity, 308
I-It relationship. *See* Buber, Martin
implicit bias, 414–16
imposter syndrome, 345, 434
improvisation, 107, 162–63, 489. *See also* empathy in jazz improvisation
In a Different Voice: Psychological Theory and Women's Development (Gilligan), 32–33
incarceration and music-making. *See* carceral logics
inclusion
   disabled students and, 375–76, 379–82
   in singing-caring relations, 271–73
   somatic self-care and, 357
inclusive ensembles
   empathy in, 247
   introduction to, 245–47
   musical empathy in, 247–48
   promoting safe environments, 249–52
inclusive excellence, 373
Individual Education Plan (IEP), 247
individualism, 28, 72, 143, 195, 234, 320, 424
individuality, 143, 197–98, 274, 377, 518
Individualized Education Program (IEP), 542–43
information channels, 436–38. *See also* core reflection
innate talent, 411–12, 416
Inner Vision Orchestra, 95, 97
inquiry in mental health, 323
Inside Out Reentry Community, 523–24
instrumental agency, 483–85
integrative diversity, 570, 578
intercultural sensitivity
   developmental model of intercultural sensitivity, 472–74, 473*f*, 478, 478*f*, 479
   ethnocentric stages, 473
   ethnorelative stages, 473

   introduction to, 17, 471–80
   knowing me, 475
   knowing students' names, 476–78
   knowing teachers, 475–76
   knowing what, 474
   knowing who, 474, 479–80
   overview of, 472–74
interest convergence, 464, 465, 466
intersectionality
   as basis of understanding, 173–74
   co-creating learning spaces and, 170–74
   core concept of care and, 168–70
   critical race theory and, 464–65, 466
   dissent and critical thinking, 9–14
   equity and, 172–73
   holistic acceptance, 17, 175
   introduction to, 17, 168–70
intimate partner violence, 294
I-Thou or I-You relationships. *See* Buber, Martin

jazz improvisation. *See* empathy in jazz improvisation; mentorship in jazz improvisation
Jim Crow segregation, 505
joy in learner identity, 513–14

Kaba, Mariame, 500, 518
Kim, Christine Sun, 549
kindness in Confucianism, 133
kinesthetic empathy, 163–64
Kleiber, Carlos, 36–37
knowing, ways of, 84–85

Larkin, Dani (Dani Carragher), 219–29
Led Zeppelin, 537
Lerman, Liz, critical response process, 524
Levinas, Emmanuel, 570
LGBTQIA+ issues in music education
   accompaniment and, 179–80, 182–89
   adaptability and, 187
   communication and, 187–88
   critical listening, 186–87
   feedback on, 188
   homophobia, 186–87, 294–95, 388–89, 414–15, 527
   implications for practice, 185–88

LGBTQIA+ issues in music education (*cont.*)
   language related to sexual orientation, 182
   queer/queerness, 12n.5, 180–82, 184–85, 186–88, 189, 197–98, 465, 495–96, 500, 514
   recent developments in, 181–82
   safe and brave spaces, 181
   singing-caring relations, 271–72
   training and professional development in, 181–82
lifelong musical engagement. *See* disabled people and lifelong musical engagement
liminal experience, 87
liminality, 424–25
literature choice, 259
Locke, John, 57–58
Lorde, Audre, 175
love
   care as, 7
   in caring about caring, 38–41
   COVID-19 pandemic and, 38–39, 202, 239–40, 495–96
   ethic of care and, 497, 498–500
   introduction to, 494–95
   meaning in music education, 556–57
   pedagogies of, 17
Love, Bettina, 500, 505–6, 518
love deeper, 501
love louder, 501
love wider, 501

magnetism, 396–97
managerialism education, 582
Manifesto for Progressive Change in the Undergraduate Preparation of Music Majors (Campbell), 558–59
Manze, Andrew, 3
marginalization, 8–9n.2, 28, 111–12, 120–21, 170, 333–34, 335, 384–85, 388–89, 408–9, 411–12, 415, 464
Marley, Bob, 554
Maslow, Abraham, 171, 297, 366
mature care, 38
mature empathy, 14–15, 135–36, 180
McDade, Tony, 511
meaning in music education
   compassion, humanity, hospitality, love, and care, 556–57

   importance of, 554–57
   interruption, suspension, and sustenance, 557–61
   introduction to, 554
   moral responsibility, 560–61
   music teachers as critical, 558–59
   narrative inquiry, 562
   Participatory Action Research, 563
   project-based curriculum, 559–61
   role of research in, 562–63
   sociological portraits, 562–63
medial prefrontal cortex (mPFC), 334
medical model of disability, 94–96
mental health
   adolescent trends, 319–20
   AIR and, 322–25
   awareness in, 322–23, 323*f*
   inquiry in, 323
   introduction to, 318
   in music performance, 15–16
   relational trust and, 321–22
   response in, 324–25
   societal influences, 319–20
   in student-teacher relationships, 320–21
mentorship in jazz improvisation, 208–9
meritocracy, 115–16, 122–23, 408–9
mindfulness. *See also convivencia* of care
   care and, 336
   emotional contagion and coordination, 329–30
   gratitude and, 333–35
   introduction to, 328
   in musical circle of care, 162–63
   non-judgmental awareness, 330–31, 334, 335–36
   oppression and, 333–35
   self-compassion and, 331–32
   shadow side of, 335–36
   STOP technique, 330–31, 334
mirror effect, 311–12
Mississippi Civil Rights Museum, 449–50
monocultural norms, 146
moral development, 9–12, 18
moral responsibility, 560–61
moral theory of caring, 233
Morris, Wesley, 450
multiculturalism, 569–71, 584–86
musculoskeletal health, 344–45

INDEX 603

music, defined, 33n.7
Music, Health, and Wellbeing (MacDonald), 423–24
musical ability development
    autonomy in, 412–14
    competence in, 412–14
    connection in, 412–14
    giftedness in, 409–12, 411f
    implicit bias in, 414–16
    introduction to, 408–9
    prodigies and, 408
    relatedness in, 413
    talent in, 409–12, 411f, 416
    understanding, 409–12
musical action, 3, 107, 109
musical asylums, 423, 425, 428
musical circle of care
    becoming aware, 162–63
    context of, 158
    extending hospitality, 161–62
    finding healing, 163–64
    introduction to, 157
    overview, 158–65
    taking leave, 164–65
    welcoming one another, 160–61
musical communities, 5, 6–7, 16–17, 33n.7, 232, 582–83
musical competence, 66, 118–19, 411, 527
musical empathy, 210–11, 247–48
musical experience, 85–87, 86f
musical habitus, 531–32
musical improvisation, 107, 162–63, 489
Music for Life (Fung, Lehmberg), 397, 399–403
musician-oriented rehearsing
    conducting approach, 260
    literature choice, 259
    pacing importance, 260–61
    rehearsal style, 259–60
    Smith, Mark Russell, 259–61
Musicians Without Borders, 219
musicking, defined, 423–24
music-making experiences
    as care, 7–8
    in community music, 108–9
    musical meaningfulness, 12–14
    muted music-making, 236–37
    trust in process of, 227–28

Music Standards (State Education Agency Directors of Arts Education, 2014), 58
music technology, 8, 16
music therapy
    community music therapy, 367–69
    continuum of, 362–64
    creative music therapy, 366–67
    defined, 362
    introduction to, 361–62
    key principles, 364–69
    relational collaboration, 369–70
    relationality and, 365, 366–69
    relationship, as change medium, 364–65
    vision for collaboration, 369–70
muted music-making, 236–37
mutuality, 12, 70–71, 73, 76, 98–99, 233, 239–40, 268–69, 277, 365, 366–68, 390, 391, 498

narcissism, 122, 498
National Alliance on Mental Illness, 324
National Association for Music Education (NAfME), 58, 451, 455–56
National Association of Schools of Music (NASM), 341
National Institute for Occupational Safety and Health (NIOSH), 342–43
National Memorial for Peace and Justice, 449–50
needs based musical education, 41
Neff, Kristin, and guided self-compassion practice, 332, 519
neurodivergent people, 196–98
New Bridges Elementary in Brooklyn, 508–9, 512–13, 514
New York Times, 450, 505
Nicomachean Ethics, 304
Noddings, Nel, 22–23, 35, 121, 130–31, 138, 375–77, 380, 471–72, 546
Noise-induced Hearing Loss (NIHL), 343
nonegoistic action *(wuwei)* in Daoism, 135
non-judgmental awareness, 330–31, 334, 335–36
nonreactive presence, 520, 523, 524, 526, 527
nonverbal collaboration, 212, 213–14
nonverbal communication in jazz improvisation, 211–14, 212t
nonverbal instruction, 213

Nordoff, Paul, 366–67
Nwigwe, Tobe, 496

Oakdale Prison Community Choir, 522–27
observation *(guan)* in Daoism, 135–36
Ocadiz, Gabriela, 589–90
Oliveros, Pauline, 80
one-caring *vs.* cared for, 14, 70–71, 76, 269–70, 277, 397, 426–27, 472, 474, 478, 544, 546
One-Handed Woodwinds program, 97
Ontario College of Teachers, 364
open-ended dialogue, 209–10
ordinariness, 464, 465, 466
othering/otherness, 15, 63, 72, 81, 82, 86, 87–88, 103, 105–6, 107–8, 333, 484, 567, 569–71, 580

pacing importance, 260–61
pain, as body communication, 344
para-musical, defined, 363
Para-orchestra, 95
participation, defined, 64–65
Participatory Action Research, 563
participatory music, 74, 105, 235–37
pathological altruism, 333–34
patience and somatic self-care a, 357
pedagogical, relational teachership (PeRT), 429
peer mentoring
    approaches to, 281–82
    brave spaces for, 283–84
    co-creating learning spaces, 285
    co-creating shared musical goals, 285–86
    as community of learning, 286–87
    compassionate learning through, 285–87
    creating opportunities for, 282–83
    discussion, 287–88
    establishing trust, 286
    introduction to, 280–81
    in jazz improvisation, 208–9
    philosophical framework, 282
peer victimization, 292–93, 294–95, 296–97
Performing Arts Medicine Association (PAMA), 341
person-first language, 197–98, 377, 378*b*
personhood, 39–40, 61–62, 143–44, 471–72, 474, 485, 518

perspective-taking, 196, 205, 206, 207, 208–9, 416
Peter Pan syndrome, 86–87
philosophical perspectives on care, 8–14
phronesis, 40, 118, 310, 314–15
physical spaces in classroom SEL, 198–99
piano class and carceral logics, 525–27
place-based pedagogy, 210
police brutality, 6, 449, 505, 509
policy practice. *See* citizenship building through policy practice
politicized care, 497
politics of care, 2–3, 116–18, 120–21, 122–26. *See also* gifted children's musical education
politics of hope, 157
positive psychology, 304, 435
post-rehearsal reflection, 433–34, 436–38, 439
post-traumatic stress disorder (PTSD), 297–99, 385
power dynamics, 170–71, 218, 467, 496–97, 500, 525–26
power of example, 27–28
practical wisdom, 310
Practicing Core Reflection: Activities and Lessons for Teaching and Learning from Within (Evelein, Korthagen), 440
Prakash, Suri, 69–70
prison music-making. *See* carceral logics
problematizing idealization of caring act, 71–73
prodigies, 408
professional learning community (PLC), 466
professional solidarity, 582–83, 587, 590
Profound and Multiple Learning Difficulties (PMLDs), 92–93
project-based curriculum, 559–61
psychological health, 345–46
psychological safety, 292–97, 299–300

QIAN (Questioning, Immersion, Active-Listening, and Negotiation) model, 566–68, 569–71
    active listening, 573*f*, 574*f*, 574–75
    cultural diversity and, 570
    cultural validation, 577–78

diversification and social
    responsibility, 568–69
immersion, 573
integrative diversity and, 570, 578
introduction to, 17, 566–67
multiculturalism, 569–71
negotiation, 575–77
overview, 567–68
questioning, 571–72, 572f
virtue of, 566–67
quality-of-life in older music participants
    caring and, 397
    caring connection in, 397, 399–403
    connection and, 396–97
    contributions to, 403
    gerotranscendence, 396, 401–2
    implications with, 403–4
    introduction to, 395–99
    music participation benefits, 398, 400t
    older adults, defined, 395–96
    older adults, psychological
        development, 396
    quality of life and, 399
    social caring connection, 400, 401–2
    temporal caring connection, 400, 402–3
queer/queerness See LGBTQIA+ issues in
    music education

racial justice. See critical race theory; hope for
    racial justice in music education
racism. See also antiracist music education
    COVID-19 pandemic and, 504
    Jim Crow segregation, 505
    police brutality, 6, 449, 505, 509
    structural racism, 464, 586
    systemic racism, 464–65, 497
    white supremacy, 69–70, 169, 456, 495–96,
        498–99, 504–7, 510, 512
Rattle, Simon, 36–37
reasonable adjustments, 91–92
reciprocal relationships, 98
recommended exposure limits (REL) for
    hearing, 342–43
reflection. See core reflection
reflection-in-action, 286, 287–88
reflection-on-action, 286, 287–88
reflective thinking model, 434

rehearsal style, 259–60
relational care
    aesthetic educational approaches, 423–26,
        429–30
    approaches to, 9n.4, 22n.2, 37–38, 429
    human flourishing and, 423–29
    introduction to, 421–23
    liminality, 424–25
    musical asylums, 423, 425, 428
relational engagement, 38n.15, 104–5,
    370, 484–85
relational ethics, 9, 314–15
relational expertise, 119–20
relationality, 73, 74, 76, 119, 165, 365, 366–69,
    423, 485, 580
relational pedagogy, 428
relational trust, 186, 206, 207, 217, 225,
    225f, 321–22
relationship, as change medium, 364–65
relationship skills, 193, 194–95
Relaxercise technique, 353–55
reliability, 14, 217, 227, 228, 341, 387
religion/religiosity, 93–94, 109–11
"Remember: Be Love" (Blackwell), 524–25
resilience in music education, 23n.4
response in mental health, 324–25
The Responsibility of the Artist
    (Maritain), 26
responsible decision-making, 193, 202
Rindale, Donald, 248
risk-taking, 7, 207–8, 212, 213, 218, 264, 294–95,
    297, 357–58, 368, 485–87, 488–89
Robbins, Clive, 366–67
Roman Catholic Church, 116–17
Rousseau, Jean-Jacques, 59
Rubinstein, Mary Jane, 80

Sacks, Jonathan, 569–70, 578
safe environments in ensembles, 249–52
safe spaces, 181
school safety, 292–93, 377–79
school-to-prison pipeline, 388, 495–96
secondary traumatic stress (STS), 321
self-actualization, 18, 171, 175, 297, 366
self-awareness, 160, 162, 193, 194–95, 209, 221,
    224–27, 228–29, 350–51, 361, 377, 414, 416–
    17, 468, 472, 510

self-care by music educators. *See also* somatic self-care
  burnout and, 321, 339–40, 341, 344, 345, 346–47, 438–39
  hearing health, 342–44
  introduction to, 339–41
  musculoskeletal health, 344–45
  planning for, 346–47
  psychological health, 345–46
  starting practices, 341–47
  vocal hygiene, 341–42
self-censorship, 308, 312–13
self-compassion
  carceral logics and, 519–21
  mindfulness and, 331–32
  somatic self-care, 350–51
  teacher vulnerability and, 14
self-determination theory (Deci & Ryan), 116–17, 304–5, 376–77, 378*b*, 381–82, 409, 412–13
self-esteem, 207, 307, 311–12, 379–80, 381, 422
self-expression, 27, 209, 211, 268–69, 271, 276, 308, 401–2, 513–14
self-identity, 270, 276, 377, 378*b*, 583
self-knowledge, 304, 350–51, 352, 355–56, 401, 439
self-love, 498
self-management, 193, 194–95, 197
self-monitoring, 198–99
self-reflection, 46, 134, 139, 209, 271–72, 313, 417, 466, 467–69, 510–12, 523
self-regulation, 162–63, 386–87, 413
sense of care, 3, 33, 73, 109, 205
Severe Learning Difficulties (SLDs), 92–93
Shakespeare, William, 23
Shearing, George, 93–94
Shelly, Mary Ann, 471
Shōbōgenzō (Dogen), 335
Shusterman, Richard, 352
signed-singing, 544, 548–51
Silent Spring (Carson), 73
Simon, Paul, 84
sincerity in Confucianism, 132–33
singing-caring relations
  balance in, 273–75
  community choral, 273, 275
  connection in, 275–77

context in, 270–71
holistic approach to, 273–77
inclusion in, 271–73
introduction to, 268–69
one-caring *vs.* cared for, 269–70
overview, 269–70
Small, Christopher, 423–24
Small Axe (2020), 554
Smith, Mark Russell, 258–66
social activism
  biological and cultural ecosystems, 145–47
  care and compassion, 5, 8–9, 16–17
  caring with, 141–43, 145–50
  culture bearing *vs.* making, 147–49
  hero narrative and, 143–44
  introduction to, 141–42, 445–47
  soulcraft and, 149–50
social awareness, 193, 194–95
social caring connection, 400, 401–2
social change, 157, 416, 506, 518, 519, 568, 590
social emotional learning (SEL)
  accessibility and, 201–2
  community and, 199–200
  compassion and caring in, 196–202
  culturally relevant pedagogy, 200
  executive functions and, 197
  IDENTITY, BELONGING, and AGENCY in, 194–96
  intentional use of, 194–98
  introduction to, 192–94
  in music education, 194
  neurodivergent people and, 196–98
  respecting individuality, 197–98
  SELF-OTHERS-DECISIONS in, 194–96
  student choice and, 201
  student empowerment, 198–99
  universal design for learning, 196–97
  white supremacist oppression, 499
social identity, 308
social inequality, 84–85, 157
social isolation, 97, 237, 296, 320
social justice. *See* hope for racial justice in music education
social model of disability, 96
social responsibility, 1–2, 568–69
solidarity policy practice, 586–89
soma, defined, 351

somaesthetics, 352–53
somatic empathy, 36–37
somatic self-care
    Alexander Technique, 344, 351–52
    authentic connection, 358
    community and, 357–58
    compassion in music teaching, 355–58
    defined, 344
    educators as sense-beings, 351–52
    empathy and, 356
    Feldenkrais Method, 344, 350–52, 353–55, 356, 357–59
    inclusion and, 357
    introduction to, 350–51
    patience and, 357
    recommendations and applications, 358–59
    somaesthetics, 352–53
    trust and, 356
The Songs of Mourning (Dowland), 80–81
songwriting and carceral logics, 524–25
sonification, 95
son jarocho music, 69, 74, 75
soul, in teaching, 328
soulcraft, 149–50
sounds of intent framework, 247–48
Speaking Proactively About Race with Kids (S.P.A.R.K.), 510
Specific Learning Difficulties (SpLDs), 92–93
spiritual experience in music, 86f, 87
spirituality in musical circle of care, 162
stage fright, 310–11
Stigma of the Giftedness Paradigm (SGP), 116
St John, Patricia, 86, 87
STOP mindfulness technique, 330–31, 334
structural racism, 464, 586
student empowerment, 198–99
student safety as caring, 377–79, 382
student-teacher relationships, 170–71, 320–21, 365
subjecthood, 143–44
suicide, 6, 320, 379
sustainability, 54, 71, 139, 141–42, 144, 145, 146, 147, 150, 345, 580–81, 582–86, 588, 589
symbolic culture, 547
symbolic violence, 17, 531–32, 533, 534–38, 539
systemic racism, 464–65, 497
systems reflexivity, 117–18, 125–26

"Take a Risk" (Pestano), 81
take care, 168–70
talent in musical ability development, 409–12, 411f, 416
Taylor, Breonna, 505, 511
teacher-student relationships. *See* student-teacher relationships
Teaching and Learning from Within: A Core Reflection Approach to Quality and Inspiration in Education (Korthagen), 440
temporal caring connection, 400, 402–3
tender loving care, 168–70
terror and wonder, 80
The Human Condition (Arendt), 555
Theory of Practice (Bourdieu), 109–10
therapy, defined, 362
Thunberg, Greta, 18
Timm, Rosa Lee, 549
transformative justice, 519
transitional object, 2
trauma
    bullying and, 293, 297–99
    changing practice narratives for, 388–91
    compassionate music teaching, 390–91
    deficit narratives, 388–89
    informing educational narratives, 193
    introduction to, 384
    justice considerations, 388–89
    lack of attention to, 15–16
    literature on, 385–88
    musical circle of care and, 158–65
    rationale of, 384–85
    reactions to, 385–88
    relational work, 389–90
    resilience and, 23n.4
    salvation narratives, 388
    student considerations, 385–87
    teacher considerations, 387–88
Tronto, Joan, 33
trust
    agency and, 218, 223–24
    authentic connection and, 218, 219, 220, 222–23, 223f, 228–29
    benevolence and, 217, 221, 222–26, 227, 228
    coding and analysis, 220–21
    competence and, 218, 221, 222–23, 224–28

trust (cont.)
   confidence and, 217, 222–23, 223f, 224–25, 226–28
   discussion, 228–29
   establishing through peer mentoring, 286
   in Feldenkrais Method, 356
   findings, 221–28
   holding space, 226
   honesty and, 218, 221–22, 224–26, 227, 228
   introduction to, 217–18
   multifaceted and dynamic nature of, 221–22
   openness and, 218, 221, 222–23, 227, 228
   procedures in, 219–20
   process of music-making, 227–28
   purpose and method of, 219–21
   relational trust, 186, 206, 207, 217, 225, 225f, 321–22
   reliability and, 217, 227, 228
   space of presence, 222–23, 223f
   vulnerability and, 217, 218, 220, 221–24, 228
Trust Matters (Tschannen-Moran), 218

unconditional positive regard, 366, 367–68
United Nations (UN), 395–96
United Nations (UN) Convention on the Rights of the Child, 64–65, 116–17
universal design for learning (UDL), 196–97
University of Iowa Liberal Arts Beyond Bars program, 523–24

Vaughan, Sarah, 36–37
virtual ensembles, 46–50
virtual music-making, 16, 46, 234–35, 237, 238, 241f. *See also* ethics of expectation in virtual music-making
virtue and wonder, 81–83
vocal hygiene, 341–42
voice, 308–11. *See also* singing-caring relations
voice shame, 308, 312–13
vulnerability
   in caring relationships, 313–15
   critical race theory and, 467–68
   introduction to, 307
   mirror effect, 311–12
   trust in music education, 217, 218, 220, 221–24, 228
   vignette, 307–8

voice as audible body, 308–9
voice as musical instrument, 310–11
voice shame, 308, 312–13

wellbeing and human flourishing
   care and compassion, 5, 8–9, 15–16
   context of, 158
   introduction to, 8–9, 157, 303–5
   relational care and, 423–29
white, educated, industrialized, rich, and democratic (WEIRD) individual, 414n.2
White Fragility: Why It's so Hard for White People to Talk About Racism (DiAngelo), 505
whiteness as property, 464, 465, 466
white supremacy, 69–70, 169, 456, 495–96, 498–99, 504–7, 510, 512
Wiggins, "Blind Tom," 93–94
with care, defined, 32, 34–35. *See also* caring with
Wonder, Stevie, 93–94
wonder in music education
   children and, 83–84
   introduction to, 79
   musical experience and, 85–87
   philosophy of, 79–84
   terror and, 80
   unknown and, 80–81
   virtue and, 81–83
   ways of knowing, 84–85
World Health Organization (WHO), 93, 339, 399
Wright, Ruth, 557–58

youth instrument ensemble
   building community of learners, 261–62
   caring with approach, 258–66
   expressive musicianship, 262–65
   fostering relationships, 257–58
   introduction to, 256–57
   musician-oriented rehearsing, 259–61
   Smith, Mark Russell, 258–66
Youth Risk Behavior Surveillance System (YBRSS) survey, 293–94

Zhou Wen Wang, 131